Typhoon to Typhoon

RAF Air Support Projects and Weapons Since 1945

Typhoon to Typhoon

RAF Air Support Projects and Weapons Since 1945

Chris Gibson

HIKOKI PUBLICATIONS

'Single Role Aircraft are simply passé.'
Air Chief Marshal Sir Richard Johns,
13 June 2018

'In the unpredictable context of a short intense European war, when there will not be time to develop new aircraft or modify old aircraft, fundamental flexibility in the performance of available aircraft will assume even greater importance than in the air campaigns of the past.'
MoD Operational Requirements Committee paper on AST.403, October 1975

Dedicated to those the fighter pilots call 'mud movers'.

First published in 2019 by
Hikoki Publications Ltd
1a Ringway Trading Est
Shadowmoss Rd
Manchester
M22 5LH
England

Email: enquiries@crecy.co.uk
www.crecy.co.uk

Line Drawings: ©Chris Gibson

Original photography: ©Peter Edwards, © Chris Lofting and © RA Scholefield
Original artwork by Luca Landino and Luciano Alviani

Layout by Russell Strong

ISBN 9 781902 109596

Printed in Turkey by Olas Solutions

Front cover illustrations:

Top: An RAF Eurofighter Typhoon in full swing-role configuration. Swing-role fighters can attack ground targets and take on enemy aircraft. This Typhoon carries two Raytheon Paveway IV LGBs, six single-mode MBDA Brimstone air-to-surface missiles, four MBDA Meteor beyond visual range air-to-air missiles, two MBDA ASRAAM short range air-to-air missiles and a pair of drop tanks. *MoD/Open Government Licence*

Bottom: Northern West Germany, September 1993. In this hypothetical scene, using their base-burners and reheat, a pair of Hawker Siddeley P.1191 Tempest GR.1s draw the fire of a ZSU-23/4 Shilka to allow a third Tempest to attack a column of *Nationale Volksarmee* (East German Peoples' Army) T-72 main battle tanks with IBL.755 cluster bombs. *Luca Landino*

Back cover illustrations:

Top: BAC TSR.2 XR219 on the ramp at A&AEE Boscombe Down being prepared for a test flight. XR219 was the only example of the TSR.2 to take to the air before cancellation. *BAE Systems via Joe Cherrie*

Centre left: Hawker Siddeley Brough artwork showing a BAC.221 fitted with base burning equipment on each side pf the tailfin. *Brough Heritage*

Centre middle: The search for a replacement for the Jaguar and Harrier produced many innovative design studies including the BAC P.103 with variable incidence wing and tilting engine pods. *North West Heritage Group*

Centre right: Another possible Jaguar/Harrier replacement was the Kingston-designed HS.1187-5 that used a modified Pegasus with a single rear nozzle. *Brooklands Museum*

Bottom: The Phantom FGR.2 had a short career in ground attack but did perform the tactical reconnaissance role when equipped with the EMI P391 reconnaissance pod, seen here on the centreline pylon. *Terry Panopalis Collection*

Rear flap top: BAC usually put on a good spread at Farnborough Air Show and in this case the BAC 167 Strikemaster is shown with the array of weapons it could carry for strike missions. *Terry Panopalis Collection*

Rear flap bottom: BAC's Lightning F.53 for the Kuwait Air Force was exhibited at the Paris Salon with the range of weapons that could be carried. *RA Scholefield*

Half Title: Tornado GR.1 in 'Desert Pink' casts its shadow on the surface of the Saudi Arabian desert during a low-level flight in the build-up to Operation Granby. Tornados conducted strike missions against Iraqi airfields and installations from the first hours of the air war. *Terry Panopalis Collection*

Title page, top: A pair of Harrier GR.3s from No 1 Sqn/Hardet Belize generate vapour trails from their wingtips in the moisture-laden tropical air of Belize in Central America. This pair were photographed in 1978 and RAF Harriers were based in Belize from 1975 until 1993. *Terry Panopalis Collection*

Title page, bottom: Two Hunter FGA.9s from No 20 Sqn on patrol over the island of Pulau Tioman, Malaya in August 1965. This pair of Hunters are carrying 3in RPs and drop tanks. *Terry Panopalis Collection*

Contents

A Harrier GR.7 is readied for a strike mission during Operation Telic 2003. This GR.7 is armed with the AGM-65 Maverick and is equipped with the nose-mounted sensors for night/adverse weather operations. *Crown Copyright via Terry Panopalis*

Acknowledgements

Typhoon to Typhoon has drawn together information from a multitude of sources and archives around the UK that are maintained by volunteers, mainly retired employees of the various companies involved, who are also experts in particular fields. The benevolence of BAE Systems PLC provides much of the funding for archives at Woodford, Brough and Warton. BAE Systems and its former employees deserve better recognition as the keepers of Britain's aerospace heritage. The Brooklands Museum, whose staff and particularly its volunteer archivists work to preserve the work of Hawker and Vickers, deserve particular recognition for their year-round efforts

These volunteers and organisations should be encouraged and congratulated for their help in allowing researchers like me to access their material, much of which has remained under wraps for years. When it comes to the professional archivists, the staff at the National Archives at Kew are always helpful and patient with a rummager like me. Internet resources have become more important and one resource that has become invaluable to aviation researchers is the Secret Projects Forum, set up and managed by Paul Martell-Mead. Since it went 'live' the Secret Projects Forum has helped researchers by allowing us to communicate and inevitably discover aspects of our research subject that would not previously cross our minds. Other important online resources are the archives of *FlightGlobal* and *Aviation Week and Space Technology*, both very welcome and useful additions to the researcher's armoury.

Firstly, I would like to thank my dear wife Kirsten, for her considerable patience and continuing encouragement. When it comes to artwork, there is no finer exponent of 'what-if' computer artwork than Luca Landino who can bring my drawings and sketches to life in living colour. Luciano Alviani brought his skill with the brush to *Typhoon to Typhoon* with his paintings of the Avro BAC P.101 and 'Rods from the Gods'. Tony Buttler and Phil Butler must be thanked for their continued guidance on matters of research and provision of images. A book like *Typhoon to Typhoon* requires photographs of a variety of subjects from aircraft to vehicles and Terry Panopalis must be thanked for allowing access to his collection and supplying many of the images for this book. Thanks are also due to Peter Edwards, Chris Lofting and RA Scholefield who supplied many of the original images for *Typhoon to Typhoon*.

Another group whose ongoing help and advice contributed so much to *Typhoon to Typhoon* are the aforementioned volunteers at the various archives who always provide a warm welcome, a brew and friendly assistance. A visit to any of these archives is always something to look forward to. Chris Farara must be thanked for his continuing work at Brooklands Museum and providing information on the Kingston studies for AST.396. Tony Wilson and the staff at North West Heritage Group at Warton have, as ever, been of great assistance. Brough Heritage provided material on many AST.396 studies, but especially on base-burning and the various configurations that Hawker Siddeley Brough examined for base-burning research and, thanks to Paul Lawson, Peter Hotham and the volunteers at Brough, the base-burning studies have been described for the first time.

Thanks are also due to a number of people who have provided invaluable help in its creation. Neil Lewis who edited the text and as ever provided guidance in all matters of book production. Gillian Richardson, Charlotte Stear and Jeremy Pratt at Crécy Publishing for their continuing support and are, as always, a pleasure to work with. I must also thank Neil Armstrong, Phil Strachan and my colleagues in the *Ocean Patriot* drilling team.

Chris Gibson, Washington
September 2019

Introduction

'The cavalry, in particular, were not friendly to the aeroplane, which it was believed, would frighten the horses.'
Sir Walter Alexander Raleigh, *The War in the Air*

Typhoon to Typhoon is a title that suggests that misused modern expression 'a journey' through time from the Hawker Typhoon of World War Two to the Eurofighter Typhoon of the 2020s. That would be correct, but this also the story of how roles and capabilities; interceptor, anti-tank, counter-air, defence suppression and bomber, tasks at which the Hawker Typhoon excelled, were taken on by the Eurofighter Typhoon seventy years later. In the era of the ballistic missile there are no massed bomber formations for Typhoons to intercept, just Russian maritime types such as Tu-142 *Bears* making incursions into UK airspace or charter flights with rowdy passengers to escort. Modern Typhoons spend most of their operational time doing what their 1940s predecessors did – attacking ground targets.

The intervening years saw the RAF fight many wars, none of which involved the nuclear 'balloon going up' but spent most of its time delivering rockets, bombs and cannon rounds on ground targets. When it comes to technology and warfare there is a chicken/egg situation. Does the technology allow certain types of weapon to be developed, for example the laser and laser-guided bomb or does warfare drive technology, such as the need for accurate targeting that produced the global positioning system that is on the mobile phone in your pocket? Wars such as Vietnam saw many developments initiated to solve particular problems, but these could only come to fruition as computers and sensors shrunk with the development of integrated circuits. In time these reached civvie street.

Typhoon to Typhoon describes some, but not all, of these technologies in relation to their incorporation in weapons. Attacking ground targets, essentially the bread and butter of any air force in the early 21st Century, has prompted the development of technologies that have entered the civilian market, from GPS to the low-light television much-loved by wildlife documentary makers. Whatever your view of drones, they now have a place in civilian life, be it for TV coverage of events or documentary making to inspection of buildings and structures; all have their origins in a UAV that can hit a 'Technical' with a Hellfire.

What should always be remembered when discussing ground attack is that there is invariably ground defence which makes this particular role the most hazardous in any air force. Those who conduct such operations deserve a better monicker than 'mud mover'. An infantry platoon in a 'situation', pinned down by the enemy, will always be happy to hear a 'mud mover' announce they are 'Rolling in now' on the RT.

In the years since World War Two the RAF has met changing strategic and tactical situations with a variety of equipment, some of which was not always suited to the task. Armed forces are always kitted out to fight the last war and having equipped for all-out nuclear war the RAF in Europe had to change to a conventional footing from 1961. As luck would have it the colonial policing tasks around the Empire had given it an expertise in ground

A Jaguar T.2 emerges from a hardened aircraft shelter at an RAF base. Air forces on both sides of the iron Curtain 'went hard' in the years after the Six Day War of 1967, building hardened shelters in locations around the main airfields. *Blue Envoy Collection*

attack and in the Hawker Hunter, an ideal type. Having re-equipped with Harrier, Jaguar and Tornado for battlefield support and interdiction, plus acquiring the weaponry to conduct a conventional war in Europe, the Iron Curtain fell, leaving the RAF with lots of kit. Fairly soon, the RAF was back to the 'colonial policing' role east of Suez and soon discovered its new kit was somewhat lacking.

The 21st Century saw the rise of the swing-role fighter, and aircraft that could at the press of a button on a multifunction display, switch from attacking tanks to dogfighting. *Typhoon to Typhoon* outlines the key aircraft and weapons developments involved in ground attack since 1945. Look elsewhere for aircraft and squadron histories or the exploits of particular pilots, these are well catered for in other books. The story told herein is how the RAF has gone from an arguably failed interceptor to a world-beating, swing-role, netcentric war-fighting machine – from Typhoon to Typhoon.

Notes on Units

Nautical miles (nm) have been used throughout this book. The RAF used statute miles until the 1960s and where these are included in quoted text from original documents, the conversions to nautical miles and kilometres are appended. In the main text, nautical miles are used throughout to allow comparison with post 1960 data. Speeds are quoted in knots (kt) and kilometres per hour (km/h), mass/weight is quoted in long tons (2,240 lb) and metric tonnes or pounds and kilograms. Metric equivalents of all units are shown for clarity. Throughout this book all-up weight (AUW) is quoted and should be taken as the maximum gross take-off weight which includes the aircraft's structure, engines, fuel and oil, crew and payload. It is quoted in pounds (lb), with its metric equivalent in kilograms (kg) alongside. From the early 1970s the British aviation industry went metric and many documents use metric units. Where used their Imperial equivalents are presented alongside.

Personal Prologue

'Do like aircraft, son?' said the lady behind me at the supermarket checkout, pointing to the aviation magazine on top of my shopping. 'Aye, I write about them' I replied, proudly, having just had my first book published. 'My son was in Tornados' said the lady. 'Really?' I replied, but before I could continue, the lady said, 'He was killed on the first night of the Gulf War.' I was speechless, completely lost for words. As you read what follows, remember this paragraph.

The RAF's ground attack aircraft in the Noughties. Seen here in 2007 are Harrier GR.9 ZD354 of 1(F) Sqn; Tornado GR4 of II(AC); Typhoon F.2 ZJ934 of 3(F) Sqn and Harrier GR.9 ZD410 of IV(AC) Sqn. *MoD/ Open Government Licence*

1 'My vas pokhoronim!' The Soviet Horde and Other Enemies

'Quantity has a quality all its own'
Attributed to Josef Stalin

'Let's keep our boots polished, bayonets sharpened, and present a picture of force and strength to the Red Army. This is the only language they understand and respect.' General George S Patton, US Army

From the end of World War Two until 1991, the period known as the Cold War, two military blocs faced each other across the Iron Curtain that stretched 'From Stettin in the Baltic to Trieste in the Adriatic'. NATO, formed in 1949 by the USA, Canada and the European democracies while the Warsaw Pact comprised the Marxist/Leninist Soviet Union and its eastern European satellite states. Each bloc feared invasion by the other, so built up armed forces that faced each other across the Iron Curtain. Prior to 1961 any incursion across the Iron Curtain, by either side, would have prompted massive nuclear attack, but from 1961 conventional weapons – tanks, aircraft and infantry – would have fought it out on and over central Europe. A fight in which ground attack aircraft would have been key.

This work mainly deals with the period from 1946 until 1991, a period known as the Cold War. This 45 year timespan saw two power blocs; the democratic capitalist 'West' and the totalitarian Communist 'East' led by the United States of America (USA) and Union of Soviet Socialist Republics (USSR) respectively, each ostensibly attempting to prevent the other gain the upper hand in the world. Each garnered support from allies willing and unwilling in the shape of various political and military treaty organisations around the world. In Europe these organisations comprised the North Atlantic Treaty organisation (NATO) and the Warsaw Pact.

From 1946 US policy was to contain what it saw as Soviet expansionism and to aid this aim April 1949 saw twelve western nations form NATO. In response the Soviets and their allies in Eastern Europe signed the Warsaw Pact in May 1955. Both blocs were armed with nuclear weapons and expanded their arsenals to ensure Mutually Assured Destruction, which was intended to prevent war. This led to a nuclear arms race as each bloc tried to 'outgun' the other.

A column of Red Army T-72 main battle tanks moves along a road in Eastern Europe in November 1983. This deployment to the field was prompted by Soviet uncertainties about NATO's Able Archer exercise that simulated NATO's command, communication and control systems under attack by the Warsaw Pact. *DoD*

By the end of the 1950s, US policy under President Eisenhower had led to the adoption of massive retaliation or 'Trip Wire' whereby NATO would launch a retaliatory strike as soon as Warsaw Pact forces moved against Western Europe. This was an apt name; the Cold War was in constant danger of becoming a hot war at the least provocation. This response worked well in deterring the Warsaw Pact, if NATO possessed superiority in nuclear forces, but by the late 1950s, the forces were becoming more balanced, or at least perceived to be more balanced. In 1961 President Kennedy, sceptical of the Trip Wire policy, adopted Flexible Response whereby by any Soviet aggression would be met firstly by conventional forces (Direct Defense), then use of tactical nuclear weapons (Deliberate Escalation) and ultimately a strategic exchange of nuclear weapons (General Nuclear Response).

Throughout the Cold War a series of treaties limited certain classes of nuclear weapon, such

Below: An RAFG Phantom FGR.2 undergoes decontamination at RAF Brüggen. The prospect of nuclear, biological and chemical warfare made such equipment necessary and training in NBC kit a must for the 'lineys'. *Terry Panopalis Collection*

Opposite page:

Always outnumbered and probably outgunned. This diagram shows the imbalance of forces in Europe in the early 1980s. Much of the Warsaw Pact firepower would be held in reserve beyond the front line, the RAF's emphasis on interdiction by Tornados is understandable.

Comparison of the air arms of the Warsaw Pact and NATO explains some of the decisions taken by the Air Staff when drawing up requirements. The imbalance on interceptors is obvious, possibly explaining the change in emphasis from close support with AST.396 to air combat with AST.403.

as the Strategic Arms Limitation Treaty (SALT), Intermediate Range Nuclear Forces in Europe (INF Treaty) or the ABM Treaty helped stabilise the strategic situation. A balance of nuclear forces helped maintain an uneasy peace but by the 1980s both sides were modernising their nuclear *and* conventional forces. The Warsaw Pact had always had large conventional forces, Stalin's quantative quality, and NATO always considered its forces qualitively superior but the Warsaw Pact forces were also improving. In modernising its conventional forces NATO was aiming at blunting any conventional attack from the eastern side of the Iron Curtain, even against modernised Warsaw Pact equipment. Preferably without resorting to nuclear weapons.

Thankfully a war in Europe did not happen during the 45 years of the Cold War but innumerable 'proxy' wars occurred around the world, typically on the back of liberation struggles. These saw developments in conventional weapons, either by the military industries of the two blocs, typified by the high technology developments in air defence and SEAD by the 'military industrial complex' for the war in Vietnam, or improvised weapons by the village mechanic in his workshop in the Middle East.

We Will Bury You

Nikita Khrushchev, General Secretary of the Central Committee of the Communist Party of the Soviet Union, was paraphrasing Karl Marx when he declared '*My vas pokhoronim!*' (We will bury you!) to assembled ambassadors at a November 1956 meeting in Moscow. Of course, eyeing the assembled Warsaw Pact tank armies from the western side of the Iron Curtain, the NATO allies, particularly the Americans, took Khrushchev at his word. The prospect of a Soviet 'horde' swarming across the North German Plain, pouring through the Fulda gap in Germany or advancing down the Vipacco Valley in north east Italy, filled the NATO allies with dread.

NATO saw their nuclear capability as the means of balancing out the WP's overwhelming superiority in conventional forces, particularly in the field of armoured warfare on a nuclear battlefield. The strategic aspects were well catered for in the B-47, B-52, Vulcan, Victor and Valiant squadrons carrying freefall atomic bombs or later, stand-off weapons, into the Soviet heartland, but these would have been of little practical help to a company commander watching a Soviet armoured unit bearing down on his position.

The Americans invested heavily in nuclear weapons ranging from the 25MT Mk-41 (also known as the B41) freefall weapon to the 0.02kT Mk-54 used on the Davy Crockett antitank spigot mortar and GAR-11 Falcon AAM. Until the mid-Sixties an armoured force crossing the Inner German Border would have been met with a hail of tactical nuclear weapons delivered by the many tactical fighters such as the F-105 Thunderchief or former interceptors like the Javelin or F-104 Starfighter, based in western Europe. With the adoption of Flexible Response, these 'tactical' fighters were now tasked with supporting the ground forces, counter-air and interdiction, roles they were not exactly suited to. For the RAF the superb Canberra, designed as a bomber but adapted to the tactical nuclear bomber and interdiction

roles, which it filled for almost three decades, while the Phantom FGR.2 had a short-lived career in ground attack.

This led to a flurry of activity in Europe to design and produce aircraft to meet the new roles, although the Hawker Hunter, originally a fighter, excelled in the ground attack role. NATO requirements such as NBMR-1 and NBMR-3 attempted to produce a bespoke ground attack fighter for all of NATO, but despite the FIAT G.91 being adopted for NBMR-1, only West Germany Italy and Portugal acquired the 'Gina'. Portugal operated the G.91R in its intended role during Portugal's colonial wars in Angola, Mozambique and, principally, Guinea. NBMR-3 fared less well, with only prototypes of the V/STOL machines being produced as its main role, tactical nuclear strike, disappeared when Flexible Response was adopted. Only one country developed a V/STOL aircraft that could lurk in the woods and farmyards as required by NBMR-3. The country with no stated interest in MBMR-3: The United Kingdom.

While the RAF's V-bombers and Canberras fielded the nuclear weapons in Europe, including US weapons under Project E, such equipment was of little use to the British in that other major pre-occupation in the 1950s and 1960s – withdrawal from Empire. Valiants and Canberras did bomb, conventionally, in Egypt in November 1956 but ground attack in the campaigns in Cyprus, Aden and the proxy war in Oman relied on the dumb bombs, guns and rockets, delivered by re-roled fighters and trainers such as the Hawker Hunter FGA.9 and BAC Strikemaster.

Only by the mid-Seventies were true ground attack aircraft appearing, the rugged, armoured A-10A Thunderbolt, Harrier and the Jaguar, plus the munitions required to kill tank formations without resorting to the nuclear weapons that had held the ring until the late 1960s. This is the period, 1965 – 75, that saw the fastest development in weapons technology since 1945, driven by two factors. The first was the Vietnam War which the USAF had entered with a range of aircraft more suited to Armageddon than fighting a 'bush war'. Oddly enough the US Navy and Marine Corps, thanks to their emphasis on expeditionary warfare were better matched to Vietnam. The other driver was the expanding Warsaw Pact conventional forces, which were not only increasing in size but in quality, on the ground and in the air. Another bush war, fought with severely limited resources, saw the Hunter and Canberra used, with new bespoke weapons, to great effect in Rhodesia.

It was weapons, unsurprisingly, that would make the difference, and by the late Seventies laser and infrared guided missiles were becoming a common sight on the pylons of western ground attack aircraft and as well a being able to drop bridges, they could now hit tanks and that was a game-changer for NATO. The Seventies saw the newfound precision and the sensors developed to destroy trucks on the Ho Chi Minh Trail applied to the Soviet Horde. This revolution in weapons – and it was a revolution – saw aircraft that were never intended to engage a ground target such as the F-15, doing just that with *élan*.

The Horde

In the 1981 edition of *Soviet Military Power*, the US Department of Defense (DoD) annual analysis of the Soviet military, the DoD stated that the Warsaw Pact forces in eastern Europe comprised 83 divisions, of which 30 were Soviet Red Army. On armoured forces alone, the

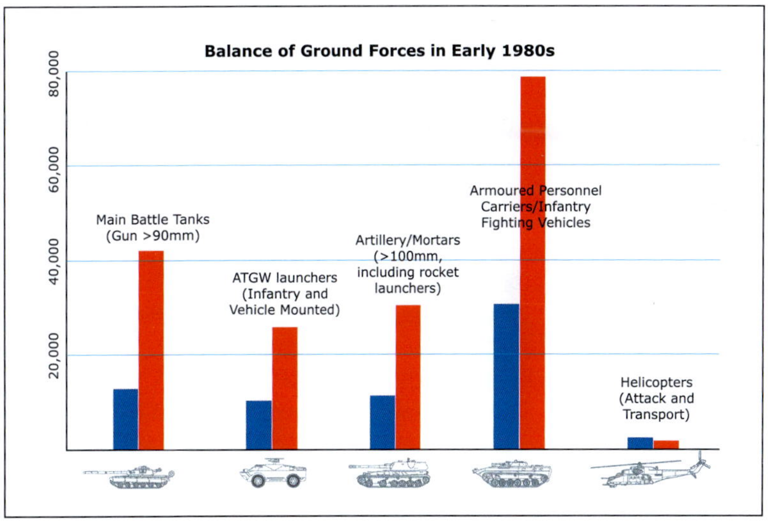

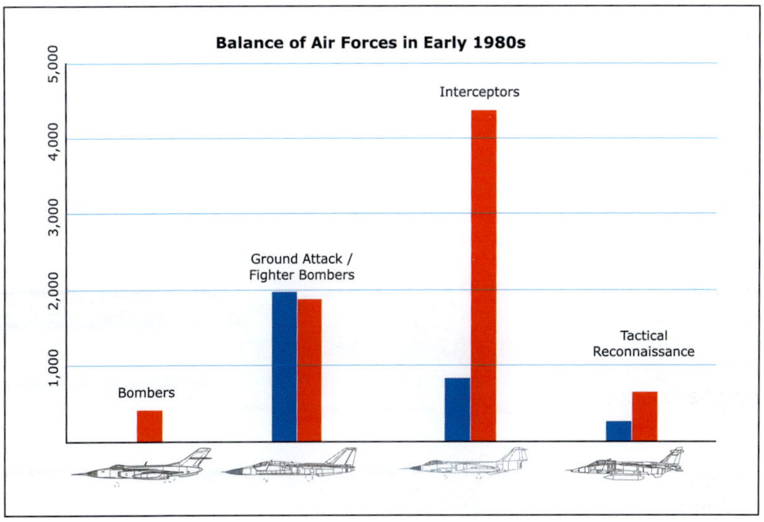

The *Hind*. Heavily armed and armoured, the Mi-24 (NATO reporting name *Hind*) posed a problem to NATO forces in western Europe. This is a Ukrainian Air Force Mi-24P (NATO reporting name *Hind-F*) fitted with side-mounted 30mm GSh-30-2K twin-barrel cannon on the port side of the fuselage. The wingtip pylons can carry the 9M114 Shturm (AT-6 *Spiral*) ATGW as well as the B-8V20A pod for 80mm rockets. *Chris Lofting*

Warsaw Pact possessed more than double the number that NATO could field with NATO possessing 31,000 tanks (not all in Europe) against the WP's 71,000 and, as with NATO, not all of these were in Europe. As for aviation, the only area where NATO outnumbered the Warsaw Pact in 1981 was helicopters, although the Warsaw Pact fielded almost double the number of attack helicopters; 700 vs 400. Whether these NATO types were true attack helicopters such as the AH-1 Cobra or armed utility helicopters such as the Scout AH.1 with AS.11 ATGWs is unclear, but the formidable Mil Mi-24 *Hind* certainly figured in that Warsaw Pact total.

NATO, especially US generals and politicians, claimed that in the era of Flexible Response, the numerical superiority of Warsaw Pact forces was balanced by the better quality of western equipment and the technology behind it, leading to projects such as Assault Breaker (see Chapter 6) and the ability to reinforce western Europe from the USA. The latter was regularly rehearsed in the Return of Forces to Germany (REFORGER) exercises but was dependent on NATO sea and air power protecting the sea lanes in the eastern Atlantic from the depredations of Soviet naval and air forces roaming the north east Atlantic.

On the European Central Front, which was essentially a line along the Inner German Border and the border with Czechoslovakia, the NATO Northern Army Group (NORTHAG) faced the Group of Soviet Forces in Germany (GSFG). NORTHAG comprised forces of the US Army, West Germany's Bundeswehr, France's Armée de Terre, Belgium's Composante terre/Landcomponent, Dutch Koninklijke Landmacht and the British Army on the Rhine (BAOR) and supported by 2nd Allied Tactical Air Force (2ATAF). The air forces of 2ATAF comprised units of the USAF, Koninklijke Luchtmacht (KLu), Belgische Luchtmacht/Force Aérienne Belge, Luftwaffe and RAF. For the purposes of this work, British forces will be the focus and these comprised the British Army of the Rhine (BAOR) and RAF Germany (RAFG).

BAOR was expected to take on five Soviet divisions in the first wave of an attack on Western Europe and while the Army could engage the first wave of any assault, RAFG was expected to deal with the second echelon and engage in the interdiction of Warsaw Pact reinforcements in East Germany and Poland. In addition to that, RAFG was also tasked with offensive counter-air and delivery of nuclear weapons to targets assigned by NATO. Offensive counter-air involves the suppression of enemy air capability through attacks on airfields, air defence systems and the aircraft themselves, the aim being to restrict, if not prevent, Warsaw Pact air operations against NATO forces. Meantime, the same Warsaw Pact air forces would be conducting offensive counter-air operations of their own against RAFG airfields.

In the immediate postwar years, the RAF operated from many former Luftwaffe bases in the British Zone of Occupation but following the establishment of the German Air Force in 1956 many of these were handed back to West German command. From 1956 the size of the RAF in Germany was reduced, thanks to the aforementioned adoption of massive nuclear retaliation and the usual lack of funds. Operational flying was mainly conducted from six bases: Brüggen, Laarbruch, Wildenrath, Gütersloh, Jever and Geilenkirchen, with the last two handed over to the German Air Force in 1961 and 1968 respectively.

Having examined the geopolitical and strategic lie of the land between the Oder and the North Sea, what would be coming across the inner German Border towards BOAR and RAFG? Tanks, certainly, but the Soviet doctrine of all-arms warfare that had served them well in World War Two had been kept up to date with modern warfare, particularly the nuclear battlefield, and the tanks would be accompanied with the BMP series of armoured personnel carrier, mobile air defence systems and, most worrying to NATO armies, attack helicopters.

When it appeared in the Soviet order of battle in 1972, Mil's Mi-24 *Hind-A* came as a bit of a surprise to NATO. There is no aircraft quite like it in the western arsenal. A heavily armoured helicopter, armed with UB-32A 57mm rocket pods, four AT-2 *Swatter* (9M17 Fleyta) ATGWs, a Yakushev-Borzov Yak-B 12.7mm Gatling-type machine gun *and* capable of carrying eight troops, the *Hind* posed a threat to NATO armoured and helicopter forces.

Impressed by the US Army's use of armed helicopters in Vietnam, the *Hind* was developed in the late 1960s as a flying infantry fighting vehicle (IFV) – an airborne BMP-2 – that combined the air support and troop transport roles admirably. The helicopter that NATO identi-

In 1955 the RAF operated from 18 bases in the north of West Germany, by 1965 this had been reduced to six by 1960 after the re-establishment of the German Air Force in 1956. By 1995 the RAF operated from four bases; three Rhine Clutch airfields (Laarbruch, Wildenrath and Brüggen) plus Gütersloh. The RAF also operated from Gatow in the British Sector of Berlin. The three Berlin Air Corridors are shown in Yellow.

The bases of RAFG hosted the full range of the RAF's fighter aircraft in the Cold War. From six bases in 1960, the RAF's strength was concentrated on four bases by 1970.

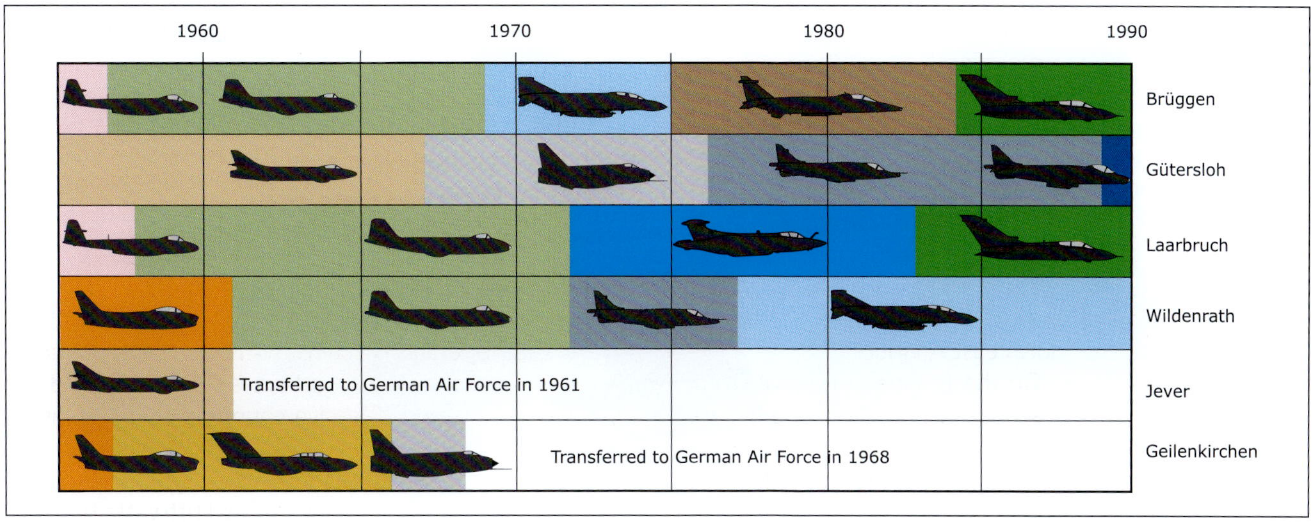

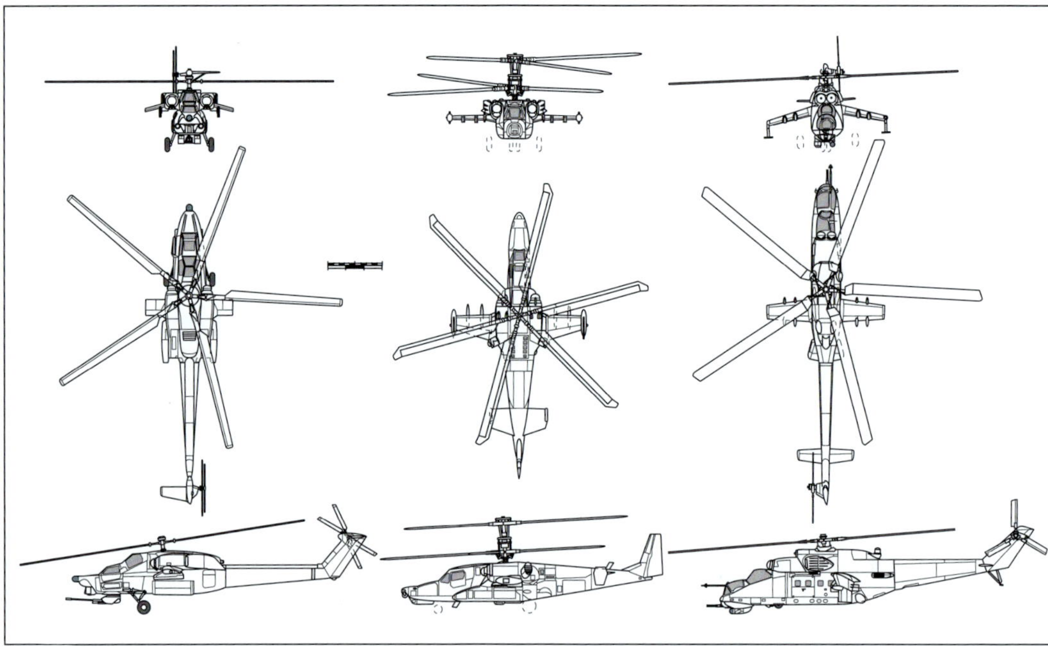

The threat from Soviet attack helicopters increased through the 1980s. Left to right; Mi-28 *Havoc* and Ka-50 *Hokum* were dedicated anti-tank helicopters while the Mi-24 *Hind-E/F* could carry eight troops as well as weapons for fire support.

fied as the *Hind-A* turned out to be the *second* production variant, the version that had superseded what NATO called the *Hind-B* and whose most obvious difference was the lack of anhedral on the wings. *Hind-C* was the unarmed training version of the *Hind-A*, but what became the ubiquitous *Hind* 'gunship' or 'flying tank' of the popular press and stalked the battlefields of the world was the *Hind-D*. Its tandem bubble canopies gave it an ominous air that the earlier 'greenhouse' lacked and with its improved anti-armour weaponry in the form of the AT-6 *Spiral* (9K114 Shturm) ATGW system it posed a formidable foe to NATO armies in the late 1970s. This was followed by the *Hind-E* in the 1980s with the AT-6 *Spiral* system and the *Hind-F* that sported a twin-barrelled 30mm GSh-30K cannon on the starboard side

The Soviet Big 7 alludes to the Big Five, the deadly big game animals of the African savanna. These were the Warsaw Pact weapons that would be spearheading any invasion of Western Europe. The main threat to ground forces were the T-72, self-propelled guns and BMP while the Shilka and *Gecko* posed a problem to aircraft. The formidable *Hind* was a threat to all. *DoD via Terry Panopalis*

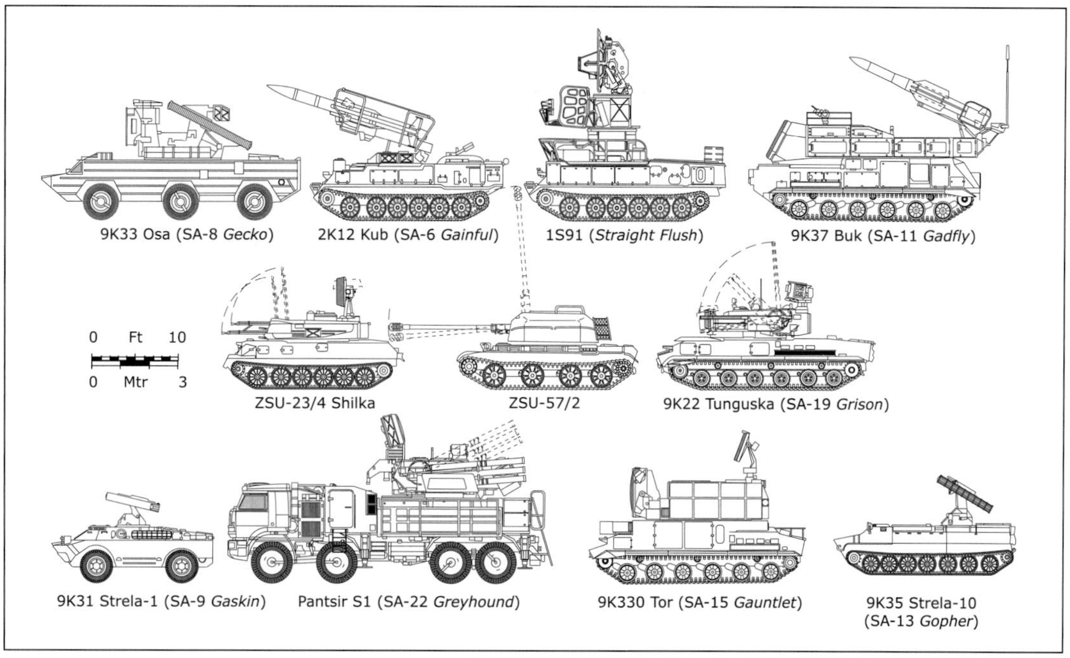

The first targets for RAF battlefield support aircraft and Army Air Corps anti-tank helicopters were the Soviet mobile air defence systems. The Shilka and *Gainful* had given the Israelis a nasty surprise in October 1973 and led to a change of tactics in NATO. The later *Gadfly*, Tor, Tunguska and Pantsir modernised and increased the threat to NATO aircraft.

of the fuselage. This made the *Hind-F* a tough ground support machine but also a formidable anti-helicopter type, capable of hunting down NATO's anti-tank (Helarm) and support helicopters. What NATO required was a counter to the *Hind*; a deer hunter.

The *Hind* was a member of what the US DoD called The Big Seven; Soviet weapons that posed a particular threat to NATO forces and included the T-72 main battle tank (MBT), BMP Infantry fighting vehicles, ZSU 23/4 Shilka self-propelled anti-aircraft gun (SPAAG) colloquially known as the *Zeus*, 9K33/SA-8 *Gecko* mobile SAM system and two self-propelled guns (SPG); the 122mm 2S1 and 152mm 2S3. These were the systems that NATO ground attack aircraft would face either through attacking them or being attacked by them. Against the ground vehicles, attack aircraft and armed helicopters would have used the traditional gun/bomb/rocket armament and be tasked to attack ground targets in the face of defensive fire. With the appearance of the *Hind*, the ATGW-equipped helicopters and ground attack aircraft would now be under attack themselves.

To NATO attack aircraft, such as Harriers, Jaguars and, of course, the A-10 Thunderbolt, the Shilka and *Gecko* posed the main threat but towards the end of the Cold War a new, more advanced threat appeared: the 9K22 Tunguska. Known as the SA-19 *Grison* to NATO (due to its missile armament it was classed as a missile system), the 2S6 combined twin 2A38M 30mm cannon and eight SA-19 *Grison* SAMs with the *Hot Shot* radar system with an E-band acquisition and J-band tracking radar on a tracked vehicle. Soviet studies had revealed that a heavier round would be more effective against NATO aircraft such as the AH-64A Apache and A-10 Thunderbolt, whose manufacturers had stated that their airframes were resistant to the 23mm rounds of the Shilka or the 12.7mm rounds from the *Hind-A's* Yak-B gun.

Interestingly, while the Apache and Thunderbolt were said to be capable of surviving a hit from a 23mm shell, one wag pointed out that these shells tended to fly in flocks. Therefore, the 30mm cannon became the weapon of choice on the Tunguska and the *Hind-E*. The 30mm cannon allowed engagements at longer ranges, out to 4,000m (4,374 yards), and trials against scrapped ground attack aircraft had shown that the 2A38M guns on the Tunguska had a 1.5x better chance of an effective hit than the 23mm of the Shilka. NATO had reached the same conclusion, fitting the 30mm GAU-8/A rotary cannon on the Thunderbolt and the 30mm M230 Chain Gun on the Apache.

The Soviets required these air defence systems due the expectation that the NATO allies would have air superiority and in turn these weapons had influenced NATO attack aircraft, be they fixed or rotary wing. The A-10A Thunderbolt was born out of the American experience in Vietnam where ground fire claimed many aircraft on ground support operations while the Apache was designed to take on well defended Warsaw Pact armoured formations in western Europe.

Another threat that the Soviets addressed was the Tomahawk series of cruise missiles being developed by the US in the 1970s and

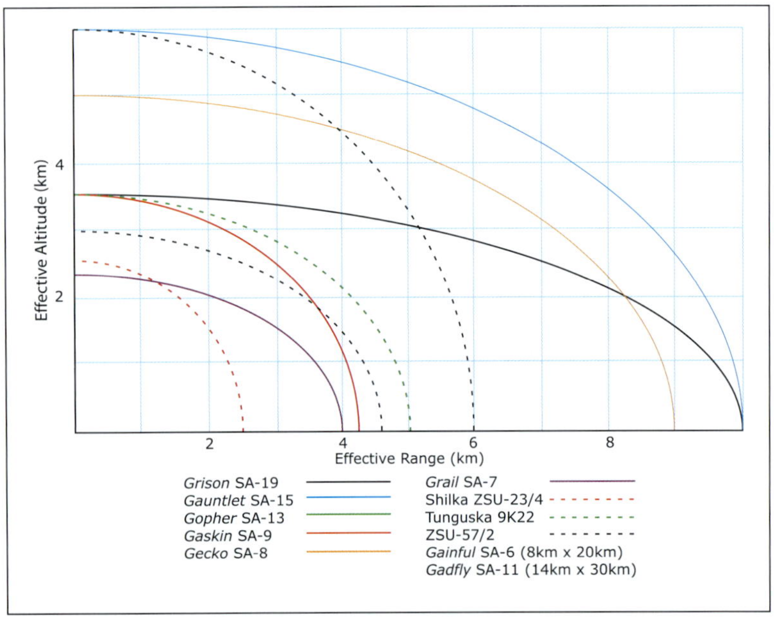

When it came to mobile air defence, the Warsaw Pact had more than adequate coverage. This graph shows the engagement envelopes of the various systems. Gun systems were for short-range threats and missile systems for longer ranges. The guns could also be used against ground targets, which has been the main use for the Shilka since 1990.

early 80s. To take on the cruise missiles the Soviets developed the Tor to replace the SA-8 *Gecko*. Known to NATO as the SA-15 *Gauntlet*, the 9K330/Tor system was designed from scratch with cruise missiles in mind but was also capable to taking on fixed and rotary-winged aircraft, UAVs and even precision guided munitions. The *Gauntlet* system can be mobile or static, but for the purposes of this book, the mobile version is examined. The Tor-M1 system is housed in a large turret mounted on a GM-355 tracked vehicle with the target acquisition radar on top and the tracking radar mounted on the front of the turret. The eight vertically-launched 9K330 missiles are housed between the radars and extend below the turret ring and into the turret basket although the later Tor-M2 carries 16 missiles.

Replacing the ZSU-23/3 Shilka and combining the mobile SAM and the SPAAG, the 26S Tunguska would have ridden shotgun for Warsaw Pact armoured divisions in the 1990s. This example has its 30mm cannon elevated and SA-19 *Grison* launchers in travelling mode. *Wiki Commons*

One of the latest mobile air defence systems developed and deployed by Russia is the Pantsir-S1, known to NATO as the SA-22 *Greyhound*. Carried by either a GM-352 tracked chassis or a Kamaz 6560 8x8 truck, Pantsir (Shell) can be used on the move, but accuracy with the gun improves if the vehicle is static, or in the case of the wheeled chassis, when raised on levelling jacks. The system was developed from the Tunguska as its replacement and shares the combined guns and missiles on the same mount configuration. The turret carries the phased-array acquisition and tracking radar, twelve 57E6 (SA-22 *Greyhound*) SAMs and a pair of 2A38M 30mm cannon.

In addition to the *Hind*, by the 1980s two new attack helicopters were under development for the Red Army's aviation arm and artists' impressions of these began to appear in western literature. The first was described as an Apache lookalike while the second was a radical departure from western helicopter doctrine. The first, assigned the ASCC reporting name *Havoc-A*, adopted the classic attack helicopter configuration – single main rotor, tandem cockpit, externally-mounted turboshafts, stub wings and tail-dragger undercarriage. The second was assigned the ASCC reporting name *Hokum-A* and was a single-seater with co-axial main rotors, retractable tricycle undercarriage and small, rather than stub, wings.

Havoc-A was the Mil Mi-28 and *Hokum* was the Kamov Ka-50 and while the *Havoc* appeared to be a dedicated anti-armour system, the *Hokum* just looked like a helicopter 'fighter' and that was pretty much how it was being described in the West. By 1989 the Cold War was thawing, and the *Havoc* was being displayed at the Paris Salon and as the Soviet Union dissolved the Russian military's focused turned to the south eastern republics, such as the war in Chechnya, where these new weapons were deployed.

The *Havoc* was armed with the AT-9 *Spiral-2* (9M120 Ataka) ATGW, plus the usual suite of rocket pods and a 2A42 30mm cannon mounted in a chin turret. It could also carry the SA-18 *Grouse* 9M39 Igla air-to-air missile for use against enemy aircraft. The *Havoc*'s target-

Mil's Mi-28 (NATO reporting name *Havoc*) had a protracted development and is a dedicated attack helicopter. Armed with a Shipunov 2A42 30mm cannon in a chin turret, up to eight 9M120 (AT-9 *Spiral*-2) missiles and rocket pods it would have been widely used on the Central Front. *Chris Lofting*

ing system would be upgraded to provide full night/all-weather capability as the Mi-28N.

The Ka-50 *Hokum-A* had in fact been developed as an anti-tank attack helicopter that used automation to allow a single pilot to fly the helicopter and operate the weapon systems. The co-axial rotor, a Kamov design bureau speciality, gave the *Hokum* a good turn of speed and agility. *Hokum's* primary armament was the AT-16 *Scallion* (9A4172 Vikhr), with up to 16 being carried on the wing pylons. The *Scallion* was a long-range laser-guided missile in the same class as the US AGM-114 Hellfire, but the system proved to be very complex and maintenance heavy, so the laser-guided version of the AT-9 *Spiral-2* was adopted. Rather than a flexible cannon in a ventral turret, *Hokum* carried the same 2A42 30mm cannon as the BMP-2 IFV, on the starboard side of the forward fuselage and despite having limited traverse in azimuth and elevation, is used like a fixed gun.

The single-seat Ka-50 was joined fairly soon by the two-seat Ka-52 *Hokum-B*, which western experts took as an indication that the single-seat attack helicopter concept had failed. In reality Kamov was reacting to changes in the post-Cold War world, counter-insurgency rather than all-out armoured warfare, and the Russian adoption of the armed scout helicopter along similar lines to the US RAH-66A Comanche.

On the fixed-wing front, the nuclear weapon-lobbing fast jets that had dominated in the 1960s and 70s were viewed as less than ideal in the era of flexible response. The US armed forces in Vietnam had learned that ground attack was a specialist role and a specialist aircraft could make a difference, which lead to the A-X competition. The A-X led to the A-10A Thunderbolt and by the early Eighties the wail of its turbofans was heard over north west Europe and the UK. This was not lost on the Soviets, who like the NATO forces had been using fast jets, such as the MiG-17 *Fresco* and Su-7/17/20 *Fitter*, that were somewhat unsuited to the ground support role. In the late 1970s US satellites observed a type that was being called *Ram-J*, under the US DoD's provisional reporting name system. *Ram-J* was soon given the official ASCC reporting name *Frogfoot* and shortly after that it was revealed as a Sukhoi design bureau development called Su-25. By the early 1980s photos of *Frogfoot* in action in Afghanistan were appearing in the western press. *Frogfoot* has been described as the Russian equivalent of the A-10A Thunderbolt, but it is less of a dedicated 'tank-buster' and more of a support aircraft in the *Shturmovik* class. In addition to its 11 pylons for stores, *Frogfoot* is fitted with a Gryazev-Shipunov GSh-30-2 twin-barrelled 30mm cannon.

From 1980 the Warsaw Pact forces in eastern Europe were undergoing modernisation, but such modernisation brings an economic cost, a cost that the Soviet Union was having great difficulty bearing. The Soviet Old Guard in the Politburo died one after another until Mikhail Gorbachev was elevated to General Secretary of the Communist Party in 1985. Gor-

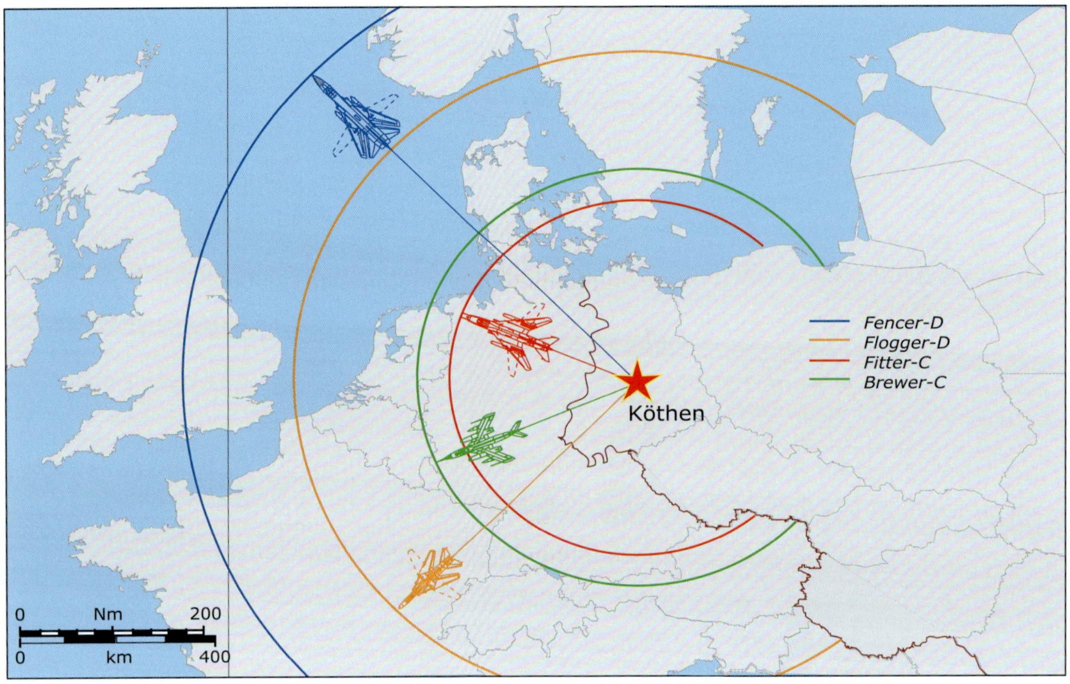

The radii of action for four of the main strike aircraft in the Warsaw Pact's air forces toward the end of the Cold War. Although not shown here, the Tu-22M *Backfire*, with a radius of action of up to 1,300nm (2,400km) and Su-24 *Fencer* could be based further east in Poland, Czechoslovakia or Romania.

Tactical air support of Warsaw Pact forces was also being updated by the end of the Cold War. The top row (L-R, Sukhoi Su-25 *Frogfoot*, Sukhoi Su-24 *Fencer* and MiG-27 *Flogger-D*) superseded the bottom row (L-R, Sukhoi Su-22 *Fitter-C*, MiG-17 *Fresco* and Sukhoi Su-7 *Fitter-A*). The new types possessed longer range and greater weapons carriage capacity.

Frogfoot – viewed in the West as a Soviet A-10A, the Sukhoi Su-25 (NATO reporting name *Frogfoot*) was smaller and less heavily armed than the A-10, but still packed a punch. While not as dedicated to the anti-armour role, it was possibly more suited to the ground support role. This pair of Su-25SM *Frogfoot-A* (05 Red, RF-95482 closest to the camera) are on approach to Chkalovsky. *Chris Lofting.*

bachev ushered in an era of *perestroika* (openness) and a series of arms control agreements were signed. Within five years the countries of eastern Europe east of the Iron Curtain were independent, Germany was unified and Soviet forces were being withdrawn. By the end of 1991, the Soviet Union ceased to exist.

A Not So Quiet Decade

In November 1989, as the Berlin Wall was being broken up for souvenirs and East Berliners gawped at the shop windows on Kurfürstendamm, RAF Germany mainly operated from four main bases: the three Rhine 'Clutch' bases west of Cologne; Brüggen, Laarbruch and Wildenrath near the border with The Netherlands and one base, Gütersloh, further east tasked with supporting BAOR operations.

RAF Brüggen was home to four squadrons of Tornado GR.1s (Nos. 9, 14, 17 and 31) plus an air defence squadron and a light armoured squadron of the RAF Regiment. This unit configuration was similar at RAF Laarbruch (Nos. 2, 15, 16 and 20 Squadrons with Tornado GR.1) One squadron (No.2) was equipped with the Tornado GR.1A and tasked with reconnaissance while the remaining Tornado squadrons were tasked with counter-air and nuclear strike operations, equipped with the WE.177A/C. RAF Wildenrath housed two squadrons for air defence (Nos 19 and 92) equipped with the Phantom FGR.2 and one communications squadron (No.60) with Andover CC.2s plus an RAF Regiment air defence squadron.

RAF Gütersloh lay halfway between the Dutch border and the East German border, close to the BOAR garrisons and played host to two squadrons (Nos 3 and 4) flying Harrier GR.5s, No 18 Sqn flying Chinook HC.1 and No 230 Sqn with the Puma HC.1 both supporting BAOR and the RAF's Harrier operations.

The RAF in 1989 had the aircraft it needed but was on the brink of a weapons revolution with that aforementioned series of new weapons and sensors in the wings. For the Counter-Air mission, JP.233 was on the brink of service, ALARM was progressing to completely change the SEAD role and to take on the Soviet tanks, Brimstone was promising sniper-like performance in a salvo-launched weapon. To direct these weapons, systems such as TIALD and new reconnaissance pod called RAPTOR were in the offing, while ASTOR's all-seeing eye orbited at 50,000ft to provide targeting information. The WE.177 nuclear weapons would soon be retired, replaced by precision weapons such as Paveway and for long range, Storm Shadow. The RAF in 1989 was acquiring new weapons and would have been well placed to take on the Soviet Horde. And then it disappeared.

The next couple of years saw the Warsaw Pact dissolve, the Soviet Union collapse and, having just concluded a major war with his neighbour, a Middle East dictator invaded his other, smaller, neighbour. Unfortunately for Saddam Hussein, he invaded a country, Kuwait, with large friends. Friends who had large armouries of weapons developed specifically to take on the Soviet weaponry that equipped Saddam's armies.

The radii of action of the five RAFG strike aircraft (including the Phantom) in service towards the end of the Cold War. The Harrier and Phantom were used for battlefield interdiction and close support while the Buccaneer and Jaguar were used for interdiction. The Tornado's longer range made it ideal for nuclear strike, counter-air and deep interdiction.

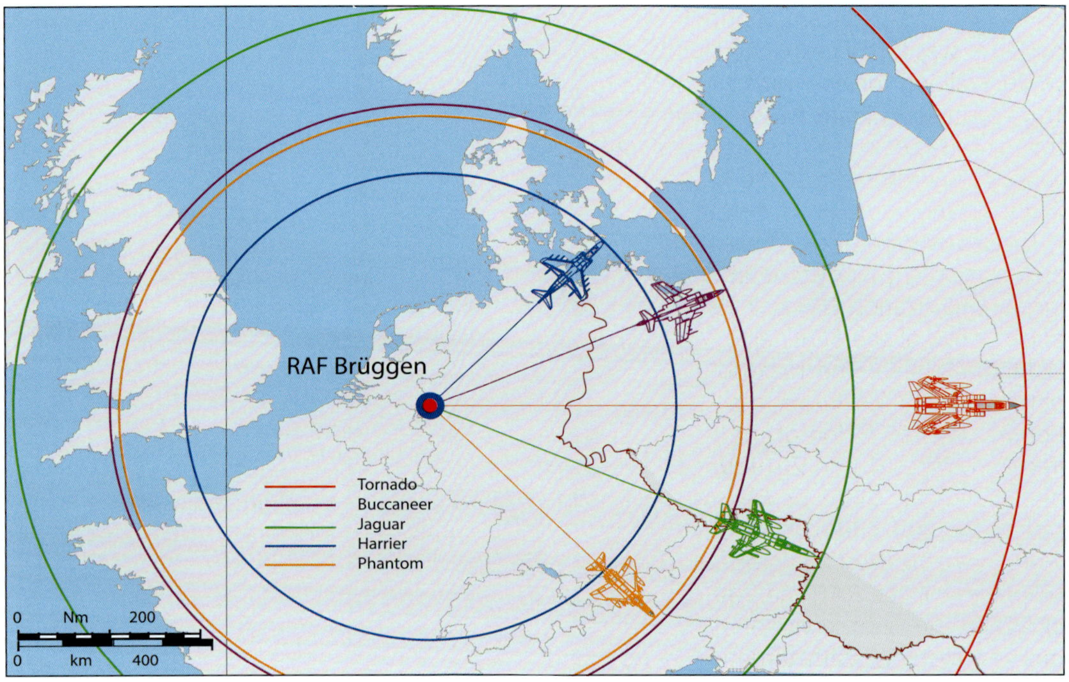

Long-range strike aircraft had concerned NATO planners with the RAF Tornado force tasked with counter-air operations against their bases in eastern Europe. Clockwise from top right: Tu-22M *Backfire*, Sukhoi Su-24 *Fencer*, Yakovlev Yak-28 *Brewer* and Tupolev Tu-22 *Blinder*. The *Blinder* and *Brewer* were being superseded by the more capable *Backfire* and *Fencer* by the end of the Cold War.

Lessons were learned, such as that RAF speciality, low-level weapons delivery, turning out to be very dangerous in a landscape with little terrain to hide behind, never mind avoid. The liberation of Kuwait proved to be the sole outing for JP.233, but the Paveway and ALARM proved to be excellent weapons. The next 10 years saw withdrawal from Germany, withdrawal of older systems, delays to the new and reduction of forces in the West to provide a peace dividend. The RAF became involved in the post-colonial equivalent of colonial policing, now called peace keeping, in Iraq, Sierra Leone and the former Yugoslavia.

The War on Terror

Catching up on my viewing after two weeks offshore and stopping between recordings to make a brew, I noticed the news was on at a very odd time. The rolling strap line stated that 'A light aircraft has crashed into the World Trade Center.' Thinking this was an action film, I continued to watch. As the coverage progressed, a Boeing 767 flew – *flew* – directly at full speed, into the other tower. 'That's no light aircraft.'

Less than a month later, on 7 October 2001, US, Australian, Canadian and UK forces, plus the Northern Alliance, were in action against the Taliban forces in Afghanistan. What became known as Operation Herrick lasted until 2014, becoming one of the longest wars in British military history. For the RAF, Herrick saw close air support become the primary task of fast jets, with an increase in the support of troops in contact. What became known as the War on Terror was further expanded in March 2003 when coalition forces invaded Iraq, Operation Telic, ousting Saddam Hussein and setting in train a series of armed engagements against various insurgents across the Middle East and Afghanistan.

These saw the RAF's first use of new kit such as Maverick and Brimstone in operations that included Operation Ellamy in Libya from 2011 and the use of the Sentinel R.1 to track Boko Haram in Nigeria. The Tornado's career culminated in Operation Shader, the RAF's participation in the destruction of the Islamic State of Iraq and the Levant in 2019. Variously known as ISIS, Islamic State or *Daesh*, this organisation had also pretty much stated that they would bury the West and proclaim a worldwide caliphate. For the RAF, the War on Terror heralded the entry into service of many new weapons and systems, with targeting sensors and precision, low-collateral damage weapons used in preference to traditional dumb iron bombs.

Imperial Affairs

Colonial policing had been a constant task for the RAF from its inception and after World War Two continued to be a major role, whether as piggy-in-the-middle (and using Japanese aircraft) in French Indochina or as a major combatant in Malaya or Kenya. These conflicts saw air power play a similar role in postwar colonial warfare to that it had in the pre-war era, although wartime experience and weaponry made it a faster, more devastating affair, with Hawker Hunters rather than Harts.

Malaya and Kenya saw strategic bombers in action while in Aden it was guns and rockets, as used in Normandy. A colonial affair of a somewhat different nature; full-scale war between nation states, that involved the RAF in Counter-Air and SEAD before it had the necessary equipment, but what the Falklands War did do was give the RAF its first martial experience of smart weapons.

Typhoon to Typhoon

The Cold War and the War on Terror that followed saw the aircraft come full circle from superannuated fighters through dedicated ground-attack aircraft to true multi-role aircraft where the weapons, also transformed from mass destruction through local area to precision. For the Royal Air Force, *Typhoon to Typhoon* sums up that transition.

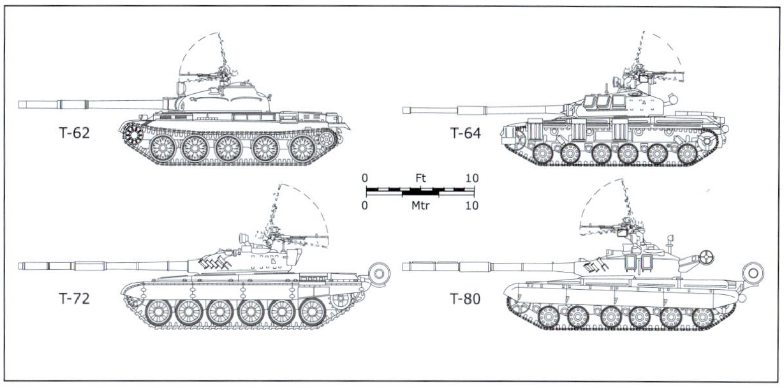

Above: The tip of the Soviet spear was the tank force. By the 1980s the primary threat would have been the T-64 and T-72, both with a smoothbore 125mm gun and composite armour. These tanks were on a par with, if not superior to, the early M60, Leopard and Chieftain operated by NATO. The gas turbine-powered T-80 was considered equal to the initial model M1 Abrams and Challenger 1.

Below: The S-75 Dvina (SA-2 *Guideline*), having brought down Gary Powers' U-2, proved to be the nemesis of US strike aircraft in Vietnam. The *Guideline* drove the world's strike aircraft to low-level, but as the Israeli Air Force found, it drove them into the face of the Shilka and *Gainful*. *DoD via Terry Panopalis*

Bottom: A fine view of a ZSU-23/4 Shilka in travelling order. The gun laying radar is folded down behind the turret. The Shilka and its four 23mm cannon was ideal for air defence in the 1970s but its lack of an early warning radar and 23mm guns meant it was outdated in the 1980s. It was outranged by the 30mm cannon that appeared on NATO aircraft and vehicles in the 1980s. *DoD*

2 Low Attack for the RAF

'Let us see what they will devise if left to themselves.' Air Marshal FJ Linnel, Controller, R&D, 29 Jan 1942

'...of value...for annoying tank crews.' Group Captain Drury, A&AEE, October 1942, recommending fitting .303 machine guns to ground attack aircraft.

The Royal Air Force has been involved in ground attack, not always willingly, from its formation in 1918. The British Army were never happy about the RAF's support but during World War Two army support evolved into an efficient machine for supporting the troops. The weapons and tactics for supporting the troops on the ground; battlefield support, precision strike and interdiction have their origins in the Second World War.

As noted above, the RAF could stand accused of using hand-me-down types for ground attack but there is a very good, and practical, reason for this. The main influence on the habitual use of interceptors for ground attack was that the British aircraft industry was at maximum capacity developing and building fighters and bombers. The Air Ministry's view was that developing a new type would affect the current work on types currently in development and, more importantly, production. This was also the case during the Cold War, at least until the adoption of Flexible Response.

Before moving on to the postwar era that is the subject of *Typhoon to Typhoon*, it would be beneficial to outline how the RAF (and other services) approached the ground support role and show how little has changed in the intervening years: Hawker's Typhoon was designed as a fighter and became a ground attack aircraft as was Eurofighter's Typhoon.

Jabo Ascendant

When it came to a bespoke ground-attack aircraft for British service, two types come to mind; the Blackburn Skua for the Fleet Air Arm and the Hawker Henley for the RAF. The Skua was a dive-bomber/fighter that was intended to intercept long-range bombers and reconnaissance aircraft far from shore bases as well as operating as a dive bomber against ships. The Henley was designed as a two-seat light

Spectre's Grandad. The Dyott Battle Plane of 1917 was to mount a 12-pounder Davis gun transversely in the forward fuselage. The Battle Plane was intended to be a flying dreadnought armed with five or more Lewis guns in a fighting compartment in the nose. By removing all but one of the Lewis guns, the Davis gun and loaders could be accommodated. The intention was to put the Battle Plane in a bank to port and fire the Davis gun at German strong points.
Luca Landino

Developed to destroy tanks in the Western Desert, the Hurricane IID was armed with a Roll-Royce 40mm cannon but this was superseded by the 40mm Vickers S gun. The 3in RP took over from the cannon as the RAF's anti-tank weapon. Its effectiveness is debated to this day. Hurricane IID prototype Z2326 was originally built as a IIA. *Blue Envoy Collection*

bomber/dive bomber to meet Air Ministry Specification P.3/34, using components of the Hurricane fighter but proved less than satisfactory in the ground support role. Much of this was down to it lacking dive-brakes, bomb crutch and sighting systems, standard kit for the dive bomber role, so it was relegated to target tug duties while the Hurricane took on the ground attack role.

In contrast, the Skua did have dive brakes, bomb sights and bomb crutch, so was a capable dive bomber and performed well until it encountered German fighter aircraft (which it was never intended to take on) and served until 1941. Like the Henley, Skuas served as target tugs, and as training aircraft.

Why were dive bombers required? Dive bombing allowed precision attacks on point targets and the type was particularly favoured for attacks on shipping. For a land war, they could in theory hit tanks and artillery pieces and the German Ju 87 – Sturzkampflugzeug (*Stuka*) – was the archetype of the dive bomber. Like the Hurricane and Skua it suffered at the hands of enemy fighters and was replaced by the Fw 190. Again, as in the case of the Hurricane, the Stuka became a tank-hunter. The Ju 87G-1 gained a more powerful engine, heavier armour – a bathtub similar to the IL-2 *Shturmovik* – and underwing pods each fitted with a 37mm BK 3.7 with 12 rounds per gun. These gun pods were also fitted to earlier Ju 87D and the type was successful in the ground attack/anti-tank role until Allied air superiority made its operations untenable and it was replaced by Fw 190A and G *Jabos*.

By January 1942 the Air Staff were aware that they were somewhat lacking the capability for the close support role demanded by the army. The Hurricane was being superseded as an interceptor and used for close support from mid-1941 while the Mosquito was under consideration for ground attack as it had been 'reported upon favourably in view of its handling close to the ground'. The thinking was that the Hurricane could be improved by adding more armour while the Mosquito (at this point in 1941/42 an unarmed bomber, with the fighters still in development) could be fitted with a pair of 40mm cannon. Oddly enough Captain Liptrot, AD/RDT1, who championed a twin-engined type for low attack, was unaware of the Low Attack Mosquito until December 1942.

The Hurricane IIC was fitted with four Hispano II 20mm cannon and wing racks for bombs, 500 lb (227kg) or 250 lb (113kg),

The 6pdr Molins gun, seen here on its wheeled carriage (with loader) alongside a Tsetse Mosquito of RAF Coastal Command. Earlier in its career the Mosquito was discussed as a possible Low Attack Aeroplane, armed with three 40mm Vickers Class S guns. The Molins gun was mainly used against ships and U-boats. *Crown Copyright*

becoming known as the Hurribomber. These conducted operations over northern France and the Low Countries but are best known for their service in the Western Desert and Far East. The Hurricane IID was a dedicated anti-tank variant that dispensed with the Hispano cannon, replaced with a single .303 Brownings (excellent for annoying tank crews apparently) firing tracer to provide aiming cues for the main armament. The Hurricane IID and IV were armed with a pair of 40mm Vickers S guns in underwing pods with 12 or 15 rounds per gun, depending on the variant. The guns proved effective against vehicles in North Africa, and were accurate, especially the high explosive (HE) rounds whose ballistics were similar to the .303 rounds fired for aiming. The armour-piercing rounds were heavier and thus slower, tending to drop more than the HE. The Hurricane IIC lacked armour, which was addressed in the Mk.IV with its low attack wing that could carry bombs, S-gun or eight 3in RP-3s but by the time it entered service in 1944 it was outclassed in the European theatre and being superseded by the Hawker Typhoon. The vulnerability of the Hurricane towards the end of its service in western Europe was graphically described by Pierre Clostermann in *The Big Show*.

Another type that came to the fore in ground attack in the Western Desert and Italy was the Curtiss P-40 series with the Tomahawk and Kittyhawk being used by RAAF, RAF, RCAF and SAAF units of the Desert Air Force. Used initially as a fighter to replace Hurricanes, from mid-1942 the P-40D Kittyhawk was not used as fighter-bomber armed with two .50 Cal M2 machine guns in each wing and up to 2,000 lb (907kg) of bombs. The Kittyhawk also served in the Far East in the India/Burma Theatre and with the RAAF in the New Guinea campaign until replaced by the P-51 Mustang.

It may have been outclassed in Europe, but the Hurricane IIC soldiered on in the Far East. Two armourers, resplendent in battered slouch hats, load 20mm rounds for the Hispano cannon into HW557 K of No.28 Sqn, Sadaung, Burma in early 1945. The two hatless men working on a camera show that this was a tactical reconnaissance 'Tac R' Hurricane. *Blue Envoy Collection*

Casting an Eye on the Enemy

The lack of a dedicated ground attack aircraft prompted the British to look at developing a Low Attack Aeroplane for the RAF and as a start, examine other forces and their weaponry. Captain Liptrot notes that the Henschel Hs 129 has lower performance, range and less armament that that demanded for the British Low Attack Aeroplane: 2 x 15mm, 2 x 7.9mm guns in the forward fuselage and a 30mm cannon in a ventral fairing as an alternative to a bombload. In reality the early Hs 129 carried 2 x 7.92mm MG 17 machine guns and 2 x 20mm MG 151/20 20mm cannon. The ventral 30mm cannon was correct, a MK 103 was fitted, but a BK 3.7 37mm cannon or in the case of the Hs 129B-3/Wa, a BK 7.5 75mm cannon. It could carry four 50kg (110 lb) bombs on a ventral rack and one 50kg bomb under each wing.

Continuing his analysis, Liptrot noted that the forward fuselage, including the cockpit is 'built up of armour plate spot welded' and this section was connected to the stressed skin rear fuselage 'via the blast tubes for the 15mm guns'. The bullet-proof windscreen was curved and 'about 3" thick' which was not the case as it was a flat plate canopy. The lack of dive brakes appears to have intrigued Liptrot and uses information from a Russian document that stated that the Hs 129 made diving attacks at around 45° and that 'if the dive is done at higher speeds aiming is inaccurate.'

Another aircraft that may have had some influence on the Air Staff's thinking was the Russian Ilyushin IL-2 Sturmovik. A heavily armoured – and armed – ground attack aircraft used by the Red Air Force throughout the Great Patriotic War and into the 1950s. Initially a single-seater, the predations of German fighters saw the two-seater with rear gunner developed. This first saw action in late October 1942 initially as outer defence for formations of single seaters.

The IL-2 was armed with up to 600kg (1,320 lb) of bombs, up to eight RS-82 rockets, two VYa-23 23mm cannon and two ShKAS 7.62mm machine guns plus a flexible UBT 12.7mm machine gun in the rear cockpit, but some were modified to carry a NS-37 37mm cannon under each wing at the expense of bombload. The original IL-2 was mainly of wooden construction, although the engine and cockpit (not the rear gunner!) were enclosed in an armoured tub that formed the structure of the forward fuselage and was proof against small arms fire. Later versions

Henschel's Hs 129B was in service with the Luftwaffe in the North African and Russian theatres. Heavily armed and armoured, the Hs 129 might well have been the Air Staff's Low Attack Aeroplane. This example, FE-4600, was evaluated by the USAAF at Freeman Field, Indiana. *DoD*

had Duralumin wings instead of wood, but the armoured structure meant that its weapons load was much less than a Typhoon or P-47 Thunderbolt. Nor was the IL-2's accuracy particularly great, although when used in numbers against large *panzer* formations its effect was devastating. Over 36,000 IL-2s were built by the time manufacturing ceased in 1945, replaced by the IL-10.

As noted above several fighters, not just the Hurricane, were being earmarked for 'low attack wings' and possibly the most famous of these was the P-51A Mustang that was modified as a dive-bomber/ground attack type. Its origins lay in the RAF's use of the Mustang I in Army Co-operation squadrons from early 1942, including over the Dieppe landings in August 1942. The Mustang's Allison V-1710 engine was at its best at lower altitudes and the Mustang performed well in the Army Co-operation role for the British and through various subterfuges by the Americans to obtain funding, the P-51 was modified to become the A-36 Apache. The changes were mainly to the wings which were strengthened and fitted with bomb shackles and dive brakes. Armament included two Browning M2 .50 Cal machine guns in each wing and one M2 each side of the nose, synchronised to fire through the propeller arc. The A-36 could also carry up to 1,000 lb (454kg) of bombs on wing hardpoints.

The A-36 Apache was a formidable, accurate dive-bomber and ground-attack type, operating in the Sicilian and Italian campaigns as well as in the China-Burma-India theatre. It was vulnerable to ground fire due to its ventral radiator for the liquid-cooled engine and so by mid-1944 the A-36 had been replaced in the European theatre by the more robust, and more heavily armed, Republic P-47 Thunderbolt.

Having watched the Hurricane perform in the ground attack role in the Western Desert, the type was found wanting in the western European theatre. Another Hawker aircraft took over the role having been found to be less than ideal as an interceptor but superb at low altitude, conducting 'Rhubarb' and 'Ramrod' raids over northern France and the Low Countries. While the Typhoon did not meet the high-altitude interceptor requirement and suffered a number of technical difficulties, by mid-1942 it was being fitted with racks to carry a 1,000 lb (454kg) bomb under each wing. These 'Bomphoons' entered service in September 1942 and a year later the Typhoon was fitted with four 3in RP-3 rockets under each wing which combined with the four Hispano Mk.II 20mm cannon provided a formidable air-to-ground capability.

The 3in (76mm) Rotated Projectile RP-3 was derived from the 3in Unrotated Projectile that was developed for use in Z Batteries, an anti-aircraft weapon that fired rockets from a mobile launcher. The rocket was powered by a 3in (76mm) solid rocket motor (hence the name) and barrage fired at enemy formations. The 3in UP was fitted with a high explosive warhead, with the fuze triggered by a photo-electric cell. The 3in solid rocket motor was used as the basis for the 3in Rotated Projectile (RP-3) that was fitted with either a 60 lb (27kg) HE warhead or a 25 lb (11kg) armour-piercing warhead. Four rectangular fins imparted spin on the rocket to stabilise it in flight but being unguided, accuracy was dependent upon the launch aircraft maintaining a steady course during the launch. The RP-3 was used on a variety of RAF aircraft ranging from the Hurricane to the Consolidated Liberator, the latter for anti-submarine use but it was its use by the

The 'Strafe masters'. When it came to attacking ground targets and being able to look after themselves in air combat, there was not a lot better than a Typhoon IB – until the Tempest V entered service. The original swing-role fighters these were arguably the first true multirole fighters. *Blue Envoy Collection*

Hawker Typhoon that brought it to fame in the Normandy campaign.

The Typhoon was a key type in the Second Tactical Air Force (2TAF) that was formed in June 1943 to support the forthcoming invasion of Europe and was operated from austere front-line strips called Advanced Landing Grounds near the front and saw the introduction of the 'Cab Rank' system whereby fighter bombers such as Typhoons could be directed onto a target by an RAF ground controller attached to the units on the ground. On receiving a call, Typhoons would take off from the Advanced Landing Grounds (or might be airborne in the vicinity) and be guided onto the target by the ground controller, if follow-up attacks were required more Typhoons would take off to provide a rotating but constant presence over the battlefield.

While there is an ongoing debate as to the efficacy of the 3in RP-3 in combat against tanks, a barrage of rockets from a flight of Typhoons had a devastating effect on German morale, forcing many vehicles to be abandoned, most famously at the Falaise Pocket in August 1944. Later research has suggested that the PIAT destroyed more panzers that the RP-3, but the sight of a salvo of eight RPs leaving the wings of a Typhoon would have more impact on the Wehrmacht than the clunk of a PIAT.

In an odd parallel, the Luftwaffe came to similar conclusions as the RAF and USAAF – a fighter can make a good ground attack aircraft, with the Germans applying the name Jagdbomber (*Jabo*) to the role. The Fw 190 A-3 was fitted with ventral and underwing bomb racks for 500kg (1,102 lb) of bombs, while the later Fw 190 F-series could carry up to 750kg (1,653 lb) of bombs.

As the Allies closed in on the Reich, *Jabos* worked hard, especially during the Battle of Berlin against the Russians and against the Western Allies in Operation BODENPLATTE on 1 Jan 1945. As related in Chapter 5 had BODENPLATTE been launched on the same day as the Ardennes Offensive as intended, that operation might have met with more success, in the short term at least.

Armourers slide 3in RPs onto the launch rails of a Typhoon IB of No 247 Sqn at an Advanced Landing Ground in Normandy June 1944. Despite the effort to start development of a Low Attack Aeroplane, Hawker's Typhoon filled that niche with ease. The Typhoon could also hold its own when faced with German fighters. *Crown Copyright*

The fighter bomber was also pivotal to campaigns in the Far East and Pacific where the RAF was still using the Hurricane, with bombs and rockets in the India/Burma theatre. Another type being used for ground attack in the Far East was the Vultee A-31 Vengeance dive bomber. These were supplied to the RAF and, deemed unsuitable for operations in Western Europe, were used from early March 1943, playing a key role in the defence of Imphal and Kohima. The RAAF also used the Vengeance but found it less than ideal and the Kittyhawk was considered more useful as it could carry a similar bombload and strafe targets while able to look after itself against Japanese fighters.

The interesting aspect of the Vengeance is that it was the only designed from scratch ground-attack aircraft acquired by the RAF; who took over l'Armée de l'Air's order in 1940 when the dive-bomber was considered a necessity for future RAF operations. The other aircraft that served in the ground-attack role were either re-roled fighters and interceptors (Hawker's Hurricane and Typhoon or Westland's Whirlwind) or light bombers (Bristol Bisley/Blenheim Mk.V or Martin Baltimore).

In the island-hopping campaign by US forces in the Pacific, fighter bombers such as the US Marine Corps' Vought F4U Corsairs were widely used and capable of carrying up to 4,000lb (1,814kg) of bombs or eight 5in (127mm) rockets in addition to six M2 0.5in machine guns. In Royal Navy service the Corsair also conducted ground attack missions against the Kriegsmarine in Norway, but mainly on Japanese targets in Indonesia and across the western Pacific as the Allies moved in on the Japanese Home Islands.

No discussion of RAF fighter-bomber operations in World War Two would be complete without mentioning the formidable twins – Mosquito and Beaufighter. Bristol's Beaufighter was conceived as a long-range heavily-armed fighter that was to use as many components as possible from the Beaufort torpedo bomber coupled with a pair of Bristol Hercules engines. The resulting machine saw initial service as a night fighter with Fighter Command but as more became available, Coastal Command acquired it and used it to great effect as a long-range fighter and strike aircraft, famously by the Banff Strike Wing operating up and down the coast of Norway. With its four 20mm Hispano Mk.II and six .303 Brownings, combined with eight RP-3 rockets or 500lb (227kg) of bombs, the Beaufighter packed a punch.

The Mosquito arrived in ground-attack from the bomber role, originally conceived as a fast, unarmed bomber it became a nightfighter before conversion into a fighter bomber. For this role the FB.VI was fitted with wing racks for up to 1,000lb (453kg) of bombs or eight RP-3s plus another two 500lb (227kg) bombs in the bomb bay. The FB.XVIII, also known as the Tsetse was fitted with the 6-pdr Molins gun with 25 rounds, but this was mainly used in the anti-shipping role rather than ground support. The Mosquito was also one of the types intended to carry the Highball anti-shipping weapon.

One notable operation where the RAF was employed in ground support of the troops on the ground was around Caen in July 1944. Over 2,000 heavy and medium bombers of the RAF (over 1000 from Bomber Command) and USAAF supported the artillery bombardment of German positions around Caen.

By the end of the war the RAF had a range of aircraft available for ground attack and since 1939 had shown that just about any aircraft could be employed as a ground support type. True, any type could be used for ground attack, even training aircraft dropping grenades on

Vought's F4U Corsair could be described as the Typhoon of the Pacific. Used by US Navy, US Marine Corps, Fleet Air Arm and Royal New Zealand Air Force, the Corsair was superb in the ground attack role. This Marine Corps F4U unleashes 5in (12.7cm) rocket projectiles against Japanese positions on Okinawa in June 1945. *Lt David D Duncan*

These aircrew from No 16 Sqn South African Air Force and No 227 Sqn RAF await their next mission from Biferno, Italy. This Beaufighter Mk.X is armed with eight 3in RPs fitted with 25 lb (11kg) armour-piercing heads. Compare these with the 60 lb (27kg) rockets on the ground to the left of the group. The ports for two of the four 20mm cannon can be seen under the nose. *Crown Copyright*

south coast invasion beaches in 1940, but was a bespoke ground attack aircraft required? That was the basis of the Air Ministry's specification for a Low Attack Aeroplane.

The Low Attack Aeroplane

The Air Staff was asked for a specification that covered a Low Attack Aeroplane and Ministry of Aircraft Production (MAP) was advised that this should be issued to a restricted list of companies. The capacity question – a firm's ability to undertake development and production – saw Air Marshal FJ Linnell, Controller R&D (CRD); NE Rowe, Director of Technical Development (DTD) and Captain RN Liptrot, Assistant Director, Research and Development (Technical), (AD/RDT.1), discuss which company could best undertake the development of the Low Attack Aeroplane. MAP was well aware that developing new designs took time and manpower, neither of which should be spared, so by 16 February 1942 MAP had drawn up a list of companies that would have capacity: those 'running out of development work'.

De Havilland were fully engaged with the Mosquito and E.6/41 that ultimately became the DH.100 Vampire. Avro could develop and produce the Low Attack Aeroplane instead of the Anson but had their hands full developing the Lancaster. Boulton Paul had no new designs in production but were deemed to be too slow at developing their designs. Armstrong Whitworth appear to be out of favour with MAP due to their 'experience with the Albemarle' while General Aircraft had no experience in fitting armament in aircraft. Airspeed were busy with the Horsa glider as in the light of British experience at the hands of the Wehrmacht's airborne forces, gliders were rightly seen as crucial to future operations. That left Percival Aircraft and Phillips & Powis, aka Miles Aircraft. Percival's experience with combat aircraft was considered insufficient but when Phillips & Powis were discussed, they were described as being able to produce new aircraft designs quicker than anyone.

Air Marshal FJ Linnell, CRD, advised that the specification should be issued to Airspeed (despite their work on Horsa) and Phillips & Powis. The specification was never numbered, but for some reason has become linked to F.6/42 a 1942 specification that called for a fighter aircraft to match the Fw 190 and replace the Hawker Typhoon/Tornado/Tempest, but possibly indicative of the Air Staff's reliance on fighters for ground attack. Evidence for these being separate specifications has been found in a letter dated 7 September 1942 from NE Rowe the DTD at MAP to the engine companies which covers the requirements for 'a) A single seater high performance day fighter to Specification F.6/42.' and 'b) A single seater ground attack fighter, design study only.'

The initial thinking was for an aircraft with better armour and armament than the Hurricane and short field performance, landing in less than 600yds (549m). All this would require a large aircraft with a correspondingly large wing fitted with full span flaps, all of which would reduce the type's manoeuvrability and lead to an aircraft bigger than the Mosquito. Not the 'comparatively simple type they may have had in mind.' By the end of March 1942 CRD was minded that a Hurricane with the 'low attack wing' would be the best solution, which later appeared as the Hurricane IV. Captain Liptrot, on the other hand, considered a pusher type to be best for carrying the battery of heavy guns intended for the low attack type. Seems CRD was on the money.

This led to the DTD to propose that the type should be designed to the Air Staff's requirements for performance and range and 'see what's left for operational equipment'. This led to 'concessions' on the requirement that included a less severe landing requirement of 850yd (777m) and simpler production, both of which saw the demise of the large and complicated high lift devices. The added advantage was that the concessions, coupled with the 'novel' configurations would allow a much smaller and cheaper aircraft to be developed.

Late June 1942 saw the AD/RDT.1, Captain Liptrot, waxing lyrical on the subject of Phillips & Powis' proposal for a tandem wing pusher design whose small size, manoeuvrability and 'perfect forward view' would 'lend itself very well indeed to the Ground Attack aircraft'. According to Liptrot the tandem wing design was superior to the twin boom pushers for 'structural reasons' while the tandem wing allowed maximum area for high lift devices on a small airframe. Liptrot also pointed out that Phillips & Powis could develop and build new aircraft quickly and the tandem wing configuration was 'the only layout which could give the desirable operational characteristics without loss of performance'.

Liptrot's enthusiasm wasn't shared by the DTD, NE Rowe, who advised the Assistant Chief of the Air Staff (Technical Requirements), ACAS (TR), Air Marshal RS Sorley at the Air Ministry not to put too much weight on the remarks as Liptrot's observations were 'not backed by any trial design'. The VCAS, Air Chief Marshal Sir Wilfrid Freeman, did appear to share Liptrot's view and asked for 'the requirements to be put out for design studies to evolve such novel types'. By the end of July 1942 Air Marshal FJ Linnell, CRD advised that the specification was to be sent to Airspeed, Phillips & Powis and Boulton Paul and that it 'would have to be made clear that this was a competitive design and that production of any of the types submitted was not guaranteed'. Mr NE Rowe advised on 28 July that Boulton Paul should be omitted but Avro be added to the list. As for Phillips & Powis and their tandem wing, Mr Rowe stated that the specification be sent with a note about their use of the tandem wing being looked upon favourably.

Boulton Paul did receive the specification and invitation to tender when these were sent out to Airspeed, Armstrong Whitworth, Boulton Paul, Cunliffe-Owen and Phillips & Powis on 15 August 1942. The gist of the requirement was that the aircraft should carry more guns of heavier calibre than a Hurricane, be manoeuvrable, a steady gun platform and provide the pilot with an excellent view. It should be robust and hardy, wooden structure and fixed undercarriage were acceptable and it should be simple to build and be in production by January 1944. One interesting aspect was 'Emergency Exit' with provision for escape by parachute it was 'essential that he be able to leave the aircraft immediately and without difficulty'.

The first brochures arrived in the first week of October 1942. Boulton Paul proposed three designs: P.99, a canard pusher, P.100 a twin-boom pusher and the P.101, a reverse-staggered biplane with fixed undercarriage. All three were powered by either a Bristol Centaurus or a Roll-Royce Merlin X engine.

Meantime, although not on the tender list, de Havilland had been busy and submitted a variant of the Mosquito aimed at the Low Attack role. Liptrot was dismissive of this, stating on Christmas Eve 1942 that it was 'only the Night Fighter with Low Attack armour and provision

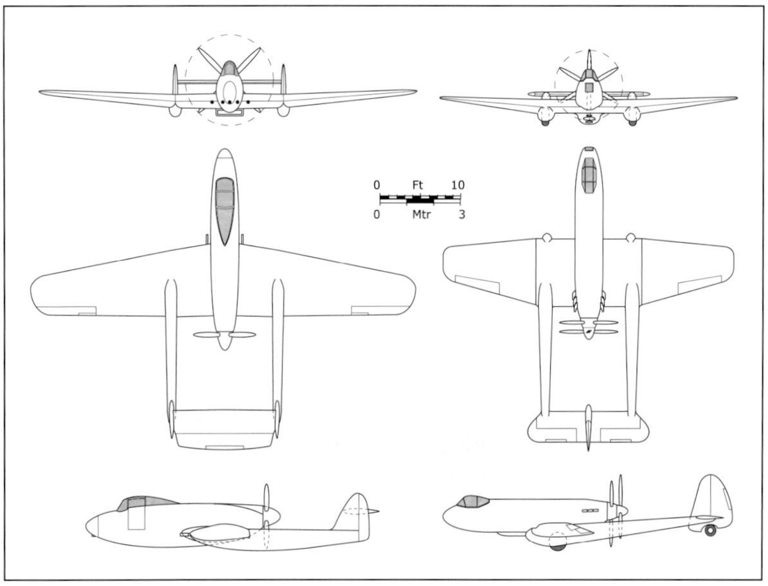

A twin boom pusher configuration was considered ideal for ground attack as it provided a good view over the nose. The Armstrong Whitworth AW.49, seen here on the left, was to use a laminar flow wing while the Boulton Paul BP.99 was to use a contraprop. Engine cooling was thought to be a potential problem with rear-engined designs.

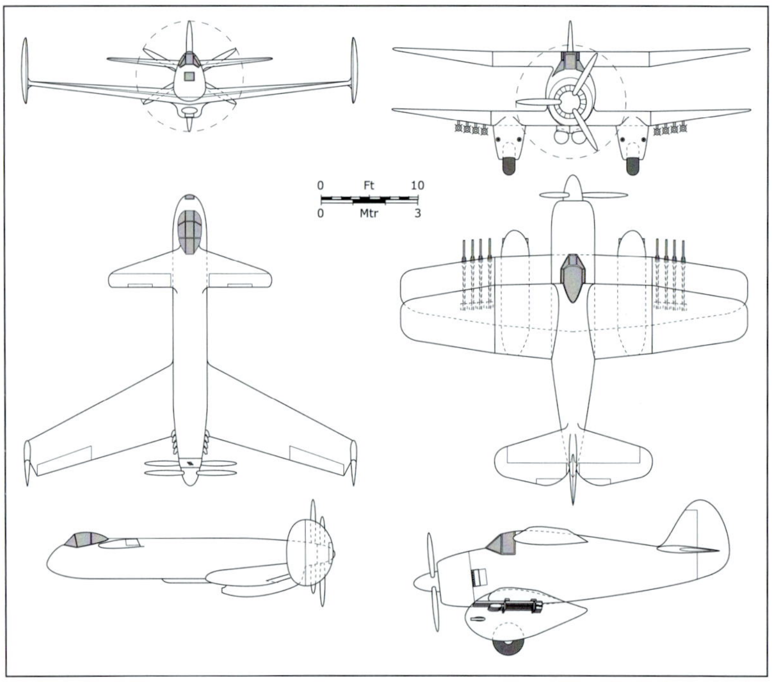

Above: Boulton Paul's designs for the Low Attack Aeroplane covered a variety of configurations. The modern-looking P.100 canard pusher contrasted with the anachronistic BP.101 reverse-staggered biplane. The BP.101 was to use many components from the company's Defiant.

for UPs' (Unrotated Projectiles – 3in rockets used for anti-aircraft work, not the RP-3 used by aircraft. Liptrot may be confusing the two) and therefore could only be viewed as an 'interim Low Attack Aeroplane'. The Low Attack Mosquito diverged from the specification, particularly in armament which four Browning .303 and four 20mm Hispano cannon, with the latter replaced by two 40mm if required. The new type was to have at least three 40mm cannon or two 40mm plus two or four 20mm, with the Brownings not being required. The Low Attack Mosquito would not meet the landing requirement, even the 850yd (777m) concession distance, as its landing run was 1,100yd (1,006m). Liptrot suggested that the features for the Low Attack role be added to Specification B.4/42, for the Mosquito replacement.

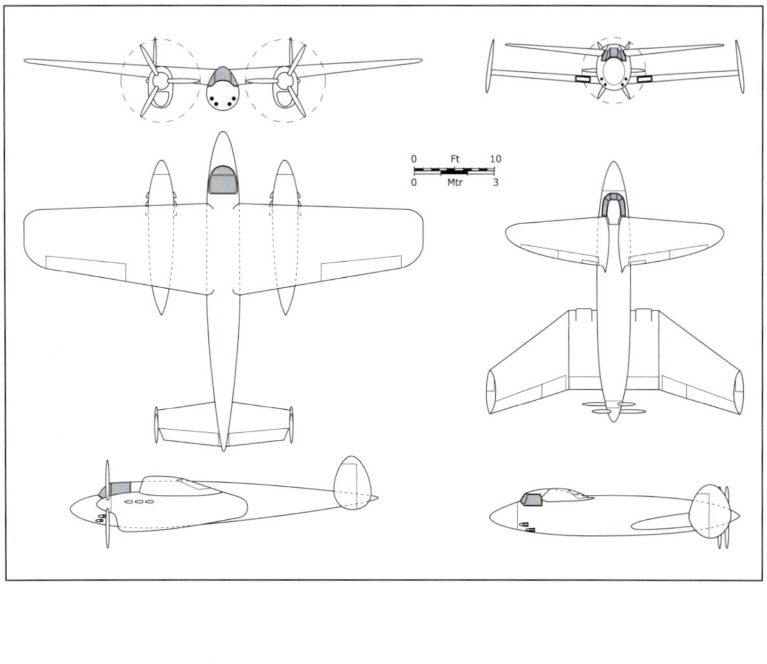

Interestingly when it came to armament and the statement that the Brownings were not required, Group Captain Drury of the Aeroplane and Armament Experimental Establishment A&AEE) was in October 1942 recommending that a pair of .303 Brownings and 500 rounds per gun be fitted on all subsequent low attack aircraft. Drury advised that the Brownings were of value not only for aiming purposes with tracer but 'also for annoying tank crews'.

Armstrong Whitworth submitted their AW.49, a twin-boom pusher powered by a Merlin X and fitted with a laminar flow wing. Liptrot suggested in early January that the Merlin 32 be installed rather than the Merlin X and pointed out that the rear-mounted engines on the AW.49, P.99 and P.100 could be difficult to cool on the ground.

The new year dawned with discussions about the urgency of the Low Attack Aeroplane as January 1943 had been stated as the production target date but experience from fighting in the Western Desert may have changed the Air Staff's priorities. Mr Rowe took the view that if there was great urgency for a Low Attack Aeroplane 'a simple twin-engined design must be the first choice, but if there is more time, then the tail first is recommended'. It appeared that Mr Rowe was coming around to the Liptrot view.

As noted above, Boulton Paul had submitted a biplane design and this had been assessed in the remarks on the design studies. These could not be dismissed as easily as might have been thought, especially in its simplicity of design, although its 'sighting angle' was inferior to that of a rear-engined type.

In total, eight proposals were submitted against the specification: from Boulton and Paul (P.99, P.100 and the P.101 biplane) the Phillips & Powis Miles M.42/43, Armstrong Whitworth AW.49, design studies by Cunliffe-Owen (one featuring up to nine 40mm cannon with seven angled downwards in the aerofoil body and one firing forwards in each outer wing) and a drawing from Martin-Baker. The Mosquito with two 40mm cannon was undergoing trials and heavier armament, the Molins 6-pounder, was also being examined. Another possibility was to convert the North American Mustang for low attack by fitting a low attack wing. This was apparently a separate design from the USAAF A-36 Apaches used for ground attack. One type that was suggested for low attack was the Tempest, but there was little enthusiasm for diverting work from its development as a fighter to develop a low attack wing.

Apparently in late 1943 the Royal Aeronautical Society (RAeS) had looked over the specification and were somewhat unimpressed as in their opinion 'it does not offer sufficient advantage over the Hurricane IV'. The Hurricane should be developed as 'an interim low attack aircraft to cover the next two or three years and a new specification should be issued on more advanced lines'. CRD advised that the Hurricane had been re-engined with the Merlin 32 'in order to obtain better performance at lower altitudes' and asked if, in the light of this, the new designs warranted further consideration.

In March 1943 a new contender appeared on the list of companies: Martin-Baker. Their design was another twin-boom pusher but this design had fixed tricycle undercarriage and a 6-pounder anti-tank gun in the long nose, giving it the appearance of an anteater. The fuselage was skinned with armour - 'The entire fuselage and engine cowling of ½in armour plate. Wt of armour plate approx. 4,800 lbs'. The aircraft had an all-up weight of 12,000 lb (5,442kg), although MAP estimated that it would be closer to 15,500 lb (7,029kg) but NE Rowe considered this 'optimistic' with 18,000 lb (8,163kg) being more likely. Propulsion was provided by a Rolls-Royce Griffon II rated at 1,760hp (kW) driving a 10ft 6in diameter propeller, all of which Rowe considered unfeasible. The large rectangular low aspect ratio wings gave the aircraft a wing loading of 25.5 lb/sq ft and the take-off run was stated to be 360yd (329m).

The 6-pounder was installed with the barrel aligned with the horizontal axis of the CoG to avoid pitch changes when the gun was fired. The gun was fitted with an automatic feed mechanism, with a magazine for 30 rounds. This is probably the mechanism devised by Molins, a manufacturer of cigarette-making machinery. The Molins Class M gun would find fame as main armament of the Tsetse variant of the de Havilland Mosquito, the FB Mk.XVIII, in operations against submarines and shipping.

How the 6-pounder was aimed was not mentioned, but the Tsetse carried a pair of Browning .303s for sighting purposes, but such guns are not shown on the Martin-Baker type, nor was the aircraft to carry any other weapons. Interestingly, given future developments, the Martin-Baker aircraft featured a novel pilot escape system in the form of a ventral trapdoor system that allowed the pilot to fall clear of the tail and propeller disc.

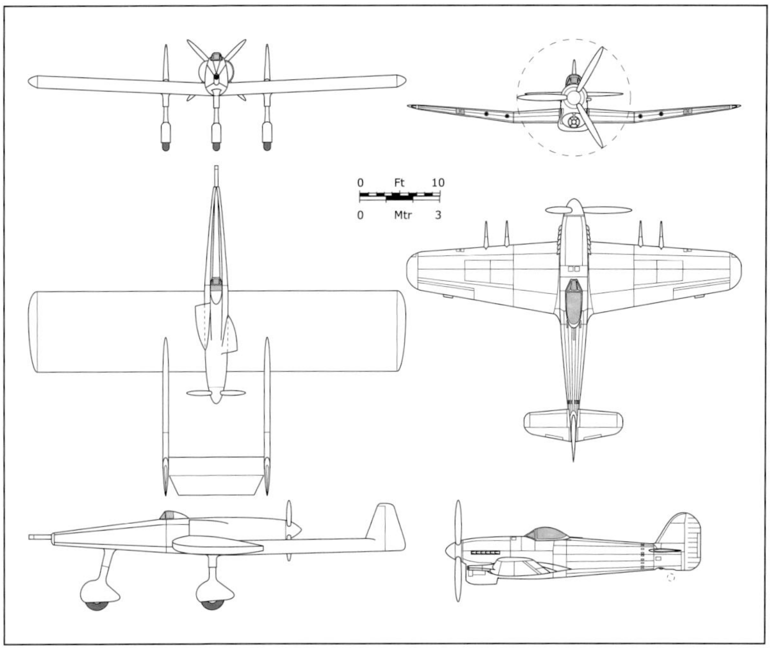

Above: Tankbuster by name and tankbuster by reputation. Martin-Baker proposed their rather peculiar Tankbuster, an armoured beast with a 6pdr anti-tank gun in the fuselage. The real tankbuster turned out to be Hawker's Typhoon IB.

By mid-May 1943 the writing was on the wall for the Low Attack Aeroplane. Hawker's Typhoon had been rushed into service as a low-level interceptor to deal with the Luftwaffe's Fw 190 and by late 1942 had shown its potential in other roles including ground attack. The Typhoon was fast, manoeuvrable and could carry two 1,000 lb (453kg) bombs in addition to its four Hispano Mk.II 20mm cannon and by September 1943 the Typhoon acquired the weapon that would make it famous: the 3in RP-3 (rotated projectile) with four on rails under each wing.

By the start of April 1943, the Director of Operational Requirements was describing the Martin-Baker type as 'not attractive' and that designing an aircraft around a single weapon that was 'only useable against one out of five or six types of targets' was 'uneconomical'. Interestingly, 30 years later, Northrop and Fairchild were doing just that with the A-9 and A-10 that were designed around the GAU-8 Avenger 30mm rotary cannon.

Liptrot's thinking was that rather than design a new low attack aircraft the Air Staff should 'make the best with such types and the TYPHOON and MOSQUITO.' As for the Martin-Baker machine, it did not 'allow for the fitment of the normal low attack weapons'. The aircraft as proposed relied on the 6-pounder and did not carry guns, bombs or rockets and to do so would make the type 'considerably overloaded'. Subsequent to this criticism, Martin submitted a second design with a 'detachable armament "bath" into which various types of armament can be fitted conveniently'. This

Opposite page, bottom: Phillips & Powis, known for rapid prototype construction and advanced designs, drew up a number of studies for the Low Attack Aeroplane based on some of their existing work. On the right is the Miles M.44, a fairly conventional twin, while the Miles M.43 employs the tandem wing of the company's Libellula.

bath could carry up to 12 x 3in rocket projectiles and could be jettisoned 'in the event of the stores igniting on the aircraft'.

On being informed that the Air Staff wasn't interested in his Tankbuster as it was too specialised, James Martin on 12 April asked CRD if the Americans might be interested and if the MAP had any objections to him showing it to the Americans. CRD replied on 15 April that he had no objections and promptly fired off a memo to Colonel HG Bunker, USAAF, of the Air Technical Section at the US Embassy 'just to warn you that you might be hearing from him in the near future'.

Air Marshal Linnell was days away from leaving the post of Controller, R+D and promoted to Deputy AO C-in-C, RAF Mediterranean and Middle East. In his letter to James Martin, Linnell wrote: 'I do not suppose I shall see you again before I leave and if not there is one thing I do ask of you. It is that you should get ahead with your own fighter with the maximum possible drive and not be led away by thoughts of Griffon editions, or 6 pounder aircraft. Unless you produce the goods soon there is bound to be another upheaval such as that we had in 1942. This is the advice of a friend – take it as such.'

The Air Marshal is referring to the Martin-Baker MB.3 that would make its maiden flight on 31 August 1942 but crashed when the Napier Sabre engine failed on 12 September, killing Captain Baker. The MB.3 was redesigned with a Griffon engine as the MB.4 but was abandoned in favour of the Griffon-powered MB.5, one of British aviation's great what-ifs.

The Air Staff cast its net widely in its search for a low attack aircraft, including examining German aircraft such as the Henschel Hs 129. This type was described in AI2(g) report No.2145, dated 6 January 1943. The Air Intelligence (AI) branch gathered the latest intelligence on enemy aircraft and passed it on to the relevant departments in the Air Ministry, RAE and MAP. In the case of the Hs 129, much of the information appears to be from German documents captured by the Soviets. Liptrot presented his view of the type based on this report, opening with 'it is interesting to note that they have accepted my often-reiterated view that the ideal layout for the duty is twin engined.'

Analysis of the Submissions

On 19 December 1942 AD/RDT.1 Liptrot presented an analysis of the various submissions for the Low Attack Aeroplane. This comprised six pages which at this point in the war and with paper being rationed, was a fairly substantial document. He conceded that his drag and weight figures were higher than the manufacturers, mainly due to his 'emphasis on simplicity of design and rapid construction' and simple high lift devices to meet a landing run of 600yd (549m).

Armstrong Whitworth

Liptrot was quite complimentary of the range of armament that the AW.49 could carry but thought the designer had not sufficiently explored alternative configurations to the twin-boom pusher. However, Liptrot stated that 'having accepted this layout, however, he has gone into the design far more thoroughly than any of the others.' Full of praise for the laminar flow wing, Liptrot was impressed by its simplicity of construction with 'relatively small amount of concentrated boom liable to be shot away, it should be less vulnerable than the more usual

Wind tunnel models of the Armstrong Whitworth AW.49 Low Attack Aeroplane. Note the unrestricted view for the pilot and twin-boom/pusher configuration. *Via Ray Williams*

This Phillips & Powis design study examined a tandem wing naval fighter armed with four Hispano 20mm cannon. A Miles Low Attack Aeroplane such as the M.43 would may have looked similar. *Via The Miles Aircraft Collection*

types.' Liptrot's criticisms of the Armstrong Whitworth AW.49 were that the twin-boom design lacked sufficient stiffness and that the engine could not be adequately cooled when running on the ground unless a cooling fan was provided.

Boulton Paul

Three configurations were proposed by Boulton Paul: a twin-boom pusher with a Griffon engine; canard pusher with Griffon engine and a conventional tractor cantilever biplane with a Centaurus engine. Liptrot ignored the biplane due to its poor view from the cockpit and 'the bad position of the armament, where firing the guns impose as heavy nose-down pitching moment'. The biplane was heavier than the other two and used many Defiant components, including its wings, which meant it could be in production sooner than the other two.

The P.99 twin-boom type was comparable with the AW.49 but was larger due to the use of the Griffon and using the fuselage nacelle rather than the wings for fuel. The bigger P.99, according to Liptrot 'does not pay for itself as regards performance' and that 'the choice of engine is not nearly so happy as the Merlin 32 would have been'. Liptrot continues his criticism of the P.99, turning to the pilot escape system, stating that the designer 'makes a great point of the arrangements for pilot's emergency exit'. On pressing a button, the floor fell away, taking the pilot and armament with it, which Liptrot viewed as 'an unwarranted piece of elaborate design and might easily prejudice the whole aeroplane'. As with the AW.49, Liptrot was concerned about ground cooling, although Boulton Paul had suggested that a fan be provided. In summing up the P.99, Liptrot saw no reason for the larger engine and larger airframe and deemed the designers' performance estimates as 'optimistic'.

Turning to the canard P.100 Liptrot states categorically that the choice of the Griffon was wrong and as with the P.99 the weight and performance estimates were optimistic. He did approve of the view from the cockpit and that the canard configuration allowed a smaller, lighter and more manoeuvrable aircraft. Liptrot considered the canard to be the better of the three Boulton Paul proposals.

Phillips & Powis

Liptrot was critical of the Miles proposals from the start 'The firm content themselves with a totally inadequate description of three possible layouts' essentially stating that the company has not provided sufficient information to 'enable any valid criticism of the designer's weight and performance estimates'.

Three types were proposed: Miles M.43, a canard with a single Griffon engine; Miles M.42, a canard powered by two Merlin 30s and the Miles M.44, a conventional twin with two Merlin 30s. This last type was proposed due to the longer time that would no doubt be needed to develop the canards. The Merlin 30, rated at 1,360hp (1014kW) was used in the Fairey Barracuda Mk.I and Fulmar Mk.II and led to the Merlin 32. Liptrot appeared to be annoyed by the lack of information from Phillips & Powis, summing up with 'I can only say that the general size and weight of the aircraft described are ridiculously low in relation to the specific requirements' which we issued as the basis to the designer.'

Cunliffe-Owen

In contrast to his remarks about Phillips & Powis, Liptrot was glowing in his praise for Cunliffe-Owen, stating that the firm had 'entered into the spirit of our enquiries on the low attack aircraft, and has made a very complete and useful design study'. The company had investigated a number of configurations: tractors, pushers, twin-booms, canard, shaft-driven tractors as well as 'unorthodox arrangements' but for various reason settled on two types. These were a small single-engined tractor type with a 42ft (12.8m) wingspan whose only unorthodoxy was that the pilot was 'accommodated below the fuselage' and a conventional twin-engine type.

Liptrot thought that the single-engined type could meet the requirement 'as well as any possible single engine layout' and that despite its unorthodox layout was 'simple and perfectly straightforward'. Similarly, the twin-engined type was 'straightforward' and clean, with Liptrot pointing out that it shared its geometry with the B.4/42 Mosquito replacement. In both cases the weight estimates were 'quite unacceptable' but that was due to the designer's 'lack of contact with modern power units' or service requirements.

Concluding his appraisals, Liptrot stated that the design studies submitted 'confirm my original opinion' that high performance, coupled with simplicity of design and construction, could only be met by a twin-engined type. Following on from this Liptrot stated that the ideal layout for a low attack aircraft 'would possibly be the pusher tailless type' but the addition of a forward tail for stability and control would provide the 'necessary handling qualities'. This canard type would be smaller, more compact and therefore more manoeuvrable than any other layout. The twin-boom types were promising but the configuration had structural problems and as a pusher, had potential engine cooling problems on the ground.

Making his recommendations, Liptrot advised that of the single-engined types, the AW.49 'promises to be the best' but that was subject to solving the engine cooling problem. The safest choice was the larger twin-engined type, a low attack version of the B.4/42 or the Cunliffe-Owen design that 'could be adjusted to meet the requirements in all respects and would promise to give better performance than any of the single engined types' being proposed.

By the summer of 1943, plans for what would become Operation Overlord were being formulated. The Typhoon was showing its mettle as a ground attack type and Second Tactical Air Force was established on 1 June 1943. There was not time to develop a bespoke low attack aircraft and the RAF went with what was available: Typhoons. These proved very successful indeed. Of course, the Army had different ideas.

Intimate Support – Spectre's Father

'He suggests a peripatetic selection of half-fledged airboys, with NO army knowledge, flying odd aircraft all over the sky, can build up as coherent a picture as a trained, senior army observer.'
Brigadier JA Churchill, Deputy Director of Technical Investigations, 18 November 1943

'It seems quite obvious that opposition from the RAF would be so strong that we should only be knocking our heads against a brick wall.' Note to CD Ellis, Scientific Advisor/Army Council, by Brigadier SF Rowell, 24 November 1943

By early 1943 the tide of the war was starting to turn, and the British were planning for an invasion of occupied Europe and this would require an assault on a fortified coast, establishment of beachheads and advance into Germany. The air support techniques formulated in the Desert Campaign would be applied to any future operations. The received wisdom laid out by Brigadier G N Tuck, Deputy Director of Science in the General Staff, was that the Allies would have air supremacy from the start of any offensive but unless Germany 'succumbs to the bombing offensive or to Soviet invasion' the defeat of the Germans would require troops on the ground and they would require support from the air. That was a particularly knotty problem in need of urgent attention as there 'would appear to be [a need] to improve our methods of supporting the advance of ground forces by air action.' Brigadier Tuck had looked at the various campaigns since 1939 and concluded that 'aircraft are the least flexible of all types of war equipment' as they are designed for 'particular purpose' and not easily adapted for another. This was particularly applicable to army co-operation and Tuck proposed that the time was right to develop and 'specially made aircraft for army co-operation purposes'. RAF aircraft had bombed and strafed in support of the Army, but the time might be right for an 'assault aircraft' rather than a traditional army co-operation type. The Westland Lysander had proven less than ideal, the Bristol Bisley (ground-attack version of the Blenheim) was showing promise, but it appeared that the Curtiss Tomahawk, a fighter, was much preferred to all other types due to its high performance.

The Hurricane IIC, another modified fighter, had been used in the Western Desert in support of troops and in tank busting, but its performance was poorer than had been hoped, especially in the anti-tank role. Tuck saw parallels with the trench fighters of the Great War and described how the Sopwith Salamander was essentially a Camel fighter with an armoured underside that 'turned out to be a death trap'. While the Tomahawk had performed well, the increased armour and defensive weapons on the new generation of German vehicles meant that something with more clout was required. The type should be able to absorb the punishment from flak and the obvious answer was a 'heavily armoured slow-flying assault aircraft' and it would be 'valuable to the army' in carrying out the following tasks:

- Close support by firepower of the ground forces
- Commander's personal reconnaissance
- Neutralising enemy batteries or for observing counter-battery fire
- Breaking up enemy counter attacks and destroying enemy armour
- Air Observation Post in the 'sustained aerial observation' role

The assault aircraft should have heavy protection from ground fire, proof against anti-aircraft fire up to 20mm armour-piercing and carry defensive armament that could out-range the guns of enemy fighters, although the type would be operating 'under conditions of local air superiority'. The aircraft's primary targets were to be personnel under cover of 'earthwork defences or gun pits' with the secondary target being 'armour and concrete e.g. tanks and pillboxes'. The weaponry was to include automatic small arms or 'small fragment' high explosive weapons, anti-personnel bombs and 'weapons firing hollow-charge projectiles, e.g. rocket or Burney Gun'. Firepower was to be concentrated for maximum effect and a heavy load of guns and ammunition was desirable. As can be imagined, this level of firepower, offensive and defensive, would require a sizeable crew comprising a pilot, signals operator and three or more gunners or bomb aimers.

There was precedent for this type of ground support aircraft. American designer George Dyott had built a biplane bomber powered by two 120hp (89.5kW) Beardmore engines.

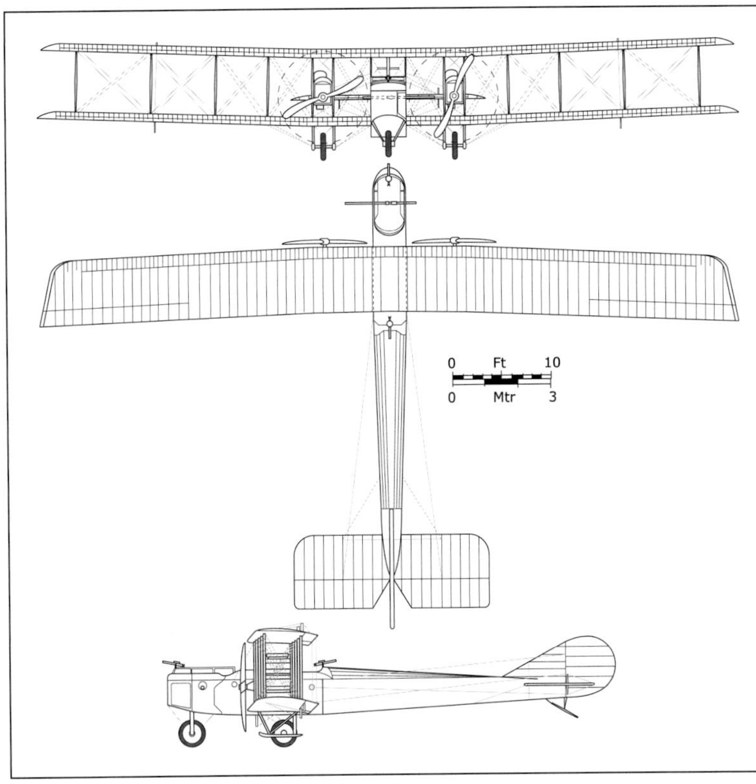

The product of the Air Ministry's views on what was a fighter, the Dyott Battle Plane was to provide a platform for up to five gunners to go toe-to-toe with German aircraft. The Air Ministry stuck to their 'guns' but the concept lost out to the 'scouts', what we now know as fighter aircraft. This variant carried a 12-pdr Davis gun transversely mounted in the forward fuselage. The gun was to be used against strong points, pill boxes and perhaps even German tanks.

The first prototype Dyott Bomber was built at Chingford in Essex for the Royal Flying Corps, making its first flight in August 1916. A second prototype was modified by fitting 230hp (171kW) Beardmore engines (almost double the power of the first prototype) and deepening the forward fuselage to accommodate four .303 Lewis guns (a fifth Lewis was in a dorsal mounting). This became the Dyott Battle Plane, aimed at the RFC's requirement for a flying dreadnought as the small single-seater scouts were not the RFC's idea of an offensive type.

The Battle Plane was further modified for the ground support role by carrying a 12-pounder Davis Gun mounted transversely in the fuselage. The Davis Gun was the original recoilless weapon and worked by firing its shell out of the muzzle as normal, with a counterweight being fired out of the rear of the weapon. The Davis Gun was fitted in the Dyott Battle Plane so that the muzzle protruded from the port side of the aircraft, with the counterweight being fired out of the starboard side. Intended for use against ground targets, the Battle Plane was to be banked into a turn to port and the whole aircraft used to aim the weapon. Aiming was helped by a co-axial Lewis gun firing tracer, a technique used for sighting large direct fire weapons since.

A Burney Gun, as suggested for the assault aircraft, was a recoilless rifle developed by Sir Denis Burney as an infantry anti-tank weapon.

Burney's weapons dispensed with the counterweight of the Davis Gun and used a ported shell casing that allowed a portion of the propulsive gasses from the propellant charge to be diverted rearwards through vents in the breach. Its official designation was Ordnance, RCL, 3.45in and fired a 3.45in (88mm) HESH (high explosive squash head) round that could be used against tanks and concrete emplacements. The Burney Gun led to the development of the BAT (battalion anti-tank), MoBAT (mobile BAT) and WOMBAT (weapon of magnesium, battalion anti-tank) used by the British Army and these could be mounted on a variety of vehicles.

This amount of firepower could only be delivered accurately if the aircraft was flying slowly enough to permit target identification and allow communication with the troops on the ground. The slow speed would also allow the aircraft to be manoeuvrable at low altitudes, also aiding gunnery. At this point in Brigadier Tuck's memo he might just show that his grasp of aeronautical matters wasn't on the same level as the Air Staff. Tuck states that the considerable weight of the armour, weapons and crew could be best carried by a slow-flying aircraft with a low ceiling. A maximum speed of 120-150mph (193-241km/h) 'should be ample and there seems no reason why reversion to the biplane or even triplane construction should not be considered'. It was also pointed out that a slow flying aircraft with heavy armament was a difficult target for an 'essentially fast fighter' citing the 'Fortress' as an example of this. All the memos and reports referenced here are dated between January and early August 1943, before the disastrous Schweinfurt/Regensburg raid of 17 August 1943 that cost the USAAF sixty aircraft with a similar number lost in the following October.

The Flakpanzer IV Wirbelwind mounted a 2cm Flakvierling 38 in a turret on a Panzer IV chassis. A forerunner of the ZSU-23/4, it was soon found wanting in range and replaced by the Ostwind with a 3.7cm Flak 43. Allied ground attack aircraft would attack these SPAAGs before hitting the tanks. *National Digital Archives of Poland*

The purpose of this aircraft would be to provide very close support, so close to friendly troops that it was called 'Intimate Support'. The General Staff were well aware that aerial bombing could be inaccurate, and the bombs carried by fighter-bombers, if they did hit, might not destroy the new generation of German tanks. To destroy these tanks and concrete pill boxes required larger bombs and these could not be dropped at low level (to ensure a hit) because the aircraft might be caught in the blast. The solution would be a low-flying 'armoured aircraft mounting close support artillery.'

What Brigadier Tuck had described is a type that would not appear until 25 years later: the AC-130E Pave Aegis version of the Spectre gunship (See Appendix 3). The General Staff's Intimate Support aircraft was to be armoured to be proof against 20mm anti-aircraft and armour piercing rounds, mount guns of sufficient calibre to disable light and medium armoured fighting vehicles (AFVs), capable of low speed and low altitude flight that would allow the guns to be accurately aimed. A further reason for the low altitude flying was to avoid heavier flak guns such as the 8.8cm Flak 18/36/37/41 series anti-aircraft guns. An over-target endurance of 30 minutes was required, which could amount to a lot of 20mm hits.

Interestingly a similar proposal had been made in 1941 by Major General Nye, Director of Staff Duties, and soon to become Vice Chief of the General Staff, to RS Sorley, ACAS(OR) at the Air Ministry. Sorley's 1941 reply concluded with what could be the aircraft designer's lament. 'It is always a bad thing to distort the natural attributes of the aeroplane to make it fulfil unsuitable and limited roles, as it always ends up in such an unsatisfactory compromise that nobody afterwards wants it.'

Another naysayer was Lieutenant-General Reade Godwin-Austen, Director of Research, General Staff, who took the view that 'We are asking aircraft to perform functions more suitable to ground weapons.' The General also voiced his scepticism of armouring the aircraft because although the fuselage could be protected 'adequate protection of its wings and tail is impossible.' As for countermeasures against the assault aircraft, the General thought smoke might 'render precision in fire effect very difficult.' As for the slow flying aspect of the Assault Aircraft, General Godwin-Austen pointed out that the slower it flew the closer it would need to be based to its objectives or to provide timely support when required. The General was a bit more enthusiastic about the assault aircraft's firepower asking 'can we guarantee equipping the aircraft with a sufficiently accurate concrete buster?' but answered his own question with 'Personally, I think that if the Burney projects develop as successfully as we hope, the answer may be "Yes".' Overall while General Godwin-Austen liked the idea, he did not think it merited submission to the Air Ministry without further examination by the Army, but also by one of the RAF liaison officers at the War Office.

How would airpower help the troops on the ground? Current types were vulnerable to ground fire and the German 20mm Flak guns, especially the four-barrelled 2cm Flakvierling 38, were seen as the primary threat to ground support aircraft. This was supported by a report from the British Military Mission in Moscow that described how attacks on heavily defended German troop formations and transport columns were carried out. Fighters and dive-bombers were not used as 'the casualties were always heavy' and the preferred tactic was level bombing from above 6,000ft (1,829m), but these rarely destroyed tanks. The Ilyushin IL-2 Sturmovik was used against enemy troops at heights between 200ft and 5,000ft (60m to 1,524m) and was armoured to withstand flak and thus enlightened, the General Staff appear quite keen on a Sturmovik-type aircraft. Oddly enough the report states that the fighting on the Eastern Front 'is nothing like as intense as that which we have met in Africa.'

By July 1943 the Assault Aircraft requirement was firming up. An RAF officer, Wing Commander Ayres completed a technical summary and Brigadier Tuck was co-ordinating the effort, including a Technical Examination of the developments the Assault Aircraft would need.

Guns would be fitted in the nose, tail, port and starboard sides of the fuselage and possibly a dorsal turret. These would be .303in, .50cal, 20mm and 'possibly a type such as a Burney gun' plus bombs, flares and 'possibly rockets'. Later, as the discussions progressed, bombs were not required as 'the limited offensive role of this aircraft does not justify the complications of installing bomb-racks and bomb-sights'. Since the aircraft 'will be in the class of the heavy bomber and therefore limited in its manoeuvrability' all weapons should be in power-operated turrets. These turrets should have the best possible downward view for the gunners who 'should also be trained observers' all issued with 'powerful optical instruments such as binoculars'.

On the question of armour, due to its 'relatively slow speed' the aircraft would be 'an easy target to flak fire and enemy fighters' especially if used offensively. Critical systems and crew stations should be armoured but 'it would not be possible to armour the control surfaces or the whole of the wing and fuselage area'. These should be designed to take severe fire without the aircraft losing its stability through the use of secondary controls. Interestingly the section on the weight of the armour remained blank, but a scribbled note requests the weight of the armour on a Vickers Wellington and the weight of a square foot of 8mm armour (as used on the Sturmovik) which is approximately 12 lb 2oz (5.5kg). Sense prevailed and by the end of September 1943 the Army was asking for armour to 'afford maximum protection to the crew, the engines, fuel tanks and other vulnerable areas'.

Even a back-of-a-fag-packet calculation showed that the amount of armour required to allow operations in daylight in the face of light flak would be excessive and therefore night capability would be required. Operation over friendly troops in daylight or over a 'wide no-man's land' out of the reach of enemy flak might be feasible, but that was more restrictive than the Army would have liked.

The next technical question under consideration was communications. To operate effectively the Assault Aircraft would need to talk to a variety of services including Army HQ, the forces they were supporting, the RAF Group Control, the fighter escort and communication between the crew and other assault aircraft. This section ends with 'it is thought probable that these communications could be manned by one operator.' Another busy chap was to look after navigation aids such as Rebecca-Eureka, IFF and 'AI (radar) or similar equipment for recording enemy fighter reaction' which would be 'of the greatest assistance for night operations'.

Once the complement was totted up, a crew of nine would be required: Pilot (RAF). Observer/Air Gunner/Navigator (also RAF), four Observer/Air Gunners (Army), two Wireless Operators and one Flight Engineer. The RAF Observer/Air Gunner/Navigator was required to help co-ordinate air operations and other support aircraft. There might even be a case for carrying a 'Commander and Staff Officer' in lieu of two of the Observer/Air Gunners, although this would be 'undesirable'. The four army Observer/Air Gunners should ideally 'represent different arms of the Army' to provide expertise on the various ground operations they would be supporting.

Truly intimate support. The Westland Apache AH.1 provides the British Army with the organic fire support Brigadier Tuck and his colleagues sought in 1943. Here an Apache unleashes as salvo of CRV7 rockets on Taliban positions in Afghanistan. *MoD/Open Government Licence*

In fact, 'supporting' was the operative word as the name 'Support Aircraft' was considered more suitable in the eyes of the RAF as 'Assault' was more associated with the Army.

Unfortunately, when the Army's ideas for a 'Support Aircraft' were submitted to the Air Ministry, the Director, Aircraft (possibly Air Marshal Bottomley, DCAS) threw it out, much to the annoyance of the General Staff. By the end of October 1943, the Army had approached the subject 'afresh from the more limited aspect of providing "eyes for the commander" by day'. This new use for a tough, long endurance aircraft was being called Sustained Air Observation. Not that this was met with a favourable response as the Air Ministry pointed out that the aircraft they currently used for tactical reconnaissance, Tomahawks and Mustangs, could do the job much better and that the Sustained Air Observation aircraft would be easy meat for enemy fighters.

This response from the Director, Aircraft, was met by a scribbled note that included a somewhat disparaging description of the RAF's Army Co-operation and their grasp of Army matters. The Deputy Director of Research wrote on 18th November and was less than complimentary about the Director, Aircraft's idea that enemy fighters posed a threat. '...nobody but a fool would launch a major offensive without a degree of local air superiority to secure this.' As for the expertise of the RAF's Army Co-operation pilots 'He suggests a peripatetic selection of half-fledged airboys, with NO army knowledge, flying odd aircraft all over the sky, can build up as coherent a picture as a trained, senior army observer.' To put it more...diplomatically...the Army took the view that a single pilot would be overworked by flying and conducting reconnaissance.

Having had the Intimate Support aircraft and the Sustained Air Observation type knocked back by the Air Ministry, Brigadier SF Rowell, Director, Technical Investigations, wrote a note to Sir Charles Ellis, Scientific Advisor/Army Council (SA/AC) on 24 November 1943, and pretty much admitted defeat. 'It seems quite obvious that opposition from the RAF would be so strong that we should only be knocking our heads against a brick wall'.

What becomes clear from these discussions is that the Army knew what it wanted; a type that could loiter over the front-line performing reconnaissance and/or air support, on demand. Unfortunately, the Air Ministry, despite what the Generals appeared to think, already knew what would be required to meet this and pointed out that the Army's ideas were unrealistic. What the RAF did provide for the Army was air superiority, the Hawker Typhoon with four 20mm cannon, eight 3in RPs and the Cab Rank system. It would be two and a half decades before the War Office's Intimate Support aircraft came into being, in the shape of the USAF's Lockheed AC-130E Spectre, specifically the Pave Aegis with a 105mm howitzer. It would take sixty years for the British Army to acquire what it had wanted all along; an organic, on-demand, heavily armed and armoured fire support platform. The WAH-64D Apache AH.1 entered Army Air Corps Service in 2004. Incidentally, it was to be proof against hits from 23mm cannon shells anywhere on its airframe just like the Intimate Support Aircraft. Happily, for the Army, the RAF were not involved in that procurement process.

3 Studied Unkindness: Replacing the Hunter

'I can't see anything worthwhile coming out of the Anglo-German study and we all sincerely hope that it will die under its own weight.' Air Commodore Ian G Esplin, Director, Operational Requirements, 14 August 1961

'Ideal replacement for the Hunter in the overseas reinforcement role.' Air Commodore EGL Millington, Central Fighter Establishment, on the Mirage IIIC, August 1962

The RAF had successfully taken interceptors and transferred them to ground attack duties but had come to a dead end with the Hunter whose replacement, the Lightning, was not particularly suited to the role change. NATO in the late Fifties was looking for a new strike aircraft to replace the FIAT G.91 and despite professing no interest, the RAF might just acquire a Hunter replacement from the process. They did, but not what they expected.

The RAF in the post was era fought a series of local wars during, and after, the retreat from Empire. The Malayan Emergency, 1948-60, saw the RAF use just about every aircraft in its inventory in the air support role during Operation Firedog. Ground attack missions were conducted with types from World War Two such as the Spitfire, Tempest and Beaufighter to modern types such as the DH Vampire and English Electric Canberra. Avro Lincolns were used for bombing suspected Communist Terrorist positions in the jungles of the Malayan peninsula. From 1963-66 the Indonesian Confrontation saw British forces deployed to the Far East to counter Indonesian incursions into the newly created state of Malaysia, whose creation had been opposed by Indonesia. The Hawker Hunter was the main ground attack type, operating from bases in Singapore

The Middle East saw many operations, most famously in Operation Musketeer in 1956. This was the first operation that involved the modernised RAF, with air support provided by Hawker Hunters, DH Venoms and Canberras,

If you go down to the woods today, you're in for a big surprise. Harrier GR.1s of No 1 (Fighter) Sqn at a dispersed WARLOC site in a West German forest. Each site could accommodate up to six Harriers and support crew. *Terry Panopalis Collection.*

The NBMR-1 process led to the FIAT G-91 light strike aircraft. This example underwent trials at Bristol Siddeley Engines and is seen here in Italian Air Force colours as MM6283 but carrying the British 'G' Registration G-45/4 for trials at Filton. *Via Phil Butler*

with bombing operations conducted by Vickers Valiants. The barren rocks of Aden formed the backdrop for another series of RAF operations with the Hawker Hunter FGA.9 being principal type used to support troops in the Radafan.

One type is common to these conflicts; the Hunter. By 1963 the Hunter F.6 interceptors had been replaced by types such as the Lightning and were converted to ground attack FGA.9s. The modifications included strengthened wings able to carry 230 Imperial gallon (1045 litre) drop tanks and a brake parachute. As ever, even before an aircraft had entered service, its replacement was being sought.

Light Strike Fighter – NBMR-1

Like Britain, France was withdrawing from its empire, leading to colonial wars in Algeria and Indochina. France had in the early 1950s attempted to produce a dedicated ground attack aircraft for overseas operations to replace the Douglas B-26 Invader and AD-4 Skyraiders. This led to designs such as the Morane-Saulnier MS 1500 Épervier and the odd-looking Potez 75. Meantime, under development in the 1950s were a series of aircraft to operate from unprepared strips, such as fields or from ramps, leading to the Sud-Est SE.5003 Baroudeur

None of these were proceeded with but by 1953, NATO had been looking at a similar capability and drew up a specification for a lightweight tactical strike fighter to operate from improvised air strips and need minimal maintenance. This became NATO Basic Military Requirement 1 (NBMR-1), issued in December 1953 and the aircraft companies of the NATO nations were invited to tender.

The Air Staff had little more than a watching brief on NBMR-1, happy to carry on with Vampires and Hunters, but British firms did submit designs such as the Folland Gnat or Avro 727. Some of the other proposals were interesting, with French companies submitting a number of studies that reached prototype stage: the Breguet 1001 Taon, Sud-Est SE.5003 Baroudeur and Dassault Étendard IV. Italian companies built prototypes of two of their proposals, the Aerfer *Ariete* and the FIAT G.91 while from the USA the Northrop N-156 was put forward. In September/October 1957 a team from the Aeroplane and Armament Experimental Establishment (A&AEE) evaluated three types at the *Centre d'Essai en Vol* at Bretigny in France as part of the NATO evaluation process. The British team of pilots and technicians flew and examined the Taon, Barodeur, Étendard IV and G-91, observing that none of the aircraft 'met the spirit of the requirement', specifically the take-off performance and take-off weight. For rough field performance 'then the Baroudeur appears to be the only contender'. If 'handling and aiming qualities were all-important, the Étendard IV is by far the best aircraft' and depending on whether 'time were available for development, the Taon could easily become a serious contender'.

If the choice 'rests upon simplicity and ruggedness' then the FIAT G-91 would 'appear to rank high' and this was what the NATO committee in charge of the requirement opted for. The G-91 entered service with the Italian Air Force and Luftwaffe, who later passed forty G-91R/4s on to the Portuguese Air Force, who used them extensively in their colonial wars, particularly Guinea but latterly in Angola and Mozambique.

Following the apparent success of the NBMR-1 process and the adoption, although not as universal as had been hoped, of the G-91, a series of NATO Basic Military Requirements emerged from NATO working parties and advisory committees. At least forty NBMRs emerged from NATO committees, covering all aspects of weaponry. Two programmes from the early 1960s era of massive retaliation go hand in glove: Hawker's P.1154 and NATO Basic Military Requirement (NBMR) 3. Although the UK had no direct interest in NBMR-3, the size of the British aviation industry meant that the UK had to have an iron in the fire. More than one iron, at least ten, depending on your definition of British.

In June 1961 NBMR-3, essentially a discussion document distributed by the NATO Advisory Committee as AC.169, replacing SHAPE GOR.3 and calling for an all-weather, supersonic, vertical/short take-off and landing strike, reconnaissance and tactical support aircraft. A snappy description that may have been a pointer to its future, but that was one of the NBMR-3 requirements. NBMR-3 was split into two: NBMR-3a (AC.169a) was the supersonic nuclear strike aircraft while NBMR-3b (AC.169b) was the same but subsonic. A related requirement, NBMR.4 and a later NBMR.22 were issued for a V/STOL transport aircraft to support the NBMR-3 fleet.

The Air Staff had no desire to be involved in NBMR-3 but kept an eye on its progress. The requirement was essentially to deliver a tactical nuclear weapon on a Warsaw Pact airfield or tank laager but the RAF wanted an aircraft for use in limited and imperial wars, a replacement for the Hawker Hunter FGA.9. They did however have an interest in V/STOL operations and at the time NBMR-3 was issued, the British were conducting two studies, which were similar to the German requirements that would lead to NBMR-3a and 3b. The first was being carried out by the Land/Air Warfare Committee, examining the general use of V/STOL aircraft and their operation. The second was by Second Allied Tactical Air Force (2ATAF) and was looking into how the TSR.2 could be used for STOL operations from dispersed sites in West Germany, which was the TSR.2's *raison d'être* and the basis of a new requirement, OR.343. By August 1961 the Defence Research Policy Committee (DRPC) recommended that a working party involving the various ministries should be set up to examine the use of VTOL and STOL aircraft in the close support role, a study that would ultimately lead to the Harrier.

The STOL aspects were taken care of by BAC's TSR.2 whose role was nuclear strike, essentially the role envisioned by the NBMR-3a type. The Air Staff were not particularly convinced by the prospect of operating such a high-performance aircraft from dispersed sites if the comments of Air Commodore RJP Pritchard, Director, Air Plans, are a summary of the Working Party's thinking. In a memo dated 9 August 1962, Pritchard stated that the dispersed sites might not be available for recovery of the aircraft after their first operation. The Air Commodore summarised the Working Party's views with 'Follow-up operations would certainly require base support and in this phase the main emphasis appears to lie in the wide choice of operating bases, rather than in true dispersal.'

A tank laager such as this British Army example would make a superb target for tactical aircraft. In wartime or a period of tension vehicles would be dispersed and camouflaged. *MoD/Open Government Licence*

Meanwhile, Air Commodore EGL Millington of the Central Fighter Establishment had been on a trip to France. During his visit to the *Centre des Expérimentations Aériennes Militaires* (CEAM) at Mont de Marsan, Millington had been given a demonstration of the Mirage IIIC, which he considered an 'ideal replacement for the Hunter in the overseas reinforcement role' especially if fitted with the Avon engine and Ferranti AIRPASS II radar, which became the Forward Looking Radar for TSR.2. The DOR, Air Commodore Esplin agreed and thought it a better option than anything that was likely to arise from the ongoing Anglo-German studies into a transonic VTOL support aircraft, which he hoped would '...die under its own weight.' He was, of course, referring to the study based on the Hawker P.1127. This summed up the RAF's attitude to the P.1127 – interesting but no use as a combat aircraft.

What really intrigued the Air Staff was the Mirage IIIV, with Esplin saying that 'We have been very interested in the Mirage 3V' although he added the caveat that 'it could also grow in weight and complexity and we might eventually find that we were having to pay too much for the ability to take off and land vertically.' Either way, Esplin appeared hopeful about the Mirage, stating 'Meanwhile the knowledge that there would be an excellent aircraft available to us in the Mirage 3V is very comforting and I am sure DCAS will regard this as his main insurance when resisting pressure from various quarters to take a sub-standard aircraft for this all-important role.' This era, early 1960s, was a time when only supersonic aircraft were considered viable as combat aircraft and a subsonic aircraft like the P.1127 was viewed as old hat, hence the Air Staff's attitude to it.

By the end of September 1961, it was becoming obvious that despite framing OR.345 around the P.1127 and 'even with the expenditure of considerable time and money' the type could not meet the full OR.345 requirement as issued in May 1960 and a rethink was required. What the P.1127 could not meet was the interceptor requirement with a speed of Mach 1.2. The P.1127's future hinged on the BS.53 engine, at that point limited to 13,500 lbf (60kN) as the Pegasus 3, and Bristol Siddeley's Stanley Hooker informed the ACAS(OR) Air Vice-Marshal Christopher Hartley that an engine, Pegasus 5, producing 18,000 lbf (80kN) would be available for the P.1127 by March 1962. Hartley pondered 'Just how useful is his aircraft likely to be?'.

By the end of November 1961, the Anglo-German activity on P.1127 had prompted some interest from the USA who would join the studies, order six P.1127 and conduct joint evaluation *if* the British and West Germans also ordered six apiece, in addition to the six already on order. The Assistant Under Secretary (Air) at the Air Ministry, RC Kent, in mid-November 1961 advised that this was an expensive course to take but the treasury was most 'unlikely to agree to the purchase...unless they have assurances from the Air Ministry that we regard it (or some form of it) as the ultimate answer to the requirement for a lightweight strike/reconnaissance aircraft.'

Esplin's view was that the P.1127 should be pursued as a study but the selection of an aircraft to re-equip the RAF should wait until 'we at least have the benefit of all the design studies and work which is going into the NBMR-3 competition.' Further to this, Julian Amery, Secretary of State for Air, on 23 November 1961

Dassault's Mirage IIIV (or to the British, the 3V) was one of the few NBMR-3 designs to take to the air. The Mirage made the last two in the NBMR-3a studies. The British viewed it as too complicated and when BAC designed their P.39, re-engined it. *Blue Envoy Collection*

Another of the NBMR-3 types that flew was the VAK 191B which began life as joint venture between Focke-Wulf and Weser-Flugzeugbau to develop the Fw 1262. Of note in this photo are the doors on top of the fuselage for the intakes to the RB.162 lift jets. *Blue Envoy Collection*

informed Harold Watkinson, Defence Secretary that 'If my fears were realised we should find ourselves saddled with an aircraft which except for short take off has an overall performance little better than the Hunter FGA.9 and which the Air Staff consider would not survive over the battlefield.'

So, what prompted this somewhat fluid situation with OR.345? The original issue of OR.345 in May 1960 should have stated that interception was a secondary role, but by November 1961, interception was becoming more important. This, according to the DCAS, Air Marshal RB Lees, was not due to the Air Staff changing its mind but 'the quality of the opposition has gone up' and proceeded to list which countries have, or were about receive, the MiG-19 *Farmer* and MiG-21 *Fishbed*.

On 1 December, at a meeting at the Air Ministry chaired by the Controller, Air, representatives from the Ministry of Aviation, Hawker Siddeley (including Sidney Camm) and Bristol Siddeley (including Gordon Lewis) to discuss P.1127 and NBMR-3, the consensus was that the subsonic aspects of NBMR-3 would be outdated before the type entered service and that a supersonic V/STOL aircraft should be developed – the P.1150. However, in Hawker Siddeley's opinion, the subsonic P.1127 could be used to gain experience of V/STOL operations. Two weeks later, OR.345 was being withdrawn and OR.356 being drawn up in its stead.

By mid-December the scheme that evolved into the Tripartite Evaluation Squadron was taking shape, with Solly Zuckermann, Chief Scientific Adviser to the MoD, sent to the US to discuss the possibilities with the USAF while Harold Watkinson was in touch with Robert McNamara, US Defense Secretary. Things were looking rosier in the P.1127 garden until on 20 December 1961 Intelligence Report No.84/61 arrived from Paris. Air Commodore GFW Heycock, Air Attaché in Paris advised that he had 'Some interesting information…from a

The first Kestrel FGA Mk.1 XS688 is seen here in the colours of the Tripartite Evaluation Squadron. It also carries Hawker Siddeley P.1127 titles on the nose. XS688 survives in the Museum of the USAF at Wright Patterson AFB, Ohio. *BAE Systems*

The EWR VJ-101C combined tilting engines in wingtip pods and lift engines in the forward fuselage. To provide supersonic performance the four RB.145 turbojets in the wingtip pods were fitted with reheat on D-9518, the X2 prototype, seen here. *Blue Envoy Collection*

reliable source concerning the West German attitude towards the P.1127 or its successors'. Apparently a German officer on a recent visit to Paris 'stated that the German Government have no further interest in the Hawker P.1127 or any derivative of that aircraft for their own air force' and that the Germans had dropped their plans for the VJ.101 VTOL fighter. Adding to the intrigue, Heycock said that this same officer was 'known to have made a carefully concealed visit of one day to the Dassault company' where he had seen the Mirage IIIV. Why this visit should be carefully concealed is odd because there was a 'continual exchange of information' between the French and Germans on NBMR-3, Mirage IIIV and the VJ.101.

By 12 January 1962 a draft requirement for a 'OR.345 Successor' was in circulation, with the major difference being that the requirement was a joint one with the Air Staff and the Admiralty, to replace the RAF's Hunters and FAA's Sea Vixens. Unfortunately, it was apparent that the Royal Navy didn't want it and were quite vocal on the matter. The Air Ministry was concerned that the Ministry of Aviation would only be interested in the subsonic P.1127 and RC Kent, AUS(A) on 19 February stated that there was a possibility that the 'Admiralty will by one means or another kill our concept of a supersonic lightweight strike fighter by studied unkindness'.

This Hawker drawing of the P.1154 shows the type armed with a tactical nuclear weapon. NBMR-3a was intended to equip the air forces of western Europe with a replacement for the F-104 Starfighter, a supersonic strike aircraft to deliver nuclear weapons onto the Warsaw Pact's installations in East Germany Czechoslovakia and Poland. *Brooklands Museum*

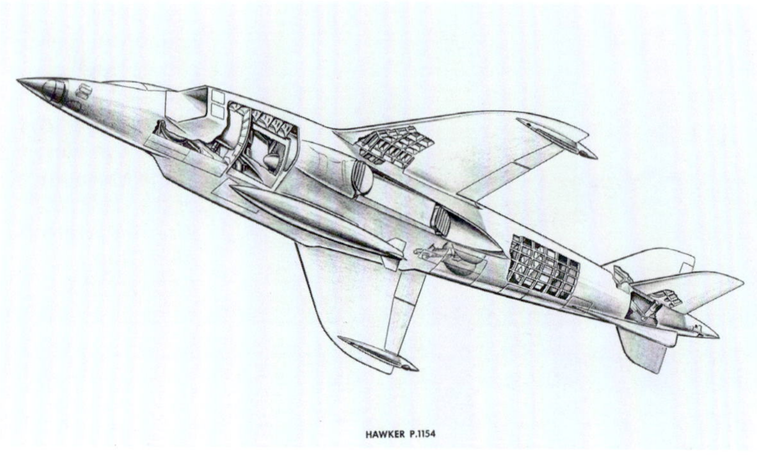

ACAS(OR) Air Vice-Marshal Hartley was also concerned and laid the blame at the door of the Ministry of Aviation for supporting three disparate programmes. These were the original Anglo-German programme based on the Focke-Wulf Fw 1161 but was essentially to show the Germans that the P.1127 is the best solution; the tripartite Anglo/German/US evaluation of the P.1127 and finally the NBMR-3 type, which the MoA suspected would fall apart leaving the French to go it alone with the Mirage IIIV.

Hartley saw two 'broad alternatives'. The first was to 'come out wholeheartedly in support of the Mirage IIIV' and use the P.1127 to gain 'early operational VTOL experience' with the Germans joining in, with the benefit that the Mirage IIIV 'would also meet the Royal Navy's needs'. Hartley also pointed out that BAC already had an arrangement with Dassault and the aircraft 'could have British engines and equipment'. The second was Hawker's proposal, the supersonic P.1154, that would meet both the RAF and RN's needs and was 'a logical development of the P.1127'. Hartley thought the Germans might be persuaded to join in its development 'though this is doubtful'.

The choice of P.1154 or Mirage IIIV was in Hartley's view 'largely political' between the Anglo-French Mirage built by BAC (as the P.39) with potentially large orders or the British P.1154 built by Hawker 'hoping to attract the majority of NATO customers, at the expense of alienating the French.' MoA's approach, according to Hartley, would either 'lead to hopeless confusion or else saddle us with an aircraft which we do not want'. Hartley hoped that the Cabinet would step in and force a decision on the MoA, with the bonus that such a move would force the Navy to toe the line and take the same aircraft as the RAF, as outlined in a letter from the First Lord of the Admiralty to the Minister of Defence back in November 1960. The result of all this would lead to the P.1154, in two different versions, that foundered for reasons described in more depth elsewhere, but the Navy got what it wanted while the RAF didn't – the McDonnell Douglas F-4 Phantom.

From December 1961, despite the RAF's stated lack of interest, the various submissions for NBMR-3 were being examined by the Air Ministry, who still required a Hunter replacement. Therefore, a brief run-down of the runners and riders would be useful. As with any aircraft procurement process, a multitude of designs were proposed and just about every aircraft design office in Europe with an interest in fast jets drew up a proposal for NBMR-3. From these proposals ten were selected for further examination under NBMR-3a (formerly Advisory Committee [AC].169a) and eleven under NBMR-3b (formerly AC.169b). Shortlists were subsequently drawn up, two types from the NBMR-3a and four from the NBMR-3b longlists. The types on these lists have become somewhat confusing and for this work many sources have been consulted and aside from the 'finalists' no consistent list of types was found.

For the supersonic NBMR-3a type, prior to drawing up the longlist, eight came from the UK (of which three came from Hawkers at Kingston, three from Vickers Supermarine at Weybridge and one each from BAC at Warton and Shorts at Belfast) and three from France (Dassault, Nord and Breguet), the Netherlands/USA (Fokker-Republic) and the USA (Lockheed) and West Germany (EWR). Hawker's submissions were at various times the P.1150, P.1154 and P.1155, all sharing the 'P.1127' configuration and four-poster vectored thrust Bristol Siddeley engines BS.100/9 for the P.1150 and P.1154 and Pegasus 5/RB.162. Vickers Supermarine's proposed the Type 583, 584 and 585, all variable-geometry types while the Warton proposal was the P.39, a much-modified Mirage IIIV. Dassault submitted the Mirage IIIV, essentially a Mirage III with eight RB.162 lift engines.

The Fokker-Republic D-24 Alliance was a mix of delta and variable geometry with a four-poster BS.100/3 engine while Lockheed's collaboration with Shorts, the CL-704, was a

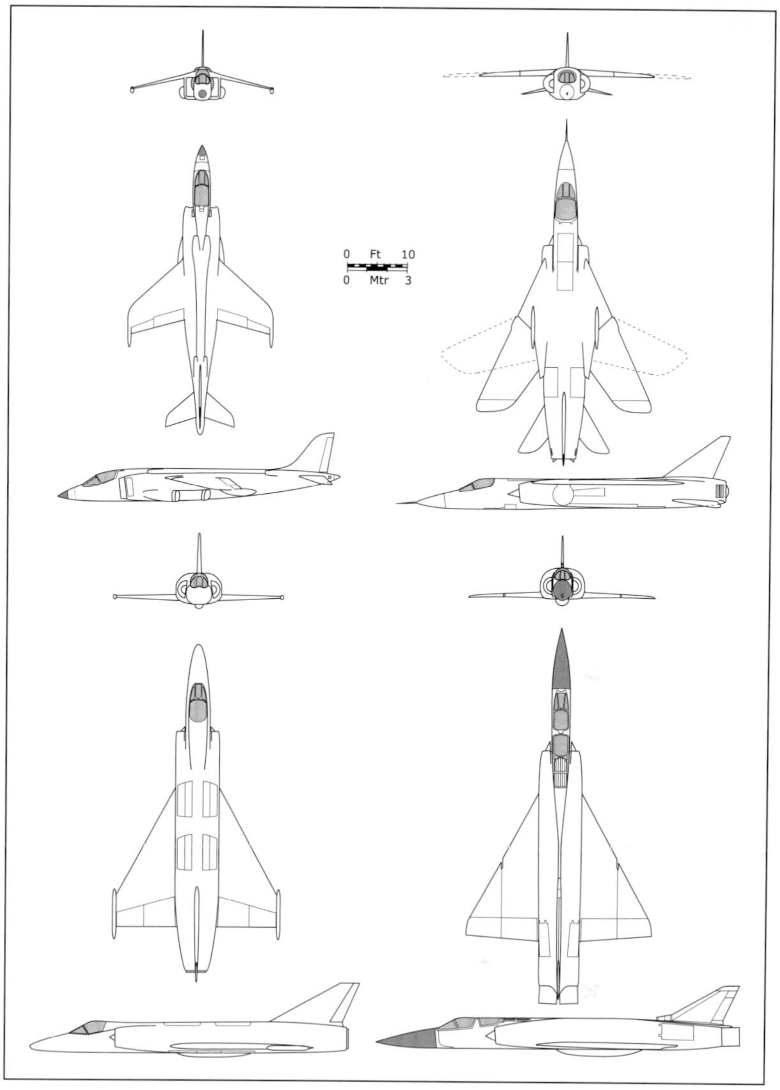

Above: The British proposals that made the 'long list' for NBMR-3a were (clockwise from top left) Hawker P.1154, Vickers Type 584, BAC P.39 and Shorts PD.56. The P.1154 and P.39 made it to the final four on the short list.

Below: BAC Warton's P.39 was also based on the Mirage III but used a pair of RB.153 with cascades in the jetpipes to deflect thrust and RB.162 lift engines for balancing thrust. The naval strike version is seen here. *North West Heritage Group*

Right: The runners up in NBMR-3a were (clockwise from top left) Fokker-Republic D-24 Alliance, Vickers Type 584, Nord N.4400, FIAT G.95/4, Shorts PD.56 and Lockheed/ Shorts CL-704. In hindsight, what NBMR-3 did show was the variety of designs and configurations that the different aircraft companies developed to meet the requirement.

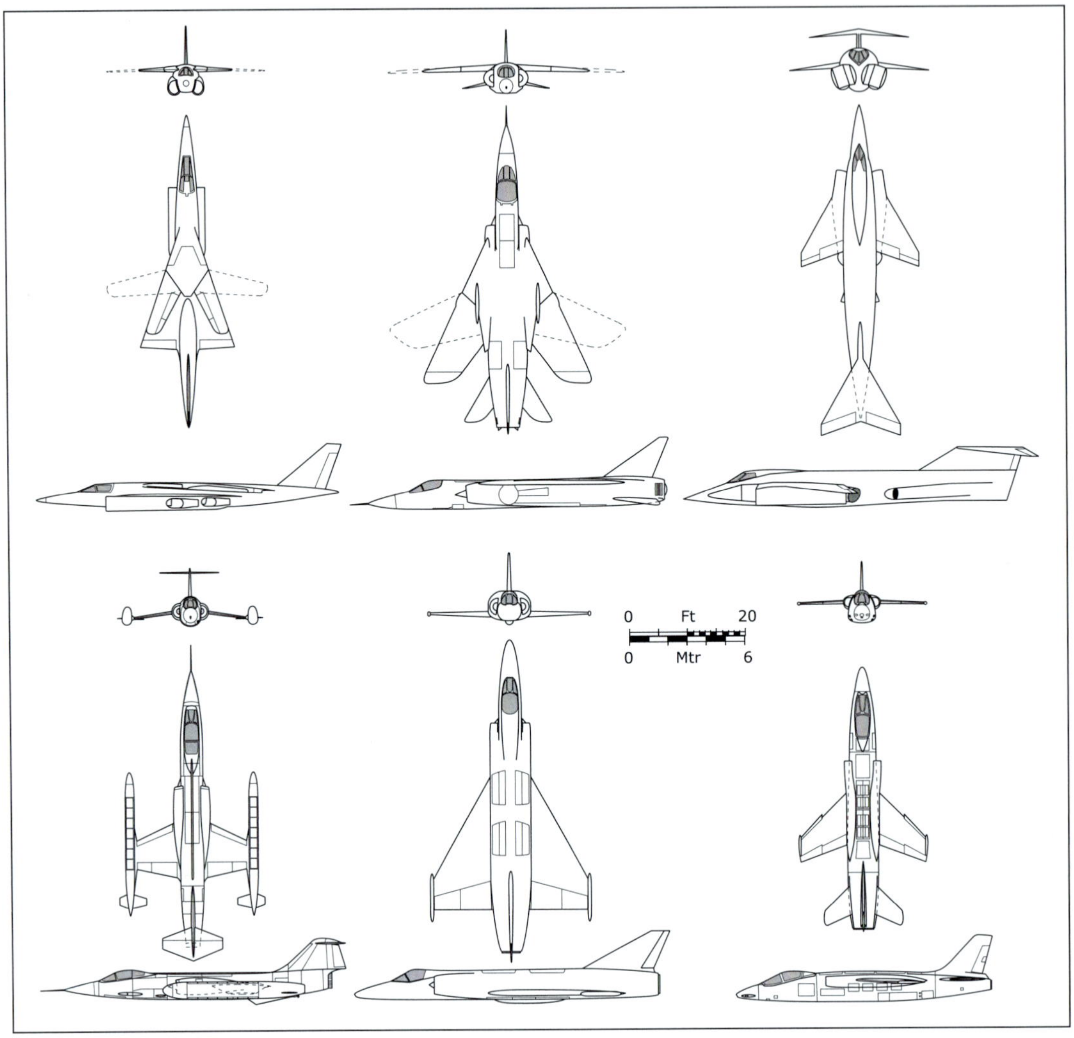

F-104 Starfighter with seven RB.181 lift engines in each wingtip pod. The EWR VJ.101 used fuselage-mounted lift engines and swivelling wingtip lift/propulsion engines. Nord's N.4400 looked unconventional in an unconventional field with BS.100 engine and small delta wings in a Delanne configuration while the Breguet Br.122 was a variable-geometry type in a similar vein to the Vickers 584. Breguet also submitted the Br.1115 delta, powered by the BS.100/3. Belgian companies may have produced studies for NBMR-3; Avions Fairey and SABCA (Société Anonyme Belge de Constructions Aéronautiques) both having built Hunter and F-104 components and upgraded F-84s.

This impressive list was whittled down to ten, Hawker P.1154, Mirage IIIV, D.24 Alliance, BAC P.39, Vickers Type 584, Lockheed CL-704,

The Fokker-Republic D-24 Alliance was a US/ Dutch proposal for NBMR-3 and featured a delta wing combined with variable geometry with propulsion from a BS.100 vectored thrust engine. Impressive, but ultimately unbuilt and superseded. *Blue Envoy Collection*

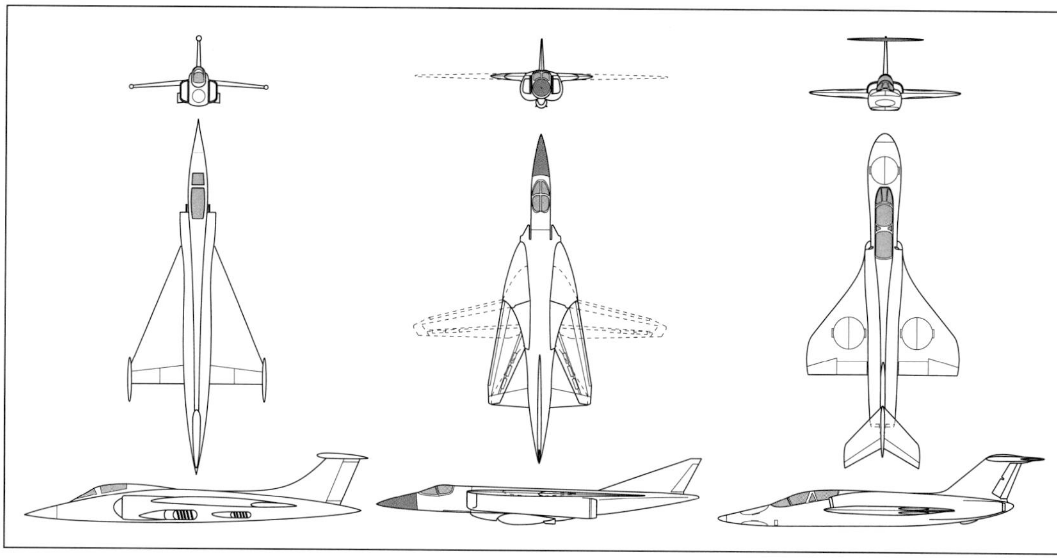

Amongst the numerous submissions for NBMR-3 some interesting configurations appeared. (L-R) Breguet Br.1115 with BS.100 engine, Breguet Br.122 variable geometry V/STOL and Ryan Model 209D.

EWR VJ.101, Shorts PD.56, Nord N.4400 and Breguet Br.122. Two types were then selected, the Hawker P.1154 and Dassault Mirage IIIV, for further development.

On the subsonic NBMR-3b front, it was no less confusing with nomenclature changes muddying the waters somewhat. The eleven initial types included the Hawker P.1127 and P.1170, Shorts PD.45 and PD.49, Focke-Wulf Fw 1262, FIAT G.95/4, Canadair CL-72, Ryan 209D, Nord N.4210, EWR.340 (the VJ.101 again) and the CL.704 (the VTOL Starfighter). The Focke-Wulf Fw 1262 and FIAT G.95/4 were similar in configuration but differed in their powerplant, with the Fw 1262 powered by a Pegasus and two RB.162 while the FIAT G.95 used four RB.162 for lift and a pair of RB.153s for propulsion. The Ryan 209D utilised Ryan's fan lift system with a fan in each wing and one in the nose, tip-driven by air bled from a pair of General Electric J85 turbojets.

Once whittled down to four, the NBMR-3 panel decided that they should be renamed, which was supposed to clarify the situation. The four shortlisted types were in August 1962 renamed Vertikalstartendes Aufklärungsund Kampfflugzeug (Vertical Take-off Reconnaissance and Strike Aircraft) or VAK 191 and designated A to D. The P.1127 was renamed VAK 191A, the Fw 1262 became the VAK 191B, the VJ.101D was renamed VAK 191C and FIAT's G.95/4 became the VAK 191D.

For NMBR.3a the ultimate choice came down to politics and performance. P.1154 was the winner in the performance stakes but as ever France had different ideas and preferred the Mirage IIIV (as if that outcome would come as a surprise). The NBMR-3a requirement was merged into the NBMR-3b requirement, hence the inclusion of the VAK 191C (VJ.101). The winner, if winner is the correct description, was the VAK 191B. In the end Flexible Response saw off the need to deliver a nuclear weapon into East Germany on Day One of a hot war, but there was still a need for the subsonic support aircraft. Flexible Response more or less meant that NATO airfields were not facing a nuclear strike from the off but could survive to allow operations by conventional aircraft, leading to requirements for what became Tornado. The irony of NBMR-3 was that the air force that had professed no interest in it was the only air arm to operate a V/STOL type the requirement called for: the RAF and its Harriers. However, before the Harriers arrived in service, the P.1154 was still a viable project for the RAF as a Hunter replacement.

The subsonic NBMR-3b 'contest' came down to two types, the Hawker P.1127 derivative (ultimately became the Harrier) on the left and the Fw 1262 on the right. These became the VAK 191A and VAK 191B respectively.

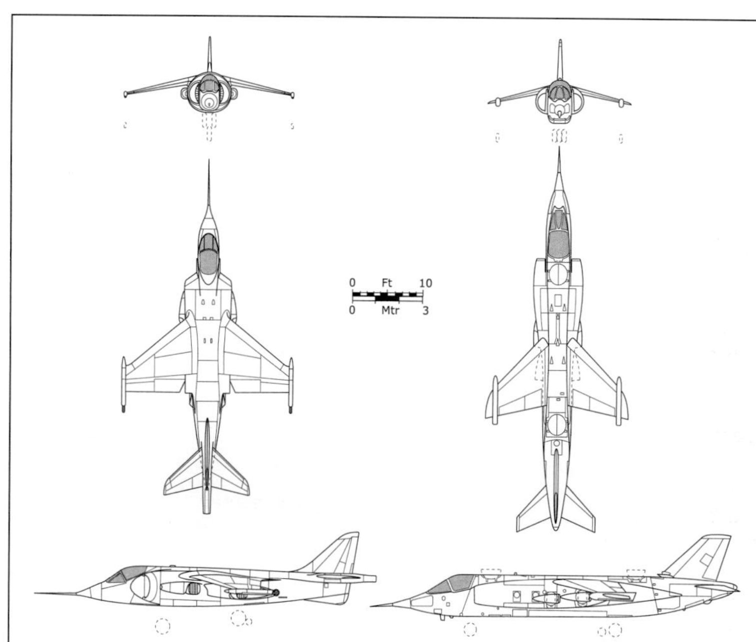

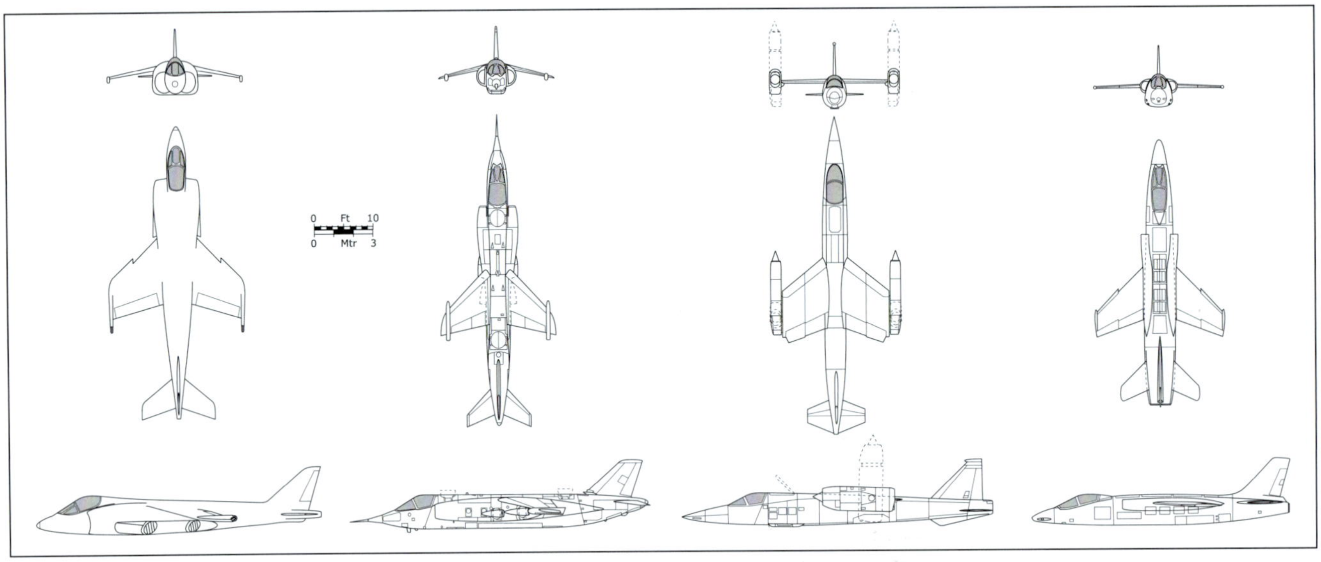

Comparable with Artillery – P.1154

'He has been brain-washed by the French.'
Group Captain Gard'ner, letter to Air Vice-Marshal Hartley, 26 October 1962

While the British were, supposedly, not closely involved with NBMR-3, they were looking for a similar capability. Unlike NBMR-3 and its NATO/Western Europe focus, the British required an aircraft that could operate worldwide and from aircraft carriers in support of British operations around the Empire. A replacement for the Hunter, which had made the usual transformation from the interceptor F.6, to the ground attack FGA.9 was required and the P.1154 looked ideal.

In a briefing note from late 1962, *The Tactical Employment and Military Validity of the P.1154 Type Aircraft,* the Air Staff outlined the background to the P.1154. The British Army had 'a requirement for tactical air support in global and limited war' and its main use would be against 'hard targets' such as tanks and APCs. The Army also required day and night reconnaissance although for limited war, visual reconnaissance would be sufficient. Interestingly, the General Staff stated that 'reaction time should be comparable to that of artillery' and that this could only be met by a 'strike support aircraft'.

The background to this was a turf war being waged between the Army, who wanted their own in-house (or to use modern parlance 'organic') air support and the RAF who were determined to keep control of all airborne offensive capability over the battlefield. This may have its roots in the Great War, but the Army's desire for their own air support increased from mid-1944 and particularly during the Ardennes offensive when much of the Allied air support was grounded due to weather. The use of the

Opposite page: The NBMR-3B supersonic short list comprised four types (clockwise from top left) the EWR VJ.101, Hawker P.1154, BAC P.39 and Dassault Mirage IIIV. The Mirage IIIV and P.39 were derived from the Mirage III but took different approaches to meeting the V/STOL requirement.

Towards the end of the NBMR-3 process the two separate requirements were merged and four types selected for further study. These were renamed Vertikalstartendes Aufklärungsund Kampfflugzeug (Vertical Take-off Reconnaissance and Strike Aircraft) 191. (clockwise from top left) The P.1127 became the VAK 191A and the Fw 1262 was the VAK 191B. The FIAT G.95/4 became the VAK 191C and the VJ.101C the VAK 191D.

This page: Hunter F.6 XF389 with drop tanks and 24 3in rockets (12 per side) on triple-tier mountings. If the 60 lb 927kg) high explosive head were fitted only eight rockets in a single tier could be carried. The F.6 was converted to the FGA.9 on relinquishing the interceptor role. *Tony Buttler Collection*

phrase 'comparable with artillery' is pertinent as Army wanted air support as and when required which led to the British Army's acquisition of long-range artillery pieces. These included the M107, M110 and later AS.90, while tactical missiles such as Honest John and Lance provided greater reach beyond the FEBA.

The RAF viewed the anti-tank role as their own and that the Army Air Corps should stick to liaison, artillery spotting and casualty evacuation. Ultimately the RAF took on the anti-armour role but graciously conceded that the Army's helicopters be allowed to carry 'bolt on' weapons which at the time were light machine guns. Imagine the reaction when the 'bolt-on' weapons became AS.11 and TOW anti-tank missiles mounted on Army Air Corps helicopters. Unfortunately, P.1154 was being designed and built to suit the British Army. Or at least that's what the British Army thought.

P.1154 for NBMR-3

Following the quick canter through NBMR-3 earlier in this chapter, an examination of the P.1154 in relation to NATO, and particularly the RAF's view of the whole business, would be helpful.

Air Vice-Marshal Christopher Hartley, ACAS-(OR) in a memo dated 8 November 1962 took the view that in a straight choice between the Mirage IIIV and P.1154, the P.1154 was the better aircraft. Hartley stated that 'We want to take full advantage of the ability to operate V/STOL aircraft from dispersed and unprepared sites' and to do this the aircraft must be 'easy to maintain in the field'. Pointing out that the Mirage IIIV had nine engines (and a complicated automatic control system) and the P.1154's 'single engine and swivel manual control' the choice was simple: 'the 1154 is by far the more practical solution'. In fact, the feeling amongst the British was that the P.1154 was the most practical solution to NBMR-3 as its performance was on a par with any of the other submissions and, being single-engined, its maintenance, logistics and pilot workload much lower than any of the others.

The German Air Force's (GAF) priorities were 'counter-air and counter-atomic', with attacks on army targets a secondary concern while an interceptor capability would be a 'bonus'. The GAF's two main areas of operation would be from the Inner German Border to the River Oder and the area east of the River Oder. Targets in the former would be small and mobile and the aircraft for use in this area must be 'capable of visual location and strike'. For the zone east of the Oder, they would be 'static and area targets' that would require 'all-weather penetration at low level and blind strike'. The Germans saw VTOL as essential, operating from hardened sites, but the UK Air Staff considered this to be folly as, for a start, the disparate roles required two types.

Oddly enough, despite their stated need for a single type, the RAF would ultimately take the same route: Harrier for close support and Tornado for counter-air and deep strike into East Germany and Poland. Another area where the RAF and GAF differed was in how to use the 'V' in VTOL. The GAF intended to operate their aircraft strictly as VTOL from hardened, pre-stocked sites whereas the RAF saw 'V' as a nice to have - 'STOL with a V capability'- and this would allow operation from unprepared sites with short strips to improve weapons load or endurance. The RAF pointed out that by opting for a VTOL strike aircraft, the capability of the new aircraft would provide little improvement over the FIAT G-91.

This led to the suggestion that West Germany's 'best interest lay in joining us in a P.1154 development programme' for which signing up for the P.1127 tripartite programme would

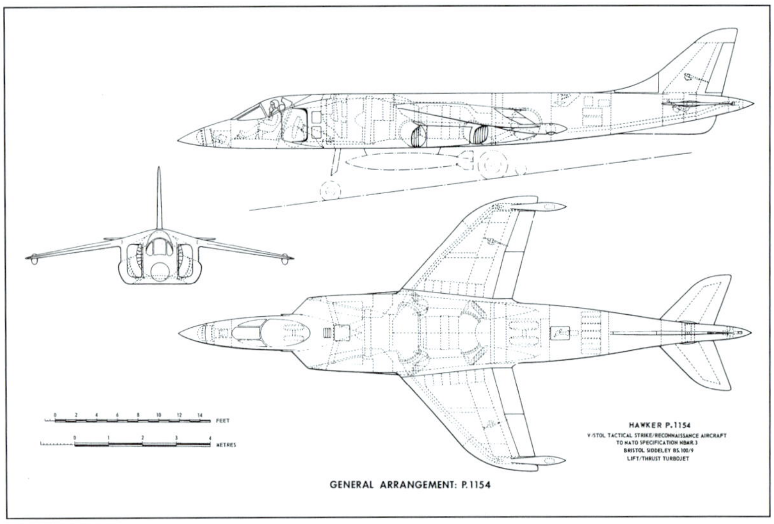

The Hawker P.1154 was to be powered by the BS.100 engine. One proposal to speed up development and to involve the West Germans in a joint project was the P.1155 that used a Pegasus and two lift engines. *Brooklands Museum*

be 'a logical first step towards introducing the P.1154'. Tellingly the document concluded with 'They are determined at the moment not to accept an imposed foreign solution which includes no identifiable trace of German ideas or technology.'

Meanwhile in Benelux...

What worried the Dutch and the Belgians was that the P.1154 would not be available before 1969, a supposition based on an article in *Interavia* magazine. In reporting his discussions with General Henry of the Belgian Air Force (BAF), Group Captain JR Gard'ner, the British Air Attaché in Brussels, on 2 October 1962 reported back to Air Vice-Marshal Hartley that the Belgians had hoped to replace their Republic F-84F Thunderstreaks by 1967. Another gem from Gard'ner was that the BAF 'had made a "big mistake" in selling 32 of its Hunters back to Hawkers'. Gard'ner also reported that if the Belgians had foreseen the delay on an F-84 replacement, they would have kept the Hunters which 'might have offered another solution to their problem i.e. by retaining some of the Hunter force until the P.1154 was ready, as the RAF are doing'. When asked about whether the BAF might opt for the Mirage IIIV, General Henry was 'non-committal' and that his study group was 'looking at all solutions'.

The upshot of Gard'ner's report was an invitation, from Marshal of the RAF Sir Thomas Pike, CAS, to make an informal visit to London by General Henry as the 'the CAS' personal guest' for discussions on the 'NBMR-3 question and the associated Hawker VTOL projects'. The CAS rounded off his invitation by saying that he and Lady Pike 'would of course be delighted if Mme. Henry could accompany you.'

Further interesting news came for the Air Attaché in Bonn, Air Commodore JN Tomes, who wrote to Air Commodore Esplin, DOR(A) at the Air Ministry to report on his informal meeting with the German Air Force's General Panitzki, Inspector of the Air Force. General Panitzki would gain fame for being fired by the Federal German Defence Minister for remarks he had made about the procurement of the F-104 Starfighter. Tomes did what an Air Attaché was supposed to do on finding himself seated beside Panitzki at lunch and engaged the General in discussion and 'he talked quite a lot'.

Of most interest was what Panitzki had to say about the current status of the German and French VTOL projects. The French Defence Minister Pierre Messmer had offered to 'tear up French ideas on the Mirage IIIV if this would help institute a Franco-German project.' This would incorporate the 'best features' of the Mirage IIIV and EWR VJ101, but the General had noted that the French team had visited the Germen defence ministry and 'Far from being willing to tear up the IIIV' suggested that the Germans should 'drop the 101D' and that in return the French would 'consider embodying certain 101D features in their IIIV'. Tomes also reported that the General had advised the West German aerospace companies 'including those old-fashioned gentlemen with Messerschmidt' that they would not 'get one pfennig more for individual projects' and that international co-operation was expected.

The ACAS(OR) took this information, which appeared to support similar material he had received in mid-October from DOR(A), Air Commodore Esplin, and passed it on to the DCAS, Air Marshal Sir Ronald Beresford Lees, and explained how Dassault had applied pressure to the French Government to withdraw the offer to 'tear up the Mirage IIIV'. Hartley also briefed the DCAS on possible British co-operation with the West Germans on P.1154 and the integration of West German 'technical ideas'. This would apparently involve fitting lift engines to the P.1154 but Hartley suspected that more would be required due to 'industrial pressures and national pride' that precluded West German acceptance of the P.1127 or P.1154. The RAF had no interest in the German 'lightweight' aircraft and believed that the requirement was 'fundamentally unsound'. In addition, the 'heavyweight' aircraft was 'unattractive' due to the Germans' 'technical ideas' (swivelling main engines and lift jets) and the performance which Hartley thought would be 'unacceptable to the Navy'.

The Hawker aircraft Hartley had in mind was the P.1155, a variant of the P.1154 with two RB.162 lift engines, one behind the cockpit and the second in the rear fuselage. The main engine was a Bristol Siddeley Pegasus 5 rated at 15,000 lbf (67kN), with this configuration drawn up to replace the BS.100 engine. Another interesting parallel is the HS.1185 intended for MinTech's Wide Speed Range Aircraft (WSRA) project that had a pair of XJ.99 lift engines installed between the Pegasus' nozzles.

The ACAS(OR) outlined how he still viewed the P.1154 as the correct type to pursue as a joint requirement with the Navy and how 'faith in the P.1154 as the right solution' was confirmed by the visit to the head office of Entwicklungring Süd. Hartley's team had a day of presentations and discussions on the VJ.101D and 'as a result are convinced that, of the Mirage IIIV, the VJ.101 and the P.1154, the best operational and technical solution to our joint requirement is the P.1154'. The team observed that the VJ.101D was 'fairly large' and based on a multi-engine solution and embodies control systems of considerable complexity'. Oddly enough, the RAF team gained the impression that 'the Germans themselves are not entirely convinced on their VJ.101 ideas' and Hartley stated that they 'admitted to me that they see little hope of developing and financing the project unaided. I think we can discount it as a serious starter'.

Hartley cautioned against dismissing the German ideas out of hand and advised they should be examined, and the RAF should 'think carefully before rejecting them and losing any chance of collaboration'. The alternatives were: attempt to 'bring the Germans round to our way of thinking' by proposing a joint study based on the P.1154 with German input i.e. lift jets (the P.1155) or embark on a joint development with the Navy.

The impression gained is that the RAF would rather co-operate with the West Germans than the Royal Navy and Hartley addressed this by stating that the way forward should be 'decided at Government level'. A meeting between Peter Thorneycroft, UK Defence Secretary and Franz Josef Strauss, Federal German Minister of Defence, was scheduled for later in the month, but the matter should be discussed beforehand.

In a memo to Group Captain Gard'ner dated 26 October 1962, Hartley summed up the situation. He was unsure where General Henry was getting his information on delays with P.1154 unless 'he has been brain-washed by the French' who had 'made a concerted attack on the BS.100 engine in the NBMR-3 committees'. The work on the P.1154 to meet OR.356 (Hunter replacement, superseded OR.345) was progressing and 'looks very like NBMR-3' albeit with 'emphasis on simplicity and reliability' so that the aircraft can 'readily be dispersed'. Hartley had informed General Henry that the aim was to have the aircraft available in 'trial squadron strength in 1967 and squadron service by 1 January 1968'. Development by Hawker of the P.1154 for the Navy to meet AW.406 would follow the RAF version, but the Navy had 'traded VTO capability (which they don't need with deck catapults) for a second seat' but vertical landing would still be required.

Turning to the P.1127, Hartley was impressed with 'the success Hawkers are making of it and (we) are very anxious to get our hands on a few'. This would be for evaluation only as the RAF 'have no interest in it as an operational aircraft'. Hartley and, of course, the Air Staff's reasoning for this was that that they did not believe 'it would be sensible to have a subsonic aircraft in the late 60s and the 70s when even the Arabs will have MiG-21s'.

As for the Germans, who were 'very keen on developing their own aircraft' and hoped to replace the FIAT G.91 and Lockheed F-104

The Hunter, Hawker's most graceful aircraft, made the transition from F.6 interceptor to FGA.9 ground attack and T.7 trainer. The search for a Hunter replacement continued for most of the Sixties. Seen here (clockwise from top) are WW664, an F.4 converted to a T.8B; XF389, an F.6, refurbished and sold to Jordan; XL614, a new-build T.7A and XE618 an F.6 converted to FGA.9. *Blue Envoy Collection*

Above: One of the many Shorts design studies for a supersonic V/STOL strike aircraft. This study is shown with different engine installations; tilting wingtip engines on the right; in-fuselage lift engines on the left. Much of this work used data gathered from the SC.1 VTOL aircraft. *Blue Envoy Collection*

with their own designs. Focke-Wulf had the Fw 1262, which Hartley described as a P.1127 with two RB.162 lift engines, to replace the G.91 and the VJ.101 for the F-104. What Hartley was pointing out was that the West Germans were coming to realise that they could not develop V/STOL aircraft 'unaided'.

Warton's Mirage

Warton's proposal for OR.356 was a variation on the Dassault submission to NBMR-3, the Mirage IIIV. Whilst this may look like a very odd Roman number, it stands for Mirage 3 Vertical and was referred to as the Mirage 3V in RAF circles, who had given up Roman numerals in 1947 and adopted Arabic numbers.

English Electric became a major constituent of BAC in 1960, but continued the P.nn series designations for its Warton projects, which had started with the P.1 in 1947 and so by 1962 Warton's work on the Mirage 3V was designated the P.39. BAC at Warton would work with Dassault on the Mirage IVK also known as the Spey Mirage. The P.39 was completely re-engined with British powerplant, with two RB.153-61, rated at 6850 lbf without reheat, replacing the single Snecma TF104B turbofan, rated at 19,840 lbf (88.2kN) with the RB.153s fitted swivelling jet pipes and only two RB.162 lift jets. Unlike the Mirage IIIV, the P.39 was a naval aircraft, intended to operate from aircraft carriers. As a V/STOL strike aircraft its inclusion in the NBMR-3 process was inevitable.

WARLOCs

NATO Basic Military Requirements 3 and 4 were intended to create a strike force dispersed across West Germany with the transport aircraft to support it. Neither came to fruition but the oddest aspect of the NBMR-3 and 4 sagas was that despite British companies submitting proposals for both, the UK government held nothing but a watching brief on the process. The real oddity lies in the fact that from 1970 the RAF operated its Harriers in the dispersed role, as outlined in NBMR-3, supported by the RAF's Puma HC.1 helicopter force rather than V/STOL transports.

Dispersed operations were, at first glance, an ideal way to operate the Harrier whose V/STOL capability was ideal for sorties from concealed locations around the countryside. At least that was how it was presented to the general public. The three squadrons of Harriers (3, 4 and 20 Sqn) assigned to 2ATAF were originally based at Wildenrath but were moved to Gütersloh, closer to the Inner German Border and the potential battle front. When 20 Sqn became a Jaguar squadron, its Harriers were absorbed into 3 and 4 Sqn with 18 aircraft each.

The reality was that the Harrier GR.1 and from 1975, the later GR.3 on a LO-LO-STOL mission profile carrying three BL.755 and two 30mm ADEN cannon had a radius of action of only 168nm (311km) which meant that the Harriers would need to be based further forward than the 'Rhine Clutch' airfields (Brüggen, Laarbruch and Wildenrath), near the Dutch/West German border. Given that Gütersloh would quite possibly be either over-run or rendered unusable through Warsaw Pact counter-air operations early in any invasion, Gütersloh's Harriers were to disperse into sites in the West German countryside. With two squadrons of 18 aircraft each, between six and nine dispersed sites would be required and the RAF estimated that with 70% availability, the 36 Harriers could generate four sorties a day for six days, producing 605 sorties.

These dispersed sites were called War Locations, abbreviated to WARLOC, and this mode of operation had been explored almost as soon as Harrier GR.1s had entered service in 1969 with 1 Sqn at RAF Wittering. Trials were conducted in the British countryside and in Norway, where Harriers would be deployed in support of NATO's northern flank. Of course, dispersed operations became the forte of RAFG as part of 2ATAF, with MoD photographers providing many photographs of Harriers lurking amongst the conifers, giving the impression this was how the Harriers would operate.

Bizarrely, to allow RAF aircraft to operate from the WARLOC sites, a change in West German law was required as they were effectively private property. The sites were covertly surveyed well before they would be required and left untouched, ignored even, and activated only when required in wartime. The sites should be flat, away from 'army concentrations' and free from the 'vagaries of German agriculture'. This may sound odd but according to one of this author's university lecturers, despite the German reputation for efficiency, German farming in the 1970s was pretty much based on the small-holding and open-field agriculture, mainly due to food shortages in both World Wars. Many urban families maintained a small plot of land for growing food – just in case – meaning that ownership of the land was very fragmented, hence the need for legislation to activate its wartime use by the RAF. Interestingly a series of training sites were established but these were within the bounds of the British Army's Sennelager training area to the east of Gütersloh. These were the sites seen in the numerous photographs of dispersed operations in West Germany.

A WARLOC should include an area that could be used as a runway at least 400m (437 yards) long, with German roads that incorporated cycle paths considered ideal. Local roads were preferred as trunk routes would be used for troop and vehicle movements as the war progressed. Autobahns were not used as these were earmarked for use by military traffic or, as was demonstrated by RAF Jaguars, used as emergency runways. Ideally there should be areas with cover nearby and these could be woodland, or on occasion supermarkets with carparks and storage sheds where the aircraft and site facilities could be concealed. In wooded areas, the aircraft would be provided

Opposite, bottom: WARLOC sites were presurveyed but would not be used until the balloon went up. Most dispersed operations by Harriers were conducted in the forests on the British Army's Sennelager training area east of the Harrier's home base at Gütersloh. *Blue Envoy Collection*

Above: Harriers did not always fly from rain-sodden German forests, the windswept Falklands or arctic Norway, they also operated from the tropics. This GR.3 of 1417 Flight is being worked on in a camouflaged revetment in Belize by a suitably dressed engineer. The RAF had a presence in Belize from 1975 until 1993. *Terry Panopalis Collection*

Below: The SEPECAT Jaguar began life as a supersonic trainer but evolved into a formidable strike aircraft as the GR.1 and later GR.3. Capable of operating from short fields it could use roadways such as German autobahns as seen here during an exercise. BAC Warton demonstrated this on a stretch of the M55 in April 1975. *Terry Panopalis Collection*

Harriers operated from dispersed sites in the Falkland Islands. This No 1 Sqn Harrier GR.3 passes the wreckage of Argentine FMA IA 58 Pucarás at Stanley Airport. It is armed with AIM-9L Sidewinders, two ADEN 30mm cannon, plus two drop tanks for the QRA role. Note the PSA (Prefabricated Surfacing Airfield) panels in use as a runway surface. *MoD/ Open Government Licence*

with a 20m x 20m landing pad comprising Prefabricated Surfacing, Airfield (PSA) panels located near enough to the aircraft hides to allow them to rapidly move out of sight. Aside from the benefit of concealment, trees offered a degree of protection from attack as bomblets from Soviet cluster bombs such as the RBK-500 would be detonated by the tree canopy.

Originally, four Harriers were to be based on each WARLOC site but eventually six Harriers were installed, mainly to ease the engineering and logistics burden of supporting the sites, producing the need for six WARLOC sites. Each site was to be within a 5-mile (8km) radius of a 'logistics park' holding six days supplies which would ideally be near to a railhead. Additionally, each Harrier site was to have an alternate location, to which the entire unit could be evacuated within two hours, resuming operations after six hours. All sites were to have air traffic control, fire/rescue, medical, catering and photo-interpretation facilities. Four out of the six sites were to specialise in photoreconnaissance, with the 4 Sqn Harriers carrying a Vinten Vicon reconnaissance pod equipped with five cameras.

Having decamped from their home base, the dispersed Harriers were considered more of less free of the threat from Warsaw Pact counter-air operations, but 'saboteurs' were considered a serious threat to the dispersed sites. The Americans had learned a hard lesson in Vietnam: a few determined individuals could wreak havoc on an airfield. The British reaction for their airfields in West Germany was to keep people away and, for the dispersed sites, that involved the RAF Regiment who would have mounted patrols around the site, established observation posts in daylight hours and listening posts for the hours of darkness. In addition to the RAF Regiment, base personnel would carry out guard duties within the site itself.

The dispersed sites addressed the Harrier's range limitations, but they were not without problems such as the need to be supported by trucks and helicopters to move material from the logistics park or the command and control problems created by dispersion, all compounded by the need to secure an area of countryside. Despite all these, dispersed operations became a standard procedure for RAF Germany's Harriers, the GR.3 through to the GR.9 and could be seen as the heirs of the 2nd Tactical Air Force Hawker Typhoons operating from Advanced Landing Grounds in Normandy in 1944.

When AST.396 was being considered, dispersed operations were examined and their

Dispersed operations ranged from the Arctic to the desert. The RAF's Harriers were not only tasked with supporting the Central Front but also the Northern Flank. These No 1 (Fighter) Sqn GR.3s are seen in arctic/ winter camouflage on exercise in Norway in 1986. *Blue Envoy Collection.*

main benefit stemmed from them being able to operate, albeit at a less intensive sortie rate, while the main bases were being attacked but this would be balanced by the proximity to the FEBA that allowed a higher sortie rate. However, the main problem with expanding the number of dispersed sites was finding enough in the first place. The existing Harrier Force was pushed to find dispersed sites for its 36 aircraft and the AST.396 Working Party stated that 'an additional consideration is the practical difficulty of finding sufficient dispersed sites'.

When required, specifically during the Falklands Campaign of 1982, Harriers could operate from locations much more austere than those purloined from West German small-holders. The Forward Operating Base (FOB) at San Carlos on East Falkland was one such site. The original pre-assault plan was to provide facilities similar to those in West Germany; a 400m airstrip plus maintenance and logistics support for 12 Harriers on or near the beachhead. This was to be constructed as soon as possible after the landings and used not only as a diversion field but provide quick reaction support. It was also intended to replace a carrier if either HMS *Illustrious* or HMS *Hermes* was lost to Argentine action or mechanical failure.

HMS *Sheathbill* (sheathbills are large white birds, endemic to the Falklands. They are opportunist feeders and scavengers, famed for stealing food out of the mouths of penguin chicks) was constructed by the Royal Engineers on the north shore of Port San Carlos and involved a 260m (284 yard) strip built using interlocking panels of Prefabricated Surfacing, Airfield (PSA) pinned into the peat. Not being the most competent of substrates, the peat did not hold the pins securely and with repeated use the PSA panels moved around. This was further compounded by panels being loosened by thrust from a hovering Harrier (which subsequently made a forced landing after ingesting FOD) and a few days later the downdraught of Chinook ZA718 lifted some of the panels. The reason for the runway being shorter than originally planned was the loss of the *Atlantic Conveyor*, which as well as carrying Chinook HC.1s, also carried most of the task force's PSA.

Despite its rudimentary appearance, HMS *Sheathbill* (also known as Sid's Strip to the RAF) increased the effectiveness of the Harriers and Sea Harriers by allowing them to maintain a ground alert on the strip and react much more rapidly to requests for air support. The aircraft carriers were operating east of the Falkland Islands, out of range of Argentine aircraft. British aircraft flying from their carriers were similarly restricted and took around 30 minutes to fly to the battlefield – and the same for return – which limited their time over the battlefield to around 10 minutes.

In the 21st Century the RAF's Harriers rarely deployed to dispersed sites, despite their almost constant operations from 1990 until they were retired in 2011. For operations over the former Yugoslavia, such as Operation DENY FLIGHT and Operation DELIBERATE FORCE, the Harriers operated either from the *Invincible*-class carriers in the Adriatic or from Gioia del Colle in southern Italy. For Operation PALLISTER in Sierra Leone in 2000, RAF Harriers again flew from carriers operating offshore. These operations from Royal Navy carriers led to the establishment of Joint Force Harrier in 2000, combining the two Fleet Air Arm Sea Harrier FA.2 squadrons with the four RAF GR.7 squadrons as a single command. Harriers were involved in Iraq, enforcing the No-Fly Zone from 1991 and in Operation TELIC, the invasion of Iraq in 2003. From late 2004, Joint Force Harrier (RAF Harrier GR.7s, GR.9s and FAA Sea Harrier FA.2s) operated from Kandahar and Camp Bastion in Afghanistan's Helmand Province during Operation HERRICK.

NATO's venture into STOVL met its end at the hands of a policy change, a change that meant the conventional aircraft and its runways would survive, at least, the initial phases of a Warsaw Pact attack. The RAF acquired its Hunter replacement in the shape of the Harrier but as the United Kingdom's focus moved from empire to north west Europe, the RAF's roles would require new equipment to meet the UK's policy change. That equipment had one aim – stopping the Soviet Horde.

Sporting winter camouflage, Harrier GR.3 XZ130 of No 1 Sqn is on exercise in Norway during the winter of 1986. The extended nose carries the laser ranger and marked target seeker (LRMTS). *Blue Envoy Collection*

4 Dead in Their Tracks

'They do not wish to diminish interest by reference to the need for "improvements" or offer the prospects too soon of better jam tomorrow'. Air Chief Marshal Sir Douglas Charles Lowe, Controller, Aircraft, August 1982

'If the tanks succeed, then victory follows.' General Heinz Guderian, quoted in *Panzerkrieg: The Rise and Fall of Hitler's Tank Divisions* (2002) by Peter McCarthy and Mike Syron, page 33

Having ostensibly bettered the tank with its rockets in Normandy, the RAF saw tank killing as its area of expertise in any European war. Tanks evolved and, with the massive tank armies the Warsaw Pact had built, the RAF needed new weapons and the sensors to take on this burgeoning threat. The argument came down to bomb or missile, shotgun or sniper.

Since their inception in 1916, tanks have been subject to, and proof from, many forms of offensive fire. As shown in Appendix 1, tanks and other armoured fighting vehicles (AFVs) were involved in a gun/armour spiral to gain an edge on the battlefield. There are two methods by which an aircraft can destroy tanks. The first is by direct attack, gun, rocket or guided weapon, or indirect, with a bomb; explosive or napalm. Essentially, any weapon that could be carried by an aircraft could be used against AFVs, even lumps of concrete on 3in RP practice rounds are rumoured to have been used against tanks.

Having used the 3in RP against tanks and other ground targets – plus ships and submarines – they were found less than ideal for the new high-performance jets that the RAF were acquiring in the postwar era. Even with modification to the rockets and launch rails, the rocket/rail installation created too much drag and the rockets themselves were too slow and not particularly accurate, so a replacement was sought. Interceptors such as the Lightning could carry the 2in RP in a 22-round pack, but this

Tornado GR.4 ZA456 of No 9 Sqn is seen here with a pair of Paveway IV LGBs, LITENING III designator pod and a single-mode Brimstone. *MoD/ Open Government Licence*

The 68mm SNEB rocket, carried in a Matra Type 155 rocket pod, was the preferred weapon for use against tanks in the 1960s. This Kestrel FGA.1 XS693 is seen here at Farnborough in 1966 carrying a Type 155 pod. *Terry Panopalis Collection*

lacked the punch for use against tanks such as the Soviet T-10 that appeared in the early 1950s. Across the Channel a company called Société Nouvelle des Etablissements Edgar Brandt had developed a 68mm (2.7in) diameter folding fin, unguided rocket that could be carried in a streamlined pod. The rocket could be fitted with a variety of warheads and if fitted with a HEAT warhead, proved ideal for use against AFVs. The rockets were loaded in a pod, with the RAF's preferred version being the MATRA Type 155 with the whole rocket/pod being known simply as SNEB, after the company that made the rockets. The Type 155 pod held 18 rockets, and these could be launched singly or in salvos.

Until 1961 the British, and NATO, weapon of choice against Warsaw Pact armoured formations was the tactical nuclear weapon. This saw the development of such weapons as the Davy Crockett nuclear spigot mortar, providing the prospect of a corporal in charge of a nuclear weapon on the battlefield. Thankfully sense prevailed and Flexible Response was adopted, making the use of nuclear weapons less of a knee-jerk reaction, although they would be earmarked for use against airfields and other targets beyond the FEBA until a new anti-runway weapon was developed. Therefore, the RAF needed a weapon that could be used against armour formations with an improved generation of Soviet tanks such as the T-54 and T-55 and the appearance of the BMP armoured fighting vehicles, all designed for the nuclear battlefield. The SNEB was not considered up to the job so a replacement was sought leading to the raising of joint Naval and Air Staff Require-

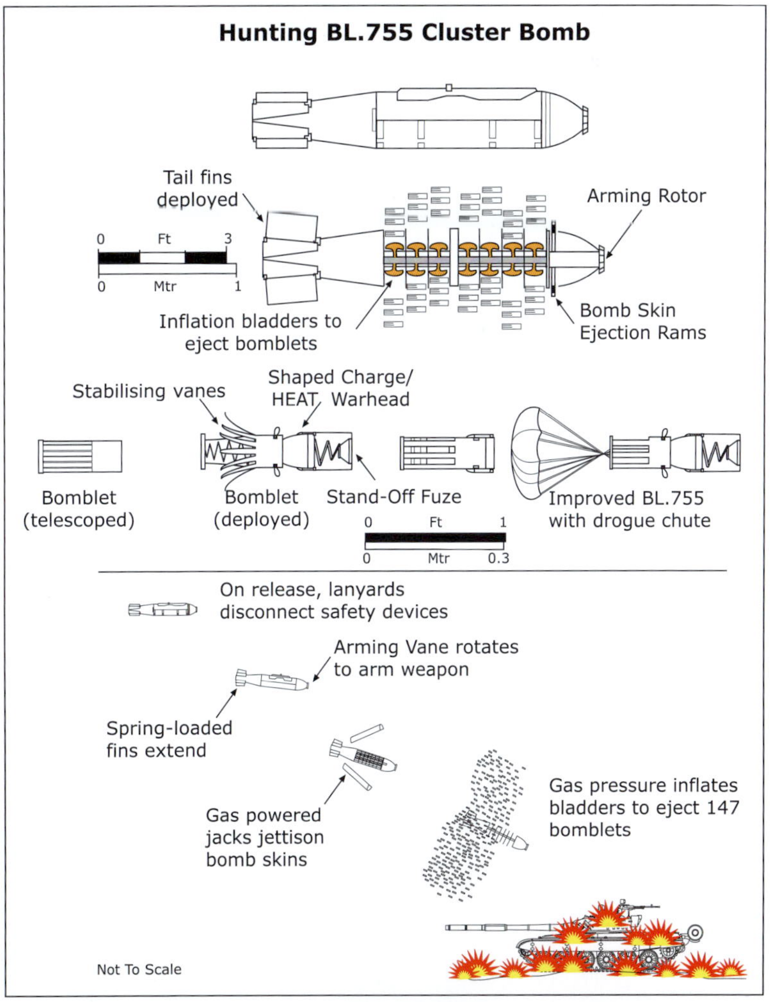

Hunting's original BL.755 was designed to tackle the T-55 and T-62 tanks of Warsaw Pact armies but needed a major update to take on the new generation of Soviet tanks such as the T-72 and T-80 producing the IBL.755. In the post-GRANBY climate, the IBL.755 had to be modified for delivery from medium altitude as the RBL.755.

Phantom FGR.2 XV499 of No 41 Sqn still carries its air superiority weapons and is carrying an almost full load of seven BL.755s. RAF Phantoms were not cleared to carry three bombs on the outer wing pylon ejector rack units, which could have increased its warload to nine BL.755. *Terry Panopalis Collection*

ment NASR.1197 calling for an anti-armour cluster bomb.

Hunting Engineering developed the BL.755, which looked like a standard 1,000lb (454kg) bomb and could be carried and delivered in the same manner. Inside, the bomb was divided into seven compartments that contained 147 submunitions (bomblets). The submunitions were 'telescoped' to reduce their length and comprised, from the front, a stand-off fuze, HEAT warhead and stabilising vanes. Ideally it should be delivered from low level and once released, a lanyard would release an arming vane in the nose, which would trigger a sequence of actions that included release of the bomb's outer skins, which in turn sequentially inflate a series of bladders to push out the submunitions, which on release, telescoped to their full length. The submunitions deploy to form a swarm that on impact forms an elliptical pattern on the ground. The size, area and density of the impacts is dependent on the height and speed of release.

This meant that the aircraft was required to overfly the target and by releasing a pair or quartet of BL.755, could destroy vehicles in an area the size of a football pitch. The submunitions worked well against the T-54 and T-55 but were marginal against the T-62 that had appeared in numbers from the mid-60s. With the prospect of the next generation of tanks using composite armour, a new anti-tank weapon would be required.

Better Jam tomorrow – AST.1227 (First Revise)

The change in doctrine from Massive Retaliation to Flexible Response in the mid-1960s had, as shown above, seen the adoption of cluster bombs and the move away from the use of tactical nuclear weapons against targets such as airfields and tank laagers. While effective against the Sixties era Soviet tanks such as the T-55 and T-62, by 1975 the Next Soviet

The main anti-tank weapon in the RAF's armoury in the 1970s was the BL.755 cluster bomb. Its 147 submunitions could cover the area of a football field and any AFV in that area was subject to its HEAT submunitions. Until the T-72 and T-80 MBTs arrived on the scene when the BL.755 was found wanting. *Blue Envoy Collection*

Tank (NST) and Future Soviet Tank (FST), the T-64/T-72 and what became the T-80 and T-90 were proving a hard target for the BL.755 and SNEB. According to the Air Force Department tanks were 'the toughest and most important target on the battlefield.'

Issued in 1975, ASR.1227 called for an air-delivered weapon that could defeat the NST and FST. This requirement led to VJ.291, a Hunting Engineering guided anti-armour cluster bomb. Targeting info was provided from the launch aircraft's navigation system allowing stand-off attacks on targets offset from aircraft track. The VJ.291 weapon comprised a dispenser that carried dual-purpose submunitions, fitted with folding cruciform wings at rear and nose-mounted cruciform canards. The submunitions were dispensed centrifugally and each had a sensor that detonated it on impact with a vehicle, but if the submunition landed on the ground, it functioned as a 'minelet'. Having reached project definition stage, VJ.291 was cancelled in December 1980 on the grounds of low cost-effectiveness.

In early 1981, ASR.1227 (First Revise) was issued for a weapon to deal with NST and FST and for carriage on the Jaguar GR.1, Tornado GR.1, Harrier GR.3 and its replacement, with the latter becoming the Harrier GR.5, the principle anti-armour type for the 1990s. A RAE study on future anti-tank weapons emphasised the 'need for autonomous operation, compatibility with single-seat aircraft and a full capability at night or in adverse weather.' In fact, there was a 'plethora of possible solutions' but most relied on 'advanced sensors which would provide a fire-and forget capability'. The gist of the RAE report was that there were two options: stand-off weapons and line of sight weapons.

An off-the-shelf solution was preferred, and a number of weapons were considered, but the field was soon reduced to three, four if laser-guided bombs were considered and in July 1982 the Air Force Department (AFD) issued its report to the MoD Operational Requirements Committee.

The laser-guided bomb (LGB), first used in 1972 during Operation LINEBACKER I, was a mature technology by the early Eighties, but against fixed installations. For use against tanks, LGBs were just not ready and the Air Staff dismissed them as anti-tank weapons. It would take a decade and another generation of LGB to make them reliable as tank killer. A number of factors worked against the LGB but the main problem was designation. In 1980 the RAF were using Paveway II kits on 1,000 lb (454kg) bombs and with the RAF's doctrine of low-level attack, LGBs would need to be tossed into the target area to provide sufficient altitude and angle of descent for the LGB to guide itself onto the target. Soviet tanks had lower profiles that NATO's MBTs, typically 8ft (2.4m),

Top: The T-72, (known as NST, Next Soviet Tank) is identifiable from this angle by its V-shaped splash guard on the glacis plate, was intended as a cheaper alternative to the T-64. It was so much cheaper that it all but replaced the T-64. This T-72 sports the 'Dolly Parton' composite armour on the front of the turret. Much of the anti-tank weapons development effort, such as the Improved BL.755, was aimed at defeating the T-72. *DoD*

Above: One of the first photographs of the T-80 (known as the Future Soviet Tank, FST to NATO planners) showed the exhaust for the gas turbine. The T-80 is fitted with the same 125mm smoothbore gun as the T-64 and T-72. *DoD*

Armourers, clad in NBC kit, load a Paveway II LGB onto the centreline pylon of a Jaguar GR.1. Early LGBs lacked the fine control required to hit tanks, especially if moving. Note that the armourers are not wearing gloves, possibly because these do not provide the dexterity for the task in hand. *Crown Copyright via Terry Panopalis*

The weapon to replace the BL.755 was to be small enough to be carried as multiple loads on the Jaguar and Harrier. In the threat environment of the 1980s and beyond, Sidewinders, jammers and chaff dispensers would also be required, reducing the warload, as would any designator that was required by a new weapon.

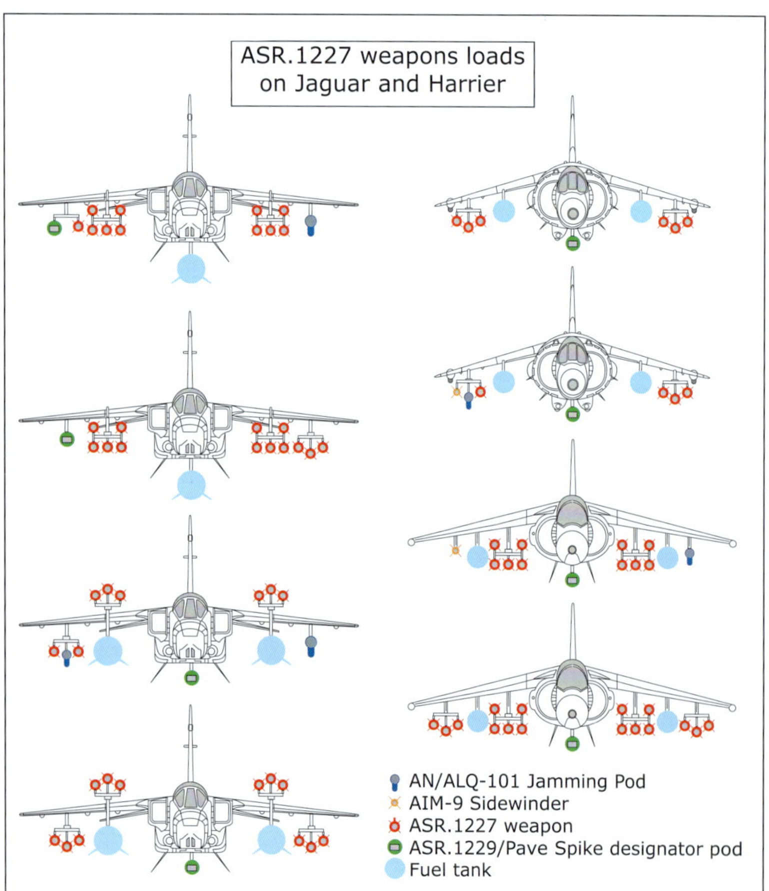

presenting a smaller target that would prove difficult to 'spike' – illuminate with the laser designator – especially if the tank was moving.

Designation itself would prove problematic as the carrying aircraft could not self-designate targets, relying on either Pave Spike-equipped Buccaneers (of which there was a grand total of six) or troops on the ground with portable laser designators. In the frontline, a soldier would rather be carrying an ATGW than a designator, while beyond the Forward Line of Own Troops (FLOT) designation would need to be conducted by special forces, an unrealistic prospect.

Paveway II guidance kits used 'bang-bang' controls to guide the bomb onto the target by deflecting the control surfaces to their full extent, resulting in an overcorrection that is countered by reversing the surfaces. This induced snaking in the bomb as it descended and since the effective radius of a 1,000 lb bomb against tanks was 10ft (3m) the chances of this sort of accuracy were about as likely as a direct hit: 'very low indeed'. Paveway III used proportional controls that allowed a smoother trajectory and thus did not snake, but it still relied on a designator keeping the laser on target and if the target went behind a bush, laser lock would be lost.

A decade on from the Air Staff's dismissal of LGBs in the anti-tank role the USAF showed that LGBs could be used against armour, with F-111Fs using their stabilised Pave Tack targeting systems to destroy Iraqi armour in the 1991 Desert Storm campaign. Of course, the F-111s were 'tank plinking' from medium altitudes against dug-in Iraqi tanks with little or no air defences rather than the RAF's *modus operandi* of low altitude attacks against mobile armour in the face of the Soviet 'dense and highly mobile air defence network'. The LGB was neither fish nor flesh – potentially accurate enough to guarantee a kill on a single tank but not covering enough area to guarantee tank kills on a tank formation – and what the Air Staff called for was maximum tank kills per aircraft per pass.

Having dismissed LGBs, the Staff looked at three other systems: Trefoil, Maverick D and Improved BL.755. Trefoil was a submunition intended for BL.755, and possibly VJ.291, that if it failed to detonate on a vehicle, acted as a mine. It was aimed at the road interdiction role, attacking Warsaw Pact second echelon formations moving forward. Interestingly, the name dates back to the origins of mining in siege warfare where a three-chambered mine was dug under a fortress and packed with gunpowder which, when detonated, caused more damage over a larger area to the structure under siege than a single-chamber mine.

Trefoil was not 'active' enough for the Air Staff, which left Maverick D and Improved BL.755 so a series of comparisons was conducted on their effectiveness. The specific Maverick under discussion was the Hughes AGM-65D with an imaging Infra-Red (IIR) seeker that made it suitable for use at night or through the fog of war. However, Maverick D was reliant on knowing where the target was, which would require either a forward air controller (FAC) or intelligence from a stand-off radar (which would not appear in the RAF order of battle until 2005) to allow the pilot to cue the weapon on the run in.

At 8ft 2in (2.5m) long and weighing in at 485 lb (220kg) Maverick D certainly had clout, as its 126 lb (57kg) shaped-charge warhead could pretty much guarantee knocking out a Soviet MBT. In fact, the warhead futureproofed the Maverick D making it capable of handling not just NST and FST, but Soviet tanks into the Nineties and beyond. At least that's what its advocates claimed. In USAF service on a type such as the Fairchild A-10A Thunderbolt, Maverick D was launched at a distance of 5 miles (8km) from the target during a pop-up manoeuvre to 500ft (152m) for 8-12 seconds. During this manoeuvre the pilot had to acquire the target on a 3in (76mm) display in the cockpit that showed the view from Maverick's IR seeker, lock on, launch and break off to return to low level at 2 miles (3km) to avoid point defences.

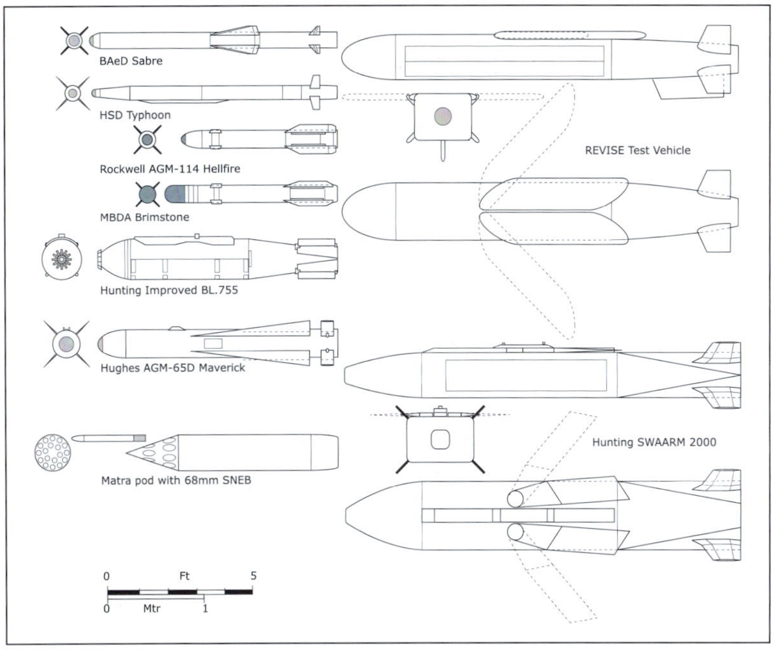

The possibilities for new antitank weapons were many and varied. Modified SAMs like Sabre; Typhoon, a modified AAM, free-flight dispensers such as REVISE and SWAARM. Ultimately Marconi's Brimstone won through, to production and service, inspiring a new family of weapons, SPEAR.

The success of the Maverick D attack was 'critically dependent on the ability to acquire targets using the displayed image from the IR sensor of the missile.' This in turn was dependent on the pilot knowing where the target was, information that would have to come from a FAC in the air or on the ground. For the Americans, three levels of FAC were available: Fast FAC (in a fast jet), Airborne FAC (in a helicopter or type such as a Rockwell OV-10 Bronco) and Ground FAC (attached to troops on the ground).

Maverick D was not suited to the RAF's fast and low doctrine – minimum exposure and sin-

This Jaguar GR.1 in Granby colours is carrying four GP Bombs in tandem pairs on the inboard pylons. While effective against Iraqi forces, the low altitude delivery required for maximum effect put the RAF's ground attack aircraft in harm's way. *Terry Panopalis Collection*

Harrier GR.9 ZD470 of No 1 (Fighter) Sqn cuts a dash, showing off its AGM-65G2 Maverick in the skies above RAF Akrotiri, Cyprus. Acquired in the light of delays with Brimstone, the G2 model was optimised for anti-armour rather than anti-bunker strikes and armed the Harriers pending delivery of Brimstone. *MoD/ Open Government Licence*

gle pass attacks – and was summed up in the AFD report with 'while the pop-up concept of operations is clearly attractive to the USAF, its suitability for use by the RAF must be rated as poor unless the full range of supportive measures is available.' What the AFD was alluding to with 'supportive measures' was the USAF's 'Route Package' tactics with defence suppression and FAC capability, not to mention the fact that the A-10A was designed to survive in the face of air defences. Maverick D would also require a completely new training and maintenance infrastructure to support it. It was also twice the cost of Improved BL.755.

Cost also influenced the adoption of Improved BL.755 in another way. At this time an Air Staff Target was being drawn up for a stand-off, direct-acting, precision-guided weapon for use against armour. This would lead to AST.1238 that was issued as ASR.1238 in 1982. The Air Staff had been observing the rise of the attack helicopter armed with, in the case of the AH-64A Apache, up to 16 ATGWs and saw this as a threat to the RAF's firm grip on the anti-tank role. The Air Force Department's view was that to 'ensure that fixed wing anti-tank operations remain worthwhile beyond the end of the decade, improved kill capabilities, as envisioned in AST.1238 will be necessary.' Interestingly the British Army was at the same time drawing up General Staff Requirement GSR.3971 for an anti-tank attack helicopter and this was issued in 1985. The debate on the pros and cons of fixed-wing vs rotary wing in the anti-tank roles continues to this day.

Despite this rivalry, a delineation between the RAF and Army zones of 'interest' appears to have formed with the Army and its TOW-armed Lynx tackling the armour on the front line and the RAF attacking the follow-on forces moving up on the road network. The RAF had a great deal of experience in the interdiction role and knew how effective it could be and was very keen to use new technology such as stand-off radar for targeting purposes, with the ASR.1238 weapon. By opting to upgrade BL.755 as an interim measure rather than developing VJ.291, the Air Force Department freed-up funds to develop the ASR.1238 Advanced Anti-Armour Weapon but like the stand-off radar, this was a long-term project.

As noted above, BL.755 was designed for attacking the T-55/T-62 generation of Soviet tanks that were in widespread service when BL.755 was introduced in 1972. A decade later the NSTs, T-64 and T-72, had improved armour protection with thicker and more steeply-sloped composite armour that presented a problem for the existing BL.755 submunition. Of course, as anyone who has seen the films *Kelly's Heroes* or *Fury* knows, even the most formidable of tanks can be more easily destroyed by attacking them from the rear. The Air Force Department pointed out that rear attacks, while more successful, would result in a higher attrition rate in the attacking aircraft as the attackers were required to overfly Soviet formations to conduct an attack on the vehicles' rear aspect. Given the increasingly widespread use of mobile air defences in Warsaw Pact formations, frontal attack with a single pass was the preferred tactic for the Harriers, the RAF's primary anti-tank platform.

While the current BL.755 submunition was more than capable of destroying the T-64/T-72 in rear attacks, it could not penetrate their frontal armour. The deficiency lay in two places: the power of the warhead and the angle of impact. Hunting Engineering advised that the former could be addressed by replacing the RDX/TNT explosive with more energetic EDC 1S and fitting a new metallic liner angled at 45° to increase the effect of the shaped-charge's plasma jet (See Appendix 1). The angle of impact was steepened by increasing the drag on the submunition. The existing BL.755 submunition used a multi-segment spring steel 'coronet' tail to stabilise it as it fell, giving an angle of impact of 15°. By replacing the coronet with a small parachute, the drag on the weapon was increased, slowing its speed of descent and increasing the angle of impact to 35° which improved the chances of a killing hit on the front and top armour of the tanks.

Improved BL.755 entered service as the BL.755 No.2 and was used in Operation Telic in 2003. One lesson learned from Operation Granby over a decade earlier, although IBL.755 saw very limited use, was that the low altitude delivery required for weapons such as BL.755 made the aircraft vulnerable to ground fire. Delivery from higher altitudes meant that the dispenser opened soon after release and the submunitions spread out while falling, creating a wider but less effective pattern. To address this, IBL.755 was modified for delivery from higher altitudes, typically above 10,000ft (3,048m), the effective ceiling of light AAA and MANPADS. The changes included fitting the radar altimeter from the WE.177 nuclear weapon that delayed release of the submunitions until the dispenser had fallen to the most effective altitude, creating a much denser pattern of bomblets. This variant became known as RBL.755 and remained in service until all cluster munitions were withdrawn from British service after the UK signed the Convention on Cluster Munitions in December 2008.

As usual, the MoD liked a bargain and for the same price as 1,000 Maverick D, the MoD could acquire 5,000 IBL.755 and so the existing BL.755s were modified with the IBL.755 enhancements made to the submunitions. As ever the MoD Defence Sales department had an eye on the export market as the original BL.755 had sold well to customers such as West Germany, India, Saudi Arabia and Iran amongst others. The MoD(PE) was concerned that if word of the need for improvements got out, sales of BL.755 might suffer. In August 1982, the Controller, Aircraft, Air Chief Marshal Sir Douglas Charles Lowe, summed this up by pointing out that 'neither Hunting nor Defence Sales are enthusiastic about a formal press release'. Huntings had plenty of BL.755 available for sale and 'they do not wish to diminish interest by reference to the need for "improvements" or offer the prospects too soon of better jam tomorrow'.

In reality, IBL.755 was the best choice for the ASR.1227 (First Revise) in 1982: affordable, deliverable in the low, straight and level attack

A Harrier GR.7 is seen during Operation Telic carrying two Paveways and a pair of IBL.755 improved cluster bombs. The T-72, main target for ASR.1227/IBL.755, was the principal main battle tank of the Iraqi Army in 2003. *Terry Panopalis Collection.*

A trio of BL.755 cluster bombs lined up alongside three Sea Harrier FRS.1s on the deck of a Royal Navy carrier. The BL.755 was used by Harrier GR.3s and Sea Harrier FRS.1s during the Falklands Conflict with the Sea Harrier carrying the store on the centreline pylon. *Terry Panopalis Collection*

by Harriers and capable of destroying the T-64/T-72. As a stopgap pending the deployment of the ASR.1238 weapon, IBL.755 fitted the bill but not everyone was convinced. Baron Orr-Ewing on 1 October 1982 penned a letter to the Minister for Defence Procurement, Viscount Trenchard, questioning the wisdom of adopting IBL.755 rather than the Maverick D, Orr-Ewing lists ten points against IBL.755. Citing losses to ground fire, Orr-Ewing stated 'I understand 3 Harriers were lost in over-flying Stanley Airfield in the Falklands. Saving one Tornado would pay for the entire Maverick programme' while pointing out that Maverick was an all-weather system with a 'deadly' shaped charge warhead.

Trenchard's reply came three weeks later and addressed each of Orr-Ewing's ten points. Trenchard's key argument was that Orr-Ewing had included the TV-guided version of the Maverick in his list, rather than the IIR-guided version. On the attrition question Trenchard advised that his staff could 'find nothing to support an estimate that 95% of aircraft shot down in the Falklands were flying at low level.' As for the 'deadly' shaped charge, Trenchard pointed out that Maverick was for use against point targets '...as it is a guided weapon' and for use against rear echelon targets, enemy territory would need to be overflown 'at an altitude that would be dangerous even with Maverick'.

Another weapon suggested for the anti-armour role, although not necessarily for ASR.1227 (First Revise), was the Bristol Aerospace CRV7 (Canadian Rocket Vehicle 7), a 2¾in (70mm) rocket carried in and launched from a pod. In March 1982 the RAE stated that its HEAT warhead was not effective enough compared with the IBL.755, with the RAE advising that it was only 30% as effective and thus incapable of defeating the T-64. Bristol Aerospace responded by describing an upgraded CRV7 with 'a new rocket motor and a heavy metal warhead'. The RAE was suspicious of this proposal and suggested that it 'may have been put together hastily' and that the new warhead would not provide the three-fold improvement required for ASR.1227 (First Revise). Even with the 'heavy metal' warhead 'a very dramatic increase in the number of rockets which could

RAF Tornado GR.4A ZG707 of No 13 Sqn refuels from USAF KC-10A Extender 85-0034 during Operation Telic. The Tornado is carrying four IBL.755 cluster bombs for use against Iraqi armour and SAM sites. *Terry Panopalis Collection*

be carried by the aircraft would be required' to approach the effectiveness of IBL.755.

Interestingly, later trials discovered that the CRV7 possessed such a high impact velocity that practice rounds with solid steel heads could penetrate the armour of an obsolete Centurion tank. When the steel was substituted with a tungsten warhead (this may be the heavy metal warhead mentioned above), the CRV7 could penetrate the frontal armour of a T-72. A development of this was the *flechette* anti-tank round with five tungsten penetrators that could punch through the T-72's side armour. By early 1983 the Air Staff were still interested in the CRV7, as a defence suppression weapon to be launched by Harriers as they made their approach for an IBL.755 attack on an armoured formation.

Another matter of concern to the Air Staff and MoD(PE) in mid-1983 was an increase in the cost of IBL.755. As noted above, ASR.1227 (First Revise) had always been intended to be cheap and the reason for that low cost was to ensure that there was maximum funding for the second stage of the RAF's two-stage anti-armour weapons development programme, ASR.1238. Despite being dismissed from the ASR.1227 (First Revise) running and being deemed incapable of destroying the T-64/T-72, Air Commodore DW Hann, ACAS-(OR) thought CRV7 might have a place in countering Warsaw Pact amphibious operations in Norway or the Baltic. In these theatres it could be used against landing craft, *Ivan Rogov*-class assault ships or the large hovercraft such as the *Aist* and *Pomornik*-class landing craft, air cushion (LCAC) vehicles.

Although Maverick D had been dismissed by the Air Force Department in 1981, the MoD ordered the AGM-65G2 for the Harrier GR.7/9 in 2000 as an interim anti-armour weapon pending delivery of Brimstone. The AGM-65G was optimised for bunker-busting, but the G2 was fitted with software modified for the anti-armour role and was deployed on the RAF's Harriers, with up to four being carried. The Harriers used Mavericks during Operation Telic, reportedly with very good results in the close support and anti-armour roles. Similarly, the CRV7 did ultimately equip British forces, and again on the Harrier, with 19-round pods being carried on wing pylons. The CRV7 was also carried by the Army Air Corps on their WAH-64D Apaches.

The massed attack by Warsaw Pact armour never materialised and thus, aside from limited use in Iraq, the IBL.755 was never used in its intended role. As for the 'rejected' weapons all three, Paveway LGBs, CRV7 rockets and AGM-65 Mavericks, found themselves being launched from Harriers against the 21st century's most numerous military vehicle – the Technical.

Smart Tank Killing

'...but on the day that Lot went out from Sodom it rained fire and brimstone from heaven and destroyed them all.' Luke 17:29

'Don't we want EO assistance for all our dumb bombs eventually?' Marginalia on a memo to Air Commodore Beddoes, DOR2, from WM Jarvis, Head Air Weapons Dept, RAE, 3 March 1978

'The prime target in the AST is the MBT. There has been speculation in the West that the key role of the MBT on the battlefield may be coming to an end... The Soviets do not appear to share this view.' RAE AST.1238 Working Paper 42, February 1984

When the policy of Flexible Response was adopted there was still a need to deal with Warsaw Pact armoured formations and preferably by a means that did not up the nuclear ante. That had been met by the BL.755 cluster bomb and the SNEB 68mm rocket but by the late 1970s new technology, the so-called 'smart weapons' were on the cards and showing promise. The BL.755 required the delivery aircraft to overfly the target, at low level, with the inherent risk of being shot down so the Air Staff had issued AST.1227 for a BL.755 replacement. By 1976 the BL.755 bomblet was '...considered to be on the small side for the successful attack of the latest assessed type of Warsaw Pact armour...'.

The RAF's current anti-armour weapons, BL.755 and SNEB were capable of penetrating 'all the armour of both T-62 and T-64/T-72 for impact angles at or near normal.' SNEB was considered to be 50% more effective than the BL.755 bomblet, but each SNEB pod only carried 19 rockets against 147 bomblets in a BL.755 dispenser. Unfortunately, the attack profiles employed saw the weapons impact at 15° to the horizontal and since the 'fuze cut-off' angle was 20°, neither munitions would penetrate the thinner top armour of these main battle tanks (MBT). In addition to this, the T-64 and T-72 were thought to employ new com-

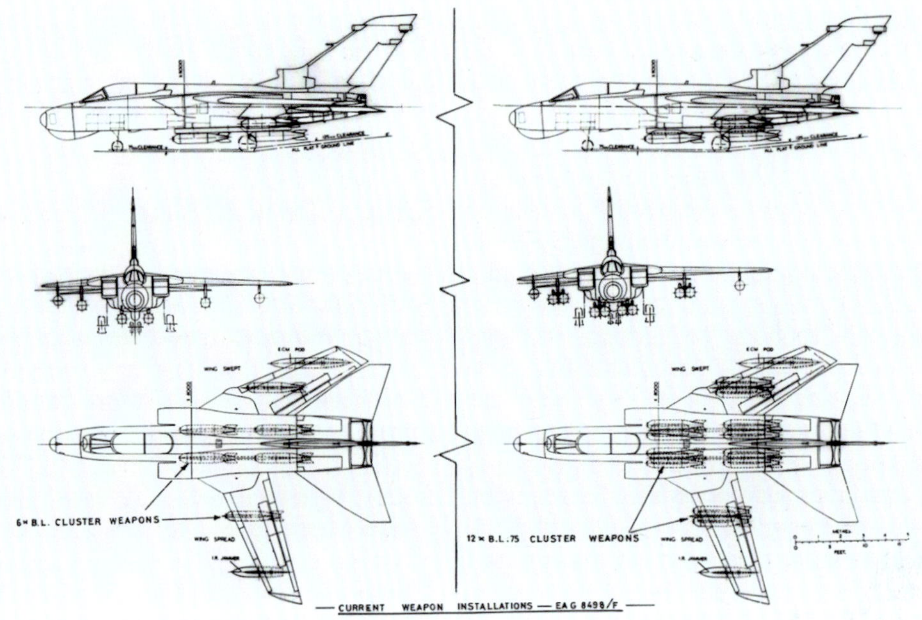

While a minimum load of six BL.755 or AST.1227 weapons was specified for AST.396, this Tornado-based design study could carry up to 12 BL.755 plus countermeasures pods. Note the new optronics nose. *North West Heritage Group.*

posite armour that was more steeply sloped, and these were expected to reduce the effectiveness of SNEB and BL.755 warheads by half. However, it was noted that air-launched weapons were not usually aimed at a MBT's glacis plate, so BL.755 and SNEB were still credible weapons, but as Soviet MBTs improved with the Future Soviet Tanks (FST), a new weapon would be required. This could be either a 'guided cluster bomb' or a 'precision guided missile' and should have 'high kill probabilities (PK) even against the most modern Warsaw Pact tanks.'

As issued to contractors in November 1975, ASR.1227 was based around a Royal Armaments Research and Development Establishment (RARDE) study called 'Tankill' that called for the weapon to be capable of 'defeating a Warsaw Pact main battle tank with the characteristics of the T-62S which is an uparmoured version of the T-62.' There was an additional requirement to defeat the T-72, although details of this MBT were sparse in October 1976, but RARDE was able to supply the contractors with information on warhead types suitable for use against these MBTs, such as the RARDE's Comprador that had been specifically designed to counter composite armour such as Burlington, a member of the Chobham armour range.

This information was particularly relevant to any proposals that involved a guided weapon, but not every proposal was a guided weapon, as Hunting Engineering were proposing '...the more sophisticated version of the cluster bomb solution....' By August 1977 the 'steered cluster weapon' was not finding favour and was being described by the head of DS9, Mr DJ Fewtrell, as neither 'feasible or indeed necessary'. This was due to the newly adopted Soviet tactic of increasing the distance between the tanks to reduce the efficacy of cluster bombs. When a line of tanks came under air attack the 'odd' tanks in the formation moved 50-100m (164-328ft) to the left and the 'even' tanks moved the same distance to the right, but the distances were to be staggered to avoid the tanks lining up as before. The Air Staff identified three types of armoured formation targets: lines of up to ten tanks forming up in the enemy rear, scattered groups of up to three tanks in the front line and denser groupings of vehicles, possibly in lines, exploiting a breakthrough.

The Air Staff took the view that the ability to attack targets 'late and off bore-sight far outweighs any apparent loss in effectiveness through fewer submunitions' which was particularly relevant to the Jaguar. If a dual purpose submunition with a steering unit was employed, the ASR.1227 project manager expected a '300% improvement over BL.755 in terms of 'exchange ratio' as the steering unit 'could offer some flexibility of pattern shape against smaller target groupings.'

As with the AST.1217 anti-runway systems, the Air Staff focused on the 'exchange ratio', specifically the number of tanks destroyed per aircraft lost, with the studies for AST.1227 showing this as ranging from 3.2:1 to 11.7:1. As with the anti-runway weapons, the main threat to the attacking aircraft were ZSU-23/4 Shilka AAA and SA-8 *Gecko* SAMs but the Air Staff expected the aircraft-mounted ECM to meet ASR.853 (Skyshadow), chaff dispenser to meet ASR.612 (BOZ dispenser) and the anti-radiation missile to meet ASR.1228 (ALARM) to increase the exchange ratio in favour of the attacking aircraft.

Staff Target AST.1227 became Staff Requirement ASR.1227 that called for a weapon with fire-and-forget capability. This was written in due to the workload on the pilot of a single-seater aircraft such as the designs for AST.396 and ASR.403 plus the existing Jaguar and Harrier. As a result, when it came to aiming and delivery, rather than the drop-and-depart cluster weapon, a guided weapon was preferred specifically one with an autonomous targeting and attack capability.

In 1978 such autonomous capability was still in the laboratory, so aircraft such as the Jaguar required a designation system such as the ASR.1229, which entered service in the shape of the Pave Spike pod, that could be carried on the outer wing pylon of the Jaguar. Unfortunately, the Jaguar only had five pylons and if the inboard wing pylons were used for fuel tanks, only the centreline pylon was available for AST.1227 weapons as the Pave Spike and an AN/ALQ-101(V)-10 jammer pod would occupy the outer pylons. To address this, there was a suggestion that the overwing pylons on the Jaguar could be used for the designator and jammer pods or fit double or triple carriers on the pylons, but another proposal involved a completely new wing with three pylons for the Jaguar. Wherever the designator was mounted, on a single-seater the designation system would have required an automatic lock-follow system to operate effectively.

This was not unique to the Jaguar as the Harrier only had five hard points so carriage of a number of weapons on multiple racks was required. In 1977 laser-guided munitions, or rather the guidance kit, were large and so were mated with larger bombs such as the 1,000 lb (454kg) bomb. While these LGBs could be used against individual tanks (a technique used by the USAF in Operation DESERT STORM) these 'would be better used to create choke points on the line of march where tank concentrations would present lucrative targets for attacks with BL.755.' If, as was suggested, Paveway kits were fitted to the BL.755, that would restrict the number of weapons that could be carried, and this was compounded by the change in the intended aircraft to carry the ASR.1227 weapon. In February 1978 the Staff Requirement was revised to have the Jaguar as the main carrier aircraft. This is mentioned in February 1978 by the CAS, Marshal of the RAF Sir Michael J Beetham who stated that '... the AFD (Air Force Department) position on this important project is not fully understood. I would like to reiterate it. There is no question that this aircraft's primary task is ground attack and it should have the maximum capability in this role.'

This was not seen as a problem in March 1978 as the preferred weapon was a 'cluster bomb with a direct-hitting submunition' or a 'Dual Purpose Submunition' (DPS) that also acted as a minelet if it failed to hit a vehicle. The proposed minelet was to be based on the HB.876 submunition for the JP.233 anti-runway system. While a guided weapon was desirable, the cluster bomb would be available sooner and could be used by the single-seat Harrier, Jaguar and AST.403, none of which had any capability with a guided weapon, but the guided weapon would be developed in the long term. Settled? Not at all. A full-blown argument ensued over

Precision teamwork during Operation GRANBY. A Victor K2 XL161 of No 55 Sqn trails its wing pod hoses for Tornado GR.1 (possibly ZA491/N) carrying three Paveway II LGBs and Buccaneer S.2B providing target designation with its Pave Spike pod. *MoD/ Open Government Licence*

whether a steered or unsteered cluster bomb be adopted although the steered cluster bomb was eventually 'dropped'.

This did not please the Air Staff as it would mean that the weapon would not possess the 'late attack' or 'off-boresight' capability. Prior to this the Air Staff had, according to the VCAS, Air Marshal Sir Peter DG Terry, been 'expecting to make a difficult choice between two very promising solutions' but were by April 1978 'likely to be presented with a poor Hobson's choice and one that would hardly be acceptable to the ORC' (Operational Requirements Committee). Nor was the VCAS pleased by the inferred 'major shift in AFD policy away from using AST.403 in the anti-armour role' repeating the CAS' statement that 'there is no question that this aircraft's primary task is ground attack and we intend that it should have maximum possible capability in this role.'

On the cluster weapon front, Hunting Engineering Limited (HEL) were proposing extensions of the BL.755 in either unsteered or steered variants. HEL stated that by 'optimising bomblet design, ground patterns and dispensing methods' an unsteered direct attack bomblet could achieve a 30% performance advantage over BL.755. HEL's other option was a steered direct-attack bomblet that would 'allow aircraft to attack targets without directly overflying the accompanying defences'. Although this variant was larger (13% fewer bomblets in the same dispenser) it would allow aircraft like Jaguar to perform off-boresight attacks, albeit only 100-200m (328-656ft) off-boresight. The steering was affected by an inertial unit in the dispenser that could control the bomblet release height, producing a tighter pattern and therefore more top attacks on armour. HEL were not particularly convinced by laser guidance, stating that it could minimise aiming errors 'on the relatively few occasions when visibility will permit' and that the designation pod would take up a stores pylon that could be used for a weapon. As for the dual-mode bomblet/minelet HEL proposed, much of its development was underway for the JP.233 system so could be transferred to ASR.1227, although the Air Staff was sceptical of HEL's assurances on fuzing and triggering the minelets, not to mention their claims of an 80% improvement in effectiveness over BL.755.

The Air Staff were pretty much convinced that a guided weapon offered a 'somewhat better mission performance than the cluster weapon, so what were the 'promising solutions' to ASR.1227? These proposals were for guided weapons, one called Sabre and the other Typhoon. Sabre was developed by BAC Dynamics using the Rapier airframe, but the airframe required modifications to handle the stress of carriage on a ground attack fighter in 'the more severe air carriage environment' and fitted with a 5kg (11 lb) shaped charge warhead guided by a laser seeker from the Copperhead shell. The other was developed by Hawker Siddeley Dynamics (HSD) based on the SRAAM, the missile that would ultimately become the ASRAAM air-to-air missile to meet ASR.1234, the Sidewinder replacement.

HSD's proposal used the thrust vector controlled SRAAM airframe to provide a highly agile weapon with the same imaging IR seeker but fitted with the 25kg (55 lb) tandem charge warhead from the Trigat-LR ATGW that due to its size did not require the precision designation of the Sabre with its smaller warhead. BAC stated that the larger warhead could be fitted to Sabre to match the effectiveness of the Typhoon against targets other than tanks. Other changes to the air-to-air weapon included a shorter, reduced power rocket motor, a radar altimeter and repositioned warhead. Interestingly at this point in the Air Staff's discussions, Hellfire is mentioned and deemed to be 'markedly inferior to the proposed UK missile solution' in short range attacks. The laser-guided AGM-65C Maverick was similarly dismissed as it needed to be locked on before launch, was twice as heavy and had three times the drag of the Sabre. Interesting observations in the light of later developments.

The Air Staff appeared to have paid little heed to the RAE's evaluation of the drag effects on a Jaguar or Harrier carrying multiple rounds for the ASR.1227 guided weapons and took the view the overwing carriage of missiles on Jaguar had 'not been adequately discussed' nor had the firing and jettison methods been investigated, particularly the double-missile mounting. The RAE considered 'relatively simple cleaning up' of the cluster weapon could have reduced its installed drag by 30% on a Harrier.

The impression gained from the correspondence on ASR.1227 is that the cluster vs guided weapon debate was never going to be resolved, indeed at one point in May 1978 the Secretary of State for Defence Fred Mulley posited the view that a dedicated anti-tank aircraft was required! Perhaps the minister had been asleep during the discussions, having famously fallen asleep in the presence of HM The Queen at the 1977 Jubilee Review of the RAF. Subsequently 'having a Mulley' became RAF slang for a short kip.

This Jaguar GR.3 departs RAF Coltishall with just wing tanks and a Sidewinder acquisition pod on the overwing pylon. This stores station was considered for any designator for the AST.1227 guided weapon, freeing up the underwing and ventral pylons for multiple racks of weapons. If a designator was not required, weapons could be carried. *MoD/ Open Government Licence*

By the end of May 1978 there were two, possibly three, options: the cluster bomb, the guided weapon and, a new option if the cluster bomb was selected, a completely new guided weapon for the 1990s. The cluster bomb was gaining ground again, as a means to attack the second echelon Soviet armoured formations massing in the rear. Squadron Leader LS Penny OR50c discussed this matter with the Director of Operational Requirements (DOR2) Air Commodore JGG Beddoes in a memo dated 7 June 1978 and took the view that a large dispenser carrying the HEL dual purpose bomblet could be used in the same manner as the JP.233 for ASR.1217, with the same dispenser carrying up to 800 bomblets. Penny also thought he had found the solution to the Jaguar payload quandary in the JP.233 dispenser as a Jaguar could 'carry the equivalent of more than four cluster bombs units (CBU), fuel and ECM pods, for less weight, drag and complexity than individual bombs on multiple racks.' The Tornado could carry two dispensers (as per the anti-runway mission) with less complexity and drag than nine BL.755 bombs.

The advantages, according to the Squadron Leader were commonality with the ASR.1217 anti-runway weapon and thus much lower risks and cost plus it could be in service much sooner than a guided weapon; 1983, the original ASR.1227 in-service date. Penny also pointed out that a fixed dispenser had two 'clear advantages over CBUs' as the forward throw was much reduced which improved weapon aiming and, with reduced target acquisition ranges, dispensers took less time and distance to aim.

Air Commodore Beddoes took the view that the scenario Squadron Leader Penny described was not in the requirement and that the dispenser system would not meet the basic ASR.1227 requirement but could be an addition to ASR.1227. DOR2 was also somewhat sceptical of the delivery method as it would require the aircraft to overfly the target and therefore lacked the off-boresight capability demanded in the requirement.

By July 1978 the MoD had received more intelligence on the new generation of Soviet tanks such as the T-64 and T-72 and Air Commodore Beddoes had a few questions on the effectiveness of the BL.755 bomblet against these MBTs. This new information prompted a re-evaluation of BL.755 and other British anti-tank weapons and added impetus to ASR.1227. On 24 July 1978 the VCAS, Air Marshal Sir Peter DG Terry, had been on a visit to RAE Farnborough to discuss the new Soviet tanks. The VCAS outlined his thoughts on the matter to the Deputy Controller, Establishments & Research (C), HW Pout, and suggested that '...our study work on air-to-surface munitions for use in the Central Region may be in need of some reorientation to recognise recent developments.' Terry also suggested that 'we should treat the situation as an operational emergency in all but name.' and that a cluster weapon would be quicker to develop than a guided weapon. The VCAS also requested that the RAE should look into improving existing munitions 'to produce in-service in a very few years a significant increase in anti-tank kill probability, particularly against the T-72.' The cluster weapon to meet

ASR.1227 was to be a 'mid-term solution to be pursued with vigour' while the research into a precision guided munition (PGM) and associated systems should be viewed as the long-term solution.

Jaguar and Harrier would require major modification to carry the PGM, specifically a cockpit rebuild to fit a video display, and these types would also be required to 'give up' a pylon for a designator. As already noted, the laser-guidance system was not suited to bad weather operations and experience had shown that laser-guided munitions worked best for single-seat aircraft when used with ground designation due to 'jitter'. And thus, by August 1978, the PGM solution to ASR.1277 was considered unfeasible, so it was back to the drawing board for a guided cluster weapon, essentially an improved BL.755. The result of this re-assessment was VJ.291, a Hunting Engineering guided anti-armour cluster munition to AST.1227, described above. As had been argued at length, the effectiveness of a cluster weapon against dispersed armoured vehicles was questionable and even when guided, it lacked the capability the Air Staff sought.

A further reassessment of the requirement was undertaken in 1981-82 by the Air Force Department (AFD) who advised that VJ.291 be cancelled and ASR.1227 revised in the light of new information on Soviet armour. A new Staff Target, AST.1238, was drawn up, calling for a weapon that was capable of destroying '5 out of a company of 10 tanks' in a single pass and able to be carried in sufficient numbers to allow two attacks in a single sortie. In comparison, BL.755 could only destroy 0.5 tanks in a 10-tank column per pass. The AFD review also drew on intelligence on the New Soviet Tank (NST) and Future Soviet Tank (FST) that was expected to be fielded in the late 1980s, this was the T-80 with composite and explosive reactive armour.

Trials Tornado GR.1T ZA326 of the A&AEE is seen here with a REVISE dispenser on its centreline pylon. The stores on the outboard pylons are camera pods to record submunition behaviour on release. *Blue Envoy Collection*

After some debate in the Operational Requirements Committee (ORC) on the relative merits of line-of-sight and stand-off weapons the ORC agreed with the AFD that, given the development timescales, a line-of-sight weapon was feasible for service entry in 1990. The AFD intended that any weapon developed to meet AST.1238 should be used for battlefield air interdiction (BAI) and close air support (CAS), with the latter considered most important in dealing with a Soviet breakthrough. One key aspect of AST.1238 was the ability to differentiate between targets i.e. identify high value targets such as MBTs in formations of trucks and other vehicles, although in a CAS situation the ratio of tanks to truck would be higher, making identification less important plus the aircraft would in all probability be under forward air controller (FAC) direction.

As for the weapon, the prospect of new armour systems such as composite and ERA would influence the warhead fitted to the AST.1238 weapon and that would affect the size of the weapon. Target acquisition was also viewed as a potential problem for AST.1238 with aircraft avionics being required to operate at low altitudes (<200ft/60m) and at high speed, with around 10 seconds from target identification to the aircraft overflying it, resulting in a very high pilot workload. Automated systems would help, but these were not mature enough to permit a no-man-in-loop system. Targeting was to be via FLIR and LLTV systems that would provide the pilot with an image of the target that could allow identification at a distance of 2 miles (3km). There was some debate on whether the cockpit was to be modified to provide this imagery as redesign of existing aircraft cockpits was frowned upon.

There was no doubt that AST.1238 was difficult to achieve, and it combined a number of features that were being developed for other systems such as laser designators, explosively formed penetrators, dual-mode and MMW seekers and pilot interfaces such as helmet-mounted sights. As with ASR.1227 there was a variety of systems under discussion be they missiles or dispensers. On the missile side, three weapons were proposed. The first was BAeD's 'conventional' A1, a transonic missile fitted with a shaped charge warhead while the A2 was a derivative of BAeD's FLAME (Future Lightweight Air-to-air Missile Equipment), a high velocity air-to-air weapon with a kinetic energy warhead but was thought too complex due to its need to perform a bunt before a top attack impact. and like the A1, it used an imaging infrared seeker with lock-before-launch. HEL's A3 missile was also transonic, used a MMW seeker with designate-before-launch and lock-after-launch. The A3 had a long minimum range and to address this HEL suggested that it should be launched 'in a backwards direction over the top of the launch aircraft', which did not impress the Air Staff. All three were carried in pods, with six of the BAeD or eight of the HEL missile missiles per pod. When loaded, HEL's pod was almost twice as heavy as the BAeD systems.

On the dispenser side, BAeD proposed two systems while HEL, dispenser experts, proposed four, all differing in seeker, guidance, warhead and propulsion. BAeD's two dispensers carried eight submunitions, the B1 type used an aerodynamically-controlled, terminally-guided submunition with inertial guidance and an IR seeker. BAeD's B2 used a thruster-controlled, terminally-guided submunition with imaging infrared guidance and a IR seeker with lock-before-launch. This dispenser was capable of climbing after launch for a top attack.

HEL's four proposals cover the gamut of techniques. The B3 used a 'simple munition' with a self-forging fragmentation warhead, inertial guidance with IR and MMW dual mode seekers. The B3 was capable of climbing and 24 could be carried in the dispenser. The B4 was an aerodynamically-controlled, terminally-guided submunition with a shaped-charge warhead, no guidance but did have an IR seeker. Only nine could be carried, in a pod half the weight of the B3. The B5 weapon was a thruster-controlled, terminally-guided submunition with inertial guidance and an IR seeker. The B5 could climb for the attack and 12 could be carried in the dispenser. HEL's B6 was the most complicated of the dispenser weapons with a aerodynamically-controlled, terminally-guided submunition, a MMW seeker and guidance with designate-before-launch and lock-after-launch. It could also climb for the attack and be fitted with a rocket motor for extended range. With twelve submunitions per pod, the B6 was the heaviest, and most complicated, of the proposals.

In the analysis, the missiles were deemed superior in the CAS situation where flexibility was important but in the BAI case with large numbers of densely packed targets, the dispensers were more suitable. Missiles, specifically the A1 and A2 were capable of attacking individual tanks but if targets other than tanks are attacked, the dispenser would be preferred.

As ever, the MoD were looking for a cheaper option and as luck would have it, the Luftwaffe and MBB were working on an simple anti-armour weapons dispenser for its Alpha Jets called Vebal/Syndrom that launched VBW submunitions, based on Panzerfaust 3 or LAW80 warheads, vertically below the aircraft as it overflew the target, triggered by automatic sensors. This harked back to the Förstersonde SG113 tested on Fw 190As in 1945.

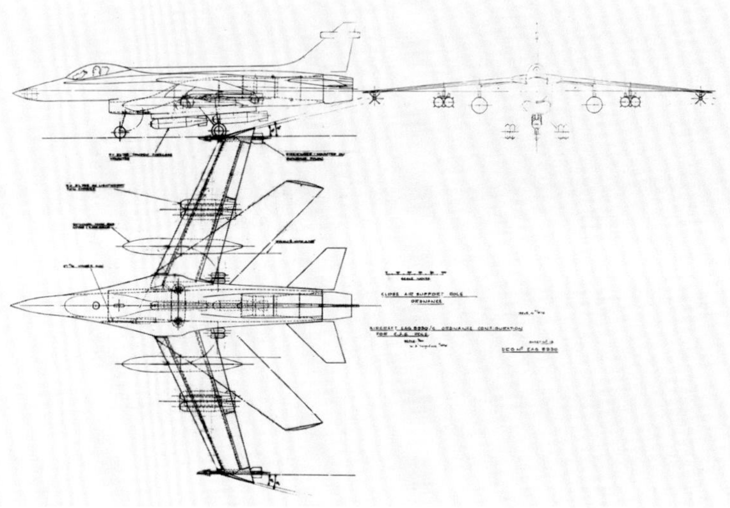

The BL.755 was to be the main armament of the aircraft to replace the Jaguar and Harrier under AST.396. This BAC Warton study, Drawing EAG.8930 carries the requisite six bombs, but the AST.1227 weapon would have replaced these. One interesting aspect of this study is the swivelling pylons at the wingtips for AIM-9 Sidewinder AAMs. *North West Heritage Group*

By the mid-1990s the use of cluster munitions, and their association with landmines in countries such as Afghanistan, Angola and Iraq, was becoming less and less politically tenable. The UK was a signatory to the 1997 Ottawa Treaty that aimed to remove anti-personnel mines from the world's armouries while a similar campaign led to the Convention on Cluster Munitions, signed by the UK in 2008. As far as Her Majesty's Government was concerned, the cluster bomb was history.

Landmines, of the anti-tank variety rather than anti-personnel, went hand-in-hand with the cluster bomb as the mined areas forced the advancing Warsaw Pact formations along narrower routes, suitable for attack by strike aircraft with cluster bombs. Landmines played such a pivotal role in the defence of western Europe that when the RAF issued new requirements for battlefield support helicopters, the requirement included the uplift and delivery of huge quantities of landmines across West Germany to create the denied areas.

Added to all these factors there was the increase in number and effectiveness of Warsaw Pact mobile air defence systems that were making the delivery of cluster bombs by aircraft overflying the armoured formations, less feasible. A new anti-armour weapon was required, one that could pick off individual vehicles at distances beyond the effective range of air

Four AGM-114L Hellfires on the stub wing of a Boeing AH-64D Apache. The AGM-114L uses a MMW seeker with target acquisition by the mast mounted Longbow radar. The outboard pylon carries a pod of 19 Hydra 70 rockets. Although externally similar, Hellfire and Brimstone are completely different. *Author*

defence weapons. This was reinforced in January 1991 when RAF Tornados were shot down, not delivering the JP.233 anti-runway weapon, but standard 1,000lb (454kg) bombs, on the first night of Operation GRANBY.

What the Air Staff needed was a fire-and-forget weapon that could be launched in salvos from outside the Warsaw Pact forces' air defence envelope and attack individual targets. This was the basis of AST.1238.

Hellfire and Forget

In the July 1971 discussions about GSR.3431, an anti-tank guided weapon for the Lynx AH.1, Col. PE Collins wrote to the Assistant Chief of the General Staff (OR) Major General Ian Gill and while decrying RARDE and EASAMs 'seemingly pedestrian predictions' on guidance systems, Collins presents what at first reading is a fairly innocuous sentence relating to guided weapons development in the USA. Collins wrote that North American Rockwell claimed to 'be producing, at the cost of £3K a round, a "fire and forget" missile which could be introduced as a helicopter weapon in the mid-1970s.' The weapon was described as having 'an optical contrast target seeker' of a type to be tested later in 1971 by the RAE. This is the earliest mention of a weapon that would ultimately become Hellfire.

Not that Rockwell were alone in applying this high technology to anti-tank weapons. Hunting and Honeywell proposed SWAARM (smart weapon anti-armour) a submunition dispenser that was to be delivered in a loft manoeuvre to avoid overflying the target formations, releasing 16 submunitions to descend on parachutes while scanning for targets. Another stand-off system delivered by lofting was BAeD's air-launched anti-armour weapon (ALAAW) that used submunitions similar to SADARM (Search And Destroy ARMour) a parachute-deployed submunition fitted with a seeker and self-forging warhead. ALAAW was tested on a RAE Buccaneer.

It would be Rockwell's system that would prevail. Originally called Heliborne, Laser, Fire and Forget Missile when development began in 1974, the weapon was initially described as a 'modular missile' that could accept a range of seekers (semi-active laser, dual-mode radar frequency/infra-red, optical contrast (TV) or imaging infra-red) but the first Hellfires in service were laser guided. The AGM-114A Hellfire is most associated with the Hughes AH-64A

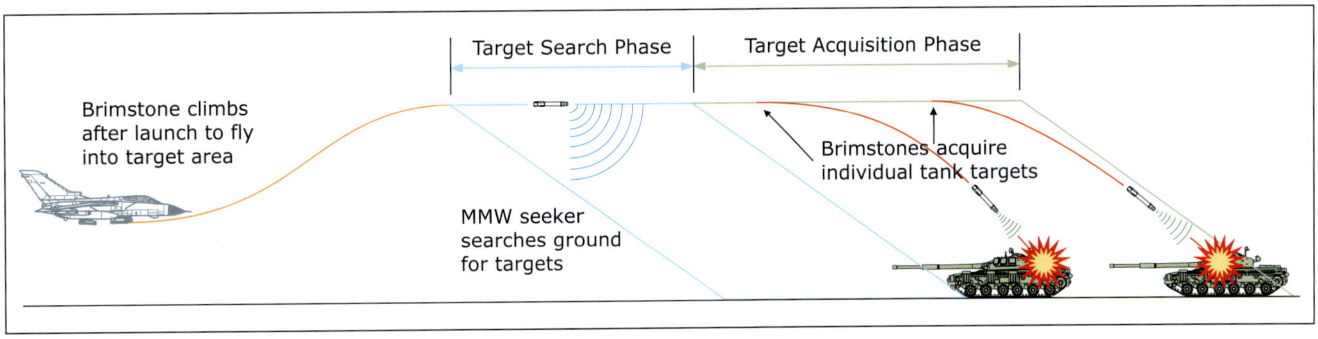

Brimstone at work. The outcome of the ASR.1238 was an autonomous weapon, capable of being launched in salvoes and seeking individual vehicles. These are the flight profiles for MMW Single Mode Brimstone. Dual Mode Brimstone can be guided by a laser designator for rules of engagement that require a human-in-the-loop.

Apache and the combination entered service as the US Army's primary attack helicopter weapons package in 1984 and in 1987 crossed the Atlantic as a counter to Soviet armoured forces in Europe.

The need to designate the target with a laser meant that the original Hellfire was not a truly fire-and-forget missile and the nose-mounted Target Acquisition and Designation Sights (TADS) required the Apache to place the bulk of its airframe above cover. Longbow Hellfire, AGM-114L, is a radar-guided variant that uses a millimetre-wave radar seeker coupled with inertial guidance and is a true fire-and-forget weapon for use against targets using smoke or other battlefield obscurants that could counter laser-guided weapons. The AN/APG-74 radar's antenna is mast-mounted above the main rotor and provides tracking for 128 targets and handle up to 16 targets at once. It was the Longbow Hellfire that the AAC acquired when the WAH-64D entered service in 2004 and was used with great success in Afghanistan on Operation Herrick from 2006.

How does a missile developed for the Apache relate to the Air Staff's ASR.1238? Marconi Defence systems first proposed a radar-guided variant of the Rockwell Hellfire in 1987, specifically to meet the Air Staff's anti-armour weapon requirement. This was based around a Marconi millimetre wave (MMW) radar seeker that the company had been captive-testing on a Hellfire strapped on a helicopter. Resistant to ECM due to its narrow beam, the MMW radar could discriminate between buildings and armoured vehicles and could be fired as a fire-and-forget weapon. These features would allow MMW-guided weapons to be launched against armoured formations and, importantly, identify and lock on after launch, so Marconi's work continued with the seeker being integrated with the Hellfire airframe. As trials continued it soon became apparent that the Hellfire, designed for launch from a helicopter, was unsuitable for carriage and launch from a fast jet. Therefore, the entire airframe was redesigned for fast jet carriage, became known as Brimstone and aside from superficial similarity, is unrelated to Hellfire.

Alternatives to Brimstone

In the post-Granby re-assessment of the RAF's weapons that followed on from the post-Cold War studies, the Air Staff examined proposals from industry. Having previously dismissed the BAe/Hughes Rapid Fire Maverick and the ML/Rheinmettal Damocles, five bids remained. Two of these were missiles, two were dispensers and the fifth was a hybrid.

SWAARM 2000 was a variant of the Mehrzweckwaffe-2, a free-flight dispenser developed for the Royal Swedish Air Force as the Dispenser Weapons System (DWS) 39 and used systems derived from the Mehrzweckwaffe (MW-1) anti-runway weapon developed for the Luftwaffe's Tornado fleet (See Chapter 5). The SWAARM 2000 was fitted with extended wings and could be powered by a Royal Ordnance rocket motor to extend its range. It carried 16 SADARM (Sense And Destroy ARMor) munitions developed for the Multiple Launch Rocket System (MLRS) that deploy on parachutes, canted to rotate the munition in the horizontal plane and since the munition now hangs at an angle, allows the sensor to scan the area below the munition for targets. These sensors comprise a MMW radar and IR sensor, plus a magnetometer to ensure the target is big and metallic i.e. a tank. On detecting a target, the SADARM fires and an explosively-formed penetrator (also known as a self-forging warhead), travelling at velocities in excess of 6,500ft/sec (2,000m/sec), punches through the top armour of the vehicle. SADARM has an effective range of 500ft (152m).

Oddly enough, despite its origins with Hunting's BL.755, it was the Thomson-Thorn Missile Electronics partnership that based its bid on the existing BL.755. The Thomson-Thorn Advanced Anti-armour Weapon System (TAAWS) used the BL.755 dispenser to carry three SADARMs

Opposite, bottom: Brimstone, developed by MBDA as an anti-armour weapon as seen here in its Single Mode guise on a three round carrier. Typhoon is the main platform for the RAF's Brimstones but can also be carried by the Protector RG.1 UAV and the Apache AH.1. The Lightning will use the SPEAR 3 variant. *MoD/Open Government Licence*

A single Dual Mode Brimstone on the port rail of a triple launch shoe. The active seeker of Brimstone operates on a narrow beam width which reduces its susceptibility to detection and jamming. *MoD/ Open Government Licence*

into the target area, boosted by a small rocket motor. The ML Aviation/Rheinmetall Damocles carried five Rheinmetall ZEPL (Ziel entdeckende projektilbildende Ladung) submunitions that were spun as they were released over the target area, scanning the area below the weapon. One variant of Damocles was interesting as it flew very low, less then 100ft (30m), dispensing its ZEPL submunitions upwards, something that impressed the MoD.

In mid-1988 the MoD selected SWAARM and Brimstone for further development which tended to suggest that the MoD didn't really know what they wanted. A further difference involved the warheads; explosively-formed in the SWAARM and shaped charge in Brimstone. The SWAARM warhead was much larger and considered pretty much future-proof while the Brimstone's might be defeated by the explosive reactive armour that was appearing on Soviet tanks (See Appendix 1). To address this Marconi pointed out that Brimstone's shaped charge was large enough to handle any foreseeable development in Soviet armour. Marconi also proposed fitting their MMW seeker to a 1,000lb (454kg) general purpose bomb fitted with a guidance kit. That would definitely defeat any Soviet tank and while it might sound like overkill, it was exactly what the USAF did in Kuwait in January 1991.

In July 1990, following the fall of the Berlin Wall the previous year, the MoD decided to shelve SR(A) 1238 and was considering 'designs to less stringent criteria' driven by the Treasury. At this point the field had been whittled down to Hunting's SWAARM and Marconi's Brimstone. The Options for Change review published in July 1990 outlined the shape of Britain's armed forces in a post-Cold War world and the Treasury was intent on the Peace Dividend, with projects such as the replacement for the Chieftain tank looking vulnerable. This left the RAF with the Improved BL.755 as its anti-armour weapon. Then, a month later, Saddam Hussein invaded Kuwait and with it came Operation GRANBY, the British name for the liberation of Kuwait.

In the fallout from GRANBY and the concerns about collateral damage and cluster weapons, dispensers had fallen from favour. GRANBY had also seen the rise of the precision guided weapon and therefore the prospect of a salvo-fired, fire-and-forget, lock-after-launch precision tank killer was attractive to the Air Staff. By 1992 SR(A).1238 was back, with dispensers off the menu. Brimstone was still in the running, but BAe were proposing an updated Typhoon called FLAME, a variant of the ASRAAM air-to-air missile with a Hughes imaging infrared seeker from the Maverick. BAeD opted for IIR as they considered the power requirements for a MMW seeker 'prohibitive'. Diagrams of FLAME show a 'shark nose' profile (also seen on SRARM, see Chapter 5) which may indicate two seekers.

Also being considered was the Hughes AGM-65G IIR Maverick and the Aérospatiale AS.30L, both having had a 'good war' in Kuwait. The AS.30L was an odd choice as it required laser designation and like the Maverick, took up a pylon for each round, unlike Brimstone that could be carried as 'triplets' on a single pylon. Also entering the fray in 1992 were the Alenia Skyshark (a dispenser system) and a variant of Maverick fitted with a MMW seeker. BAeD were also offering Medusa, an air-launched version of the Merlin smart anti-tank mortar bomb, that also used an MMW seeker.

By 1995 the on-again/off-again SR(A).1238 saga had reached a point where a decision was required as the RAF's fleet of Harrier GR.7s, the intended main user of the SR(A).1238 weapon, were in service. The final five contenders were MSDS Brimstone, Hunting's SWAARM, Thorn EMI's Terminal Guided Warhead (TGW3), Texas Instrument's Joint Stand-Off Weapon (JSOW) and the BAe Typhoon/FLAME. Interestingly BAe claimed that Typhoon retained some of the ASRAAM's air-to-air capability.

Texas Instrument's bid for SR(A).1238 was the AGM-154B, the anti-armour version of the JSOW that had been developed for USN and the USAF (to fit in the F-117A's weapons bays). The AGM-154B dispenser carried six BLU-108/B submunitions that deploy on parachutes and as it descends ejected four Skeet warheads, each fitted with a laser (for active target acquisition) and an IR detector (passive acquisition) and self-forging warhead.

By November 1996 the Air Staff had selected Brimstone to meet SR(A).1238 to arm Tornado and Harrier. Meantime, MSDS had become GEC-Marconi and by 1998 what had been the missile seeker development arm had been bought out by BAe to form BAE Systems. BAE System's Dynamics division had merged with other European guided weapons companies to form MBDA and it was under MBDA that Brimstone entered final development and production. After ground firings and initial flight trials in 2000, Brimstone was put on the back-burner while the Storm Shadow cruise missile was given priority (see Chapter 5).

Brimstone entered service in early 2005 and its first use in combat was in 2009 during Operation Herrick in Afghanistan. Operations in Libya for Operation Ellamy saw Brimstone in action, especially against 'technicals' - pick-up trucks armed with a variety of weaponry ranging from the *Dushka* (sweetie) the 12.7mm DShK heavy machine gun to the UB-32 57mm rocket pod. The Brimstone missile was used in a variety of modes including salvo fire against armoured columns. Brimstone also saw action during Operation Shader, with the RAF attacking forces of ISIS in Iraq, again taking on the technicals.

The aircraft weapon system allows the Brimstone to be programmed with a target signature that it will search for when it arrives in the target area. The targeting data can be supplied by pre-mission reconnaissance or as an update from surveillance platforms such as Sentinel R.1 (ASTOR) or the traditional means, troops on the ground. The MMW seeker on Brimstone operates on the 94GHz frequency and although it is an active emitter, GEC-Marconi stated that due to its low output and narrow beam, had low probability of interception by a potential target. The high frequency of the seeker not only allowed the missile to discriminate between vehicles and structures, as development continued, it could not only identify types of vehicles but also where on the vehicle its tandem-charge warhead would have most effect.

Brimstone can be salvo-fired into the target area to select and attack individual targets but can also be used in direct and indirect fire modes. In terms of effectiveness, Brimstone was estimated to be at least three times more effective than Maverick and seven times deadlier than BL.755. Dual Mode Brimstone was the result of an Urgent Operational Requirement for the RAF and added laser guidance to the MMW seeker to allow the weapon to be used in theatres where the rules of engagement required human intervention in the firing sequence. This might include a manual abort to avoid civilian casualties or in urban areas where the MMW seeker might suffer from a multitude of returns. The MMW seeker works best when engaging moving targets such as vehicles, the targets it was originally designed to attack. These new variants were called Dual Mode Brimstone and can be identified by their transparent 'radomes'.

RAF Tornado GR.4s could carry up to twelve Brimstone on four triplet carriers on the ventral

Tornado GR.4 ZA542 of No 31 Sqn loaded with what had become the standard load-out for operations over Afghanistan, Iraq, Libya and Syria. This comprises two Paveway IV LGBs, three Dual Mode Brimstone and a LITENING III designator pod. *MoD/Open Government Licence*

The Technical Hunter. An MQ-9 Predator UAV loaded with a mix of Single and Dual Mode Brimstones. The Dual-Mode allows a 'human-in-the-loop' capability for use in built-up areas. *MBDA*

pylons leaving the wing stations for fuel tanks, ALARM and countermeasures pods such as Skyshadow and BOZ. Typhoon can carry up to 18 Brimstone plus Meteor and ASRAAM for air-to-air. The Harrier force was to carry Brimstone, in fact it was the Harrier that Brimstone was originally intended for, but its integration with the Harrier was underway when the Harrier force in the Joint Strike Wing was stood down in 2011.

SPEARheading development

Aside from Dual Mode Brimstone, developments included a new range of variants developed from a MoD requirement to improve Brimstone's performance. The programme, Selective Precision Effects At Range (SPEAR) lead to Brimstone 2 that had an updated seeker, new insensitive munitions (explosives and propellants that burn, rather than explode, when subjected to shock or heat) and simplified modular construction. Brimstone 2, also known as SPEAR 2, entered service in 2015. MBDA also tested Brimstone 2 on the AH-64E Apache attack helicopter with another proposed version known as Future Attack Helicopter Weapon (FAHW) which is a Brimstone 2 modified to allow selectable trajectory (line-of-sight or 'lob' to reach behind structures) and warhead modes such as airburst, proximity and impact.

On the maritime front, navies had noted Brimstone's capability against small moving targets such as technicals (Brimstone 2 had successfully intercepted a speeding pick-up truck during trials) which might make the weapon useful against small boats. A maritime variant, named Sea Spear in the usual British style, was developed and a test organised, with a Tornado GR.4 launching a Sea Spear at a 6m (20ft) rigid hulled inflatable boat (RHIB). The weapon destroyed the RHIB.

Perhaps the ultimate development of Brimstone is SPEAR 3 a stand-off weapon with a range of 80 miles (129km) thanks to a wing kit and a Hamilton Sundstrand TJ-150 turbojet with a INS/GPS guidance system. Up to 18 SPEAR 3 can be carried by Typhoon on the triplet carriers or eight in the weapons bays of the F-35 Lightning.

Intended to blunt a massed armour spearhead of the Red Army on the North German Plain, the weapon that met SR(A).1238 endured an extended gestation before meeting, if not exceeding, all aspects of the requirement. The T-72 and T-80 may have been its original target but in the third decade of the 21st century Brimstone will handle not only the latest MBTs but a Toyota Hilux with a *Dushka* motoring along in a built-up area.

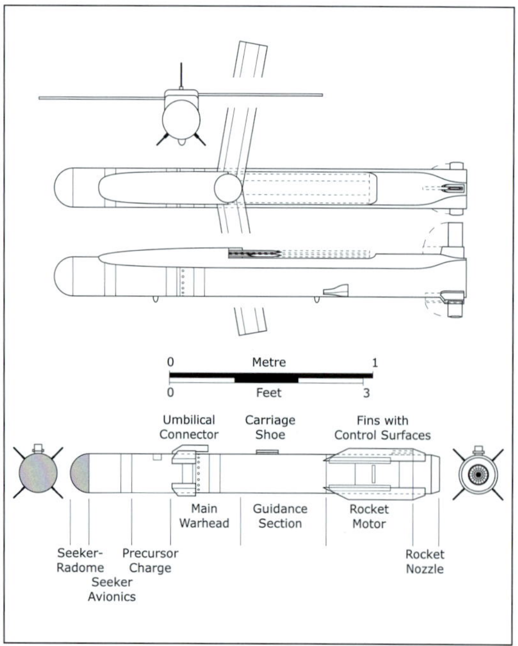

Brimstone is a compact millimetre-wave radar guided rocket-powered weapon originally designed for use against tanks. In the years between the issue of ASR.1238 and Brimstone's service entry the targets, and rules of engagement, changed. SPEAR added wings and replaced the rocket motor with a turbofan to produce a compact stand-off weapon.

5 Countering the Air Threat

'There is an obvious gap in Warsaw Pact defences, which if the UK developed a second-generation cruise missile, could be exploited well into the future.' Lieutenant General Sir Maurice Robert Johnston, Deputy Chief of the Defence Staff (OR), Chiefs of Staff Committee, February 1981

'Hitherto the attack of aircraft protected by substantial concrete shelters has been considered as an unrewarding occupation.' EW Lawrence and CD Coxhead, DOAE paper (Air)/98, March 1974

Perhaps the biggest challenge facing NATO was the Warsaw Pact air forces that would support any invasion of western Europe. NATO could fight them in the air, but a more effective tactic was to destroy their airfields and offensive counter-air became a primary role for the RAF. These airfields would be hardened and heavily defended which in turn required some means to getting the counter-air types to their targets with minimal losses. These roles required specialist weapons and great effort was expended to develop these and ultimately only one survived.

While the obvious threat to western Europe was the Warsaw Pact tank force that would spearhead any invasion, these would be supported by air forces that were, as time passed, becoming increasingly effective. The potential of surface-to-air missiles (SAMs) had been shown on May Day 1960 when Gary Powers' U-2 had been brought down over Sverdlovsk in the Soviet Union. While this demonstrated the lethality of SAMs against high-altitude aircraft, driving NATO air forces to low altitudes operations, the Soviets soon saw to the low-level threat. The war in Vietnam and the 1973 October War demonstrated that short-range, low-altitude mobile air defence systems could be lethal against strike aircraft. Suppression of such air defences became a critical task in the operations of interdiction and close air support aircraft.

The improvement in Warsaw Pact combat aircraft mirrored that of NATO, who had opted to continue the use of conventional aircraft operating from airfields. As a result, another role that became essential to the survival of NATO aircraft was to destroy, or at least prevent the use of, Warsaw Pact airfields in eastern Europe. While tactical nuclear weapons had been ear-

Panavia Tornado IDS seen during trials of the Hunting Engineering JP.233 anti-runway dispenser. Tornado could carry a pair of the two-part dispensers. *Hunting Engineering via Terry Panopalis*

The S-125 Neva/Pechora (SA-3 *Goa*) was capable of operating at lower altitudes than the *Guideline*. Transportable rather than mobile, the *Goa* would have been deployed on the Warsaw Pact airfields that would be attacked by the RAF. These examples are on their transport vehicle. *DoD via Terry Panopalis.*

marked these counter-air missions, by the late 1970s conventional weapons were being considered for this mission.

With a need to operate from conventional airfields and facing attack from the start of any conflict, both sides' airfields went 'hard'. Aircraft and servicing facilities were placed in hardened aircraft shelters (HAS) and command and control centres were housed in bunkers, all built in steel-reinforced concrete. Where previously a single, or in the case of WE.177C, a pair of nuclear weapons would suffice to put an airfield out of action, hardened facilities now required a more focused, surgical strike. Stand-off weapons had come a long way since the days of Blue Steel and the days of a ½ mile (1km) accuracy were long gone. Technology had made it possible to destroy a point target from a considerable distance.

The modern RAF strike force would be unable to operate without a new generation of weapons which like Brimstone (see Chapter 4) have their origins in the 1970s and now fight a completely different kind of war. Having examined anti-tank weapons in the previous chapter, weapons for use against air defences and airfields – offensive counter air – will now be examined

ALARM – Surviving the High-Tech, High-Threat Battlefield

'In this two-horse race I believe both must win.' Sir Kenneth Warren MP, Letter to Prime Minister Margaret Thatcher, 17 May 1983

'You would be faced with making up a suit of clothes on your judgement of whether it was likely to fit and be of the right material.' Air Marshal Sir Douglas Lowe, Controller, Aircraft. Memo to Texas Instruments, 30 April 1982

As noted elsewhere, many of the tactics, roles and weapons described herein have their origins in the conflicts of earlier years. This is certainly true of suppression of enemy air defences (SEAD), which has evolved into a specialist role, especially in the US armed forces, but for the RAF having more emphasis on small formations rather than the large packages of the US Air

Warsaw Pact mobile SAMs included the SA-6 *Gainful* that had given the Israelis a shock in October 1973. This photo shows a *Gainful* providing cover for a convoy of BMP-1 infantry fighting vehicles and, on the road, four BM-21 Grad 122mm multiple launch rocket launchers. *TASS*

Force, SEAD was more of a self-defence capability. SEAD could range from a fighter strafing a flak emplacement as a target of opportunity to B-52s launching AGM-69 Short-range Attack Missiles (SRAM) ahead of their formations on a Cold-War-turned-hot mission into the Soviet Union, blasting a route through the Soviet defences.

One of the earliest SEAD missions took place during the Battle of Britain when the Luftwaffe attacked RAF Chain Home radar stations. By failing to follow up these missions against the Chain Home stations and the associated command and control systems, the Luftwaffe contributed to the ultimate success of the RAF. SEAD did not necessarily mean destroying the enemy's weapons and associated air defence systems but hindering their operation on a temporary basis while a mission was underway could work just as well, which is where jamming and other countermeasures enter the fray.

The first practical application of electronic warfare was the Battle of the Beams in 1941 when Luftwaffe bombing aids were detected and countered by the British. What became known as electronic countermeasures (ECM) and SEAD is rooted in Bomber Command's radio countermeasures and intruder operations from 1942 and specifically with 100 Group from November 1943. Many of the peculiarly named bits of radio countermeasures (RCM) kit fitted to 100 Group aircraft came from the Telecommunications Research Establishment at Malvern and included *Piperack*, *Mandrel* and *Airborne Grocer* jammers and *Serrate*, *Lucero* and *Perfectos* homing equipment. The jammers disrupted a coherent picture of a raid or prevented German radars such as Freya and Würzburg from working while other systems such as *Tinsel* disrupted communications by transmitting engine noise on the same frequencies as Luftwaffe nightfighter (*nachtjager*) ground controllers. The passive homing equipment allowed RAF intruders and nightfighters to home in on the emissions from the Liechtenstein radars of their Luftwaffe counterparts.

While the above systems were mounted on specialist aircraft such as 100 Group's Fortress IIIs, standard aircraft could be equipped with kit such as *Fishpond* to detect nightfighters (a very early airborne early warning system) and the *Monica* tail warning radar. The most widely used RCM equipment was Window, now known as chaff. First used on Operation GOMORRAH, the July 1943 Battle of Hamburg, Window was very effective in blinding German radars. On the suppression front, 100 Group's Mosquito nightfighters carried homing systems to seek and destroy *nachtjagers* or conduct intruder missions against their bases, destroying the *nachtjagers* as they landed.

All these measures and the constant move and countermove in the night skies over Germany had by May 1945 produced in Bomber Command an integrated fighting machine whose SEAD arm had developed to such an extent that it could counter any threat to its operations.

On the tactical front, RAF Typhoons carried the Abdullah homer for use in attacking German radar sites in the run-up to OVERLORD and post D-Day operations. SEAD operations were not solely an airborne task, artillery could be used in what the British Army called Apple Pie missions in support of operations such as VARSITY, although these were of mixed success. This lack of success was due to two deficiencies: lack of intelligence and lack of firepower. The first could be solved by the applying the material gained from radio reconnaissance, now called Elint, while the second could be improved not by increasing firepower but making it more focused. This boiled down to identifying the target radar, pinpointing its location and hitting it. Since, by their nature, radars give away their location, finding them should not pose a problem similarly hitting them could be achieved by using their own emissions to guide a weapon onto the radar emitter.

Postwar, much of the RCM/ECM effort went into countering the Soviet air defences ranged against the RAF and USAF strategic bombers in what was very much a continuation of the British work over Germany. USAF night bomber operations over North Korea suffered at the hands of radar-directed M1939 52K 85mm and KS-19 100mm anti-aircraft guns. The USAF fitted Douglas A-26 Invaders with radar detectors to attack the SON-9 (NATO reporting name *Fire Can*) radar directing these AA guns. Despite this, the effort against air defences was predominantly aimed at getting strategic bombers

The USAF and USN developed anti-radiation missiles (ARM) to tackle North Vietnamese air defences. The larger AGM-78 Standard is mounted on the inboard wing pylon of the F-105G Wild Weasel while the AGM45A Shrike is on the outboard pylon. These are exhibited in the National Museum of the USAF. *Author*

to their weapons release points over the Soviet Union.

This all changed from early 1965 when US forces in Vietnam encountered an increasingly effective integrated air defence system that included radar-directed AAA (from 37mm to 100mm) and the S-75 Dvina (NATO reporting name SA-2 *Guideline*) SAM. The next decade saw a process of measure and countermeasure as tactics for each side to beat the other evolved, with the US developing jammers, chaff dispensers and anti-radiation missiles plus the tactics for their use. The North Vietnamese developed tactics of their own while their Soviet patrons improved the missiles and (along with other nations such as the UK) learned lessons that would be applied in future, and potential, wars.

The US Navy and Air Force applied different doctrines to the air war in Vietnam. The USN and Marine Corps favoured the quick in and out operation with small formations whereas the USAF opted for the package; large formations that, by the end of US involvement in 1973, saw the strike aircraft outnumbered by the support types. The Navy developed the AGM-45A Shrike missile for attacking radars such as the *Fan Song* used by the SA-2 and this was adopted by the USAF. Its limitation was that its range, around 9nm (16km) was less than the effective range of the *Guideline* (25nm/45km) which was well inside the *Guideline's* engagement envelope. Added to that, the launch aircraft had to fly towards the radar (and ever-increasing chances of being attacked) to launch the Shrike and if the *Fan Song* fire-control and tracking radar was switched off, the Shrike would not guide. The later AGM-45B variant possessed longer range, 21nm (40km) which was an improvement but still within the *Guideline's* range.

This basic countermeasure of switching off the radar (usually by putting the transmitter onto dummy load rather than off) was overcome in 1967 by the AGM-78 Standard ARM, a larger weapon based on the naval SAM, which was faster than the Shrike, had longer range (43nm/80km) and a memory module with an inertial guidance system to 'remember' the radar's location. Switching off the radar remains a useful, but not 100% effective counter to ARMs. Radio frequency emissions are not the only part of the electromagnetic spectrum available to anti-radar weapons as the radar system and its power generator become hot and if not suppressed, an IR seeker can be used to guide an inbound weapon. The other benefit of the Standard ARM was its larger warhead, 215 lb (98kg) rather than the 149 lb (68kg) of the Shrike, that could cause considerable damage to a SAM site rather than just shred the radar antenna.

SEAD became a specialised role in the USAF and US Navy with the advent of Operation IRON HAND in 1965. US Navy units flew A-4 Skyhawks supported by F-8 Crusaders and A-3 Skywarriors, with the Skyhawks launching Shrikes at the SAM radars and dropping cluster bombs on the sites themselves. The USAF units were equipped with F-100 Super Sabres or F-105 Thunderchiefs also armed with Shrikes and cluster bombs.

The USAF's IRON HAND operations came to involve a new class of aircraft, the Wild Weasel, a dedicated SEAD variant of the F-100 (Wild Weasel I) or most famously, F-105G called the Wild Weasel III (the F-105D formed the basis of the short-lived Wild Weasel II). The F-105G Thunderchief was based on the F-105F two-seat trainer and was adopted after the F-4C Phantom proved unsatisfactory as the Wild Weasel II. Since the F-105 was out of production and suffering high attrition in Vietnam, another attempt at modifying the F-4C was made, with more success. This became the Wild Weasel IV but only 36 were produced before being superseded by the F-4G Wild Weasel V. One reason the F-4C proved unsatisfactory as a Wild Weasel was its inability to carry the Standard ARM. The lack of Standard ARM capability on the Phantom was solved when the next generation of ARM entered service on the F-4G, which carried the HARM and that combination remained in service until 1996 when the role was taken over by the F-16, which brought the reign of the custom-built Wild Weasel to an end. The only true SEAD type in service as of 2019 is the Tornado Electronic Combat/Reconnaissance (ECR) in service with the Luftwaffe and Italian Air Force.

While the Vietnam War would mould the tactics and equipment of the US services, another war added to the West's knowledge of Soviet air defence doctrine, one more applicable to any RAF operations in a western European war. The October/Ramadan/Yom Kippur War of October 1973 saw a joint Egyptian/Syrian two-front offensive against Israel. Initial gains by the Arab armies were helped by the prewar build-up of a SAM belt along the 1967 ceasefire lines comprising SA-2 *Guideline* and S-125 Neva (NATO reporting name SA-3 *Goa*). The *Goa* had a shorter range than the *Guideline* but could engage more manoeuvrable targets at much lower altitudes and was more resistant to US ECM systems, thanks to lessons learned in Vietnam. It was ideal for intercepting the Israeli strike aircraft such as McDonnell Douglas F-4E Phantoms, A-4N Skyhawks or Dassault Super Mystères.

Once beyond the SAM belt, Egyptian and Syrian ground forces were protected by mobile, vehicle-mounted systems such as the ZSU-23/4 Shilka and, to the great surprise of the Israeli Air Force, the 2K12 Kub (NATO Reporting name SA-6 *Gainful*). With the capability of engaging targets down to 300ft (100m), if not lower, the *Gainful* gave the Egyptian and Syrian forces the upper hand against Israeli strike aircraft that were flying low to avoid the *Goa* and *Guideline* systems. In addition, the Israeli threat warning systems were initially incapable of warning pilots that they had been illuminated by the *Gainful* SAM's *Straight Flush* radar. Even if the SAMs were detected, evasion by flying lower put the Israelis into the engagement envelope of the Shilka's four 23mm cannon.

Israeli countermeasures included retuning the radar warning receivers on the aircraft, using chaff (lack of pods saw chaff stuffed into air brakes) and updated jamming pods hastily despatched from the USA. This diminished, but did not remove, the threat but allowed Israeli aircraft to conduct aggressive SEAD operations against the mobile air defences with gun, rocket and cluster bomb.

What did become clear was that once an army, whichever side, advanced beyond its air defence 'umbrella', it was vulnerable to air attack by the opposing side. This was the case on the Golan Front when Syrian ground forces advanced beyond SAM coverage and suffered heavy attrition at the hands of the Israeli ground attack units once the Shilkas and *Gainfuls* had been dealt with. A second lesson learned from the October War was that intelligence was crucial to the SEAD role. Up to date information on threats, ECM that could be retuned to meet new threat and multi-threat chaff dispensers were all required. If only one lesson from the Middle East and Vietnam was learned it was that the Warsaw Pact divisions would be carrying umbrellas and these air defence umbrellas would be multi-layered.

The multi-layered nature of the Soviet air defences required weapons that could be flexible enough to deal with the various threats. In the 1970s, the West had three anti-radiation missiles: The US Shrike and Standard plus the French AS.37. All three shared a common trait: seeker modules that had to be fitted or reprogrammed before the mission to deal with specific radars. They were, especially the Standard and AS.37, large and heavy and what was needed was a lightweight, programmable-in-flight weapon that could cope with the countermeasures, such as emitter shut-off.

The American approach involved two weapons with the first being a quick, lightweight solution based on the AIM-9C Sidewinder. The Sidearm was developed by the US Navy as the AGM-122A with the AIM-9C's semi-active radar seeker replaced with a seeker tuned to the radars of mobile air defence systems. Its main user was the US Marine Corps on its AH-1W Cobra attack helicopters and AV-8B Harrier STOVL attack aircraft from 1986. The other American system, whose development was also led by the US Navy, was intended to replace both the Shrike and Standard ARM and was sized between the two at 780lb (354kg) and 13ft (4m) long. It possessed the range of the Standard and high speed and as a result was called the High-speed Anti-Radiation Missile – HARM.

Whither the British?

Radio directed aircraft – drones – in British service date back to the Larynx naval bombardment weapon of the 1920s, back to 1916 if the Lowe AT is included. By the 1930s the possibility of swarms of 'wireless directed' bombers attacking the UK was a concern to the Air Ministry. Countering these 'wireless-directed aircraft' had been discussed at a meeting of the Committee for the Scientific Survey of Air Defence on 15 March 1934. A Mr Barton of the RAE described a system whereby a pilotless aircraft would home in on enemy wireless transmitters and it would be 'a fairly simple matter to provide that "homing" aircraft reach the neighbourhood of their targets'. Unfortunately, radio transmitters in the 1930s were large, comprising tall masts with wires, the antennae, strung between them. The Committee was sceptical 'the chances that one aircraft would effect important, and not easily repairable, damage to a transmitting station are so small that a very large number of [homing aircraft] would need to be used.' Accuracy in azimuth was not seen as a problem, but elevation was, given that the towers could be 100ft (30m) tall and the chances of the homing aircraft hitting a mast fairly slim.

As noted above, the RAF's 100 Group used homing systems to attack German nightfighters, which in turn were probably homing in

Buccaneer S.2 XK527 banks away from the camera ship to show its quartet of AS.37 anti-radiation missiles. The AS.37 was a large weapon and like its anti-ship variant AJ.168 Martel, not particularly successful. *Terry Panopalis Collection*

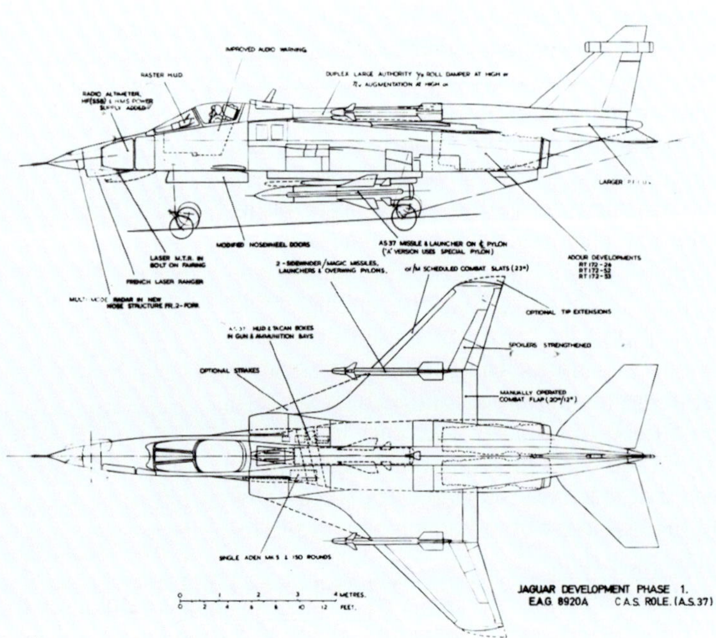

The size of the AS.37 more or less precluded its use by tactical aircraft like Jaguar. This Jaguar study, EAG.8920, shows a single AS.37 on the centreline pylon. The missile's ancillary equipment would be housed in the starboard gun bay. *North West Heritage Group*

on RAF bombers using H2S ground-mapping radar or *Monica* tail-warning radar. Hawker Typhoons fitted with *Abdullah* attacked German early warning and targeting radars and therefore by the end of the war the RAF were well-versed in using a radar's own emissions for targeting weapons. All this experience does not appear to have survived the immediate postwar period as the services' focus moved to strategic and colonial matters neither of which required active countermeasures in the form of anti-radar weapons.

The US Navy's interest in an anti-radiation missile led to the Shrike in 1962, but the French Air Force and Royal Air Force were in the market for a new air-to-surface weapon to arm their next generation of strike aircraft, with the RAF's F-111Ks to carry it as an anti-ship weapon to meet ASR.1168. De Havilland Propellers were working on their RG.10 missile while France and Germany were developing the AS.33 and AS.34 missiles. France and Germany went their separate ways, with Messerschmitt-Bolkow-Blohm developing the AS.34 as the Kormoran 1 and Matra developing the AS.37. De Haviland Propellers, by 1963 part of Hawker Siddeley Dynamics (HSD), and Matra joined forces to use the AS.37 airframe as the basis for a British weapon, the TV-guided AJ.168 MARTel while Matra concentrated on the AS.37, an anti-radiation missile for l'Armée de l'Air, which the RAF also adopted. Neither version of the weapon fared well in RAF service and HSD proposed a number of variants, but only one of these came to fruition, the Sea Eagle. Such was the RAF's dissatisfaction with the Martel/AS.37 missiles that when an Argentine AN/TPS-43 air defence radar on the Falkland Islands was identified as a threat to British air operations in May 1982, a request was sent to the USA to supply AGM-45 Shrikes rather than use the AS.37 Martel.

Well before the events of May 1982 the British had been apprised of the American and Israeli experience in the early Seventies. With the focus on operations against Warsaw Pact land forces in western Europe, the Air Staff came to appreciate that SEAD would be a key to future operations and that the existing kit was not up to the job.

AST.1228 – Drones, Decoys and Delayed Action

The Operational Requirements Committee recognised the need for a SEAD system for the Central Front in Europe and endorsed AST.1228 in November 1975. The Staff Target had arisen from studies and simulations carried out by the Air Staff into 'RAF offensive sorties carried out in Central Europe in the face of the postulated ground defences which may be deployed by the Warsaw Pact'. These studies concluded that aircraft attrition rates would be very high 'unless positive steps are taken to reduce the effectiveness of the defences' prompting a two-year study into making these 'positive steps'.

The April 1978 report described a multi-faceted study conducted under the direction of Directorate of Future Systems DFS(PE) and the Defensive Weapons Department, RAE (the Co-ordinating Research and Development Authority, CRDA) and involved delivery vehicles, decoys, glide bombs, air-launched projectiles, ground-launched projectiles and a harassment drone. The intended targets were 'front line defences, say about 20km (11nm) from the FEBA' especially the SA-8 *Gecko*, ZSU-23/4 Shilka, SA-6 *Gainful* and S-60 AA gun with the *Gecko* viewed as the most effective against low-flying aircraft 'perhaps by a factor of 5'. In the reserve area, 20-100km (11-54nm) the targets would be the same plus the SA-3 *Goa* and SA-4 *Ganef* but dug in or protected by revetments and possibly employing decoys and 'guard radars'. Guard radars were secondary, lower-powered radars designed to detect incoming threats and automatically shut down the main radar when necessary. A further requirement was discussed; support of offensive counter-air and deep strike missions up to 250km (135nm) beyond the FEBA.

The munitions under consideration were the anti-radiation Sub-Projectile, anti-radiation Glide Bomb and the Self-Defence Decoy. The Sub-Projectile (SP) was the basic building block of the AST.1228 proposals, delivered into the target area by a variety of means. On release from these delivery systems, the SPs deployed parachutes allowing them to hang vertically, 'listening' for radar signals with a BAeD homing head while descending at 15m/sec (50ft/sec). The delivery systems were to climb after launch and release their SP payload at 12,000m (39,370ft) a height deemed to be above the effective ceiling of low-level air defences such as the SA-8 *Gecko*. At 12,000m (30,370ft) the seeker on an SP had a footprint with a diameter of 15km (8nm) reducing to a diameter of 12km (6.5nm) by the time it had descended to 8,500m (27,887ft). The SP could hang on its parachute for up to four minutes, descending and listening. On detecting a radar, the parachute was jettisoned, and the SP dropped free, descending on a controlled trajectory. This trajectory used the passive radar seeker that guided the SP under proportional navigation and controlled by the rear four of eight flip-out fins, onto the target radar in a vertical attitude, maximising the damage from its 25kg (55 lb)

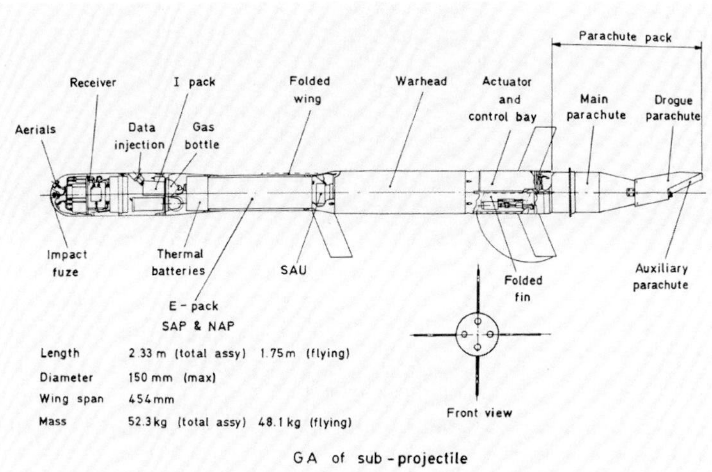

The anti-radiation Sub-Projectile was the basic component of BAeD's AST.1228 studies. On release, the Sub-Projectiles would deploy a parachute and slowly descend 'listening for radar emissions'. *Blue Envoy Collection.*

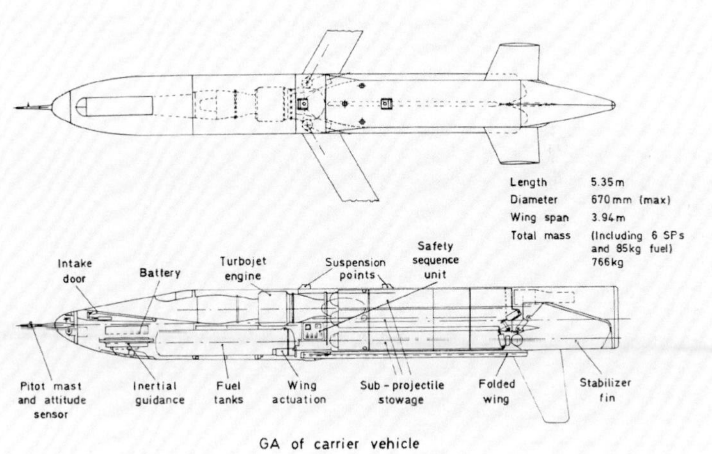

The turbojet-propelled Air-Launched Carrier Vehicles allowed stand-off deployment of up to six Sub-Projectiles, although four was the preferred payload. *Blue Envoy Collection.*

blast/fragmentation warhead. The SP was considered a low technological risk as its configuration, folding fins and aerodynamics had been proven on an anti-tank weapon.

First delivery system to be examined was a powered dispenser, to keep the aircraft well out of harm's way, for which a large, 5.35m (17ft 6in) long, air-launched Carrier Vehicle (CV) was examined. This could be launched at low altitude from a strike aircraft and could carry up to six anti-radiation SPs to an altitude of 12,000m (39,370ft) above the target area where they would be released. The CV was fitted with flip-out wings and tail surfaces with the wings having a span of 3.9m (13ft) and powered by either a Turbomeca Arbizon IV turbojet or a Microturbo TRI 60 turbojet with a bifurcated jet pipe and guided by a Ferranti FIN2000 inertial navigator.

The Carrier Vehicle was deemed far too expensive and complicated, so two other delivery systems were examined. The 4m (13m) long Air-Launched Sub-Projectile (ALSP) bore a resemblance to an enlarged Rapier SAM and carried a single Sub-Projectile in the forward portion of its airframe whose skin formed a sabot around the projectile. On reaching the target area the combined boost/sustain motor cut out and a first stage parachute deployed to slow the missile followed by a second parachute to further slow the missile and swing it into a vertical orientation. This direction of attack could be especially useful against radars protected by revetments. The sabot would then uncover the Sub-Projectile, which would separate and deploy its own parachute. The ASLP had a range of 26.5km (14nm) on a ballistic trajectory that saw it climb to 17,000m (55,774ft) before deploying its retardation system at 12,000m (39,370ft) and releasing the Sub-Projectile.

A Ground-Launched variant, GLSP, was the same diameter, sharing the same sabot/sub-projectile section but was longer than the ASLP, 5.5m (18ft), due to an extended boost/sustain motor and a three-stage retardation parachute section. The GLSP was to be launched from a Stonefield 4x4 truck (with 12 launch rails) towards a target area 55km (30nm) away on a ballistic trajectory, climbing to 26,000m (83,300ft) before deploying the parachutes/Sub-Projectile at 12,000m (39,370ft). In this case the SP lacked parachutes and relied on the parachutes on the delivery vehicle for deceleration and orientation. As with the Carrier Vehicle, the sheer number of mechanical devices, rocket motors, parachutes, release mechanisms and control systems involved in the ALSP and GLSP raised concerns about reliability. The failure of one device in the complex sequence of events would cause the entire weapon to fail and thus neither was proceeded with.

In pursuit of simplicity, the next weapon examined was a Glide Bomb. This weighed in at 500kg (1,100 lb) but to allow more to be carried on aircraft, was reduced to 254kg (560 lb) including a 180kg (397 lb) warhead, a radar seeker and basic compass-based guidance unit. Since any glide bomb relies on height and glide angle for range, the weapon had to be released at high altitude, typically 12,000m (39,370ft) which posed a problem to the launch aircraft.

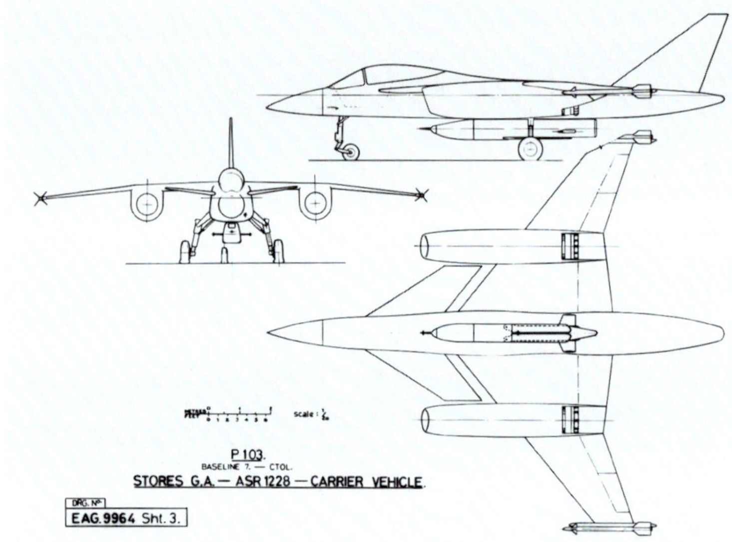

This drawing (EAG.9964-3) Shows the BAC P.103 carrying the Air Launched Carrier Vehicle (ALCV) on its centreline pylon. The ALCV would have allowed attacks of air defence systems at longer range, but once launched, its four Sub-Projectiles were used. *North West Heritage Group*

The Air-Launched Sub-Projectile, looking like a BAeD Rapier, could carry a single Sub-Projectile. Its range was up to 14nm (26km) when launched from a strike aircraft. *Blue Envoy Collection.*

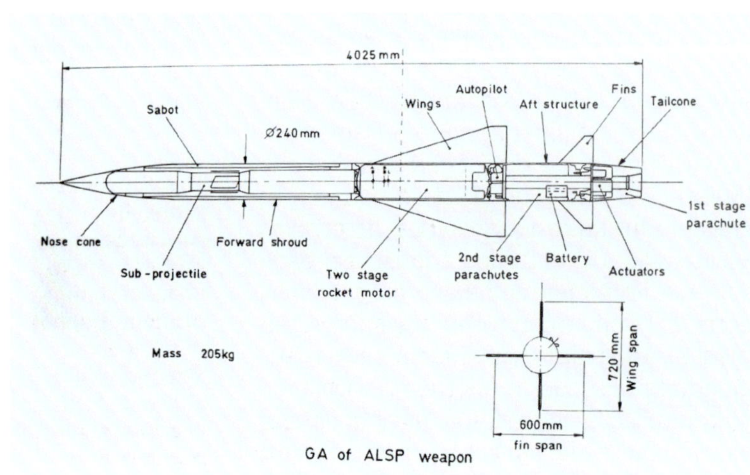

An aircraft at such an altitude presents air defence systems with an excellent target, so to reduce the aircraft vulnerability the Glide Bomb was to be launched from 30km (16nm) behind the FEBA and with a glide range of up to 70km (38nm) allowed targets up to 40km (21.5nm) beyond the FEBA to be attacked. Once over the target area the Glide Bomb seeker selected a target radar, switched guidance to the seeker head and performed a bunt into a vertical dive onto the radar. The Glide Bomb was fitted with simple twist/steer (polar) control and was borne on flip-out wings.

Having examined systems that could destroy enemy radars, attention turned to alternatives that could either spoof the air defence systems or keep them so busy that they would be unable to engage NATO strike aircraft. This was the role of the Harassment Drone, a small UAV, launched in large numbers to overwhelm the defences. The Harassment Drone weighed in at 30kg (66 lb) with a 5kg (11 lb) warhead and a radar seeker installed in a 1m (3ft 3in) long cylindrical fuselage with a 10hp (7.5kW) piston engine driving a three-blade pusher propeller. The drone's cruciform wings spanned 1.3m (4ft 3in), with the vertical 'wings' spanning 0.8m (2ft 8in) with control by canard foreplanes, The Harassment Drone was to be launched on rocket boosts from trucks sited 10km (5.4nm) behind the FEBA and fly at 200m (656ft) or lower for up to 70km (38nm) beyond the FEBA. Massed launches of drones at a rate of 600 per hour were envisaged, using ten twin-rail launch trucks.

The Harassment Drone, flying at 250km/h (136kt), would be 'easy meat' for systems such as the ZSU-23/4 Shilka, and if the cruciform wings acted as a corner reflector for radar, might present a strong radar return for the SAM systems, which would perform a precautionary switch-off. Either way, the Harassment Drone would occupy the defences and possibly keep the heat off the strike force. The basic concept of the Harassment Drone had been demonstrated by a project at BAe Filton where a Stabileye drone had been fitted with an anti-radiation seeker.

One aspect of note from these studies was the warhead, whose casing was pre-cut tungsten alloy with a Misnay–Schardin plate (as used in the Claymore mine) at the base. The barrel shape and Misnay–Schardin plate ensured the blast was focused into a narrow band with a 'beam angle' of 20° for the annular blast. In the Sub-Projectile and Glide Bomb the long axes of the warhead and projectile are aligned while in the Harassment Drone the warhead is inclined at 35°. The Harassment Drone was to impact the target at an angle whereas the SP and GB 'arrived' in a vertical orientation.

The Israeli armed forces used drones to spoof Syrian air defences during Operation Mole Cricket 19, part of the 1982 campaign over the Bekaa Valley in Lebanon. A direct result of their experience in 1973, the Israelis, saw the destruction of Syrian air defences as the key to any operations in the Lebanon. IAI Mastiff UAVs were used to either prompt the Syrian SAM operators to fire at them, turn off their radars or track the UAVs long enough for the SAM site's position to be triangulated by sigint aircraft. Israeli success was replicated in Operation Desert Storm in 1991 when the US Navy deployed the ADM-141 Tactical Air-Launched Decoy (TALD) to trigger the Iraqi air defence system, with many of the radars hit by anti-radiation missiles when they were activated.

The final system examined was the Self-Defence Decoy (SDD) that was to be launched from pods in the strike aircraft and then

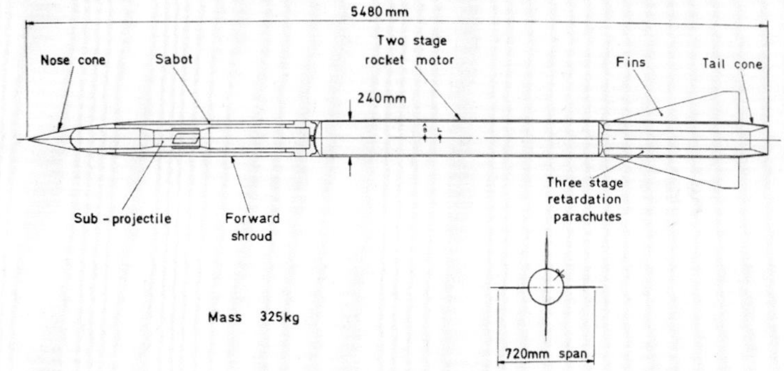

GA of GLSP weapon

The Ground-Launched Sub-Projectile shared the forward section of the ALSP in a longer airframe designed for ground launch. *Blue Envoy Collection.*

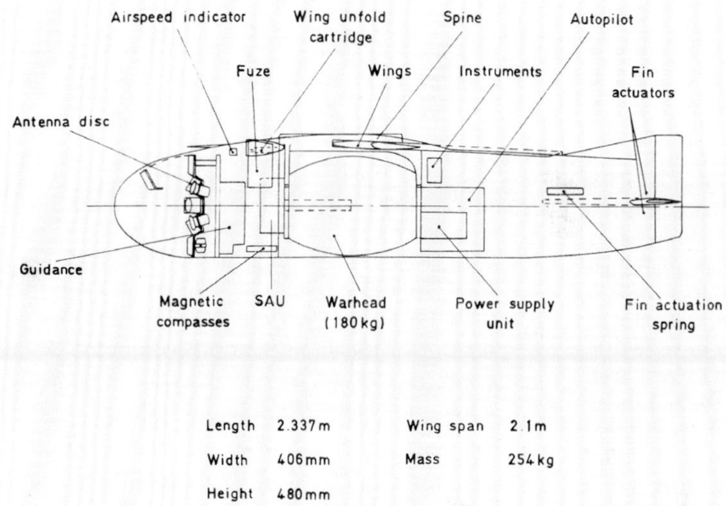

GA of glide bomb

The anti-radiation Glide Bomb allowed an increase in warhead size to 180kg (397 lb). The consequence of this was a reduction in the number of weapons carried. *Blue Envoy Collection*

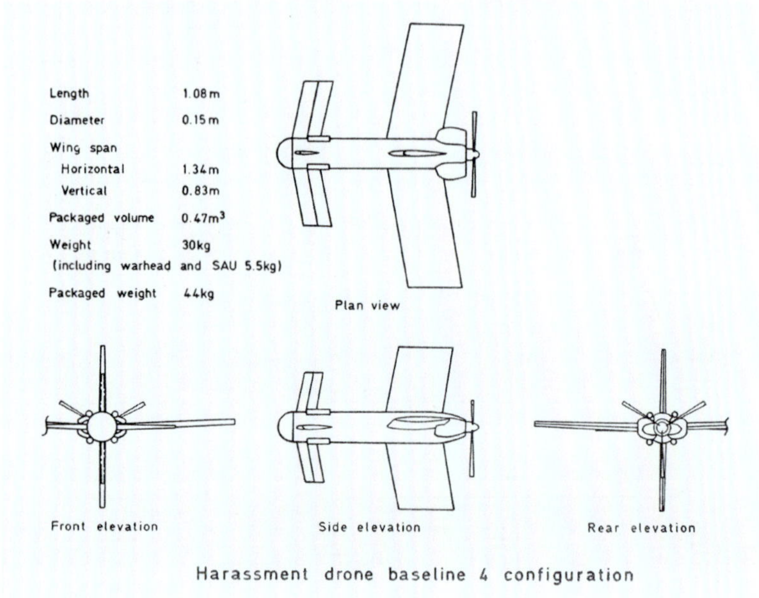

Above: The Harassment Drone was designed to be shot at. Its aerodynamic surfaces were almost perfect corner reflectors and be acquired by the radars of Shilka and SA-8 *Gecko* systems. The drone's purpose was to either draw fire away from the strike aircraft or force a radar shut down. *Blue Envoy Collection*

accelerate and climb away retransmitting the incoming signal. An active transmitter for the decoy was preferred as a passive system on the small decoy would not provide a large enough radar cross-section. The decoy was intended to be triggered by the aircraft's radar warning receiver or by the ECM pod to meet ASR.853 (entered service as Skyshadow) to protect against gun-laying or missile guidance radars. The decoy was intended for use in conjunction with such ECM systems, especially against the SA-8 *Gecko*, and could switch the decoy between pulsed or continuous-wave modes. On launching the decoy, the 'Decoy System Management Unit' (DSMU) in the pod would instruct the ASR.853 jamming pod to shut down while the decoys were in flight as 'jamming and deploying against the same threat would be mutually non-productive'.

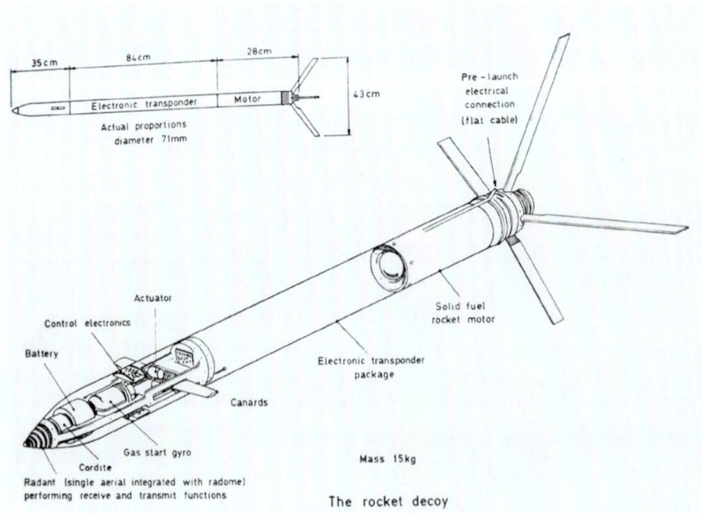

Weighing in at 15kg (33 lb) and with a diameter of 70mm, the decoy was intended to be fitted in a rocket pod similar to SNEB such as the 19-round MATRA LAU51, with one tube allocated to the DSMU. Smaller 7-round pods could be used to carry six decoys. As well as the standard four flip-out stabilising tailfins, the decoy was fitted with very simple canard controls to stabilise the decoy and make it climb to around 60m (200ft) above the line of flight to keep station with the launch aircraft throughout its short flight time.

The decoy was for use against pulsed radars and took each pulse and retransmitted it as an 'extended return' of up to 10µs to produce a return that appeared to be 10km (5.4nm) away. Since it would take at least 20 seconds for the radar to resolve the return(s) as separate and reacquire the aircraft, a new decoy would be automatically launched if radar lock-on was regained. This, effectively, had the same effect as making the radar switch off, but the corollary to this to make the guns and SAMs switch to optical mode, which in good visibility could be as good as radar at low altitudes. Another use for the SDD could be to shut down an air defence system at a 'vital point' such as an airfield to allow a counter-air mission to be conducted with minimal air defences to engage them.

On examining each system, the CRDA listed the potential problems that would need to be addressed during development. For the SP, the warhead was marginal and would need 'barrelling' to enhance damage. The ALSP would need careful management of its mass and size to maximise the number of rounds that could be carried by strike aircraft. The GLSP's retardation parachutes would need careful design if they were to handle the deceleration from Mach 3. The main concern with the Carrier Vehicle (CV) was the tail surfaces, which if retracted while on the aircraft made the aircraft unstable and if extended reduced the number carried from five to three. Other concerns were the 'novel' intake and the bifurcated jetpipe. What concerned the CRDA most, and in all schemes, was the reliability of the various systems involved in the vehicles and sub-projectiles: there was a lot to go wrong. In summing up, the GB and GLSP was too inflexible and of limited range, the CV was far too complex, costly and heavy while the ALSP was complex but most flexible and probably had an earlier in-service date. The Harassment Drone was cheap but heavily dependent on logistics and lacked flexibility. The favoured systems were the Sub-Projectile as a concept and ALSP as the delivery system while the Harassment Drone could be attractive if it was feasible. Self-Deployed Decoys only gave temporary protection and was an 'expensive throwaway' solution whose interfacing with the ASR.853 (or RWR) is likely to require as difficult development and proving programme.'

By April 1979 the process had moved on to focus on homing heads from Marconi Space and Defence Systems (MSDS), warhead studies and an air-launched anti-radar missile 'similar to ALSP but without the requirement to retain the identity of the sub-projectile within the overall design'. This missile was called ALARM – Air Launched Anti-Radiation Missile. ALARM retained the essential features of the ALSP with the features of the SP, including the new MSDS seeker, incorporated into the missile body. This allowed a larger seeker and warhead diameter, 200mm (8in) rather than 150mm (6in).

In operation ALARM shared ALSP's dual-phase boost/sustain rocket motor to propel it to 12,000m (39,370ft), two-stage retarder parachutes and the four-minute frequency search before dropping onto the target. ALARM differed in having side-venting nozzles on the sustainer motor and a forward-looking laser proximity fuze. The warhead 'beam angle' was increased to 40° (by replacing the original warhead with two warheads) and the tungsten alloy fragments increased in size to 7mm (¼in) while the 'manoeuvrability envelope' was increased to allow attack at the very edge of the 15km (8nm) diameter detection footprint. The new seeker was intended to operate 'in a wide band and dense radar environment' which made target selection difficult. Of course, ALARM had one advantage over the

Opposite, bottom: The Self-Defence Decoy was carried in the same pod as 70mm folding fin rockets. It was to be used against the SA-8 *Gecko*, cued by the Skyshadow ECM pod. *Blue Envoy Collection*

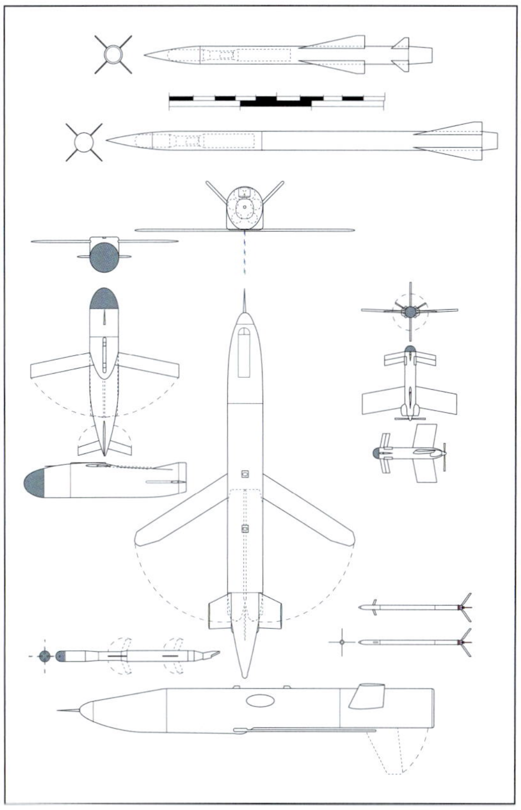

Left: The size range of the AST.1228 proposals is evident in this diagram. The ALSP led to the solution to AST.1228 which became ALARM.

Tornado GR.1 in the desert pink colour scheme adopted for Operation Granby, carries a pair of ALARM on its ventral pylons. ALARM was intended to be carried by any strike aircraft, not just dedicated defence suppression types. *Terry Panopalis Collection*

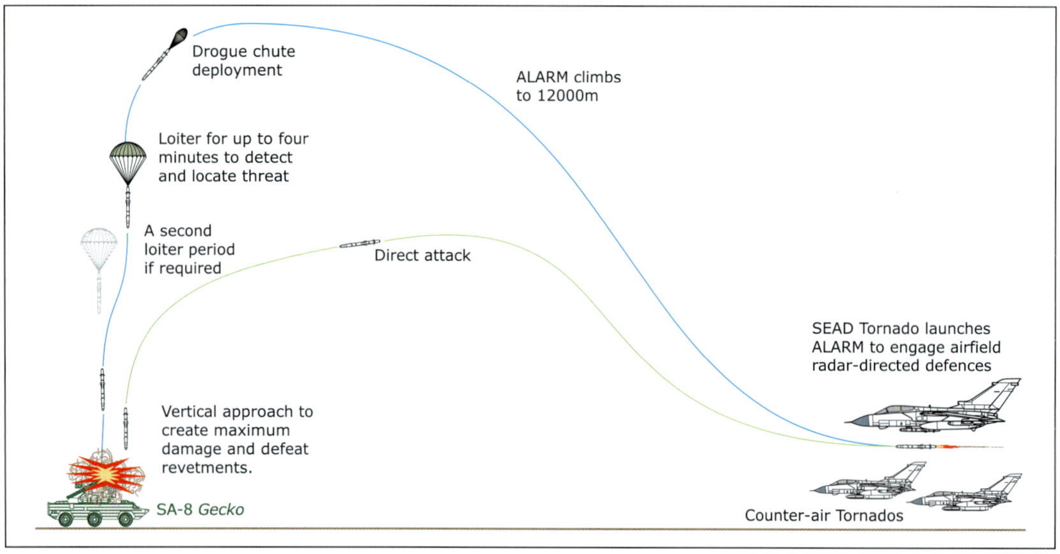

ALARM in operation. The loiter capability gave ALARM an edge over other ARMs and its vertical attack trajectory was intended to cause maximum damage to the target.

CV/SP and GLSP – the carrying aircraft could prompt the defences to activate.

There was, as ever, a catch. The CRDA identified a couple of disadvantages in ALARM's *modus operandi* (climb, loiter, attack) for attacking radars which was a completely different tack to that taken by HARM. On a dedicated 'Wild Weasel' type aircraft, it 'would need to precede the offensive strike formation by around 5 minutes' which introduced co-ordination problems and 'a potential increase in aircraft vulnerability.' If ALARM were to be used as part of a weapons load for an offensive strike aircraft the time delay in using ALARM might require flying a dogleg while the missile attacked the air defences. This reduced the operational range and increased vulnerability. The solution, according to CRDA, was to make the navigation system programmable, delete a parachute phase or add an offset to the trajectory based on Precision Emitter Location Systems (PELS) data (see Chapter 6).

Two generations of Wild Weasel. The F-4G and its F-16C replacement from the 52nd Tactical Fighter Wing based at Spangdahlem, West Germany. The F-4G was the last dedicated Wild Weasel type, the F-16C took on the defence suppression as one of its multiple roles. *Terry Panopalis Collection*

In essence the choice of ARM depended on how they would be used. The Americans preferred to operate a dedicated SEAD type, which by the early 1980s was the McDonnell Douglas F-4G Phantom Wild Weasel V, the replacement for the F-105G Wild Weasel III or by the late 1990s, the Lockheed F-16C. The RAF (lacking the resources for a dedicated version of a strike aircraft) preferred a weapon that could be carried by just about any aircraft and in mixed loads.

AST.1228 Applications

This led to a discussion on the scenarios to which an AST.1228 weapon such as ALARM or CV/SP could be applied. ALARM and CV/SP were designed as 'campaign weapons' for use in pre-planned operations against targets whose defences were known and those where the defences were mobile and locations only revealed to attacking aircraft as they opened fire. The missions earmarked for the RAF on the Central Front were Counter-Air and Battlefield Air Interdiction and such campaigns were modelled.

A Counter-Air campaign would see 100 Tornados pitched against six airfields on Day 1 and returning every 12 hours with ten aircraft each with two JP.233 initially then five aircraft thereafter. Penetration would be over a 20km (11nm) wide corridor with two ALARMs per aircraft using what was called the 'roll back' technique; using the ALARMS in sequence to deal with the air defences each side of the flightpath. In essence the Tornados were to use ALARM to open their own path to the target. Given the size of the CV/SP, dedicated SEAD Tornados would be required and this would

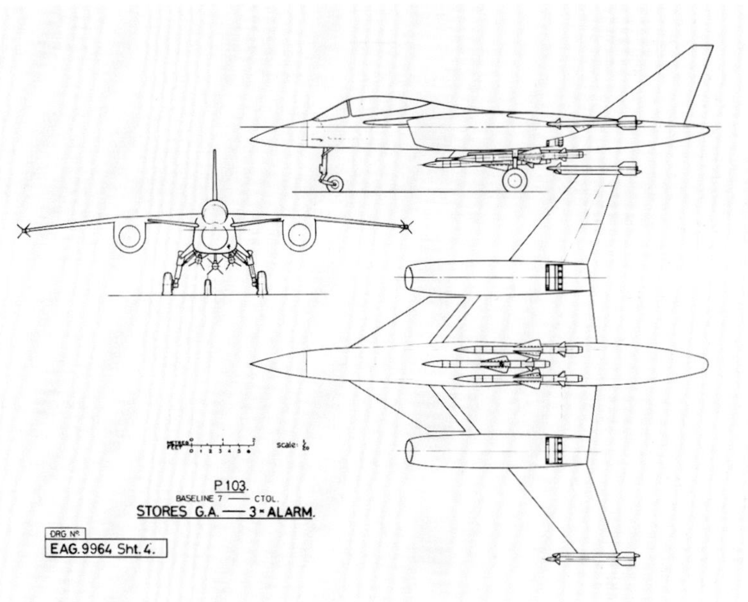

Above: Drawing EAG.9964-4 Shows a BAC P.103 with three ALARM. Unlike the ALCV, individual missiles allowed flexibility in operation and avoided unnecessary expenditure of weapons. *North West Heritage Group*

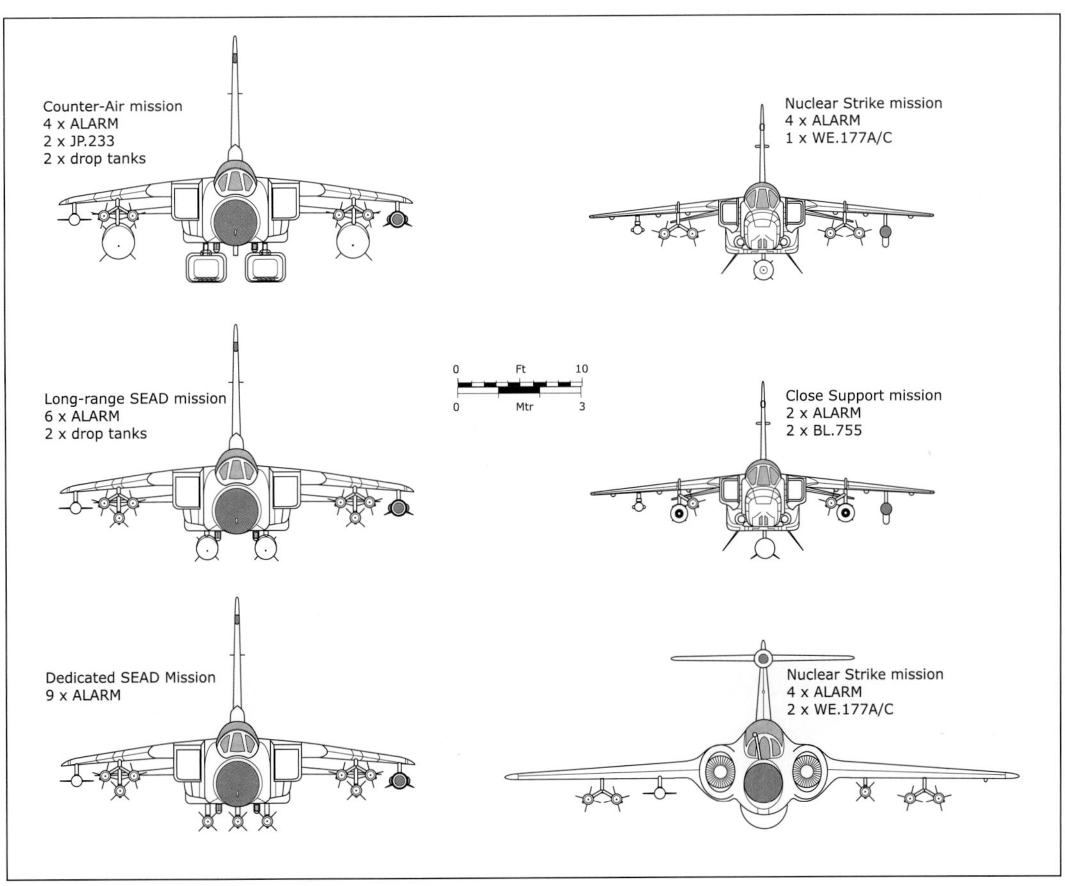

ALARM load-outs for various aircraft and missions. Had the Cold War continued into the 1990s ALARM would have been part of the load-out on Tornado, Buccaneer and Jaguar.

a) decrease the number of aircraft with JP.233 and b) increase the number of aircraft required for the same Counter-Air effort.

Battlefield Interdiction would involve 105 Jaguars and 48 Harriers attacking Warsaw Pact armoured formations either on the battlefield or, more likely, moving into the battlefield area along roads beyond the FEBA. In this case, only the Jaguar could carry ALARM, so would provide a SEAD escort for the Harriers. The air plan envisaged four sorties/day by strike aircraft crossing the FEBA and dealing with Warsaw Pact air defences as they engaged the RAF aircraft. This would mean that 100 missiles would be required for each 'battlefield corridor' along which the strike aircraft would fly. As with the Counter-Air mission, the need for aircraft dedicated to carrying CV/SP would affect the weapons loads of the attacking force.

From these studies the inevitable conclusion was drawn: Counter-Air and Battlefield Air Interdiction campaigns could be sustained for longer if ALARM, rather than CV/SP, was used against Warsaw Pact air defences. ALARM would provide a much more flexible SEAD capability without the need for a Carrier Vehicle, especially in the Battlefield Air Interdiction role. ALARM was selected and the Air Staff Target became a Requirement, ASR.1228.

Having decided on ALARM, a major spanner landed in the works in the shape of lack of funding. ASR.1228 was set aside on cost grounds in 1979 but that lasted less than three years, during which BAeD and MSDS had continued work on a private venture basis. Lessons from the Falklands War and Israeli experience in Lebanon gave ASR.1228 a new impetus. However, by 1982 there were some new players on the field.

This Tornado GR.1 carries five ALARM for a SEAD mission or 'campaign' sortie in support of counter-air Tornados. The Tornado could carry up to seven ALARMs, nine if ALARMs were substituted for the inboard fuel tanks. *Terry Panopalis Collection*

Alternative ARMs

In 1979 the only completely new defence suppression weapon on the stocks in 1979 was a US/West German anti-radar drone, but a drone had been dismissed early in the AST.1228 process. The logical alternatives to ALARM were the AGM-45 Shrike 9A with an upgraded broadband seeker and the AGM-85 HARM (High speed Anti-Radiation Missile), which as noted above applied the lessons learned from Vietnam and Yom Kippur Wars. The RAE took the view that Shrike had been overtaken by HARM and its 'poor performance in the event of switch-off countermeasures' made Shrike the least favoured alternative, leaving HARM and ALARM. HARM procurement had two options: British HARM produced in the UK with Lucas Aerospace as the UK partner to TI, who would still provide the seeker, or a straight buy of HARM from the US Government. Interestingly, TI refused to release details of the seeker to Lucas Aerospace.

The respective companies were invited to tender, not to meet the Staff Requirement, but to offer 'whatever solution it thought would best meet a need for defence suppression and to itself write the technical and performance specification'. This process was described to the companies by Air Marshal Sir Douglas Lowe. Controller, Aircraft, as 'you would be faced with making up a suit of clothes on your judgement of whether it was likely to fit and be of the right material instead of being given all our measurements and specific details of cloth, buttons, threads etc.' This according to Lowe would 'answer criticism that MoD does not give industry a big enough say in what we ought to procure.' How bizarre, but more of a Request for Proposals than a request for tender. TI read this letter as an invitation to tender on a strictly commercial basis i.e. lowest cost wins.

By early 1983 HARM and ALARM were both in the running to meet what had become Air Staff Requirement ASR.1228 but as with every weapons procurement undertaken by the British Government it was not at all cut and dried. HARM was being offered, but when the MoD asked for performance data on HARM from Texas Instruments (TI), it was not released. This raised suspicions amongst the Air Staff who took the view that HARM could not meet the requirement. While this might appear to be the Air Staff jumping the gun, one of the reasons HARM had been rejected was its state of development – ready for service – and therefore would need a mid-life update sooner than

ALARM. It was deemed to lack growth potential, unlike the brand-new ALARM which as a clean slate to work on, could be tailored to the RAF's specific needs, rather than rely on US modifications to come through. This would be important in wartime whereby modification could be quickly incorporated. Another reason for selecting ALARM over HARM was industrial; retention of seeker head expertise in the UK as the only company considered capable of designing and building a seeker was MSDS. If ALARM was not selected, the MSDS seeker development team would break up, with consequences in later years for weapons such as BVRAAM, ASRAAM, Sea Eagle and their replacements.

During this to-and-fro of letters and memos, a letter emerged from Air Chief Marshal Sir Douglas Lowe, Controller, Aircraft, dated 30 April 1982 and addressed to Mr Grant Dove of TI in Dallas. Lowe outlined the presentation made to MoD Ministers on the AST.1228 but mentions a weapon not discussed before – SHARK. This was apparently an alternative to ALARM and may have been the MSDS proposal for AST.1228. No further information on SHARK has come to light.

The pros and cons of HARM and ALARM were argued well into 1983 with the MoD arguing for ALARM and the Treasury arguing in favour of the cheaper HARM. Oddly enough despite the MoD making the case for ALARM, an alternative case was made for *both* missiles, based on the possibility that the Warsaw Pact might produce a counter to either weapon. On 17 May 1983 Sir Kenneth Warren MP wrote to Prime Minister Margaret Thatcher (Via Lucas Aerospace for some reason) advocating this approach based on his 'defence experience'. Warren informed the PM that 'Whilst it would be unacceptable to deliver our anti-radar defence solely into the hands of the Americans, they can deliver a capability we need quickly.' In Warren's view, ALARM was 'beyond [BAeD and MSDS] threshold of experience' and thus both weapons were required, so 'In this two-horse race I believe both must win.'

ALARM was selected, surprisingly not on cost but operational grounds: growth potential to meet evolving threats and flexibility. By flexibility BAeD advised that ALARM, unlike HARM, could be carried with other weapons rather than instead of – with four ALARM in addition to a standard weapon load. Not that this met universal approval with the Treasury and TI expressing displeasure about BAeD's more expensive bid. The price difference was being described by BAeD as the 'cost of continuing the technology in the UK, but the hoo-hah prompted BAeD's Managing Director Admiral Sir Raymond Lygo to offer a fixed price contract and 'absorb up to £100M (1982 prices) of the development and initial production costs' in exchange for an undertaking that 'buys beyond the initial 750 missiles would be obtained at the commercial export price'.

In the light of this TI cried 'Foul!' and pointed out that Controller, Air's letter had pretty much said that lowest bid would win, so HMG was moving the goalposts. TI's (or possibly the US Government) response on 13 July 1983 was to allow Lucas access to the seeker technology, allowing them to build seekers in Britain and TI would open a repair facility at Bedford. All this would mean that HARM would be £60M cheaper than ALARM, which some at the MoD saw as an opportunity: Buy HARM and sink the saving into a new missile that also used BAeD and MSDS technology – SRARM, the Short-Range Anti-Radiation Missile for deployment in the 1990s. SRARM was to be 'smaller, faster and more accurate than HARM/ALARM'.

Of course, this being a British Government contract for an aerospace item, Shorts became involved, albeit indirectly, in what was becoming a political football. With the Government apparently 'wobbling' on selecting ALARM the implied threat from the US Government on UK/US military/industrial co-operation entered a new phase. Mr Richard Haggett of Lucas Aerospace phoned the Permanent Secretary at the Northern Ireland Office (NIO). Haggett explained that the ALARM decision had 'gone to Cabinet three times and was due to be discussed [again] next week'. The gist of Haggett's argument was that if ALARM was selected, 'for blatantly political reasons' this would be viewed as protectionism by the US Government and they 'might retaliate in the UK'. Haggett pointed out to the NIO that the 'first opportunity would probably be the proposed European Distribution Systems Aircraft (ESDA) in which Short Brothers Limited allegedly have a $800M stake.' The EDSA was a military variant of the Short SD.330-UTT Sherpa that the USAF in Europe bought as the C-23 Sherpa to transport items such as F100 engines around its bases.

At the Cabinet meeting on 26 July 1983 the Northern Ireland Secretary Jim Prior explained that Shorts might be vulnerable to pressure from the States if ALARM was selected and the US felt 'snubbed by a decision in favour of ALARM' and that 'difficulties facing Shorts on their employment record will be of higher significance.' In fact, Prior believed that employment discrimination in Northern Ireland might

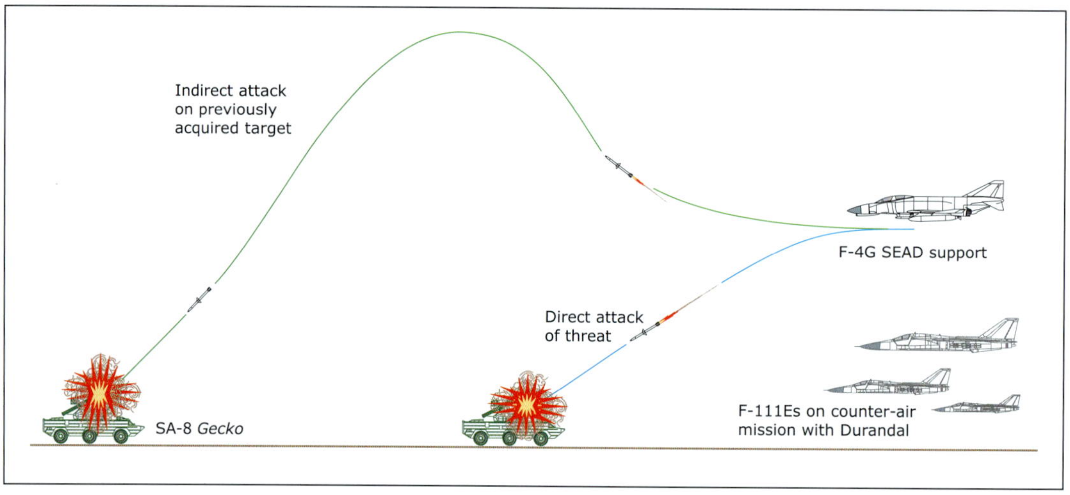

The HARM in action. The High-Speed Anti-Radiation Missile lacked ALARM's loiter mode (although it could conduct an indirect attack to deal with radar shut-off) and was much bigger than ALARM. It also required a dedicated aircraft, such as the F-4G Wild Weasel.

have more influence with the Americans than an order for ALARM. In summary the NIO thought 'the Shorts contract is in any case vulnerable to other political pressures.'

Despite this, ALARM was ordered in early August 1983, with the decision being made at Cabinet level rather than by the MoD alone, such was the concern amongst the various Ministries with an interest in the process. The USAF took 18 C-23A Sherpas but the option of another 48 wasn't taken up although 16 C-23Bs were acquired.

Government-funded development of ALARM resumed including carriage trials with up to nine dummy ALARMs being carried by Tornado GR.1s at Warton and by late 1985 powered but unguided trials were underway. Development continued and aside from problems with the Nuthatch rocket motor, all went well. A powered terminal phase was required after the ability to power the final attack was added to the Requirement during development. The burn/loiter/burn Bristol Aerojet Nuthatch was replaced with a simpler Bayer Chemie Bayard motor after problems with the Nuthatch. For development firings, pending availability of the Bayard, the Linnet motor from the Firestreak AAM was fitted.

ALARM's operational modes had been modified to include a direct attack/loiter mode whereby the missile could abort its attack if it lost target acquisition and climb to altitude and loiter on a parachute until the radar switched on again. ALARM entered service in 1990, in time for Operation Granby, the 1991 Gulf War during which 121 rounds were launched with great success. Post-Granby the missiles underwent a mid-life update under SR(A).1247 to incorporate lessons learned from Granby.

Although the RAF had shown little interest in a dedicated SEAD aircraft they had by 2003 embraced such a machine in the form of the Tornado F.3 which from 2003 was modified to carry ALARM on its stub pylons in the SEAD role. The modified Tornado F.3's Emissions Location System used the existing radar warning receivers to provide the navigator with a picture of the radar environment allowing targets to be selected for ALARM. These modified Tornado ADVs served from 2003 with No 11 Sqn, reportedly designated Tornado EF.3, which may not be an official designation. ALARM was withdrawn from RAF service in December 2013, but as of early 2019 was still in service with the Royal Saudi Air Force and in the end it could be argued that HARM won.

Well...not exactly. ALARM's finest hour came during Operation Allied Force, the 1999 NATO campaign against Serbia. One success story attributed to ALARM involved a Serbian radar that had stayed online after around 100 attempts to shut it down by F-16C, EA-6B and Tornado ECR using HARM. A RAF Tornado GR.1 was called in and shut the radar down with a single ALARM. Whether it was the ALARM's loiter, vertical attack or combination of both that produced a successful engagement hasn't been released, but ALARM turned out to be considerably cheaper than 100 HARMs.

As for a replacement, at the time of ALARM's withdrawal the MoD in 2013 stated that there was a more than enough weaponry capable of destroying air defences by which they meant Brimstone and Storm Shadow. The former would be outranged by 9K37 Buk (SA-11 *Gadfly*) or 9K37M1-2 (SA-17 *Grizzly*) unless the turbofan-powered/wing kit fitted SPEAR 3 was used, while the latter would be a somewhat expensive solution. Meantime the stated policy is that the UK would only ever operate in a coalition and the SEAD mission left to other air forces. With HARM.

Alarm Clocks, Concrete and Maps: Counter-Air

'There is nothing better at destroying a runway than a Durandal.' Captain George Kelman, Flight Commander, 20 Tactical Fighter Wing, 1991

It had been done before, famously during Bodenplatte on 1 January 1945 and again on 5 November 1956 as part of Operation Musketeer. Göring's August 1940 plan was looking successful before being sidetracked by an angry Führer and the Japanese achieved little with their endeavours in the field in July 1944. However, the Israeli Air Force did it with élan. 'It' was offensive counter-air, defined in an online encyclopaedia as 'the suppression of an enemy's military air power, primarily through ground attacks targeting enemy air bases, disabling or destroying parked aircraft, runways, fuel facilities, hangars, air traffic control facilities and other aviation infrastructure'.

Offensive counter-air wasn't new, but only entered the public imagination on 5 June 1967, Day 1 of the Six Day War when the Israelis all but destroyed the Egyptian Air Force on the ground. That prompted two changes, the first of which saw the Pakistan Air Force fail to emulate that Israeli success in Operation Chengiz Khan on 3 December 1971 while the second saw a flurry of research and development activity.

From the middle years of the Great War, the aircraft were seen as a key technology in winning battles and ultimately, wars. As aircraft became increasingly complicated and more difficult to destroy in the air; requiring radar, guided weapons and a great deal of time, the expedient of destroying them on the ground with bomb and bullet appealed. At first glance all you need are those keys to offensive warfare – an alarm clock and a map – the first to get going before your enemy and the second to find them. In reality the 'luck of the generals' would be a huge factor in a successful operation.

There had been operations against the enemy's airfields in the Great War that could be described as counter-air operations, such as the prelude to the Battle of Messines in June 1917, but it was the Second World War, a conflict in which the aircraft came to dominate the battlespace, that counter-air operations became a major aspect of campaigns. The Wehrmacht took two attempts to perfect counter-air tactics; Poland, where the Polish aircraft were saved by being dispersed on the eve of the German attack, and the Battle of Britain where on the verge of a counter-air success, the Luftwaffe was diverted to attacking cities on the orders of the Führer. One interesting aspect of this point in the chronology of World War Two was British counter-air measures against their own airfields. During refurbishment of the airfield at Lee-on-Solent, twenty 60ft (18.3m) pipe bombs were discovered, laid cross-wise under the runway to be detonated in the event of invasion and prevent German aircraft landing.

In July 1941 the Luftwaffe got it right, destroying much of the Soviet Air Force in the opening phase of Operation Barbarossa, contributing to the rolling up of Soviet forces and gaining territory. The Luftwaffe also got it right in January 1945 for Operation Bodenplatte but the numbers game was against the Germans; the Allies could replace losses far more easily than could the Germans.

The Western Allies' counter-air operations were on a grander scale with Operation Pointblank, covering the period from June 1943 until April 1944. Pointblank saw strategic bombers attacking aircraft manufacturing plants and drew the Luftwaffe fighter force into battle. In response, the Luftwaffe High Command moved fighters from the Russian, Mediterranean and eventually, western fronts, to defend the Reich over an extended period. What Pointblank did achieve was to force German weapons manufacturing underground and this relocation process and the impact of the Allied operations saw the Luftwaffe fighter force almost cleared from the skies by spring 1945. Despite Pointblank, the Luftwaffe did mount a classic counter-air operation when on 1 January 1945 they launched Operation Bodenplatte.

Offensive counter-air: hardened aircraft shelter at Al Salman air base destroyed by coalition forces during Operation Granby/Desert Storm in Iraq during January/February 1991. Much of the Iraqi Air Force's infrastructure was wrecked along with much of the Iraqi Air Force's capability, either destroyed on the ground or departing for Iran. *DoD*

BODENPLATTE was intended to be a classic counter-air operation timed to coincide with the ground offensive of Unternehmen Wacht am Rhein (Operation Watch on the Rhine), more widely known as the Battle of the Bulge. On 1 January 1945, the Luftwaffe had the alarm clocks, but unfortunately Unternehmen Wacht am Rhein had commenced on 16 December 1944. The reason for the disparity was the weather, as BODENPLATTE was also originally timed for 16 December to destroy the Allied tactical air forces in France, Holland and Belgium thus removing the threat posed by the Allied *Jabos*.

Luckily for the Wehrmacht, the same weather that grounded the Luftwaffe grounded the Allied air forces, but from 23 December the weather began to clear. With better weather the Allies could support their hard-pressed troops on the ground and the German offensive stalled. In an attempt to restart their operations, the German High Command drew up Unternehmen Nordwind (Operation Northwind) with the rescheduled BODENPLATTE to start on 1 January 1945. Despite the weather, the Luftwaffe had not been idle in the previous two weeks, conducting numerous operations that had led to the loss of many aircraft and aircrew. This had diminished the number of aircraft, mainly Bf 109s and Fw 190s, available for BODENPLATTE and this was compounded by routing the Luftwaffe aircraft over V-2 launch areas in Holland. These were protected by a lot of flakartillerie and due to the security around the operation, these units had not been informed of BODENPLATTE, so opened up on their own aircraft.

Not that BODENPLATTE failed, at least not in its immediate effect, but in the long term it could be described as a pyrrhic victory. It did great damage to the Allied tactical air force, with almost 300 aircraft destroyed, but the losses inflicted on the Allies were replaced by mid-January whereas the Luftwaffe's losses could not. BODENPLATTE was the last gasp of the Luftwaffe as the losses of aircraft, aircrew and lack of fuel, all a consequence of POINTBLANK, meant that the Germans lacked the capacity to launch further large-scale aerial operations in the war.

These counter-air operations used fighters and bomber aircraft, but what would latterly be called special forces were also used in counter-air operations. The British Special Air Service (SAS) tore around the Western Desert in Jeeps, shooting up German and Italian airfields and laying bespoke demolition charges in aircraft. The SAS repeated the feat in the 1982 Falklands Conflict by destroying Argentine Air Force aircraft on Pebble Island in a heliborne raid from Royal Navy vessels.

The Japanese also mounted counter-air operations during WW2, initially at Pearl Harbor and again three years later when faced with an onslaught against the Home Islands by USAAF B-29 Superfortresses. In the initial operation on 7 December 1941 the Japanese Navy aimed to remove the US Navy carrier force and its aircraft from the US order of battle before embarking on expansion of the Empire. This was a classic counter-air operation that failed due to bad timing and lack of intelligence; the US carrier force was at sea when the Japanese strike force went in. A later Japanese counter-air operation took place on 6 December 1944 by Teishin Shudan (Japanese Army Air Force Raiding Group) units against American airfields on Luzon and Leyte in the Philippines. A second operation by Giretsu Kuteitai (Japanese Army Heroic Paratroopers) was also carried out against B-29 bases in the Marianas Islands. In both cases special forces were to be airlanded but the aircraft, Mitsubishi Ki-21 *Sally* and Mitsubishi Ki-57 *Topsy*, were either shot down before delivering their troops or crash landed on the target airfield.

Aside from nuisance raids by 'Bedcheck Charlie' – North Korean Polikarpov Po-2 *Mules* – attacking United Nations bases at Pyongyang and Suwon airfields at night during the Korean War, the next counter-air operation was during Operation MUSKETEER. Representatives of the British, French and Israeli governments met at Sèvres in France during October 1956 and the resultant Protocol of Sèvres saw the three countries collude in taking back control of the recently nationalised Suez Canal. Initially known as HAMILCAR, then MUSKETEER, and eventually Operation MUSKETEER REVISE, the gist of the plan drawn up at Sèvres called for the Israelis to commence operations against Egypt in Sinai, with British and French forces intervening under the pretext of separating the Israelis and Egyptians while 'securing' the canal.

The RAF was tasked with counter-air operations against the Egyptian Air Force (EAF) but almost as soon as the Canberras and Valiants from Malta and Cyprus began operations late on 31st October, some of the missions were aborted. HM Government had been made aware that American citizens were being evacuated from Cairo West Airport, a primary target for the RAF, so the eight Valiants tasked with attacking Cairo West were recalled. The Canberras and Valiants had attacked at high altitude and subsequent reconnaissance showed that the 'results were disappointing' and therefore RAF strike aircraft, Meteors, Venoms and Hunters from Cyprus and FAA aircraft such as Wyverns, Sea Venoms and Sea Hawks from carriers took over the counter-air task. Meantime, the disappointing results and aborted sorties had allowed some EAF aircraft to escape to the south, out of strike range. Despite this, over 250 EAF aircraft were destroyed and EAF operations were pretty much non-existent during the period of hostilities.

Operations were ended when the economic pressure on the UK forced the Government to apply for a loan from the International Monetary Fund. Given that this organisation was heavily influenced by the US Government, the British had no choice but accede to a cease fire. Concurrently, the Soviet First Secretary, Nikolai Bulganin, had threatened to attack London and Paris with nuclear weapons. Militarily, the Suez adventure was over. Politically, the fallout would see the British Prime Minister, Anthony Eden, resign for health reasons.

While the British counter-air operations in November 1956 had followed the now standard routine of attack with bomb, cannon and rocket, the next major counter-air operation caused the major powers to sit up and take notice. Again, it involved Israel and Egypt, but with the latter having the alarm clocks and the former having very detailed maps plus a new weapon that had been developed in France for the Israeli Air Force.

On 5 June 1967 the Israelis launched Operation Focus. Rather than following standard military procedure of a dawn attack, the Israelis relied on the Egyptians' alarm clocks. As usual, the EAF mounted their dawn patrols and once these sorties had returned to base, the perfectly-timed Israeli strike aircraft hit ten airfields at once from the north west. The Israelis also possessed very good maps, so good that they knew where aircraft, specifically Tupolev Tu-16 *Badger* bombers, would be parked. For Operation Focus the Israelis sortied at 'maximum effort' with two waves separated by ten minutes, ultimately attacking 18 airfields. Each flight of four aircraft carried a mix of bombs and rockets, with one aircraft in each flight carrying the Israeli Air Force's secret weapon: the Dibber Bomb.

Dropping bombs on runways was old hat, but while the grass strips of 1940 could be easily cratered by general purpose bombs, the reinforced concrete runways of the 1960s, required to support operations by high-perfor-

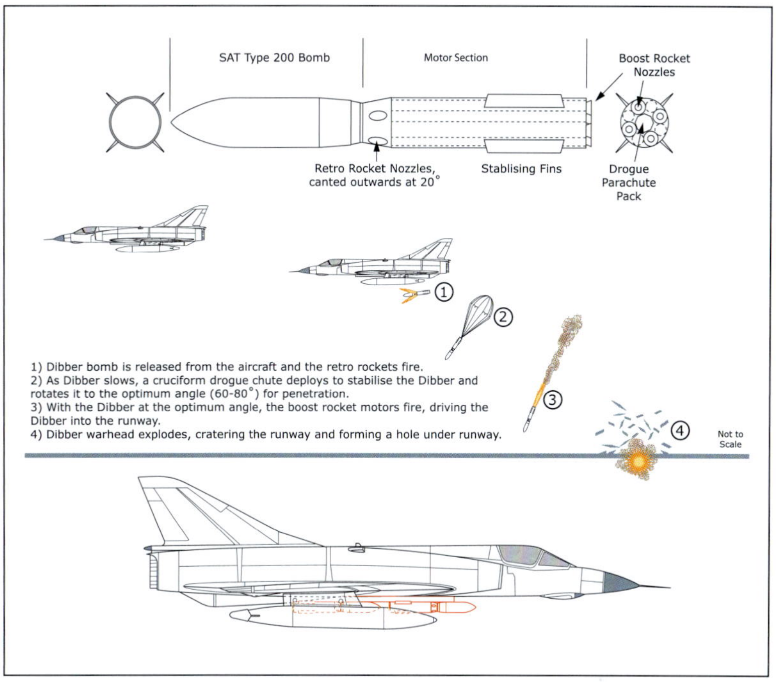

mance jets, were a different kettle of fish. They could be cratered, but their inherent strength meant that craters could be rapidly patched up. The Dibber changed that.

As the Israeli Mirage IIICJs streaked in, on the deck at 500kt (926km/h), three of the flight assaulted the parked EAF aircraft with bombs, rockets and 30mm DEFA cannon. The fourth aircraft was armed with two types of Dibber: a 70kg (154 lb) type and a larger 500kg (1,102 lb) version called *Ollar Had* (Sharp Knife) The Dibber used two sets of rockets and a parachute, all mated with an armour-piercing bomb to attack runways and taxiways, thus rendering the airfield unusable. Once released and clear of the aircraft four retro-rockets fired to slow the bomb before deploying a drogue parachute. The drogue further slowed the bomb, stabilised its attitude and once the bomb had reached an angle of 60-80°, a second set of rockets fired, driving the armour-piercing bomb through the concrete and into the hardcore beneath before exploding below the concrete. This not only made a crater but heaved up the surrounding area and created a cavity under the runway, thus further complicating the repair process.

Op. Focus destroyed the Egyptian Air Force, removed the threat to Israeli cities posed by the *Badgers* and freed the Israeli air force to support the ground troops as they swept across the Sinai Peninsula. Air forces around the world took notice and, well aware that they could suffer the same fate, decided something should be done.

Although a generic term for a runway penetrating weapon, 'Dibber' has become most associated with the Matra runway penetrator developed for the Israeli Air Force as the *Ollar Had* and used to great effect on the first day of the Six Day War in June 1967.

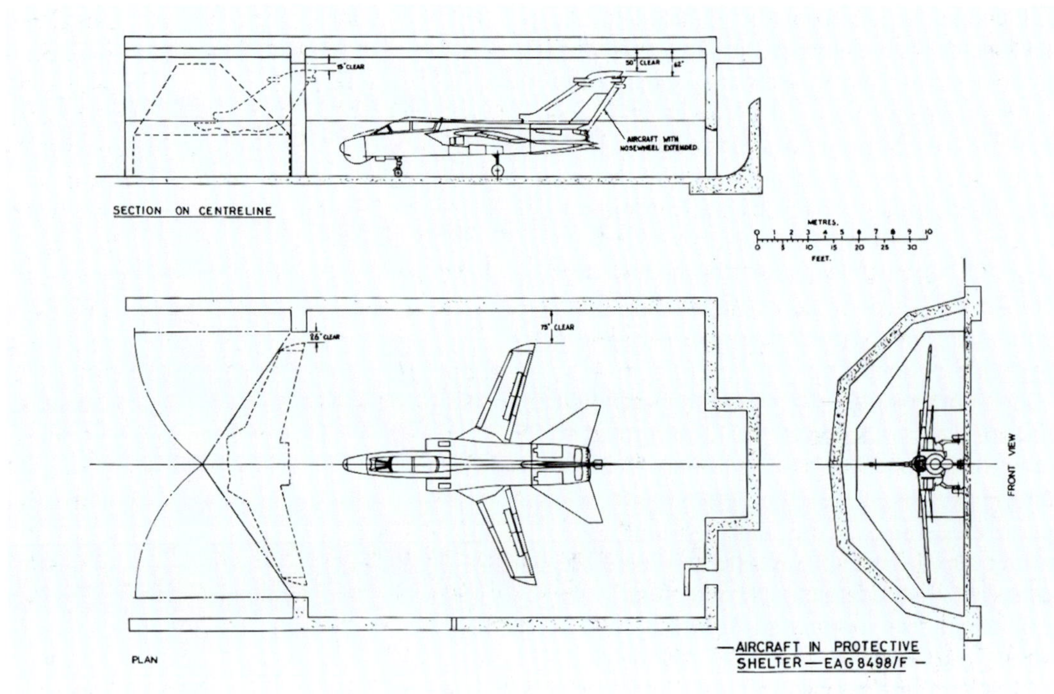

This interesting drawing shows a Tornado-based AST.396 within a HAS. The Tornado is a tight fit and close examination of the drawing reveals an extendable nosewheel oleo to tilt the aircraft and reduce the height of the fin. Also of note in this drawing is how narrow the door is to allow passage of a fully-spread Tornado. *North West Heritage Group.*

India was the first beneficiary of the fallout from Operation Focus. The destruction of the Egyptian Air Force was partly due to the Israeli intelligence knowing exactly where the aircraft were parked; the map, and when they would be parked there; the clock. When the Pakistan Air Force (PAF) launched Operation Chengiz Khan on 3 December 1971, they lacked the numbers and intensive training of the Israelis. In addition to these, the Indian Air Force (InAF) had built reinforced hangars, the forerunners of the hardened aircraft shelters (HAS), to house their aircraft and the PAF didn't launch its attack until 1745hrs. With the Indian aircraft secure in their HAS the PAF bombed the runways but the time of the attack made follow-up attacks, critical to the earlier Israeli success, impossible and allowed the InAF to repair the runways overnight.

As shown above, the pre-emptive strike against airfields was nothing new and air forces, particularly in western Europe, had been planning for such an attack by the Warsaw Pact. Up until the adoption of Flexible Response in 1961 the main threat to NATO airfields was nuclear strikes. The answer to this was to disperse the aircraft around small simple airstrips. Given that in the Fifties nuclear weapons were expensive and few and far between, dispersal to numerous airfields would work. This was how the RAF's V-force operated and the herring-bone operational dispersal points (ODP) appeared at airfields around the United Kingdom. Strategic Air Command's bombers also dispersed around Europe to bases like RAF Elvington, home of what is probably the largest concrete slab on Earth at 47 acres (19 hectares), perfect for parking Convair B-36 Peacemakers, but Elvington never saw SAC's bombers.

While that took care of the strategic force, the tactical air forces based in western Europe were a different matter. By the late 1950s nuclear weapons were becoming more readily available in the form of tactical nuclear weapons that could be used against NATO airfields to the west of the Iron Curtain. In the mid-1950s NATO had drawn up a NATO Basic Military Requirement (NBMR) 1 for a lightweight strike aircraft. This led to the FIAT G.91, a small strike fighter that could be bought in large numbers and dispersed around the airfields of western Europe, but the spread of nuclear weapons made these, known, dispersal fields vulnerable. What was needed was more dispersal to forest clearings, playing fields and other open areas.

Once again, NATO stepped in with NBMR-3 for a V/STOL strike aircraft to operate from short and unprepared strips and NBMR-4 for a V/STOL transport to support the dispersed fighters. Further information on NBMR-3, see Chapter 3 and for NBMR-4 please refer to this author's *On Atlas' Shoulders*.

The gist of the NBMR-3 and 4 stories is that although the British Air Staff showed little interest in them, being focused on the wider role around the soon-to-be shrinking Empire, the British aircraft companies did tender designs suitable for NBMR-3 and 4. The irony is that the type of aircraft required for NBMR-3 – V/

STOL strike – failed to make headway in the NATO air forces but eventually entered service with the RAF as the Hawker Siddeley Harrier GR.1 and its successors.

With the failure, probably through lack of interest from the RAF and USAFE, of NBMR-3 and the rise of sensors such as infrared linescan that could detect aircraft hidden away in forests, the various Air Staffs concluded that protected facilities at airfields were the best answer to counter-air operations and this was reinforced by operations FOCUS and CHENGIS KHAN. Aircraft parked in the open were vulnerable, but aircraft parked in a protected shelter were safe and so the cement mixer became the weapon of choice.

Hardened shelters for aircraft were not new, having been a German speciality during WW2, especially once Bomber Command and 8th Air Force formations began laying waste to the German economy. With a taste for the massive, the Luftwaffe placed its aircraft in caves and eventually the aircraft factories themselves went underground. The Germans excelled at the construction of enormous structures and as these grew larger, so did the bombs, with Barnes Wallis' 'earthquake' bombs for the RAF and, oddly, the Admiralty's Disney Bomb for the USAAF.

Cold War Runway Wrecking

The lessons from the Vietnam and Six Day Wars were not lost on the Air Staff and these events coincided with a strategic reappraisal of Britain's place in the world. The 1970s saw the focus of Britain's armed forces move from East of Suez to an emphasis on North West Europe and the Eastern Atlantic. The change led to the development of the Tornado, in its IDS and ADV guises, and the Type 42 guided missile destroyer with the latter two intended to provide air defence for convoys reinforcing western Europe had hostilities broken out.

While the challenges in the maritime theatre were clearly defined as the Soviet submarine fleet and anti-ship platforms such as the Tupolev Tu-95/142 *Bear* and later, the Tu-22M *Backfire*, the threats to Western Europe were more diverse. The most immediate threat was the massed formations of Soviet armour ranged across the countries of the Warsaw Pact which when combined with infantry and air support, posed a formidable problem.

The Soviet 'horde' and its armoured divisions would ideally be beaten back by NATO Chieftain, M60 and Leopard main battle tanks supported by Harriers, F-16s and A-10A Thunderbolts. Obviously, the Warsaw Pact forces

Tupolev's Tu 22M (NATO reporting name *Backfire*) was tasked with long range strikes into the NATO rear area, including the UK, from bases in the western Soviet Union. The airfields would have been targeted by RAF counter-air operations. This example, Tu-22M3 (*Backfire-C*) 37 Red, RF-94145, is carrying a Kh-22 anti-ship missile (NATO reporting name AS-4 *Kitchen*) on its port wing glove pylon. *Chris Lofting*

Weapons fit was one of the many reasons for constructing a mock-up of a new aircraft. This photo shows two WE.177 Lay Down Bomb 'shapes' in the weapons bay of the TSR.2 mock-up at Warton. *North West Heritage Group*

would not be operating in isolation but supported by the well-honed support machine that was the Soviet Air Force's Frontal Aviation. Given the lessons learned, and forgotten, since 1917 – specifically that the air support of ground forces was key to a successful operation – Frontal Aviation's activity had to be curtailed and offensive counter-air was the solution.

Attacking the enemy's airfields in their rear areas wasn't new but was a decedent of intruder operations whereby long-range fighters operated over enemy airfields and attacked aircraft using the bases. The Luftwaffe's Nachtjagd 2 successfully operated Junkers Ju 88Cs over the RAF's airfields in England during 1941 and 1942 before (as had happened to the Kampfgeschwader in 1940) being pulled out by Hitler and sent elsewhere. The finest exponents of intruder operations were RAF Fighter Command squadrons and their Mosquito night fighters that from May 1942 patrolled German airfields across occupied Europe, attacking the Luftwaffe's night fighters on their home turf.

The success of RAF intruder operations in World War Two made the role a must-have capability, leading to the development of the intruder variants of the Canberra, initially with converted B.6 as the B(I).6 and later the new-build B(I).8. Modifications for the intruder role included a ventral gun pack in the bomb bay with four 20mm Hispano V cannon and underwing hardpoints for bombs or rockets. The B(I).6s and B(I).8s were fitted with the low altitude bombing system (LABS) for the delivery of nuclear weapons providing nuclear capability to 2ATAF from late 1959.

Prior to 1961 any movement of Warsaw Pact forces across the Inner German Border would have been met with a massive nuclear response and the intruder aircraft would have been putting their LABS kit to use delivering nuclear weapons; US-supplied Mark 7 and B43s in Europe and British Red Beards east of Suez, these being installed in the bomb bay in lieu of the cannon pack. After 1961, with President Kennedy in the White House, NATO moved from a Trip Wire massive retaliation footing to Flexible Response whereby rather than unleashing all-out nuclear war, a series of escalations would need to move the warring forces from the first shots to what would ultimately be Armageddon.

This change necessitated an acceptance by NATO governments that a war against the Warsaw Pact with conventional weapons was required from the start. NATO armour would be required to hold back the Soviet mechanised divisions while NATO air forces would need to support the ground troops and reduce the effectiveness of Warsaw Pact air support aircraft and helicopters.

Once the escalation had reached Deliberate Escalation with nuclear weapons readied for use, the bombs were to be tossed onto targets, typically airfields in eastern Europe in what was recognised as an effective counter-air technique, also used by the Soviets. For this the Soviet arsenal of tactical ballistic missiles such as the *Scud-A* and the later SS-23 *Spider* were tasked with attacking NATO airfields with nuclear warheads. The *Scuds* were not precision weapons, but an airfield is a large target and the warheads were of sufficient yield to be effective. As nuclear weapons became smaller and could be carried by smaller strike aircraft, a different technique was developed. Red Beard was designed around technology developed for Britain's first atomic bomb, Blue Danube and as such was being superseded by US weapons. Operational Requirement OR.1177 was issued in August 1959 for a nuclear depth bomb but was also intended to be what was described as a laydown bomb. In the laydown technique the carrying aircraft flies across the target at low level and releases the weapon. The bomb is slowed by a parachute and falls to the ground, travelling along the surface for a short distance. This delivery requires the weapon to be rugged enough to withstand the shock of impact and subsequent bouncing across an airfield before detonating.

The resulting weapon was WE.177, which came in three variants. The initial WE.177A was a 10kT fission weapon to be carried by TSR.2. Its relatively low yield was the result of a diktat from Prime Minister Harold Macmillan who was concerned that bombs with higher yield could provoke escalation in a nuclear war. WE.177A, or Bomb, Aircraft, HE 600 lb MC, became a variable yield depth bomb (0.5-10kt) for the Royal Navy. Given the size of Soviet airfields and the hardening of facilities, the RAF opted to deliver the WE.177A in sticks of up to four bombs. WE.177B and C or in RAF parlance Bomb, Aircraft, HE 950 lb MC, weighed in at 1,008 lb (457kg) but the WE.177B carried a 450kT warhead while the WE.177C carried a 190kT warhead and it was the C model that was carried by the Jaguar and Tornado aircraft of RAF Germany. The 190kT yield was considered more than enough to destroy an airfield.

Oddly enough the laydown delivery method led to a debate at a conference which the author attended. The question under consideration was what would an AAA gunner do if he saw a bomb skidding to a halt in front of his position? The balance of opinion was that they'd have a go at it with the four 23mm cannon to violently disassemble it. Worth a shot. Wouldn't you?

As Flexible Response became established in the mid to late 1960s, conventional weaponry for counter-air were being sought, especially after the Six Day War prompted the proliferation of hardened aircraft shelters across the world, particularly in Europe. The drive for V/STOL aircraft and a 'runwayless' air force typified by NBMR-3, 4 and 22 had all come to naught (see Chapter 3) with only the RAF, who had been disinterested in all these NBMRs, fielding a V/STOL type with the Harrier. Rather than create an entire air arm that did not rely on runways, the RAF had four Harrier squadrons plus an operational conversion unit (OCU) while the remainder of RAF Germany's forces were based at the four 'Rhine Clutch' airfields. These, like their NATO allies, were dependent on runways but more importantly for NATO, so were the Warsaw Pact air forces.

Counter-Air Weapons

The Defence Operational Analysis Establishment (DOAE) produced a paper, *Air/98, The Attack of Take-Off Surfaces and of Aircraft in Shelters* that examined the effects of potential anti-airfield operations by Warsaw Pact forces on NATO airfields. This data was applied to NATO attacks on Warsaw Pact airfields and how such attacks could be conducted in future. The paper described the Warsaw Pact order of battle of the forces facing the 2ATAF (2nd Allied Tactical Air Force) area of the Central Region of Allied Command Europe (ACE). By 1985 these forces were estimated as being 225 *Backfire* and *Blinder* bombers, 85 *Fencers* and 270 *Fishbeds* and *Floggers*. The paper pointed

The MiG-27 (NATO reporting name *Flogger-D*) had a similar capability to the RAF's Jaguar GR.1s and was introduced around the same time, 1975. This example, 24 Yellow, is a later MiG-27M *Flogger-J*, armed with B-8M1 rocket pods and a Gryazev-Shipunov GSh-6-30, 30mm Gatling gun. *Chris Lofting*

A Rapier fire unit on a RAF airfield in West Germany. These were the 'active' defences for the RAFG Clutch Bases. These SAMs protected the bases but just as important were the 'passive' defences – the rapid repair units assigned to each base. *Terry Panopalis Collection*

Jaguar GR.1 XX759 of 226 OCU outside its HAS at RAF Lossiemouth. Some air forces camouflaged their HAS, but perhaps the RAF couldn't afford the paint. Apparently on one occasion hardstands were painted, producing an increase in first aid cases as 'Lineys' skidded on the slippery surface. *Terry Panopalis Collection*

out that the *Fishbeds* and *Floggers* could not reach the 'Rhine Clutch' airfields of the RAF with a useful bombload but could attack NATO forward bases.

These types would attack at 200ft (60m) using 1,000lb (453kg) bombs, guided weapons and anti-runway weapons similar to the UK's AST.1217. NATO airfields would be defended by Rapier and Roland SAMs (RAF bases had eight Rapier fire units apiece) and low altitude visual CAP by NATO fighters. These were described as 'active' defences, but what the paper concentrated on was the 'passive' defences such as hardened shelters and rapid runway repair units. These repair units were well-drilled and thought capable of repairing the 7m (23ft) diameter crater from a 1,000lb (454kg) bomb in four hours and the damage from a weapon along the lines of AST.1217 in three hours.

This posed an interesting question: why attack the runways if the aircraft, secure in their shelters, could be using the runways within four hours? Realistically it served to 'defer an enemy's ability to generate sorties' for a short period and at 'great cost' in aircrew and aircraft. Attacking the shelters and the aircraft therein, although also costly, had a greater effect on the enemy sortie rate in the long term than attacking the

The F-111E/F could carry up to 24 Durandal on six-round pylons on each wing pylon. The McDonnell Douglas F-15E can carry at least ten Durandal for the runway cratering role. *Wiki Commons*

runways. In fact the paper's authors opined that attacking runways cost the attacker more than the attacked, and that NATO ground-attack resources would be expended very rapidly if anti-runway operations were pursued but attacking the shelters with 1,000 lb (454kg) bombs had a longer term impact on enemy operations than attacking runways.

The conclusion was that it was better to spend money on airfield defences, passive and active, than weapons to attack runways. Why did the Air Staff continue to pursue the anti-runway weapon? The basic truth was that finding and hitting shelters was difficult and damaging the aircraft within was even more difficult. RAE studies conducted at RAF Laarbruch in 1966 had shown that visual acquisition of an airfield at low altitude was difficult in a fast jet, with the airfield only visible at 4.5km (2.5nm) in an aircraft flying at 80m (262ft). The tower and hangars were visible before the runways and identifying camouflaged HAS and aircraft was extremely difficult, with shelters only visible at 3km (1.6nm), or 1.5km (0.8nm) if camouflaged. That did not leave a lot of time for target selection and attack.

The result was the continuing work on a counter-air system to meet AST.1217, a system that evolved from an anti-airfield (i.e. shelters and runways) to solely anti-runway weapon.

A Dibber for the Eighties

By the 1970s Flexible Response was well established and the opposing forces were less likely to 'go nuclear', with a 'no first use' policy becoming the status quo. This led to the development of non-nuclear weapons for counter-air operations. As with the BL.775 anti-armour cluster bomb that replaced small nuclear weapons (see Chapter 4) the aim was to deny the enemy its airfields without resorting to nuclear weapons. As noted above, runways are rather hard targets for conventional weapons, hence the development for the Israelis of the specialist Dibber by Matra. Not that Matra had been resting on their laurels; they had since 1971 been developing a follow-on system called Durandal, named after the sword of the Frankish warrior, Roland.

Durandal could be carried on standard ejector racks, six to a pylon, with an F-111 carrying a load of up to 24 on its wing pylons. Released at 200ft (60m) and 550kt (1019km/h) the Durandal was slowed by a small parachute that also stabilised it and as it swung to an angle of

'There is nothing better at destroying a runway than a Durandal.' The USAF withdrew from JP.233 but took on the Matra Durandal, heir to the Dibber's crown as runway destroyer, with the designation BLU-107.

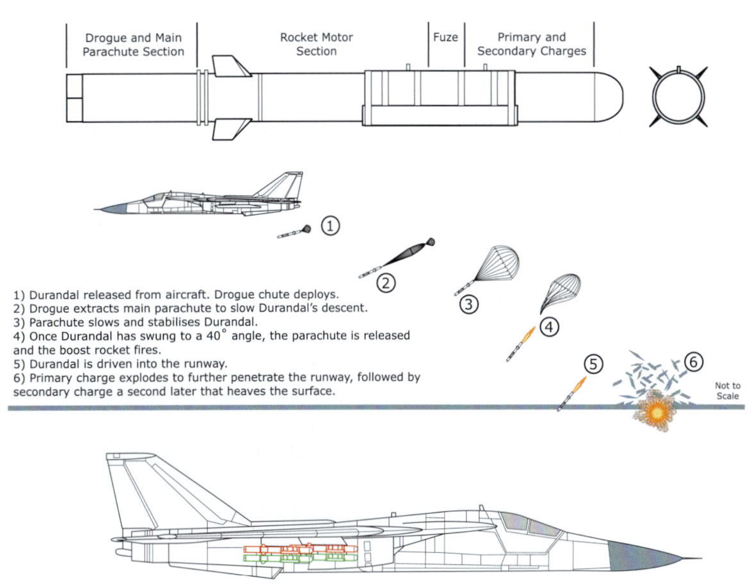

Six Durandal on Multiple Rack Ejector rack on General Dynamics F-111F

Within the confines of a hardened aircraft shelter (HAS) RAF Armourers and 'Lineys' in full NBC kit prepare a Jaguar GR.1 for a sortie. Of note in this image is the anti-spall lining and a fuel bowser. *Terry Panopalis Collection*

40°, a rocket motor fired, driving the weapon into the concrete surface. Once through the runway surface, the 100kg (220 lb) primary warhead detonated which in turn drove the weapon deeper, where the 15kg (33 lb) secondary charge exploded. The secondary charge could also be fitted with a delay fuze to hamper repair work. In all, Durandal could damage an area with radius of 25ft (7m), which if the entire stick of 12 hit its target, could heavily damage a runway.

Durandal is the most widely used anti-runway weapon in the world and when acquired for their F-111Es and F-15E Strike Eagles as the BLU-107, the USAF requested a higher delivery speed, 630kt (1167km/h) and steeper firing angle.

Deep Strike, Deep Thought

Rather than reproduce the Dibber, which in reality merely made a better job of cratering than a 1,000 lb (454 lb) general purpose bomb, the British thought about what the aims of counter-air operations were. The objective was to deny the enemy the use of their airfields for as long as possible. The answer to a cratered runway was a bulldozer to refill the hole and a road roller to flatten the surface. In theory a cratered runway could be back in operation in a few hours.

The British approach was to maximise the damage through using a variety of weapons that would create different types of damage requiring greater effort to repair. This produced some original thinking. Techniques for cratering runways were well established: punch through the concrete and heave the surface or leave a cavity that could not bear the weight of an aircraft. Techniques for repairing such damage were also well practiced so why not develop a system to kill two birds with one stone?

Air Staff Target 1217 had called for an air-delivered weapon to deny the Warsaw Pact the use of its airfields, essentially a Dibber for the 80s. Since Israel's success in June 1967, airfields had been hardened, with the construction of hardened aircraft shelters (HAS) on pretty much every military, and some civil, airfield across Europe. A HAS is a bunker for an aircraft, designed to protect it from bomb and shell and in its most sophisticated form is fitted with equipment to protect the ground crew from nuclear, biological and chemical (NBC) weapons while they work on the aircraft. Most HAS housed a single aircraft, usually a strike aircraft or interceptor, but RAF Alconbury in Cambridgeshire had the largest HAS structures in Europe, built to shelter the USAF's Lockheed U-2Rs, the true identity of the TR-1As used for stand-off radar reconnaissance. (See Chapter 6).

The threat to the 'Rhine Clutch' airfields was not the Warsaw Pact tactical aircraft such as *Flogger, Fitter* and *Frogfoot* but long-ranged types such as *Blinder, Backfire* and *Fencer,* the equivalent of NATO's F-111, Tornado and Buccaneer, so NATO could expect heavy attacks on its airfields and to deny this capability to Warsaw Pact air forces required innovative weapons. As noted, when it came to destroying airfields, NATO and Warsaw Pact forces were thought to possess comparable systems.

Hardened shelters posed a knotty problem to both sides, requiring a precise hit from a heavy weapon, in the form of the 2,000 lb (907kg) Paveway, which also required a designator. On the F-111F this was provided by the onboard Pave Tack system in the weapons bay, but this capability was not available across the western air forces as most types, such as the RAF's Tornados, lacked self-designation. Therefore, rather than attack the shelters, it was the runways, taxiways and hard stands that became the target. If this meant the enemy aircraft were safe and sound in their HAS, that was where they would stay as they could not move if the taxiways were damaged or take off from a cratered runway.

Warsaw Pact airfields were, as might be expected, bristling with defences; AAA and SAMs. NATO air forces had since 1960 made the low level, typically <200ft (<60m) - their operating environment and therefore a weapon that could be delivered at low altitude and at high speed, preferably without the need to reduce speed or increase altitude, was preferred. In May 1982 the RAF proved just how difficult it was to hit a runway with freefall bombs from high altitude when a Vulcan B.2 attacked Port Stanley Airport in the Falkland Islands in Operation Black Buck 1.

AST.1217

The basic aim of AST.1217 was to produce a series of cuts across, or along, the take-off and landing areas of Warsaw Pact airfields and destroy aircraft in hardened shelters. The latter aim proved to be difficult, so the former became the core of the target. The weapon was to cut the runways with a pattern of 1m (3ft 3in) diameter craters each with a depth of 15cm (6in) and no more than 15m (48ft) apart so that no part of the runway was more than 500m (547 yards) long. Each cut was to be 625m (684 yards) long to allow taxiways and secondary grass strips to be cut at the same time.

Aside from Dibber-type weapons other systems were examined such as the caltrop, a tetrahedal spike that had been used against cavalry and infantry since Roman times. Caltrops were dismissed as they lay on the surface and could be swept away on concrete areas or rolled into the soil on grass strips. The application of sticky tar-like substances was also dismissed as being difficult to deliver and no use on grass areas.

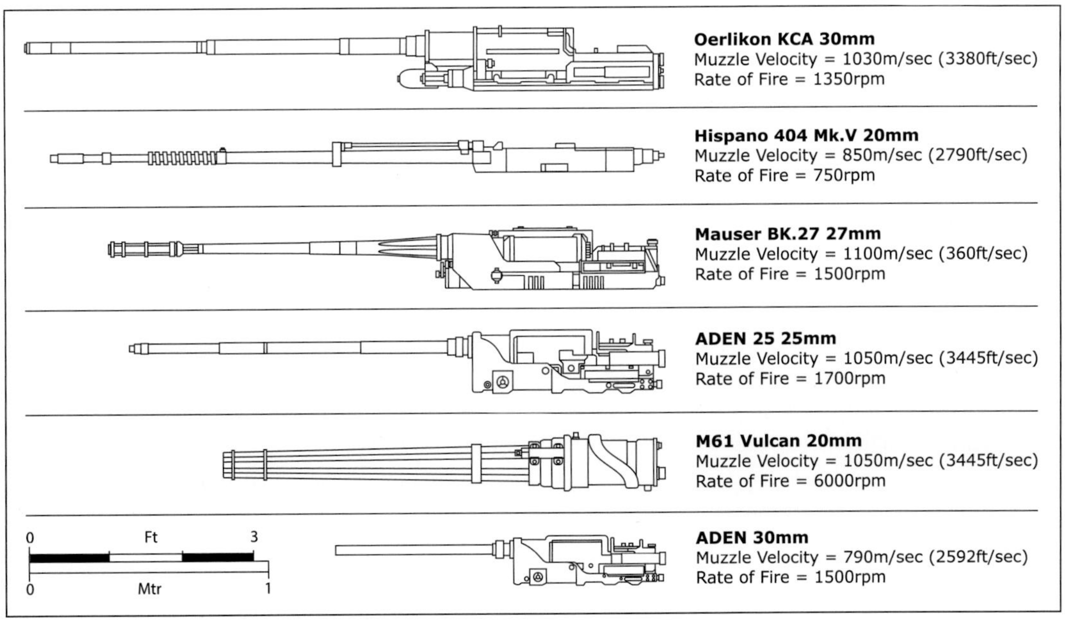

Guns were also considered for the anti-runway mission but only the Oerlikon KCA 30mm cannon could provide a 1m diameter crater but was too big for any of the aircraft that would be in RAF service beyond 1990. All of these guns can be used to strafe ground targets in support of troops.

Guns were examined, particularly the RAF's old favourite, the ADEN 30mm cannon. With a muzzle velocity of 800m/sec (2,625ft/sec), the ADEN's 250g (8oz) round with 40g (1oz) of explosive produced a crater 0.6m (2ft) in diameter. Around this time Oerlikon were developing their 304 revolver cannon (30mm, 4 chamber) that would become the KCA as used on the SAAB JA-37 Viggen. The KCA's muzzle velocity of 1,030m/sec (3,400ft/sec) and 395g (12.7oz) shell with 50g (1.6oz) of explosive produced a crater 24cm (9.5in) deep and 0.8m (2ft 8in) in diameter. The standard shell performed better than armour-piercing rounds in cratering the runway, mainly due the former's reduced penetration and larger explosive charge.

In the anti-runway role, the cannons had to be fired at a fairly steep angle into the runway, typically 60° from horizontal. Given that the attacking aircraft would be flying low, typically 200ft (60m), a diving attack would not be feasible. Nor would installing the weapon at an angle as this would require either a large pod or a weapons bay. This would be especially difficult with the KCA which was 2m (6ft 7in) long and the only aircraft with a bomb bay capable of conducting these operations were the Buccaneer or Canberra, but the KCA would not fit the Buccaneer.

Attention returned to more feasible, and effective, weapons with four schemes being examined: A) dispenser for downward-firing rocket penetrators, B) dispenser for parachute retarded penetrators, C) cluster bomb and D) dispenser for shaped charge bomblets.

For Scheme A) tests by Hunting Engineering had shown that a 25mm (1in) rocket fired downwards and backward at 40° from vertical was feasible. Trials also had shown that a 50mm projectile worked best but could damage the aircraft unless the aircraft was flying at high speed.

For Scheme B), a parachute retarded 50mm projectile with a 100mm diameter rocket motor allowed the aircraft to escape damage while producing a 1m crater. The parachute would ensure the projectile was in the ideal orientation before firing its rocket.

The cluster bomb for Scheme C) was based on the BL.755, but its 57mm (2.2in) diameter bomblets produced craters of 0.3m (1ft) in diameter and 8cm (3in) deep, which could be repaired in 'tens of minutes' using rapid-setting cement such as Bostik 276 magnesium phosphate cement or RASH – rapid hardening asphalt. RARDE reported that a larger diameter bomblet, 114mm (4.4in), could produce the 1m crater, but only 28 rather than 147 bomblets could be carried in the BL.755 body. This new bomblet had five flip-out fins and an extendable stand-off for the fuze. A variant with a fixed tail was also proposed.

The same bomblets could be used in a fixed dispenser in Scheme D) which produced a narrower pattern than BL.755 as the wider elliptical pattern of cluster bomb was not required. Each

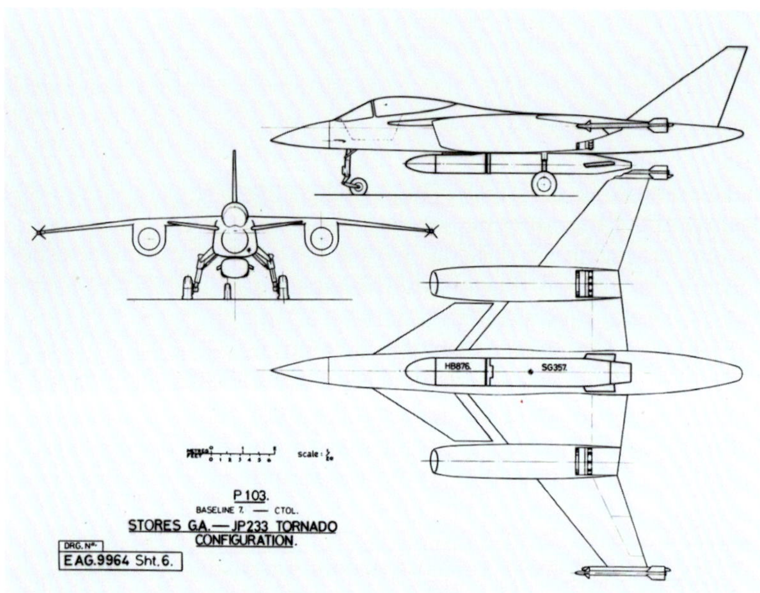

Warton's P.103 aircraft to meet AST.403 was a candidate aircraft for the JP.233 dispenser system. It could carry a single Tornado-style dispenser on the centreline pylon. *North West Heritage Group*

Boomerang was a name applied by BAC Warton to a UAV designed for road interdiction and airfield attack. This example is carrying six BL.755 for the road interdiction role. It was to be powered by a single (scaled) Pratt & Whitney Canada JT15D turbofan and launched from a ramp by rocket motor. *North West Heritage Group*

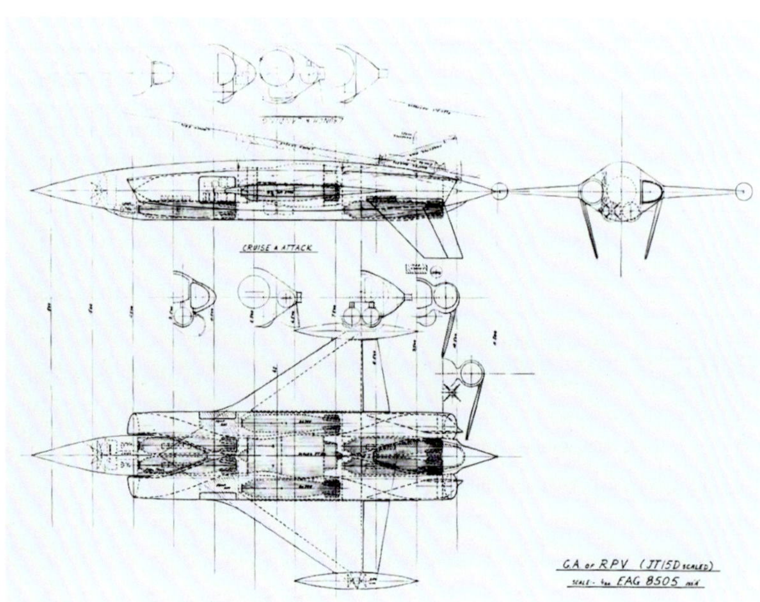

dispenser could carry up to 69 of the lighter fixed-tail bomblets or 81 collapsible bomblets. These had the advantage of impacting at the best angle for the shaped charge to work.

When comparing the effort required to cut a runway, one cut using 1,000 lb (454kg) bombs producing 7m (23ft) diameter craters would require 5-6 aircraft meaning that to perform a complete airfield closure with five cuts would require 25-30 aircraft. If the weapon was used in attacks along the runway, one aircraft could feasibly wreck a runway. The preferred method was to make a series of cuts across the runway. With a dispenser system as described above five aircraft could do the same operation, although the 1,000 lb bombs would cause more damage on the airfield in general. As for the dispenser systems, these were very much single purpose weapons – runway attack – whereas the cluster bomb had an anti-armour role as well. Ultimately what the Air Staff wanted was for one aircraft to make one cut and a dispenser was looking at the best method, with a retarded shaped-charge weapon.

The next item to be discussed was how to extend the period the airfield was out of action. As noted above, with well-drilled rapid repair teams, runways could be repaired in 2-3 hours. The RAE had produced a paper *A Study of Area-Denial Weapons for Airfield Attack* in July 1972 that examined ways to hamper runway repairs. The first suggestion was to add a time delay to the penetrators to explode over a period, thus adding to the repair teams' workload. An alternative was to attack the repair teams and their plant, but the most favoured option was to deliver anti-vehicle and anti-personnel mines with the cratering charges. These area denial munitions were meant to prevent the repairs being made rather than cause casualties, more of a psychological weapon, or destroy equipment. The conclusion was that the mines should be in and around the runway cuts with other areas of the airfield – taxiways, buildings – as a secondary target.

As for attacking the repair plant, British trials had shown that to repair three 7m (23ft) craters caused by 1,000 lb bombs in under four hours required 65 vehicles of 14 different types, with three types critical to the initial work on the damage. These were a wheeled hydraulic excavator (JCB or Gradall type); a tractor, medium, articulated (Michigan 275) and a tractor, fully-tracked, medium (Caterpillar D6) while for the final phase sweeping vehicles were required. The studies showed that against the vulnerable parts of vehicles; tyres, radiators, engine sumps and driver's cab, a 2g (0.06oz) fragment from a mine could cause enough damage to cripple the vehicle or crew but also be useful against parked aircraft. To produce a more effective damage pattern a cylindrical, self-righting munition was used, flipped upright by 12 spring-loaded legs.

Fuzing and triggering was also discussed with time, contact, influence and tripwires being examined with the conclusion that a combination of timed and contact fuzing on a cylindrical mine provided the best solution. If that mine was a combination of fragmentation for anti-personnel and a self-forging warhead for use against vehicles, even better. This was the combination of features the led to the HB.876.

Having delivered the cratering charges and leaving a wrecked airfield in their wake, the strike aircraft headed back to their own, hopefully relatively intact, bases, be they east or west of the Elbe. As soon as the strike package had departed, the runway repair teams would have sprung into action. These would be equipped with excavators, graders and road rollers, essentially road building kit and, interestingly, the specifications for postwar RAF transport aircraft were drawn up to accommodate such equipment rather than military vehicles. Cra-

To meet the ASR.1217 requirement for a 1m diameter, 15cm deep crater, a range of cratering munitions were proposed. These included rocket-propelled penetrators and freefall submuniitons, including variations on the BL.755's armour piercing bomblet. To deliver these, a number of dispensers were considered. Including BL.755.

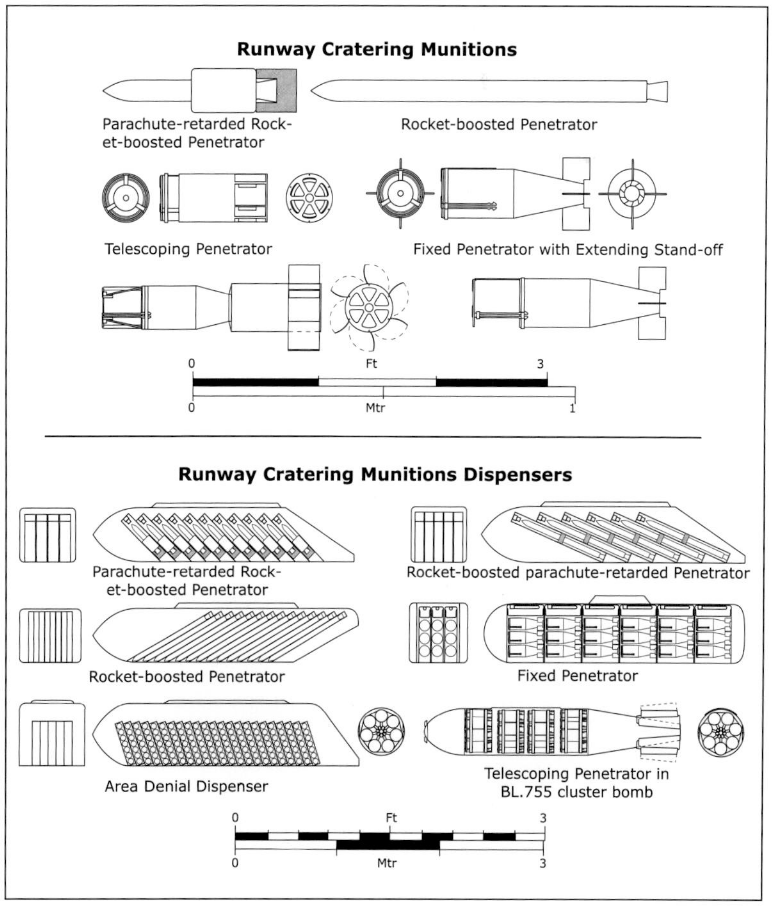

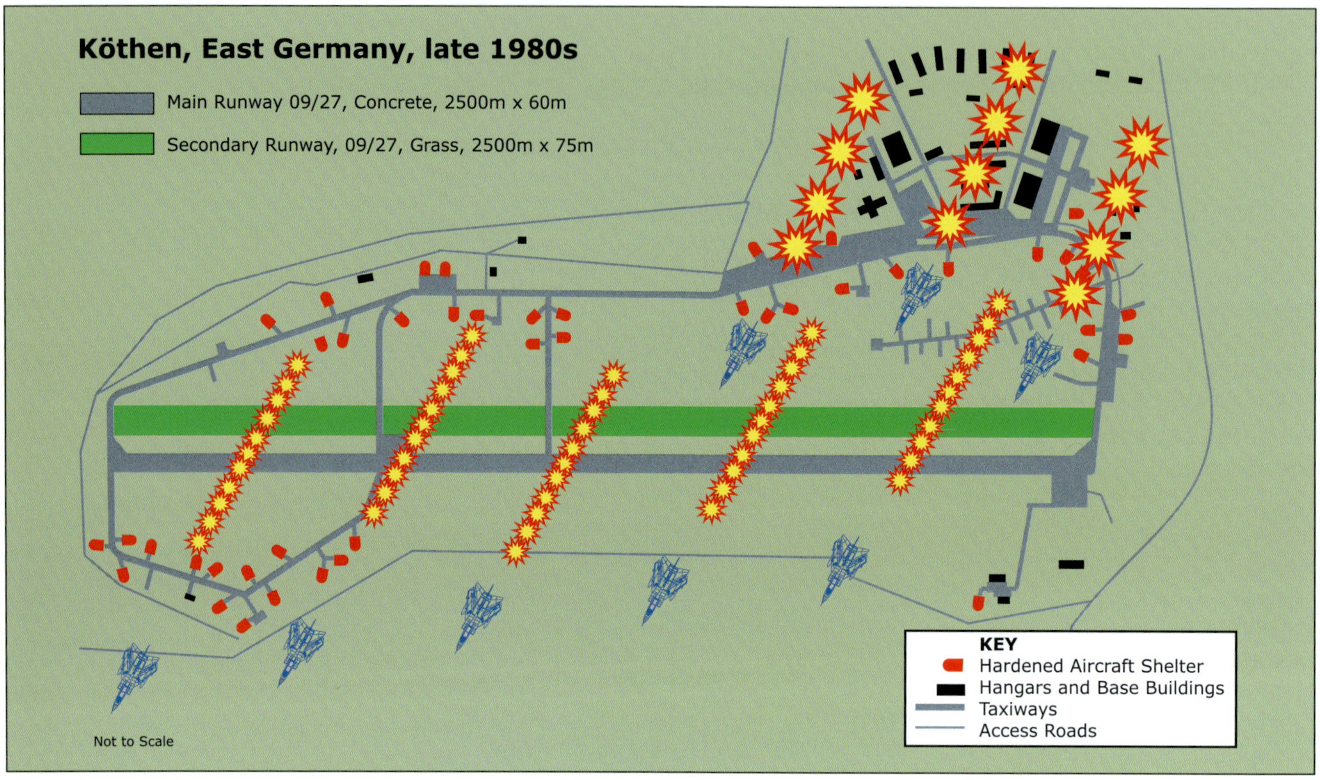

Köthen was a typical Warsaw Pact airfield in East Germany. Given its proximity to the Inner German Border, shorter-ranged types such as *Fitter* and *Fishbed* would have been based here. The airfield was defended by guns and SA-3 *Goa* SAMS. A RAF attack would have used JP.233 to cut the runways and taxiways and 1,000 lb bombs to destroy buildings.

ters would be backfilled with the rubble blown out when the runway or taxiway was cratered or stockpiled hardcore material. The surface would be levelled by the grader and finally compacted by the roller. Sounds easy and with a well-trained team, could be a fairly quick process but another aspect of the anti-runway weapon was to give the repair teams plenty of work by delivering a large number of cratering weapons.

Runway repairs, and the time taken to conduct them, also depended on the repair crews being able to work efficiently. Harassment raids by intruder-type aircraft were by the 1980s no longer feasible, but the anti-runway systems to meet AST.1217 had addressed this aspect.

Rods from the Gods

Amongst the studies for AST.1217 is a RAE report, mundanely titled *'A Surface-to-Surface Missile for Airfield Attack'*. This author opened the report, dated May 1970, expecting a modified Lance or a variant of the Foil artillery rocket system but was surprised to see a drawing of a UGM-27 Polaris A3 SLBM. This, however, was not to be launched from a Royal Navy *Resolution*-class submarine cruising under the North Atlantic, but from the back of an 8x8 truck in a forest clearing in West Germany. So far, so straight forward – ballistic missile used to drop a weapon on an airfield target – standard procedure for the Soviets with their R-17/R-300 Elbrus (NATO reporting name *Scud-B)* and OTR-23 Oka (NATO reporting name SS-23 *Spider*) tactical missiles.

The difference was that the Polaris would not be carrying nuclear warheads. The RAE proposed taking the first stage of the Polaris and replacing the second stage and warhead bus with a cluster weapon dispenser to deliver 2608 anti-runway or 258 anti-shelter bomblets. From space.

The Ministry of Technology had first proposed using ballistic missiles to deliver non-nuclear payloads in 1969, a year before Polaris entered RN service as the deterrent carrier. The study concluded that an 'inertially-guided ballistic missile with a cluster warhead for the attack of airfields' would be promising and looked at the Black Arrow and Blue Streak satellite launchers and the Polaris submarine launched ballistic missile (SLBM). The satellite launchers were quickly dismissed as they used liquid propellants, kerosene and High Test Peroxide (HTP) for the former and liquid oxygen (LOX) and kerosene for the latter. These were deemed unsuitable due to logistics and mobility difficulties. These same considerations had also been one reason Blue Streak was not adopted as the UK nuclear deterrent carrier; a role ultimately filled by Polaris.

By 1968, a year before Polaris went to sea with the Royal Navy, the RAE was quite familiar with the missile and was investigating various improvements, but for the counter-air weapon, a British manufactured missile might be cheaper than buying Polaris vehicles from the US, given the number that would be required. For the purposes of the AST.1217 study, a missile of similar performance and characteristics was assumed.

The existing Polaris first and second stages were examined and it was noted that the first stage 'could carry an effective payload of 11,023 lb (5,000kg) about 155 miles (250km) or 7,937 lb (3,600kg) to 311 miles (500km)'. The second stage was considered unsuitable for extending the range to attack more distant targets. Since the system was to be mainly operating from West Germany, a missile based on the Polaris first stage was deemed acceptable. If a bit more range was required, a slightly larger rocket motor based on the Polaris motors could be developed in the UK. One aspect that could have an effect on the motor was the impact angle of the submunitions. RAE investigations in the Polaris Improvement Programme (PIP, eventually became known as Chevaline) were examining cutting the motor to control range and 'fly the missile above the minimum energy trajectory'. This would steepen the re-entry angle (more than 60° to the horizontal was required) and reduce the potential for ricochet on impact with a shelter or runway. The RAE also examined fitting the thrust vector control system from the second stage on the first stage (which used swivelling nozzles) to reduce the missile weight and thus increase range or payload.

When AST.1217 was issued, the RAE examined a series of proposals to use ballistic missiles against airfields with submunitions designed to destroy runways and hardened aircraft shelters on airfields in East Germany, 9-155 miles (15-250km) east of the Inner German Border, which corresponded to 311-994 miles (500-1,600km) from East Anglia, Lincolnshire or East Yorkshire. The typical target airfield comprised a concrete runway and taxiways, hardened shelters distributed along the taxiways and a grass auxiliary strip alongside the main runway. The system could also be used in the SEAD role against airfield defences, blazing the trail for manned aircraft to attack the runways and shelters with specialised weapons such as LGBs and dispensers.

As with the dispenser weapons described above, the intention was to produce craters 3ft 3in (1m) in diameter with a spacing small enough to prevent the runway being used by aircraft. The shelters were assumed to be a concrete arch 2ft (0.6m) thick covered with 6ft (1.8m) of soil. Given that the submunitions would impact at an angle, the effective thickness would be greater in a similar fashion to slopped armour on an AFV. If Warsaw Pact shelter designs mirrored NATO's, there would be an anti-spalling lining inside the shelter so the most effective submunition would be one that penetrated the structure before detonating to damage or destroy the aircraft within.

The missile would be launched from an environmentally-controlled tube mounted on a truck or a trailer. Each truck would have a number of pre-surveyed launch sites and these would be clustered to allow one fire control unit to handle several missiles.

As with the Polaris SLBM the missile would comprise a first boost stage, but no second

The Polaris-boosted endo-atmospheric 'bus' deploys its warheads as it plunges through the atmosphere onto an East German airfield. The shrouds have been released and the bus spun up on its long axis to throw the warheads outwards to form a circular pattern. *Luciano Alviani*

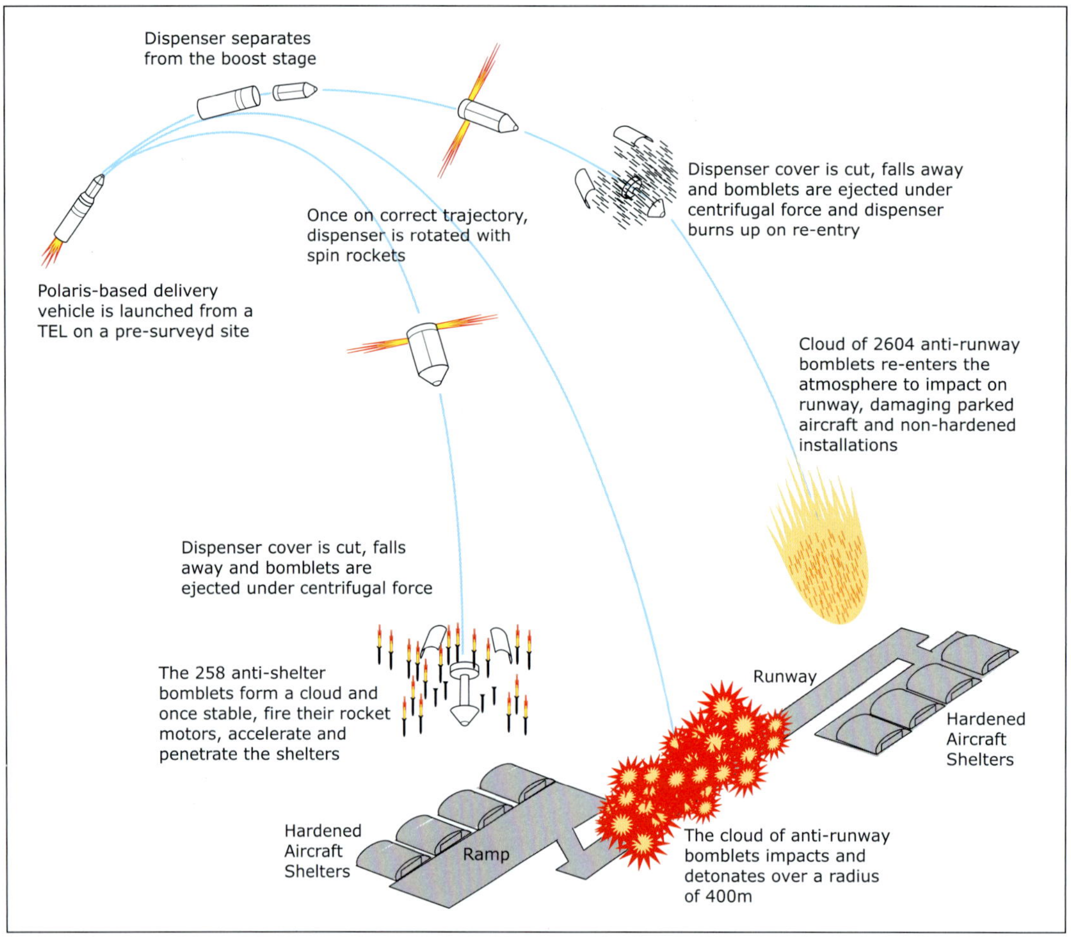

Rods from the Gods. The Polaris sub-orbital airfield denial system relied on kinetic energy as well as explosives to destroy Warsaw Pact airfields. The system could operate by deploying its submunitions in space (exo-atmospheric) or in the atmosphere (endo-atmospheric) depending on the target and mission. One downside of such a system would be the potential for escalation.

Two 'buses' were proposed for the Polaris Counter-Air System. The first carried 258 Anti-shelter submunitions while the second, with the same diameter as the Polaris missile, carried 2604 runway cratering bomblets. The 'bus' was to be spun up by six tangentially firing rocket motors to throw the submunitions outwards.

stage, and a dispenser. The fire control system would input target location, launch location and relevant environmental data. On launch, the missile would be ejected from the tube by steam pressure, the rocket motors ignite at around 98ft (30m) and the missile turn onto its programmed course. At motor burn-out, the dispenser would separate, and the attitude control system stabilise the dispenser until it reaches 'a sensible vacuum' in space. Just prior to re-entry into the atmosphere the control system would align the dispenser with the re-entry flight path 'to reduce impact point errors' and once aligned, a series of spin-up rocket motors would ignite to spin the dispenser, which would throw the submunitions outwards once the dispenser shrouds fell away.

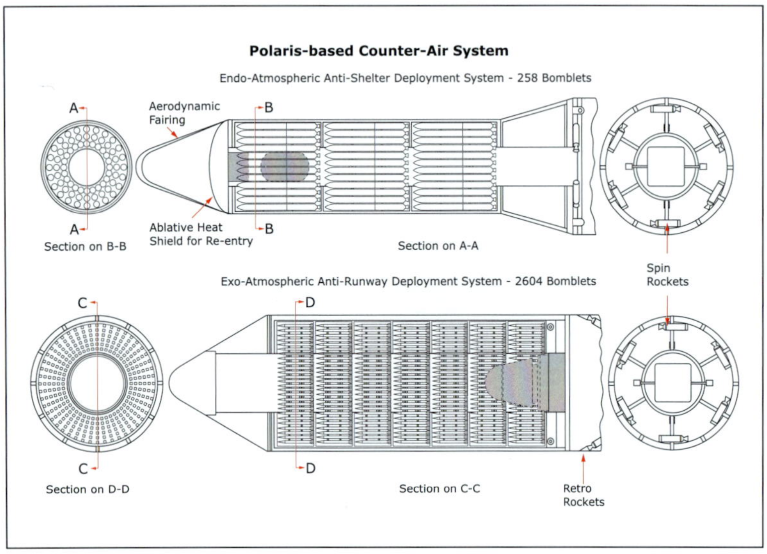

For the anti-runway role, the dispenser would carry up to 2,608 submunitions and these would 're-enter the atmosphere individually, impacting over an area of 1,312ft (400m) radius'. For attacks on shelters, the dispenser would carry 258 larger rocket-boosted submunitions which could be deployed in two modes – exo-atmospheric and endo-atmospheric. The former would operate in a similar manner to the anti-runway dispenser, but for the latter, the dispenser would re-enter the atmosphere before deploying the submunitions at an altitude of 16,404ft (5,000m). The intended benefit of the endo-atmospheric deployment was a tighter pattern but the bomblets would be slower, Mach = 0.97, so rocket boost would be required to further increase the impact velocity of the submunitions, which were fuzed to detonate inside the shelters. The tighter pattern was intended to reduce the number of submunitions that impacted on runways/taxiways as these would 'penetrate too deeply to produce useful craters'.

Exo-atmospheric deployment was deemed to have a few benefits including that the dispenser could be less robust, i.e. lighter, as it would not need to survive the rigours of re-entry. Its main benefit was that the bomblets impacted at an angle close to vertical.

The bomblets differed in many ways with the anti-shelter submunition 'an order of magnitude different in total mass' from the anti-runway weapon. The anti-runway weapon was designed to impact at around 1400ft/sec (426m/sec) and its warhead would create a 3ft 3in (1m) diameter crater with a depth of 11in (27cm). The cone/cylinder/flare design enhanced the submunition's stability while optimising its drag characteristics. The cone and flare were to be made from ceramic which allowed the warhead to differentiate between concrete and grass. By selecting the correct ceramic, the nose cone would be made to shatter on impact with concrete but remain intact to penetrate grass. While these warheads would have little effect against shelters, they would '...cause damage to parked aircraft and installations. They would also have some effect as an anti-personnel weapon'.

Anti-shelter submunitions were designed to penetrate the soil and concrete of a typical Warsaw Pact HAS and was rocket-boosted to provide an optimum impact velocity of 1970-2625ft/sec (600-800m/sec). If the weapon impacted on a runway or grass, it would penetrate too deep to produce a useful crater or camouflet and therefore of little use against runways. To stabilise the submunition in the atmosphere, it carried flip-out fins that also allowed more to be carried in the dispenser.

For endo-atmospheric deployment the dispenser was to be fitted with barometric sensors, similar to those used on Polaris, to initiate deployment at a predetermined altitude. Firing the rocket-booster would be by a clockwork timer mechanism as electrical timers would require a power source such as a capacitor that would need charging. Firing the main explosive charge inside the shelter would also be triggered by a timer, but in this case the time would be around 1.5msec after initial impact. This type of fuze could be based on those designed for anti-aircraft shells during WW2, but being of fixed delay, could not account for different material thickness or construction techniques. A second type of fuze was proposed, one that 'started on impact and stores energy during deceleration; this energy is given up to fire an igniter when deceleration has finished.'

How effective would the 'Rods from the Gods' have been? The assumed target for the studies involving the anti-runway weapons was a typical Warsaw Pact airfield comprising a 9,842ft (3,000m) concrete runway, a compacted soil/grass strip and a taxiway parallel to both. For purposes of the design study this was treated as a rectangular target area 1,568 x 9,842ft (478 x 3,000m) and that a STOL aircraft would require a contiguous strip 49 x 2,126ft (15 x 648m) to take off. The 2608 anti-runway weapons from a single dispenser would produce a circular pattern of 3ft 3in (1m) craters over an area with a radius of 1,312 – 1,509ft (400-460m) with each crater approximately 49ft (15m) apart. Therefore, one weapon could cover the entire width of the target but would leave more than enough runway undamaged for STOL operations. As a result, at least two dispenser loads, with aim points 3,871ft (1,180m) apart would be required.

For attacking hardened aircraft shelters, the studies assumed that an airfield had forty HAS, fifteen arranged down each side of the main taxiway and five along each side of a taxi-way extension at one end of the main taxiway. They are distributed over two areas: one 7,874 x 656ft (2,400 x 200m) and a smaller area 1,968 x 646ft (600 x 200m). The 300 bomblets impact more or less vertically and are evenly distributed in a circular pattern.

The Polaris Counter-Air System would have required different submunitions for hardened shelters and runways. The Anti-shelter round was designed for endo-atmospheric deployment and used a rocket motor to drive it into the shelter before detonation.

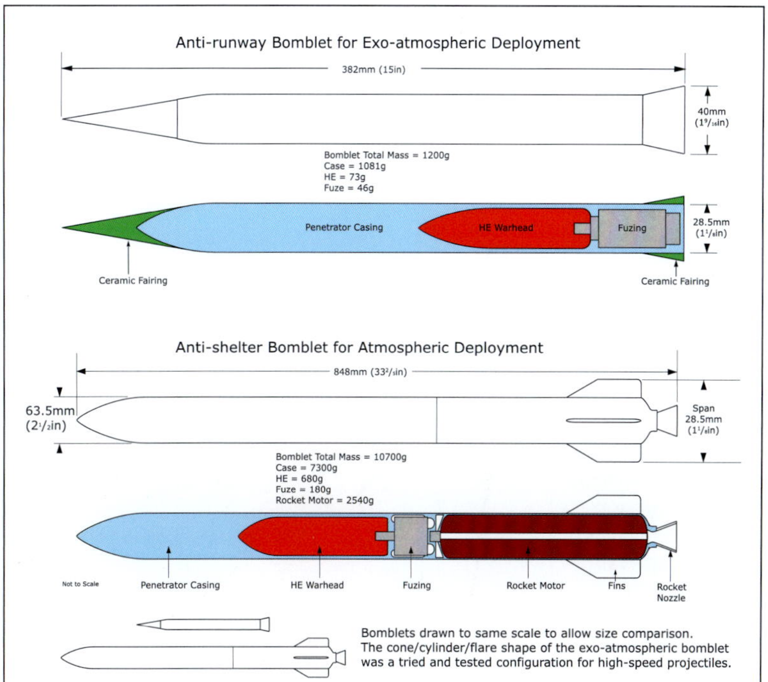

Bomblets drawn to same scale to allow size comparison. The cone/cylinder/flare shape of the exo-atmospheric bomblet was a tried and tested configuration for high-speed projectiles.

The studies proved disappointing as they showed that only 20% of the anti-shelter submunitions would fall in the target area and of these only one out of 125 would hit a shelter i.e. only one weapon out of 600 would hit a HAS. Therefore, it was noted that if HAS are spaced far enough apart, an area attack such as the SSM would not be very effective on an airfield.

The conclusion was that while the counter-air SSM was feasible only the anti-runway version could have worked as hoped and it appeared that it would take six missiles to have an 80% chance of disabling an airfield. One aspect of the proposals that raised concern was the need for two submunitions, which was seen as a problem as the dispensers and attack profiles were different. A dual-purpose submunition was highly desirable and should be considered if the concept was to enter development and it should be based on a modified anti-shelter weapon.

Launchers

As noted above a number of launchers were examined to loft the counter-air dispenser but only Polaris and Black Arrow were deemed suitable. A RAE study advised that Black Arrow's first stage was capable of boosting a 4,600 lb (2,086kg) warhead to 350nm (648km) and an 8,600 lb (3,900kg) warhead to 210nm (389km). If the first and second stages were used then a 1,000 lb (454kg) warhead could be delivered to a range of 2,000nm (3704km) and a 4,000 lb (1814kg) warhead to 1,100nm (2037km). Unfortunately, the British preference for HTP/Kerosene made Black Arrow unsuitable for a weapon that was to be trucked around the byways of North West Germany, competing with the RAF's Harriers for the best dispersal spots.

Counter-air Polaris

The intended use for the counter-air Polaris system was to disable thirty Warsaw Pact airfields and with a minimum requirement of six missiles per airfield, possibly even twelve, that would require between 180 and 360 missiles. This would require around 500 presurveyed and prepared launch sites. If only the 23 airfields defended by the formidable S-125 Neva (NATO reporting name SA-3 *Goa*) were attacked, the numbers reduced to 138 and 276 respectively. The effort involved in developing a British equivalent of the Polaris rocket motors, the dispensers, warheads and associated equipment would have cost £32M in 1970, which equates to £486M in 2018. Ultimately it was precision weapons such as Paveway or Storm Shadow that would be used against HAS, the former in Iraq during Operation Granby in 1991 and the latter in the 2003 Operation Telic.

Below: Tornado GR.1 delivers the contents of a pair of JP.233 dispensers during trials in the mid-1980s. JP.233 required the aircraft to overfly the airfield at low altitude (200ft/60m), which made the aircraft vulnerable to AAA and SAMs, especially on the vast Iraqi airfields during Operation Granby. *Hunting Engineering*

Opposite page:

The SG.357 submunition in operation. The parachute orients the weapon for optimum penetration. A hollow charge warhead punches a hole in the runway forming a pathway for the cratering charge. A similar principle is used in the BROACH warhead for Storm Shadow.

The HB.876 area-denial mine was to land in the rubble left by the SG.357 cratering munitions. On landing the 12 sprung-steel triggers would flip it upright to expose the self-forging/explosively-formed penetrator warhead. This was intended to damage or destroy the construction plant used for runway repairs. The casing of the mine was prefragmented to act as an anti-personnel mine.

Low-Altitude Airfield Attack System – JP.233

Having examined the research work on anti-airfield systems, the Air Staff concluded that attacking the runways with a dispenser loaded with anti-runway munitions and area denial mines was pretty much the most viable counter-air option. AST.1217 became ASR.1217 and development contracts were let. The initial effort was made under the codename Pavercock, and a further Staff Requirement was issued; ASR.1225 to cover the minelet that became known as HB.876 while the anti-runway munition was designated SG.357.

By 1977 the US Air Force had also become interested in an anti-runway weapon and took on a 50% share on the system known as the Low-Altitude Airfield Attack System (LAAAS) to be developed by Hunting Engineering Ltd. Under the MoD's designation system, the LAAAS was renamed JP.233 and development of the system progressed until 1982 when the USAF became alarmed by rising costs and withdrew from the programme.

The JP.233 system comprised a long, 21ft 7in (6.56m), pannier divided into two main sections. The forward section held 215 HB.876 area denial mines while the aft bay held 30 SG.357 cratering munitions. These dropped from the pannier's underside and were retarded and stabilised by parachutes.

The SG.357, weighing 57 lb (26kg) was a sophisticated weapon with four sections: parachute bay, penetrating shaped-charge, cratering charge and stand-off fuze. The SG.357 were carried 'upside down' in the pannier bays and on released tumbled for a short period before the stabilising 'chute deployed to slow the munition and orient it to an angle of 30° from vertical. The spring-loaded stand-off fuze in the nose deployed to ensure the penetrating charge was triggered at the most effective distance from the runway surface. On impact, the shaped charge triggered and formed a plasma jet that passed through the hole in the annular cratering charge to form a channel in the runway into which the cratering charge passed before detonating under the pavement in the subgrade creating a camouflet and heaving the surface.

As the SG.357 munitions fall away from the rear of the dispenser, HB.876 area denial mines drop from the front section and descend on small parachutes to land in the newly cratered runway. A series of 12 spring steel strips, held flat against the cylindrical body, are released by a small charge to form a 'crown' of metal

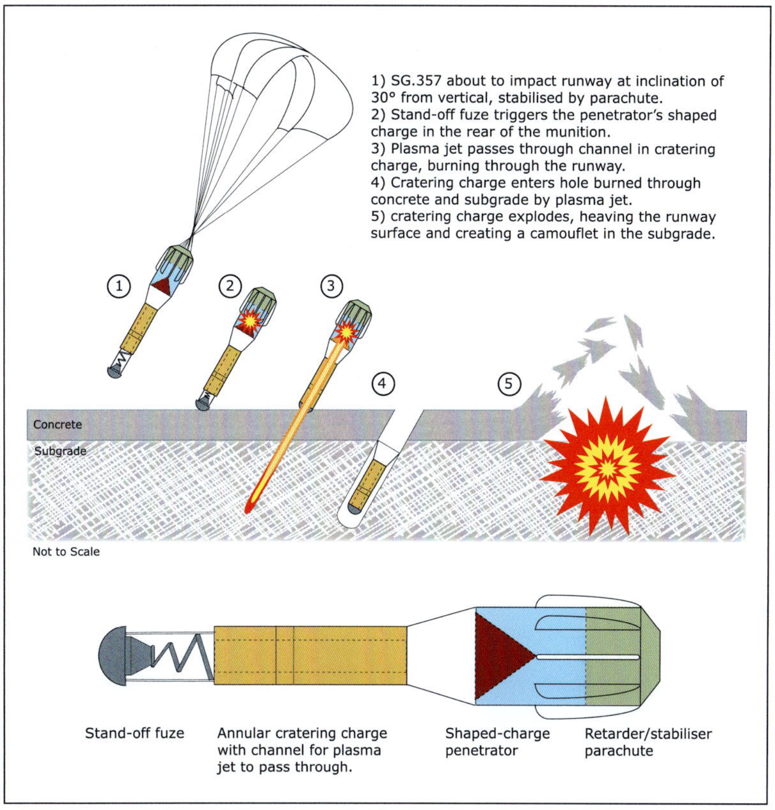

loops that act as stabilising legs for the mine, keeping the top facing upwards. The body of the HB.786 is segmented to create small pieces of shrapnel on detonation while the top of the cylinder is a self-forging forging warhead for use against vehicles such as bulldozers. As rec-

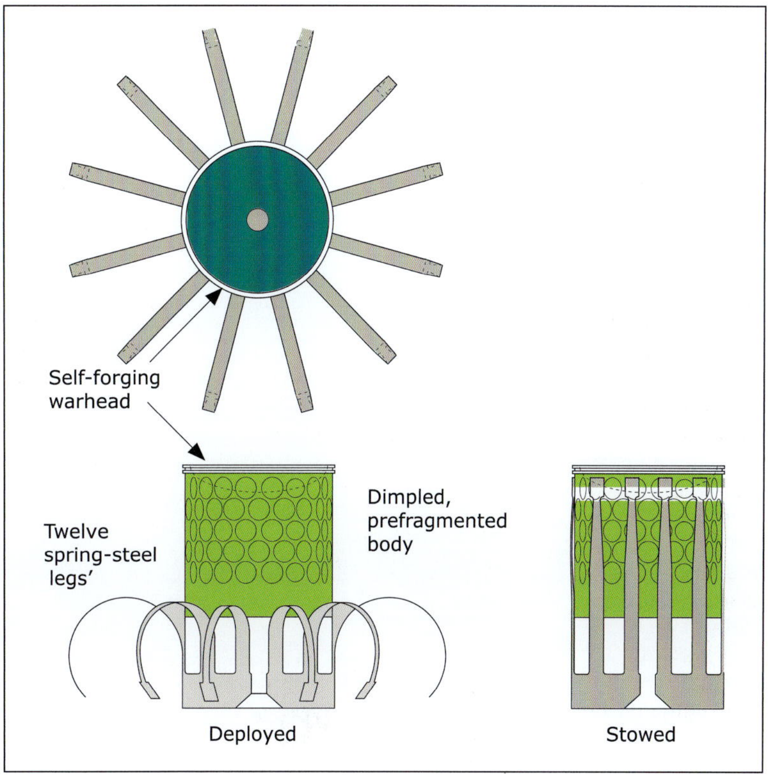

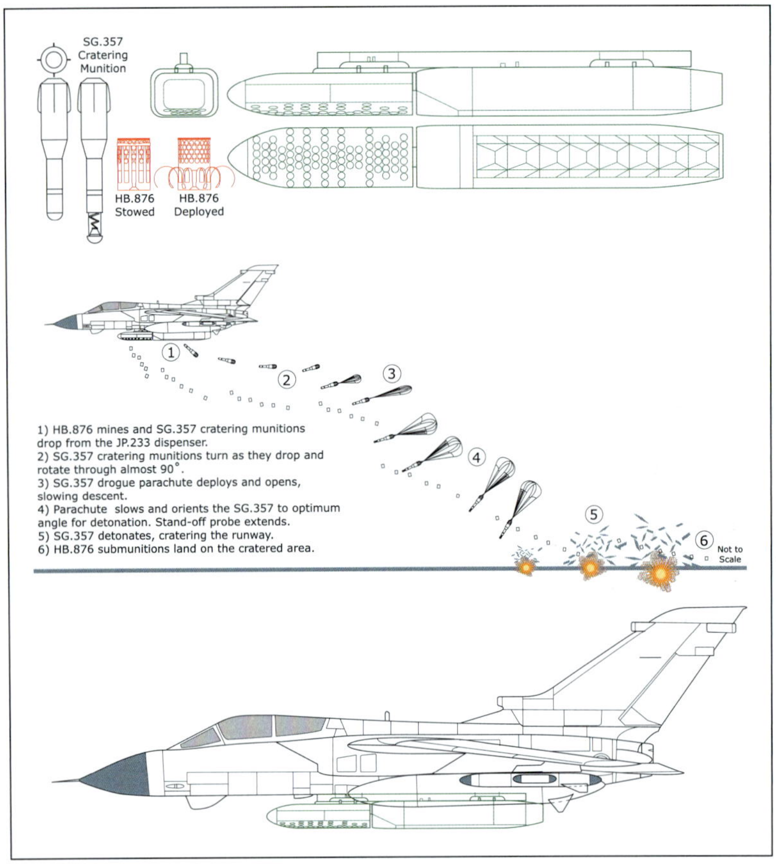

Hunting Engineering's JP.233 was the culmination of much research into runway cratering and area denial/repair hindering submunitions. The system comprised two tandem dispensers, the forward dispenser holding 215 HB.876 area denial mines while the aft section held 30 SG.357 runway cratering submunitions. The aim was to produce a 'cut' across a runway with the SG.357s and use the HB.876 to hamper repair operations.

A pair of Hunting Engineering JP.233 dispensers being loaded onto the ventral pylons of a Tornado GR.1 prior to a sortie during Operation Granby. The size of the dispenser is evident. *Terry Panopalis Collection.*

ommended by the studies, the 5.3 lb (2.4kg) HB.876 used a combination of time delay and contact fuzes.

The two-part pannier for JP.233 was intended for use on Tornado GR.1, as a single unit. No other RAF aircraft could carry these panniers, but alternative panniers, with the addition of fairings, could be carried by other aircraft such as the Buccaneer, Jaguar and Harrier as a two-pylon load-out with the SG.357 under one wing and the HB.876 under the other. The Buccaneer carried the SG.357 panniers on its inboard wing pylons, with the HB.876 pannier on the door of the rotary bomb bay, although the bay could not be closed. Other proposals included a powered stand-off system based on the pannier or UAV delivered munitions including the Boomerang.

Operation Granby saw JP.233 (designated L2 by the RAF) used in action during the first six days of the 1991 Gulf War. Contrary to popular belief, losses on operations involving JP.233 were no higher than those on other low-level ops, with the only JP.233-related loss in 100 sorties incurring after the attack. The system required the Tornado to fly straight and level at 200ft (60m) at around 500kt (926km/h) and continue that for the 15 seconds it took to deliver the submunitions. As noted elsewhere, Warsaw Pact airfields were furnished with a great deal of AAA and SAMs, including the SA-3 *Goa* (S-125 Neva) that was designed to defend against low-level intruders such as the Tornado.

The system's apparent withdrawal from use after six days was more due to the Iraqi air force's decimation rather than from the need for repeated attacks on the Iraqi airfields. The entire system was withdrawn as the new generation of stand-off weapons could be used to attack airfields and due to the Ottawa Protocol against anti-personnel landmines. Despite the adverse publicity around the JP.233, it was an effective weapon. The SG.357 and HB.876 worked well and JP.233 meant the least number of aircraft could provide maximum damage to a runway.

In the fallout from Operation Granby the lesson from operations was that aircraft flying at low level were vulnerable and that the PGBs were the future. As had been observed as far back as 1972, the best way to prevent sorties by enemy aircraft was, as the Israelis had demonstrated, to destroy them on the ground. By August 1982 a Staff Target had been drawn up for a weapon that could do that, even if they were in a HAS: Storm Shadow.

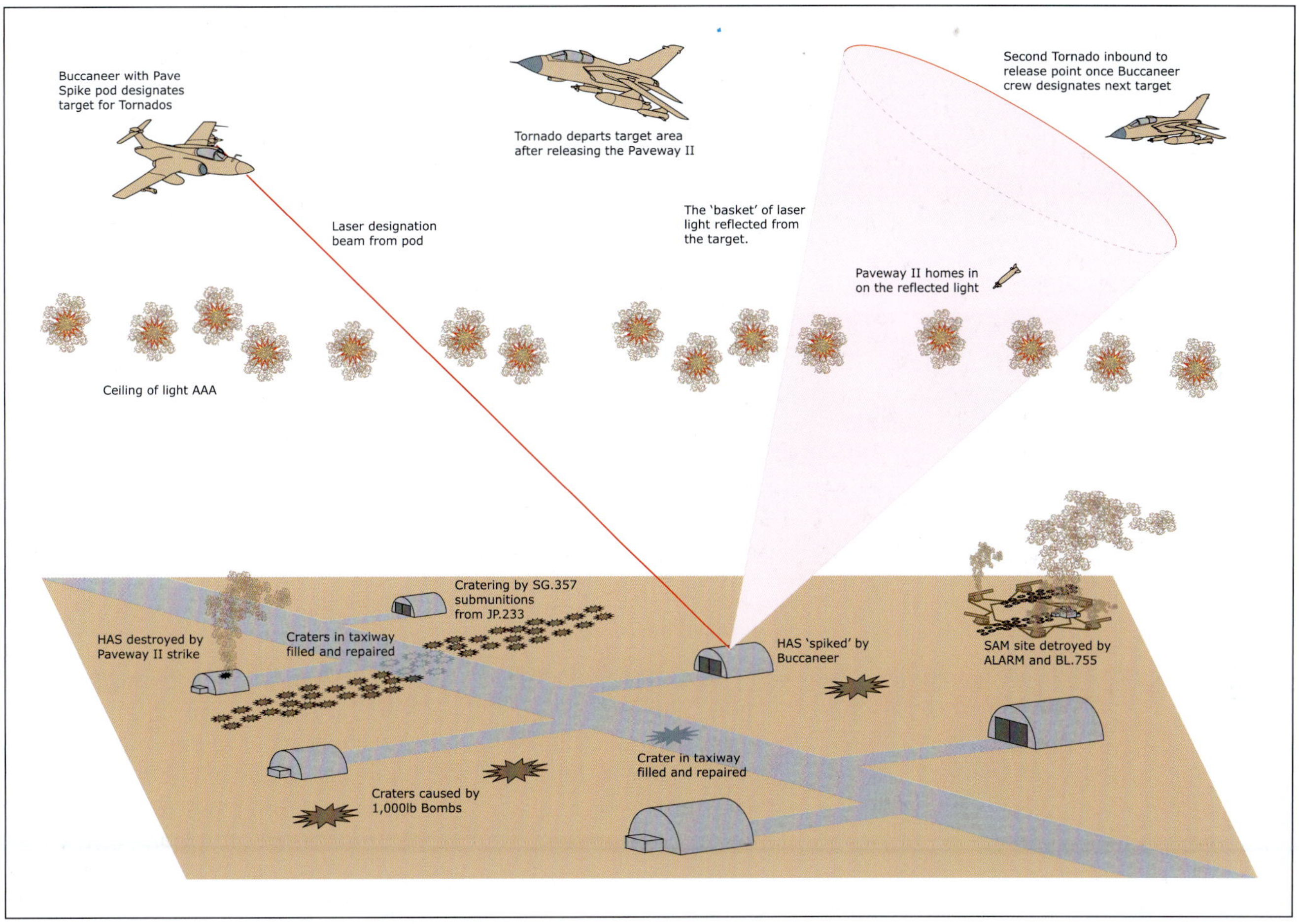

RAF anti-airfield operations, Iraq 1991. By the later stages of Operation Granby, with the heavy SAMs destroyed by ALARM, the RAF were operating above the AAA using Paveway LGBs 'spiked' by Buccaneer S.2s. The earlier strikes with JP.233 and 1,000lb bombs have been repaired.

Storm Shadow

'The case for, and application of, this weapon is limited to the NATO area, the Central Front and Northern Flank in particular. In view of current operations in the South Atlantic is perhaps pertinent that the operational Studies should not exclude employment in other areas.'
Rear Admiral Peter M Stanford, Assistant Chief of the Naval Staff (OR), memo to Air Vice-Marshal Kenneth W Hayr, ACAS(OR)27, May 1982

The Soviet Horde, as noted in Chapter 1 was expected to charge across the Inner German Border at any time. The Warsaw Pact was expected to field up to 180 divisions against the 30 of NATO with the respective air forces numbering 4,000 and 2,000. In the event of a Warsaw Pact invasion of western Europe, planners estimate that of the 2,000 aircraft at NATO's disposal, only around 25% of these would be available for interdiction missions beyond the Forward Edge of the Battlefield Area (FEBA). In a zone beyond the FEBA, to a depth of 173nm (320km), NATO estimated that there were 2,000 fixed targets plus the mobile vehicle formations moving forward. The scale of the task was monumental as the war planners estimated that to destroy 60% of a single Soviet armoured division over 2,000 sorties would be required and the Soviets alone were thought to have almost 70 tank divisions. Previously, such targets would be attacked with tactical nuclear weapons, but in the age of Flexible Response and with the constant improvements in guidance systems, conventional weapons could be considered.

NATO intended countering these numbers with technologies such as the multiple launch rocket system (MLRS) with smart munitions to attack the first echelon to a distance of 20 miles (32km) beyond the FEBA but the second echelon required delivery of munitions into the Warsaw Pact rear areas. This deeper interdiction would be the RAF's responsibility. The principle of Follow-On Forces Attack and Assault Breaker are described in Chapter 6. The Americans took the view that ballistic missiles armed with up to 2,500 submunitions were the best method for attacking airfields and other fixed targets, but the European allies, especially the British and West Germans thought the use of

ballistic missiles, even with conventional warheads, could lead to escalation. This had been discussed in the Ministries and was raised by Dr Geoffrey Pope, the Assistant Chief Scientific Advisor (Projects), ACSA(P) at the RAE, in a memo to the ACAS(OR) Air Vice-Marshal David Harcourt-Smith, in March 1982, stating that 'The political implications of using conventional ballistic missiles have yet to be considered'.

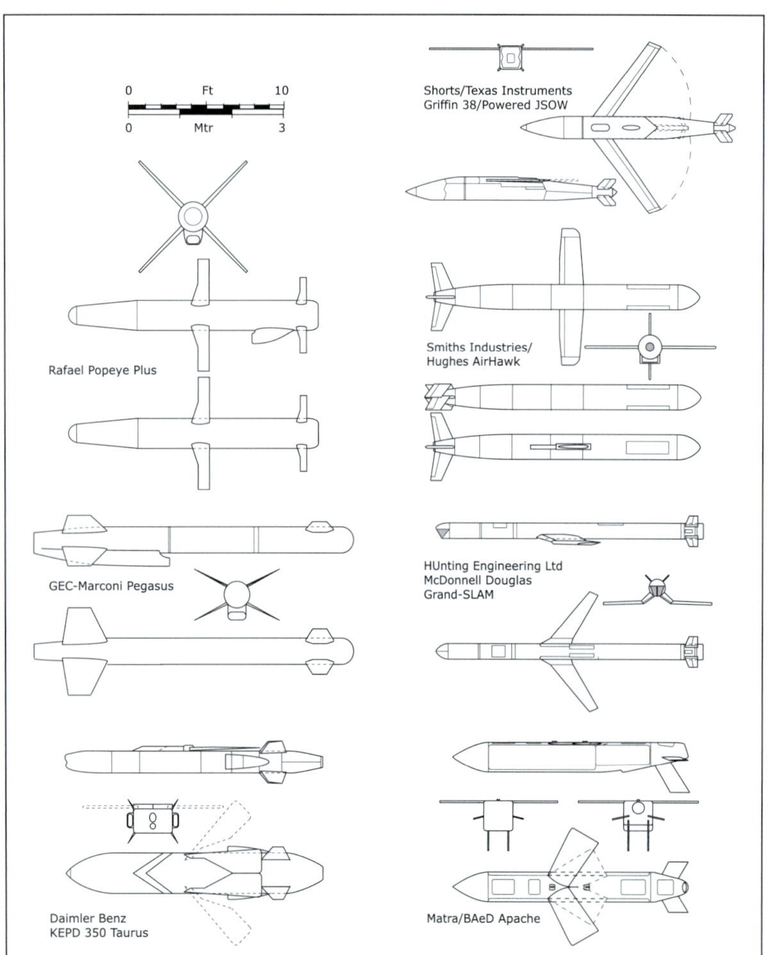

The weapons currently available in the late 1970s required the carrying aircraft to overfly the target, Warsaw Pact aircraft were benefitting from improved range and could be based further beyond the FEBA deep in Warsaw Pact territory which in turn required deeper penetration of Warsaw Pact air defences. From 1979 a series of studies were funded by the USA, West Germany and the UK to examine the possibilities for a Conventional Cruise Missile whose primary role was to deliver conventional explosive. During the initial discussions, the possibilities for alternative warheads arose and the weapon became the Long-Range Stand-Off Missile (LRSOM). Two teams became involved: the first included Boeing, MBB, BAe Dynamics (BAeD) and Marconi Avionics while the second comprised General Dynamics, Dornier and Hunting Engineering Ltd (HEL). These studies were for weapon systems to attack fixed and mobile targets beyond the FEBA and included ballistic, boost-glide, supersonic and subsonic vehicles. Ballistics could be problematic but had the best attrition rates, boost-glide vehicles such as the Lockheed Axe were unproven, supersonic missiles were likely to be large and heavy, which left the subsonic cruise missile. This would also be the least risky to develop.

For the subsonic cruise missile, the Boeing-led team drew on work for the recent AGM-86 air-launched cruise missile and BAeD's P4T Sea Eagle derivative, particularly the terrain profile matching (TERPROM) guidance systems. The General Dynamics team based their work on the BGM-109 Tomahawk and the Tactical Airfield Attack Munition (TAAM). Hunting Engineering contributed their expertise in anti-runway submunitions and dispenser systems. Hunting also contributed to development of a shorter-range standoff weapon called LOCPOD (low cost powered dispenser) although the British saw this more as a system better suited to the ASR.1238 anti-tank weapon.

With the selection of the cruise missile platform, a Staff Target could be drawn up and issued, with NGAST.1236 endorsed on 5 August 1982 covering a requirement for 1,500 LRSOM as a conventionally-armed cruise missile (with a potential for a nuclear warhead) with a 324nm (600km) range and a 500kg (1,102 lb) warhead against point targets. The range restriction was ostensibly to remain within the rules of the second Strategic Arms Limitation Treaty (SALT II) that was under negotiation and might lead to a range restriction for weapons that could be fitted with nuclear warheads, although the UK was not bound by these treaties. As noted above, LRSOM was proposed as a carrier for a nuclear warhead, NAST.1231, the replacement for the warhead on WE.177A and C nuclear weapon. Interestingly, at the same time LRSOM/NGAST.1236 was being discussed and another requirement for a stand-off weapon and replacement for WE.177 was being discussed. To meet SR(A).1244 a weapon called the Tactical Air-to-Surface Missile (TASM) was being studied but was cancelled in 1993 possibly as a result of the adoption of 'Sub-Strategic Trident'.

LRSOM was to be capable of launch from the ground, ships, submarines and aircraft (hence the NGAST designation covering all arms of the UK forces) and be capable of launch from Tornado, the next generation of offensive aircraft, B-52s, C-130, LRCA (Long Range Combat Aircraft, became the Rockwell B-1), F-111, F-16 and any large aircraft that could be modified to carry it. Possible targets included second echelon formations, airfields, POL (petrol, oil, lubricant) storage facilities, transport hubs, bridges and harbour facilities. Particular attention, priority in fact, was given to attacking the airfield facilities of the Soviet Naval Air Forces in the Kola Peninsula, from where Tu-95 *Bears* and Tu-22M *Backfires* would sortie into the north east Atlantic to attack NATO convoys.

As noted above, although destruction of runways was a key task for the deep interdiction units, destruction of the enemy's aircraft in their hangars and the associate support infrastructure would prove more beneficial in the long run. Despite the effort that had been put into the JP.233 anti-runway system, this was described in a March 1982 HEL report as problematic and represented a 'cost-effective approach for the present decade: but there-after some form of stand-off weapon is essential if Tornado is to continue to attack Warsaw Pact airfields without experiencing unacceptable attrition rates.' Therefore, it appeared that even HEL, the developer of JP.233 saw no future for it beyond the 1980s which is effectively what happened when JP.233 was withdrawn after Operation GRANBY, the 1991 Gulf War.

As issued, in August 1982 NGAST.1236 stated what the the Naval (i.e. the Admiralty), General and Air Staffs wanted the Air Launched Missile (ALM) as LRSOM was now known, to do. The Admiralty and General Staff had less interest in the weapon and eventually the 'NG' prefix was lost. The primary use of this missile was to deliver a 500kg (1,102 lb) conventional explosive, or nuclear, warhead to a point target at a range of up to 600km (324nm). It was to be subsonic, powered by a gas turbine and of modular construction to ease maintenance, allow midlife update and changes to warheads. Its guidance system was to be autonomous and allow the ALM to impact a point target 24 hours a day in all weathers, over land and water, and the flight profile was optimised to the target and variable to take obstacles and defences into account. Survivability was to be enhanced by being 'as electronically quiet as possible' with high ECM resistance and reduced radar, infrared, visual and acoustic signatures. It should be stealthy. The engine, such as a the Microturbo TRI-60, should also be smoke-free. The ALM was to be optimised for carriage on the Tornado but a surface-launched version, to replace the British Army's Lance, was still a possibility and commonality between the versions was to be maximised.

As the Eighties progressed the ALM was absorbed into the Modular Stand-Off Weapon (MSOW), a NATO programme supported by the UK, USA, Canada, France, Spain, West Germany and Italy. As the name suggests, MSOW was to be modular and come four versions: short-range anti-tank weapon dispenser on the same lines as LOCPOD and two long-range versions one for use against static targets and another for mobile targets. As usual, France withdrew over workshare differences, as did Canada, but the MSOW's biggest impediment was that the USAF already had a long-range

Opposite page:

Fencer was viewed as the major air threat to RAF airbases in Germany, resupply operations in western Europe and even the UK. The Sukhoi Su-24 (NATO reporting name *Fencer*) has been a very capable interdiction and strike aircraft since the 1970s. This Su-24RF *Fencer-B* 23 White, RF-33768 is seen on approach to an airfield in Crimea. *Chris Lofting*

SR(A).1236 attracted a number of proposals, some derived from existing missiles such as SLAM-ER from Harpoon, but it was the bespoke SCALP-EG that would become Storm Shadow.

cruise missile, the AGM-86, which could be modified to carry a conventional warhead as the AGM-86C conventional ALCM. The USAF and RAF had operational differences on how the ALM was to be used, which did not help the situation. The consortium fell apart and by 1989 the MSOW project was dead and buried.

By 1993 NGAST.1236 had become SR(A).1236 for a Conventionally Armed Stand-Off Missile (CASOM) and was re-issued as a requirement for a missile for use against hardened facilities such as command bunkers, hardened aircraft shelters and other point targets. CASOM was to be carried by Tornado and its replacement, what would ultimately become the Eurofighter Typhoon. Meanwhile, from 1992 the aerospace companies of the UK, France Germany and Italy began discussing the merger of their guided weapons interests and in December 2001 MBDA was formed.

In response to SR(A).1236 a number of guided weapons developers submitted proposals to the MoD to meet the requirement, all subsonic apart from the Aérospatiale Asura. This was an ASMP (Air-Sol Moyen Portée) ramjet powered nuclear missile fitted with a 240kg (530 lb) conventional warhead from the AS-30L missile and an imaging infrared (IIR) seeker. GEC-Marconi had been working on a guided weapon for the United Arab Emirates under the name Al Hakim as the PGM series, with the PGM-500 and PGM-2000 being 500 and 2,000 lb (227kg and 909kg) respectively. The PGMs could be guided by IR, laser or TV seekers and when the Air Staff were looking for a modern laser-guided bomb to meet SR(A).1248, GEC-Marconi proposed the Al Hakim under the name Lancelot. For SR(A).1236 GEC-Marconi proposed stretching the airframe to accommodate fuel and a Teledyne Ryan gas turbine, calling it Pegasus.

Prior to merging with GEC-Marconi and taking on the Pegasus, BAe had a few irons in the fire over the period between the requirement's issue and issuing the contract. BAe, in partnership with Rockwell, had proposed an extended range variant of the AGM-130E, fitted with a Williams P8300 turbofan rather than the original rocket motor. In-house designs included the P4T Golden Eagle, a long-range version of the P3T Sea Eagle fitted with larger fuel tanks and a dual/kinetic charge warhead. BAe, as noted above had examined the Revise and Mantis dispensers proposed for SR(A).1238 and proposed fitting them with turbofans to provide the range.

The list went on, with Israel Aircraft Industries proposing the Popeye 2, a lightened version of Popeye with extended range while a version with a Williams turbofan was being aimed at the SR(A).1236 range requirement as the Popeye Turbo. Sweden were also in the market for a long-range weapon and the RBS-15 III with a 250km (83nm) range was developed to be carried on AJS-37 Viggens and JAS-39 Gripen in Swedish service.

Possibly the most unusual bid for SR(A).1236 came from Kentron in South Africa. The Kentron modular stand-off weapon (MUPSOW) was described as 'somewhere between an Apache and a Tomahawk' and was derived from the H2 extended-range glide bomb developed by the South Africans in the 1980s for their war in Angola and South West Africa (now Namibia). The turbojet-powered MUPSOW was under development from 1991 and tested on the Atlas Cheetah fighters.

The Serious Contenders

As the tendering progressed, seven weapons were selected for further, more detailed examination. Daimler Benz Aerospace and SAAB proposed their Kinetic Energy Penetrating Destroyer (KEPD) 350, a 5m (16ft 5in) long boat-shaped weapon with flip-out wings spanning 2m (6ft 9in) and powered by a Williams P8300 Turbofan. Weighing in at 1,500kg (3,307 lb), the KEPD 350 carries a 481kg (1,060 lb) MEPHISTO warhead (see below) for over 500km (270nm) under inertial, GPS and TERPROM guidance. KEPD 350 entered service with the German, Spanish and South Korean air forces as the Taurus from 2005.

Shorts Missile Systems' bid for SR(A).1236 was Griffin 38, a collaborative effort with Texas Instruments to modify the AGM-154 Joint Stand-Off Weapon (JSOW) to meet RAF requirements, specifically range and warhead. Designed to fit the Lockheed F-117A's weapons bays, the JSOW was unpowered and relied on altitude to provide its range; for example if released at low altitude could hit a target at a distance of 12nm (22km) but if released from high altitude could fly for up to 70nm (130km). As noted in Chapter 4, JSOW was originally designed as an anti-tank munitions dispenser but for SR(A).1236, a larger 'unitary' warhead was required to tackle the bunkers and hardened shelters outlined in the requirement. To address the range question, Shorts proposed fitting a propulsion system in the form of a Williams WJ24-8 turbojet, as used on the BQM-74 Chukar target drone, with 'fuel bladders in every nook and cranny.'

Although Rafael lacked a UK partner for their bid, their proposal of a gas turbine powered variant of the Israel Aircraft Industries Rafael Popeye prompted interest. Popeye had been in service with the Israeli Air Force, Royal Australian Air Force and the USAF as the AGM-142 Have Nap, famously to provide stand-off capability to the B-52H. Popeye Turbo as proposed for SR(A).1236 was to have a range of up to 300km (162nm) and carry a 360kg (800lb) I-800 penetrating warhead. Propulsion was to be provided by the same Teledyne CAE J402 used on the AGM-84 Harpoon, but a Williams/ Rolls-Royce engine might be a better option for a British procurement. Although Popeye for SR(A).1236 never came to fruition, Rafael did produce a turbofan-powered cruise missile in the form of Popeye Turbo ALCM. This shared the standard Popeye's 20in (53cm) diameter and folding cruciform wings spanning 7ft 6in (1.98m) but was 26ft 6in (6.25m) long.

The main contender from the USA came from McDonnell Douglas, with Hunting Engineering as the UK partner, in the shape of the AGM-84H SLAM-ER, (Stand-off Land Attack Missile – Extended Range) as the RAF-SLAM. Derived from the AGM-84E SLAM which was itself based on the successful AGM-84 Harpoon already in British service, SLAM-ER differs in having flip-out wings spanning 8ft 3in (2.5m) rather than folding cruciform trapezoidal wings but is powered by the Teledyne CAE J402, a combination that provides a range of 146nm (270km). An inertial guidance system is used, backed up by GPS with terminal guidance via the same imaging IR seeker as the AGM-65D Maverick or command guidance from an aircraft.

The SLAM-ER weighs in at 1,598lb (725kg), had a diameter of 14in (35cm) and a length of 14ft 5in (4.4m). Aside from its long wings, which may be folded away and thus not obvious, the SLAM-ER's most distinctive feature is the chisel-nosed sensor window in the nose. Hunting Engineering Ltd and McDonnell Douglas hoped that the RAF would opt for a two-tier procurement with a large weapon for Tornado GR.4 and RAF-SLAM for the Sea Harrier FA.2, Harrier GR.7/9 and the Jaguar GR.3, although SR(A).1236 did not mention these types. This is an example of how weapons development can improve the capability and efficacy of a particular aircraft. By August 1994 Huntings had renamed the RAF-SLAM, with the suitably apt moniker 'Grand SLAM', but the changes were more than just a label.

Grand-SLAM featured a fuselage stretch to 17ft 5in (5.3m) to accommodate a longer fuel tank, to provide 160nm (300km) range, and a new increased-penetration hard-target warhead. To improve its penetration of concrete structures, the new, larger (400kg/882lb) longer warhead had a steel jacket rather than aluminium while the charge itself was encased in aluminium for increased robustness. All these changes produced a weapon that was 2,425lb (1,100kg) in weight. Grand-SLAM had been fit-checked on Tornado GR.1 and Harrier GR.7 along with simulations and windtunnel studies. McDonnell Douglas also offered the RAF a shorter, increased diameter version being developed for the USAF's Joint Air-to-Surface Standoff Missile (JASSM), but that would probably have lacked the range for SR(A).1236.

Not content with stretching the SLAM-ER, McDonnell Douglas reshaped the fuselage into a shorter (less 21in/530mm) ingot shape whose flat surfaces reduced radar signature and allowed conformal carriage. This odd configuration was the result of a USAF programme called Have Slick and resulted in a more compact store with almost double the range of the Grand-SLAM. Named Grand-SLAM Plus this new weapon was proposed for CASOM, but may have been too late, due to Grand-SLAM Plus being delayed by its submission to the JASSM requirement. Have Slick was intended to examine low-drag stores carriage on strike aircraft and on the next generation of stealthy aircraft.

Smiths Industries tied in with Hughes to develop the AirHawk, which was essentially an AGM-109 Tomahawk, shortened by 34in (85cm) and fitted with a large unitary warhead. Hughes believed they were in the running for the CASOM contract because the Royal Navy was buying Tomahawks and therefore the support infrastructure would be in place. One of the reasons AirHawk was shorter was to reduce its fuel capacity and consequently its range. Why might too much range be a problem? The existing AGM-109 Tomahawk in its tactical land attack missile (TLAM III) guise possessed a range of 900nm (1700km) but any weapon to be procured for CASOM was to fall into a range bracket under 480km (260nm) to keep within the spirit of the Strategic Arms Limitation Treaty (SALT), although the UK was not a signatory.

As noted above, GEC-Marconi had been a somewhat mysterious player in the precision weapons game since the late 1980s, developing what could be described as bespoke smart bombs for the United Arab Emirates. GEC-Marconi's engineers had developed larger weapons and eventually produced a stand-off weapon called Centaur which was offered to the RAF.

One of the many weapons proposed for CASOM was Air Hawk, a shortened, reduced range version of the AGM-109 Tomahawk cruise missile. General Dynamics thought AirHawk was a shoo-in for CASOM as the Royal Navy was procuring the Tomahawk Land Attack Missile for its submarines. *Blue Envoy Collection*

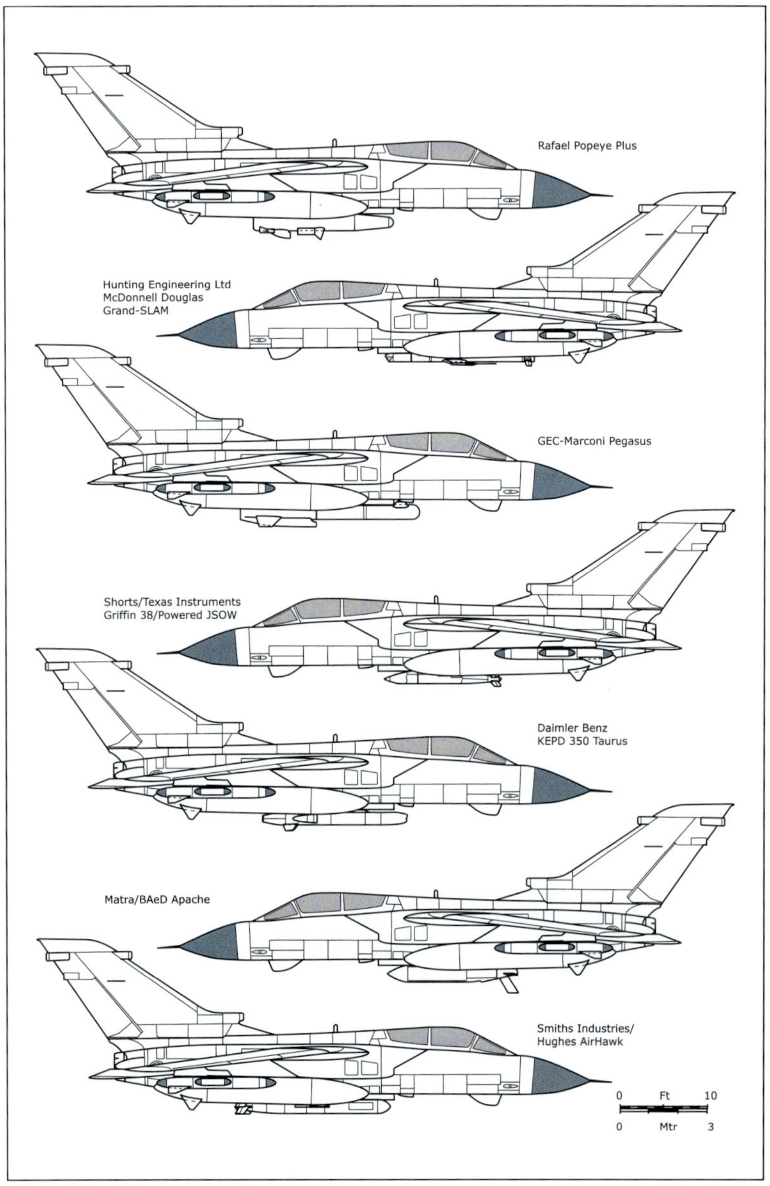

The CASOM contenders would have been carried by Tornado GR.1/4 on deep interdiction missions against Warsaw Pact, command and control centres, airfields and nuclear facilities. The SCALP-EG/Apache would be the ultimate winner, becoming the MBDA Storm Shadow.

This led to GEC-Marconi bidding on CASOM with a different weapon. A somewhat odd situation arose with a set of photographs appearing showing an RAF Tornado GR.1 sporting a rather large store that wasn't a fuel tank on its starboard inner wing pylon. This store was soon revealed to be Pegasus, a powered stand-off weapon developed jointly by BAeD and GEC-Marconi to meet SR(A).1236. Pegasus soon became the talking point of a political row between Whitehall and the Quai d'Orsay, and the appearance of Pegasus on the pylon of an RAF Tornado, rekindled the fire.

The gist of the row was that BAe Dynamics and Matra were negotiating a merger, but the French Government would not agree to the merger unless Matra's Apache was selected for SR(A).1236, all very cosy when BAeD and Matra were collaborating on bidding the Apache. GEC-Marconi's Pegasus used a number of components sourced from France, such as the Microturbo TRI-60 engine, Sagem guidance system and the warhead from SNPE but the French Government was reluctant to provide export licences for the equipment to be used on the British missile.

Et le gagnant est...

While the British were discussing CASOM and examining possibilities for a Tornado weapon, Aérospatiale and Matra were taking different views on a stand-off weapon with similar capability for l'Armée de l'Air. Aérospatiale proposed ASMP-C, later known as Asura, a supersonic ramjet-propelled dart that would fly at high altitude and dive onto its target from high altitude. Matra on the other hand took their Apache anti-runway submunitions dispenser, changed the engine, added more fuel in a fuselage stretch to extend its range to over 120nm (220km) and fitted a unitary warhead. This produced the Apache-C to meet the l'Armée de l'Air's APTGD (l'armement de précision tiré à grande distance –

Tornado GR.4 ZA600 of No 617 Sqn is readied for a mission with two Storm Shadow stand-off missiles. The weapon was successfully used against a Syrian chemical weapons facility in April 2018. *MoD Open Government Licence*

long range air-launched missile) so could rightly claim CASOM was being successfully built upon French work. As noted earlier, the Air Staff were aiming for a range of 400km (216nm) for CASOM, but the Storm Shadow/SCALP-EG has a range of over 300nm (560km) when flying a lo-lo mission profile.

Storm Shadow/SCALP-EG is propelled by a Microturbo TRI-60 turbojet rated at 1,200 lbf (5.4kN) and flies to its target at low altitude under TERCOM and GPS guidance until, as it closes on the target, it climbs to obtain a better view of the target area. As it climbs, the nose-cone is shed to reveal a thermographic camera that observes the target area and compares the view with imagery in the targeting database. This is called Digitized Scene-Mapping Area Correlator (DSMAC) and when used in conjunction with TERCOM, allows pinpoint attacks by a missile that would have been unheard of twenty years before.

By July 1995 the final bids for SR(A).1236 had been submitted to the MoD for selection of a shortlist of two or three in spring 1996 before selecting the successful weapon in early 1997. By August, Matra and BAeD had teamed up as MBD (the A came later when Alenia joined) and Apache-C was renamed Storm Shadow for the British and SCALP-EG for France (Système de Croisière Autonome a Longue Portée – Emploi Général – Long Range Autonomous Cruise System – General Employment), with Matra and BAeD divvying up the export markets for Storm Shadow.

Storm Shadow is a low-observable, long range air-to-surface missile for use against large and hardened structures. Targets include blockhouses, hardened aircraft shelters (HAS), port and airfield facilities, communications hubs and of course, command bunkers. Operation GRANBY had shown that many high value targets in Iraq had either gone underground or acquired a thick layer of reinforced concrete. This had not come as a great surprise as NATO observers had seen similar activity in eastern Europe, prompting CASOM and SR(A).1236. The RAF used Paveway and dumb bombs against Iraqi

Typhoon was cleared for Storm Shadow well before the Tornado was retired in April 2019. Storm Shadow provides Typhoon with a stand-off, precision strike capability that in earlier times was the responsibility of a specialist unit.

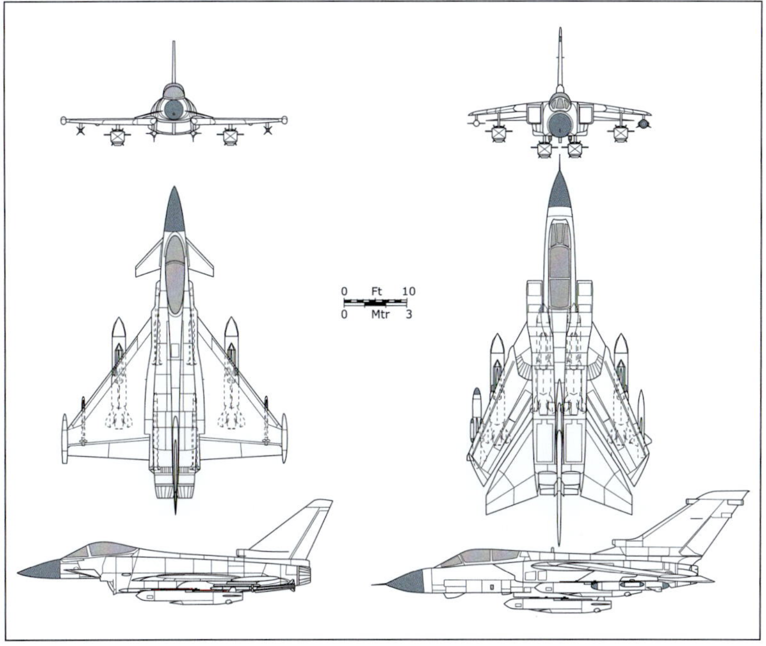

The Tornado GR.4, such as ZA614 of No 41 Sqn, could carry four Storm Shadow stand-off weapons for deep strike against point targets such as hardened shelters and bunkers. The BROACH warhead is designed for use against such targets. *MoD/ Open Government Licence*

bunkers, but these could only be effective if an air vent or similar opening was struck.

As for the development of CASOM, discussions were well underway by 1991 and but it took until 1996 for the Matra/BAe Apache-C to be selected for development as Storm Shadow/SCALP-EG, with the contract placed with the newly formed MBDA in 1997. The first guided firing took place from a Mirage 2000 in December 2000, with the first British firing from a Tornado in May 2001 and service entry six months later. Storm Shadow trials were considerably advanced to ensure the weapon would be available for any action that might be taken against Iraq in 2002/3.

The RAF took Storm Shadow to war in March 2003 in the opening hours of Operation Herrick with 617 Sqn launching 27 Storm Shadows against Iraqi targets. Storm Shadow/SCALP-EG was next in action during Operation Ellamy against pro-Gaddafi forces in Libya, including airfields and bunker complexes. This campaign also saw the Italian Air Force launch Storm Shadow from their Tornado IDS. RAF Tornado GR.4s used Storm Shadow against ISIS forces in Iraq, the weapon's recently earned reputation making it the preferred weapon against the bunkers that ISIS favoured. Storm Shadow was also employed to attack a chemical weapons storage facility in the Homs region of Syria in April 2018.

The first flight of a Storm Shadow on a Typhoon took place in 2013 and by 2015 the integration and flight trials were complete. With the withdrawal of Tornado in 2019, Typhoon was the sole RAF platform for Storm Shadow as the F-35 Lightning is (at time of writing in June 2019) not earmarked for Storm Shadow integration.

The Business End of Bunker Busting

When it came to bunker busting, the approach was very similar to that of sinking battleships – punch a hole through the armour and explode inside. During World War Two, the British had two approaches to the bunker problem, both involving aircraft-delivered ordnance. The first, and most famous are the Earthquake Bombs, Grand Slam and Tallboy, designed by Barnes Wallis and developed by Vickers and used successfully against German hardened sites such as the V-weapons bunkers at Watten, Wizernes and Mimoyeques amongst others, but also (echo of the battleship analogy) against the *Tirpitz*. The Earthquake Bombs worked by falling at high speed and penetrating deep into the ground before exploding, creating a 'camouflet' or void that on collapsing, destabilised the foundations of the target structure. Tallboys could penetrate 16ft (4.9m) of reinforced concrete if they hit the bunker but did not necessarily need to hit the target to damage it beyond practicable repair.

The other less well-known 'demolition' weapon was the Disney bomb, designed by

Captain Edward Terrell RN (which may explain its non-adoption by the RAF) and was also built by Vickers. Terrell's bomb was not intended to destroy the bunker itself but its contents, such as the U-boats in a fortified pen complex, by penetrating the roof, entering the building and then exploding. As such the amount of explosive was less than might be expected at 500 lb (227kg) but the casing was thick and very long, providing a high 'sectional density', the key principle in the kinetic penetrators of anti-tank rounds.

The Disney bomb was long, 16ft 6in (5m) and thin, with a diameter of 15in (38cm) for the forward 60% of the weapon with the rear 40% slightly larger, with a diameter of 17in (43cm). The larger diameter rear portion held a cluster of 19 x 3in rocket motors. These boosted the Disney bomb onto its target with an impact speed of 1450ft/sec (440m/sec). The USAAF adopted the Disney bomb and used it in combat from early 1945, with B-17s carrying a pair, one under each wing root. The bombs were aimed with the Norden bombsight and as the bomb fell the rockets were triggered by a timer or a barometric switch. The weapon worked best when dropped from a predetermined altitude, typically 20,000ft (6,096m) and could penetrate up to 16ft (4.9m) of concrete. The main advantages the Disney bomb had over the earthquake bombs were smaller size, two bombs per aircraft and minimum modifications required to the carrier aircraft.

The 'earthquake' and Disney bombs, worked differently, applying civil engineering principles and unsettling the foundations of structures or driving an exploding armoured spike through a roof. The Germans, of course, took a rather more technological route, not having four-engined bombers to carry 22,000 lb (9,979kg) bombs around, used either railway guns such as *Schwerer Gustav,* 80cm (31½in) to deliver high-explosive onto emplacements such as the Soviet defences at Sebastopol or for more mobile, tactical applications, vehicles such as the *Sturmtiger* with its 38cm (15in) Raketen-Werfer 61 L/5.4 breech-loading mortar. The rocket-boosted shaped charge fired by the *Sturmtiger* could penetrate up to 2.5m (8ft 2in) of steel reinforced concrete.

Having examined how bunkers were bust in the Forties, how are they bust today? Exactly the same manner – dense penetrators, shaped charges or a combination of both. The accuracy has improved but the basic principles are the same. There was little need in the Cold War inventory for a specialist deep penetration bomb like those designed for the RAF in World War Two but by 1990 and Iraq's occupation of Kuwait, the Coalition realised that during the eight years of the Iran-Iraq War from 1980-88, much of Saddam Hussein's kit had gone underground and/or into hardened facilities many of which had been built by western construction companies.

To tackle these deep, hard targets the USAF turned to artillery. Unlike the Germans who shot shells through them, the Americans took the gun barrels and converted them to bomb casings by turning them to a constant outer diameter on a lathe, filling the bore with explosive, adding tail surfaces and LGB guidance kit to produce the GBU-28. Since 1991 the US has produced a number of freefall bombs designed to attack deeply buried or hardened installations and as ever, have pushed the boat out with the GBU-57 Massive Ordnance Penetrator, a 30,000 lb (13,605kg) weapon delivered by a B-2A Spirit or B-52 Stratofortress.

The brute force of the 3,970 lb (1,800kg) GBU-28 or MOP cannot be matched by the Europeans, but the ordnance companies of Europe have produced some very clever – and effective – bunker busting warheads for their missiles. Throughout the CASOM procurement process the words 'unitary warhead' appear on a regular basis. Ostensibly this meant that the missile was to carry a single, rather than a cluster warhead to separate the CASOM role from the anti-tank or anti-runway dispenser systems upon which many of the CASOM bids were based (including the winner).

What the ordnance developers were working on were specialist warheads designed to tackle the hardest of bunkers using the highest of technology both in explosives and in targeting.

The original bunker busters were Barnes Wallis' Earthquake Bombs such as the 22,000 lb (9,979kg) Grand Slam seen here with an Avro Lincoln. Designed not to destroy but destabilise or topple structures, earthquake bombs were effective against bunkers, submarine pens, canals and viaducts. *Blue Envoy Collection.*

Hit an installation at the ideal position and it can be destroyed. Experience in Iraq had shown that as well as concrete and 'rebar' (reinforcing bar), a thick covering of soil (or buildings) could considerably reduce the effect of a bomb on a bunker. The solution was to remove the covering before the main charge impacts the bunker structure itself. This was effectively a larger version of the tandem charge used on anti-tank guided weapons. The blast effect of the initial stage is also highly effective against area targets such as airfields.

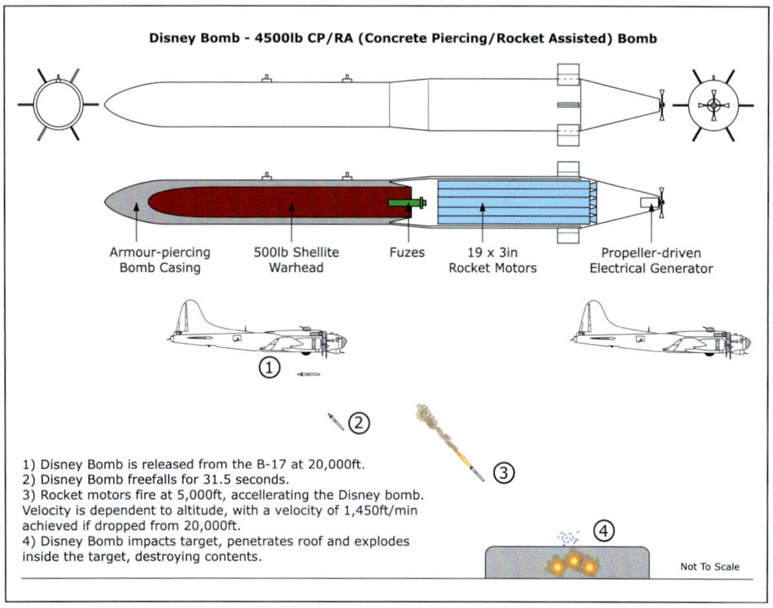

Applying different principles to earthquake bombs, the Disney Bomb was developed by the Admiralty, built by Vickers and used by the USAF. It used 19 rocket motors from the 3in (76mm) rocket projectile to propel it through bunker roofs to explode within the structure and destroying its contents.

The GBU-28 was developed to penetrate and destroy deeply buried and hardened bunkers. Essentially an 8in (203mm) naval rifle barrel turned down to a constant diameter, filled with explosive and fitted with Paveway guidance kit. It worked like a kinetic penetrator by having maximum mass over minimum area.

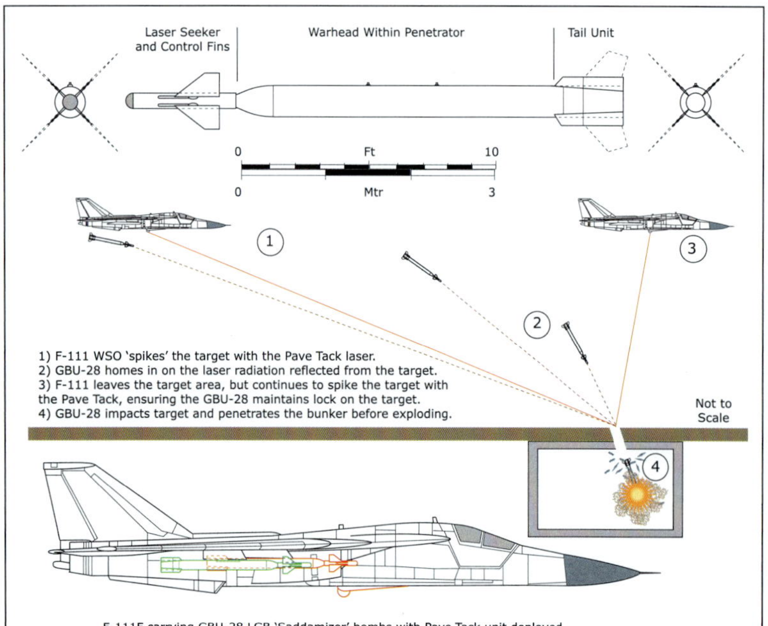

F-111F carrying GBU-28 LGB 'Saddamizer' bombs with Pave Tack unit deployed.

Two warhead types came to prominence in the conventional stand-off missile saga: MEPHISTO and BROACH, used in the KEPD 350 and Storm Shadow/SCALP-EG respectively. MEPHISTO (Multi-Effect Penetrator Highly Sophisticated and Target Optimised) is the warhead used on the KEPD 350/Taurus and features a two-stage charge with the first used to clear a path through earth or a bunker roof before the second charge detonates inside. MEPHISTO weighs in at 481kg (1,060 lb) and is fitted with a 'void-sensing' fuze than can be programmed to detonate after passing through a number of walls or floors and rooms before reaching its 'hard and deeply buried target'.

The BROACH warhead (Bomb, Royal Ordnance Augmenting CHarge), followed similar two-stage principles with the initial, or precursor, shaped charge. This charge forms a plasma jet that cuts a hole in the structure and allows the follow-on charge to enter the void and detonate. Weighing 400kg (882 lb) the BROACH charge is capable of penetrating structures that previously could only be breached by the 3,970 lb (1,800kg) GBU-28 described above. Storm Shadow's BROACH warhead is effective for another reason – the accuracy of its targeting. In the deep strike role, deep meaning 250km (135nm) rather than the hundreds of miles of earlier years, Storm Shadow flies at low-level under the power of a Microturbo TRI 30-30 turbojet, using GPS and TERPROM guidance. On approaching the target, Storm Shadow performs a bunt and jettisons its nose cone to reveal an imaging-IR seeker. The seeker searches the scene below for a match with an image of the target in its memory. On finding a target that corresponds to the image in the database, the missile will dive onto the target, triggering the missile's BROACH warhead on impact.

In 1944 if a bunker or special structure was earmarked for destruction, a special weapon on a special aircraft with a special unit was required: Tallboy on the Lancaster B.I Specials of 617 Sqn. In 2019, with the target selected, Storm Shadows are loaded on a Typhoon FGR4 of 617 Sqn. Of course, before any target can be attacked, it must be found, identified and assessed, all of which require reconnaissance assets.

6 To See Beyond the FEBA

'The whole art of war consists in getting at what is on the other side of the hill.'
Arthur Wellesley, Duke of Wellington

'CASTOR is essential in order to help fill the 50-150km corps surveillance gap.'
GSAR.3956: Joint Surveillance Working Party Terms of Reference, March 1984

'Decisions on the employment of our limited air assets, therefore, need to be founded on the availability of an accurate and comprehensive database.' Report on 2ATAF Intelligence Requirements, March 1984

New weapons required not only new sensors and targeting systems but the means to identify and track threats and plan missions. Air defences had used radar for this purpose since World War Two and in the 1960s battlespace management by airborne early warning aircraft became the norm. The advances in computing and radar technology had, by the 1980s, enabled similar systems to be applied to the ground war.

Reconnaissance – finding out what lies on the other side of the hill – is an essential function in warfare and is especially important in the land battle, be it an infantryman peeking around a corner or a satellite gazing on the movement of armoured formations in the enemy's rear areas. As a discipline, reconnaissance has evolved into intelligence gathering with the initial aim being to understand the enemy's intentions and acquire the information to plan air and ground operations. This is now called 'battle management information'. A second category of intelligence allows planning of operations to engage the enemy which requires targeting information: accurate locations, identification of targets and timely reporting of this information.

In land warfare reconnaissance was traditionally the job of cavalry units but by the start of the Great War these were trading their horses for armoured cars and, with the advent of the static trench lines, aircraft. Despite the assertion that aircraft would scare their horses, cavalry officers transferred to the Royal Flying Corps (or Deutsche Luftstreitkräfte*)*, using aircraft in lieu of chargers to gather information on the enemy's dispositions. By 1939, with the RAF deeply committed to the strategic bombing role, the Army Co-operation role was seen as

Raytheon Sentinel R.1 ZJ692 of No 5 (Army Co-operation) Sqn on approach to RAF Waddington in 2006. The Sentinel provided a capability that had been missing from UK's order of battle and like AEW in the air war, its contribution to battlefield management and reconnaissance is widely appreciated. *MoD/ Open Government Licence*

a side-show whereas the Luftwaffe had placed great emphasis on supporting the *Heer*.

By the end of World War Two tactical reconnaissance and artillery observation post (AOP) had become pivotal in the prosecution of the land war, identifying targets and calling down fire, from artillery or ground attack aircraft, onto those targets. The pilots of the wartime AOP aircraft were officers in the Royal Artillery, although the aircraft were maintained by the RAF. After 1957 and the establishment of the modern Army Air Corps (AAC), the army co-operation role – liaison with the Army – fell to the AAC while tactical reconnaissance remained with the RAF.

Radar had by 1945 become a key technology in warfare but mainly used for air warfare although one aerial radar, H2S, was showing potential for other uses from its introduction to service. In its original role the H2S radar was used for ground-mapping and allowed RAF heavy bombers to identify landmarks such as rivers, coastlines and cities. Fairly soon after its introduction, crews noticed that other aircraft could be seen on the H2S display and this was further developed as Fishpond, probably so named because the display was like a pond with the aircraft like fish swimming around in it. Fishpond used an extra plan position indicator (PPI) displaying airborne returns and was the first airborne early warning (AEW) radar system to enter service on its introduction in 1943. Fishpond was used to give warning of Luftwaffe night fighters and crews soon discovered that the system's range could be extended by banking the aircraft.

Ground-mapping radars and AEW radars remained pretty much separate entities with development teams grappling with what they called 'clutter'. Airborne radars for target identification became standard kit on bombers with the sideways looking airborne radar (SLAR) becoming a requirement on aircraft such as TSR.2 and in service with the US Army on the Grumman OV-1 Mohawk. Meanwhile the AEW radar developers were being troubled by clutter, unwanted returns from the ground, with the most famous being the Marconi radar on the Nimrod AEW.3. AEW radars were designed to reject static or slow-moving targets and present the returns from fast-moving aircraft on the displays. The Marconi radar had actually been designed to detect and track slower airborne and surface targets, specifically ships in a maritime surveillance role and helicopters in the airspace control role. This meant that the Nimrod AEW.3 could also detect ground vehicles and this caused the system's computers to become overloaded and shut down. Improved computers cured this but by the time this had been implemented the Boeing E-3A Sentry (which the Air Staff had wanted all along) had been ordered and the Nimrod AEW.3 scrapped. The sole remnant of the entire programme is a cockpit section in the Solway Aviation Museum at Carlisle Airport.

Assault Breaker

The numerical advantage enjoyed by the Warsaw Pact would have allowed them push forward into western Europe *en masse*. NATO air power had been viewed as the key to slowing the rate of Warsaw Pact advance, but these large armoured formations were defended by air defence systems whose effectiveness had been demonstrated during the 1973 Yom Kippur War. Another lesson learned from the Yom

The Auster AOPs had served since 1942 and Taylorcraft Aeroplanes (England) Ltd had high hopes for continuing to supply AOP and liaison aircraft to the British Army into the 1960s. These roles were taken on by helicopters and the Auster AOP.11 XP254, converted from an AOP.9, was the last of the AOPs and only one was built. *Blue Envoy Collection*

The AGM-124 Wasp anti-armour missile was under development as a ground support weapon for the USAF. Wasp was to be carried in a 12-round pod and fired in salvoes towards the target area. A MMW radar seeker then guided the weapon onto individual targets. This artwork shows Boeing's bid for Wasp being launched from an F-16. *Blue Envoy Collection*

Kippur War was just how fast modern warfare consumed weapons, requiring a massive logistics effort to maintain operations. This would lead to the use of nuclear weapons sooner than military planners and politicians had anticipated, effectively a return to the Trip Wire strategy.

Meanwhile in the USA, a Defense Advanced Research Project Agency (DARPA) programme called Assault Breaker was underway with the aim of blunting any Warsaw Pact attack by delivering precision munitions into the Warsaw Pact armoured formations and rear areas – follow-on forces. This project involved various munitions programmes and sensor/targeting systems under development in the US. One of these, the Precision Location Sensor System involved Lockheed U-2Rs (designated TR-1 – Tactical Reconnaissance) fitted with a sensor suite to detect and categorise emitters such as SAM radars but this relied on the passive detection of emitters. Once targets had been detected they were to be attacked by systems such as the Martin-Marietta T-16 or Vought T-22 tactical missiles carrying dispensers with smart munitions such as the Avco Skeet, a smart mine with an IR seeker and SADARM warhead (See Chapter 4) that could attack armour as it descended on a parachute or once on the ground, as a 'active' landmine flicked at the target like a clay pigeon. Another weapon was the Boeing/Hughes AGM-124 Wasp, a millimetre wave (MMW), active radar-guided missile that could be fitted in a pod weighing 2,000 lb (907kg) with strike aircraft such as the F-111F carrying up to four 12-round pods. The 120 lb (54kg) Wasp was to be released in swarms (hence the name), fly to the target area before using the MMW seeker to attack individual targets.

Other, related, programmes were Tacit Blue and Tactical Air Weapons Direction System (TAWDS), that was given the USAF designation Pave Mover and these platforms and radars could be used to produce a radar picture of the enemy's ground forces. Tacit Blue was an odd-looking type, designed with low observable techniques such as blended wing/fuselage, a recessed dorsal intake and shrouded exhaust to allow it to operate behind enemy lines. The Hughes and Grumman/Norden versions of the Pave Mover radar on the other hand were intended to work with the Assault Breaker weapons from behind the friendly lines in a stand-off mode to provide mid-course correction for smart munitions and each was mounted on a F-111 for competitive trials. The airborne element of the Pave Mover was merely a transmitter/receiver, with the data transmitted to a ground station for processing and analysis.

General Dynamics F-111E, 67-0115, was used for Pave Mover radar trials as part of the Assault Breaker programme. The radar data was transmitted to a ground station for analysis as the F-111 lacked the capacity to handle processing. *Blue Envoy Collection*

When asked about its priorities for surveillance, 1(Br) Corps (most likely to face the brunt of a Warsaw Pact invasion) identified the zone 50-100km (31-62 miles) from the Inner German Border (Iron Curtain) and the area beyond of most interest. These would be where the Warsaw Pact formations would be forming up and moving forward.

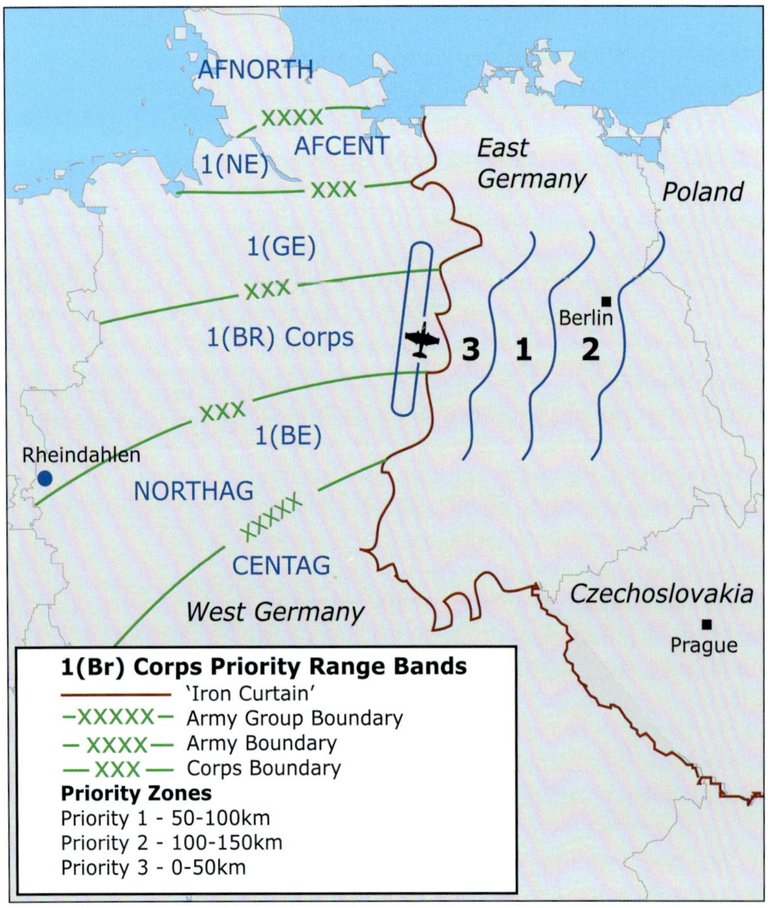

When Assault Breaker foundered, the focus moved to a radar mounted on a modified Boeing 707 which became the Joint Surveillance Target Attack Radar System (JSTARS). Two trials JSTARS aircraft were sent to Saudi Arabia during Operation Desert Shield, the build-up to the campaign to eject Iraqi forces from Kuwait, Operation Desert Storm and Desert Sword in 1991. This proved the worth of the ground surveillance radar and 16 Boeing 707s and a CC-137 were converted to E-8s, with 16 E-8Cs and a TE-8A being produced.

Meanwhile in the UK, a similar British Army requirement, GSR.3956, was drawn up in 1978 for a battlefield surveillance system that would be capable of, via moving target indicator (MTI) technology, providing a radar picture of Warsaw Pact armoured formations up to 30 miles (48km) beyond the Iron Curtain or in wartime, the FEBA. Known as the Corps Airborne Stand-Off Radar (CASTOR) the data gathered by the radar would, like Pave Mover, be transmitted to a ground station for analysis and distribution. This was originally to be based on a modified Ferranti Blue Kestrel carried by the Westland Lynx AH.1 helicopter but by 1983 a Thorn EMI X-band sideways-looking synthetic aperture radar (SAR) was installed in Canberra WT327's bomb bay for trials. A year later, a second I-band 360°-scanning system from Ferranti was undergoing flight trials in the nose of a Britten-Norman Turbine Islander G-DLRA/ZG989 for comparative trials under the CASTOR programme but both projects were subsequently cancelled.

In 1987 the Army's CASTOR requirement for a battlefield surveillance radar was merged with an RAF requirement for a new ground mapping SAR and the resulting programme became Airborne Stand-Off Radar (ASTOR) which required a new radar to operate at high altitude to provide combined SAR and MTI data for transmission to ground stations. The system was to have a useful range of up to 300km (162nm) and operate in the SAR 'strip map' mode with a resolution of 3m (10ft) while being capable of a 'spotlight' mode with a resolution of 0.5m (1ft 6in) to examine specific fixed targets. In MTI mode the radar was to be capable of detecting and tracking targets moving at speeds between 10 and 270km/h (6-167mph), with the higher speed for the detection of helicopters.

Thorn EMI were given the contract to examine the feasibility of such a radar and a trials set was installed in Canberra WT327 with test flights beginning in 1989. By 1991 the concept was shown to be viable and a Staff Requirement SR(L/A).925 issued in 1993 with a specification issued the following year. The contract for ASTOR was let to Raytheon Systems Ltd whose ASARS-2 radar when installed on the Bombardier Global Express bizjet was to form the basis of the Sentinel R.1 (ZJ690-ZJ694) that entered service with No 5 (Army Co-operation) Squadron in 2008.

As shown in Chapter 7 CASTOR was a role envisaged for the BAe P.1239 Versatile SABA. The equipment would have been palletised and installed in the dorsal compartment of the P.1239 and in that case the aircraft was fitted with a rotodome, suggesting that the Ferranti I-band system was intended for the SABA.

CASTOR Origins

By the late Seventies the General and Air Staffs concluded that managing the defence against an invading Warsaw Pact force would require more intelligence and a degree of early warning that was hitherto missing. What commanders required was the location and composition of enemy forces and their direction of movement. A system to provide these would also allow identification of potential targets, moving and static, out to a considerable distance beyond the forward line of own troops (FLOT), deeper into enemy territory than previously possible. Another factor was the new generation of smart and long-range weapons that needed precise targeting information to be available for planning offensive air support, battlefield air interdiction, counter-air operations or long-range artillery and multiple launch rocket systems (MLRS). These roles would be effective only if and when targeting data was available as the new guidance systems would require target location within 100m (109yd), day or night, and without that precision, targets might as well be attacked by 'Harriers with BL.755'.

Commanders really did want to know what lay on the other side of the hill and that was a distant 150km (80nm) away. What did they require? For a start, in peacetime the Generals wanted the Warsaw Pact order of battle to ascertain what they would be up against, any movement of units and signs of build-up in rear

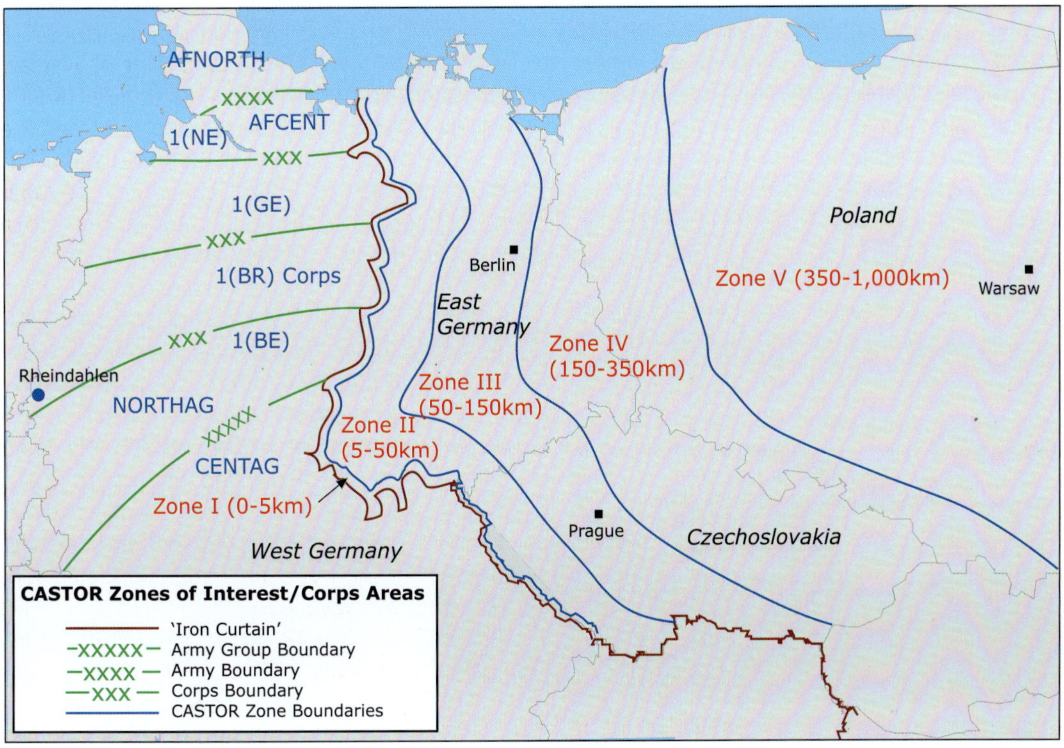

The Joint Surveillance Working Party outlined the needs of a Corps level surveillance system. Five zones of interest were described, each with their own particular requirements for radar and platform type.

areas, hence the requirement for 150km depth of surveillance by the General Staff. The Air Staff's peacetime wishlist was the location of and activity on airfields, air defence units and nuclear weapons stores to allow targeting of these and route planning in the event of a war.

In wartime the Army wanted to know where the enemy was, what direction they were moving in and the progress of what were called follow-on forces. The RAF wanted to be able to assess the serviceability of airfields, activities of runway repair teams, location of AAA and SAM sites for SEAD missions and any other on-route threats for mission planning. In addition to these, the RAF also wanted to use the information to task tactical reconnaissance sorties since these optical systems required precise cueing as their sensors, photographic and linescan, only covered a swathe 1-5km (½– 2½nm) wide. Tactical reconnaissance provided the positive identification, precise location and classification of targets and in the 1970s and '80s tactical reconnaissance units were crucial to effective offensive air operations.

The key to these was surveillance and until the late 1970s the capabilities available to the UK were passive systems either short-range sigint gained by ground stations or from 'radio proving flights' by 51 Sqn Comet 2Rs and Nimrod R.1s. While these could triangulate the location of systems that happened to be emitting, such as radars and communications systems, the location of non-emitting potential targets was very difficult. Air defence systems could be located by sigint but their precise location, ascertained by triangulation, was not always available and without such information, optimum penetration routes could not be plotted.

There were other sources of intelligence, US satellites and other reconnaissance systems, but these were strategic assets and as such not necessarily available for what became known as battlefield management. Nor were they timely enough for use by commanders on the ground, particularly those planning offensive air operations into eastern Europe along routes that could be rapidly equipped with replacement air defence units thanks to the large number and variety of mobile air defence systems available to the Warsaw Pact forces.

Without detailed information on the enemy's air defence units (ADU) along these routes, strike packages were to be directed into areas thought to have 'weak' defences. The lead aircraft would have been Tornados equipped to launch ALARM defence suppression missiles 'without necessarily knowing precisely where the ADUs are located'. As described in Chapter 5, ALARM operated by being fired into the airspace above a target area and loitered on a parachute until the ADU's radar operated and 'the ALARM seeker-head footprint is sufficiently large to cover an area in which likely targets are known to be', detect an emitter and attack it. However, at this time a UAV was being investigated for the suppression of enemy air defences (SEAD) role. Called Cuanca, this vehicle was possibly related to the Harassment Drone (See Chapter5) and was to be armed with CLARM (Cuanca-launched anti-radiation missile) and would require much more precise targeting data than ALARM.

What the Army wanted was a system that could provide 'timely information' on follow-on Forces, assess this and allow attacks on these forces (Follow-On Forces Attack – FOFA) by the RAF. Both services needed a sensor or sensors that could add detail to the sigint material and provide precise locations for potential targets, be they for attack or investigation by tactical reconnaissance.

The RAF's sigint force triangulated the locations of Warsaw Pact emitters in Eastern Europe. Nimrod R.1 XW666 of No. 51 Sqn in the original white over sea grey colours applied to all R Mk.1s and MR Mk.1s when they entered service. XV666 was lost after ditching in the Moray Firth. *Terry Panopalis Collection*

Phantom FGR.2 XV407 of No 41 Sqn from RAF Conningsby banks away from the camera to show the EMI Reconnaissance Pod on its centreline. It is also carrying four BL.755 cluster bombs on the inboard wing pylons, drop tanks on the outboard pylons and four AIM-7 Sparrow AAMs on the fuselage stations. *Terry Panopalis Collection*

The answer was radar, but the question was what type of radar? The use of ground-mapping radar dates back to the H2S bombing aid that Bomber Command used from early 1943. In the intervening years to 1984, the Royal Radar Establishment (RRE) had developed a number of ground-mapping radars for reconnaissance and navigation. H2S was a radial-scanning radar whose antenna was installed in a ventral radome but by the time the V-bombers entered service it was in the aircraft's nose. By 1953 the RAF's Canberras were being fitted with Blue Shadow, an X-band radar used for navigational fixes by producing a radar image of the terrain to the side of the aircraft track, with its output on thermal paper. This is called a sideways-looking airborne radar (SLAR) and Blue Shadow could display features in the landscape, such as river mouths, that could be matched to maps. The success of Blue Shadow as a navigation aid led to a project called Sky Shadow that matched the output from Blue Shadow with a cathode ray tube and a camera to photograph it. This allowed higher resolution reproduction and recording which in turn allowed more detail to be seen out to a distance of 40nm (74km) on the starboard side of the aircraft.

The next development involved two Blue Shadow systems, installed port and starboard to cover either side of the aircraft track. Developed as an interim system under the codename Yellow Aster, this was to be used pending development of a new SLAR for the next generation of reconnaissance aircraft. Yellow Aster was tied into the aircraft navigation system to provide the location data for the analysts, but it was soon discovered that Yellow Aster could not distinguish between runways and grass.

A new SLAR was required to provide the V-force with high-resolution targeting information for a Mach 2.5 reconnaissance aircraft to meet specification R.156. The primary sensor for the R.156 type was to be the Red Drover X-band (later J-band) radar that used a 50ft (15.2m) long, vertical scanning antenna to observe a swathe of terrain on either side of the aircraft flight path. In the case of Red Drover, it could 'look' out to 75 miles (121km) on each side of the aircraft when flying at 70,000ft (22,336m). Another high-resolution SLAR for use in navigation and weapons aiming was the X- or Q-band Red Setter that was test flown but superseded by Red Neck, to meet OR.3595, that used two radars, X-band for long range and Q-band for short range.

While neither Red Drover, Red Setter nor Red Neck reached service, other SLARs did, including the Blue Shadow used on Canberras and P.391 on the Phantom FGR.2. Originally intended for installation on the forward fuselage of TSR.2, what became the Q-band P.391 radar could scan each side of the aircraft but on the demise of TSR.2, was fitted into a pod carried by the RAF's Phantom FGR.2. These Phantoms were replaced in the tactical strike and reconnaissance role by the Jaguar in the mid-Seventies. Where the P391 differed from its predecessors was in its use of a moving target indicator to allow vehicles to be detected.

In some applications, rather than scan the terrain either side of the aircraft track as described above, the radar can scan to one side to pick up returns from structures and features deep inside

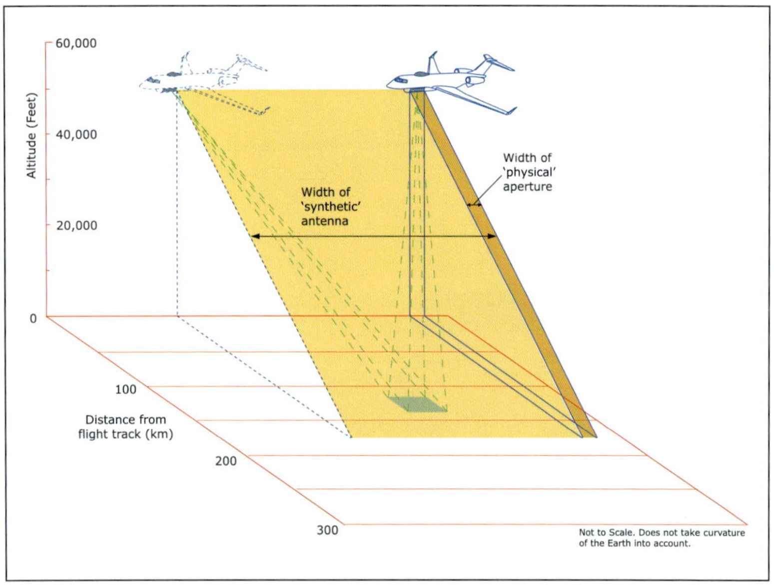

This much-simplified diagram shows how a synthetic aperture radar (SAR) works by building a 'picture' from a series of radar returns to provide a highly detailed – almost photographic – image of the ground below. The ASARS radar on Sentinel can work in wide area or spot scan.

denied territory. This is called an airborne stand-off radar (ASOR) and allows an aircraft to fly along a border and 'look' into enemy territory.

When radars were being developed, especially airborne radars, the system's performance suffered due to 'clutter' – unwanted returns from the ground that could mask the item the radar was to detect. One way to overcome the effect of clutter was a moving target indicator (MTI) that allowed the radar, through processing, to identify returns from a moving object. Aircraft and helicopters could be detected due to their high speed (MTI systems initially used an acoustic delay line, but later systems used Doppler effects) but by the late 1970s slower targets such as ground vehicles could be detected. The radar on the Nimrod AEW.3 famously detected traffic on the roads around Aberdeen, much to the amusement of the lay press.

An advanced variation on the SLAR/SOR is the synthetic aperture radar (SAR) that can produce radar images almost on a par with photographs. SARs work best on a moving platform such as an aircraft or satellite and use the craft's movement to synthetically increase the size of the radar antenna. This has the effect of increasing the resolution of the radar image produced when compared with a scanning radar. By moving the antenna along the flightpath a number of radar returns, from slightly different angles and therefore apparently different relative locations, are processed to build up a more detailed image. The development of SARs began in the late 1950s and have become increasingly sophisticated, especially with the reduction in size/increase in power of computers.

A synthetic aperture radar can operate in swathe or stripmap mode, covering a region abeam of the flightpath. In spotlight mode, by steering the antenna (and beam) to keep the radar on the same point of interest, even more detail of the target area can be revealed. The SAR was ideal for showing large features such as the airfields, roads, bridges, weapons storage areas and fixed SAM sites, and as far as the RAF was concerned, SAR was ideal as it picked up airfields with ease.

Both the Air Force and Army Departments appreciated the need for a surveillance system for use in the European theatre and shared 'a long-standing interest in ASOR for surveillance'. The Army were involved in the development of a UAV for surveillance to meet GSR.3846 under project Phoenix but were also interested in a SOR. The Air Staff were keen on a joint requirement, but the Air Force Department and Army Department could not agree on a Competitive Engineering Definition for the surveillance system. A Joint Surveillance Working Party (JSWP) was established in 1984 and examined the state of the game, assessed the technologies,

The GEC Phoenix (ZJ348 seen here on its launch vehicle) was not particularly successful. That could be mitigated by observing that it was not designed for the rugged terrain of the Balkans. One of the factors in its delayed development was its stabilised sensor package. *MoD/ Open Government Licence*

defined the surveillance needs of the respective commanders and advised on a way forward.

Prior to 1980 all the technologies relevant to the surveillance requirement had been research projects and from 1980-82 these formed the basis of studies with a view to developing a system for service. This coincided with the advent of the concept of Follow-On Forces Attack (FOFA) and the realisation of the complexity of the systems required to take on the Soviet second echelon. The Working Party was aware that 'existing systems do not allow commanders to read the battlefield in sufficient detail and depth to achieve optimum deployment of their forces'. The Working Party also pointed out that a new generation of precision weapons was on the horizon, such as the multiple launch rocket system (MLRS3). Meantime at NATO, the National Armaments Directors had identified a SOR as a key capability for nuclear targeting purposes but also as a system for monitoring Warsaw Pact territory for signs of build-up during periods of tension.

The JSWP looked at the current activity in the NATO countries and the projected systems that would emerge from any development work. In France, Electronique Serge-Dassault was working on a SOR called Orchidée that was carried aloft by an Aérospatiale SA 332 Super Puma. The antenna for the X-band radar folded up to the rear to lie under the root of the Super Puma's tail boom. The JSWP assessed the Orchidée system as 'an expensive helicopter-based MTI system' that would not meet British requirements. Interestingly a similar proposal was proposed by Ferranti and Westland that involved fitting a Westland Lynx AH.1 with a Ferranti Blue Kestrel radar.

As expected, the Americans had the most projects in development and the JSWP examined these. First to be examined, and dismissed, were the US surveillance satellites mainly because they could not provide 'continuous area coverage or coverage of specific targets. They were also 'national assets that will respond to national requirements'. The Working Party did point out that the UK 'has very

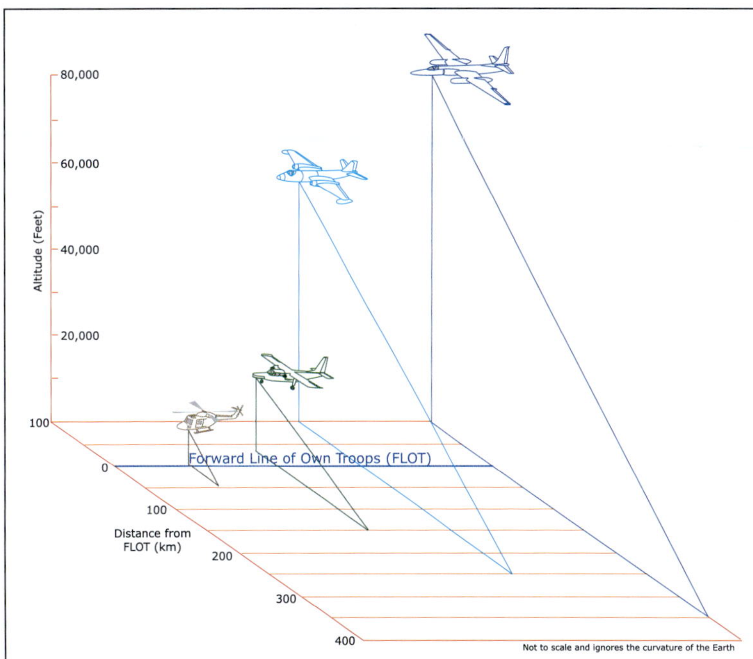

Top: A Royal Artillery M270B1 MLRS launches a round on the Otterburn range in Northumberland. One of the new weapons that would benefit from a CASTOR system was the M270 Multiple launch Rocket System (MLRS). The rockets have a range of up to 70km (43 miles) and carry a variety of warheads. The guided GMLRS in service with the Royal Artillery has a range of 60km (37 miles). *MoD/Open Government Licence*

Above: Fly higher, see further. A powerful radar does not always guarantee greater coverage, but a radar like ASARS mounted on a high-flying platform allows the radar to denied territory. The key to systems such as the U-2 or Sentinel is processing power, which has revolutionised battlefield management.

good access to the product' thanks to its 'special relationship' with the USA.

The second US system examined was the Precision Location and Strike System (PLSS) that used three TR-1A aircraft in the air at the same time with passive sensors that could perform triangulated ELINT and ESM to a depth of 350km (189nm) into Warsaw Pact territory. The TR-1A was essentially a Lockheed U-2R with sensors intended for the Assault Breaker programme but these reverted to the U-2R designation in 1992. On being re-engined with the General Electric F118 the U-2R became U-2S. The PLSS could triangulate an emitter to an accuracy of 50ft (15m), which made it ideal for planning defence suppression missions as a 'valuable contribution to achieving the SEAD task.'

Unfortunately, the Working Party saw limitations in PLSS, specifically its complexity in operation and support while they were alarmed by the need to have crosswinds of less than 15kt (28km/h) for the TR-1A to operate from the runway at RAF Alconbury in Cambridgeshire. The main drawback for the British was that PLSS, being passive, could not reliably confirm the enemy's disposition nor could it be used for targeting to the degree required by the RAF. To maintain the three aircraft on constant patrol would require 18 TR-1As based at Alconbury with the associated infrastructure that included the largest hardened aircraft shelters (HAS) in Europe to accommodate the TR-1A's 105ft (32m) wingspan.

A second TR-1A project in development was the TR-1A fitted with the Advanced Synthetic Aperture Radar System (ASARS) whose origins lay in a 1972 US requirement to observe the Warsaw Pact's second echelon forces in eastern Europe. The intention was to apply the intelligence acquired by ASARS to Follow-On Forces Attack and the Assault Breaker programme.

This system had a 3m (10ft) resolution at a distance of 160km (86nm) plus a spotlight mode with very high resolution, but no MTI. The Working Party considered this 'very high capability' system very close to meeting the UK's needs, but pointed out that the 'data is controlled at highest level' to which one reader has responded by scribbling the word 'Rot' in the margin of the JSWP report. The British had good reasons to work with the Americans as neither had developed an application for the intelligence gained by a system such as ASARS. In 1984 the only emitter location US system in service in Europe was the Guardrail based on the Beechcraft RU-21 from 1971 and from 1983 the Beechcraft RC-12, a comint/elint platform that has been described as a Super King Air that has flown through a fence. Despite its apparent age, Guardrail, as the US Army' tactical sigint platform, has been continually upgraded over the decades of service.

While the Guardrail conducted comint/elint, the US Army had another platform that was equipped with a SLAR with a MTI. The Grumman OV-1D Mohawk was, like the Guardrail, a twin turboprop type but unlike the Guardrail had been designed as a warplane rather than an executive transport. The OV-1D Mohawk was equipped with a AN/UPD-7 radar under the port side of the nose.

Overall, the Working Party was less than enthusiastic about relying on American assets for their surveillance intelligence; access to the data 'from US assets was not guaranteed' nor would it 'meet the essential requirements' of the UK forces. Another factor working against US systems was the sheer volume of data that would need to be processed if the British were supplied with the US intelligence 'take' with

U-2S, 80-1083, on approach at Fairford in August 2017. The ASARS-2A (Advanced Synthetic Aperture Radar System 2A) is housed in the extended nose. The large dorsal pod houses a Senior Span satellite datalink (or Senior Spur, depending on mission) and the wing pods carry mission equipment. The previous U-2R was also known as TR-1 when assigned to stand-off reconnaissance in Europe in the early 1980s. *Chris Lofting*

the JSWP stating that 'UK processing of US raw data is beyond our resources'. The UK MoD had been working on a project called GEMINI, a 'joint intelligence fusion centre' to analyse and disseminate intelligence to the Army and RAF from a site at Rheindahlen and an unspecified 'hardened facility'. On the bright side, a bespoke British battlefield surveillance system would provide a complementary system with redundancy if the US systems were not available. Making the case for a UK CASTOR, the JSWP pointed out that only a British system was 'capable of meeting I(Br) Corps essential requirements' or those of 2ATAF but conceded that the TR-1A sensors would 'make a major contribution to the database'. The Working Party concluded that only national systems could satisfy the requirements of the Army and RAF.

Platforms for CASTOR

As noted above the Army required the locations of moving targets whereas the RAF wanted data on what were essentially static targets with the joint requirement calling for coverage across a 65km (35nm) front, essentially the I(Br) Corps area of responsibility, and to 150km (81nm) beyond the FLOT. For the Army, a MTI was required to determine speed and direction of enemy movement whereas the RAF wanted a SAR with secondary MTI capability. The RAF's SAR was to have a resolution of 6m (19.7ft) at a distance of 250km (135nm) and a location accuracy of 100m (328ft) for targeting purposes. The range requirement of 250km was to allow the SAR platform to cover the battlefield into Zone IV while remaining 100km (54nm) behind the FLOT.

The UK had more experience of SAR than in MTI and while the developers saw no problems covering Zones I to III with ease, but Zone IV might pose a problem. They did however state that computer processing power was increasing and pattern recognition (for targeting purposes) was improving.

Two platforms were proposed: A Britten-Norman Islander (ZG989) with a radar fitted with MTI and an English Electric Canberra (WT327) with a SAR and secondary MTI. The Canberra was considered ideal as it had the performance; patrol altitude of 50,000ft (15,420m) to achieve the ideal grazing angle and speed to achieve the desired coverage. The latter was important as timely and up to date intelligence was required to provide targeting information for the estimated wartime rate of 1000 sorties per day.

The Army preferred a low altitude system that used a moving target indicator and used a Ferranti radar fitted in a Britten-Norman Islander, ZG989. The radar (CASTOR-I) was based on the Blue Kestrel radar. This radar was also considered for installation on a Westland Lynx AH.1. *Terry Panopalis Collection.*

Having recommended the Islander and Canberra, the JSWP began to look at their vulnerability to Warsaw Pact air defences, of which there were many. The Islander would have patrolled at 15,000ft (4,572m) on a line 30km (18.6 miles) behind the FLOT while the Canberra would patrol at 50,000ft (15,420m) 100km (54nm) behind the FLOT. In the case of the Islander it would be within the engagement envelope of SA-5 *Gammon*, SA-10 *Grumble*, SA-11 *Gadfly* and SA-12 *Gladiator/Giant* while being a 'target of opportunity' for any roving Warsaw Pact fighters or fighter-bombers that encountered it. The Canberra on the other hand, being higher, faster and farther back would be vulnerable only to the longer-ranged SA-5 *Gammon* and a SA-12 *Gladiator/Giant*. *Gladiator* was derived from the SA-10 *Grumble* but has a range of 75km (47 miles) while *Giant* has a range of 100km (54nm). These SAMs could intercept the Canberra if deployed at the front, which in the case of the SA-5 *Gammon*, was unlikely as it was 'transportable' rather than mobile.

Having pointed out the vulnerability of the Islander and Canberra, another type was proposed as a SAR platform. The Harrier GR.5 was in development as a replacement for the Harrier Force's GR.3s and so was identified as a candidate CASTOR aircraft. The advantages of the Harrier were its agility, survivability in the face of SAMs and fighters, its flexibility and familiarity with the I(Br) Corps forces in West Germany. The radar would be installed in a centreline pod and to extend the Harrier's endurance, extra fuel would be carried in underwing tanks. To maintain one aircraft on patrol would require three Harriers. Acquiring and converting a dedicated flight of CASTOR Harriers' would be an expensive operation while wiring the entire Harrier force to carry the radar would lead to diversion of Harriers from their essential strike role, which would be a 'heavy price to pay'. This

The RAF was intent on a high-altitude, long range surveillance system using a synthetic aperture radar. Canberra WT327 was fitted with a Thorn EMI SAR designated ASTOR (Airborne Stand-Off Radar, CASTOR-C to the Army) with trials beginning in 1989. Requirement SR(L/A).925 was issued to cover the development of ASTOR in 1994. *Via Dave Forster*

proposal hinged on the great unknown that was whether the radar could be fitted in a pod in the first place never mind whether it could operate effectively from the Harrier.

Air defence missiles were not the only counter to the CASTOR systems as the Soviets were more than capable of detecting, direction-finding and jamming radars. The Working Party pointed out that although adept at these, the Soviets only had one equipment capable of jamming a SOR and that most jamming was used for point defence. Another field the Soviets excelled in was CCDM – camouflage, concealment and deception measures.

The Islander trials system was designated CASTOR-I, the 'I' unsurprisingly standing for Islander, and CASTOR-C for the Canberra testbed. CASTOR-I was a Pilatus Britten-Norman BN-2T Turbo-Islander fitted with a Ferranti MTI radar while CASTOR -C was a fitted with a Thorn-EMI SAR designed for detecting fixed targets. Designated the Demonstration Synthetic-Aperture Radar (DEMSAR), this was derived from the American AN/UPD-7 radar used on the OV-1D Mohawk. Neither testbed was fitted with a data transmission system, but the data was recorded for download and analysis once back on the ground. At least one CAS-

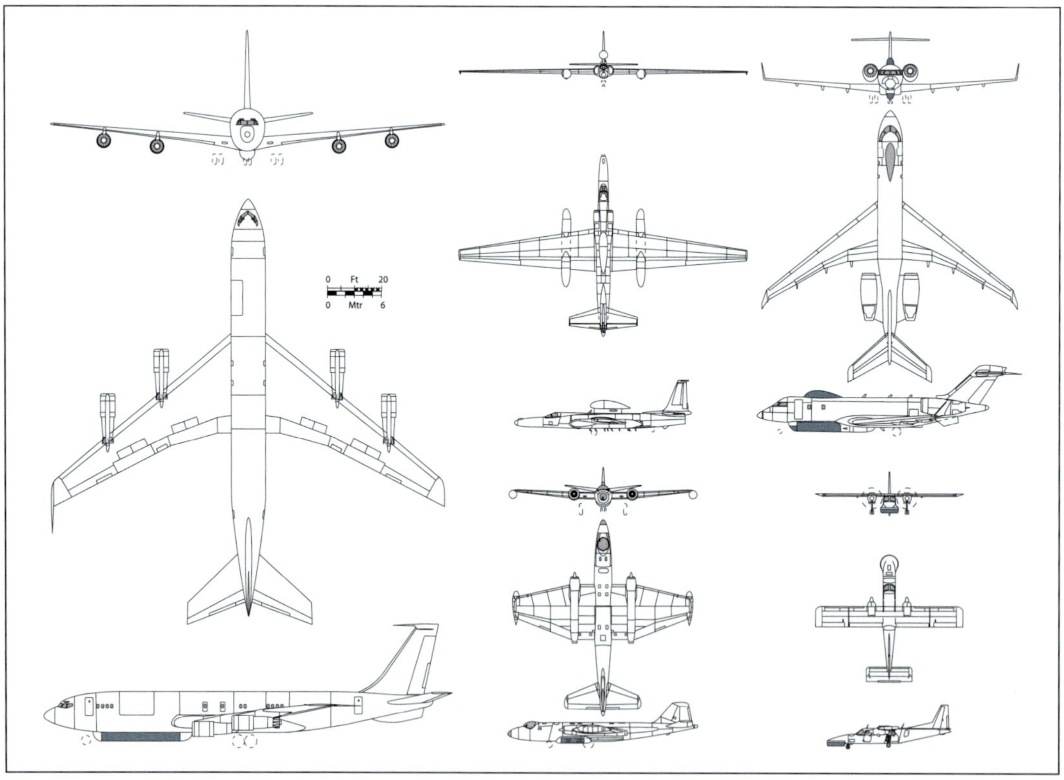

The S(LA).925 procurement process involved a number of types, although most were unsuitable for the RAF. The Boeing E-8 and Canberra were too old, U-2S probably too susceptible to the British weather and the CASTOR Defender too small. The choice fell on the Raytheon Sentinel, based on the Global Express executive jet.

TOR-I test series saw the Islander fitted with a Control Data Link from the US JSTARS to transmit data to a Ground Station Module (GSM) via the Surveillance and Control Data Link (SCDL) used for JSTARS.

By 1987 the MTI radar aspects of CASTOR-I had two rival radars. Ferranti fitted a variation of its Blue Kestrel radar for the EH-101 naval helicopter in a flattened nose radome, lending the Islander the look of a duck-billed platypus. The Thorn-EMI proposal was a variant of its Skymaster airborne early warning radar that had also been fitted in an Islander airframe for trials in the process of meeting ASR.400. Meantime a Staff Requirement had been issued as Staff Requirement (Land/Air) 925 for a battlefield surveillance system with invitations to tender issued in 1994.

With the issue of a requirement, competition hotted-up with new bidders such as BAe and GEC-Marconi. BAe had teamed up with Grumman to offer a UK-JSTARS, known as Wizard, fitting the E-8 system in an Airbus A320 (no doubt the MoD saving money by buying secondhand) although a Gulfstream V was the preferred type. Of the old guard, Thorn-EMI teamed up with IBM for their bid while Ferranti had been swallowed up by GEC-Marconi who become prime contractor for their bid, although GEC had won the SAR processing contract in 1992, which seemed to augur well for their bid. The move towards a JSTARS style system with a SAR pretty much forced the MoD into a jet answer to the platform question with an aircraft in the Gulfstream V class required. Lockheed opted for the Gulstream V modified by Marshalls of Cambridge, while Raytheon would fit their radar in the Bombardier Global Express. As for the radar, Lockheed Martin and Raytheon were in the running for the ASTOR contract but in 1997 Northrop Grumman, previously rejected, were back in the running.

The reason the Northrop Grumman AN/APY-3 radar used in the JSTARS E-8 was rejected was that the radar was deemed much too 'slanted towards MTI' to meet the MOD's SR(LA).925 requirement. Northrop Grumman we now proposing that their radar be installed in a Global Express but the proven ASARS was looking like a shoo-in.

In the end, Raytheon's bid was selected in 1999, using a modified ASARS-2 radar that would prove to have higher resolution than the ASARS-2 fitted to the U-2S. Five aircraft were ordered, plus ground stations, to enter service in 2005. The radar was a dual mode SAR/MTI with swathe and spot modes plus the capability to combine SAR and MTI to provide tracking of moving targets.

ASTOR entered service as the Sentinel R1 in 2008 with four aircraft surviving with V(Army Co-operation) Sqn at RAF Waddington, the main base for the RAF's ISTAR assets. The fifth aircraft, ZJ693, was placed in storage in May 2017. The Sentinel fleet operated in Afghanistan from 2008 until 2018, Libya in 2011 and from 2015 deployed in support of coalition forces fighting against Daesh in Iraq and Syria. The Sentinel has also operated in support of French forces in Mali from January 2013. When the Nigerian Boko Haram militants kidnapped 276 schoolgirls from Chibok in April 2014, a Sentinel was despatched to provide surveillance support. The Sentinel is said to have found the schoolgirls within two days, but ground forces were unable to rescue them.

Sentinel R.1 ZJ690 of No 5 (Army Co-operation) Sqn climbs out from RAF Waddington. The ventral canoe fairing houses the SLAR antenna while the radome aft of the cockpit is for the datalink to a ground station, via satellite. *MoD/ Open Government Licence*

Tactical Reconnaissance

The RAF's photoreconnaissance (PR) during the Second World War and afterwards, was the finest of any of the combatants and even into the 21st century, types such as the Canberra PR.9 could give any imaging platform a run for its money. This was mainly what would now be described as strategic reconnaissance or targeting and battle damage assessment tasks by PR versions of the Mosquito and Spitfire while missions conducted in direct support of the ground forces, tactical reconnaissance, is what will be examined here.

In the tactical reconnaissance field, two sensors prevailed in the Cold War: wet film photography and infrared linescan. For over a century wet film ruled the imaging world, be it still or moving pictures, and by the last three decades of the 20th Century digital photography became the means of acquiring imagery. Much of the advance imaging technology was developed for reconnaissance satellites. Digital imaging had the added benefit of being quicker and easier to disseminate, with real-time, or minimal delay, systems appearing in the late 1980s. As imaging sensors improved, so did the associated optics and stabilisation systems and ultimately all these technologies entered civvie street in the early 21st Century, appearing in consumer digital cameras and phones.

Infrared linescan had a very different background, with a Radar Research Establishment project called Yellow Duckling that was aimed at using changes in water temperature to detect the wake of submerged submarines. While its use in detecting submarines proved unsatisfactory, it was used in trials to detect EOKA forces on Cyprus with encouraging results. The IR sensor scanned across the aircraft flightpath and built a thermal image of the ground below, revealing the heat signatures of concealed targets. This was further developed into the IR Linescan (IRLS) systems that became standard fit for RAF tactical reconnaissance aircraft from the early 1970s.

RAF tactical reconnaissance aircraft such as Jaguar GR.1 and Tornado GR.1A would have been tasked with photographing Warsaw Pact SAM sites and other potential targets. This USAF tactical reconnaissance photograph shows a *Guideline* site in North Vietnam. The North Vietnamese became adept at camouflaging such sites. *DoD via Terry Panopalis.*

At the beginning of World War Two tactical reconnaissance was the realm of the Army Co-operation squadrons, using techniques that would be familiar to their fathers in the Great War: handheld cameras pointed out of the rear cockpit of an aircraft except in this case it was the Lysander rather than the RE.8. By the war's end, the Spitfire PR variants were conducting tactical reconnaissance against specific targets, providing supporting photographic material for ground forces, but the bulk of the tactical PR was undertaken by Curtiss Tomahawks, Mustang I or IIs, although one squadron, No 268, operated the Typhoon FR.IB for a period, only to be replaced with the Mustang II.

Post war, the latest jet fighters such as the Gloster Meteor FR.9 and PR.10 were modified for PR work in which by fitting cameras in lieu of guns. In the case of the Supermarine Swift FR.5, to meet Specification PR.105D&P, that was the role it served with four RAF squadrons, but the days of the dedicated tactical reconnaissance aircraft were numbered. The last of the converted fighters was the Hawker Hunter FR.10, to meet specification FR.164D, but unlike the Meteor and Swift, the Hunter retained its four cannon. For the reconnaissance role the Hunter F.6 airframe was to be equipped with three F95 Mk.2 70mm cameras comprising one forward-facing with a 12in (30cm) lens in the extreme nose and two in the nose with 4in (90mm) lenses mounted for oblique photography. The Hunter FR.10 replaced the Swift FR.5 and served with 2nd Tactical Air Force in West Germany throughout the 1970s.

While the USAF in the late 1960s opted to continue converting fighters as dedicated tactical reconnaissance types with designs such as the McDonnell RF-101C Voodoo and McDonnell Douglas RF-4C and RF-4E Phantoms, the RAF opted for a pod system for its new F-4M Phantom fleet. The F-4M Phantom in RAF service was known as the Phantom FGR.2, with the 'R' standing for reconnaissance and two squadrons were assigned to the reconnaissance role from 1972, with the Phantoms modified to carry the pod.

The EMI reconnaissance pod on the RAF's Phantoms was fitted with the EMI P391 (ARI.5960) sideways-looking radar based on

Hawker Hunter FR.10 prototype XF429 at Dunsfold carrying four underwing tanks. The transparency for the nose-mounted F-95 camera can be seen, with the windows for the port side oblique camera just visible forward of the nose cone joint. *Hawker photo HDT 2/59 via Phil Butler.*

work for the cancelled TSR.2 and F-111K. This Q-band radar used a pair of 15ft (4.6m) long multi-slotted antennae to cover a swathe of ground up to 10 miles (16km) either side of the aircraft. The pod also held an X-band radar linescan unit and the five-camera optical suite included four Vinten F.95s with 3in (76mm) lenses in a forward, vertical and oblique arrangement and a F.135 stereoscopic camera. The package was rounded off with a Texas Instruments RS-700 (AN/AAS-18UK) IR linescan unit. For night photography a separate pod carried four F.135 cameras with an electronic flash unit. The system weighed in at 2,300 lb (1,043kg) and fitted in a pod with dimensions similar to the Phantom's 500-gallon drop tank.

As described in Chapter 8, the Phantoms were supplemented, then replaced in the ground attack role by the SEPECAT Jaguar GR.1 and by 1976 these had replaced the Phantom FGR.2s in the reconnaissance role, but as before this was a podded system. The EMI pod for the Phantom had a reputation for unreliability and such were its problems, it was only operational for around a year, so when a pod for the Jaguar was proposed, only the cameras and IR linescan system were used.The BAC pod was 18ft 8in (5.7m) long with a diameter of 2ft 2in (65cm), weighed in at up to 1,230 lb (560kg) and held camera arrays and an EMI 401 IR linescan with film recorder. The camera suite included five F.95s; one forward-facing with a 6in (150mm) lens in the nose and the other

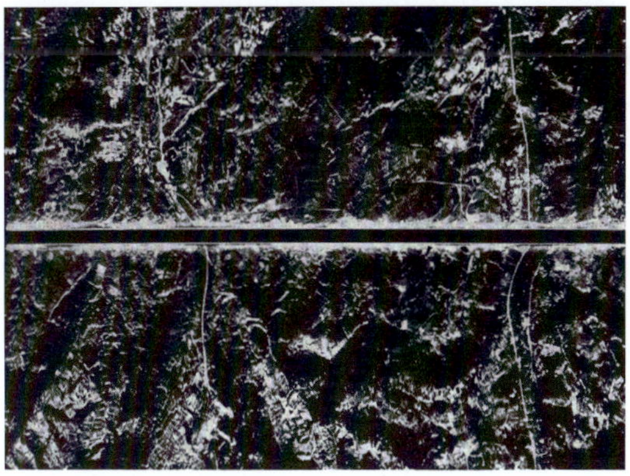

The EMI P391 sideways looking airborne radar fitted to the reconnaissance pod of the Phantom FGR.2 produced an image of the terrain either side of the aircraft's track. The black strip across the image is the blind spot below the aircraft. The P391 had been developed for TSR.2. *Blue Envoy Collection.*

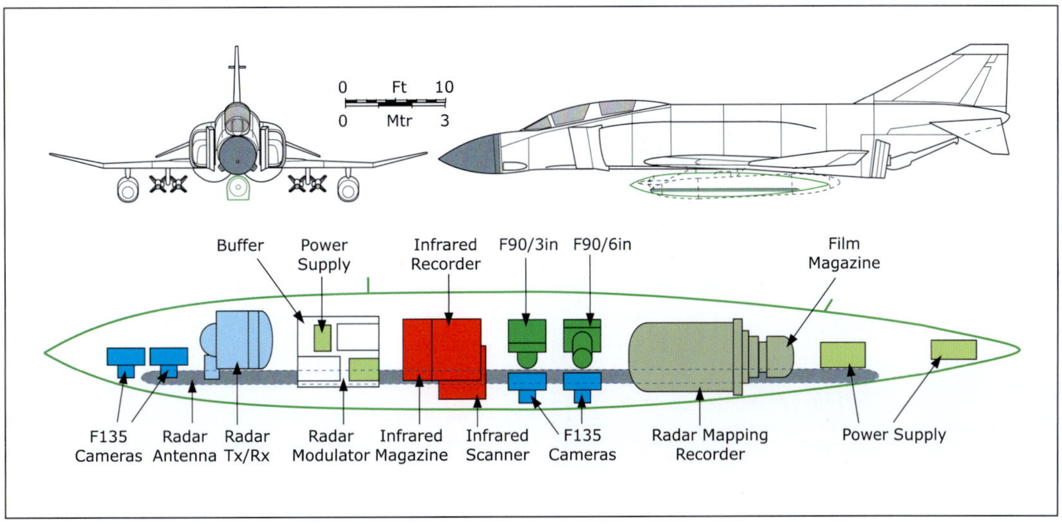

The P391 pod was developed for the Phantom FGR.2 to provide a tactical reconnaissance capability for the RAF. In reality it was unreliable and the Phantom's time in the ground attack/ reconnaissance role was short.

Tornado GR.4A ZG729 (note the window below and aft of the roundel) is fitted with a TIALD (Thermal Imaging Airborne Laser Designator) designator pod. Although rushed into service for GRANBY, it was widely used in TELIC, as seen here. *Terry Panopalis Collection*

four with 3in (76mm) and 1½in (38mm) lenses arranged to cover vertical and oblique fields of view. The pod was integrated with the Jaguar's nav/attack system to allow navigation data to be recorded on the film.

The 1990s saw the rise of digital photography, becoming mainstream in the field of consumer photography by the end of the 20th Century. Digital imaging dated back to the 1950s and was utilised as a means to transmit images from space since the 1960s, initially by scanning 'wet' film for radio transmission but later by direct acquisition with sensors such as charged coupled devices (CCD). This technology soon became small enough to fit into a pod and a new generation of reconnaissance systems entered service with the western tactical air forces. Vinten produced the Jaguar Replacement Reconnaissance Pod (JRRP) and subsequently entered RAF service in the 1990s, becoming known as the Digital Joint Reconnaissance Pod (DJRP). The DJRP was fitted with Vinten 8042 EO and Super Vigil IR sensors and was 7ft 8in (2.3m) long and had a diameter of 18in (46cm) with a weight of 595 lb (270kg).

Having opted for podded reconnaissance systems to replace the Hunter PR.10s in 1970, the RAF returned to the converted fighter in the 1990s. The Tornado Infra-Red Reconnaissance System (TIRRS) replaced the two BK-27 cannon in the forward fuselage of the Tornado GR.1, producing the GR.1A and after the upgrade of Tornados to GR.4 standard, the GR.4A. The volume previously taken up by the cannon was filled with a trio of Vinten infra-red linescan units in the forward fuselage and the GR.1A and GR.4A could still carry a full warload on sorties. TIRRS-equipped Tornados can be identified by a small window on the forward fuselage below the canopy.

Tornado and Typhoon can also be fitted with the Northrop Grumman/Rafael LITENING III pod that provides targeting capability via a laser designator plus a forward-looking IR (FLIR) system for target search/acquisition. In addition to the standard targeting systems, LITENING III incorporates a stills camera to capture visible light imagery in a reconnaissance role.

The next system applied to the Tornado was the Reconnaissance Airborne Pod TORnado – RAPTOR – pod. RAPTOR was the name applied to the procurement process that led to Goodrich winning the contract for the system. The principal sensor on RAPTOR is a long-range oblique photography (LOROP) Goodrich DB-110 visible/IR system that combines visible light images with infra-red to identify targets in real time and transmit imagery to a ground station. This combination of visible and IR imagery became particularly useful in the identification of improvised explosive devices (roadside bombs) in Afghanistan, disturbed and undisturbed ground having different heat signatures.

Close-up of a Raptor pod on the port shoulder pylon of a Tornado GR.4A. Note the radome for the forward data link and the large door covering the optics aperture. *MoD/ Open Government Licence*

The RAPTOR pod is a large store, carried on the port shoulder pylon of the Tornado GR.4A, whose most obvious feature is the sliding shutters on each side and on the bottom of the pod. These protect the DB-110's lens system which can be oriented to either side and downwards for oblique and vertical imaging. In the oblique mode the system can be used in the LOROP mode, producing high resolution images of targets at up to 100km (54nm) either side of the aircraft track. In vertical orientation the system can acquire stereoscopic imagery or lock onto a target and maintain surveillance as the aircraft overflies the area. The RAPTOR pod also carries equipment to transmit data to a ground station for detailed analysis.

In the late 20th century the term 'Netcentric Warfare' came into common usage in military circles, meaning that the various aspects of warfare; intelligence gathering, analysis, targeting and attack, were connected to streamline the war-fighting process. This wasn't new, an early example being the British Operation Elgar in late 1944 with sigint (the Y-service), analysis (Bletchley Park), targeting (Fighter Command) and attack (Mosquito night fighters) seeking to intercept the Heinkel He 111s that were launching V-1 flying bombs at the English Midlands. In recent years Netcentric warfare involved operations in Afghanistan with Nimrods performing the sigint role and their Wescam electro-optical system helping ground troops identify Taliban insurgents for attack by Harriers. Into this network of war fighting systems and operators came a rather familiar bit of kit. The difference was it was persistent and armed.

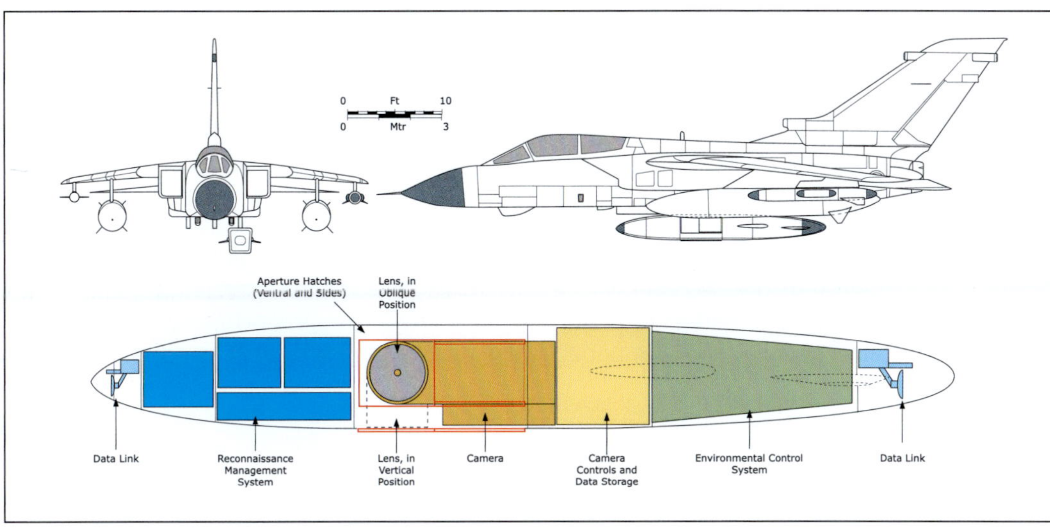

The RAPTOR pod is usually carried on the port shoulder pylon of a Tornado GR.4A, with a balancing store, typically a Paveway IV LGB om the starboard pylon. RAPTOR provides, in a self-contained pod, a capability that once required an aircraft the size of a Canberra PR.9.

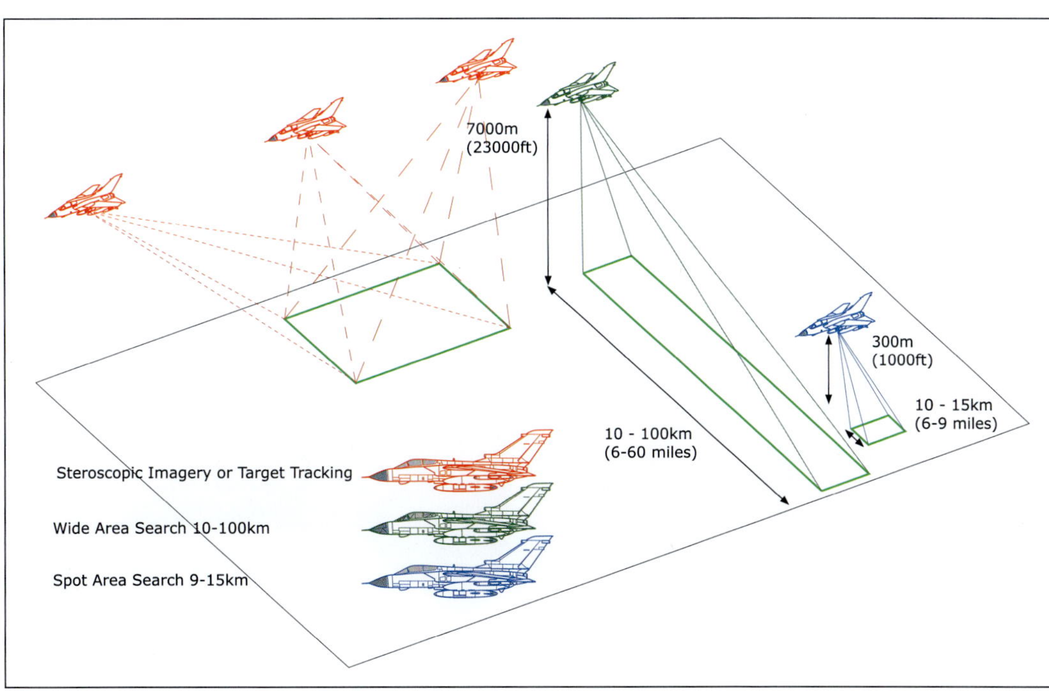

RAPTOR works in different modes depending on the tasking. close-up or spot search at low altitude, wide area across a swathe up to 100km (62 miles) wide and in the traditional photo-reconnaissance stereographic mode with overlapping images for stereo pairs.

Deadly Persistence

Much of the RAF's reconnaissance work throughout World War Two involved repeat photography of targets to detect any changes in layout such as new buildings, equipment or aircraft movements. The ideal reconnaissance system would be able to watch the target indefinitely, but that was not viable until recently with the advent of the high technology version of one of the oldest flying machines. Uninhabited Aerial Vehicles (UAV) or Uninhabited Aerial Systems (UAS), popularly known as drones, have become the *bête noire* of early 21st Century warfare. Their origins lay in the Lowe AT (Aerial Target) of 1916 which was ostensibly a guided weapon but essentially a remotely piloted aircraft. Until the early 1960s, UAVs were mainly used as targets for guided weapons and gunnery, but the USAF began using modified Ryan Firebee target drones for reconnaissance in the form of the Model 147 Fire Fly and Lightning Bug.

In the UK, aside from those operated by the Royal Artillery, the UAV was mainly used as a target, with the GAF Jindivik being the most widely used alongside drone variants of the Meteor and Canberra. In the reconnaissance role, Avro at Woodford had conducted design studies for strategic and tactical unmanned reconnaissance systems including two-stage systems such as the TRM series of radar reconnaissance UAVs. On the tactical front, Woodford drew up the short-range Z.112, Z.113, Z.114 and Z.118 that could transmit TV images over short ranges, but this led to a vehicle that was too large for frontline use.

The Royal Artillery had used UAVs for target identification since the early 1960s and the Avro W.150 was designed in 1962 to replace the Royal Artillery's first UAV, the Northrop Radioplane SD-1 Observer. The W.150 took advantage of IR linescan systems, allowing a much smaller vehicle that could transmit its data back to a ground station for printing and analysis. Unfortunately, the data transmission system failed to impress the British Army but there was a similar system under development by Canadair as the CL-89 and this was selected for the British Army, entering service as the AN/USD.501 Midge (Military Intelligence & Data Gathering Equipment). The Midge was boosted into the air by a Wagtail rocket motor rated at 5,000 lbf (22kN) and sustained in flight by a Williams International WR2-6 turbojet rated at 125 lbf (0.6kN). On a reconnaissance sortie the Midge flew a pre-programmed course, up to 37 miles (60km) long, capturing images with Vinten and Zeiss cameras using monochrome film. The Midge was also fitted with an IRLS

Tornado GR.4A ZA404 of No 2 Sqn climbs out carrying a RAPTOR pod and a Paveway IV LGB (possibly as a balancing store). The LOROP camera's optics are concealed behind the rectangular sliding panels on the port and ventral surfaces of the pod. *MoD/ Open Government Licence*

data. The Midge was recovered by parachute with the film processed at the launch station.

The Royal Artillery's next UAV, the GEC Phoenix, was a piston-engined, tractor propeller, twin-boom monoplane that carried its payload in a ventral pod. Phoenix grew out of a late 1970s project for a rotary wing surveillance drone to meet GSR.3494, issued in February 1971 under the catchy name of MRUASTAS (Medium Range Unmanned Aircraft Surveillance & Target Acquisition System) which was soon changed to Supervisor. Westland Helicopters proposed the Wide-Eye, an ellipsoid surmounted by co-axial rotors. Supervisor failed to meet the Staff Requirement, so the focus turned to a fixed wing UAV, Phoenix. Project Phoenix involved designs from Ferranti and GEC, with the requirement stating that the surveillance payload be installed in a stabilised platform. Ferranti's bid was called Firebird.

Phoenix acquired the nickname 'Bugger-off' during its service with KFOR in the Balkans, but in reality, it was not designed for use in the deep valleys of Kosovo where signals could be masked by terrain, thus losing the Phoenix. The Phoenix was to be replaced in Royal Artillery service by Watchkeeper WK450, based on the Elbit Hermes 450 but fitted with a synthetic aperture radar with moving target indicator. For its operations in Afghanistan, the British Army has acquired a variety of UAVs, ranging from the smallest, the 4in (100mm) long Black Hornet Nano helicopter, through the Desert Hawk with a wingspan of 4ft 4in (1.32m) to the Watchkeeper WK450 with a wingspan of 34ft 5in (6.1m).

The Royal Navy were great users of UAV as targets for guided weapons trials but took delivery of the Boeing ScanEagle surveillance system in 2014 as an urgent operational requirement under a three year contract with Boeing. The ScanEagle was operated from a variety of ships and provided 'game-changing, persistent surveillance and reconnaissance' and was seen as an adjunct to a warship's Wildcat helicopter. The ScanEagle could be controlled from the launch ship or from the Navy's Sea King ASaC.7s. In 2017 the Boeing contract was extended, and it was announced that a replacement for ScanEagle would be sought under the FDUAS (Flexible Deployable UAS).

Aside from target drones, the RAF had never been a great user of UAVs, certainly not to the same extent as the Army, but with the advent of new UAVs in the 1990s that was to change. The US armed forces invested heavily in UAVs, which they referred to as RPA, Remotely Piloted Aircraft. The first and most famous dividend from that investment was the General Atomics RQ-1 Predator, intended as a reconnaissance platform, it and its armed MQ-1 variant with its AGM-114 Hellfire payload, soon became renowned for their precision strikes out of the blue. Predator provided US forces (military and intelligence services) with a persistent and fairly discreet surveillance system, which if required, could attack targets on the ground. With an endurance over a task area of 14 hours up to 400nm (741km) from base and armed with two Hellfire, the Predator provided the US with a new capability. The CIA's operations with the Predator attracted criticism in the press, with particular scorn poured on the perceived 'armchair' or 'computer game' aspects of their operations.

With the success of the Predator, General Atomics began to investigate a more capable type that they called the Predator B-001, which could be described as a MQ-1 Predator scaled-up by around 30%. The B-001 was powered by a Garrett TPE331 turboprop rated at 950shp (710kW) rather than the 115hp (85kW) Rotax piston engine of the MQ-1. A jet-powered version, B-002, was fitted with a Williams FJ44 turbofan rated at 2,300 lbf (10.2kN). The USAF opted for the B-001 and this became the Predator B, later known as the MQ-9A Reaper. The larger airframe and increased power allowed the Reaper to carry more ordnance, faster and for longer periods, providing what the USAF called 'deadly persistence' with an endurance of over 40 hours with 1,000 lb of ordnance on seven hard points. Weapons include the Hellfire, GBU-12 Paveway LGB, AIM-9 Sidewinder and the GBU-38 JDAM (Joint Direct Attack Munition).

The RAF had been interested in the Predator B as a replacement for the Canberra PR.9 as an interim reconnaissance platform pending the outcome of the Dabinett programme to replace the venerable Canberra. The RAF ultimately acquired the MQ-9A under an urgent operational requirement (UOR) for use in Afghanistan and operated it as the Reaper, by No 39 Sqn in a control centre at Creech AFB in Nevada but moved to Waddington in 2007. The squadron's five Reapers were soon in action in Afghanistan in the surveillance role but by 2013 were using their four Hellfire and two Paveway II weapons against the Taliban. In 2013 the MBDA Brimstone was being integrated into the Reaper, with successful trials undertaken in the USA. A second squadron, XIII Sqn, began Reaper operations in October 2012 with a further five

An RAF MQ-9 Reaper carrying a pair of Paveway IV LGBs and four AGM-114 Hellfires. The chin turret houses the multi-spectral targeting system with visual and IR optics plus a laser designator for the Hellfires. The 'cockpit' covers a satellite datalink to the ground station at RAF Waddington or Creech AFB, Nevada. *MoD/ Open Government Licence*

Reapers. The Reaper also saw action against Islamic State as part of Operation SHADER in Iraq and over Syria.

Having acquired the Reaper under a UOR, i.e. funded directly by the Treasury, the MoD decided that given their success, Reaper should become core equipment and therefore funded by the MoD from 2014. A follow-on to the Reaper was sought and the MQ-9B SkyGuardian was selected and designated the Protector RG.1 (Reconnaissance Ground attack Mk.1). Also known as Certifiable Predator B (CPB), the SkyGuardian was intended to meet European civil aviation certification regulations to improve its sales prospects in Europe. The Protector (General Atomics have stated that they wanted to get away from names that suggested the aircraft only had a strike role) has increased endurance, 40 hours at 50,000ft (15,240m) and nine hardpoints, but the Protector's most distinctive feature is the curved winglets on its wings whose span is increased by 13ft (4m) to 79ft (24m).

The General Atomics MQ-9B SkyGuardian will replace the Predator in RAF service as the Protector RG.1. The Protector will be able to carry Brimstone, SPEAR and Paveway systems in addition to reconnaissance and surveillance payloads. *General Atomics*

UK UAVs – always in the background

The impression might be gained that US companies have been setting the pace on UAVs, but development of pilotless air systems had also been underway by the UK's aerospace companies. Design studies for remotely piloted surveillance and strike vehicles made regular appearances over the decades of the Cold War in about any role imagined.

Many of these were remotely piloted interceptors intended to operate either within a new air defence system as was the case with the BAe P.1224 UFA or carried as a force multiplier by interceptors such as the Panavia Tornado F.3. Many of these design studies were also aimed at ground attack and reconnaissance, particularly against well-defended targets in the enemy's rear area or against armoured formations.

BAe's Kingston Division in 1983 drew up the P.1224 Unmanned Fighter Aircraft (UFA) as a counter to the new generation of Soviet fighters such as the Su-27 *Flanker* and MiG-29 *Fulcrum*. The UFA came in two basic variants: high subsonic powered by an unreheated Rolls-Royce Viper turbojet and supersonic, powered by a reheated Rolls-Royce Adour turbofan. The basic airframe and control systems were similar for both types, as was the launch and recovery system, which involved being rocket-boosted from a truck-mounted 60° ramp by a pair of externally-mounted Blackcap rocket motors, rated at 12,500 lbf (55.6kN) apiece, as used in the Sea Wolf SAM. Recovery involved a system similar to Ryan's X-13 Vertijet but with the UFA entering a vertical attitude, aided by a 3D engine nozzle with 17° axial deflection, deploying a 'hoop' at the nose and latching onto a hook on the launch/recovery truck.

In the interceptor role, UFA was to carry passive electronic support measures (ESM – radar and IR detectors), a FLIR and AIM-120 AMRAAM, cued from the ESM systems before going active after launch. Alternative roles saw the systems for low-level flight installed, including a radar altimeter and TERPROM (Terrain Profile Matching), a BAE navigation system that used onboard terrain elevation data and a radar altimeter to calculate the vehicle's location. Of the low-level roles envisioned for UFA, all involved flight into the face of air defences, so the obvious role would be suppression of enemy air defences (SEAD) using a pair of ALARM or six of the short-range ARM to meet ASR.1240, ASRARM. The ASRARM was intended for use against the SA-11 *Gadfly*, specifically its *Snow Drift* target acquisition radar and *Fire Dome* fire control radar. In the counter-air role the UFA could carry BL.755 cluster bombs or dispensers for HB.876 and SG.357 submunitions. For operations against enemy armour, the UFA would use its FLIR to detect vehicles and attack these with the BL.755 or the weapons to meet ASR.1238, which ultimately became Brimstone. Other missiles considered for ground attack roles were the AGM-65 Maverick and rocket dispensers.

Dating from 1972, Boomerang (See Chapter 5) was an BAC Warton design study for an anti-runway/runway denial system that was potentially cheaper than Tornado/JP.233. A squat single-engined delta aircraft, it featured a bifurcated jet pipe to create space to house its internal bombload of six BL.755 cluster bombs. Two of these were installed side-by-side in the rear fuselage, flanked by the jet pipes, with another BL.755 either side of the engine in the centre fuselage. Behind the terrain following radar in the nose, yet another pair of BL.755s were housed in the forward fuselage. The Boomerang was launched 'inverted', boosted from an inclined launch rail by a pair of rocket motors that were jettisoned on burn-out.

This was examined with interest by BAC at Warton who commenced their own unmanned aircraft (UMA) studies, beginning with work on the pros and cons of expendable vs reusable systems, deciding that a reusable system had benefits, but in a shooting war all systems might be expendable anyway. Another area under examination was control and guidance systems that involved a large model aircraft called CYCLOPS and a modified Jet Provost. BAC's Stevenage plant became involved, examining aspects related to guided weapons including a harassment drone and anti-radar system that could 'sneak up on' and attack an emitter even when it was switched off. Some of this work may have found its way into ALARM.

By 1973 Warton's initial studies on the offensive use of UMAs involved systems that could use existing geographical data to fly a preprogrammed route that would allow it to attack fixed targets such as airfield, roads and the traffic on them in the enemy's rear areas. The Road Denial System carried a low light TV (LLTV) transmitting to a ground station that allowed identification of targets and attacks on enemy vehicles. Against fixed targets such as airfields and shelters, the UMA studies were to use new technologies such as TERPROM and millimetre wave (MMW) radar with TERPROM guiding the vehicle to the airfield and MMW radar to identify shelters and buildings for attack.

The appearance of the Tomahawk ALCM in the United States prompted work on cruise missiles that could be used for stand-off attacks on armoured formations. This led to the medium-range air-to-surface missile (MRASM) and long-range air-to-surface missile (LRASM), which also tied in the RSRE work on SARs and their Canberra testbed. The work on LRASM led to an anti-airfield system using JP.233 components that allowed airfields to be attacked from stand-off ranges but the ultimate outcome from LRASM was ASR.1236 and the resultant Storm Shadow.

The work on reconnaissance and surveillance systems, now called ISTAR (Intelligence, surveillance, target acquisition and reconnaissance), has allowed the West's armed forces to see over the hill and not for the briefest glimpse. Modern UAVs and stand-off reconnaissance systems provide persistence, allowing a target to observed for long periods and patterns of activity recorded. This has been especially useful in the various wars fought since 2001 and yet another system designed for observing T-72s on the Central Front has been applied to track 'Technicals' and insurgents on mopeds.

7 The Deer Hunter and MinTech's Harrier

'Many of the enemy were killed...the remainder put to rout during gun and rocket attacks by Strikemaster aircraft.'
David Watkins, p117, *From Jet Provost to Strikemaster*, Grub Street, 2017

While the massed ranks of Warsaw Pact tanks would be brought to a halt by NATO's anti-armour weapons, the armour would be accompanied by air-mobile units that would include the Mi-24 *Hind* gunship. These posed a threat to NATO armour and anti-tank helicopters so what was required was a small, agile anti-helicopter type that could also conduct battlefield support when required. Such roles, traditionally filled by armed versions of training aircraft, prompted a number of design studies to find an aircraft that could operate like a helicopter *and* an aeroplane.

The main thrust of this book is that the RAF has not fielded a dedicated ground attack/battlefield support aircraft, relying on retired fighters such as the Hunter F.6 and ultimately multi- or swing-role aircraft. For a brief period in the 1970s and 80s bespoke aircraft were being discussed by the aircraft companies. Whether the Air Staff were remotely interested is moot as is whether the finance was available, but two roles stood out.

The light attack aircraft has been an area that British aerospace companies have constantly examined since 1945, usually with training aircraft putting their weapons training capability to offensive use. Occasionally, dedicated light attack versions of training aircraft have been developed, which was the case with the Strikemaster and Hawk 200. Then there is the Jaguar whose origins lay in a French requirement for a supersonic trainer but evolved into an excellent strike aircraft. Of course, there are exceptions to this and on each occasion the burgeoning Warsaw Pact tank forces has prompted action from the Ministries or, seeing an opportunity, the companies themselves.

The increase in the quality of Warsaw Pact mobile air defence systems and the concerns

This page: A BAC P.101 Blitz Fighter leads a formation of BAe P.1233 against a Warsaw Pact armoured division, knocking out tanks and Shilka air defence vehicles ahead of the main formation. The wing man in the P.1233, armed with ASRAAMs, is dealing with fighters and attack helicopters. The P.101 was to be armed with the 30mm GAU-13/A Gatling gun, a four-barrelled variant of the A-10 Thunderbolt II's Avenger. *Luciano Alviani*

Opposite, top: The Ministry of Technology were pushing a few envelopes when the Wide Speed Range Aircraft was discussed. The combination was probably best met by a combination of attack helicopters such as the Cobra or Apache and V/STOL aircraft, Harriers, which was essentially what happened.

these caused the Staffs and MoD, prompted the Ministry of Technology (MinTech) in 1968 to request proposals for a battlefield aircraft to replace the Harrier from 1980. This was to incorporate aspects of high-subsonic fixed wing and VTOL rotary wing aircraft in a single airframe and allow it to operate over a wide speed range, hence the name 'Wide Speed Range Aircraft' (WSRA). The range in question was 50-500kt (93-930km/h) carrying a weapons load of 2,000 lb (907kg) over a low altitude radius of action of 100nm (185km).

The specification called for a 'comparative conventional aircraft of the same (i.e. 1980) technological standard' with 'relaxation' permitted in the take-off (a 2,500ft/762m take-off roll) and the search speed (150kt/278km/h), but the 'target acquisition and vulnerability were still fluid'. In fact, the upper end of the range may be increased to 600kt (1,111km/h) with 20 minutes search at 50kt. This meant that the specification was an 'early approximation' of what might form the basis of the of the 'MoD likely requirement' and therefore any resulting design studies might 'only give a broad indication of the performance and engineering feasibility' of satisfying the requirement. The main factor was that the need for a high transit speed and prolonged flight at slow speed were 'mutually conflicting'. This conflict led to compromises in aircraft design with attendant weight, and cost, penalties relative to a conventional aircraft.

Addressing this speed range would require lift/propulsion systems at each end of the speed range i.e. rotors and jets, with the stowed-rotor providing the best solution with the aircraft changing from a helicopter to a conventional jet aircraft. Unfortunately, none of the aircraft companies considered the stowed-rotor a viable proposition! Another approach examined by BAC, combined vectored thrust lift/cruise engine for high-speed flight with lift fans to supplant the main engines at low speed. The upshot of the range-end engines would be an aircraft with an all-up weight almost double that of a conventional aircraft or helicopter.

If the requirement was relaxed at each end of the range as described above, single vectored thrust engine could be feasible and alternative rotor-driven designs became viable. Stowed rotors had to be stopped, folded and stowed away at speeds above 500kt as they were susceptible to damage at high speeds when folded and stowing them required doors and actuators that increased airframe weight. The lightest configuration for the relaxed requirement

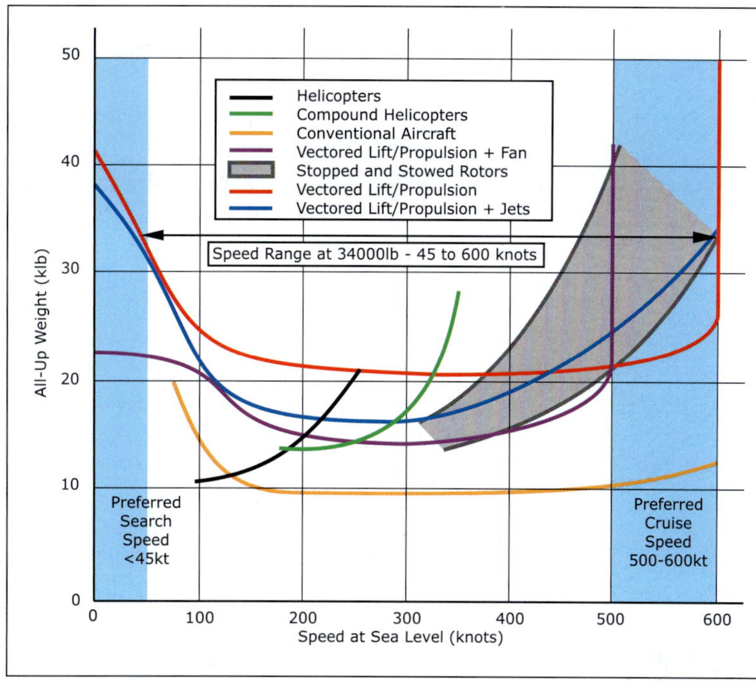

was the tilt-wing and might even be capable of speeds greater than 500kt.

BAC drew up four design studies using Rolls-Royce Pegasus-type vectored thrust lift and cruise engines: the first with vectoring cruise engine; one with a vectoring cruise engine and lift engines that could be used for manoeuvring at the search speed; another with vectoring cruise engine and vectored lift fans and

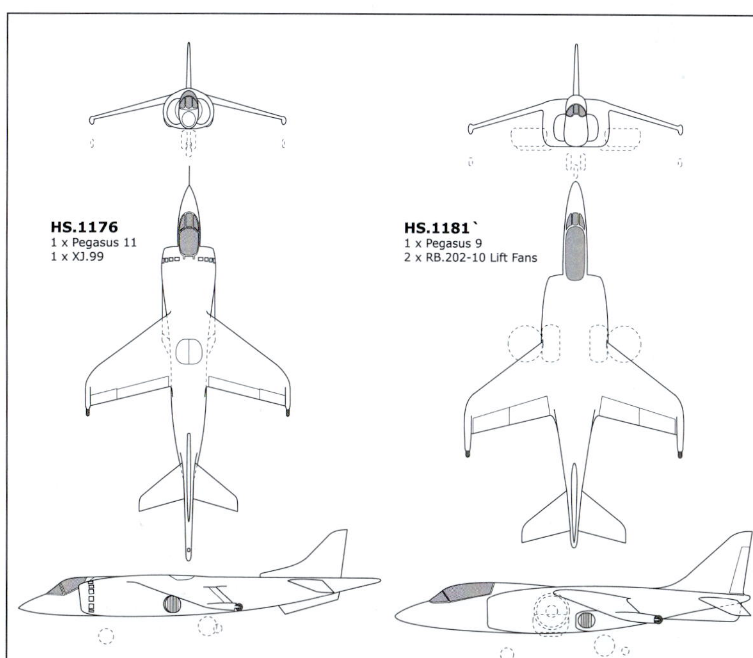

Hawker Siddeley's Kingston designers applied their Harrier knowledge to WSRA with the P.1176 being fitted with a Pegasus 9 and XJ.90 lift jet while the P.1181 added a pair of retractable RB.202 lift fans in the intake trunking.

a fourth with a cruise engine and separate lift fans. In the third and fourth examples the cruise engine was small whereas in the first and second, the vectored thrust engine is large. BAC also examined fan-lift aircraft for WSRA but does not appear to have tendered that to MinTech. On examining the BAC proposals, the MinTech assessors did not think there was much to choose from in the four studies.

The three HSA studies included two with vectored thrust turbofans and one with circulation-controlled rotors (CCR). The first study was designated the HS.1176-2 and was essentially a Harrier with a larger Pegasus 9D while the HS.1181, another developed Harrier with the Pegasus 9D, included a pair of retractable RB.202 lift fans, one fitted in each intake trunking forward of the vectoring nozzle. The third study was the HS.807-03, one of a series of studies by HSA Woodford applying the CCR to various roles, including the HS.807-3, a sleek tandem-cockpit design with a shoulder mounted wing. To provide VTOL and low speed manoeuvrability, at mid-span on each wing a two-bladed rotor was mounted. Forward propulsion was provided by a pair of RB.203 under the wing roots while the rotor propulsion and gas for the CCR system was provided by an RB.162 installed in the fuselage.

The HS.1176-2 did not meet the payload requirement and only carried a single crew member, despite two crew being preferred for workshare reasons. Range and endurance were less than required and the search speed was 65kt (120km/h). The HS.1181 also lacked range and endurance, especially the search time at a range of 100 miles, which was only 3 minutes. MinTech did not appear to view these studies as being much of an improvement over the Harrier.

Turning to the HS.807-3, the proposal was based on a body of work carried out by HSA Woodford and NGTE on the circulation-controlled rotor (CCR) system and its application to military and civil transport aircraft. CCR uses hollow elliptical blades with a slot along the trailing edge and as the rotor is turned, high pressure air is pumped into the blades and is forced out of the slot and by varying the volume of air blowing out of the slot, the aerodynamic properties of the blade change to provide cyclic and collective changes, and therefore control, in the rotor. The rotor, as a result, can be simplified with no relative movement between the rotor blades and the hub and no moving parts in the blades. They can also be rigid and robust enough to be stopped and aligned to present minimum frontal area to allow wing-borne flight. There was some concern about buffet when the rotors were stopped, wing/rotor interference and 'whirl-flutter'. One area that required further examination was the manoeuvre envelope while the rotor was being parked and MinTech was not convinced that aircraft could perform this while manoeuvring in a combat situation.

The study that utilised the circulation-control rotor used a configuration similar to that of the podded fan aircraft. The 24ft (7.3m) diameter two-bladed rotors were installed at mid-span on the shoulder wing. The propulsion system comprised two Rolls-Royce Adour turbofans for propulsion and to supply HP air for the rotor circulation system and reaction control, with a modified XJ.99, mounted vertically in the fuselage, feeding a gearbox to drive the rotors.

Westland Helicopters proposed tilt-wing aircraft for the role but MinTech were concerned about aero-elastic actions between the large propellers and the wings, stability in the tran-

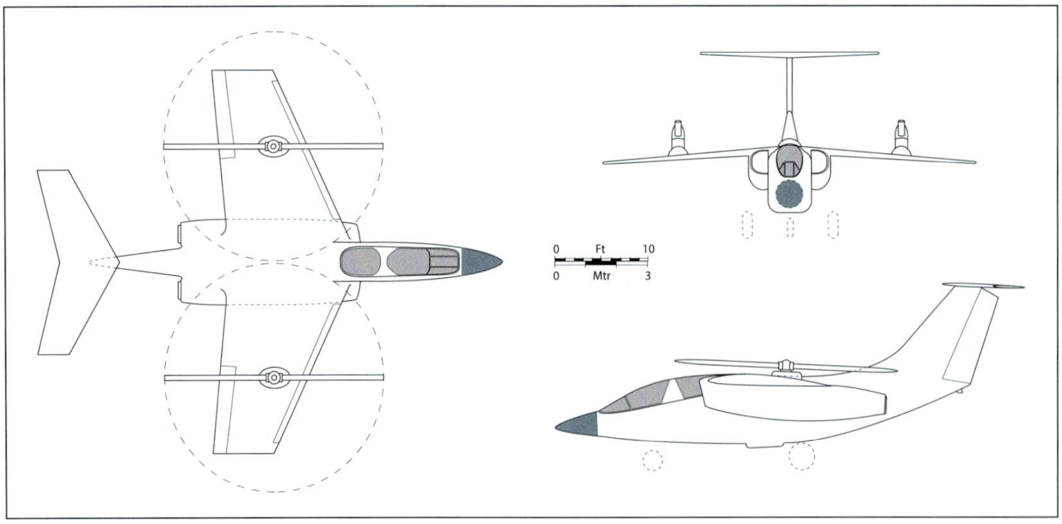

This page:

This study, part of the HS.807 series, used the circulation-controlled rotor (CCR) to provide high speed VTOL. Hawker Siddeley at Woodford applied CCR to a variety of types ranging from small combat aircraft to V/STOL airliners. The circulation-controlled rotor was developed by the National Gas Turbine Establishment (NGTE) at Pyestock.

Opposite page:

Top: The fan-lift WSRA was to be powered by a single RB.168 Spey for propulsion and a Rolls-Royce XJ.99 with a power turbine to drive the six lift fans in the inboard section of the wing. *North West Heritage Group*

Centre: Another WSRA employed two Rolls-Royce RB.202 lift fans in wingtip pods plus another modified RB.202 in retractable mounting on each side of the rear fuselage. These two fans could be rotated through 90 to direct thrust for lift or low speed propulsion. High speed propulsion was provided by a single Rolls-Royce RB.168 Spey turbofan. *North West Heritage Group*

sition from rotor to wingborne flight and gust response of the rotors during manoeuvres. Aside from these, MinTech appeared quite happy with Westland's performance figures, declaring them 'quite realistic'.

The WSRA Studies

The studies outlined above and analysed by MinTech were the initial submissions from the aircraft companies who used these as a basis for further, more detailed studies. BAC at Warton was particularly interested in the WSRA and produced a number of design studies using the range of techniques described above. To apply fan lift, the designers used a high-wing double-delta planform with three 54in (137cm) diameter lift fans buried in the inner wings. The fans were turned mechanically by a power turbine driven by a modified Rolls-Royce XJ.99 lift engine while forward propulsion was provided by a Rolls-Royce RB.168 Spey installed in the lower rear fuselage. The Spey was fed by D-shaped box intakes on the fuselage sides with the XJ.99 fed by a dorsal intake aft of the cockpits, covered by a retractable door when not in use. Control at low speed was by reaction controls at nose, wingtips and tailcone, using bleed air from the Spey. The two crew were accommodated in tandem, with the gunner in an extensively glazed front cockpit controlling a gun turret in the extreme nose. The aircraft had an all-up weight of 25,000 lb (11,338kg) and a wing loading of 70 lb/ft² (341.7kg/m²).

The second fan lift type also employed six fans and a Spey but employed a completely different configuration, a high-mounted straight wing with large, flattened wingtip pods carrying two fans. Unlike the delta type described above, these fans were RB.202 self-contained lift fans with two mounted in tandem in each pod. The last two RB.202s were mounted on either side of the rear fuselage on rotating mountings that allowed them to swivel through 90° to act as lift or propulsion fans. The main propulsion engine was an RB.168 Spey in the lower rear fuselage fed by an annular intake that wrapped around the lower fuselage below the aft cockpit. No details of weapons can be seen on the drawing, but the wings were clear for pylon-mounted stores.

Some aircraft configurations are driven by the engine installation and that is certainly true of the Pegasus in its 'four-poster' guise that lends itself to the Harrier configuration. For Warton's four-poster WSRA, the type looked not unlike a Harrier T.2 with angular wing and dihedral tail

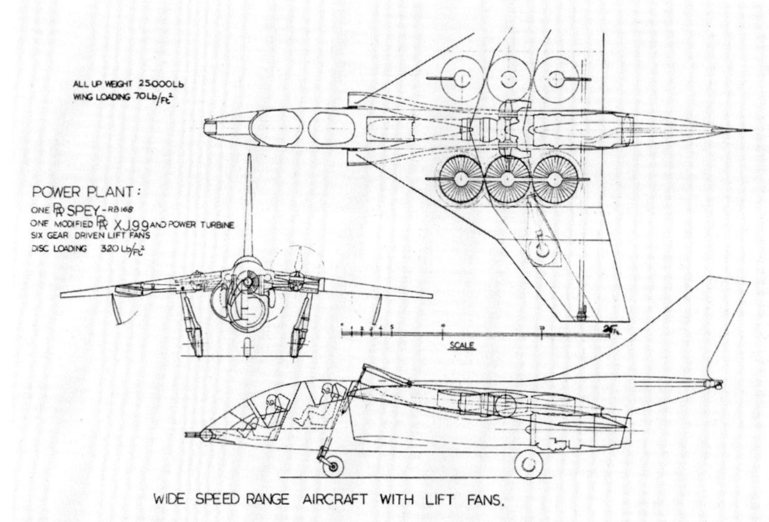

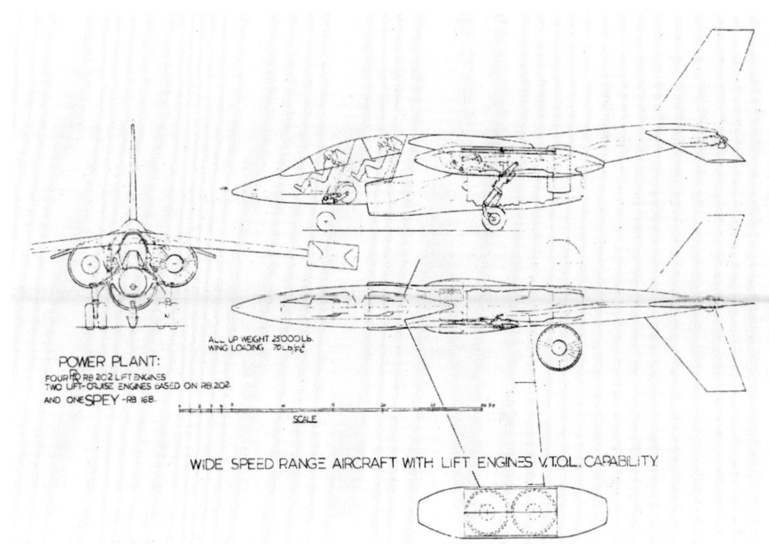

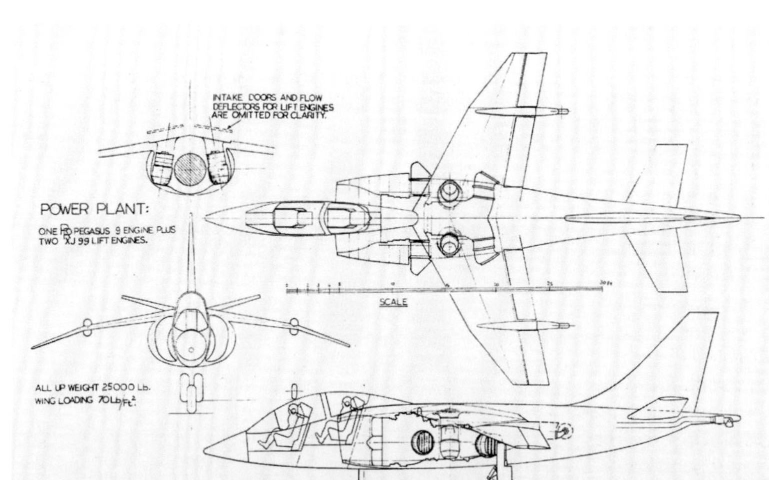

Above: **Harking back to the Hawker P.1155 of NBMR-3 days, this used a Pegasus 9 vectored thrust turbofan plus two XJ.99 lift engines installed between the nozzles of the Pegasus.** ***North West Heritage Group***

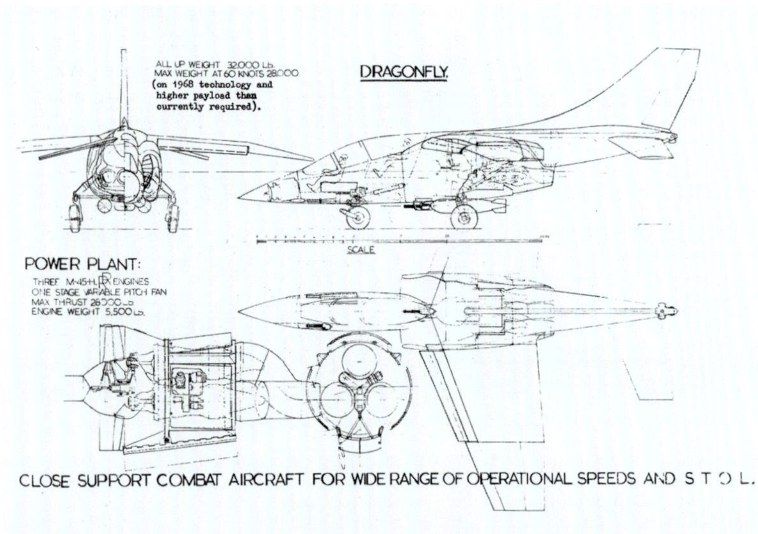

BAC Warton's Dragonfly was powered by three Rolls-Royce/ SNECMA M45H turbofans, driving a large single stage fan. The Dragonfly would have been heavily armed with weapons that include a 7.62mm minigun in a ventral turret plus another Minigun and a 40mm grenade launcher in the forward fuselage. The Dragonfly could also carry BL.755 cluster bombs on ventral hard points. *North West Heritage Group*

surfaces. To provide additional lift for VTOL and low-speed flight, a Rolls-Royce XJ.99 lift engine was installed in the fuselage either side of the Pegasus 9, between the vectoring nozzles. The intakes for these were on the upper fuselage, covered by retractable doors and flow deflectors.

One BAC design study that did receive a name was the Dragonfly, whose conventional high-wing, tandem cockpit configuration belied a novel propulsion system. The powerplant for the Dragonfly was listed as three M45H engines, two for propulsion and a third to provide HP air for flap blowing and to drive a large 72in (183cm) fan that generated thrust for the lift system. These were arranged in a cloverleaf installation, but the jetpipes fitted with vectoring nozzles, were ducted to align across the rear fuselage. The Dragonfly was heavily armed with a fixed 7.62mm Minigun and a 40mm grenade launcher mounted in the lower forward fuselage. The underside of the rear fuselage carried a turret with a second Minigun and hardpoints for stores such as BL.755 cluster bombs.

Woodford also drew up the HS.812 VTOL Battlefield Aircraft, rather handsome machine with a mid-mounted swept wing and three-blade CCR. The HS.812 differed from the other CCR types in that it used a single rotor, a ducted fan propulsor and an anti-torque tail rotor. The anti-torque rotor was required because the rotor was driven mechanically, producing torque whereas when two rotors are fitted the rotate in opposite directions, cancelling out the torque. The rotor on the HS.812 does not appear to be capable of stopping in flight, with the wings acting to unload the rotor rather than lift the aircraft in its entirety. The HS.812 had a rotor diameter of 51ft 11in (15.8m), a wingspan of 44ft 2in (13.5m) and weighted in at 26,000 lb (11,791kg).

Of the many Westland Helicopters tilt wing proposals, the one that appears to have progressed for WSRA is the WG.21 tilt-wing. This was a sleek swept-wing machine with propulsion systems set under the wings at a distance 30% inboard from the tips. Driven by turboshaft engines, the six-bladed propeller/ rotors were 24ft (7.3m) in diameter and this precluded the carriage of underwing stores, although a cannon or 40mm grenade launcher was mounted in the nose. Stores such as BL.755 cluster bombs or SNEB rockets may have been carried on ventral pylons.

The Wide Speed Range Aircraft was like its sponsor, MinTech, very much a child of its time, the era of Harold Wilson's white heat of technology. Under way in 1968, WSRA was a prod-

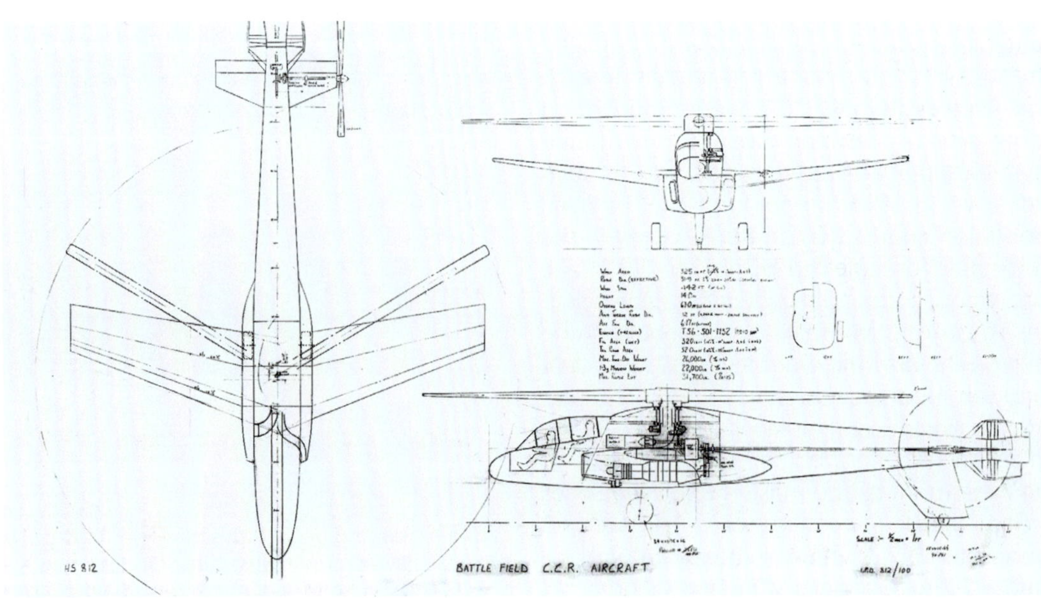

While dated after the demise of the WSRA studies, Hawker Siddeley's HS.812 CCR battlefield support aircraft may have provided a solution for the role. It was to be powered by a single T56-501, which was similar to that used on the C-130 and later, the V-22 Osprey tiltrotor. *Avro Heritage*

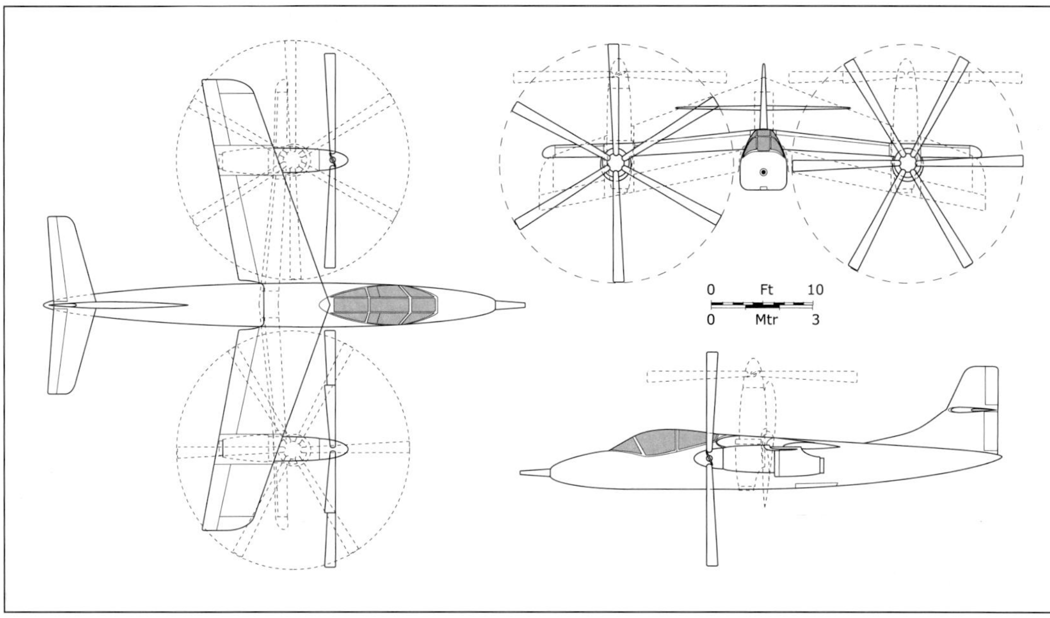

Westland's WG.21 employed a tilt-wing with large six-bladed rotoprops. While the low-speed end of the speed range would pose no problem, the high end would need further investigation.

uct of Tony Benn as Minister of Technology and the takeover of the aircraft supply functions from the Ministry of Aviation. The WSRA was a complicated machine, as are all modern military aircraft, but the width of the speed range was just too much for the late 1960s.

MiniCAS

In the mid-1970s Hawker Siddeley Aviation at Kingston was working on design studies for a small, lightweight ground-attack aircraft to meet a 1970 specification called MiniCAS (Mini Close Air Support). As ever, the Staff Target had but one simple objective – knocking out Soviet armour as it charged across the North German Plain. By the 1970s the use of nuclear weapons was the last option; conventional means were preferred. Smart weapons were in their infancy, so rockets, guns and cluster bombs were the weapons of choice, to be delivered by swarms of small MiniCAS aircraft.

The MiniCAS design studies produced a variety of configurations for small single-seater types with dorsal-mounted engines, usually the Rolls-Royce RB.199 turbofan or the Viper turbojet. One of these, the HS.1194, sported a canard and a variable incidence 'Kasper Wing' (that allowed slow speed by producing strong lift-generating vortices) with endplate fins and a rotary augmenter for the RB.199 turbofan. These subsonic (typically Mach 0.75) aircraft had an all-up-weight around 10,000 lb (4,536kg) of which around 700 lb (317kg) was weapons load.

One rather handsome shoulder-winged design (handsome for a role not normally associated with good looks) was the HS.1196. This sported the typically Hawker curved tips to the wing and tail surfaces that were mated to a beaver-tailed fuselage carrying a Rolls-Royce RB.401-06 rated at 5320 lbf (23.7kN) which, to protect it from ground fire, was housed in a dorsal pod. Apart from a ventral 30mm ADEN cannon, rockets and cluster bombs, the HS.1196 could carry four QC.434/SRAAM missiles for use against Soviet attack helicopters and enemy ground-attack aircraft.

MiniCAS fell by the wayside, as such ideas do; only to be re-invented in 1987 in another guise as the Small Agile Battlefield Aircraft (SABA). Hawker Siddeley Aviation was convinced that highly manoeuvrable lightweight aircraft were ideal to give ground support for troops, especially if they had some STOL capability. The Harrier had shown how such a type could perform, deployed close to the Forward Edge of the Battlefield Area (FEBA in the jargon of the era). Hunting Engineering's VJ.291

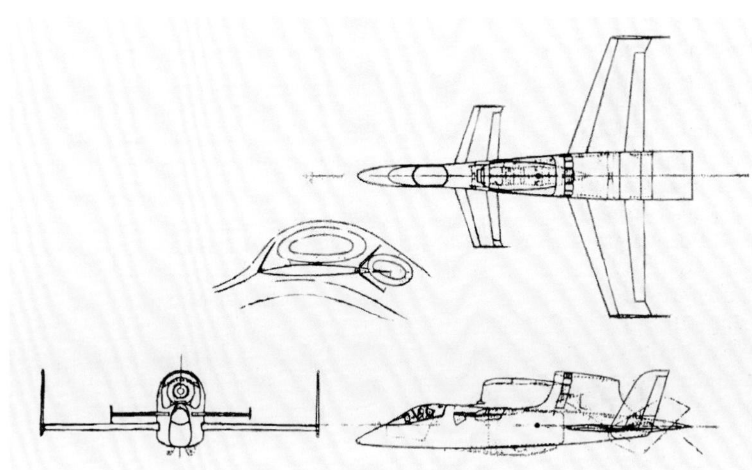

The HS.1194 MiniCAS used the Kasper wing, a means of achieving higher lift by trapping a vortex between a flap on the upper surface of the leading edge and split flaps on the trailing edge of a variable incidence wing. This effectively creates a thicker leading edge and 'wing'. *Brooklands Museum*

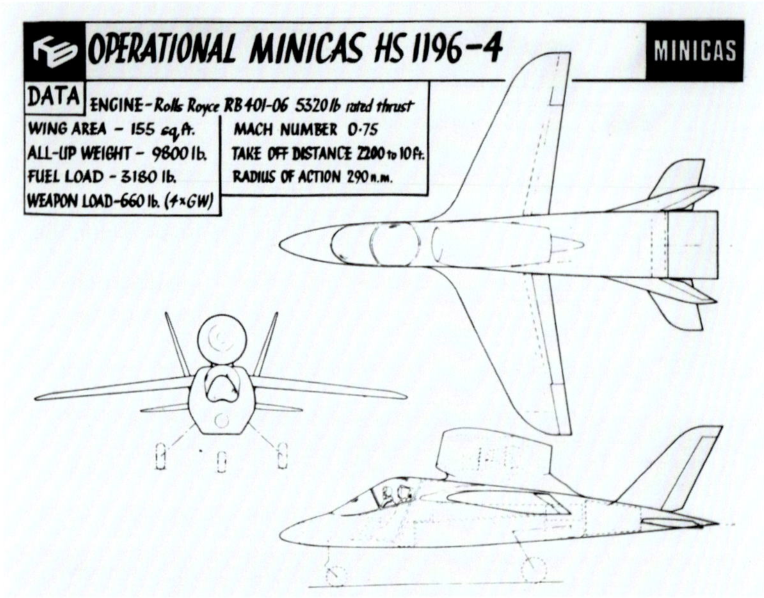

Above: The HS.1196-4 was powered by a dorsally-mounted RB.401-06 turbofan. Note the flat 'beaver tail, a feature also used on design studies towards AST.396. *Brooklands Museum*

Below: The P.1239 SABA was intended to use modular weapons packages that could be swapped out depending on the role. This example is armed with 14 Starstreak HVMs. The P.1239 could also be configured as a UAV, shown here as an interceptor with swept wings and two S225 AAMs.

Opposite, top: BAe Kingston's P.1239 Versatile SABA was intended as a light close support type that could carry its weapons in dorsal modules. The nearest example is launching Medusa anti-tank 'smart' mortar rounds while the P.1239 on the left is firing its turret mounted KCA 30mm cannon and the aircraft on the right is firing Starstreak HVMs. *Adrian Mann*

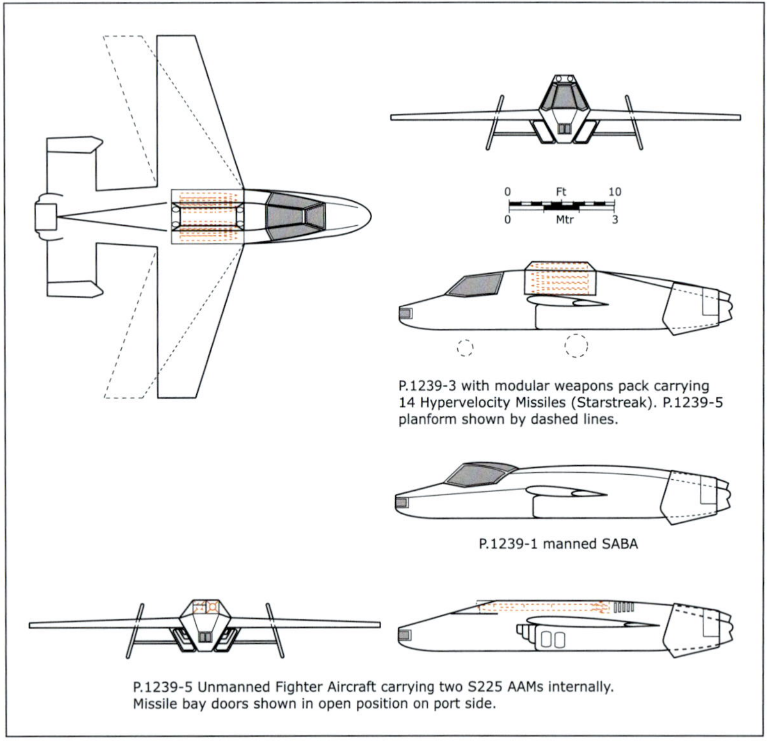

P.1239-3 with modular weapons pack carrying 14 Hypervelocity Missiles (Starstreak). P.1239-5 planform shown by dashed lines.

P.1239-1 manned SABA

P.1239-5 Unmanned Fighter Aircraft carrying two S225 AAMs internally. Missile bay doors shown in open position on port side.

anti-armour cluster bomb had used a guided dispenser to fly over the FEBA, but HSA put the VJ.291 submunition to use in one of its SABA studies. The HS.1239, 'Versatile SABA' was a squat, shoulder-winged aircraft whose weapons were carried in a removable dorsal module. Amongst the weapon fits, which could include a turret with an Oerlikon KCA 30mm cannon, was a dispenser for the VJ.291 or HB.876 minelets and a magazine holding fourteen Shorts Hypervelocity Missiles, later known as Starstreak or its BAe competitor, Thunderbolt.

The HS.1239's modular payload system allowed a wide variety of roles. One intriguing application was battlefield surveillance, with a radar system and 8ft 4in (2.54m) diameter rotodome fitted. This was intended to be a successor to the CASTOR system then under development for the Army (see chapter 6). Given that the HS.1239 was a single seater, some means of datalinking the radar picture to a ground station must have been intended.

Of most interest was the intention to fit the HS.1239 with a module carrying 72 Medusas, modified Merlin guided mortar bombs. One of the modifications was no doubt a rocket booster, due to the heavy recoil associated with a mortar and its effect on the airframe. The HS.1239 would have been a formidable foe, capable of wreaking havoc on Soviet armour formations as they poured through the Fulda Gap but, like most design studies, it elicited little official interest.

SABA – The Deer Hunter

Soviet Frontal Aviation was the arm of the Soviet air force tasked with ground attack and air support of the Red Army, which in northern Europe was the 16th Air Army Group of the Group of Soviet Forces in Germany. A formidable force with its roots in WW2, Frontal Aviation posed a major threat to NATO forces in western Europe. Throughout the 1980s, Frontal Aviation underwent a re-equipment programme that saw the re-roled interceptors (this was not just a British habit) replaced with dedicated ground support aircraft.

The close support projects developed in the Sixties and Seventies such as WSRA (Wide Speed Range Aircraft) and MiniCAS were soon, like the US Army's AH-56 Cheyenne, overtaken by developments in attack helicopters. The US and UK projects were aimed at anti-tank operations, but as noted above, the Soviet 'Flying BMP' in the form of the Mi-24 *Hind* prompted a new role – anti-helicopter operations.

The first air-to-air helicopter combat was in the Iran-Iraq War (1980-88) when Iranian Islamic AF AH-1J Sea Cobras shot down two Iraqi AF *Hind-Ds* with their TOW ATGWs. Such combats occurred throughout the war, with the Iraqis claiming ten Sea Cobras for six *Hinds* lost. A similar situation would have arisen in western Europe had the Cold War turned hot, with NATO's 'Helarm' anti-tank helicopters such the Army Air Corps Lynx AH.1(TOW), Bundeswehr Bo 105 PAH-1 using their inherent speed and agility to good advantage against the *Hinds*

The original Ka-50 *Hokum-A* was a single seater but later versions such as this Ka-52 *Hokum-B*, 96 Yellow, has two seats and all-weather capability. It can carry a variety of weapons on its six wing pylons including the 9K121 Vikhr anti-tank missile. The partially-trainable 30mm Shipunov 2A42 cannon can be seen on the port side of the fuselage. *Chris Lofting*

while the US Army's AH-64A Apaches and USAF A-10As could probably slug it out with the *Hinds*. The advent of the *Hokum*, which was viewed in the West as a fast and agile foe, posed a more difficult target for an ATGW or 30mm cannon more suited for use against ground targets.

The RAF had conducted trials using ground attack aircraft, including the Harrier force, against helicopters, but even the Harriers were too fast. What was required was a small and agile type that could hunt the *Hinds*. It was to operate over the battlefield and take on the *Hinds*, *Havocs* and *Hokums*, releasing the ground attack aircraft to support the troops and the Helarm machines to destroy Soviet armour.

BAe Kingston in late 1987 revealed the results of a series of design studies carried out to investigate a dedicated anti-helicopter aircraft that could operate just behind the forward line of own troops (FLOT) and intercept any Warsaw Pact helicopters crossing the FLOT. The type was to be agile and fast, but able to loiter over the battlefield for up to four hours and it became known as SABA – Small Agile Battlefield Aircraft. In addition to its anti-helicopter role, SABA was to provide 'surgically accurate' close air support for the troops on the ground, with a laser designator fitted in the nose to support heavier ground attack types.

STOL performance was a prerequisite, allowing operation from austere strips close to the front line and SABA was to take off with a full load of AAMs and a 25mm cannon in 1,000ft (305m) at an all-up weight in the 10,000-11,000lb (4,535-4,989kg). The type was to be able to transit to the front line at a speed of 400kt (741km/h) and be capable of performing a 180° turn in under five seconds in a radius of 500ft (152m). Even this level of agility was considered insufficient to counter the *Hokum* and *Havoc*, so the SABA's weapons could be mounted in turret providing a wider arc of fire. When combined with a helmet-mounted sight, the pilot could aim these weapons off the SABA's flightpath. In the close support role SABA was to be armed with four AGM-65F imaging infrared Maverick or up to eight AGM-114 Hellfire anti-armour missiles, plus a pair of ASRAAMs and the internal cannon. The type was to be fitted with a full defensive countermeasures suite suitable for use over the battlefield.

The SABA's internal gun was to be the ADEN 25 cannon, a 25mm calibre, modernised version of the venerable 30mm ADEN that the RAF had used since the early 1950s. The weapon was a development of the ADEN Mk.V STRADEN (STRetched ADEN) and chambered for the NATO 25mm round as used by the GAU-12 rotary cannon fitted to the US Marine Corps' AV-8B Harriers. The ADEN 25 had a rate of fire of up to 1,850 rounds per minute and a muzzle velocity of 3,445 feet per second (1,050 m/s), both greater than the ADENs fitted to RAF aircraft. The Harrier GR.5/7/9 was to carry the ADEN 25, but development problems led to its cancellation in 1999. As a result, RAF Harriers GR.5/7/9s flew without guns, unlike the Royal Navy's Sea Harrier FA.2s, which retained the original 30mm ADEN pods from the FRS.1.

Guided weapons were intended as SABA's primary weapons had it entered service, specifically the Advanced Short-Range Air-to-Air Missile, an infrared guided weapon developed as the AIM-132 to replace the AIM-9 Sidewinder series. It was designed to have greater agility, range and speed than existing 'dogfight' AAMs which when combined with an imaging infrared seeker produced a weapon that could acquire its target in difficult conditions and manoeuvre as soon as it left the launch rail.

The other guided weapon earmarked for SABA in the air-to-air role is described as 'HVM', which stands for High (or occasionally Hyper) Velocity Missile. Development of the HVM began in the early 1980s in response to General Staff Requirement GSR.3979, which was drawn up in the light of a series of studies that had shown how a high-velocity weapon could replace both gun and MANPADS (MAN Portable Air Defence Systems) while being capable of mounting on vehicles and aircraft. BAe Dynamics and Shorts Missile Systems were given contracts to develop HVMs in 1984, leading to the BAe Dynamics Thunderbolt and Shorts Starstreak. Shorts were given the contract for development and production of Starstreak, as a replacement for that company's Blowpipe and Javelin MANPADS.

The HVM Starstreak used a laser guidance system as originally fitted to the Starburst SAM by which the operator tracked the target with the aiming unit, the system calculated the target's flightpath and computed a trajectory for the missile. On firing, a small rocket motor pushed the missile out of the launch tube and once it reached a pre-set safe distance, typically 13ft (4m), the boost motor lit and accelerated the missile to Mach 4. When the boost rocket burned out, three 0.9in (22mm) diameter by 15.6in (39.6cm) long tungsten alloy darts separated from the boost motor and flew towards the target. In the rear of each dart was a laser sensor and control package that kept the three darts within a laser 'matrix' projected on the target by two lasers in the fire unit. The unpowered darts penetrated the target and detonated, fragmenting the tungsten alloy body to maximise the effect of the 1 lb (450g) warhead within the target's airframe. BAe's Thunderbolt worked differently; it had no warhead but relied on the dart's kinetic energy to disrupt the target. With a velocity of 4,100ft/sec (1,250m/sec) the projectile can also be used against lightly-armoured vehicles, effectively if you can 'paint' it, you can hit it.

HVM has a range of more than 4 miles (7km), covering that distance in just over 5 seconds, with small canard controls bringing the penetrator onto the target, even a target manoeuvring at 9g. A dedicated version for use by helicopters such as the AH-64A Apache was developed under the name Helstreak but was renamed ATASK – Air To Air Starstreak.

Kingston's SABA

BAe Kingston proposed five variants of SABA; two propfan types designated P.1233 and P.1238, and three turbofan types, P.1234. The P.1233-1 study was a low-wing canard type powered by an engine derived from the Lycoming T55 driving a rear-mounted contra-rotating 16-blade propfan. The light wing loading of 50 lb/ft^2 (242kg/m^2) combined with the canard produced an agile type, but the pusher propfan would have adversely impacted the effectiveness of rudder and elevators on a conventional empennage so along with the canard, a 'chin rudder' was fitted under the forward fuselage. These, when combined with the latest 'fly-by-light' computerised control systems, were intended to 'outmanoeuvre an armed helicopter'. With a combat weight of 10,879 lb (4,934kg) carrying six ASRAAMs plus a 25mm ADEN 25 cannon with 150 rounds, the P.1233-1 could engage Soviet helicopters and fighters. Interestingly the P.1233-1 was to be fitted with a 'flat plate' canopy as used on attack helicopters since the early 1980s. Such cockpit glazing reduces the amount of glint from the canopy, something that was found to give away a manoeuvring aircraft's position.

Another feature of the P.1233-1 (and P.1238) that could give away the aircraft's position, or at least its approach, was the powerplant. Propfans were all the rage in the late -1970s and mid-1980s, an era of increasing fuel prices and the quest for more efficient aeroengines. Many of the transport and maritime patrol design studies of this era featured propfans. Also known as UDF (unducted fan) and 'open rotor' propulsion systems, propfans promised a lot, but foundered on the rocks that claimed many an aerospace advance – noise. Turbofans shroud the noise of their exhausts in a jacket of slower, cooler air. Propfans on the other hand had a multitude of exposed blades spinning at high speed and generating a loud whine. Apart

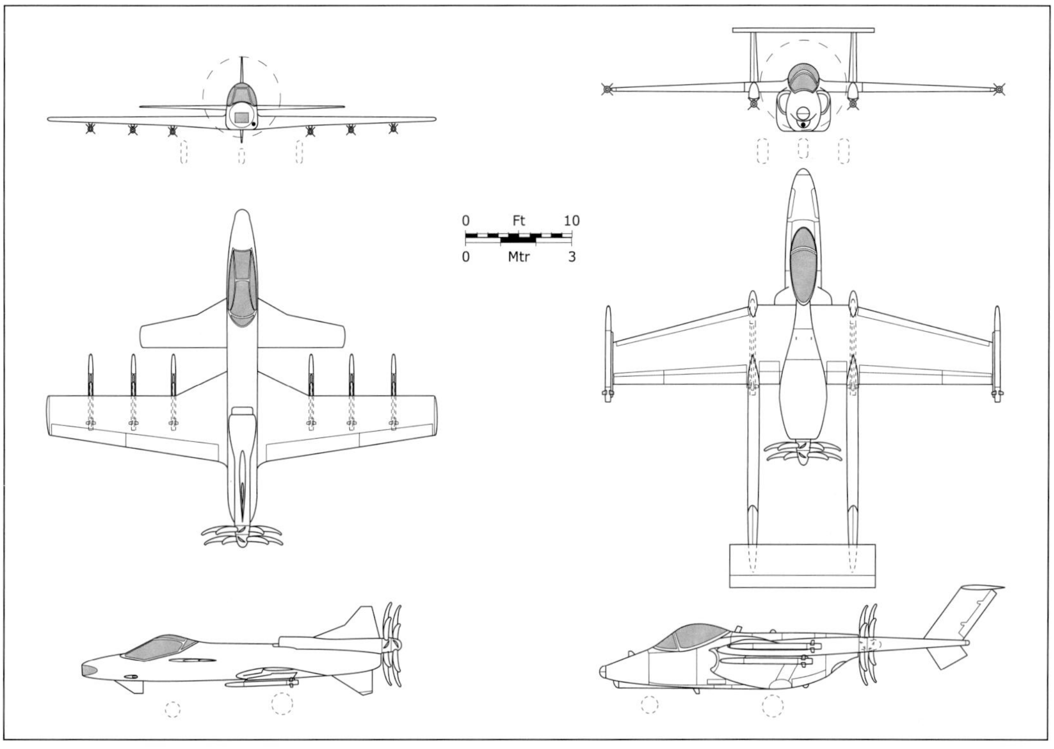

The Kingston designers drew up two propfan powered designs. Both were rear-engined pushers, differing in configuration, with the P.1233-1 a low-wing canard while the P.1238 was a shoulder wing, twin-boom type.

from testbeds such as the McDonnell Douglas MD-80 UHB, only the Antonov An-70 adopted the propfan and it fell from favour as turbofan technology advanced in the 1990s. As a powerplant for SABA, the propfan may have provided the combination of speed and endurance required, but the ominous whine of the propfan would probably let the enemy know you were coming. Of course, the same could be said of helicopters, but their noise signature had already been addressed in the use of the non-coplanar 'scissor' to reduce the noise signature of tail rotor on the Apache and *Havoc*.

Turbofan SABA

While the P.1233-1 is an interesting design from the configuration point of view, the three P.1234 design studies represent the application of various 1980s innovations to the battlefield aircraft, particularly sensors, weapons, instability, fly-by-wire and low observability. The studies that led to the P.1234-1, a dedicated anti-helicopter rather than ground attack type, were based around a cannon in a turret, aimed by the pilot using a helmet-mounted sight. These were used on attack helicopters such as the AH-64A Apache and utilised a series of sensors to detect where the pilot was looking and point the turret in that direction. The draggy chin turrets of the attack helicopters could not be applied to a fast and agile aircraft, so a wide, low-profile turret was required. This more or less dictated the aircraft's configuration, requiring a flat surface unobstructed by pylons and weapons.

The turbofan-powered SABAs such as the P.1234 studies show a variety of configurations (L-R) P.1234-1 with ventral turret for HVMs, P.1234-2 with conventional wing pylons for ASRAAM and P.1234-3 with HVM turret and sensor array.

The concept was intended to produce 'spherical' coverage by combining the 360° training in azimuth of the turret with the 360° roll in the vertical plane of the aircraft. The chosen configuration was a tailless design whose planform comprised a slightly swept leading edge with a forward-swept trailing edge. This produced a very flat and wide blended wing/fuselage with the inner wings merging into a leading-edge root extension (LERX) providing the large flat area for the turret to be installed on the underside. The P.1234-1 was to be powered by a single Turbomeca Adour rated at 5,715 lbf (25.4kN) fed by shallow intakes in the LERX. The P.1234-1 was to have a maximum take-of weight of 12,685 lb (5,753kg) with the ADEN 25 and two ASRAAMs, the turret making up much of the extra weight.

The P.1234-2 was a much more conventional mid-wing design with an unswept tapered planform, twin outward-canted fins and slab tailplanes. The aircraft was fitted with large Harrier-like intakes that fed a single Avco Lycoming ALF-502 turbofan (based on the T55 and used on the BAe 146 airliner) and rated at 7515 lbf (33.4kN). As with the P.1234-1, the -2 was unstable and used FBW controls although manual controls could be used. Loaded with full fuel, six ASRAAMs and an ADEN 25 cannon with 150 rounds, the P.1234-2 was to have a maximum take-off weight of 12,396 lb (5,622kg).

If the P.1238 represented a simple battlefield aircraft, the P.1234-3 sat at the opposite end of the spectrum. The P.1234-3 was a tailless mid-wing delta with a broad fuselage and long,

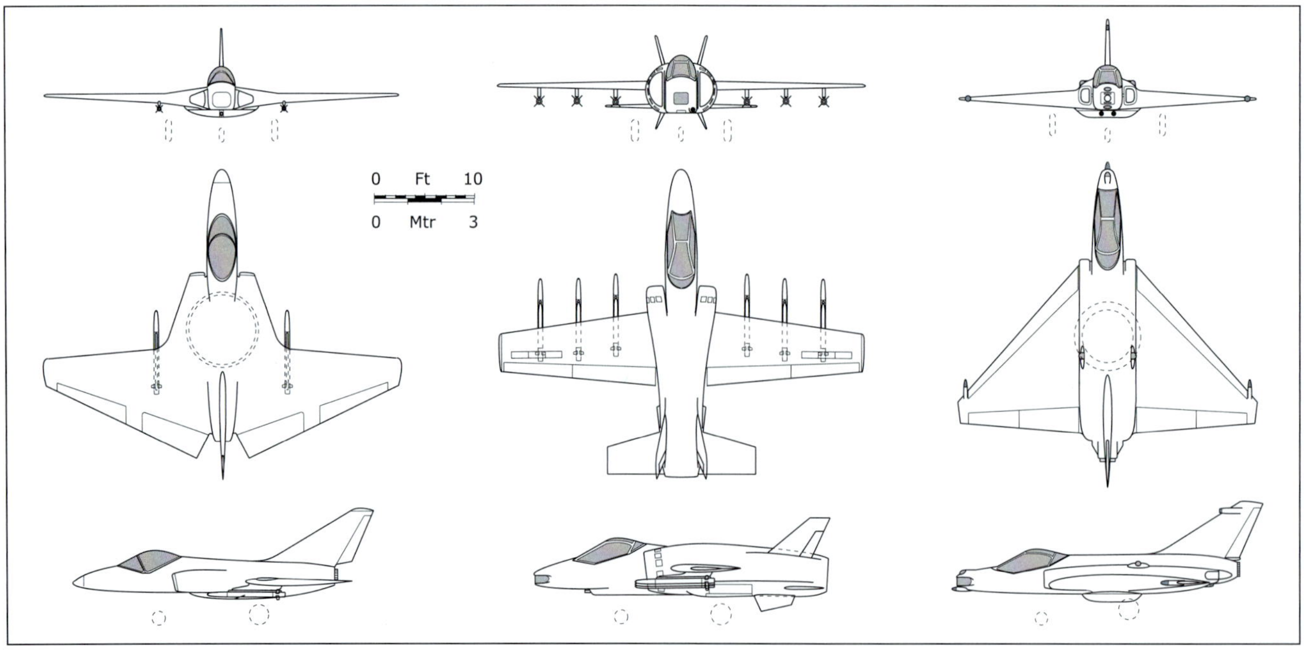

shallow intake trunking for the single Turbomeca Adour turbofan, differing from the P.1234-1 by not being as blended. The -3 weighed in at 12,750 lb (5,782kg) with full fuel and weapons. The P.1234-3's weapon system was a high technology approach to the late 20th Century battlefield where Soviet armoured formations included their own air defences such as the ZSU-23/4 Shilka self-propelled anti-aircraft gun (SPAAG) and mobile SAMs such as SA-9 *Gaskin*. Therefore, in addition to taking on the other aircraft and helicopters, the SABA had to defend itself against anti-aircraft systems.

Most modern aircraft designed to counter other aircraft are fitted with a radar of some description, but by the early 1980s another – passive – system that had been missing from the fighters of the 1960s was returning. Infrared search and track (IRST) systems dated back to before World War Two when Dr RV Jones experimented with infrared detection of aircraft and submarines. Germany fielded IR systems such as the Kielgerät on its Junkers Ju 88G nightfighters. Postwar, they featured on the USAF's interceptors such as the F-101B Voodoo, F-102A Delta Dagger and F-106A Delta Dagger, but as air interception radars improved, IRSTs became less common on interceptors, although they were still in use. They would see a resurgence in the 80s with the new Sukhoi Su-27 *Flanker* and MiG-29 *Fulcrum* seen with IRSTs on their noses ahead of the cockpit.

British avionics and optronics (equipment utilising optical technology) companies such as Thorn-EMI had not been idle and had developed IR equipment for the military. One such system was Air Defence Alerting Device (ADAD) that could detect potential airborne threats up to 5 miles (8km) away and pass this information to the Close Air Defence Weapon System (CADWS) to cue SAM systems such as Starstreak. This technology would find itself in an IRST that ultimately became the PIRATE (Passive Infra-Red Aircraft Tracking Equipment) for the Eurofighter Typhoon.

Flying over a battlefield whilst emitting radio frequency (RF) energy would make any aircraft a target for anti-aircraft systems, so when BAe looked at SABA, passive infra-red was viewed as a potential warning and targeting system. As noted above, the P.1234-3 deployed some of the highest technology with passive sensors distributed at key points on the airframe to provide all-round detection of IR and RF sources. The P.1234-3 also had radar warning receivers at the wing tips and under the nose to detect and locate the fire control radars of

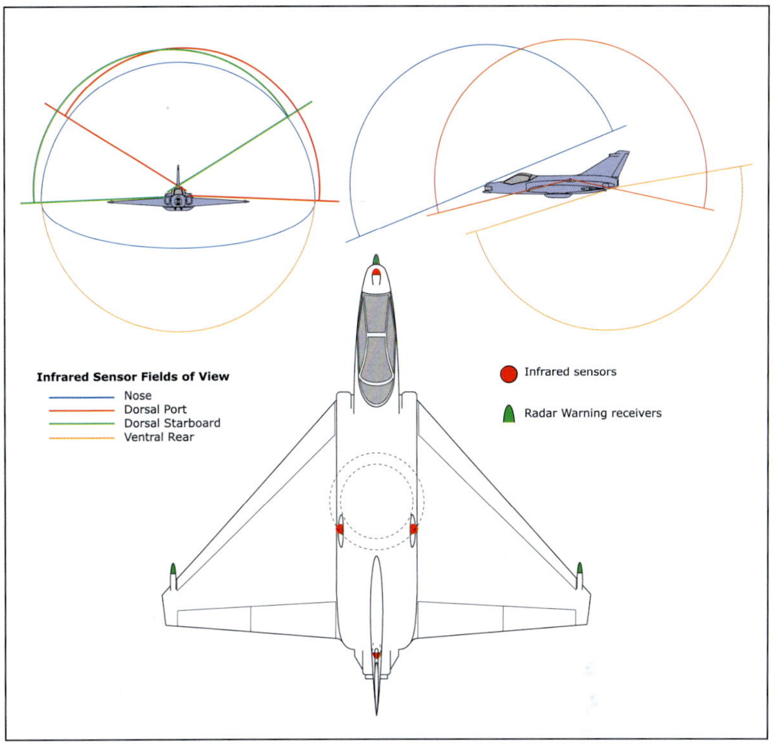

The Deer Hunter. The P.1234-3 used IR and radar warning receivers to cue its weapons. The upper diagram shows the fields of view for the sensors while larger plan view shows the locations of the sensors.

Soviet SPAAGs and SAM systems while IR sensors were installed on the nose, either side of the dorsal spine and under the rear fuselage.

These sensors not only warned the pilot of any threats but by integrating the inputs from the various sensors, onboard systems similar to CADWS could triangulate the position of the emission source, classify it and, if required attack it. The P.1234-3 was, like the other SABA design studies, armed with an ADEN 25 cannon but it was also intended to carry twelve Starstreak HVMs. The Starstreaks were to be mounted in a ventral turret with two launch tubes, with a magazine of six rounds for each tube.

As described above, Starstreak was laser-guided and possessed a velocity on a par with, if not greater than, a cannon shell and as with the turret-mounted cannon on the P.1234-1, combined the turret's azimuthal movement with the aircraft's roll to put the HVM on a heading towards the target. Using a helmet-mounted sight, the pilot placed the 'pipper' on the target and launched the HVM, keeping the pipper on the target for the 2-3 seconds flight time. Alternatively, the pilot used the helmet-mounted sight to select the target which the laser designator in the nose tracked via cues from the IR sensors to keep the target painted during the few seconds of the Starstreak darts' flight. With two launch tubes and rapid reloads, the P.1234-4 could have taken a variety of targets in quick succession, effectively operating in an 'engagement bubble' within which any targets in a five-mile radius could be engaged.

The P1233 and P.1234 studies produced very interesting designs with very advanced control and weapons systems, but as with any type intended for the battlefield, simplicity, ruggedness and flexibility were key aspects, hence the P.1234-2. A second propfan design study was drawn up as the P.1238 which employed a twin-boom configuration with a shoulder-mounted wing and a 4,500shp (3357kW) Lycoming T55 propfan mounted in the rear of the fuselage pod. The P.1238 represented a simpler approach to SABA, with manual controls rather than the fly-by-wire systems (FBW) of the P.1233-1. The P.1238 design was heavier at 11,000 lb (4,989kg) and armed with six ASRAAMs and a fixed 25mm ADEN 25 cannon in the lower port side of the forward fuselage, plus the same range of air-to-ground stores.

Kingston's designers approached increasing the SABA's flexibility by extending the range of weapons available. In the early 1980s, British companies had developed a number of innovative weapons for all three British services, but for the RAF and Army, the emphasis was on anti-armour and anti-runway systems. The resulting P.1239-1 study produced a basic mid-wing, single-engined type that also formed the basis of an unmanned type designated P.1239-5, an Unmanned Fighter Aircraft (UFA) with swept wings and armed with two S225 AAMs.

On the SABA front, the P.1239-3 study incorporated a dorsal bay that could take a variety of weapons and equipment modules, producing what was called the 'Versatile SABA'. One interesting aspect of the Versatile SABA was its shape; angular flat surfaces, inward-canted endplate fins and engine intakes under the wing roots that curved into the single turbofan whose shrouded exhaust was also shielded by the tail fins. These would later become more familiar as a means of reducing the radar and IR signatures of an aircraft and, concurrent with the Kingston studies, Westland helicopters were applying similar techniques to their attack helicopter studies.

The P.1239-3 Versatile SABA and its modular payloads would have allowed the SABA to switch roles rapidly depending on the frontline requirements. For the anti-helicopter role, the P.1239-3 could be fitted with a module for the HVM Starstreak SAM that included two launch tubes and fourteen rounds. This could be lifted out and replaced by a cannon module with a turret-mounted 30mm KCA that could turn 15° either side of the centreline but did not appear to elevate. The KCA cannon is a large piece of kit so elevation would take some heavy equipment. Another module was to carry a turret fitted with a variety of weapons including 7.62mm machine guns, 20mm, 25mm and 30mm cannon such as the STRADEN and ADEN 25 and, being more compact than the KCA, these could be elevated.

Guided weapons and cannon would be expected on any 1980s ground attack aircraft, so with the name 'Versatile SABA' some other weapons and equipment might be expected. In the late Eighties one of NATO's main concerns was the armoured formations of the Group of Soviet Forces in Germany, so any new NATO aircraft should have an anti-tank capability. Action against armour can be direct attack or indirect action. Direct attack by the P.1239-3 would have involved two different weapons carried in the dorsal modules. The first used the VJ.291 anti-armour bomblet or the submunition from the BL.755 cluster bomb, dispensed upwards into a pattern that delivered over an area the size of a football pitch.

The second direct attack weapon was a modified mortar bomb called Medusa. This had started off as a guided 81mm mortar round called MORAT (MORtar Anti-Tank) developed by BAe Dynamics that matched a top-attack warhead with a millimetre wave (MMW) radar seeker. MORAT was to be fired from a standard 81mm mortar to drop onto armoured vehicles, guided by the MMW radar. Marketed as Merlin, the weapon showed promise, but the British MoD lost interest and it became a private venture. An air-launched version called Medusa was proposed, launched from an array of 72 mortar tubes in the P.1239-3's dorsal module.

Indirect action involved the area denial weapons developed for the JP.233 counter air system (See Chapter 5) to channel the armour into choke points where they could be attacked by other means. While the HB.876 minelet was not a dedicated anti-tank weapon, it was designed to damage the heavy plant used to repair runways and could therefore cripple the Soviet support vehicles while denying the use of an area to the enemy. P.1239-3 could carry a mix of HB.876, VJ.291 and BL.755 submunitions to inflict damage over a wide area.

How far SABA could have progressed is a moot point, given the events of the two years following its unveiling. By late 1989 the Cold War was effectively over, and the threat of the Soviet horde diminished. Fast-forward another two years and the submunition weapons that would have armed SABA would be mired in controversy and effectively superseded in the anti-armour role by PGMs – precision guided munitions.

Sharpening the Blunty

The Percival Jet Provost was originally intended as an *ab-initio* trainer for the RAF but became the primary jet trainer of the RAF from 1957 and as with most training aircraft it could also be used for weapons instruction. The logical progression from weapons trainer was light strike and that is exactly what BAC did with the Jet Provost T.5 to produce the T.51 and the T.51 armed version for export but ultimately led to the BAC.167 Strikemaster. The Strikemaster, or 'Blunty' as it was known to the RNZAF, proved a rugged light attack aircraft in service with a number of air forces around the world with the largest user being the Royal Saudi Air Force with 45 Mk.80/80A and the Royal Air Force of Oman with 24. The Omani Strikemasters saw a great deal of action during the Dhofar Rebellion while the Ecuadorian Air Force used them for close air support during the short Cenepa War with Peru in 1995.

One rather interesting design study for a ground attack aircraft based on the Jet Provost was Warton's P.101 'Blitz Fighter'. This study took the Jet Provost T.5 or Strikemaster wing and centre section which was to be mated with a new fuselage, tail unit and propulsion system to produce what was essentially a 'mini-Thunderbolt II'. Like the Fairchild A-10A, the P.101 was built around a large 30mm rotary cannon, in this case a GAU-13/A, which was a lighter, four-barrelled derivative of the General Electric GAU-8/A Avenger. The GAU-13/A used the same PGU-14 armour-piercing incendiary (API) round with a penetrating core of depleted uranium as the GAU-8/A. Although its rate of fire was 2,400 rounds per minute due to pneumatic drive (the GAU-8/A rate of fire was 3,900 rounds per minute thanks to its hydraulic drive) it packed a similar punch with a muzzle velocity of 3,600ft/sec (1,100m/sec).

BAC Strikemaster Mk.81 of the South Yemen Air Force releases two 500lb bombs. Derived from the Jet Provost T.5 trainer, the Strikemaster was widely exported and was extensively used in the close support role in Oman. *Blue Envoy Collection*

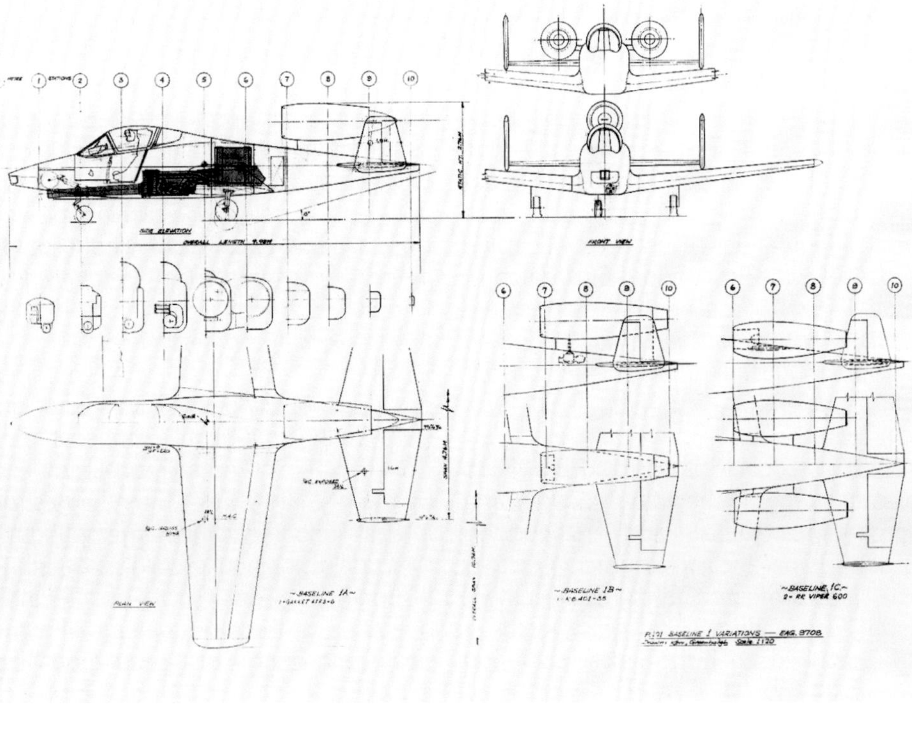

The P.101 Blitz Fighter's Jet Provost heritage is evident, and it does have the look of a mini-Thunderbolt II. The P.101 could be fitted with two Rolls-Royce Viper 600s, one Rolls-Royce RB.401 or a single Garrett ATF3. The P.101 is also fitted with an LRMTS in the nose. *North West Heritage Group.*

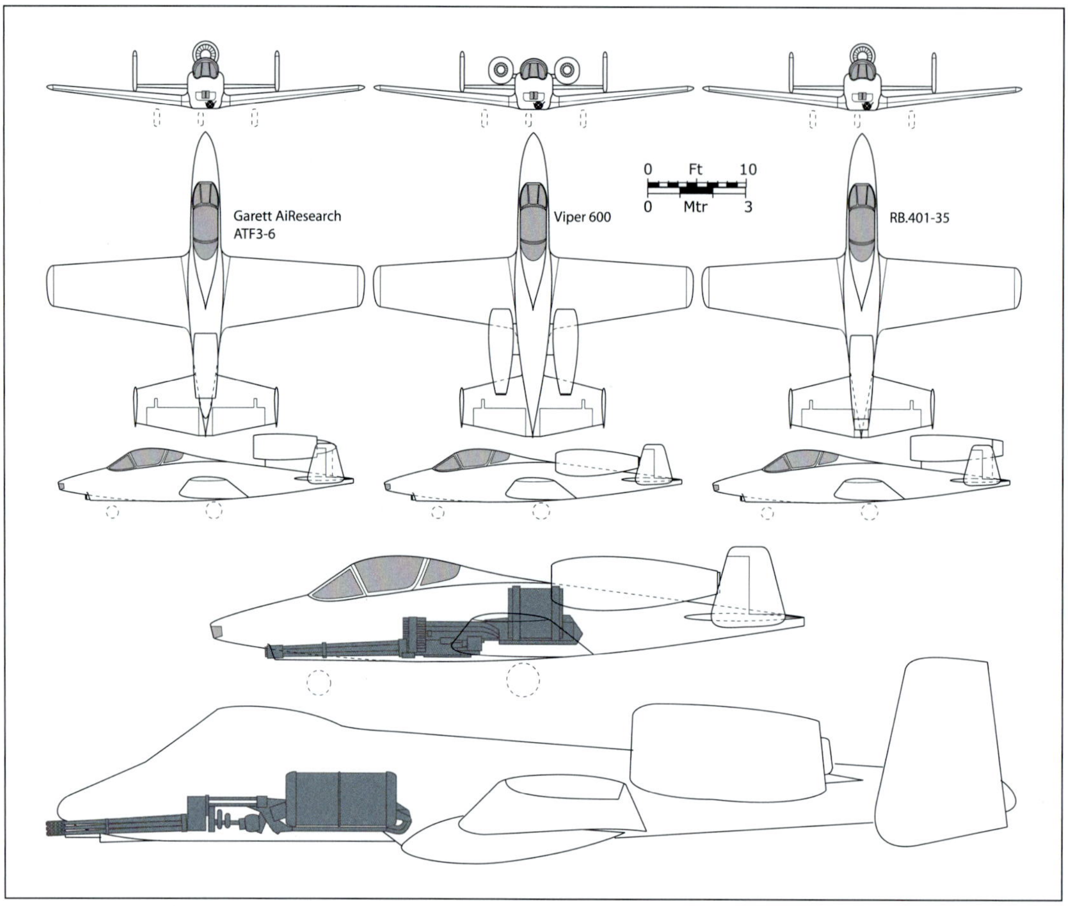

The P.101 used airframe components from the Jet Provost T.5 and was proposed in three variants differing mainly in engine type and number. An A-10A Thunderbolt II and its GAU-8 cannon is also shown alongside a P.101 to gauge the relative size of the gun and airframes.

As noted, the fuselage was pretty much designed around the gun, with the gun offset to port allowing the firing barrel to be as close to the centreline as possible. As a result, like the A-10, the nose wheel was to be offset to starboard. The gun's muzzle was below and around 3ft (0.9m) aft of the nose, which was fitted with a laser ranger and marked target seeker (LRMTS). Other similarities with the Thunderbolt II included endplate empennage and dorsal-mounted engines. Three baseline variations on the design were proposed by Warton and these differed mainly in their engine type and configuration. Baseline 1A was fitted with a pair of Rolls-Royce Viper 600, rated at 4,000 lbf (17.8kN), Baseline 1B was powered by a single Garrett AiResearch ATF3-6, rated at 5,440 lbf (24.2kN) and Baseline 1C was fitted with a single RB.401-35 rated at 5,540 lbf (24.6kN).

The Blitz Fighter could have provided a cheap and plentiful type in the MiniCAS vein and could probably carry BL.755 and SNEB pods on wing pylons as per the Strikemaster. Whether the P.101 was armoured to the same extent as the A-10A is unknown, but this would no doubt be required given the similar operating environment.

Realistically a completely new close support aircraft in the late 1970s/early 1980s was not feasible while a major ground attack type, AST.396, was being contemplated, the funds were just not available for a USAF-style force structure. However, to address the perceived lack of ground attack aircraft in RAFG, the Air Staff did propose a solution that used the weapons training capability of the Hawk. Prior to acquiring their secondary interceptor role in 1983, up to 36 Hawk T.1s from the RAF's Tactical Weapons Units and Operational Conversion Units at RAF Chivenor and RAF Brawdy were considered for the close support role. These were to be deployed in times of tension to RAF Germany, fitted with four BL.755 and their 30mm ADEN cannon and put to work in the battlefield interdiction role. Hawks have since used with this same weapons load, notably by the Air Force of Zimbabwe (AFZ) during its 1998 intervention in the Second Congo War. One notable operation conducted by the AFZ's Hawk 60s was the destruction of a rebel armoured column attempting to occupy Kinshasa, the capital of the Democratic Republic of Congo. This was the classic road interdiction operation of the type that 2ATAF would have been conducting had the Cold War turned hot in Europe.

HS Hawk XX191 of 1 Tactical Weapons Unit banks away from the camera to show off its wrap-around camouflage and a weapons load of Matra 155 (SNEB) pod, 30mm ADEN cannon and light stores (practice bomb) carrier. These aircraft would have been sent to West Germany in a war situation. *Blue Envoy Collection*

The types described above were designed for specific roles, such as close air support and the usual mantra goes that you need the right tool for the job, which is what dedicated designs are. The RAF had a history of using superannuated fighters for ground attack, of which some were successful – Typhoon and Hunter – and some were not – Swift. Despite not being provided with bespoke equipment, the RAF put the equipment it did receive to excellent use.

Training aircraft have been armed from the origin of air fighting. Hawk demonstrator G-HAWK/ZA101 is shown here with 500 lb and 250 lb (227kg and 114kg) low-drag bombs and centreline ADEN cannon. Prior to being tasked with a secondary air defence role in 1983 the Tactical Weapons Units were to be sent to West Germany and armed with BL.755 cluster bombs to attack Warsaw Pact armour. *Blue Envoy Collection*

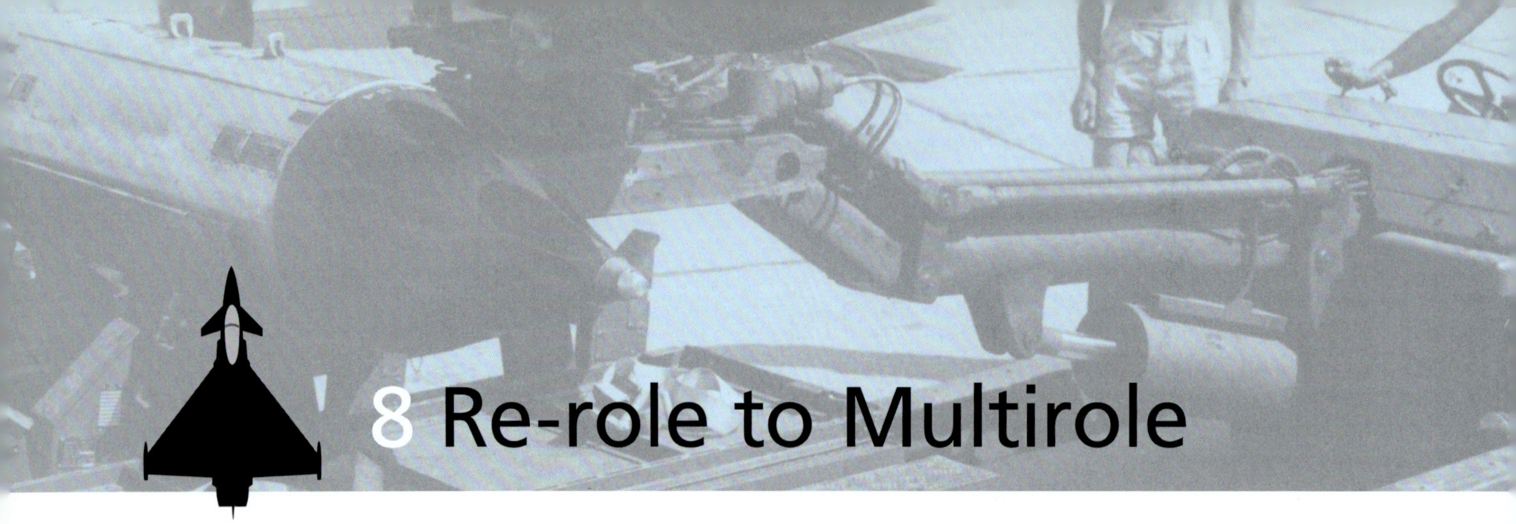

8 Re-role to Multirole

'Unless we abandon almost all our current commitments outside Europe, we shall need an aircraft of the TSR.2/F-111A class for the strike/reconnaissance role in the 1970s and no alternative aircraft will suffice.' Denis Healey, 31 March 1965

British military aircraft were usually specified to fill a role and only later in their service career did they take on new roles with interceptors becoming dive bombers and tankbusters in World War Two and ground attack aircraft in the Cold War. Some types, having an inherent flexibility, fared better than others and the success of these led to types designed for flexibility from the drawing board.

Is there such a thing as a ground-attack aircraft? Republic A-10A Thunderbolt? Sukhoi Su-25 *Frogfoot*? As shown in Chapter 2, the RAF only acquired one dedicated ground-attack aircraft, the Vultee Vengeance, during World War Two and although the term 'multirole' could be applied to RAF fighters in the ground attack role, the term was not adopted until the 1970s. Certainly there had been multirole aircraft during WW2, the Mosquito for example, but the bomber, reconnaissance, maritime strike and fighter bomber versions differed whereas a true multirole fighter such as the Typhoon can switch roles with a change of stores and mission mode. Typhoon could be described as a swing-role fighter as it can use its air-to-air capability on ground-attack missions.

The demarcation between fighters (as in interceptors) and fighter-bombers only appeared in the late 1940s and early 1950s, specifically in the Century Series fighters, when air interception radars and air-to-air missiles were large and required a dedicated platform. Those aircraft also lacked that most useful of weapons for ground attack, the gun, as the future of fighter weaponry was the guided missile. Oddly enough the only US interceptor with a gun, the Lockheed F-104 Starfighter, was not adopted by the USAF as an interceptor but

Tornado GR.4 ZG750 from XV(R) Sqn, RAF Lossiemouth, is seen in its element – at low level in North Wales. *Peter Edwards*

adopted by the Luftwaffe as a ground-attack type although it was essentially only intended to deliver nuclear weapons. A further oddity in the Century Series was the Republic F-105 Thunderchief, a nuclear strike aircraft with a gun, that in the Vietnam War gained many air-to-air kills with its guns.

In Britain, in the immediate postwar period the de Havilland Venom FB.1, as the Fighter Bomber designation suggests, was developed as a ground attack aircraft to replace the DH Vampire but soon became an interceptor/all-weather fighter. Gloster's Javelin was an all-weather fighter with guns and missiles which, despite proposals to use it as a strike aircraft with nuclear weapons, whistled away its career as an all-weather fighter. English Electric's Lightning, that out-and-out scramble-off-the-deck interceptor, began as a missile-only type, but soon acquired ADEN cannon, for use against the *Bears*, then lost them, only to regain them. Of course, adding a gun doesn't make an interceptor a ground attack type, but as the Shackleton proved in Aden, have gun, will strafe. In the 1980s the RAF's close support types, Harrier and Jaguar, gained air-to-air missiles as did most on NATO's 'fast movers', in the face of improving Soviet fighter forces in eastern Europe, but an air-to-air missile does not a fighter make.

Thereafter the RAF's close air support types, until the Harrier, were derived from interceptors, or types intended as interceptors. Some were by accident, some due to being unsuitable for the interceptor role or just a hand-me-down from the interceptor squadrons. Accident would be the Whirlwind, unsuitable would be the Typhoon and hand-me-down would be the Hurricane, although none of these could be described as lacking in either their intended or ultimate roles. The Whirlwind never got a chance at its intended role as a bomber interceptor.

Postwar, the Gloster Meteor and de Havilland's Vampire and Venom became ground attack types while the Hunter, superb in just about every role, was particularly favoured for ground attack in the RAF and other air arms. Gloster developed the Ground Attack Fighter, a version of the Meteor F.8, as the Reaper with strengthened wings to carry four 1,000lb (454kg) bombs or up to 24 3in RP, plus tip tanks. One Reaper, G-7-1, was built as a demonstrator and was flown in a spectacular display by Gloster test pilot Squadron Leader Janusz Zurakowski in the 1951 SBAC show at Farnborough.

One type that epitomised the move from interceptor to ground-attack is the Hunter. Developed as the Hawker P.1067 to meet fighter specification F.43/46 for a gas turbine-powered interceptor, which was itself superseded by F.3/48, what became the Hunter was intended to intercept Soviet Tupolev Tu-4 *Bull* bombers. As development progressed the P.1067's original armament of four 20mm Hispano cannon was replaced with four of the new 30mm ADEN cannon, with 150 rounds per gun, all fitted in a removable gun pack. Interestingly, the barrels of the ADENs remained fixed in the fuselage with the cannon mechanism and ammunition boxes were removed as a single unit.

From its introduction to RAF service in 1954 the Hunter F.1 and subsequent interceptor versions enjoyed success as a Fighter Command interceptor, with the ultimate fighter version being the F.6. Despite a successful career as a fighter, the pace of aircraft development overtook it, with supersonic types such as the Lightning entering service from December 1959. This saw the Hunter F.6 rendered more or less redundant in its original role, retired by 1963, but made it available for a role that needed a more capable aircraft – ground attack. A total of 128 Hunter F.6 were converted to FGA.9 standard with brake parachute, wing strengthening to allow the carriage of bombs and 230 gallon (litre) drop tanks.

Hawker also drew up a proposal for a tactical nuclear strike Hunter. Based on the F.6 this variant was to carry a '2,000lb Target Marker', the MoA euphemism for the Red Beard, designated Bomb, Aircraft, HE, 2,000lb, Mk.1, No.2. The weapon would be carried under the port wing, with a 230 Gallon (1045 litre) drop tank on the starboard wing. Range could be further increased by fitting a 100 gallon (454 litre) drop tank under each wing.

Prior to the adoption of Flexible Response, the tactical nuclear bomb on a fighter bomber was the weapon of choice on both sides of the Iron Curtain. This Hawker study shows a Hunter F.6 carrying a Red Beard bomb. *Brooklands Museum*

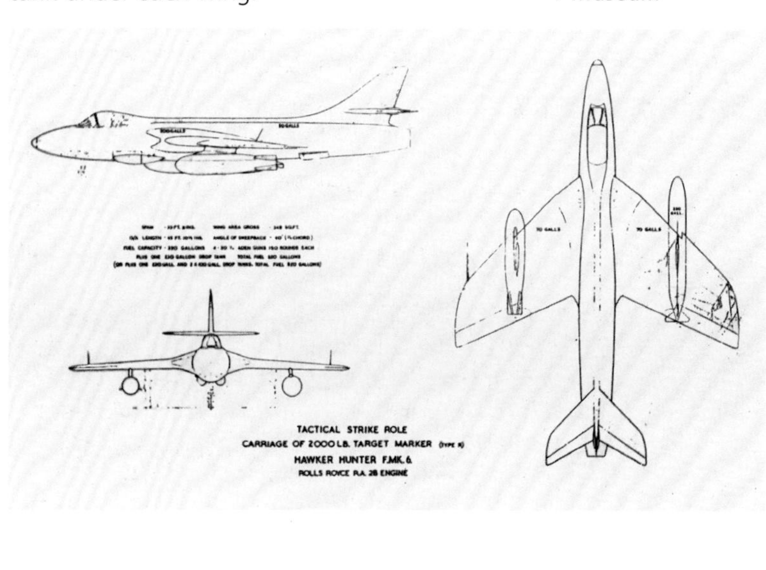

This Hawker Hunter, XG168, is an FR.10. Externally similar to the FGA.9, it carried three cameras and was fitted with extra armour to protect the pilot from small-arms fire at low altitude. *Via Tony Buttler*

Hunter FGA.9s went to war, cold and hot, around the world with most of the action for RAF squadrons being in Aden in 1964 and in the Indonesian Confrontation from 1963-66. Other air arms used their ground attack Hunters in action including the Iraqi Air Force's F.59s during the Six Day War of 1967 and subsequent War of Attrition. The Indian Air Force used its Hunter F.56s in the fighter role against Chinese air forces in 1962 and Pakistan's F-86 Sabres and F-104 Starfighters in 1971. Probably the heaviest user of the Hunter was the Rhodesian Air Force (RhAF), using their Hunter FGA.9s in the strike and ground support roles. The Hunter came full-circle and back to its fighter roots when the Republic of Singapore Air Force fitted its Hunter FGA.74s with additional outboard pylons for AIM-9 Sidewinder AAMs.

Lightning F.53 and PL1

The initial Lightning F.1 and F.2s were fitted with two 30mm ADEN cannon, but these were removed on the F.3. The Lightning F.6 acquired a removable gun pack carrying two ADEN in the forward portion of the ventral fuel tank. To improve the Lightning's export potential (at least exports to Saudi Arabia) a ground attack capability was developed, with a F.3A acting as the trials aircraft, making its first flight as a F.53 in October 1966. The Lightning F.53 could carry weapons on underwing pylons, one each wing, outboard of the wheel wells. These included a single 1,000 lb (454kg) bomb or two SNEB pods. The overwing pylons, normally used for fuel tanks, could carry Type 155 SNEB pods or two Matra JL100 combined SNEB/fuel pod with 18 SNEB 68mm (2.7in) rockets in the front section and 50 gallons (227 litres) of fuel in the rear. Another somewhat ambitious store for the overwing pylon was the 1,000 lb (454kg) retarded bomb. This had to be delivered in a toss manoeuvre, with an explosive ejection system on the pylon. Trials showed that this was a less than practical proposition, so overwing bomb carriage was discarded. With a full load of eight Type 155 SNEB pods plus another 44 2in (5cm) rockets in retractable trays, the F.53 could unleash up to 188 rockets on a ground target.

The F.53 could certainly carry out the ground attack role with bombs and rockets, and Saudi Arabia operated its Lightnings against South Yemen forces from late 1969 until mid-1970, with one Lightning being lost to ground fire. BAC at Warton in January 1961 embarked on a design study to increase the 'range and versatility' of the Lightning, specifically in the ground attack and reconnaissance roles, but also in the interception role.

The resulting PL1 study was based on the two-seat Lightning T.5, modified by adding a cambered leading edge to the wings, overwing fuel tanks, twin main wheels, wingtip stores carriage and new ventral packs. These packs could either be 'long' or 'short' and comprise extra fuel tanks and interchangeable weapons

The Lightning, that out-and-out interceptor, was festooned with rockets and bombs for the ground attack role. This Kuwaiti Lightning F.53 (with dual markings G-AXEE/512) carries four Matra JL100 combined fuel tank/rocket pods on the overwing pylons. The Microcell 2in RP tray under the forward fuselage is also fitted in lieu of the Red Top/Firestreak missile pack. *RA Scholefield*

A mock-up of the BAC PL1 short ventral pack was built and installed on F.3A XN735, seen here with a Bullpup air-to-surface missile on the weapons pack pylon. This may also have been proposed to the RAF as the P.34. *North West Heritage Group*

pallets. The fairings were not unlike extensions of the Lightning's ventral fuel tank (which on the F.6 would also carry a pair of 30mm ADENs in the forward section) although in the case of the PL1, known to Warton as the P.33, the fore and aft sections held fuel. The central section held the weapons pallets similar, but not identical, to those on the Lightning F.1 and F.2, and more fuel if required. Further weapons could be carried on underwing and wingtip pylons, with the underwing pylons ultimately appearing on the F.53.

Wingtip pylons had been investigated as part of the P.8 studies for Specification F.155 and a part of the P.23 design study towards carrying the Douglas AIR-2 Genie, which the RAF designated the RP.3. Whether this was deliberate to confuse the Genie with the 3in RP is not known but is plausible. Another British designation applied to the Genie is Store F, possibly related to US nuclear weapons supplied under the Project E plan. Aside from the usual British flair for secrecy when it came to weapons of any type, the reason for the apparent subterfuge in naming the Genie was that it was an American weapon fitted with a US warhead, the 1.5kT W25. Ultimately the Genie/RP.3/Store F was not acquired for reasons that included a British preference for British rather than American explosive in nuclear weapons, British fissile material was in short supply and earmarked for the deterrent and, of course, lack of funds.

On the PL1, the RP.3 was to be carried on a bespoke weapons pallet that also held 104 gallons (473 litres) of fuel. Other pallets for the ground attack role allowed carriage of a pair of Bullpup air-to-surface missiles or three Mk.N1 1,000 lb (454kg) bombs. The official designation was MC, 1000 LB, MK N1 and the Mk.N1 was a low-drag bomb not unlike the American Mk.82 intended for carriage by high-performance naval aircraft such as the Blackburn Buccaneer.

As described above, the PL1 could be fitted with 'long' and 'short' ventral packs depending on the mission requirements. The forward and rear sections were faired into the Lightning airframe to keep the design aerodynamically clean. The 'long' pack stretched almost the full length of the Lightning PL1 from a point below the cockpit to the tailplanes and was split into five sections. The forward pack held 150 gallons (682 litres) of fuel, the second bay carried a Doppler navigator and 'fixed assessment cameras' plus more fuel or an engine hatch tank holding 206 gallons (936 litres) of fuel, The fourth section was the armament section carrying, for ground attack, the Mk.N1 bombs or Bullpup missiles plus 104 gallons (473 litres) or a ferry tank holding 195 gallons (886 litres) of fuel.

The 'short' ventral pack extended from just aft of the wing root leading edge to the same point on the rear fuselage as the 'long' pack. In place of the forward fuel tank, a flush-fitting package carrying the Doppler navigator and

The BAC PL1 with the short ventral pack. Consideration was given to fitting wingtip stores and, to handle the increased weight, a new two-wheel main undercarriage with an underwing blister fairing to accommodate the wider main undercarriage. *North West Heritage Group*

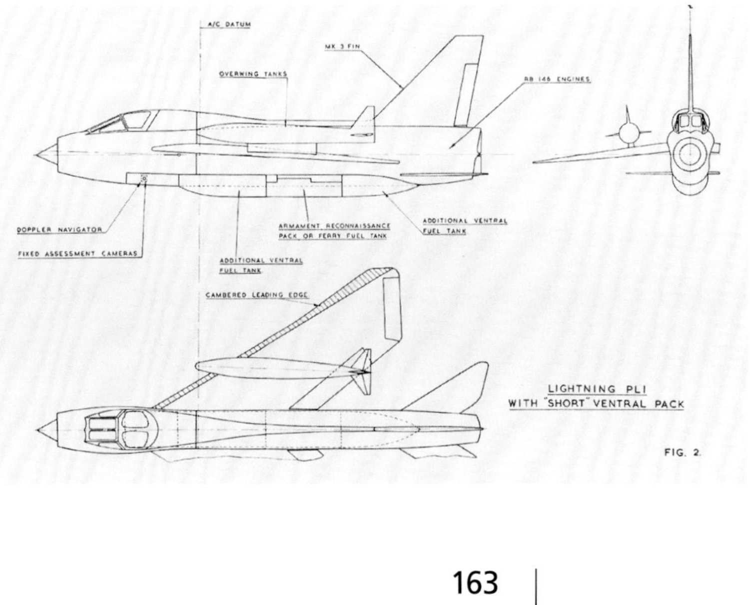

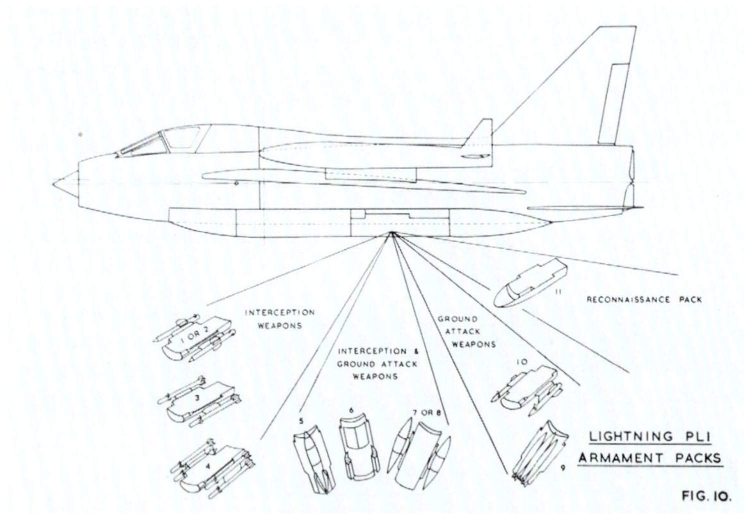

BAC at Warton proposed the PL1 multirole variant of the Lightning interceptor. This was based on the T.5 trainer, fitted with RB.146 engines, a new cambered leading edge and the fin from the F.3. The most obvious modification was the ventral pack containing fuel, weapons or reconnaissance equipment. This was available in short and long versions, with the long shown here. *North West Heritage Group.*

cameras was installed in the fuselage bay. The engine hatch tank was faired-in and as a result, only held 172 gallons (782 litres) of fuel while the armament pack and rear ventral tanks were the same as the 'long' pack.

The fuel in the ventral pack added to the 840 gallons (3,819 litres) in the wing tanks and 270 gallons (1,227 litres) in each of the over-wing tanks. All this extra fuel, plus underwing weapons if carried would have increased the all-up weight of the PL1 to such an extent that the undercarriage's rating would have been exceeded, not just the weight limit but the braking capacity. The answer was to fit a twin-wheel main undercarriage, but since the Lightning wing was rather thin (as were the original wheels) the new undercarriage would not fit. Since adding depth to the wing was not possible, an aerodynamic fairing 10in (25cm) deep was added to accommodate the new undercarriage.

Of interest, from the point of view of the Lightning's subsequent career, is the proposal to fit the AIM-9 Sidewinder to the PL1. The Sidewinder was listed as a weapon for the interceptor role and the armament pack could carry two or four missiles. The strange aspect of this is the positioning of the missiles, quite far back on the fuselage. While this might have limited the acquisition of the target by the missile's seeker, Sidewinders lock on before launch, this may not have posed a problem for the early versions that would have required the Lightning to tailchase the target for a clear view of its jet pipe.

While in no means a fighter, the English Electric Canberra was, like the Mosquito it was to replace, employed in the ground attack role. Although not intended to mix it with the MiGs over the FEBA and deliver BL.755s on tank formations, the Canberra did have an important role in the RAF's Cold War as an intruder. The first Canberra intruders were the B(I).6 that carried a cannon pack in the bomb bay and were fitted with a hard point under each wing. The B(I).6 was fitted with the LABS (low altitude bombing system) that allowed loft (also known as toss) delivery of nuclear weapons such as American Mk.7, provided under Project E. The B(I).6 used the basic Canberra B.6 airframe, but after 22 were converted, the B(I).8 entered production, with 72 being produced, including 17 exported to New Zealand and South Africa. The B(I).8 shared the B(I).6 weapons systems but was fitted with a new forward fuselage with a 'fighter-style' canopy for the pilot.

Canberra B(I).8s were declared operational for the nuclear strike role in late 1959, but as a conventional interdiction type it could be fitted with bombs in the forward portion of the bomb bay and on the wing pylons or carry SNEB pods under the wings. Of course, the four Hispano 20mm cannon were ideal for strafing. The Canberras were replaced in the nuclear strike and interdiction roles by the Tornado GR.1, one multi-role aircraft replacing another.

This page: While it could carry seven BL.755 at low level, the Phantom FGR.2 was more at home as an interceptor putting its radar, Sparrow and Sidewinders to better use. Phantom XV499 of No 41 Sqn carries its full warload. In the interceptor role it would have substituted the bombs for drop tanks and a SUU-23/A cannon pod. *Terry Panopalis Collection*

The Jaguar

The story of the Harrier and Jaguar are, and have been, subjects worthy of books in their own right. Both types have their origins in the fallout for the 1965 cancellations of TSR.2, P.1154 and later, F-111K and AFVG. The RAF was intending to acquire a strike/trainer aircraft as a lead-in to the F-111K/AFVG fleet and the subsonic Breguet Br.121 was, in the era of Anglo-French collaborative projects, deemed a feasible basis for the RAF's advanced trainer. On the cancellation of the F-111K and AFVG, the RAF required a tactical strike aircraft capable of close support and delivery of nuclear weapons. The RAF wanted a supersonic type so powered their version of what would become Jaguar with the reheated Rolls-Royce/Turbomeca RB.172 Adour turbofan and fit advanced targeting and navigation systems. In short, the aircraft for the RAF would be completely different from the original Breguet Br.121.

The Jaguar S, known as the GR.1 to the RAF was fitted with the NAVWASS (Navigation And Weapons Aiming Sub-System) and, its most visible difference from French variants, the Ferranti LRMTS (Laser Ranger and Marked Target Seeker) giving the GR.1 a glazed chisel nose. The Jaguar entered RAF squadron service in 1974 and steadily replaced the Phantom FGR.2 in the ground attack and reconnaissance role. As shown by Hawker Siddeley's Brough Division during the later AST.396 studies, the Phantom was designed as a carrier-borne interceptor and, although capable, was never at its best in the ground attack role. The Jaguar on the other hand was in its element in low-level attack and its state-of-the-art navigation and attack systems, it proved adept at ground-attack with updates to its avionics and weapons systems maintaining its capability. The Jaguar underwent numerous upgrades starting with the GR.1A that improved the NAVWASS (further improved by the FIN1064 system) and ECM systems while adding the capability to use the AIM-9 Sidewinder. Ten Jaguar GR.1s were upgraded to carry the GEC-Marconi TIALD (Thermal Imager and Laser Designator) to become the GR.1B, providing designation for Paveway LGBs. From 1996 the Jaguar fleet was given significant avionics update in the Jaguar 96 programme to become the GR.3 and the GR.1Bs were upgraded to Jaguar 97 standard, becoming GR.3B.

One role performed by Jaguars at RAF Brüggen in West Germany was tactical nuclear strike with the WE.177A while those based at RAF Laarbruch replaced the Phantoms, and their P391 pods, in the tactical reconnaissance role using the EMI reconnaissance pod. This pod was replaced by the Vicon 18-601 electro-optical pod in the 1990s.

The Jaguars were retired at the end of 2007, not long after that last Jaguar GR.3A had been returned to service after the major upgrade that modernised the cockpit with a new HUD, night vision goggles-compatible displays, GPS and TERPROM (Terrain Profile Matching) navigation systems and new electro-optical reconnaissance pods. At the time of its retirement the Jaguar was a state-of-the-art strike aircraft just as it had been on its service entry 33 years earlier. The Jaguar formed the basis of many design studies over the years, many of which were related to AST.396, which is covered in Chapter 9.

Opposite, bottom: Canberra B(I).8s XM278 and WT346 of No 14 Sqn display their weapons in a hangar at RAF Wildenrath. The large item under the nose is a gun pack with four 20mm Hispano cannon, under the wing are rockers and 1,000 lb General Purpose bombs. The large light-coloured store with fins on the left is a Mk.7 nuclear weapon. These were supplied to the RAF under Project E. *Terry PanopalisCollection*

Free to go back to what it did best, Phantom FGR.2 XV486 flies in formation with its replacement, Jaguar GR.1 XX762, both of No 14 Sqn during the transfer of types in 1975. *Blue Envoy Collection*

Jaguar GR.1 XZ384 of No 20 Sqn shows its carrying capacity with eight 1,000lb (454kg) General Purpose bombs. This would rarely be the case as in a war situation the Jaguar would carry a Phimat chaff dispenser and AN/ALQ-101 jammer pod on the outboard pylons. *Terry Panopalis Collection*

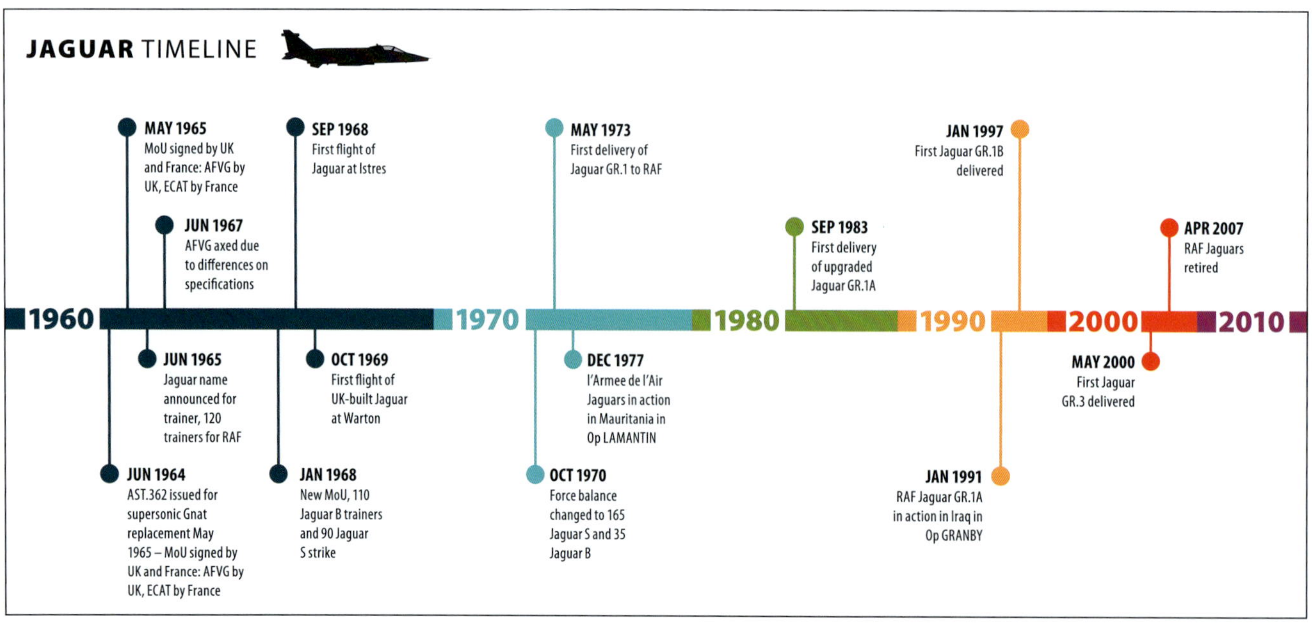

The Harrier

The aircraft that entered service with No 1 Squadron in 1969 was not originally intended as an RAF ground attack aircraft. In fact, it wasn't even supposed to be a service aircraft, merely a technology demonstrator and then a trials aircraft. The service type was to be the P.1154, a supersonic STOVL type to deliver nuclear weapons on the Warsaw Pact armoured formations and airfields in eastern Europe.

The Harrier took advantage of Bristol Engines' work on a vectored thrust engine, the Pegasus, which in turn was derived from components of the existing Olympus and Orpheus turbojets. The Pegasus, a turbofan, split the mass flow from the bypass and core to produce a 'four-poster' lift engine whereby the (cool) bypass flow exited from two nozzles near the front, one on each side of the engine while the core exited to the rear through a bifurcated jet pipe, directed to nozzles on each side. Aside from that basic innovation, the other key component was swivelling nozzles that allowed the mass flow, and thus the thrust, to be directed or vectored and this became known as vectored thrust.

Hawker's Senior Project Engineer Ralph Hooper drew up an aircraft to use the Pegasus and designated as the P.1127 and its basic configuration set the style for the entire Harrier series. The P.1127 made its first (free) hovering flight in November 1960 and first wing-borne flight three months later in February 1961. As it stood, the P.1127, a subsonic jet with little useful payload, was of little interest to the UK military but Hawker believed that with development, especially increasing the power of the engines, the P.1127 had potential.

This changed when the USA and West Germany expressed an interest in the P.1127 and thus the British Government reached an agreement to split the cost of a nine-aircraft trials programme. The nine Kestrel FGA.1s formed the basis of the Tripartite Evaluation Squadron at RAF West Raynham where the methods of operating such an aircraft were developed. These trials included operations from rough strips and aircraft carriers.

The ultimate aim for the STOVL effort was a supersonic strike aircraft that would not rely on two miles of concrete, but a combination of cost, technical difficulty, withdrawal of French co-operation and adoption of Flexible Response saw off the P.1154 and associated NATO Basic Military Requirement (NBMR)-3. In the light of this the RAF issued ASR.384, covering a requirement for a V/STOL ground attack aircraft. Hawker and Bristol Engines produced a redesigned P.1127 that became known as the P.1127(RAF) which in turn became the Harrier GR.1 and entered service on 1 April 1969.

The Harrier's career is well documented, evolving from the GR.1, upgraded to GR.3 with more powerful Pegasus 11, improved targeting and defensive countermeasures systems. The GR.5 was a powerful and capable type based on the McDonnell Douglas AV-8B Harrier II (the original Harrier had been the AV-8A for the US Marine Corps) and employed new engines, composite structures, an additional pylon forward of the outrigger wheel fairing plus UK-specific systems.

The Harrier GR.5 entered service in December 1989 but was under constant development

This trials Harrier GR.1 is carrying the maximum anti-armour load-out from the early 1970s, comprising five BL.755. In reality the Harrier GR.1 would not have sufficient range to use them. *Terry Panopalis Collection*

High over the mountains of Afghanistan, Harrier GR.9 ZG505 of No 4 Sqn, banks away to show its stores including two Paveway IV LGBs, two LAU-5003 rocket pods (each with 19 CRV7 rockets), Thales Digital Joint Reconnaissance Pod and a Sniper designator pod. *MoD/Open Government Licence*

to produce the GR.5A aimed at the interdictor role. Harrier GR.7s entered service in August 1990 and included night capability with a Forward-Looking Infra-Red (FLIR) in the nose and a cockpit compatible with night vision goggles. The Harrier GR.9, an upgrade of the GR.7, built on experience in the Balkans and included improved communications, avionics and weapons systems including the Sniper targeting pod and AGM-65 Maverick missile. The Sniper was adopted due to the TIALD pod's FLIR lacking the resolution for operations in urban areas as it could not distinguish between individual insurgents and coalition troops. The GR.9 made its first flight in May 2003 and entered service in September 2006.Further weapons trials included integration with the Brimstone, which was well underway when the RAF Harrier force was prematurely retired in 2011.

One interesting aspect of the Harrier II variants in RAF service is that once the Harrier GR.7 entered service in 1990, the RAF finally had the capability it had originally specified for AST.396 in 1971. The Harrier-based design studies towards AST.396 are examined in Chapter 9.

The Eagle

The name alone would have inspired awe; Eagle GR.1. Sleek, fast, able to carry a pair, if not four, WE.177B or C into deepest eastern Europe, it is better known as TSR.2. Put any number of British military aviation enthusiasts in a room (preferably in a pub) or a Welsh mountainside and two things invariably happen: The conversation turns to TSR.2 and that conversation turns into a heated agreement on two matters. The first is that TSR.2 was wonderful and

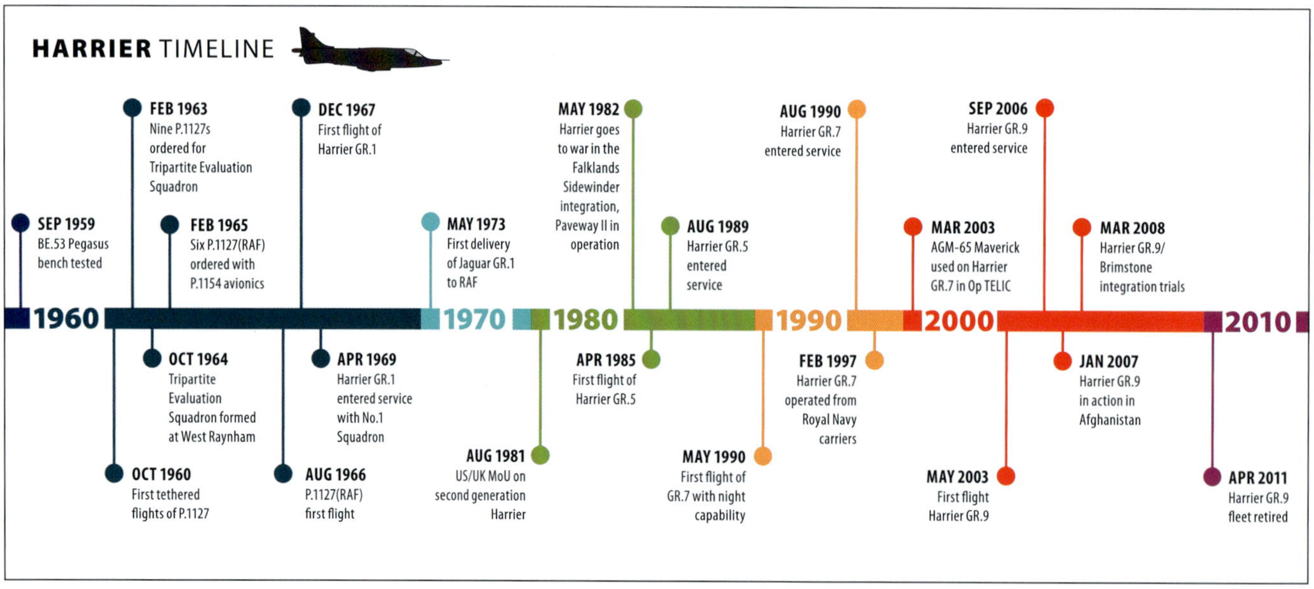

the second is that Messrs Wilson, Healey and Callaghan should have been tried as enemies of the aerospace industry, if not the people. Yes, it becomes animated and of course 'The Americans' also figure in the argument. Oddly enough many of the great defenders of the TSR.2 also, quite bafflingly, make the case for the American F-15 or F-14 rather than the Tornado ADV, but that is addressed in *Battle Flight*.

More than enough has been written on TSR.2, much of it hagiographic, so look elsewhere for your favoured spin on the story. The substance of that story is that the aircraft was designed for a different kind of war in a different kind of world. The war was all-out nuclear and the world was one where Britain had an empire east of Suez. Both were the case when GOR.339 was issued in March 1957, but within a decade, half a decade in fact, the situation had changed to one of stemming the Soviet horde with SNEB and bombs in West Germany for as long as possible before loading the WE.177s.

Intended as a Canberra replacement, TSR.2 followed the trend set in the 1950s whereby aircraft became faster, bigger and more complex with the associated increase in cost. The Australians noted that TSR.2 was an expensive way to deliver iron bombs, something not lost on HMG, who cancelled the TSR.2 in April 1965.

Would TSR.2 have been a useful type for the RAF? Impossible to say given that many aircraft have been touted as the next big thing and failed to deliver when circumstances changed. Could it, like the F-105 Thud, have made the transition from nuclear strike to tactical support? Would it have suffered the same fate as the Thunderchief in Vietnam, littering *Adler Grat*, an East German version of Thud Ridge or ultimately be as successful as the F-111. We will never know.

BAC TSR.2 XR219 opens its speed brakes on a test flight high above the clouds. The Australian Air Staff described it as an expensive means of delivering high explosive. By the time it entered service, that would have been the TSR.2's main role: low altitude, long-range interdiction.

Sunset on TSR.2. No-one will ever know how TSR.2 would have fared in service as the world, and the roles it was designed for, had disappeared by the time it flew. *Both: North West Heritage Group*

After the Eagle

While ostensibly a replacement for the cancelled TSR.2, the General Dynamics F-111K was tailored towards the 'East of Suez' theatre, particularly the anti-shipping role armed with the AJ.168 Martel TV-guided air-to-surface missile (ASM). With the withdrawal from Empire and the commitment to north west Europe, the F-111K and its maritime strike role was less relevant but the AFVG was. While the F-111 struggled in its early operations during Combat Lancer, Operation Linebacker II showed the F-111's potential and it would go from strength to strength with the USAF as a deep strike aircraft and strategic bomber as well as a strike and reconnaissance type with the RAAF. Did the RAF miss out? Probably not, as the RAF's European focus from 1970 saw the adoption of interdiction and strike missions against airfields, nuclear sites and assembly areas the Warsaw Pact's rear in Eastern Europe.

The Peculiar F-111K

The United Kingdom's long relationship with the General Dynamics (GD) F-111 started with a rather intriguing visit in December 1964 to GD's Fort Worth plant by a 20-strong RAF technical team headed by the Deputy Chief of the Air Staff (DCAS) Air Marshal Sir Christopher Hartley. The purpose of the visit was to investigate the possibility of making the F-111 a joint US/UK project.

The following April, Denis Healey announced that the TSR.2 would be cancelled and that an option had been taken on ten F-111As, to be procured at a considerable cost saving, quoted as being around half that of the TSR.2. The Air Staff Requirement for TSR.2, ASR.343 Issue 2, was effectively rewritten around the F-111A as Issue 3 and in June 1965 General Dynamics at Fort Worth received a visit by a four-man team headed by Minister of Aviation Roy Jenkins who informed the Americans that 'Britain's chances of buying F-111s would be better if we could sell some British-made products' such as ejection seats and 'weapon systems' to the US aerospace industry.

The British Government signed for the first ten F-111As in March 1966, with the designation F-111K being used in correspondence between representatives of the Ministry of Aviation and British aviation companies who were in discussions about which 'peculiar' components could be built in the UK. By September 1966 the F-111K received the go-ahead for production, but then came the 'peculiarities'.

The F-111K was to be the F-111A, as projected for the USAF's Tactical Air Command, modified to operate at higher gross weight thanks to components from the Strategic Air Command's FB-111A and would incorporate British Furnished Equipment (BFE). Two variants were envisioned; Strike/Reconnaissance, of which 40 were to be procured, and Trainer/Strike, comprising the balance. The first two F-111Ks off the line were to be examples of each; UK1 a Strike/Recon and UK2 a Trainer/Strike. UK1 was to be used for airframe and weapons separation testing while UK2 was to be an avionics testbed.

As for the peculiarities – described by GD as configuration departures – of the F-111K, the main change was the incorporation of the FB-111A main and nose landing gear for the higher gross weight, eight wing pylons (with the inboard pairs pivoting) and a BFE reconnaissance pallet for the weapons bay, which could be fitted with a centreline pylon. Many of the changes were forward of the cockpit, with the radome based on that fitted to the F-111D and FB-111A plus a new forward equipment bay. This bay housed a retractable in-flight refuelling probe on the upper centreline plus a trio of F95 cameras, one vertical and two oblique, in its lower section.

The weapons bay doors on the Strike/Recon variant were to be modified to allow a centreline pylon to be fitted. This pylon was to be mounted on four tubular supports that formed a truss to place the top of the pylon flush with the inboard bay doors that were to have cutouts to seal around the pylon. This new pylon was to carry the datalink pod for the AJ.168 TV Martel, the F-111K's weapon for its main role of long-range anti-shipping strikes East of Suez.

Below: General Dynamics artwork showing the F-111K in RAF service in dark earth/light stone colour schemes used on RAF aircraft 'East of Suez'. The F-111 order was cancelled in 1968. *General Dynamics via Joe Cherrie*

Opposite, top: Derived from the F-111A, the F-111K's 'peculiarities', shown here in blue, included: undercarriage from the FB-111A, a new forward equipment bay with in-flight refuelling probe, removable reconnaissance pallet in the weapons bay and a centreline pylon extending from the weapons bay. *General Dynamics via Joe Cherrie*

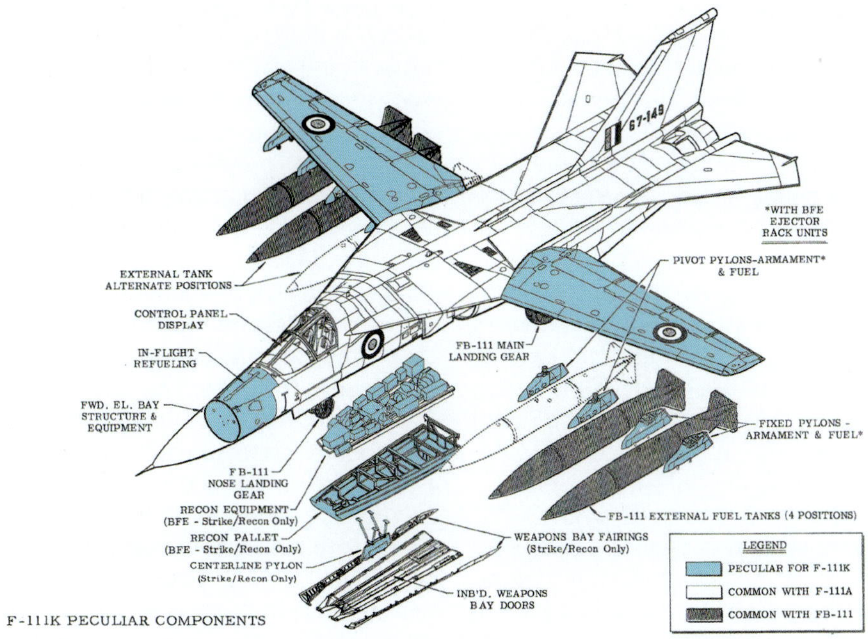

Below: Shown here are the various alternatives, successors and proposals to follow the cancelled BAC TSR.2. These in include types considered by the Air Staff. The ultimate alternative for the RAF was the Buccaneer S.2B. From the top: F-111K (with Martel) Mirage IVK, F-105F Thunderchief (suggested, but not taken seriously), Buccaneer S.2B and English Electric P.28.

The British and the F-111

Realistically the F-111 was the only game in town when it came to meeting ASR.343 (Issue 3). Healey's order for the replacements for the 'Big Three', including the F-111, suggests that it was a foregone conclusion the F-111 would be bought but that was not necessarily the case. Alternatives, some more plausible than others, were available.

F-105F Thunderchief

The 'Thud' might be unfamiliar in the TSR.2 saga and, in reality, it wasn't exactly a direct replacement but provides an interesting example of the machinations of the British Government. Republic's two-seat F-105F was suggested by Conservative MP Sir Theo Constantine on 1 April 1964 as a possible TSR.2 trainer, what would be the mid-Sixties equivalent of a LIFT (Lead-In Fighter Trainer) for strike aircraft. The Thud would be fitted with TSR.2 systems and in the light of a series of studies, the Olympus B.Ol 21 engine. As a trainer, according to Constantine who was parroting a Republic sales representative, the F-105F could 'provide the most advanced tactical training under all-weather conditions'. The F-105F was fully combat-capable and possessed high performance at sea-level with terrain avoidance and with its advanced bombing modes it 'would give the RAF early and realistic experience for TSR.2 crews' with the bonus that it could be fitted with TSR.2 subsystems. It could also provide ground crews with training in the 'handling of integrated weapons systems'.

Sir Theo, or rather Republic, may not have been too wide of the mark as a pair of British types were earmarked as TSR.2 trainers: the BAC Lightning for pilots and the two-seat Hawker Hunter (or the putative Folland Gnat T.2) for navigators. The F-105F Thunderchief could have provided a pilot and navigator training in a single platform.

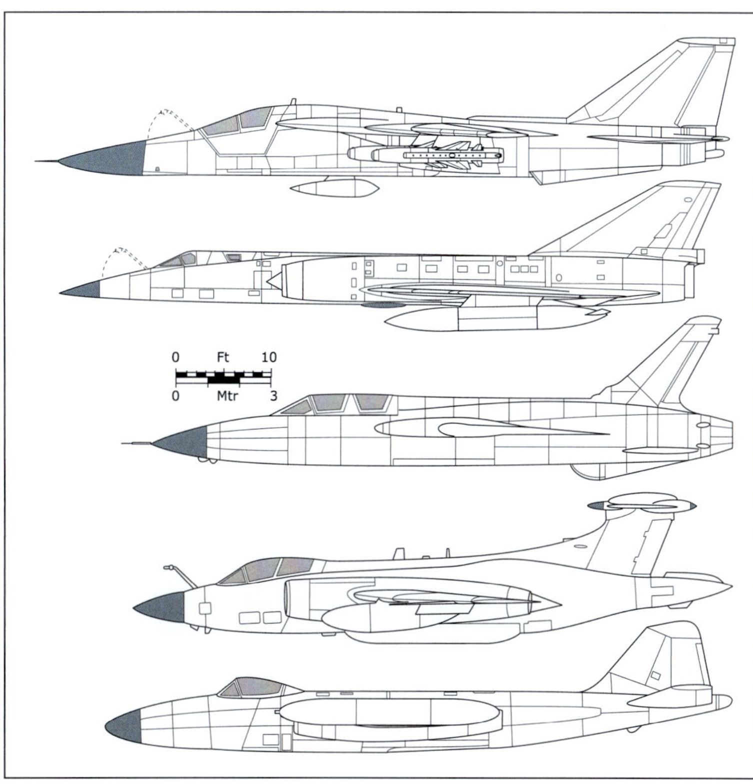

Warton's P.28

Canberra could never be described as the poor man's version of anything, but perhaps Warton's P.28 variant of the Canberra comes closest to the poor man's TSR.2. The P.28 dated back to the OR.339 period around 1958 and in the fall-out from TSR.2's cancellation in 1965, the P.28 was briefly resurrected as a Canberra B.2 re-engined with Speys. The most obvious change was to the wings, with 6ft (1.8m) clipped from each wing which were fitted with powered ailerons and new 500-gallon (2,273ltr) fixed tip tanks that replaced the 122-gallon (555ltr) drop tanks. The engine nacelles would be redesigned to take the larger Rolls-Royce Spey turbofan, probably the 201 as used on the F-4K. The forward fuselage was based on the PR.9's fighter-style cockpit, but with a terrain-following radar in the nose. At the rear the tailplanes were from the PR.9 with an extended tailcone fitted.

Mirage IVO and IVS

While not quite in the same class as the TSR.2 or F-111, the Mirage IVO ('O' a Dassault identifier for an Australian variant) had been proposed to the RAAF as a Canberra replacement, but the RAAF were never convinced by it, stating that it lacked range and was a 'more old-fashioned type of aircraft that merely flies rather fast into the waiting anti-aircraft missiles.' In the Mirage's defence, the RAAF studies and analysis predate those conducted by the RAF and l'Armée de l'Air. It was to be fitted with a Cyrano II radar in the nose, with the refuelling probe relocated to forward of the cockpit.

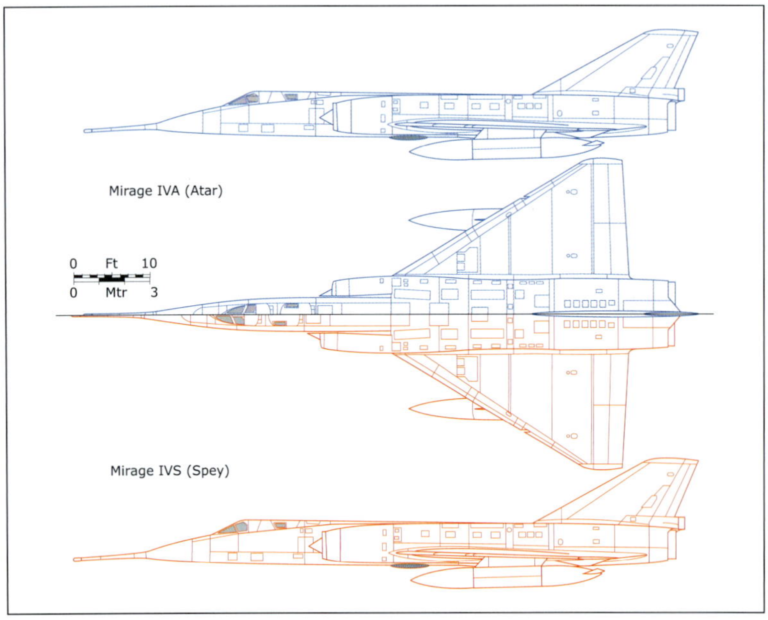

The Spey Mirage, variously described as the Mirage IVK or Mirage IVS, took the basic Mirage IV and replaced its ATAR engines with Speys. A further development, studied by BAC Warton involved further modifications to airframe, engines and systems, with the refuelling probe replaced by a retractable probe.

Mirage IVS Spey

Dassault and BAC's proposals for a Spey-powered variant of the Mirage IV in the aftermath of the TSR.2 cancellation have been described as a 'spoiler' to prevent the UK buying the F-111 for the RAF. Variously described as the Mirage IVK (no evidence has been found of this designation in official use), Mirage IVS (for Spey) or Mirage IV* (in UK designation systems '*' identifies a modification made to an existing variant), France's big delta was to be modified for British use in the usual style – fit British engines, weapons and systems – with airframe modifications to suit. Systems were to be based on those used on the Hawker P.1154 V/STOL fighter, plus the Antilope terrain-following radar rather than the Ferranti terrain following radar (TFR) being developed for TSR.2. The radar would no doubt be installed in the nose cone, as per the Mirage IVO proposal, with a refuelling probe relocated to forward of the cockpit.

The Atar 09K, rated at 11,000/15,960 lbf (49/71kN) - second figure is with reheat – would be replaced with the Spey, rated at 12,250/20,500 lbf (55/91kN) which required a 2ft (0.6m) fuselage extension and modified intakes to handle the almost 30% increase in mass flow of the Spey turbofan. The fuselage stretch would allow more fuel to be carried but still not enough to meet the 1,000nm (1,852km) range requirement of ASR.343. Of course, the Mirage IV had been designed from scratch as a high-altitude supersonic bomber rather than a low-altitude strike aircraft. The ride at low-level would be bumpy, but in tests conducted in 1963, its performance in the low altitude environment proved better than expected.

Buccaneer – Ideal Alternative

Mountbatten's 'bird' took the place of the cancelled TSR.2 and F-111K mainly because it could conduct the Western Europe/North East Atlantic-focused roles that the UK's new NATO-oriented defence posture demanded. It was also available for the RAF as the carrier force wound down, with the Fleet Air Arm's force of Spey-engined Buccaneer S.2As being transferred to the RAF with additional new-build S.2Bs acquired for the RAF in Germany to meet ASR.391.

While the Buccaneer S.2A and S.2B provided the strike capability, Hawker Siddeley produced several design studies that were aimed at the roles intended for the cancelled TSR.2 and

Blackburn's Buccaneer S.2, unwanted by the RAF, soon earned the respect of its users and enemy alike 'down in the weeds'. Buccaneer XX895 of No 12 Sqn is shown here carrying the full suite of Martel kit comprising two AJ.168 TV Martel, one AS.37 anti-radiation missile and a guidance pod for the TV Martel. The Buccaneer ended its days flying high, at war in Iraq, dropping Paveways and spiking targets for Tornados. *Terry Panopalis Collection*

F-111K, although none of these came to fruition, possibly due to Air Staff bias against the original naval Buccaneer. The P.145 built on the experience with the Buccaneer S.2B but with a new radar and bogie undercarriage, combined with rocket boosters, allowed operation at higher all-up weights. Blackburn's P.149 added a Q-band ground-mapping radar, Ferranti's FLR and a RB.162 turbofan replaced the rockets in the rear fuselage. The P.150 that followed, also known as the Buccaneer 2**, was a supersonic variant of the Buccaneer with a new thinner wing, stretched fuselage and reheated Speys combined with new nav/attack systems. As alternatives to the cancelled TSR.2 and F-111K, none of Brough's proposals found favour until the Treasury strong-armed the RAF to accept the Buccaneer S.2.

AST.355 – Super TSR.2?

As ever, as soon as an aircraft was under development to meet an Air Staff Requirement, its replacement was already being examined. This was the case with TSR.2/F-111K that were under development to meet ASR.343 (Issues 2 and 3 respectively). In mid-1961 a draft Staff Target, AST.354, was being discussed for a follow-on to TSR.2. To avoid confusion with AST.345, for what became the P.1127 Harrier, the designation was changed to AST.355. The basic premise of the Staff Target was that the resulting aircraft, and one aircraft it would be, should be multi-role and capable of application to a range of roles including nuclear strike, battlefield interdiction, suppression of enemy defences and 'destroyer' in the air defence role – air-to-air operations against enemy aircraft – effectively a Super TSR.2. Or perhaps MRCA.

AST.355 also suggested that the low/fast flight regime might be too vulnerable to improved air defences, so a high/fast regime, 70,000ft/Mach 2.5, might be more apt but the type should be capable of high-speed automatic terrain-following flight and STOL! In addition, some form of compatibility with the Royal Navy was required although the DCAS, Air Marshal Sir Ronald Beresford Lees, saw little future for the carrier force. As with all Staff Targets, AST.355 was a wish list for the future and used to identify areas for research. Amongst the items on the list were satellite communications and data distribution, no doubt to exploit new sensors such as reconnaissance radar, infrared linescan and high-resolution cameras.

Having read the Air Staff's wish list, the impression gained is that AST.355 would have been very ambitious and repeat the perceived mistakes made with TSR.2. This was not the case, as AST.355 was sent back to the drafting team with the advice that it lacked ambition! The Air Ministry's Assistant Scientific Advisor (Operations) JE Henderson went as far as stating that 'We must make a bold and major step forward, instead of asking for the marginal increases in speed and altitude of this AST.' In similar vein, Air Commodore IG Esplin, Director, Operational Requirements (Air) wrote that in AST.355 'we had set our sights too low.' What Henderson and Esplin wanted was higher and faster – 150,000ft/Mach 3.5 – and as the DCAS had said, forget about the carriers and Mounting Bases. On the offensive side, new weapons were required such as stand-off missiles but the 'newly discovered "Laser" techniques should be carefully examined' especially for illuminating and the destruction of materials. The 16,000lb (7,257kg) weapons load should be mainly air-to-surface guided weapons rather than bombs for the strike role or air-to-air guided weapons in the destroyer role. This perceived lack of ambition prompted the withdrawal of AST.355 in December 1962 and the drafting of a new, unnumbered, AST incorporating the higher performance figures and new technology outlined by Henderson and Esplin.

Armourers prepare Matra 155 SNEB pods for loading onto Phantom FGR.2s. The Phantom closest to the camera also carries a SUU-23/A Vulcan cannon pod on its centreline. *Blue Envoy Collection*

With the arrival in RAFG of the Jaguar, the Phantom FGR.2 transferred to the air defence role that they were more suited to. This FGR.2 is seen in air superiority 'Barley grey' colours. It shares a ramp with a Royal Danish Air Force F-104 Starfighter. *Blue Envoy Collection*

The End of the Eagle

All this work on replacing TSR.2 was fruitless, as by late 1967 its role had all but disappeared and there was no need for TSR.2, F-111K or a direct replacement. The commitment to East of Suez had been scrapped. Western Europe and the North East Atlantic was the RAF Buccaneer's operational area for much of the Cold War. Inadvertently successful or ideal from the start? The Buccaneer is yet another question that the UK enthusiasts can debate at length, but until the Tornado arrived in the eighties, the Buccaneer was the ideal alternative.

Short-lived Spook

Any reader of aviation magazines in the 1970s will be familiar with photographs of the Phantom FGR.2, festooned with kit. Unfortunately, as was discovered when the F-4M was assessed for AST.396, it couldn't go very far with all those BL.755s and Sparrows. The original F4H Phantom had been designed as a naval interceptor – catapulted off a carrier to accelerate towards an incoming *Badger* and use its Sparrows to bring that *Badger* down. Planning for the future,

Panavia MRCA P02 XX946 was the second MRCA to fly and the first British-built example, making its first flight on 30 October 1974. Sporting trinational markings XX946 is seen here carrying a quartet of low-drag bombs. *Terry Panopalis Collection*

McDonnell had fitted the Phantom with five hard points and these soon became loaded with fuel tanks and bombs in the Vietnam War.

Oddly enough the Phantom took a 'reciprocal course' to that of most RAF fighters in being used for ground attack *then* as an interceptor. In the ground-attack role the Phantom's RAF career was short by RAF standards, 1969 to 1974, replaced by the Jaguar GR.1, which was more suited to the ground-attack and strike roles. Despite the image of a hardware hauler, Air Staff assessors for AST.396 in 1973 discovered that with the requisite weapons (Six BL.755 and SUU-23 Vulcan gun pod) and countermeasures pods, its radius of action was only 100nm (185km) *with* external tanks!

Tornado – Devastating by Name, Multi-Role by Nature

The cancellation of the 'Big Three' and subsequent scrapping of the F-111K left a gap in the RAF's plans for the 1970s. Replacements for the Vulcan, Canberra, Buccaneer and Phantom would be required. As noted above, and elsewhere in this work, the counter to the Warsaw Pact had by 1965 become Flexible Response and escalation rather than nuclear exchange of the Trip Wire era. The RAF was also drawing in its horns, looking to North West Europe and north east Atlantic rather than worldwide commitments.

The type that had been selected as the lighter partner to the F-111K, the Anglo-French Variable Geometry (AFVG) aircraft foundered in 1967 but evolved into the UK-only UKVG, a BAC Warton project. UKVG was larger than AFVG and would be more or less a dedicated strike aircraft for the RAF rather than aimed at both the RAF and Fleet Air Arm, who by this time in the 1960s were facing the loss of their large carriers.

Another aspect of the UK aerospace industry in the late 1960s was the Government's drive for collaboration with Europe and the use of funding as a carrot for this, the stick being little or no funding for national projects. The gist of the story is that BAC, Aeritalia and Messerschmitt-Bolkow-Blohm (MBB) formed a company called Panavia to develop a multi-role combat aircraft (MRCA). On the engine, Rolls-Royce, Motoren-und Turbinen-Union Gmbh and FIAT co-operated and formed Turbo-Union to develop a new turbofan for the MRCA. Two versions were envisioned; the single-seat Panavia 100 for the Luftwaffe and the two-seat Panavia 200 for the RAF and Aeronautica Militare, but the Luftwaffe ultimately opted for the two-seater. Initially named Panther, the Panavia 200 became better known as Tornado, with the strike aircraft known as the Tornado IDS to meet Air Staff Requirement AST.392 issued in July 1968.

TORNADO TIMELINE

1960

MAY 1966
UK and France agreed to develop AFVG

JUN 1967
France withdrew from AFVG due to differences on specification and requirements

AUG 1967
Belgium, Netherlands, West Germany, Italy and Canada form Multi Role Aircraft 1975 group (MRA-75)

NOV 1967
UKVG commenced as a UK-only strike aircraft

JUL 1968
UK joins MRA-75, AST.392 issued by Air Staff. UK signed MoU leading to MRCA

MAR 1969
Multi Role Combat Aircraft (MRCA) configuration adopted with two designs: Sigle-seat PA100 and two-seat PA200. Panavia formed to develop MRCA.

JUNE 1969
Turbo Union formed to develop MRCA engine

SEP 1969
RB.199 engine selected for MRCA. NATO Multirole Combat Aircraft Development and Production Management Agency (NAMMA) formed

1970

FEB 1970
Workshare finalised (UK: 42.5%, FRG: 42.5%, Italy: 15%)

OCT 1971
Texas Instruments selected to develop Ground Mapping Radar (GMR) and Terrain Following Radar (TFR) radar

NOV 1972
Construction of first airframe begins

APRIL 1973
Vulcan testbed XA903 flew with RB.199-34R

AUG 1974
14 August, first prototype, D9591, flies from MBB, Manching.

SEP 1974
Name 'Tornado' adopted for MRCA by all patricipants

OCT 1974
30 Oct, first UK-built Tornado, XX946, flew at BAC, Warton

NOV 1974
Buccaneer began trials of Tornado avionics

DEC 1975
5 Dec, first Italian-built Tornado, MM586, flew at Aeritalia, Caselle

APR 1978
Tornado Trinational Training Establishment set up at RAF Cottesmore

AUG 1979
1 August, first Tornado F.2, ZA254, flew at BAC, Warton

1980

JUL 1980
TTTE received first Tornado

JAN 1981
TTTE opened

JAN 1982
First Tornado GR.1 delivered to IX Squadron at Honington

APR 1982
First Tornado GR.1 delivered to 617 Squadron

JUL 1983
First Tornado GR.1 delivered to 15 Squadron

JUN 1984
SR(A).417 issued for midlife update (MLU-88)

NOV 1984
First Tornado F.2 delivered

MAY 1985
JP.233 entered service. Tornado F.3 entered service

AUG 1985
Test flights of Tornado GR.1A commenced

NOV 1988
First Tornado GR.1A with TIRRS delivered

DEC 1989
MLU-88 cancelled, superseded by MLU-91

1990

JUL 1990
ALARM entered service on Tornado

JAN 1991
Tornado went to war, Op GRANBY TIALD entered service.

AUG 1991
MLU-91 issued

MAY 1993
First Flight of Tornado GR.4

JUL 1993
Sea Eagle entered service on Tornado GR.1B

OCT 1997
Tornado GR.4 entered service

2000

NOV 2001
Storm Shadow entered service

MAR 2005
Brimstone entered service

AUG 2007
RAPTOR pod entered service to meet SR(A).1368

2010

MAR 2011
Tornado F.3 retired

JAN 2019
31 January final Tornado GR.4 operation

APR 2019
1 April Tornado officially retired from RAF service

Although intended as a strike and interdiction aircraft, the also RAF needed an interceptor (bomber destroyer is a more accurate description) to operate over the Greenland/Iceland/UK gap in the north east Atlantic. This led to two versions of MRCA for the RAF, the IDS to replace Vulcan, Canberra and Buccaneer and the Air Defence Variant (ADV) to replace the Lightning and Phantom. This is an unusual change of role for an RAF aircraft as usually the interceptor became the ground attack aircraft for various reasons while in the case of Tornado the ground-attack the became the interceptor but the Phantom had proved this was feasible. See this author's *Battle Flight* for the background to the Tornado ADV.

The first MRCA prototype flew in August 1974 and deliveries of the Tornado GR.1 to the RAF started in June 1979 with the Tri-National Tornado Training Establishment formed at RAF Cottesmore in January 1981. The Tornado GR.1 fleet in West Germany was assigned to Supreme Allied Commander, Europe (SACEUR) and tasked with nuclear strike using the WE.177A and C, but also available for the counter-air and SEAD roles with JP.233 and ALARM.

The Tornado went to war on 17 January 1991 on Operation Granby, attacking Iraqi airfields with the JP.233 counter-air weapon and 1,000 lb (454kg) bombs, delivered at low altitude. The RAF lost six Tornado GR.1s during Operation Granby, most in the early phase before the decision was made to move to medium and high altitudes. Due to lack of self-designation, Tornado acquired the Thermal Imager and Laser Designator (TIALD) as an urgent operational requirement in 1991 but official service entry of TIALD occurred in 1995.

Tornados were at war almost continually from January 1991 until retired in March 2019, be it in Operation Southern Watch over Iraq or in the Balkans in 1999 or Libya and Iraq in the 2010s. The GR.1 was upgraded to GR.4 standard from 1993 to meet SR(A).417 and a decade later were conducting missions in support of Operation Telic, the invasion of Iraq in March 2003. The Tornado GR.4 replaced the Harrier GR.9 in 2009 as the RAF air support component for Operation Herrick in Afghanistan, finally being withdrawn in November 2014. During 2011 Tornados (with a newly acquired Brimstone capability) were tasked with enforcing a no-fly zone during Operation Elamy in Libya. The Tornado was in action almost up to its retirement date of March 2019, engaged in Operation Shader, strikes against the Islamic State/Da'esh in Syria and Iraq until early Febru-

The ultimate version of the Tornado in RAF service was the GR.4, seen here being prepared for a reconnaissance mission with the RAPTOR pod. The Tornado fleet was retired in March 2019. *Terry Panopalis Collection*

ary 2019. Although retired by the RAF, the Tornado continued to operate with the Luftwaffe and Aeronautica Militare. As of June 2019, the Tornado was in still action with the Royal Saudi Air Force attacking targets in Yemen.

The Tornado GR.1 was upgraded to GR.4 as a mid-life update and built on the experience of Operation GRANBY by integrating Paveway II and updating the communications and datalink systems. The GR.1B was a dedicated anti-ship variant armed with the BAeD Sea Eagle ASM serving from mid-1993. The GR.1A and GR.4A were reconnaissance versions fitted with Tornado Infra-Red Reconnaissance System (TIRRS). The GR.1A reconnaissance variant saw its two BK-27 cannon replaced with reconnaissance kit, entering service in mid-1985. The Luftwaffe acquired 35 Tornado ECR (Electronic Combat Reconnaissance) variants to operate in the SEAD role with the AGM-88 HARM. The RAF used standard IDS and latterly the F.3 ADV as the Tornado EF.3, both with ALARM. Design studies for advanced Tornados, particularly for the export market were varied and included a Panavia study from the mid-1970s called AD-PAC (Air Defence PACkage). This started life as RAD-PAC (Radar ADditional PACkage) based on the Tornado IDS with a multimode radar featuring track-while-scan capability against air targets and moving target indicator for ground targets. Two variants were proposed; AD-PAC 1 with an upgraded radar and AD-PAC 2 with a completely new radar. In addition to the air interception capability on the radar, the AD-PAC aircraft was to be fitted with pylon-mounted air-to-air missiles, possibly Skyflash or Sparrow.

Tornado was proposed for the USAF's Enhanced Tactical Fighter (ETF), the replacement for the F-111E/F. The ETF was to conduct strike missions into the Warsaw Pact rear without the need for fighter escorts and electronic warfare support in all weather conditions. The Tornado was up against tough competition in the shape of the McDonnell Douglas F-15E Strike Eagle and General Dynamics F-16XL. The programme was renamed the Dual-Role Fighter (DRF) programme and the F-15E was adopted with the Tornado deemed to lack a 'credible air superiority capability'. The F-15E, based on a fighter that had 'not a pound for air-to-ground' as its tagline stated, proved an excellent choice and as well as sales to the USAF, has sold well across the world.

Another proposal from 1989 saw the Tornado ECR pitched to the USAF as Follow-On Wild Weasel (FOWW), a replacement for the McDonnell Douglas F-4G Wild Weasel. Panavia teamed with Rockwell and made the case for the Tornado ECR as an alternative to the F-16 and F-15, stating that the Tornado could operate at low level with its terrain-following radar, in all weathers and at night. Rockwell's Larry Holdridge stated that 'Almost all Wild Weasel missions are performed on the deck' and that the 'Tornado was ideally suited to the mission'.

'Not a pound for air-to-ground' did not last long. Boeing F-15E Strike Eagle 98-0133 of the 492nd squadron 'Madhatters' 48th REF, USAF shows its sensors including the LANTIRN pods: AN/AAQ-13 navigation pod under the starboard intake and AN/AAQ-14 targeting pod under the port intake trunking. The Strike Eagle remains a formidable interdiction type. *Peter Edwards*

The Tornado had a better performance at low level and provided a more stable platform for launching HARM, which had been cleared for Tornado in the Luftwaffe's ECR programme.

Tornado variants for the RAF date back to the origins of the aircraft with many variants being proposed for AST.396, with the attack radar replaced by optronics turrets. One version proposed in 1977 for AST.403 was to be lightened, simplified and fitted with the RB.409-7, a cropped fan RB.199 and, as an air combat type, was considered more that capable of giving the MiG-23 *Flogger* a run for its money.

The Tornado, like all military aircraft, underwent Mid-Life Update (MLU), with the first Tornado MLU being MLU-88 under SR(A).417 issued in 1984. This was intended to equip the Tornado for delivery of tactical nuclear weapons such as WE.177 and its successor into the Warsaw Pact rear with few or no active emitters such as terrain following radar. New sensors and systems were to be installed, including terrain comparison (TERCOM) navigation and FLIR. With its emphasis on nuclear strike, MLU-88 was effectively redundant in 1989 when the Berlin Wall started to come down. The next MLU was -91, based on the lessons learned in Operation Granby (the 1991 Gulf War) that included the addition of GPS navigation and the thermal imaging and laser designator (TIALD) pod combined with night vision goggles-compatible instruments. The nuclear strike capability was lost, alongside the loss of the RAF's nuclear capability when WE.177 was retired from 1992. The result was the Tornado GR.4, but perhaps a more radical Tornado could have been developed.

In the 1980s, low observability (LO) was the next big thing in military aircraft, a belief furthered by the performance of the Lockheed F-117A in the 1991 Gulf War. Tornado 2000 was a design study for an extended range, stealthy Tornado with modified, slightly stretched rear fuselage, faceted nose, intakes redesigned to reduce radar cross-section and a conformal ventral tank with semi-recessed missiles. The demise of Tornado 2000 may have been prompted by a desire to avoid diversion of funds from what became the Eurofighter 2000. Tornado 2000 may have been a precursor to a Warton study known as the Long-Range Penetrator, a stealthy forerunner to the Future Offensive Air System.

Studies towards replacing the Tornado had been ongoing as soon as the type entered service in the 1980s but a Staff Target was only issued in the early 1990s. Staff Target (Air).425 became a Staff Requirement in 1995 and the studies were grouped under the Future Offensive Aircraft to replace Tornado. Amongst the types suggested as Tornado replacements were the Lockheed F-117X for the US Navy albeit with GEC-Marconi avionics and the EJ200 engine from the Eurofighter. This was treated with scepticism due to the F-117's very limited weapons load compared with the Tornado. Possibly of most interest was another naval aircraft, the McDonnell Douglas/General Dynamics A-12 Avenger II, but this was cancelled in 1991 after problems with weight gain and massive cost overruns. The legal fallout from the cancellation saw litigation continuing until 2014, lasting almost three times longer than the A-12 programme itself!

On interesting design study worked on in the Warton project office during the late 1980s was the P.125, a low-observable, STOVL interdiction aircraft. Intended for the RAF and RN, the P.125 employed a number of advanced features including a submerged cockpit whereby the pilot had no direct view of the world outside his cockpit. The pilot would be presented with a series of images on displays or a helmet-mounted display to allow them to fly and fight the aircraft. Such devices dated back three decades to the Avro 730 supersonic bomber for OR.330. the P.125 was to be powered by a single reheated turbofan, fitted with a vectoring nozzle, plus two Pegasus-style nozzles taking mass flow from the fan. The MoD's interest in the P.125 waned as the US Joint Strike Fighter programme gained momentum and the UK became a Level 1 partner in the Lockheed F-35 programme in 1995.

By 1996 the lie of the land had changed, and drones were becoming feasible as a weapon system. The studies were now to include uninhabited air vehicles (UAVs) and the programme's designation changed to Future Offensive Air System (FOAS). The scope of FOAS was wide, including aircraft (uninhabited and inhabited), UAVs, (autonomous and remotely piloted) and cruise missiles. Work on FOAS continued until 2005, replaced by a programme called Deep and Persistent Offensive Capability (DPOC) which was in turn cancelled in the strategic Defence review of 2010.

Designed from the start as a multirole aircraft, albeit in the interdiction and strike role, combining SEAD, counter-air and anti-shipping, with a major redesign as an interceptor the Tornado truly was multi-role. On its retirement in 2019 one retired RAF officer asked the former Chief of the Air Staff if the RAF would ever have another bomber. Air Chief Marshal Sir Richard Johns' reply forms the opening statement of this work: 'Single role aeroplanes are simply *passé*.'

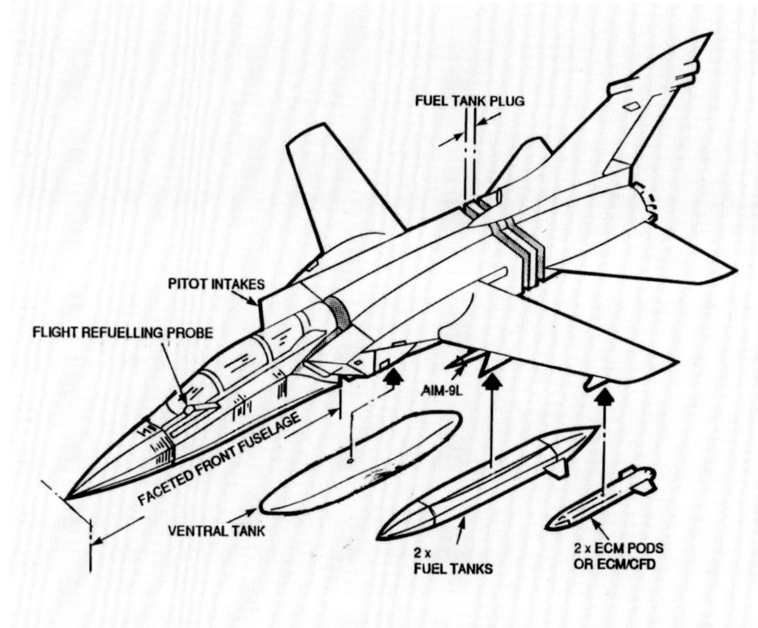

Tornado 2000 was intended to add low observability to the Tornado at a mid-life update. The forward fuselage was to be faceted, intakes changed to pitot types with the compressor faces obscured, a ventral fuel tank and fuselage stretched to accommodate more fuel. *North West Heritage Group*

This model of Tornado 2000 prepared for BAe Warton shows what the mid-life update of the Tornado GR.1 might have looked like had the Cold War continued. Faceted fuselage and drop tanks combined with a conformal ventral weapons/fuel package. *North West Heritage Group*

9 A Hunter for the Nineties AST.396

'Has any thought been given to a "simplified" MRCA for 396?' Marshal of the Royal Air Force Sir Denis F Spotswood Chief of the Air Staff, 24 July 1973

'The most cost-effective way of meeting these revised objectives is likely to be in further development of the existing Jaguar or Harrier.' Air Chief Marshal Sir Denis G Smallwood, Vice Chief of the Air Staff, 20 March 1973

As night fighting equipment was fitted to armoured fighting vehicles in the Sixties, the need to attack Warsaw Pact formations at night or in bad weather became imperative, leading to AST.396. Sensors developed to destroy trucks in Vietnam were specified for attack aircraft and these new technologies became key to fighting the night/all-weather battle that would unfold in the Eighties.

With the service entry of the Harrier and Jaguar in the early 1970s, attention turned to their replacement and in May 1971 the Operational Requirements Committee endorsed the drawing up of a Staff Target for a 'Battlefield Short Range Interdiction/Short Range Reconnaissance Aircraft' (although 'Battlefield' was subsequently deleted from the title) for the Central Front in West Germany.

The aim of the Staff Target was to assess the feasibility of developing and producing an aircraft that was suitable for 'operations at night and in conditions of poor visibility'. Any resulting aircraft was to 'Attack with weapons to impair the enemy's military potential and to disrupt the movement of his forces into and within the battlefield area.' In addition to that main task, the type was to conduct short range reconnaissance and 'Battlefield attack. Direct support of land forces in the battle area' with the in-service date for the type being 1987.

The aircraft was to engage a Warsaw Pact army 'including about a thousand tanks and APCs, deployed in battle groups of 10-13 vehicles to a depth of 5 miles (8km) behind a typical 46 miles (75km) front'. Behind that, for 31 miles (50km) moving up in convoys along roads, was

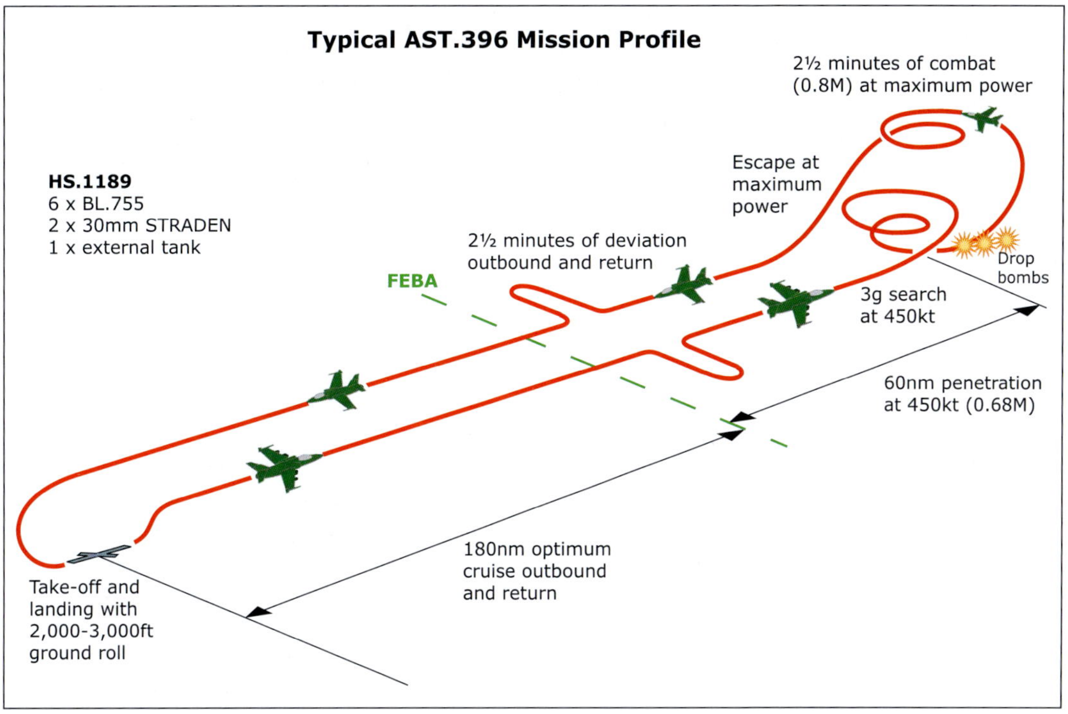

This page: As laid out in the Staff Target, the aircraft, in this case Brough's HS.1189 with six BL.755 was to perform the mission outlined in this diagram. The Staff Target advised that the objective would be 60nm (11km) beyond the FEBA. From a base 180nm (333km) inside friendly territory.

a similar number of AFVs and support vehicles.

To allow operation at low altitude by day or night the type was to be equipped with sensors that would enable it to fly at up to 450kt (833km/h) at altitudes as low as 100ft (30m). The night flying requirement was for operations in light levels equivalent to a moonless clear night (0.001Lux) but hoped to extend this to moonless overcast nights (0.0001Lux). The Staff Target also called for the ability to operate in weather with 'meteorological visibility' down to 1.5nm (2.8km). Such systems existed, with low light level TV (LLLTV) and forward-looking infrared (FLIR) being considered. Target acquisition was to be capable of night/adverse weather operation with first-pass capability against predetermined targets and targets of opportunity. The ability to operate in conjunction with Forward Air Controllers (FAC) near the FEBA was also desirable.

The Staff Target specified that first-pass attacks against predetermined targets using an inertial navigation/attack system was to be possible, especially when combined with the LLLTV and FLIR sensors on the aircraft. The plethora of systems for low-level flight, target acquisition and operating with FAC might increase the pilot workload to such an extent that a second crew member was required, so this must also be investigated. A second crew member might also make another of the Air Staff's wishes possible – attacks on moving targets. One aspect of the attention being paid to pilot workload was that 'centre stick aiming' was required whereby the pilot can select the target and release the weapons using switches on the control column. This would become known as Hand-on-Throttle-and-Stick (HOTAS) and is standard on modern combat aircraft.

Given the nature of battlefield support, targets of opportunity comprised a major portion of the task, requiring target acquisition and weapons sighting systems that were quick and preferably uncomplicated. Successful first-pass attacks on such targets were required so the 'weapon aiming system must have a short solution settling time and provide a continuously computed mode'. For the predetermined targets, such as those destined to receive 'special weapons', the aircraft must be capable of laydown and loft delivery.

As noted above, the type was to operate at low altitude at speeds of 450kt (833km/h) but the Air Staff wanted to be advised of the 'maximum continuous level speed likely to be achieved in the "weapons gone" configuration'. While this is a fairly obvious request, high speed for escape after an attack, it may have prompted Hawker Siddeley's studies into base-burning and the internal carriage of the BL.755s. Base-burning involved injecting fuel around a flat 'base' mounted on the rear of an aircraft. The aim was to reduce, or even eliminate, the base drag at transonic speeds allowing the aircraft increase its speed. Base-burning and its development is examined in Appendix 2.

Up to 6,000lb (2,721kg) of stores were to be carried, with the aircraft's principal weapon to

Opposite page: September 1993, northern West Germany. approaching from different directions at low level, two Hawker Siddeley Tempest GR.1s draw fire from a Shilka while a third attacks a *Nationale Volksarmee* (East German Peoples' Army) armoured column with IBL.755 cluster bombs. The T-72s have 'herring boned' off the road and a Shilka has opened up. This fictional artwork by Luca Landino shows three HS.1191 ground attack aircraft using base-burning in an attack.

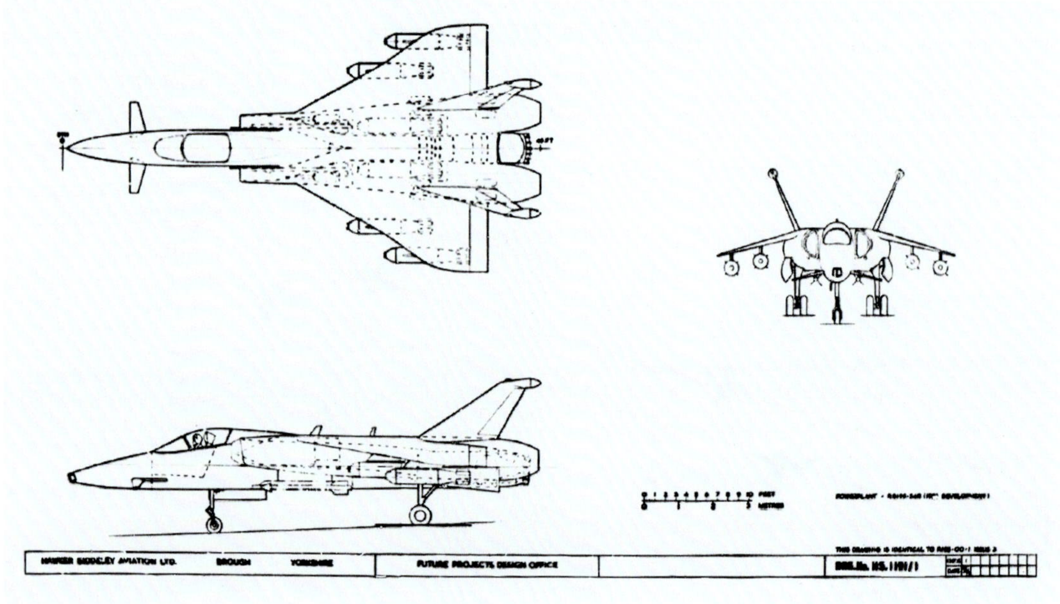

The HS.1191 was a small delta-winged type with folding foreplanes to increase manoeuvrability. The odd feature of the HS.1191 was the pair of bulbous afterbodies each side of the jetpipe. These are burning bases for the base-burning drag reduction system. See *Appendix 2* for further information. *Brough Heritage*

be the Hunting BL.755 cluster bomb, but also any existing or future air-to-ground weapons, to be used for attacks on armoured formations. This in turn prompted the Air Staff to advise that 'Regardless of the type chosen, a high-grade aiming and attack system will be essential. The effective attack of armour with BL.755 cluster bombs required an advanced inertial platform and a full solution weapon-aiming and delivery system with laser ranging.'

A gun or guns were to be fitted for use against light armour, motor transport, light watercraft and air-to-air if necessary, although the type was not to be equipped with air-to-air

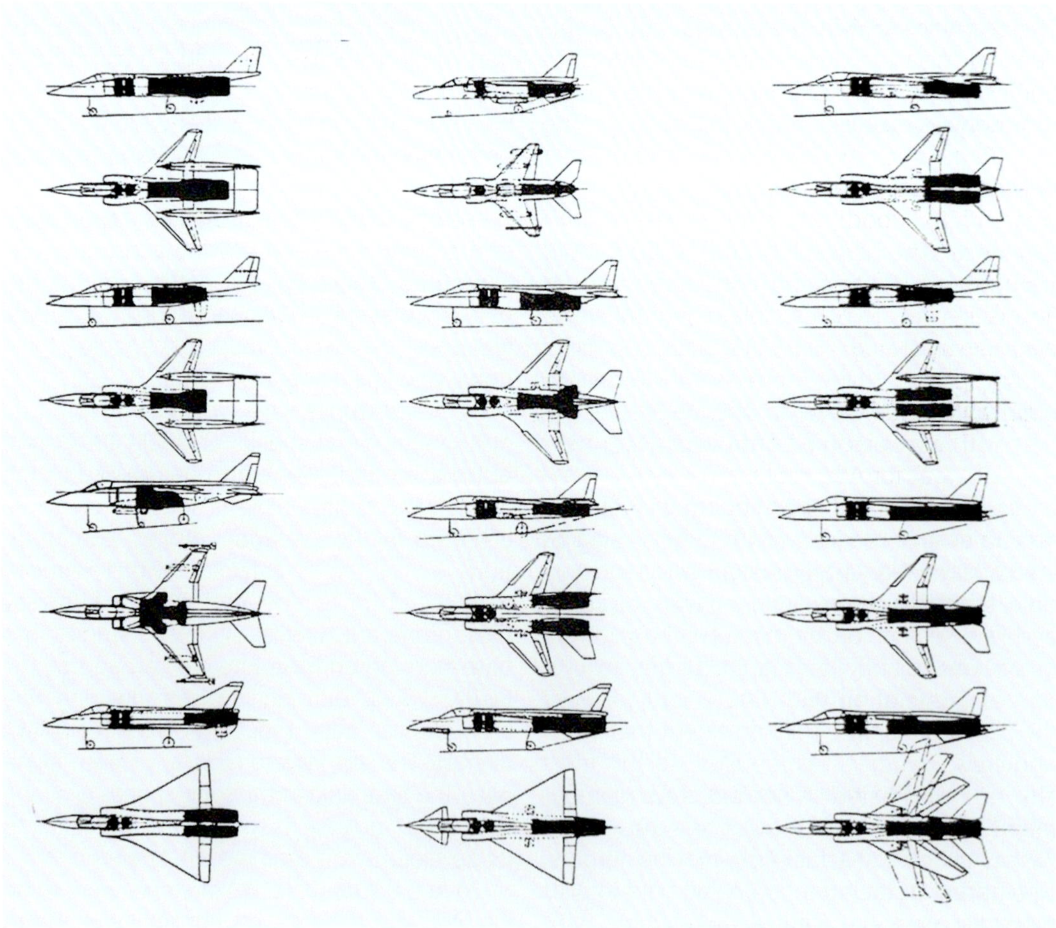

This diagram outlines the number of studies undertaken by BAC Warton towards the AST.396 programme. This is a fraction of the studies as it does not include the MRCA-based work. *North West Heritage Group*

missiles. Provision was to be made for carriage of a reconnaissance pod such as the EMI pod for the Jaguar or a 'special weapon' - Bomb, HE, 600 lb MC or Bomb, HE 950 lb, MC i.e. the WE.177A and C tactical nuclear weapons.

As for the defensive aspects, the Air Staff had taken note of the recent war in the Middle East, specifically the impact on Israeli air operations of Egyptian and Syrian air defences. The AST.396 type was to carry a passive warning system capable of indicating the 'nature and direction of threatening weapon systems and the launch of missiles but, if possible, should not display transmission from friendly AI radars.' Active countermeasures were to be carried only if they were 'found to be justified'. The type was to be flown at very low level to reduce exposure to ground defences and 'will aim to evade enemy fighters rather than match them in air combat.' The targeting systems, LLLTV, FLIR and LRTMS were to be protected against 'any likely countermeasures' while the possibility of using the LRMTS for air-to-air tracking and ranging was to be investigated.

The type was to be operated from 'established, defended bases with paved runways' and carry its full load of six BL.755, two guns and 10 seconds-worth of ammunition to a target 60nm (111km) beyond the Forward Edge of the Battlefield Area (FEBA). If operating from the 'Clutch Airfields' (see Chapter 3) this would require a radius of action (RoA) of 240nm (444km). To allow operations from potentially damaged runways, the aircraft was to have good take-off and landing performance. The ability to conduct operations from dispersed sites with 'soft' fields such as 'prepared grass' or 'prefabricated surfaces' was desirable assuming it can be acquired with little cost increase.

Pretty much any fast jet type available in the early 1970s was proposed, or formed the basis of a proposal, for AST.396, 'from developments of the HS.1182 to the MRCA and new supersonic designs.' These included vectored and unvectored engines, combinations of lift and propulsion engines either in existing designs or incorporated into conventional designs to meet the take-off and landing requirements. An all-up weight of around 45,000 lb (20,408kg) was predicted although weight saving and new materials could see that reduced to 35,000 lb (15,873kg). The main performance requirements were Mach = 0.9 without reheat, clear 50ft (15m) in 1,200ft (366m) on take-off, 7.5g turn capability at Mach = 0.8 and a weapons load of six BL.755 or its replacement.

Of the types to be replaced by AST.396, the Jaguar GR.1 came closest to the requirement, with a lo-lo RoA with six BL.755 of 130nm (241km) from a take-off roll of 3,600ft (1097m) whereas the Harrier GR.3 with six BL.755 had a lo-lo RoA of 85nm (157km) from a ground roll of 1,130ft (344m) and could only meet the AST RoA of 240nm (444km) with one BL.755 and two 330 gallon (1500 litre) ferry tanks. Two of the proposed replacements from Warton and Kingston were the Advanced Jaguar and the HS.1184-7. With six BL.755 the Advanced Jaguar had a RoA of 318nm (589km) from a 2,000ft (610m) ground roll while the HS.1184-7's RoA was 240nm (444km), again with a 2,000ft (610m) ground roll. Warton also proposed a modified MRCA with performance similar to that of the Jaguar but with a longer take-off roll of 2,700ft (823m). All of these capabilities would be of little or no use without the ability to acquire targets in low light or bad weather. The crew would need to see in the dark.

High-Tech Carrots – AST.396

Ostensibly an aircraft staff target, AST.396's success would hinge on sensors. Prior to Air Interception (AI) radar being revealed to the general public, RAF Fighter Command allegedly issued a cover story that the pilot of the first night fighter to shoot down a German bomber using AI, Squadron Leader John Cunningham, ate a lot of carrots. All nonsense of course, as Cunningham and his radar operator Jimmy Rawnsley were using AI Mk.IV in their Beaufighter IF.

While AI radar proved pivotal in the nocturnal air-to-air conflict, air-to-ground was a different matter. Roland Beamont provided an example of night-time attacks on ground targets – night *Rhubarbs* – with Typhoons in *Typhoon and Tempest at War.* When it came to strafing trains, the search was conducted at an ideal altitude of around 1,500ft (457m) from which locomotives could be seen in the moonlight and shot up to produce plumes of steam visible for miles. The flak car at the end of the train would open up, revealing its position for subsequent strafing and therefore anything between these two 'beacons' would be shot up with 20mm Hispanos.

The Eyeball, Human, Mk.1 could find targets in moonlight in a Typhoon, but the increased speed of jet aircraft, particularly against radar-directed defences made this more difficult. Technology would provide the key. Use of air-to ground radar in the 1940s was hindered by ground clutter – unwanted returns

Tropic Moon III. B-57G 53-3865 FK in a revetment at Ubon AB, Thailand in 1971. The large orange panel covers the aperture for the AN/AXQ-7 LLLTV and AN/AAS-26 FLIR. The B-57G used Paveways to destroy trucks but could only carry four bombs. *Terry Panopalis Collection*

from buildings, trees and the ground, masked specific targets. Since this clutter was mainly returns from buildings, the clutter was the target and useful for radars such as H2S, H2X and Eagle to find cities, but it was only when computing power became available that targets such as trucks and tanks could be resolved. Infra-Red showed potential and was used in the Korean War, fitted to B-26C Invaders, but could only detect large heat sources such as locomotives. Of course, destroying locomotives was a not a problem that afflicted the West's tactical fighters delivering their nuclear weapons but would soon prove knotty in South East Asia.

Tropic Moon

The United States became involved in Viet Nam from the late Fifties and American tactical aircraft were not particularly suited to the role of ground attack by day never mind by night. Aside from the Douglas A-1 Skyraider and A-26 Invader (the Invader was designated as an Attack aircraft during WW2, a Bomber in 1948, then Attack from 1965), soldiering on after operating in World War Two and Korea, ground-attack aircraft were soon found lacking in supporting the troops and interdicting supplies. The Americans soon discovered that

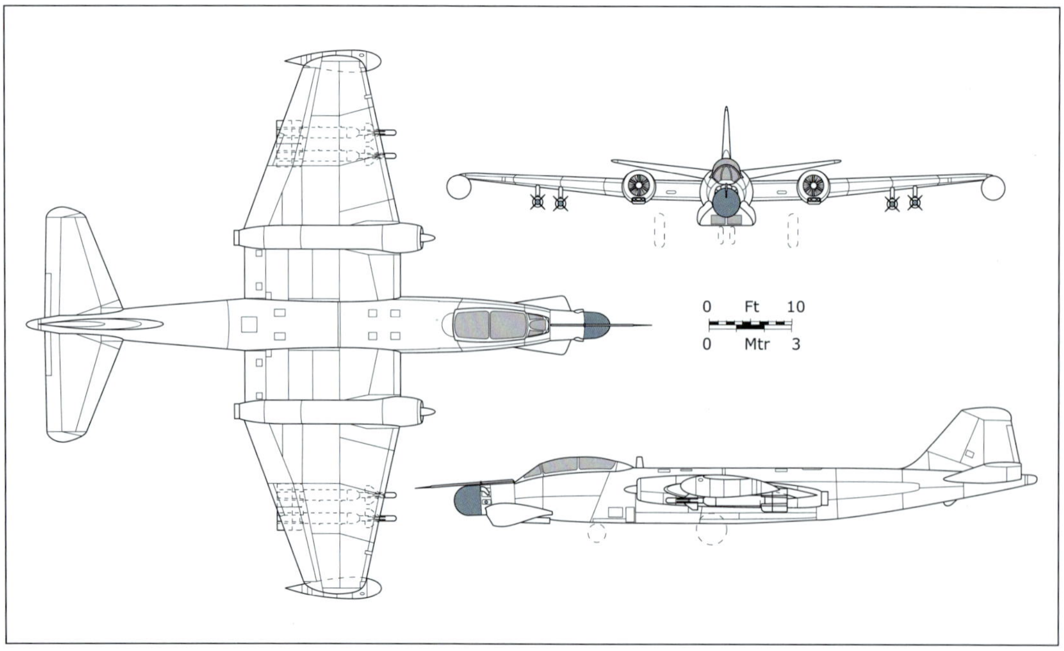

The Martin B-57G Tropic Moon III was designed for interdiction on the Ho Chi Minh Trail. The nose carried (housed implies that the equipment is inside the aircraft) LLLTV, FLIR and a laser designator.

the Viet Cong and North Vietnamese forces, especially their logistics, operated at night and bad weather, epitomised by the Ho Chi Minh Trail. For this war, going on a root vegetable binge would not help, but technology would.

As in Korea, infrared was set to work, even the infrared search and track systems of the Convair F-102 Delta Dagger interceptor were used to detect ground targets and aim 2.75in (70mm) rockets against targets on the Ho Chi Minh Trail. While not particularly successful it was a pointer to the future. The USAF in 1966 commenced a programme descriptively named Shed Light whose aim was to see in the dark and see through foliage and allow attacks on traffic on the Ho Chi Minh trail. To do that, Shed Light was required to develop the technologies and tactics. On the technology front the effort was divided into three key technologies: Infrared, radar and low light level television.

The first to enter operational trials was low light level TV (LLLTV) in a pod called Project 1533 fitted to the A-1 Skyraider as Tropic Moon I which was combined with a newly-developed laser rangefinder to become Project 698DF or Tropic Moon II. The latter was fitted under the wing of a B-57B Canberra but the results against trucks on the Ho Chi Minh Trail were disappointing. The B-57 formed the basis of the next phase, Tropic Moon III, that used the B-57 fitted with an AN/APQ.139 forward looking radar, AN/AAS-26 forward-looking infrared (FLIR) and AN/AXQ-7 low light level TV (LLLTV) to detect targets and a Philco AN/AVQ-10 Pave Knife laser designator for four Paveway II LGBs carried under the wings and cluster bombs and incendiaries in the bomb bay. Unfortunately, four LGBs proved to be the limiting factor in truck hunting when compared with the AC-130A and its battery of Vulcans, the Spectres destroying almost 12,000 trucks to the B-57G's 2,000. To address this, a project called Pave Gat, saw an Emerson turret with 20mm Vulcan cannon fitted in the bomb bay of the B-57G but this proved no match for the Spectres' firepower. The development of the Spectre is examined in Appendix 3.

What is obvious from an examination of the Tropic Moon III is the size of the sensor suite, which required a Canberra-sized airframe and operator (two when laser designation was used) to make it all work. When it did work, it could be effective, but Tropic Moon III has been described as a 'crash' programme and this may have led to a 'make-do-and-mend' approach. As ever, nothing ventured, nothing gained and Tropic Moon III, deemed a failure, was one such venture and the lessons learned contributed to future programmes. Tropic Moon III was developed to attack trucks and other vehicles, not unlike the British Air Staff requirement for AST.396, although its main target was armoured vehicles, but the problems were the same.

AST.396 was issued when Tropic Moon III was in service and no doubt at the time of its writing the Air Staff expected the systems to improve in capability and reduce in size. The Air Staff had issued Air Staff Targets 604 and 610 for a FLIR and LLLTV respectively, with both superseded by ASR.1006 and ASRs 1010 and 1011 which covered night vision goggles (NVG). The sensor suite for AST.396 was to provide a capability on a par with Tropic Moon III and even with development and miniaturisation, the sensor suite would be sizeable.

The effect of its installation on a strike aircraft can be seen in the numerous design studies, especially Brough's HS.1190-6 and Kingston's HS.1184-22 – it dominates the design. Warton designs are shown 'clean' perhaps in the expectation that such sensors would be pod-

The size of the Tropic Moon III sensor suite is apparent in this view. The B-57G was successful in destroying trucks but the AC-130 Spectres racked up a much higher number of truck kills. The key to night interdiction on the Ho Chi Minh Trail was finding the enemy and that required sensors. *Terry Panopalis Collection.*

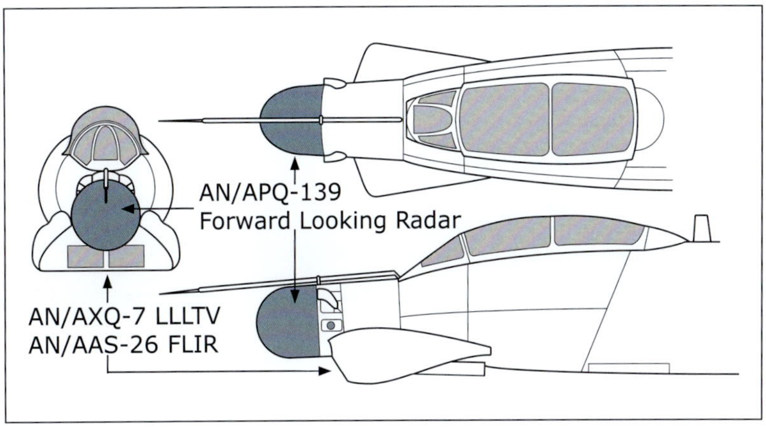

This scrap view of the B-57G Tropic Moon III forward fuselage shows the size of the sensor suite required for night operations in the early 1970s.

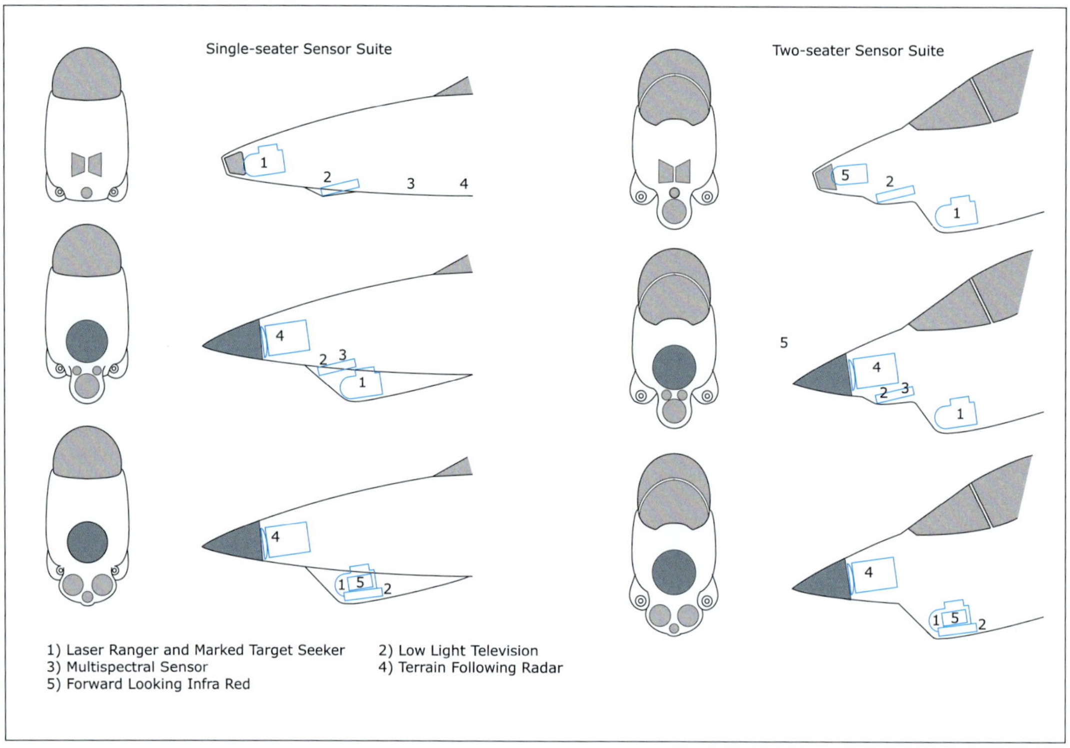

Nasal congestion was the term used to describe the sensor suite of the AST.396 aircraft such as the HS.1190-6. While great advances in miniaturisation had been made since Tropic Moon, the LLLTV, FLIR and TFR still took up a lot of space in the nose of the aircraft. Sensors were beginning to become the key to war fighting in the late 20th Century.

mounted, especially since the pace of development on such equipment would make planning for internal installation difficult. The intended sensor fit on these aircraft would be carried over into the later AST.403 and the impact on the design of the mix of AI radar, FLIR and LLTV systems 'creates problems of "nasal congestion" and the resulting ungainliness of the aircraft nose leads to performance penalties'.

When Issue 2 was endorsed on 21 May 1971, study contracts were placed with the British Aircraft Corporation (BAC), Hawker Siddeley

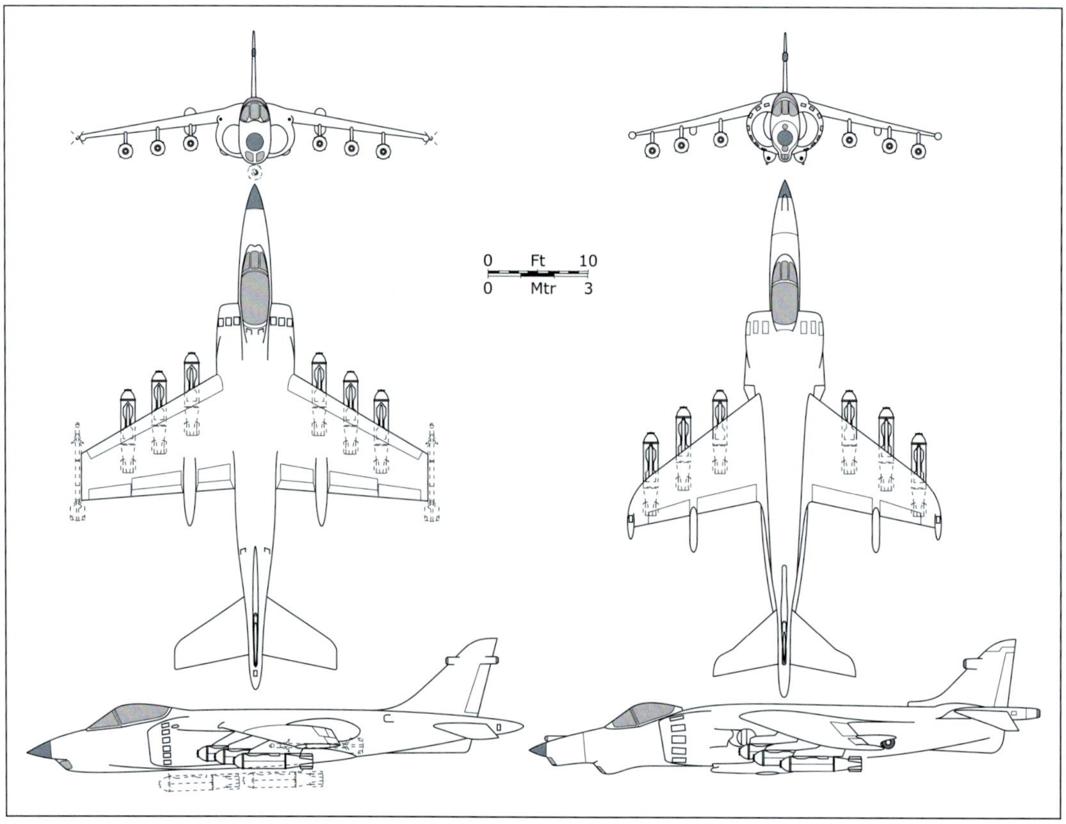

With a look of the Sea Harrier FRS.1 about it, the HS.1184-18 had a new wing with three pylons, tip rails and larger wing pods at midspan for new main undercarriage. This new tricycle undercarriage allowed carriage of ventral store. The HS.1184-20 retained the bicycle/outrigger undercarriage but moved the outriggers inboard to midspan although the wing retained the original Harrier planform.

Aviation (HSA) and Rolls-Royce (1971). Given that the Harrier and Jaguar were the aircraft to be replaced, AST.396 presented the aircraft companies with an opportunity to update, or rather further develop, existing designs or draw up new design studies.

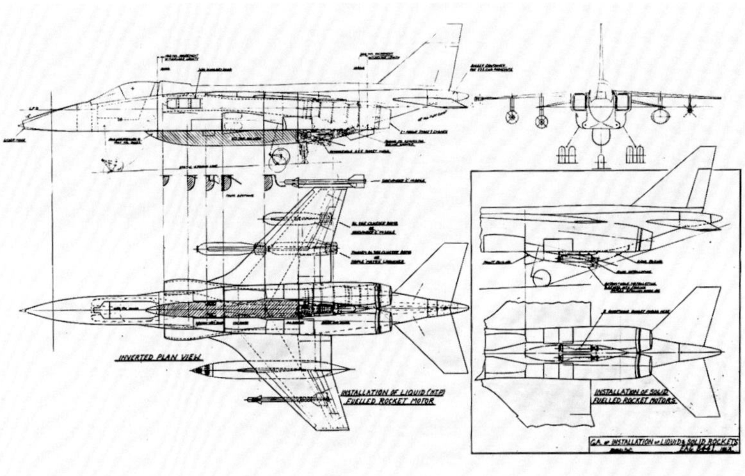

An early Jaguar-based study, EAG.8441, addressed the STOL and egress requirements by using liquid-fuelled rocket engines or solid rocket motors. The rocket engines required a tank for HTP on the centreline. *North West Heritage Group*

Warton's Anti-tank Jaguar

The existing Jaguar was entering service when AST.396 was being discussed and formed an obvious basis for an aircraft to meet the Staff Target. BAC at Warton embarked on design studies designated P.69 that involved fitting new engines and the avionics to meet the AST or allow it to be met as closely as possible. The first of these, drawn up as EAG.8530, took the Jaguar T.2 and replaced the existing avionics with new systems that could allow it to approach the capability outlined in the AST at an AUW of 29,260 lb (13,272kg).

The second study, based on the standard Jaguar GR.1 airframe, used the more powerful Adour Stage 2, rated at 9,430 lbf (41.9kN) with reheat, with the extra thrust seen as key to meeting the AST. The third study, EAG.8441, beefed up the airframe and engines while adding booster rockets, to achieve the post-attack egress speed. Solid and liquid-fuelled rockets were examined, with a pair of solid rocket motors in a retractable ventral fairing installed forward of the jet pipes. After use, rather than being discarded, the all-burnt motors were retracted. The rocket engine was the liquid-fuelled Bristol Siddeley BS.605 as used on the Buccaneer S.50, installed at the rear of a long ventral fairing containing the HTP propellant while the kerosene fuel came from aircraft's tanks. The combustion chamber and nozzle were retractable and being liquid-fuelled, the BS.605 could be started and stopped dependent on operational conditions, unlike the solid motors. The addition of rockets to achieve the egress speed is interesting as it shows a different approach to that of the company across the Pennines in Brough, Hawker Siddeley, of which more later.

The EAG.8669 possibly the most interesting of the P.69 studies as it was a major redesign of the Jaguar airframe involving a deeper/wider fuselage (the 'wide-bodied' Jaguar) with larger intakes to cater for re-engining with a pair of the MRCA's RB.199-34R, rated at 8,100 lbf (36kN) and 15,950 lbf (71kN) with reheat or two General Electric YJ101, rated at 9,500 lbf (42.2kN) and 14,300 lbf (63.6kN) as used on the Northrop YF-17. The extra weight of the revised airframe and new engines required a new undercarriage and the modified wing from the earlier study was retained. With all these modifications this design weighed in at 35,476 lb (16,092kg). Interestingly, the original Jaguar A had a maximum

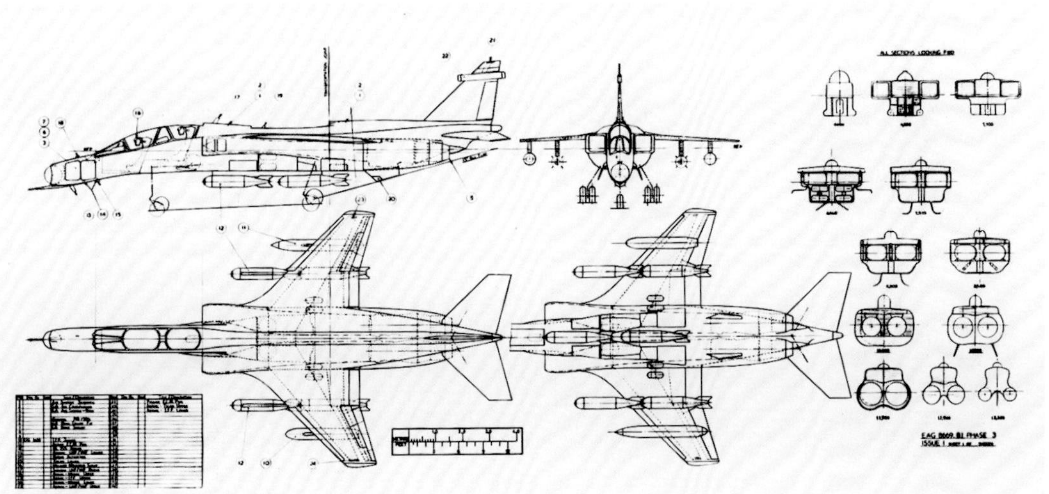

The RB.199-powered EAG.8669 was an example of the wide-bodied Jaguar with the tandem two-seater forward fuselage and larger intakes. *North West Heritage Group*

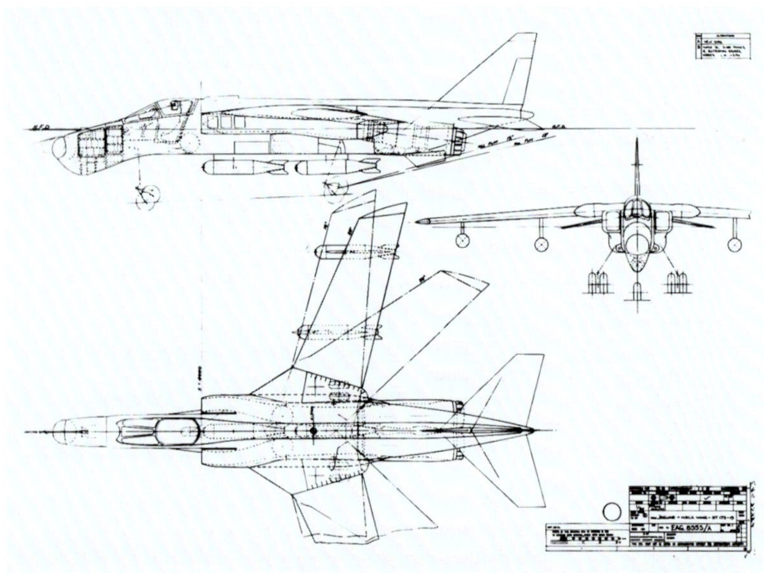

Top: This AST.396 study took the Adour-powered Jaguar and added the wings from the MRCA.

Below: Warton appreciated the impact of the AST.396 sensor suite on its airframes. The Hughes Target Recognition Attack Multi-sensor (TRAM) had the least impact on the nose of a Tornado. *North West Heritage Group*

Opposite, top: BAC at Warton proposed basing an AST.396 type on the MRCA Air Defence Variant (ADV) rather than the Interdiction Strike (IDS). The AST.396 variant would have fixed intakes. Of note in this drawing is the LLLTV, shown here as VAS – Visual Augmentation System. This sensor had been specified on the ADV but dropped on cost grounds. *North West Heritage Group*

take-off weight of 34,612 lb (15,700kg) with reheated thrust of 14,610 lbf (64.9kN) while the last of the P.69 studies had almost twice the thrust for a similar take-off weight.

One particularly interesting study was drawn up as EAG.8555 and comprised a Jaguar fitted with the variable-geometry wings from the Tornado but retaining the Adour while EAG.8593 shows a Jaguar, with the Tornado wings and a single RB.199 engine. Other interesting Jaguar variants included the EAG.8662, a shortened wide-bodied Jaguar with a single RB.199 and a similar study, EAG.8668, powered by a RB.431 (a 'straight through' Pegasus). Perhaps the most radical variant of the Jaguar was the study drawn as EAG.866, that used standard Jaguar T.2 cockpit, intakes and tail fin mated to nose 'A' with Phase 2 sensors, new wings and tailplanes with a rear fuselage designed for a single RB.199.

To address the sensor fit, the Warton design teams proposed completely changing the nose of Jaguar, Tornado and the Harrier by fitting a spherical turret in the nose and installing a terrain-following radar (TFR) in a chin fairing. Some variations of the sensor fit moved the TFR from the chin to a pod on the port outboard pylon that also contained a jammer.

The nose turret contained the optical sensors, FLIR and LRMTS and, as is still the case today with such sensors, was rotated to the rear until required. Three sizes of turret were examined, with diameters of 26, 22 and 16 inches (66, 56 and 40cm), fitted in the extreme nose. Other fits were similar to those on the HS.1190, TFR in the nose and FLIR/LRTMS in side-by-side chin mountings but a further development was to use the Hughes AN/AAS-33 TRAM (Target Recognition and Attack Multi-sensor) as fitted to the Grumman A-6E Intruder. TRAM comprised a FLIR and laser designator/rangefinder in a trainable turret installed under the nose, while the TFR was installed in the extreme nose. The results, when the spherical turret was applied to Jaguar, produced a deep, down-swept appearance while the Tornado and Harrier look somewhat snub-nosed.

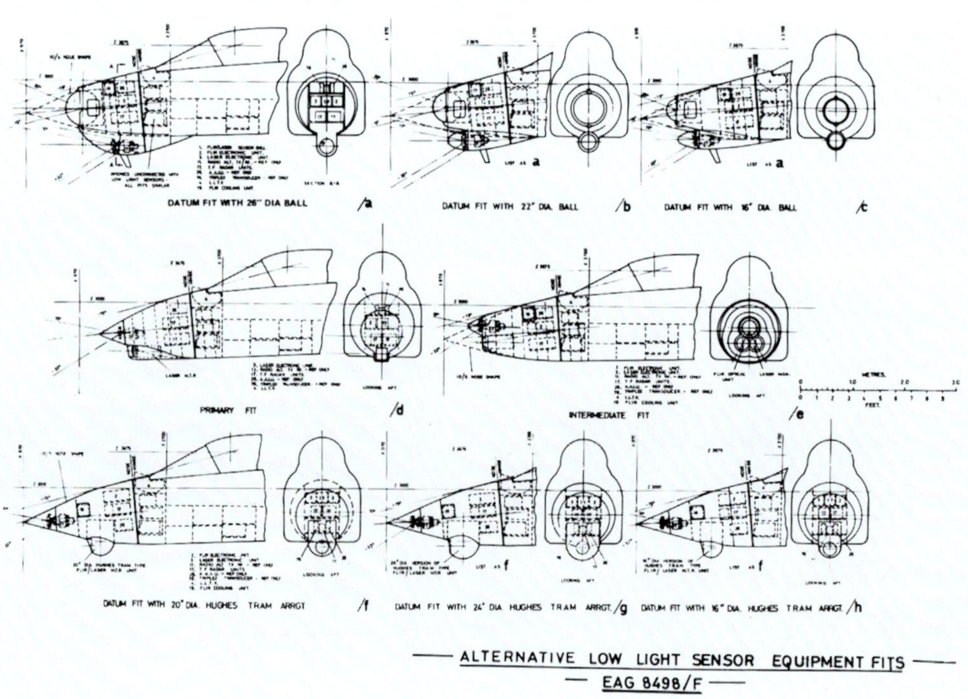

Putting the Wind Up Armour

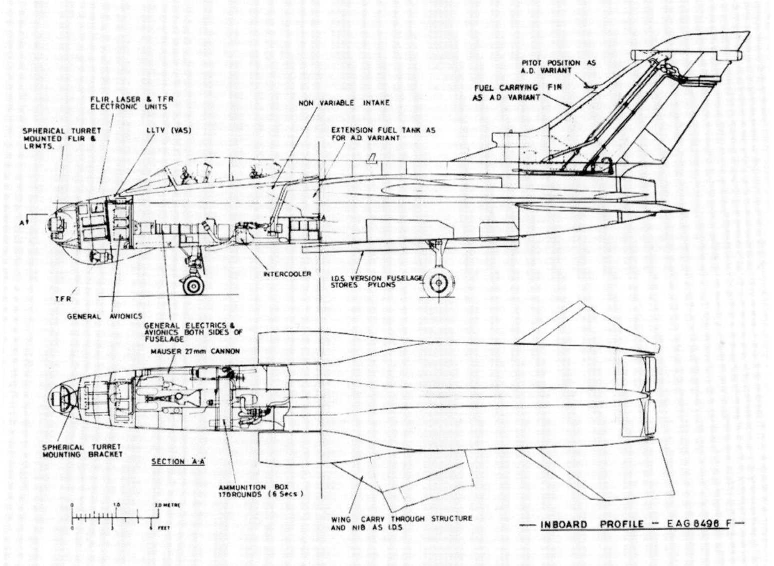

As a deep interdiction type designed for fast and low ingress, delivery on a point target and a fast and low egress, the Tornado might not sound the ideal type for the close air support or battlefield interdiction role. Tornado IDS was fitted with a TFR and LRMTS but lacked the FLIR and LLLTV required for attacking armour in the dark. For AST.396, drawn as EAG.8498, Warton proposed removing the Texas Instruments attack radar and replacing it with the spherical FLIR/LRTMS turret and fit the LLLTV just forward of the windscreen. As described above, various sensor fittings, including the TRAM turret, were proposed for the AST.396 Tornado, all with the LLLTV ahead of the cockpit. This is labelled 'VAS' on some drawings, which was a Visual Augmentation System intended for the ADV but deleted from the operational Tornado F.3s on cost grounds. Interestingly for AST.396 the cockpit/forward fuselage and rear fuselage/engine bays and tail surfaces (with fin fuel tank) were to come from the Air Defence Variant. Another modification for AST.396 was to fit larger tyres, which required changes to the undercarriage bay and bulged doors to accommodate these, which were designed for use on chemically stabilised surfaces or PSA. The centre section, non-variable intakes and wing box/carry through structure were from the IDS, with the fuselage pylons retained for stores.

The Tornado could carry up to 12 BL.755 or VJ.291 anti-armour weapons, with an ECM pod and IR jammer on the starboard and port outboard pylons. Being based on the ADV, the AST.396 Tornado was fitted with a single Mauser BK-27 cannon on the starboard side of the forward fuselage, with 170 rounds, enough for 6 seconds of fire.

Another design study based on the Tornado was drawn as EAG.8498, a single-seater with changes to the wing sweep angles, 15-55° compared with 25-66° on the IDS. The intakes were to be changed from wedge type to simpler pitot intakes. The undercarriage was to be

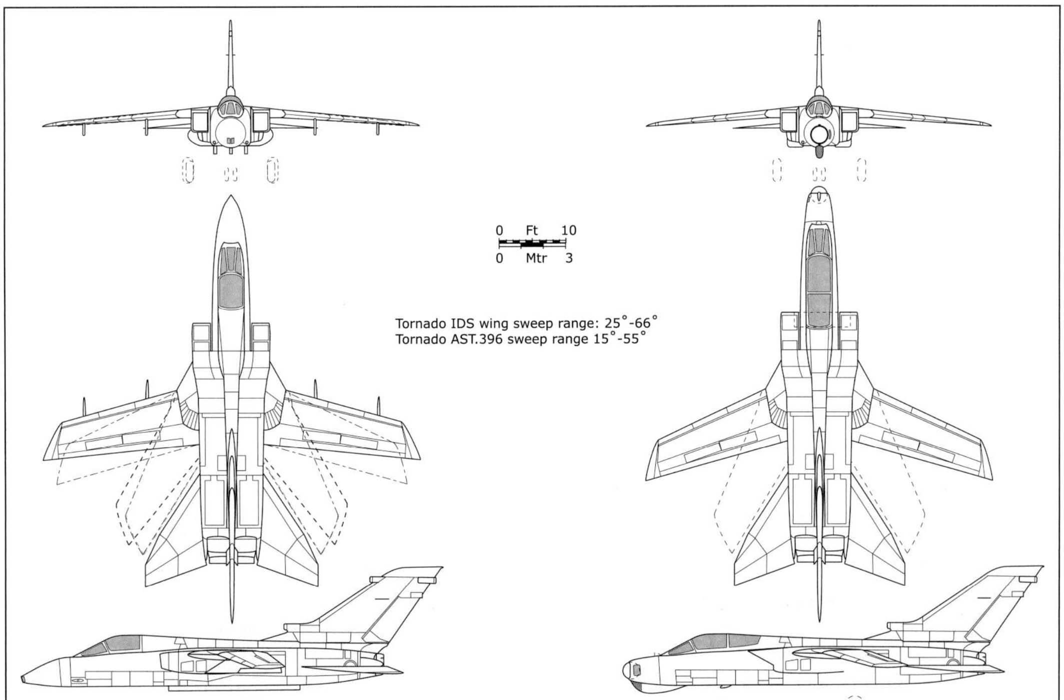

Left: When Chief of the Air Staff, Marshal of the RAF Sir Denis Spotswood suggested a simplified MRCA for AST.396, these might have been what he had in mind. The attack radar was to be replaced with night/bad weather optronics. A single-seat variant was also proposed with extra fuel, but reduced optronics. One major change for the single-seater was the range of sweep on the wings 15-55° rather than 25-66° on the IDS.

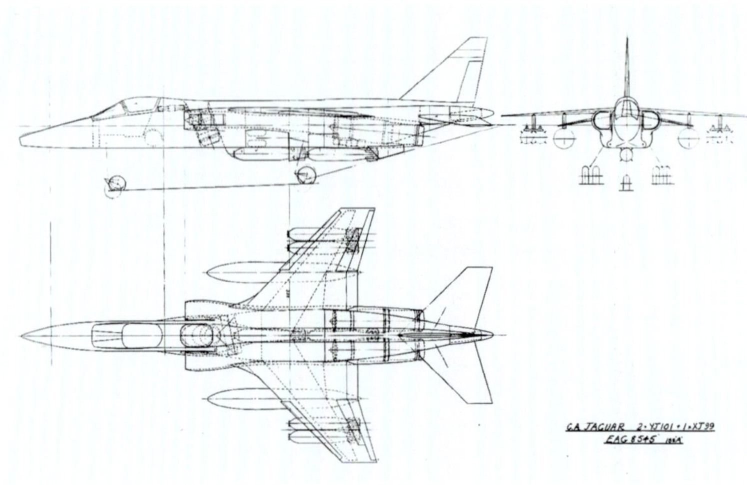

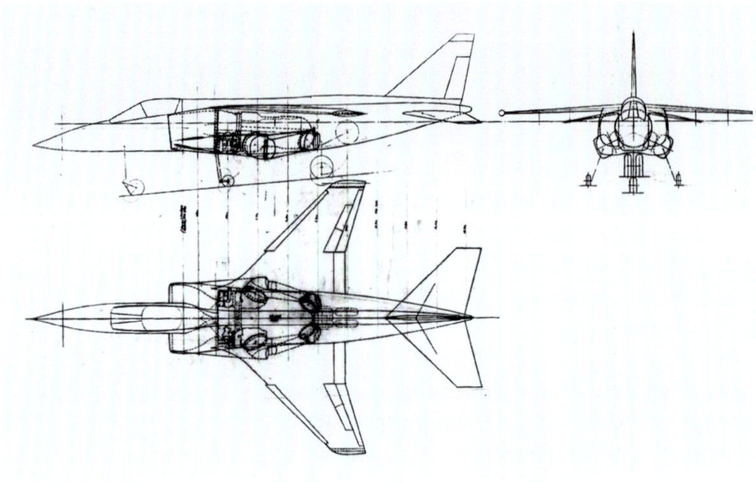

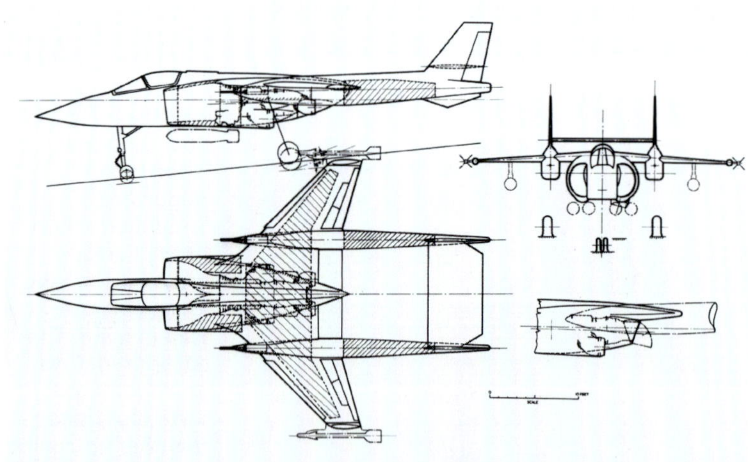

Top: To address the STOL requirement in AST.396, BAC re-engined the Jaguar with two General Electric YJ-101 turbofans plus a single XJ.99 lift engine behind the cockpit. *North West Heritage Group*

Centre: This P.70 study, EAG.8404 combined Jaguar wings with a new fuselage accommodating a Rolls-Royce Pegasus engine. *North West Heritage Group*

Bottom: Further P.70 studies with the Pegasus included the EAG.8450 that adopted the twin-boom configuration with a 30mm ADEN cannon in the forward portion of each boom. *North West Heritage Group*

fitted with larger low-pressure tyres and the second crew member's position deleted and replaced with a fuel tank. The drawing shows a Jaguar-style chisel nose with a LRTMS, but no doubt the full AST.396 sensor suite to be fitted for operations.

STOVL Anti-Tank

To achieve STOVL performance for AST.396, Warton examined fitting the Jaguar with a lift engine to shorten the take-off and landing runs. Drawing EAG.8545 shows a Jaguar GR1 with a fuselage stretch aft of the cockpit to accommodate a XJ.99 lift engine, while the Adours were replaced by a pair of General Electric YJ101 reheated turbofans in the 15,000lbf (66.7kN) class. Study EAG.8546 shows a modified wing, with blown flaps, leading edge slats on wing and tailplanes plus a large leading-edge root extension.

Having examined derivatives of the Jaguar, the Warton design team's P.70 studies took the Pegasus or RB.422 vectored thrust turbofans as the powerplant for a series of new designs. Both engines were to be fitted with plenum chamber burning (PCB) whereby fuel was added into the front bypass duct (the plenum) and burned to produce extra thrust. PCB was intended to provide V/STOL aircraft with sufficient thrust for supersonic flight and had been bench tested on the Bristol Siddeley BS.100 engine for the Hawker P.1154, with its first run in 1960. Another type earmarked for the BS.100 was the Fokker/Republic D-24 for NBMR-3.

The first P.70 study used Jaguar wings, tail surfaces, forward fuselage mated to a new fuselage from the cockpit aft to the empennage. The new fuselage was wide enough to accommodate the Pegasus engine and the large semi-circular intakes and the fairings for the forward vectoring nozzles. The use of a conventional fuselage required the rear nozzles to be wider apart than was necessary, resulting in a configuration like the Harrier with the hot efflux passing close to the rear fuselage. The next P.70 design study solved this by adopting the twin boom configuration producing an aircraft reminiscent of a de Havilland Sea Vixen. The twin-boom P.70's 30mm ADEN cannon were installed in the forward end of each tail boom which also held the main undercarriage and fuel tanks. The BL.755 cluster bombs were carried in pairs on ejector racks under the intake trunking, with single BL.755s on wing pylons, bringing the total to the required six bombs. Despite there being no requirement for self-defence, the P.70 could carry an AIM-9 Sidewinder on each wingtip.

In parallel with the Pegasus/RB.422 studies, BAC examined using separate lift and propulsion engines. The Warton design team were experienced in designing such systems having co-operated with Shorts on lift platforms such as the SC.1 and P.17D and for V/STOL transports such as the P.36 studies for NBMR-4 in the early 1960s (see this author's *On Atlas' Shoulders*). On the high performance V/STOL aircraft front, Warton had co-operated with Dassault on the Mirage IIIV (see Chapter 3) but had further developed that design into the P.39 naval strike aircraft which employed two lift jets combined with swivelling cascades that diverted the thrust from the main propulsion engines to provide lift.

Warton applied this knowledge to the P.71 studies that used the Rolls-Allison XJ.99 that had been developed via the RB.108, RB.162 and RB.189 lift engines to improve the power to weight and volume ratios, with small volume being preferable in a strike aircraft. The XJ.99 was rated at 9,000 lbf (40kN). An alternative lift engine was the more powerful RB.227, rated at 10,780 lbf (48kN) or the RB.228, rated at 15,500 lbf (69kN). The main propulsive engines on the P.71 series were the YJ101, RB.199-42R or Pratt & Whitney F100. One design that used the latter engine was EAG.8464 that combined the Jaguar's forward fuselage and wings with a new rear fuselage incorporating a F100 complete with a pair of cascades. The two XJ.99 lift engines installed behind the cockpit were fitted with bifurcated jetpipes, with the efflux being directed by cascades mounted on the lower quadrants of the fuselage.

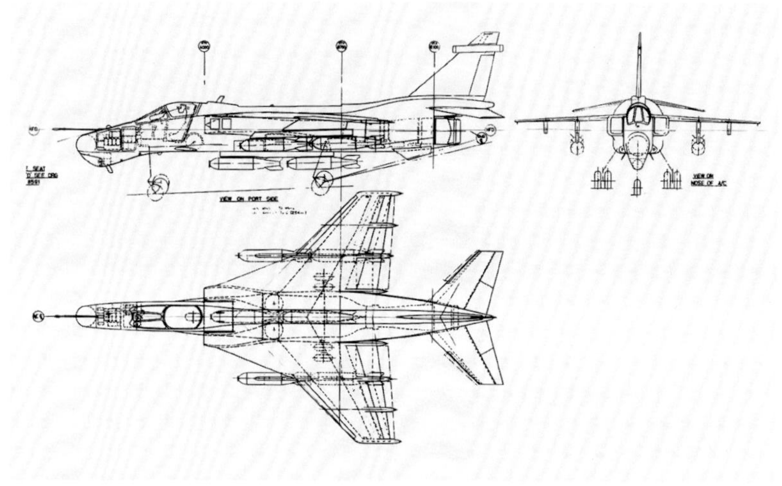

Considered to be the smallest airframe that could meet AST.396, the study shown in drawing EAG.8522 combined a single RB.199-34R with the new high-lift wing and Nose D with associated avionics suite. *North West Heritage Group*

The Jaguar-based design studies appeared to be the best route to an aircraft that could meet the AST and possibly the penultimate AST.396 study from Warton was a single-engined design that used a RB.199-34R, high-lift wing and Nose D. This design, EAG.8522, was considered to be the smallest aircraft able to meet the Air Staff Target. AST.396 prompted some interesting proposals from BAC at Warton, using just about every fast jet configuration imaginable including delta wings (P.72), variable-geometry wings (P.73) and returning to the Jaguar with upgraded avionics and new engines.

Kingston's Variety

As was the case with Warton and their Jaguar, HSA at Kingston was interested in developing the replacement for their Harrier. Kingston's 1972 report examined a number of candidate aircraft that ranged from HSA's P.1182 Hawk modified for ground attack, through Dassault's Mirage F1, to the heavier end with the SAAB AJ 37 Viggen, all of which were about to enter service. Oddly enough, in this variety of types, Kingston included BAC's Jaguar!

The Viggen might appear to be an odd choice, but it possessed the STOL performance called for in AST.396, with 1,500ft (457m) claimed as a take-off run although this would increase when carrying a heavy payload of up to 19,800 lb (9,000kg) on nine hardpoints. In Flygvapnet (Swedish Air Force) service the Viggen would operate from dispersed sites under the *Bas 90* programme whereby Viggens would operate from stretches of road 2,600ft (800m)

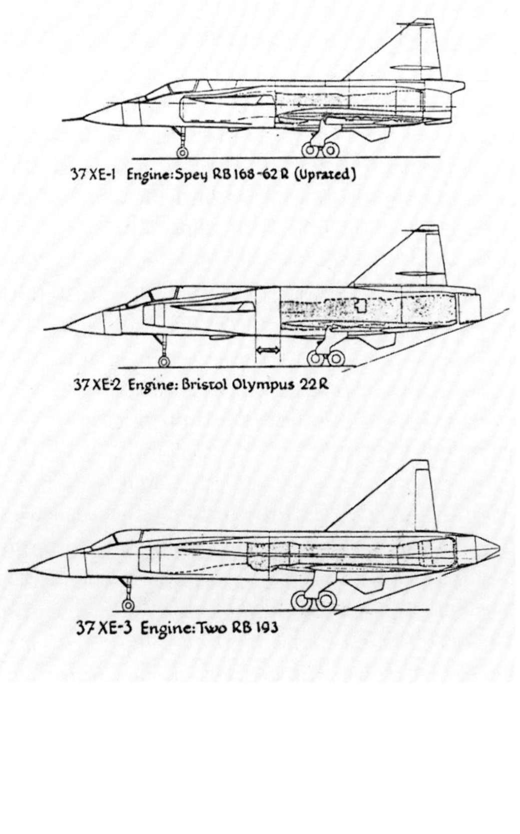

Thanks to its STOL performance, the SAAB Viggen was briefly considered for AST.396 and examined by the Hawker Siddeley design team. Meanwhile Rolls-Royce had been examining re-engining the Viggen with the Rolls-Royce RB.168-62R Spey, Bristol Olympus 22R or a pair of Rolls-Royce RB.193. *Rolls-Royce Heritage, Bristol*

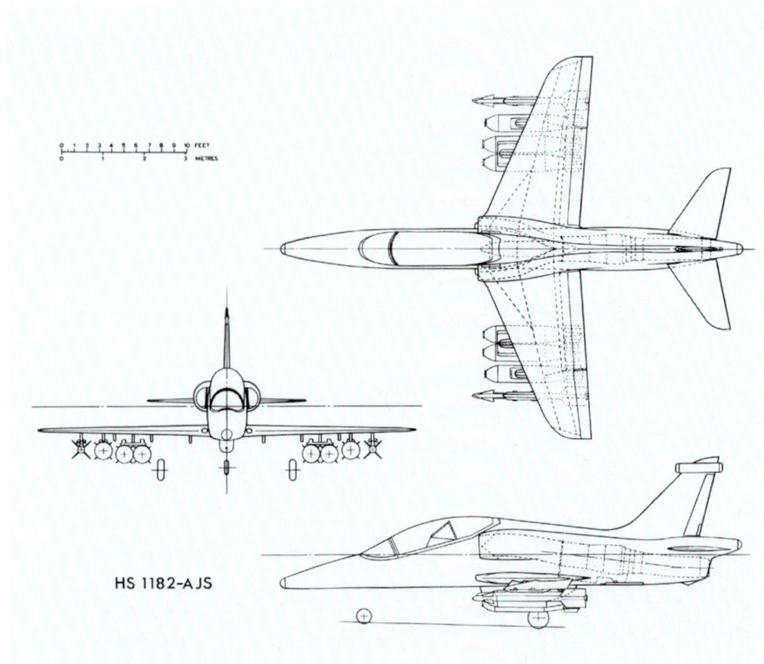

Above: HSA Kingston based their AJS on the Hawk trainer, seen here with six BL.755 and two Sidewinders. The airframe was considered too small for the sensors required for the role. *Brooklands Museum*

Below: The Hawker Siddeley Hawk was proposed for AST.396 as the AJS but was deemed too small for the role. Single and two-seat variants were studied. The two-seat variant had a more complex sensor suite, operated by the back-seater. The single-seater's sensors were much simpler and designed for single pilot operation.

Opposite, top: Hawker Siddeley Kingston's designs studies towards AST.396 included many V/STOL designs (clockwise from top left): HS.1184-1, HS.1185-9, HS.1187-5 and HS.1186-1.

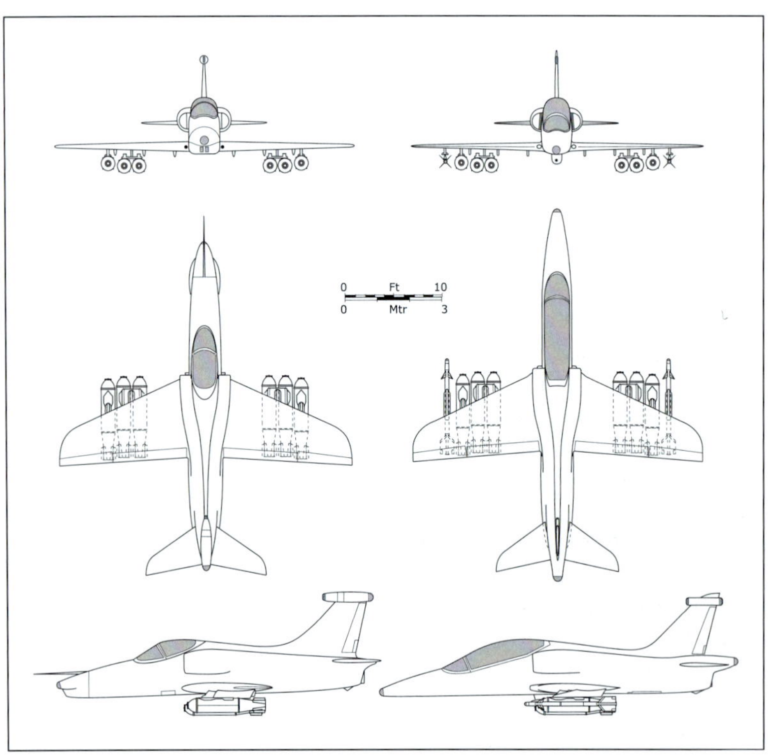

long. The AJ 37 Viggen lacked a gun but for the JA 37 interceptor variant the hard-hitting KCA 30mm cannon was fitted, a weapon also being considered for the Panavia Tornado. The Viggen had been the subject of British paper studies to re-engine it with a RB.168-62R Spey, an Olympus 22R or two RB.193 with the latter rated at 10,270 lbf (45.7kN) or 17,630 lbf (78.4kN) with reheat.

The Mirage F1 could be viewed as Dassault's response, if not spoiler, to the SEPECAT Jaguar, but for the AST.396 role, it lacked the STOL performance (although take-off and landing performance was better than the Mirage deltas) and radius of action. None of these stopped the Mirage F1 being used for ground attack by its many export customers while the Mirage F1CT was a conversion of the type from interceptor to ground attack, capable of using smart weapons. It wasn't only the RAF that used hand-me-down interceptors for ground attack.

As mentioned above, the HS.1182 was considered for AST.396, in single and two seat variants. The two-seat AJS version carried the same ventral ADEN cannon pod as the Hawk weapons trainer but was fitted with six, rather than four, wing pylons for the cluster bombs. Note that the 'HS.1182 AJ' was the HSA designation for the design variant that became the Hawk T.1. The AJS variant carried a fairly simple sensor suite, operated by the navigator in the back seat. A single-seat version of the AJS incorporated a more complex sensor suite that would allow single pilot operations on moonlit nights.

As for the Jaguar, another 'foreign' design examined by Kingston, Hawker Siddeley suggested new engines such as the RB.199, but realistically, like the other existing aircraft examined, Kingston regarded the Jaguar as not particularly suitable for AST.396. Designs, such as the Jaguar, from the early to late Sixties, could not accommodate the additional fuel, new sensors and, of course, the weapons load of six BL.755 to meet the Staff target.

Harrier and Hawk for Night Flight

By the early 1970s the Harrier GR.1 was well established in the close air support role and being upgraded to GR.3 standard by adding the Ferranti Laser Ranger and Marked Target Seeker (LRMTS), radar warning receiver system and Pegasus Mk.103 engine.

For AST.396 the Kingston designers drew up the P.1184-1 that incorporated minimal changes from the GR.3 to meet the AST, but these included a stretched fuselage (plus a longer tailboom for more effective reaction control) and modified wing with extended wingtips (as per the 'ferry tips' on the GR.1/GR.3) and drooped leading edge. The wing also incorporated overwing hardpoints for pylons carrying Sidewinder AAMs. HSA proposed many studies in the HS.1184 series with the HS.1184-7 the most suitable for the AST. The HS.1184-7 was almost a complete redesign incorporating new wings with pod-mounted main wheels and tip rails for Sidewinders or SRAAM and would be re-engined with the RB.422-1 rated at 26,000 lbf (116.6kN) or Pegasus 15, rated at 28,600 lbf (127kN). By moving the main undercarriage to the wings, the fuselage was available for stores carriage, with two of the required six BL.755 bombs carried in tandem on ventral centreline pylons. The many HS.1184 studies proved to be forerunners for the later AV-16 studies conducted in co-operation with McDonnell Douglas, bridging the gap between the original GR.1/GR.3 and the later advanced Harriers.

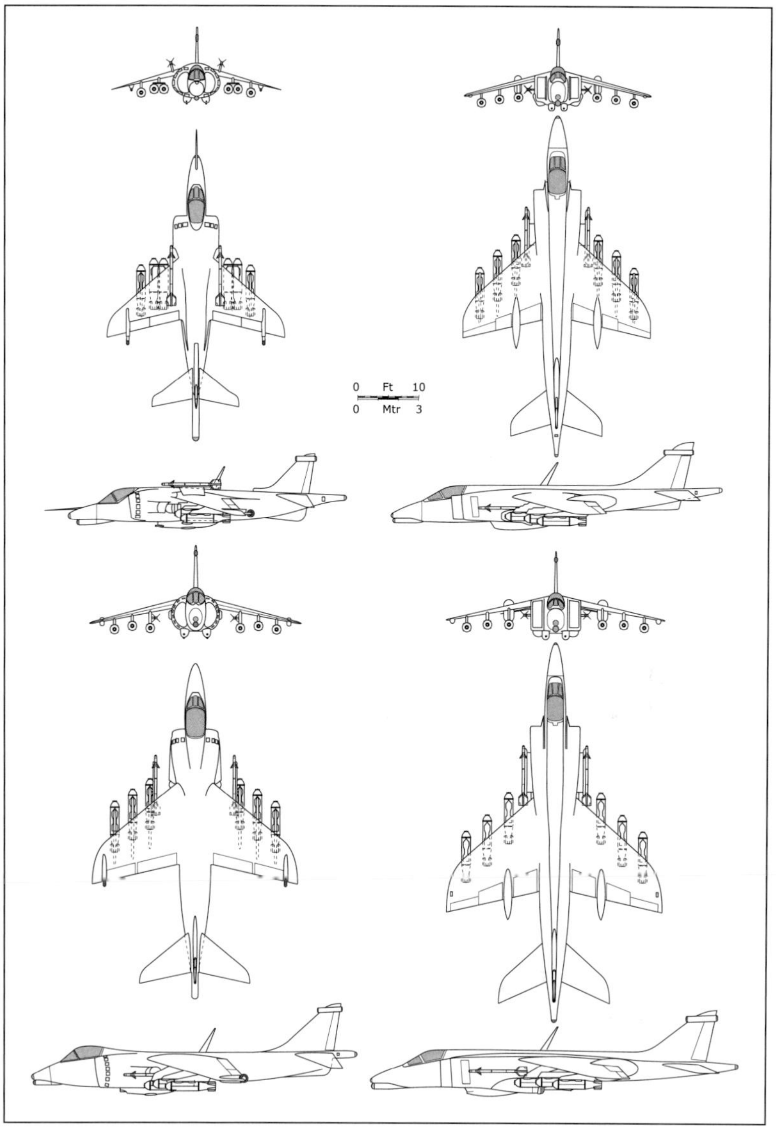

Two of the most interesting HS.1184 proposals are the -18 and -20 drawn up to meet Issue 2 of AST.396 and which carried the full suite of mission sensors. The HS.1184-18's most obvious feature was its angular wing with tip rails for Sidewinders, although AAMs were not a requirement. Interestingly the -18 is show with eight BL.755, six underwing and another two in tandem on a ventral pylon. The additional two bombs are shown in outline only, as are the Sidewinders, suggesting these are an additional capability, as eight bombs and the self-defence weapons were beyond the capability called for in the AST. The HS.1184-18 is also notable for dispensing with the 'bicycle/outrigger' under-

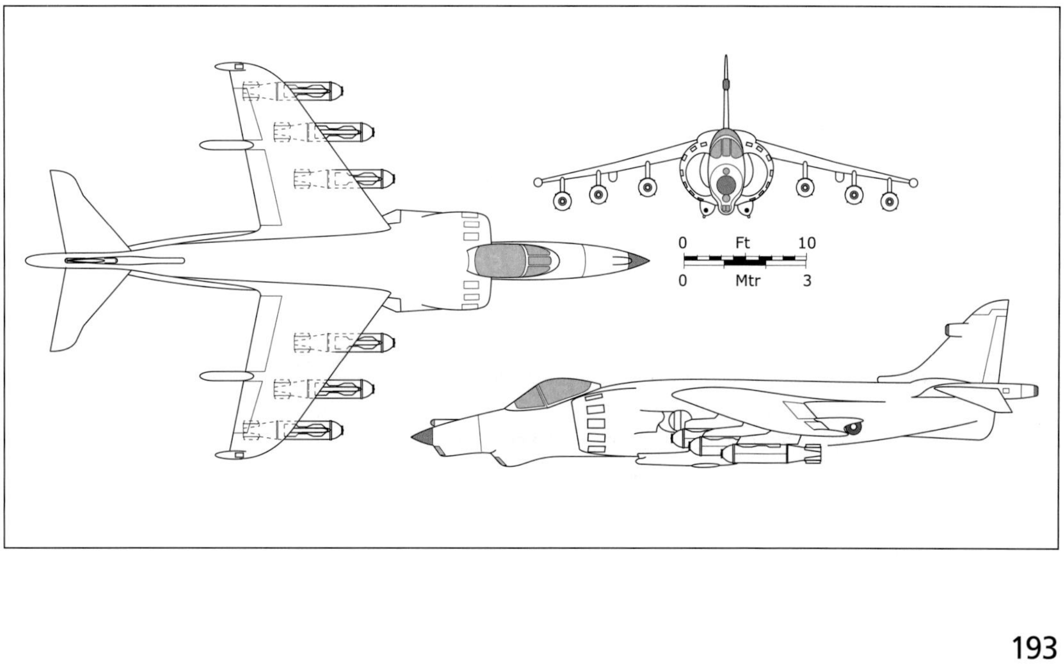

Left: Examples of 'nasal congestion' include the HS.1184-20 which is reminiscent of a Sea Harrier FRS.1 with a new nose and modified wing with six pylons. The HS.1184-20 could carry the requisite six BL.755 and guns but appears to lack the air-to-air missiles required for AST.396 (Issue 1) so may have been aimed at the later AST.396 (Issue 2).

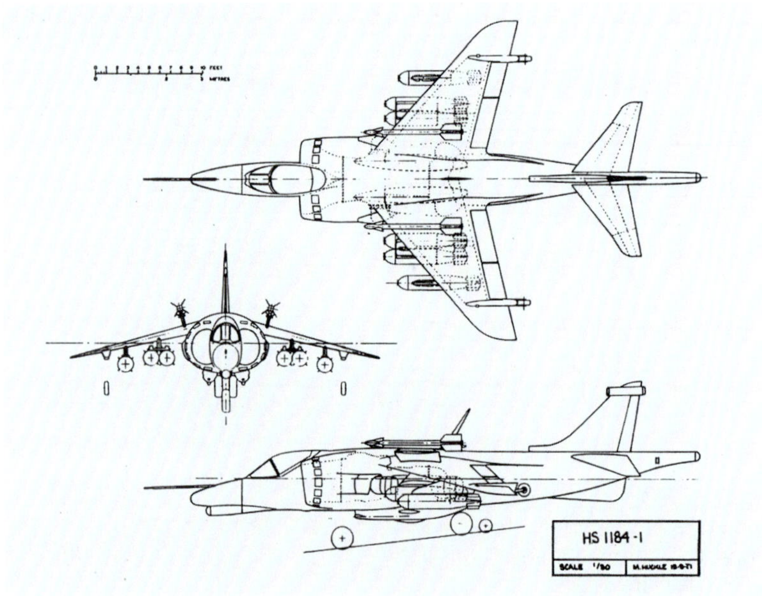

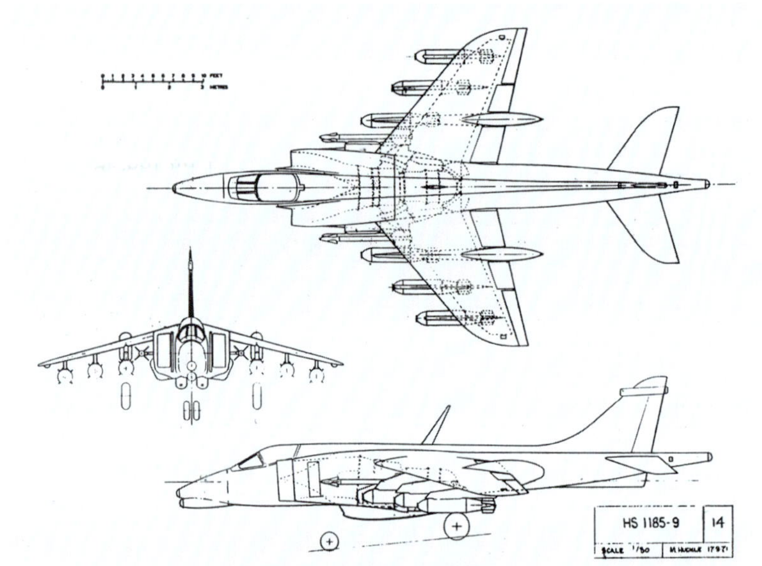

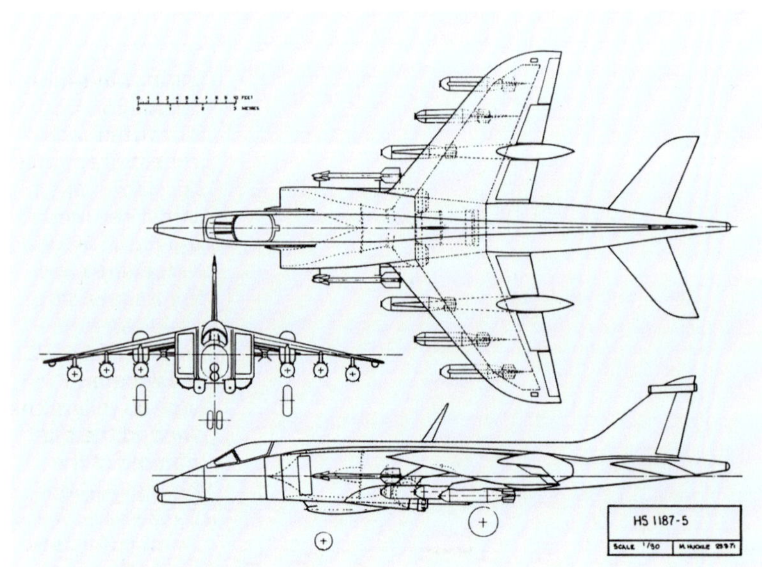

carriage and providing a tricycle undercarriage with the mainwheels on the wings, retracting into trailing edge fairings.

The HS.1184-20 is a very interesting study and at first glance it resembles a Sea Harrier FRS.1, sharing that type's raised cockpit to improve rearward visibility for the pilot. The -20's wing was modified with three hardpoints, each with a pylon for a BL.755. The undercarriage outrigger was moved inboard from the wingtip to a position at approximately mid-span on the trailing edge between flaps and ailerons. The wingtip now carried a small fairing for the reaction control valves. The term 'nasal congestion' could have been coined for the P.1184-20, with a sensor array that dominated the nose and forward fuselage. A small radome for the terrain-following radar forms the extreme nose, with LRTMS above and LLLTV below and just aft of the radome. A large fairing under the forward fuselage, almost as large as the cockpit canopy, housed the FLIR equipment.

As baseball player Yogi Berra once said, 'It's *déjà vu* all over again.' and that might be the feeling readers get when looking at the HS.1185 studies as they bear a very close resemblance to the Hawker P.1154 of a decade earlier. The HS.1185 shared the P.1154's configuration, rectangular intakes with splitter plates and plenum chamber burning systems although the weapons carriage differed significantly with six underwing pylons for stores and a stub pylon for Sidewinders on the intake trunking. As with the P.1154 and HS.1184-18, the main undercarriage was housed in wing pods with a twin-wheel nose gear. The Pegasus 15-03 was to be fitted with PCB on the forward nozzles to produce a thrust rating of 34,850 lbf (159.4kN). Installing such an engine would have impacted the airframe design by requiring heat resistant material, such as titanium, in the areas affected by the hot efflux from the PCB. One interesting design in the HS.1185 series was the HS.1185-13 with a wider, flattened rear fuselage and a

The HS.1184-1 was very similar to the Harrier GR.3 but with ferry tips and overwing Sidewinders. *Brooklands Museum*

HS.1185-9 was reminiscent of the P.1154 of a decade before with longer fuselage, tricycle undercarriage and box intakes. The Sidewinder pylons were now on the intake sides. *Brooklands Museum*

Kingston's HS.1187-5 followed the HS.1185 configuration but the rear fuselage was scalloped along the bottom to allow a single jetpipe. *Brooklands Museum*

pair of tail fins although the reason for the twin fins is not clear.

Also sharing the P.1154 configuration was the HS.1187 series that was unusual in its use of what at first glance looks like two vectoring nozzles and a single jetpipe on its Pegasus engine. The jetpipe was in fact split into two back-to-back 'D-shaped' reheat nozzles. The 'hot' rear jetpipe incorporated a deflector and downward blowing nozzle that led to the 'D' shaped nozzles and to accommodate this, the rear fuselage was much shallower.

As for aircraft from Kingston that were not Harrier derivatives, the Hawk was a new design, could carry the weapons but was too small to carry the sensors to meet the full AST, so clean sheet designs were looked on more favourably. Kingston's designers drew up the HS.1189-1 as a single-seat strike aircraft that looked like a 'beefy' Hunter. At least three variants were proposed; two differing in engine type and a third with reduced sweep on the wings. The -1 was powered by an unreheated RB.199-36 while the -3 was powered by an RB.172-19R, a reheated Adour and had reduced wing sweep. The -5 was the most attractive from the point of view of meeting the Staff Target and was to be fitted with an RB.199-41 and wing and tail surfaces of greater area. Unfortunately, the HS.1189-5 lacked the field performance required of the Staff Target.

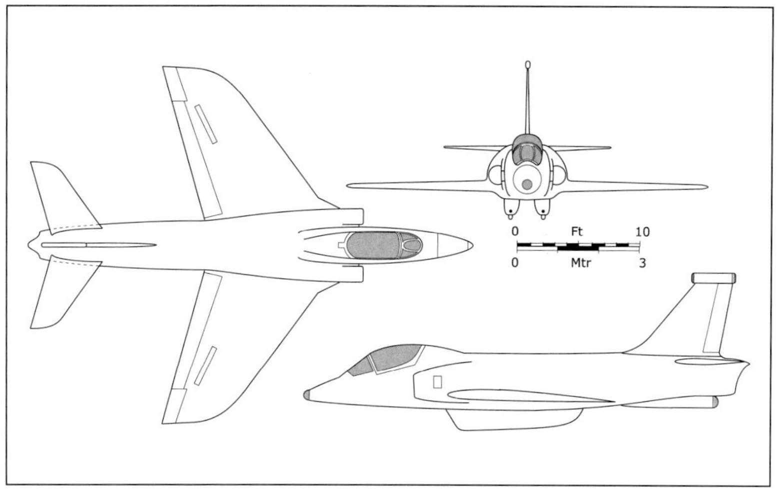

Not all Kingston design studies were based on the P.1127/Harrier configuration. This study, HS.1189-1, is reminiscent of the Hunter and was to be powered by an unreheated RB.199-36.

Brough's HS.1190

One of the many proposals to meet AST.396 was the HS.1190, based on Brough's P.153 Small Combat Aircraft. This shoulder-winged type had been designed as a single-seat lightweight fighter with a battlefield support capability and powered by a single RB.199-34R engine. This was the same engine used on the early versions of the Tornado IDS and rated at 8,100 lbf (36kN) and 15,950 lbf (71kN) with reheat. The resulting aircraft bore a startling resemblance to the Aeritalia/Embraer AMX of the 1990s.

For Issue 1 of AST.396, two versions, HS.1190-1 and -2 were proposed, both weighing in with AUW around 25,000 lb (11,340kg) but their STOL performance was less than required by the Staff Target, despite showing promise in all other areas. With the issue of AST.396 Issue 2 another two versions were proposed: the single-seat HS.1190-5 and two seat -6 powered by either RB.199-34R or RB.199-42R turbofans rated at 9,700 lbf (43.1kN) dry and 17,000 lbf (75.6kN) with reheat and two avionics fits: Simple and Conformal. The -5 was essentially the P.153 with new avionics and supersonic capability and weighed in at 25,500 lb (11,567kg) with six BL.755 cluster bombs. The -6 weighed in at 27,500 lb (12,473kg) and the two types shared wings, tail surfaces and rear fuselage/

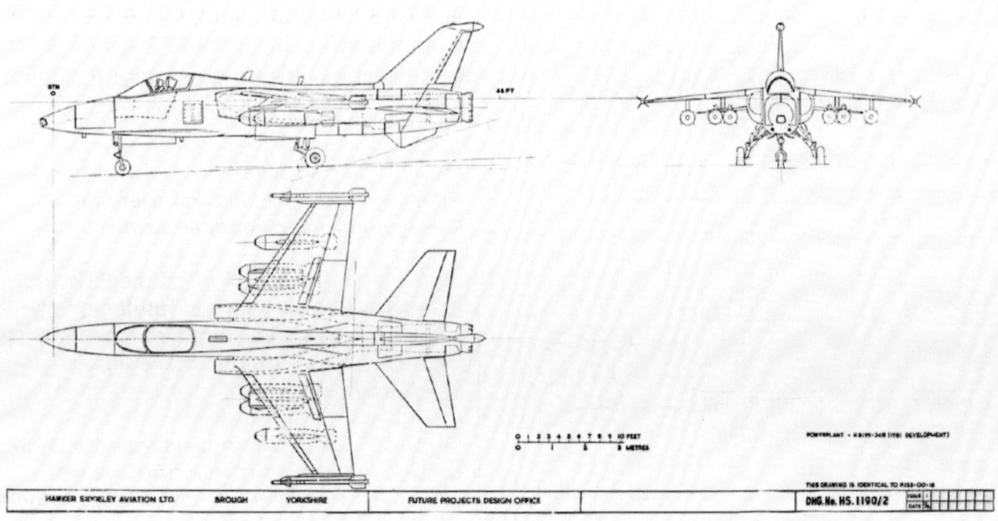

The HS.1190 series was similar to the HS.1189 but fitted with reheated engines for the extra boost required for egress from the target area and thrust reversers, as shown here on the HS.1190/2 (designated P.153 at Brough) which formed the basis of most of the Brough AST.396 studies. *Brough Heritage*

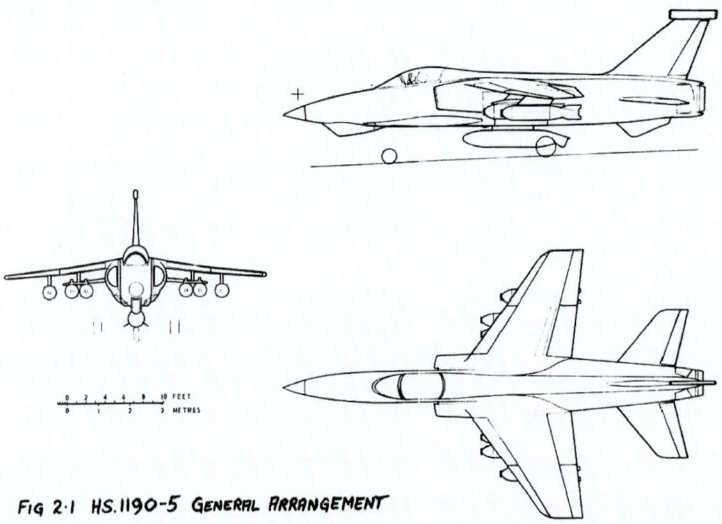

FIG 2·1 HS.1190-5 GENERAL ARRANGEMENT

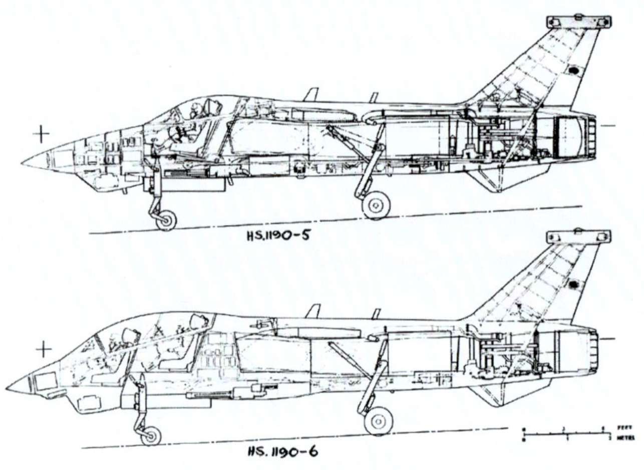

FIG 2·2 INTERNAL ARRANGEMENTS

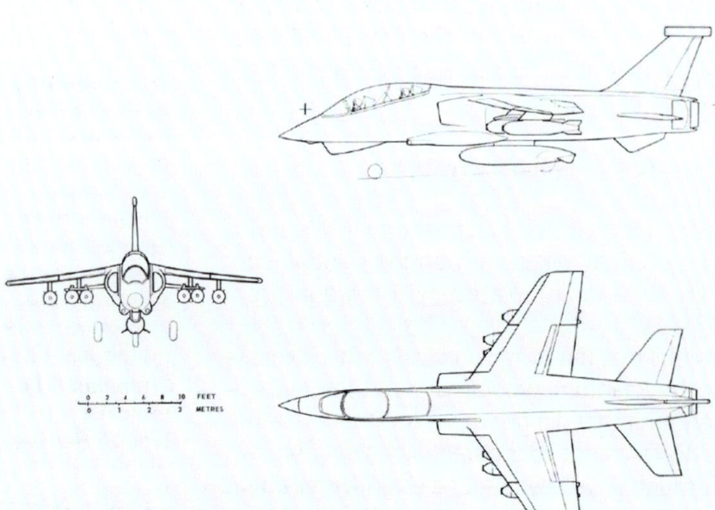

FIG 2·4 HS.1190-6 GENERAL ARRANGEMENT

engine installation with four underwing pylons and a ventral stores station plus wingtip rails for AAMs. This variant was 'considered the most attractive in the spirit of the AST.' The next iteration, the HS.1190-7 used a pair of unreheated RB.199-41, without thrust reversers, rated at 6,160lbf (27.4kN) followed by the single-engined -10 (single seat) and -11 (two seat) intended as the lightest and smallest proposal to meet AST.396. The -11 variant was more or less a lengthened -5 version described above.

All versions used boundary layer control, i.e. blown surfaces, based on those developed for the Buccaneer and Phantom which allowed the use of simple hinged control surfaces rather than complex mechanical high lift devices. The system would use bleed air from the bypass section of the engine, which would simplify the design and allow lighter material to be used for ducts and blown air slots.

Vulnerability to air defences was assessed, with IR-guided weapons such as the 9K32 Strela (NATO reporting name SA-7 *Grail*) and 9K34 Strela-3 (NATO reporting name SA-14 *Gremlin*) deemed the greatest threat in the attack and egress phases with flares as the active countermeasure. As might be expected, the aircraft would be most vulnerable when reheat was engaged and there was no countermeasure apart from cutting the reheat. In the transit to, (particularly when external stores were being carried) and from the target, the SA-6 *Gainful*, seen as the main threat. Against such radar-homing SAMs and other radar-directed weapons, countermeasures were to include the ARI.23246 Skyshadow active ECM pod (originally known as Ajax) developed to meet ASR.853.

For target acquisition and attack, various sensor suites were proposed, based on equipment being designed for the MRCA, although the size of the HS.1190's forward fuselage might mean some of the sensors were mounted in

Top: The larger HS.1190/5 had a slightly different planform without the tip rails for AAMs, as the air-to-air role was no longer required. *Brough Heritage*

Centre: Inboard profiles of the single-seat HS.1190/6 and two-seat HS.1190/6 show the amount of equipment required for the sensor suite, especially for the two-seater. *Brough Heritage*

Bottom: The two-seat HS.1190/6 had a longer fuselage and more capable sensor suite. The second crew member could use it to full advantage. *Brough Heritage*.

A flight of HS.1195s approach out of the rising sun to attack a column of T-72s and BMP-1s. The IBL.755 was intended to be used to attack armoured vehicles from the rear, which would have required the attacking aircraft to approach Warsaw Pact formations from the east.
Luciano Alviani

a chin fairing. These included a low-light level television system (LLLTV), laser ranger and marked target seeker (LRMTS) as used on Jaguar GR.1 and Harrier GR.3, forward-looking infra-red (FLIR) and a terrain following radar. These would be combined in an avionics suite that included head-up and head-down displays in the cockpit, a helmet-mounted sight and a Ferranti Digital Inertial Navigation System (DINS). Three configurations were examined: 'Simple', comprising LRMTS, FLIR and LLLTV; 'Candidate', comprising LRMTS, LLLTV, a multi-spectral sensor (in lieu of FLIR) and TFR; Conformal, comprising LRMTS, LLLTV, TFR and FLIR. FLIR and LLLTV are mounted side-by-side to ensure that the length of the forward fuselage is minimised, although proximity to the cannon muzzles could pose a problem for the sensors. To counter the effect of blast on the sensors, the cannon were repositioned aft on the HS.1190-6.

Another Brough design study for AST.396 was the HS.1195, 'evolved from a scaling up of the HS.1190-6' as the HS.1190-9 before being redesignated as HS.1195-6 and 'incorporating some features of the Buccaneer and optimised to the AST.396 mission.' The aircraft was a two-seater and with six BL.755 bombs and two ECM pods, it was to have an AUW of 34,500lb (15,649kg) and be powered by a single RB.168-72 Spey turbofan rated at 17,500lbf (77.8kN) or if the reheated version the RB.168-73R, rated at 27,670lbf (123.1kN) was fitted the AUW rose to 40,000lb (18,144kg) although this was deemed unsuitable for a subsonic aircraft. The RB.168-72 was an uprated version of the Allison TF41-A2 used in the A-7D Corsair while the RB.168-73R was proposed for the Grumman F-14 as an alternative to the Pratt & Whitney F401, rated at 28,100lbf (125kN) intended for the F-14B.

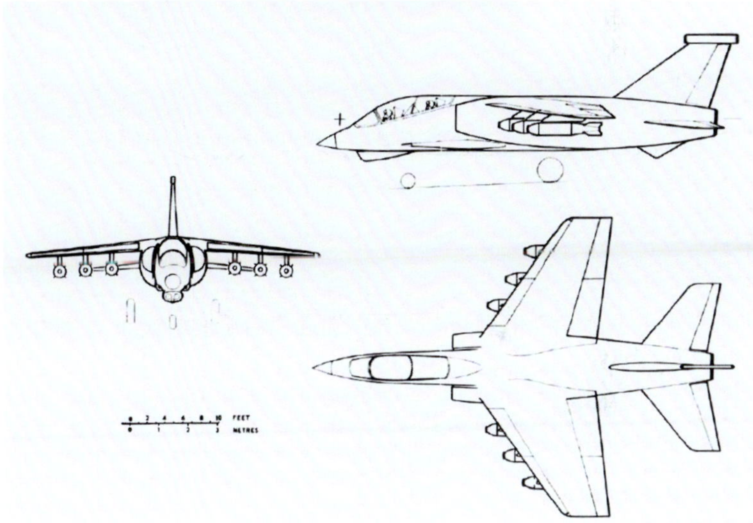

The HS.1195 was scaled up from the HS.1190 and used features such as blown flaps from the Buccaneer. They were powered by versions of the Spey that were intended for American types such as the LTV A-7D Corsair II and Grumman F-14 Tomcat.
Brough Heritage

The AST.396 Phantom

The Phantom FGR.2 had been the RAF's principal ground attack aircraft on the Central Front from 1968 until replaced by the Jaguar from 1974. When AST.396 was issued it was fairly obvious that the 'Tomb' (an early RAF nickname for the Phantom) would not meet the requirement, but that did not mean McDonnell Douglas' F-4 was not considered, albeit very briefly.

Brough's Aerodynamics Design Department 'briefly examined' the 'suitability of the British Phantom for AST.396'. The note, drawn up by Mr Neville Beckett, Principal Project Aero-

Hawker Siddeley at Brough had built the RAF's Phantom FG.1 and FGR.2s. Although designed as a carrier interceptor, the Phantom could carry a lot of air-to-ground ordnance, such as the seven BL.755 seen here but for AST.396 it would require too many modifications to even come close to the Staff Target. *Blue Envoy Collection*

dynamicist described how the main difficulty was 'evolving a loading configuration for the aircraft to enable it to approach the specified RoA with the required store load'. It was feasible but with various changes to the stores carried or with modifications that could in no way be described as tweaks.

In the anti-armour role AST.396 called for a strike aircraft capable of carrying six BL.755 and a gun, operating from an improvised runway 3,000ft (914m) in length. The Phantom's 'full mission load' for the anti-armour role was six BL.755 carried on triple ejector racks (TER) on the inner wing pylons, a SUU-23A pod with a M61 20mm Vulcan cannon on the centreline and an ECM and IRCM pod on the outer wing pylons. The Phantom would only carry its internal fuel giving a RoA of 100nm (185km) so this configuration could not meet the required RoA.

When configured for maximum fuel, adding two 370 US Gallon (1,400 litre) tanks on the outer wing pylons and a 600 US gallon (2,271 litre) tank on the centreline, the Phantom RoA was 281nm (403km) but carried no gun nor ECM pods. The next configuration exchanged the 600 US gallon (2,271 litre) tank for a SUU-23a pod to give a RoA of 185nm (342km). The last load-out examined saw the IRCM pod moved to the forward starboard Sparrow recess and a 370 US gallon (1,400 litre) tank on the port outer pylon. This configuration produced a RoA of 228nm (422km), which almost made the RoA requirement but with a 600 US Gallon tank rather than the SUU-23a gun pod.

Although the Phantom looked as if it had a plethora of locations for stores carriage, if external tanks were required, the number of pylons available was much reduced. Interestingly the TER on the RAF's Phantom was only cleared for two BL.755 rather than three, reducing the weapons load further, although this would have been addressed to meet the AST.

Take-off and landing performance were scrutinised as the standard brakes on the RAF's Phantoms could not bring the aircraft to a halt in under 5,000ft (1,524m) rather than the 3,000ft (914m) required. To meet the requirement, new brakes, thrust reversers and a larger brake parachute were considered but only the former was feasible. Adaptive brakes and two types of thrust reverser were considered; an internal eyelid type fitted between the Spey turbofan and its reheat section or an external 'target' type that was mounted on the rear fuselage. The internal eyelid type, as installed on the Hawker Siddeley Trident, could not be fitted as the Spey and its reheat section were 'closely coupled' so there was no room for the thrust reverser. As for the external target, as fitted to the Gulfstream bizjet, the shape of the Phantom's rear fuselage and the arrangement of the nozzles made fitting a thrust reverser extremely difficult. A good example of a target-type thrust reverser is the Panavia Tornado that uses two 'buckets' that deploy from above and below the jet pipe and close across the jet efflux, directing the efflux over and under the rear fuselage to slow the aircraft. When considering a larger brake parachute, Beckett noted that 'its behaviour in cross winds was not acceptable'.

Modifications to the Phantom undercarriage were examined as the Phantom was designed to operate from aircraft carriers with steel decks or from concrete runways and as such it was fitted with high pressure tyres, inflated to 300psi (21bar). For AST.396, the Phantom would be required to take-off and land from austere strips near the frontline and would be rudimentary at best. California Bearing Ratio (CBR) is a measure of the load bearing and susceptibility to penetration of a road or runway. The Phantom's undercarriage needed a CBR of 20 while AST.396 called for operations from runways with a CBR of 4. Beckett made an interesting comment, observing that the Buccaneer needed a two-wheel bogie main undercarriage to allow the type to operate from a runway with a CBR of 6. The standard Buccaneer could operate from runways with a CBR of 11.

When all these factors were considered, there was no prospect of the Phantom meeting AST.396. The Phantom had been designed as an interceptor to operate from an aircraft carrier and intercept bombers at high altitude. It was, as had been shown in Vietnam from 1965-73, Sinai in October 1973 and the Iran-Iraq War of 1980-88, an excellent attack aircraft. Unfortunately, it was not suitable for the role outlined in AST.396.

Buccaneer for AST.396

The next type from Brough under consideration was the Buccaneer, in the form of the P.1197. The Buccaneer S.2 was to form the basis of Brough's HS.1197 proposal to meet AST.396 and is outlined in Brough Note YPO.860. The HS.1197-1 weighed in with an AUW of 48,966 lb (22,210kg) and was to incorporate Rolls-Royce's latest developments on the Spey 101 including a quick start facility. The wings were to be fitted with quick-acting flaps while the main undercarriage was to be replaced with two-wheel tandem bogies for improved braking effect as well as a braking parachute. The weapons bay was to be shortened to hold two BL.755 with two ADEN 30mm cannon installed in what had been the forward portion of the rotating bomb bay. The avionics fit would have been the 'Conformal' suite along with a new reconnaissance system. The HS.1197-2 was to be the -1 with booster engines added to improve take-off performance while the -3 replaced the braking parachute with thrust reversers on the Spey 101s.

Concerns were raised about the AUW of the HS.1197-1 so a weight reduction programme was initiated. A lighter arrester hook from the S Mk.50 (Buccaneer for the South African Air Force) saved 82 lb (37kg), new Martin-Baker Mk.10B ejection seats would save 35 lb (15.8kg) while changing from stainless steel to titanium bolts would save around 150 lb (68kg) with another 160 lb (72.6kg) saved by using titanium rather than steel in hydraulic pipes and boundary layer control pipes. The greatest weight saving would come from replacing the wing pylons (stressed to carry the Martel) with new lighter pylons for the BL.755, saving 88 lb (40kg) for each pylon i.e. 352 lb (160kg) on pylons. These pylons, designed for AST.396 stores, could be changed if Martel carriage was required.

The Buccaneer S.2B, being a naval aircraft, had a number of features pertinent to carrier operations including the holdback and catapulting structure plus a robust tail bumper. By redesigning the structure to omit the first two and fitting a lighter bumper, a further 100 lb (45kg) could be saved. Removing the hydraulics for the wing folding system could save 134 lb (61kg) straight off the bat and even more if detailed design changes were incorporated in

Brough, Home of the Buccaneer (and British Phantom) examined the Buccaneer as a potential AST.396 type designated HS.1197. Modifications included a gun pack with two ADEN 30mm cannon in the forward section of the bomb bay, braking parachute, tandem bogie undercarriage and boost rocket. *Brough Heritage*

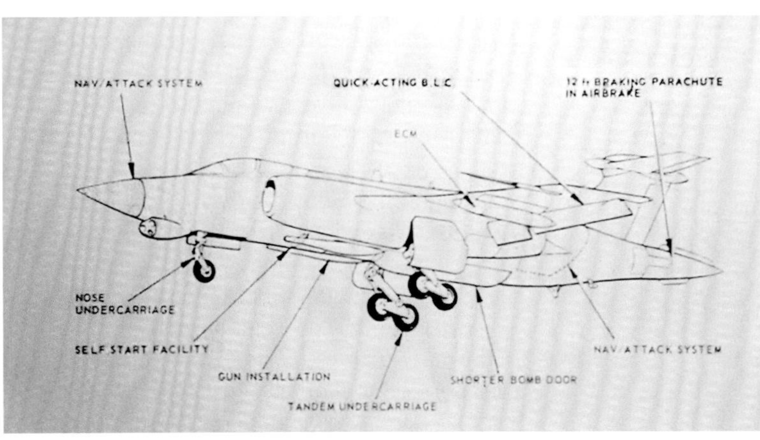

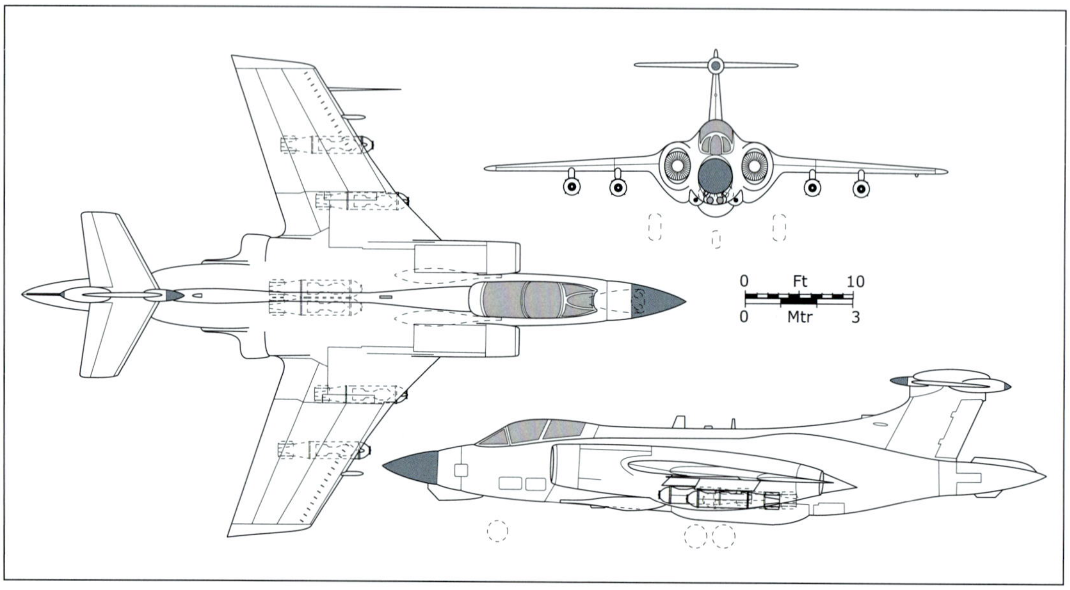

The HS.1197 Buccaneer was also put through an extensive weight-saving programme that involved substituting existing steel or Duralumin components for titanium or carbon composite. Some features not required for the AST.396 role, such as catapult kit and wing folding would be removed altogether to save weight.

the new aircraft. If wing folding was completely removed from the Buccaneer, Brough's engineers estimated another 700 lb (317kg) could be saved. New materials such as carbon fibre composites and evaporated aluminium alloys showed promise, although the latter would not be available in the AST.396 timescale. Carbon fibre could be incorporated but for a 1950s vintage design this would be limited to access doors and panels, possibly saving 42 lb (19kg) with another 30 lb (13.6kg) saved if the dorsal spine was fabricated in carbon fibre. If undercarriage doors, engine cowlings and control surfaces were in carbon fibre a further 300 lb (136kg) could be saved.

In all, Brough estimated that an aggressive weight saving programme could save 1868 lb (847kg) bringing the AUW of the HS.1197-1 down from 48,968 lb (22208kg) to 47100 lb (21,360kg). If the project's timescale were to be extended, an additional weight saving of 230 lb (104kg) might be possible.

The End of AST.396

Larger HS.1195 proposals were little better than the HS.1197 Buccaneer but what really did for AST.396 was the night and all-weather capability as the sensors and systems were not mature enough; too heavy and very expensive to develop. This was the early 1970s and while Operations Linebacker I and II had shown that smart weapons and sensors had great potential, such equipment would only reach maturity in the 1980s and prove to be a game-changer in the subsequent decade.

The Working Party on the Battlefield Support Aircraft (WPBSA) examined the proposals and reported their findings. Between them, BAC and HSA had submitted 27 design studies to the MoD/Air Staff, most derived from existing designs; Buccaneer, Harrier, Hawk, Jaguar, MRCA and Phantom, plus the clean sheet HS.1190. The aircraft that would meet the Staff Target at the lowest AUW was a 'Jaguar with a single RB.199-34R and a modified wing'. If V/STOL performance was required 'the only aircraft of those considered would be one of the Harrier variants, probably developed a stage beyond the AV-16' – one of the HS.1184 studies. As for the MRCA, it met the 'performance targets completely without major modifications, however weight and cost would be high'. The Buccaneer, HS.1197, also met the AST 'with minor modifications' aside from airfield performance but was 'heavy, relatively expensive and shortly going out of production'.

The Hawk variants fell 'well short of most of the requirements including range, take-off roll and speed'. The HS.1190 attempted to combine air combat capability with ground attack (this was the premise of AST.403 which superseded AST.396) but did not 'show up well in either role. The larger HS.1195 was included in the assessments at HSA's request. The HS.1195 had been 'tailored specifically to the AST.396 requirements and could be competitive with single-engine Jaguar variants'.

The avionics for all-weather/night missions, as described above, proved 'to be much more demanding', especially at low level in poor visibility. The WPBSA identified resolution as the main problem as 'the degree of resolution necessary to recognise small battlefield targets such as tanks can only be achieved at present in conjunction with a narrow field of view'. To recognise a tank at 3km (1.6nm) a state of the art FLIR would need a field of view of 'about 5° which would narrow the strip of ground covered by the sensor to 262m (286 yards) at 3km (1.6nm). This could be improved by 'hot-spot cueing' whereby the FLIR field of view was widened to 20° and any heat signatures displayed and selected for closer examination with the FLIR set at 5°, but this incurred a time penalty in selecting likely targets.

The WPBSA concluded that flight at the altitudes called for, in poor visibility, with the current sensors was not feasible and were concerned about the 'aerodynamic effects of the large protuberances required by the EO sensor fit'. The committee also pointed out that the aircraft to meet AST.396 would be 'a 2-seat aircraft fitted with auto-FLIR and a FLIR sensor system'.

Both BAC and HSA emphasised the difficulties in developing suitable avionics for AST.396 and the WPBSA stated that 'the avionics problems exposed are sufficient to raise major doubts about the fundamental feasibility of the Issue 2 target'. The AST would require 'an aircraft of considerable complexity, size and cost'. The Air Staff's concern about the lack of air combat capability had increased since the issue of AST.396, mainly due to evidence of improvement in the Warsaw Pact fighter threat. This meant that the AST.396 type, intended as an out-and-out ground attack aircraft would lack the performance to defend itself against the old, never mind the new generation, of Soviet fighters.

The outcome of the WPBSA's report was the withdrawal of AST.396 and the 'termination of any further studies related to it'. Harrier and Jaguar were not replaced in the 1980s, although new versions of the Harrier – GR.5, GR.7 and GR.9 – entered service and the Jaguar underwent extensive refurbishment at the end of the 1990s to become the GR.3. Their ultimate replacement was the Typhoon, a multi-role fighter whose capability lay in the weapons and ability to integrate with battlespace assets as diverse as a squaddie on the ground to a Sentinel R.1 at 50,000ft, 50 miles from the FEBA. However, there was an intervening programme on the route to Typhoon: AST.403.

The Harrier GR.7A, seen here on HMS *Illustrious*, was essentially what AST.396 should have been. The cluster of sensors on the nose includes most of those specified in AST.396, although the Harrier lacks a terrain following radar. The difference in size is testament to the miniaturisation of sensors. *MoD/ Open Government Licence*

10 AST.403 Typhoon and Beyond

'The possible merits of the F-16 would need to be balanced against other aircraft procurement decisions and the political and industrial considerations.' MoD Operational Requirements Committee paper on AST.403, October 1975

'AST.403 would in effect be the F-16 of the 1990s, the main improvement over the F-16 being runway performance.' Mr RLL Facer, Permanent Secretary, MoD to Rt Hon Fred Mulley, Secretary of State for Defence, 12 May 1978.

'You can see that the (Staff) Target represents a considerable jump in performance over what we or the Russians have now.' Presentation to AST.403 Policy Review Board, 2 August 1977

'The FAF (Armée de l'Air) had what M. Dassault dictates.' Report by Controller, Air on a conference call with Freddie Page and Denis Spotswood, 12 May 1978

The late Eighties saw the Cold War end and technologies mature to the point that true multirole aircraft could be developed, leading to AST.403 and ultimately AST.414. The evolution of the Eurofighter Typhoon was convoluted but led to a new category of fighter aircraft – swing role.

Issued in July 1975, and endorsed in August 1976, AST.403 superseded AST.396 and pretty much reversed the roles laid out in AST.396 Issue 2. Rather than the destruction of Warsaw Pact armour, air combat was now the priority for the retitled 'Offensive Aircraft to Replace Harrier and Jaguar', ground-attack was secondary, with reconnaissance as an auxiliary role. The rationale for this change was that NATO intelligence services were aware of an increase

Warsaw Pact aircraft such as MiG-27 *Flogger-D* Red 05, posed a threat to NATO ground attack aircraft. Having delivered their stores, *Flogger-D* could use their 30mm rotary cannon in the air-to-air role against heavily laden NATO aircraft. *Chris Lofting*

in the capabilities, and numbers, of Warsaw Pact fighters, such as the MiG-23 *Flogger* and future types that would enter service in the 1980s, such as the MiG-29 *Fulcrum*. These were 'likely to be operating over the battlefield and therefore likely to jeopardise the NATO air support programme in particular'. Another factor was that Warsaw Pact strike aircraft such as the Su-7/17/22 *Fitter*, Su-19 (later identified as Su-24) *Fencer* and MiG-27 *Flogger-D* were fitted with guns and 'even those returning from penetration missions to the west constitute a threat'.

Conversely, fielding an air combat type would support the ground forces by providing a threat to Warsaw Pact forces and cause them to divert resources to tackling that threat. By operating beyond the FEBA, the type would also deny the Warsaw Pact a safe haven from which to operate and, when required, provide local air superiority for the land forces.

The burgeoning Warsaw Pact air forces were also seen as a major threat to the deployment of NATO forces moving forward into the battle area from the west, with choke points being 'exposed and allied ground defences overstretched'. These would provide 'excellent targets for all forms of Warsaw Pact offensive air activity' and NATO fighters would probably 'offer the only effective means of protection'.

The aircraft required would be 'considerably removed from that of a pure interceptor' and need to tackle not only 'laden attack aircraft but also the most agile and effective of its contemporary Russian fighters.' Therefore, the first requirement of AST.403 was to 'incorporate within the AST fully effective air combat performance' as well as the ground attack capability that had been called for in AST.396. The aircraft that the AST.403 type was to replace – Harrier and Jaguar – required fighter escort in the shape of the Phantom FGR.2 and Lightning F.6. and neither would be effective against the next generation of Soviet fighters and strike aircraft.

Another factor considered in drafting the AST was the proliferation of mobile air defence systems such as the ZSU-23/4 Shilka and SA-8 *Gecko* plus man-portable SAMs such as the SA-7 *Grail*. These, according to the Air Staff, made operations over the FEBA untenable and therefore the ground attack effort should be concentrated 'in the area beyond the FEBA, and that in future available RAF attack effort could be more profitably employed in this area than in the FEBA'.

Another consideration in drafting the new AST was an increased emphasis on counter-air operations by Warsaw Pact air forces. This would have the effect of 'bottling up' NATO aircraft and these airfields in turn would be heavily attacked, possibly with a Soviet equivalent of the UK's ASR.1217 weapon that became JP.233. This would be best addressed by an aircraft with V/STOL performance but would (in 1975) mean adopting an aircraft that lacked the required flight performance. This was changing, as the YF-16 had demonstrated the capability of carrying 4,000lb (1814kg) of weapons and fuel for a 240nm (444km) Lo-Lo radius of action from a take-off roll of 1,580ft (482m). The key to the YF-16's performance was high thrust/weight ratio, with its Pratt & Whitney F100-100 engine, rated at 23,400lbf (104.1kN). As noted in Chapter 3 there had been problems finding sufficient dispersed sites for the existing Harrier force of 36 aircraft, never mind

Opposite page: Lightning ZM137 from No 617 Sqn leads a mixed vic comprising two USMC Lightning II (168726 and 168727) from VMFAT-101 and Typhoons (ZK329 and ZK310) from No.1 Sqn. Note that the RAF does not use the 'II' suffix for its Lightnings. *MoD/ Open Government Licence*

Above: The Forward Edge of the Battlefield Area – FEBA was the zone in which Warsaw Pact formations would be advancing and NATO forces would be in contact. This zone would be rich in targets, such as tanks, for support aircraft but would also have the full range of air defence assets. Therefore AST.403 was to attack targets beyond the FEBA. *DoD*

an expanded STOVL force of over 100 aircraft.

The gist of the draft AST was that the aircraft would be complementary to the Tornado GR.1, which would be reserved for attacking Warsaw Pact airfields, nuclear facilities and rear echelon targets. The resultant AST.403 type should be capable of intercepting Warsaw Pact fighter and strike aircraft and be able to defend itself while attacking ground targets in, and beyond, the FEBA without the need for a fighter escort. The aircraft's characteristics might 'overlap the Tornado GR.1 and possibly even 'whatever may emerge from the study of the armed helicopter', which in 1978 was GSR.3971. It would be 'much more than a Harrier/Jaguar replacement for offensive support'.

One Aircraft or Two?

Single Aircraft – Produce a new multi-role aircraft, possibly STOVL, or 'run on' with Harrier improvements such as the 'Big Wing' Harrier (eventually led to the GR.5) or the Super Harrier (a separate development with redesigned wing and PCB for supersonic performance), although this would produce 'no dramatic improvement in inbuilt air combat capability' against the Warsaw Pact fighter threat. Arming the aircraft with the agile SRAAM 'would be advantageous'. A third solution would be to procure a fighter aircraft that could be modified to the offensive strike role. This could be a UK/West German project, a UK/US/West German project or off the shelf in the shape of the F-16 or F-18L. Fourthly, accept an aircraft designed to European requirements, specifically the West German TKF90 (Taktisches Kampfflugzeug 90), which emphasised air combat capability or the French ACT (Avion de Combat Tactique) 92.

Two Aircraft – By its nature this option had the potential for multiple solutions but 'a feasible solution' lay with a Harrier derivative such as 'Super Harrier' combined with any of the types listed in the Single Aircraft solution.

Of the options, the Two Aircraft Solution was viewed as easier, as the multi-role aircraft of the Single Aircraft Solution would be more complex and expensive. As of September 1978, the

The General Dynamics F-16 was also under consideration for AST.403, labelled as AST.403 in hardware form by some members of the Air Staff. This Royal Danish Air Force F-16A, E-008 of Esk 727, is armed with the AIM-120 AMRAAM on its wingtip rails. *Author*

two aircraft force solution is one which 'merits serious consideration'. This was the historic approach to offensive support, with ground attack aircraft operating under an air superiority 'umbrella' and was the USAF's approach for the future, F-15s or F-16s providing air cover for A-10s engaging ground targets.

Industry saw no point in developing a new design that was 'not much advanced over F-16 and F-18' as that ran the risk of being outdated by a US design in the 1990s.

The type's radius of action was to be 240nm (445km) and its missions were to be flown at high subsonic speed carrying four AAMs, such as SRAAM, six BL.755 and a cannon. The aircraft was to be fitted with an advanced multimode radar suitable for air-to-air and air-to-ground operations. These radars, analogous to the APG-66 radar in the General Dynamics F-16, would allow the AST.403 type to carry missiles such as BAe's Skyflash. One example was Ferranti's Blue Vixen which was under development for the Sea Harrier FA.2.

The lesson learned by the Americans in Vietnam was that ground attack aircraft should either be quick and agile or slow and heavily armoured – but agile. These philosophies led to the F-16 and A-10 respectively, with the A-10 being the tank killer while the F-16 was viewed as more or less AST.403 in hardware form. The Americans could afford two classes of aircraft for the battlefields of western Europe but the British could not, so opted to concentrate on the quick agile aircraft, with the RAF implying that they would like the F-16. As for the anti-armour role, BAC Warton did conduct the P.101 study that examined a Blitz Fighter: a mini-A-10 derived from the Jet Provost as described in Chapter 7.

Collaboration: US vs Europe

By 1978 the machinations of the government and aerospace companies of France were familiar to the UK government and aerospace industry. On 15 May 1978 the Chief of Defence Procurement, Sir Clifford Cornford, took calls from Frederick Page, Chairman of BAe and Sir Denis Spotswood, Deputy Chairman of Rolls-Royce, to 'discuss industrial views on AST.403'. The Controller, Aircraft, Air Chief Marshal Sir Douglas Lowe, reported on the discussion, which is quite enlightening. Frederick Page thought it was a pity to rule out a 'national programme' as there was a size at which collaboration made sense – civil programmes – but for smaller aircraft such as Hawk and Strikemaster, a national approach was beneficial. Page declined Cornford's request to 'say where he thought AST.403 would come in such a scale'.

Page and Spotswood were asked about collaboration and agreed that they 'felt sceptical about the substance of the reported close agreement between the British and French Air Staffs on the requirement'. Both believed that France was attempting to hold everyone off until they had the new Mirage family launched'. These types were the 2000 with a single M53, 'a 3000 with two RB.199s' and the large 4000 with two M53. When Cornford enquired where they thought the French Air Staff replacement for the Jaguar lay in this scenario, both observed 'that the FAF had what M. Dassault dictates'. Page 'stressed the difficulty of collaborating with France on exports – citing the Mirage F1/Jaguar as prime example – and how in his, and BAe's, opinion 'the French aim to have the largest European export record'.

Opposite, bottom: Two US Navy F/A-18C Hornets on operations over Afghanistan in 2008 refuel from RAF Tristar K.1 ZD751 of No 216 Sqn. The land-based version of the Hornet, the McDonnell Douglas F-18L, was one type considered as an off-the-shelf solution to AST.403. *Terry Panopalis Collection*

As for the Germans, according to Page and Spotswood, West Germany was aiming for 20-30% of the civil and military markets by 1995. MBB wanted Panavia to be the focus of any future military aircraft whereas the Federal Government couldn't decide whether to 'work independently or with the US'. The West Germans refused to discuss AST.403 as the aerospace industry considered Tornado to be essentially a British specification and a British dominated programme and 'they were not going to fall into the same trap again'. The West Germans were currently working on a Tactical Combat Aircraft (TCA), it was their programme and any collaboration would be on their terms.

Asked where Britain's best interests lay, Spotswood 'considered it better to be in bed with Germany rather than trying to meet them head-on' and that France would always 'put the interests of Toulouse and SNECMA first'. Page agreed and took the view that there would be little 'prospect of getting anywhere with France until Dassault, Vallières and Ravaud had gone'. These were, respectively, Marcel Dassault, Benno-Claude Vallières, CEOs of Dassault Aviation and René Ravaud, President of SNECMA.

Looking across the Atlantic, Page saw McDonnell Douglas as the only logical company to work with as BAe already had association with them on Harrier. Page thought that German interest in AST.403 might sharpened by 'frightening them with the thought of a linked McDonnell Douglas lead on AV-8 and a BAe lead in a PCB 403', PCB being plenum chamber burning. A further 'twist' would be to suggest a 50/50 UK/US share in the F-18L (land-based version of the Hornet). Spotswood disagreed on the F-18L for AST.403 as it 'did not meet the landing requirement' and it was expensive. The F-16 and F-18L, if procured, would require some relaxation in the aims of AST.403 and as such would provide few benefits over a similar British design, apart from earlier service entry.

The Ad Hoc Group

On 18 October 1978 Lieutenant General Sir Hugh Patrick Cunningham, Deputy Chief of the Defence Staff (OR), issued a paper on AST.403 that laid out the various aspects of the Offensive Support Aircraft and its possible development. The paper noted that BAC and HSA had been active in seeking collaboration but found that France was committed to the Mirage 2000 which 'left little effort for other aircraft' and West Germany was 'not prepared to enter into any detailed discussions'. Despite these differences, the British, French and West German defence ministers had met at Ditchley Park in July 1978 and emphasised the importance of 'early discussions between the Air Staffs leading to procurement studies' on a European venture. The British has also encouraged European co-operation to 'discuss authoritively concepts of operation and operational characteristics of a TCA for Europe'. To this end an 'Ad Hoc Group' had been established, under UK chairmanship in mid-1976 and members included Belgium, France, West Germany, The Netherlands and the UK. Turkey, Greece and Italy were members but by late 1978 had yet to attend meetings. Tellingly (in the light of future developments) General Cunningham's paper notes that 'None of these three is expected to make any significant input'.

The paper describes the design studies undertaken to meet the Staff Target in the

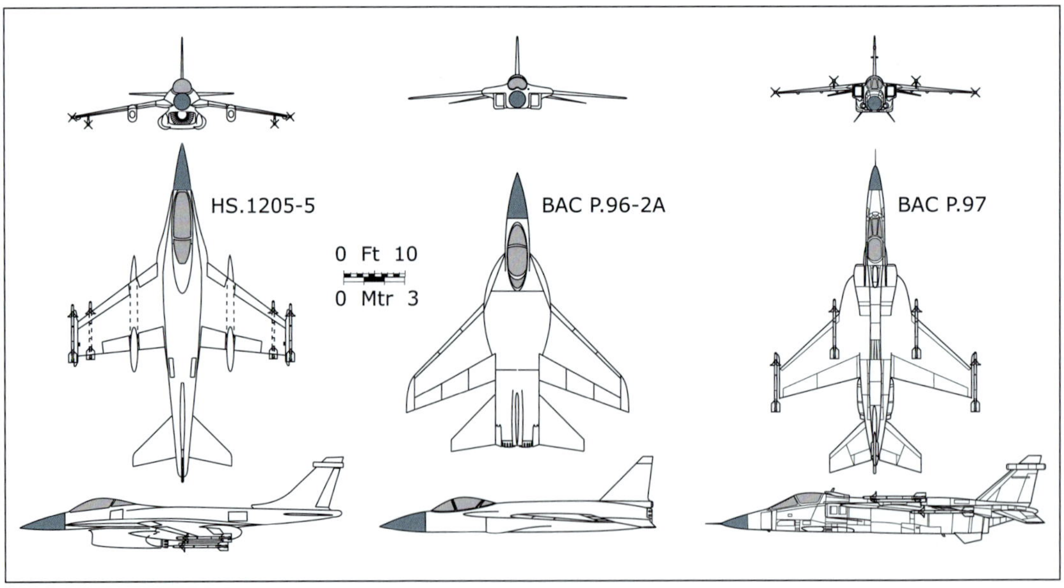

Three of the final six for AST.403 included (L-R) the HS.1205-5 STOVL type from Kingston and the P.96-2A and P.97 from Warton. The BAC P.97 was derived from the Jaguar.

period since AST.396 had been cancelled. Over 30 designs were submitted to the tendering committee and after examination, six were deemed to merit further study:

Design 1) HS.1207-2 – 36,000 lb (kg) AUW with two RB.199.
Design 2) HS.1202-6 – Similar to above but powered by a reheated RB.431 'straight through' Pegasus
Design 3) BAC P.96-2A – twin reheated RB.199
Design 4) HS.1205-5 – vectored thrust STOVL type with Pegasus/PCB
Design 5) BAC P.97 – Super Jaguar with twin RB.409-7 (Cropped fan RB.199)
Design 6) HS.1200-6 – minimum cost, lightweight type powered by a single RB.199.

General Cunningham commented on the submissions: 1) too costly, 2) similar performance to 1 but with 9% lower SEP (specific excess power). 3) Similar costs and performance to 2. The RB.409-7 was a development of the RB.199 intended to be 'virtually interchangeable with the Adour'.

Design 1 was shelved as too costly. Design 4 was cost-effective, but doubts existed about PCB. Design 5 had higher cost for less performance than Design 2. Design 6 performance failed to meet the AST. Designs 2, 3 and 4 were attractive with Design 4 meriting further investigation

While Cunningham's paper was circulating, the Chief of the Defence Staff, Marshal of the RAF Sir Neil Cameron penned a memo to the Secretary of Defence, Fred Mulley expressing disappointment about the lack of a decision from the Ditchley Park meeting on a joint venture on the TCA and how the need for progress on AST.403 was quite pressing. Some form of agreement would be required by July 1979 to commence development as 'the Jaguar force will be a wasting asset from 1986 and the Harrier from about 1988, unless topped up'. The lead time from Instruction To Proceed to in service would be around 11 years, based on experience and ideally, the In-Service Date for AST.403 should be 1990.

As for a US purchase, Cameron suggested that Mulley make a formal request to his West German and French counterparts to evaluate the YF-17 with a view to making a tripartite evaluation of it and other US types. Cameron continued with 'If this suggestion were rejected, as seems possible, we could feel free to examine US options openly and without fear of being accused of prejudicing the chances of success in European discussions.' This would leave the UK's options open and allow changes based on the numerous studies that were underway.

BAC at Warton and HSA at Kingston and Brough produced a plethora of design studies towards AST.403 but unlike AST.396 most were clean-sheet designs. The design teams intended powering their studies with available, and projected, engines. These included the RB.199-52R, a projected design rated at 9,220 lbf/14,810 lbf (41kN/65.9kN), Rolls-Royce Olympus 22R rated at 19,600/30,600 lbf (87.2/136.2kN), RB.409-50 rated at 9,700 lbf/16,595 lbf (43.1kN/73.8kN) which was a development of the RB.199 and Pratt & Whitney F100 in the 20,000 lbf/30,000 lbf (89/133.4kN) range.

The Ad Hoc Group had identified four Hawker Siddeley studies for further work, but the Kingston and Brough design teams produced many studies for AST.403, with conventional take-off and STOVL configurations

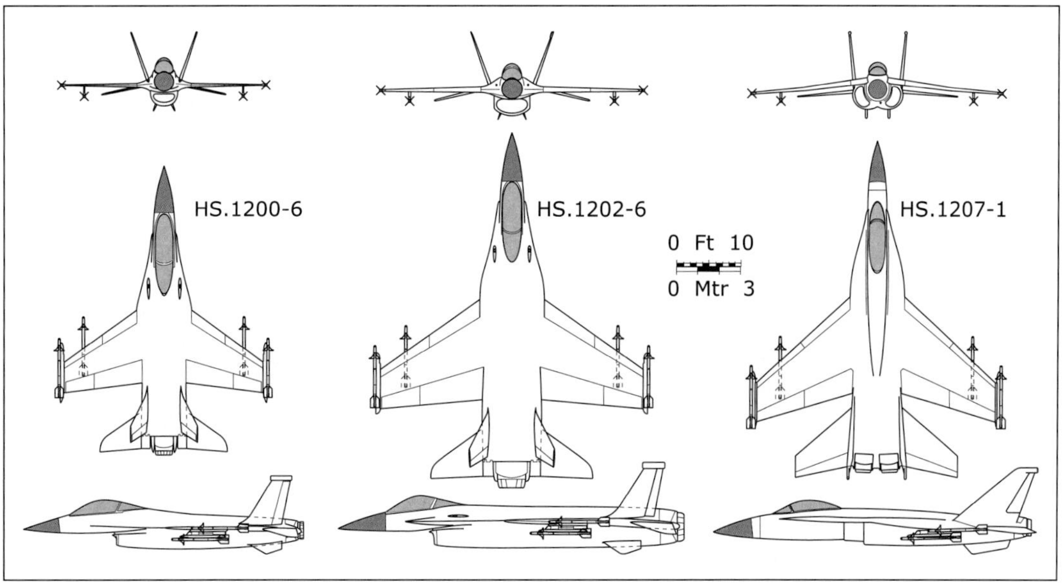

HSA at Kingston drew up four of the six final designs for AST.403. Reminiscent of twin-finned F-16s, the HS.1200-6 and larger HS.1202-6 required twin fins due to their engines being fitted with bucket-type thrust reversers.

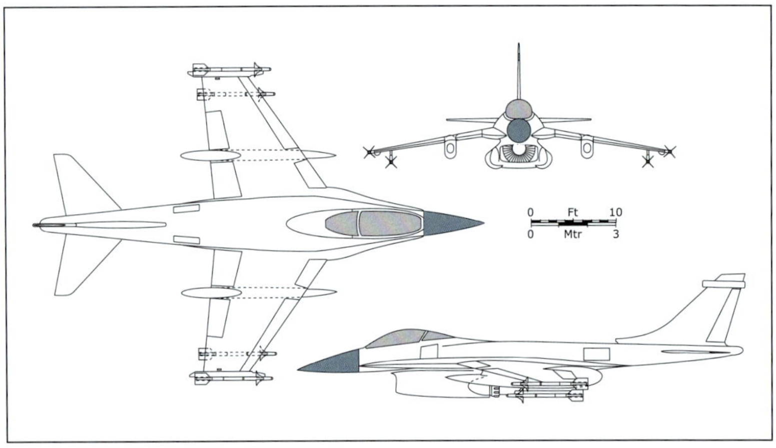

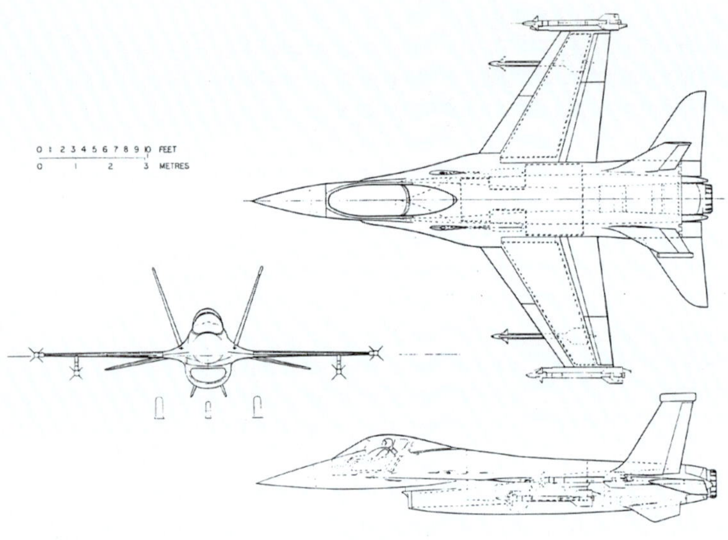

The Hawker Siddeley Kingston HS.1205 was powered by a Pegasus 11 with plenum chamber burning for higher performance. The rear fuselage was reduced to what was effectively a tail boom.

The HS.1200-6 was a minimum cost, lightweight fighter in similar vein to the F-16. The twin fins were to allow the use of a bucket-type thrust reverser. *Brooklands Museum*

examined, using engines listed above. The HS.1200-6 could be mistaken for a twin-finned F-16, with the twin fins allowing a Tornado style 'bucket' thrust reverser on the RB.409-50 engine. The slightly larger -7 was powered by the RB.246, which required a larger intake and wing. So far, so conventional.

Kingston's next study was decidedly unconventional with the HS.1201-7 that sported a butterfly tail and a RB.199 or RB.409 mounted on a dorsal pylon, positioned so the tail could obscure the jetpipe from IR-homing missiles, particularly low-level SAMs. The HS.1201 incorporated further innovative features such as the minimum diameter needle-like fuselage, made possible by inclining the pilot's seat at 65° from vertical. The wing incorporated large leading-edge slats but what was most interesting was variable incidence, not specifically to improve take-off performance but to ensure that the intake on the dorsal engine was in undisturbed airflow whenever possible. The main undercarriage was installed in pods at the 30% span point on each wing, with the pods also housing a Mauser BK-27 cannon.

If the HS.1201 boasted a minimalist fuselage, Kingston's canard HS.1202 study was completely at odds with that, thanks to its use of the large diameter RB.431, essentially a Pegasus without the vectoring nozzles but with a reheat section added. The engines were fed by large wedge intakes either side of the deep fuselage that featured a ventral recess to house six BL.755 or VJ.291 cluster bombs. Further weapons or external tanks could be carried on four underwing pylon, plus a Sidewinder or SRAAM on wingtip rails.

HSA returned to STOVL for the HS.1205, powered by a 'four-poster' Pegasus 11 with plenum chamber burning but fed by a chin intake. The rear fuselage was reduced almost to a boom that supported the tail surfaces. The anhedral wing was fitted with pylons at the wingtip and just inboard from the tip for carrying AAMs. The main undercarriage and a 27mm cannon were housed in long wing pods at approximately 30% span. If the HS.1200 could be described as F-16-like, Brough's HS.1207 (designated P.158 under the Brough nomenclature) was F-18-like, or rather YF-17. The HS.1207-1 was to be powered by a pair of RB.199-34R as used on Tornado while the -2 was to use the higher powered, but unproven, RB.409-50.

Hawker Siddeley's studies appear to have found more favour with the Ad Hoc Group than BAC's, by a four to two split, but what were the differences that prompted that split? Difficult to identify but the Warton designers appeared to focus on variable-geometry at a time when that configuration – very 1960s – was being superseded, thanks to advanced flight control systems, by fixed-wing designs such as the F-16 and F-18, designs favoured by Hawker Siddeley.

BAC at Warton also conducted a great deal of work for AST.403, covered by studies designated P.91 through P.97 with a variety of engine options to match, using the powerplant listed above. Warton's P.91 studies were based on variable-geometry wing with a shape similar to that of the Tornado. All were single-engined, powered by the F100, RB.199-52R, RB.409 or Olympus fed by chin intakes or inlets mounted under the V-G wing glove or chine. The EAG.8945 studies examined variations on the basic design, encompassing a wide but shallow fuselage and single engine. Studies -22 and -23 were powered by the RB.199-52R and differed in the length of the chin intake with the -23 having a short intake producing a side profile reminiscent of the F-16. One interesting aspect

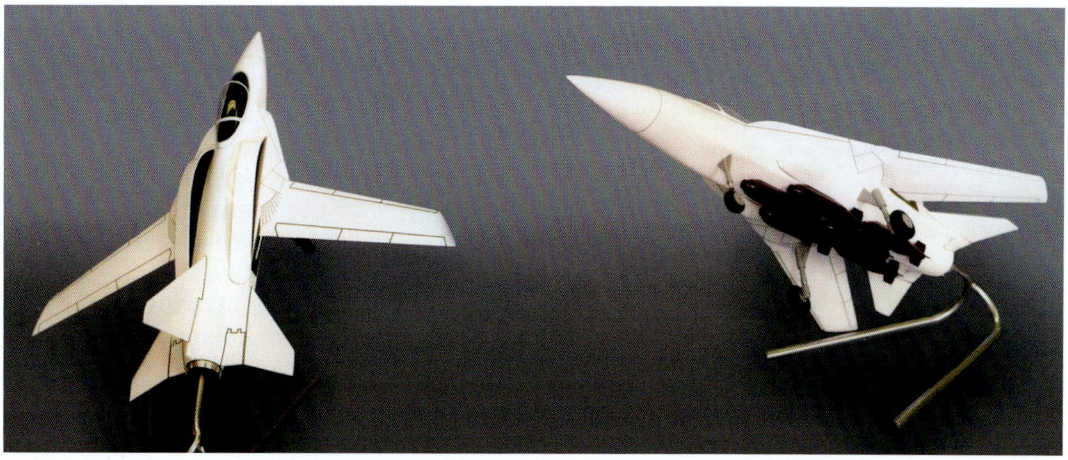

The variable-geometry P.91 carried its extra fuel in conformal dorsal tanks while its six BL.755 were mounted on ventral weapons stations. *North West Heritage Group*

of the EAG.8945 series was its dorsal stores carriage. Due to the small size of the aircraft the six BL.755 or VJ.291 bombs took up the ventral stores pylons and to avoid the complexity of swivelling wing pylons, the wings were kept clean. The wide fuselage that lent itself to three-abreast carriage of bombs also made it ideal for dorsal stores, with two SRAAMs in a retractable launcher on the dorsal centreline. Two conformal fuel tanks could be carried either side of the SRAAM launcher. SRAAM was a tube-launched IR-guided 'dogfight' missile that would ultimately lead to ASRAAM.

Many of the P.91 studies were described as 'lifting body' with wide, flattened fuselages and have an overall look of a single-engined Grumman F-14. One of the first such studies, EAG.8945-110, was powered by an RB.409 and is notable for lacking tailplanes. It is described as an 'Aircraft with twin fins and lifting body' and has an 'internal blocker door inflight thrust reverser'. The tailplanes/tailerons are replaced by control surfaces either side of the jet pipe. Weapons, two AIM-9 Sidewinders or four SRAAMs, are dorsally mounted, but the SRAAMs are not in the retractable launcher seen on other studies. Two very interesting studies are EAG.8945-130 that is similar to the -110 but has a '2 Dimensional Multi-mode Nozzle' and EAG.8945-140, a fixed-wing variant with a leading edge sweep of 45° and curved tips and root or alternatively a 50° sweep with angular tips and roots.

The dorsal SRAAM installations on P.91 were unusual as they could be installed side-by-side in a box, elevated on jacks at the front and hinged at the rear, with a door to allow exhaust gas to escape on launch. The alternate mounts saw SRAAM launch tubes mounted on a retractable rail that swung up and outwards to move the launch tubes clear of the fuselage.

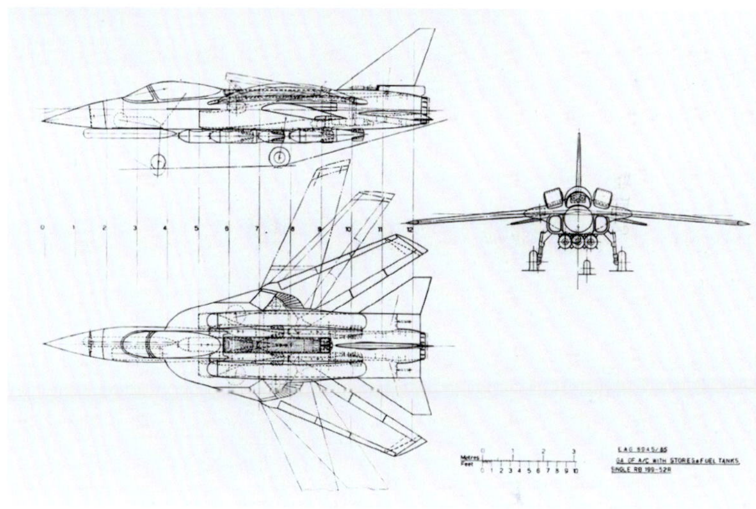

This P.91 variable geometry study, drawing EAG.8945-85 to AST.403, was powered by a single RB.199-52R turbofan. Of note are the dorsal fuel tanks either side of the fuselage spine and the six BL.755 or VJ.291. These may be VJ.291 as the aircraft has a designator pod under the forward fuselage. *North West Heritage Group.*

This P.91 study for AST.403, drawing EAG.8945-130 is described as having a lifting body. Note that it lacks tailplanes and the surfaces either side of the single RB.409 turbofan may act as elevators. Also of note in this study is the two-dimensional jetpipe with deflection system. *North West Heritage Group*

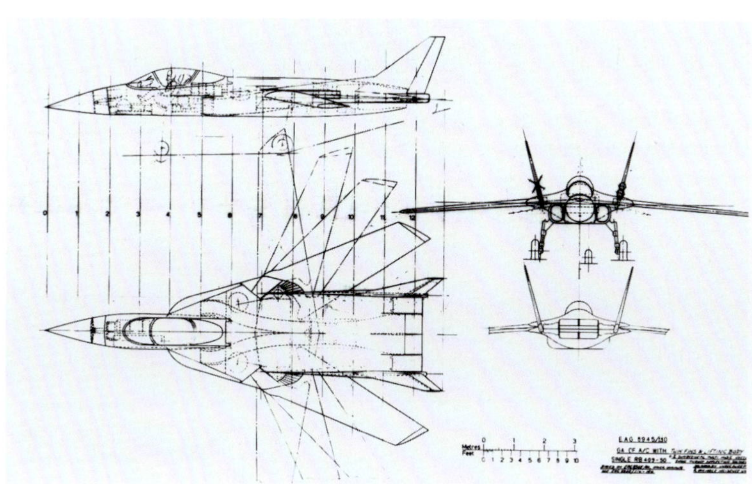

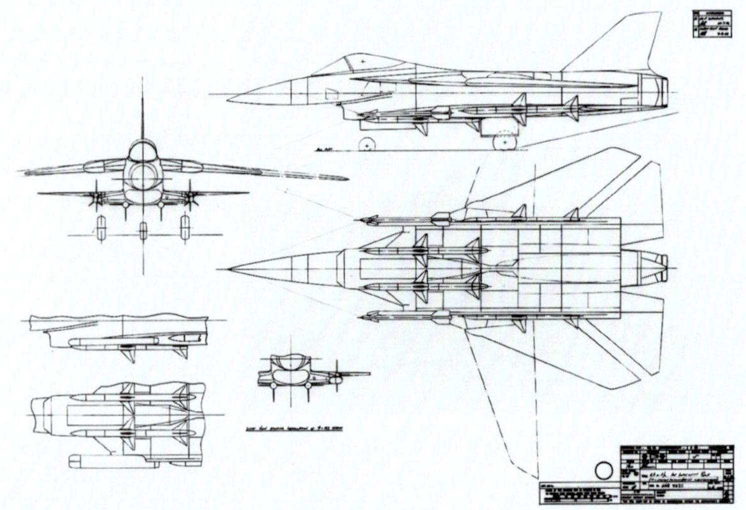

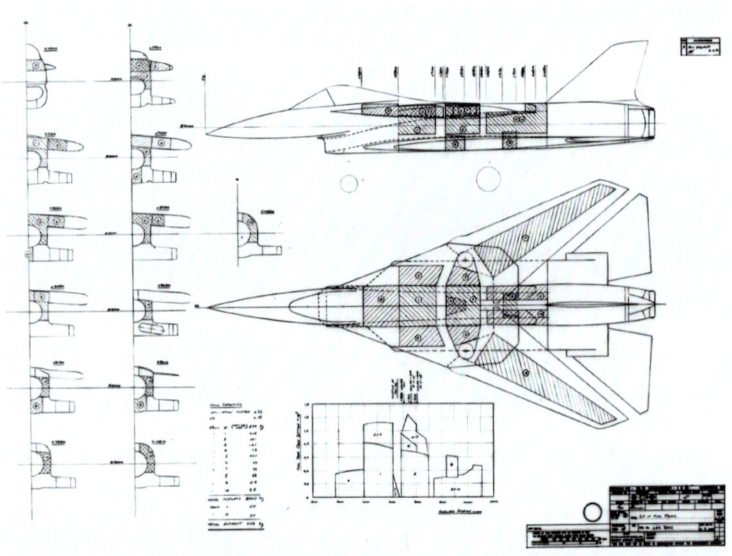

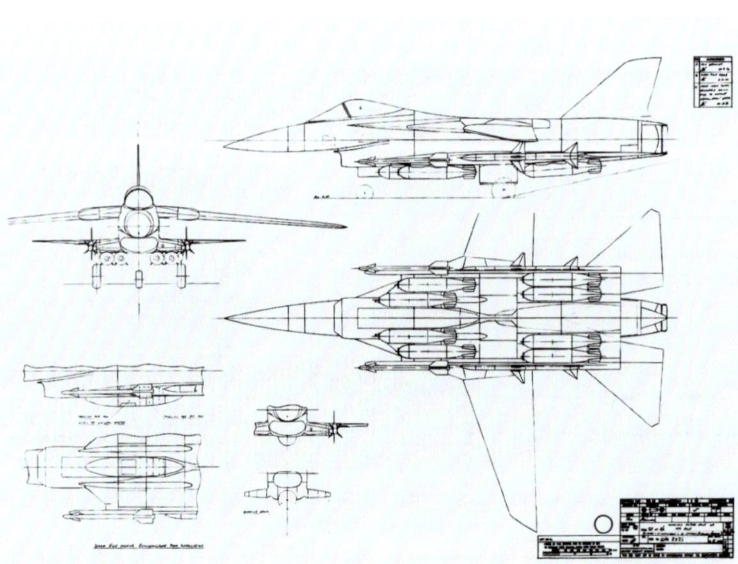

One of the most fascinating design studies for AST.403 is EAG.8985, with an innovative, if not elegant, configuration. The fuselage was conventional, wide enough to accommodate the cockpit, chin intake and the engine with the variable-geometry wing and glove set high on the fuselage but the innovative aspect of the EAG.8985 was its weapons carriage. Along the length of the lower fuselage, on each side, from just aft of the intake to forward of the jet pipe ran a fairing. Each fairing was as wide as the fuselage and allowed the carriage of eight BL.755 or VJ.291 anti-armour weapons plus a pair of XJ.521 Skyflash MRAAMs. Due to the need to provide the maximum field of view, Sidewinders or pairs of SRAAMs were carried on hardpoints at the forward end of the fairings. The EAG.8985 drawings also show a reconnaissance pack on the centreline just aft of the nose wheel bay. This configuration provided the area required to carry the eight cluster bombs called for in the requirement while avoiding the need for a large fuselage seen in earlier design studies, reducing structural weight and wetted area.

The P.92 studies continued the theme established with P.91, albeit mainly with two engines, such as the EAG.8909-20 with two RT.172 (Adour) or EAG.8909-30 with two RB.199-34R (as used on Tornado). Perhaps the most interesting, aesthetically at least, of the Warton AST.403 studies are the P.93 deltas with large LERX stretching forward beyond the windscreen. All featured a 55° leading edge sweep and 13° reverse taper on the trailing edge and differed mainly in their propulsion, with the EAG.8944-1 powered by a F100, the -30 by a

This P.91 proposal, EAG.8985 Issue A, is very interesting because of its unusual configuration. Ostensibly a normal single-engined, variable geometry type with a chin intake, it has a broad chine along the bottom of the fuselage carrying fuel and housing the undercarriage. It also serves as a mount for the armament, in this case air superiority weapons, four Skyflash and two twin launchers for SRAAM. *North West Heritage Group.*

This diagram showing the location of the P.91's fuel tanks also shows the shape of the fuselage in cross-sections along the long axis of the aircraft. *North West Heritage Group*

In the battlefield interdiction and close support roles the P.91 EAG.8985 Issue C was to be equipped eight BL.755/VJ.291 plus two Skyflash. This drawing shows the type armed with AIM-9H Sidewinder rather than SRAAM launchers. A reconnaissance pod was also planned for this type. *North West Heritage Group.*

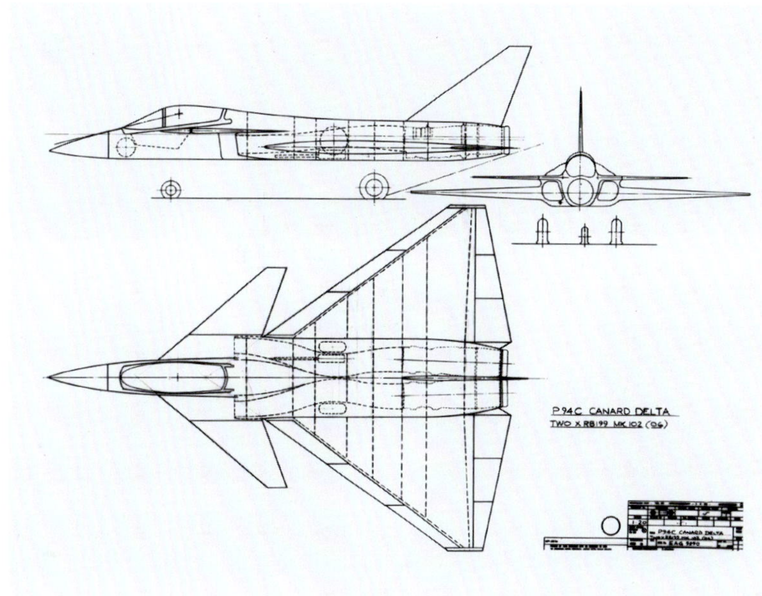

Showing the way to the future, the P.94C canard delta was to be powered by a pair of RB.199 Mk.102. Small, with a lot of power the P.94C would have been agile. The earlier but similar P.94B was powered by a pair of scaled RB.246-11. *North West Heritage Group*

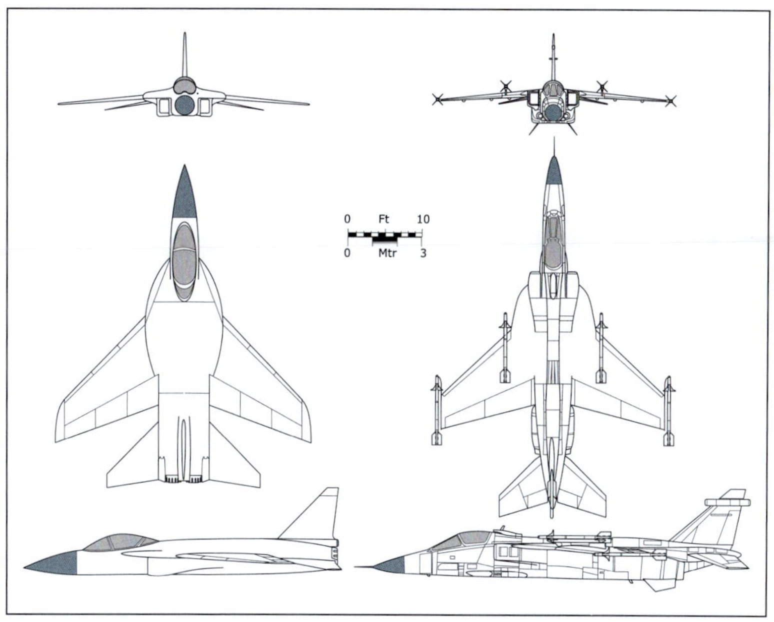

The two Warton designs selected for the last six were the P.96-2A (left) and the P.97 (right) The P.97 was also known as the Super Jaguar and used the RB.409 engine which was effectively a cropped-fan RB.199.

This BAC P.96F model shows the broad, swept wing that became the norm for fighter aircraft once variable geometry had fallen from favour in the mid-1970s. *North West Heritage Group*

pair of RB.199-34R and the -70 with a single RB.409-50. All variants of P.93 featured intakes under the LERX and the wide fuselage aft of the cockpit carried hardpoints for SRAAM or Sidewinder AAMs. Interestingly the -70 featured a tailfin whose 'Warton shape' was seen on TSR.2 and would become familiar on the Typhoon.

The P.94 studies are pointers to the future as they match the delta wing of the P.93, mounted lower on the fuselage, with canards. The P.94B (EAG.9888) was powered by two RB.246 engines and featured a large canard mounted just aft of the windscreen. The similar P.94C (EAG.9890) was to be powered by the RB.199 Mk.102, whose intakes, like the P.94B, were mounted under the canards aft of the cockpit. Following on from P.94, the P.95 studies were essentially fixed wing versions of the P.91, with similar powerplant and weaponry but it was the P.96 that would be selected for further study carried on the P.95 fixed wing designs. The P.96 designs were evolutions of the earlier studies, but AST.403 gave rise to some interesting configurations, exemplified by EAG.8982. This design featured a low-set swept wing, canards and its engines place in long nacelles over the wing, extending from the trailing edge of the canards almost to the end of the fuselage, with a tailfin mounted on each nacelle. The fuselage, as might be expected by not being required to house engines, was minimised.

The outboard engine configuration led to the P.103 studies for a STOVL fighter. The baseline design for P.103, EAG.9910, was a conventional take-off (CTOL) type with a fuselage, canards and a single fin mounted on the fuselage. The high set trapezoidal wing had compound sweep on the leading edge, 40° inboard of the engine nacelles and 30° outboard. The trailing edge was straight but did have a slight sweep outboard of the nacelles. The engines were set

at 50% span and featured flaps set in the mass flow to deflect the thrust to reduce take-off and landing distances.

This led to the ultra-short take-off and landing (USTOL) P.103 with swivelling nacelles, that

Left: This odd-looking beast is the vertical/short take-off and landing (V/STOL) variant of the ultra-short take-off P.103. The engine pods could swivel into a 60° orientation for U/STOL take-off and landing while for V/STOL landings the wing incidence could be increased to 30° to produce vertical thrust. *North West Heritage Group*

Below: The P.103 came in several configurations CTOL, V/STOL and USTOL. Some variants used fixed engine nacelles with 'post-exit deflectors' for the efflux, some used swivelling nacelles as shown here and one version, with a butterfly tail (right hand side view) applied swivelling nacelles and variable incidence wing.

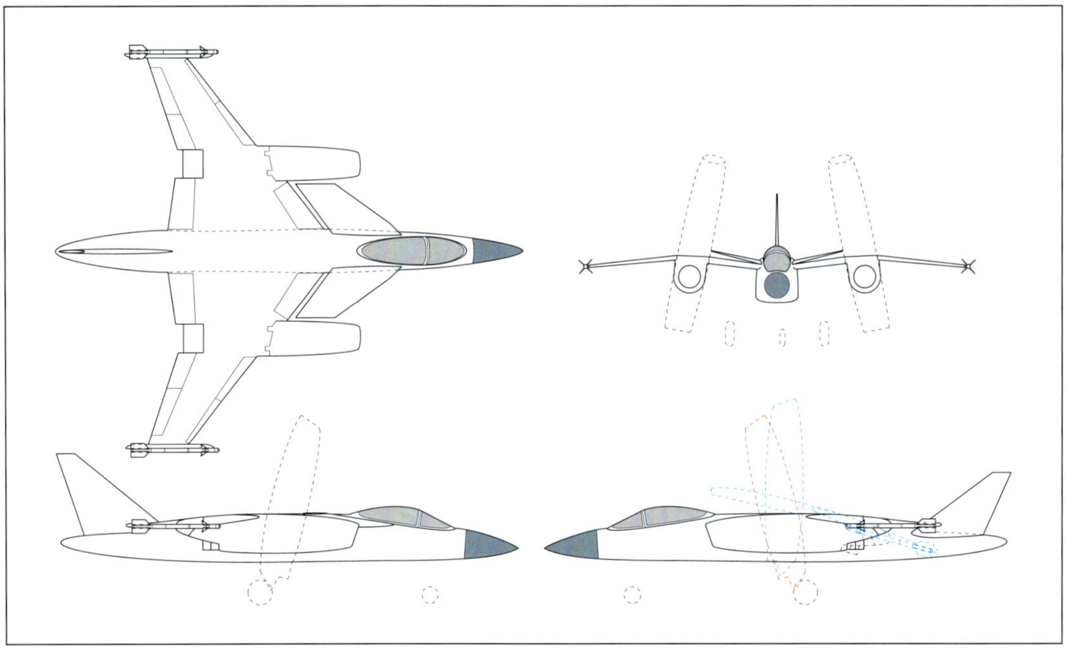

Below left: This P.103 Baseline 7 study, Drawing EAG.9964, is described as a conventional take-off and landing variant. It is armed with nine BL.755/VJ.291, although AST.403 called for six, and two AIM-9H Sidewinders.

Below right: This P.103 Baseline 7 is armed with four Paveway II with a Pave Spike designator pod under the cockpit. *Both: North West Heritage Group*

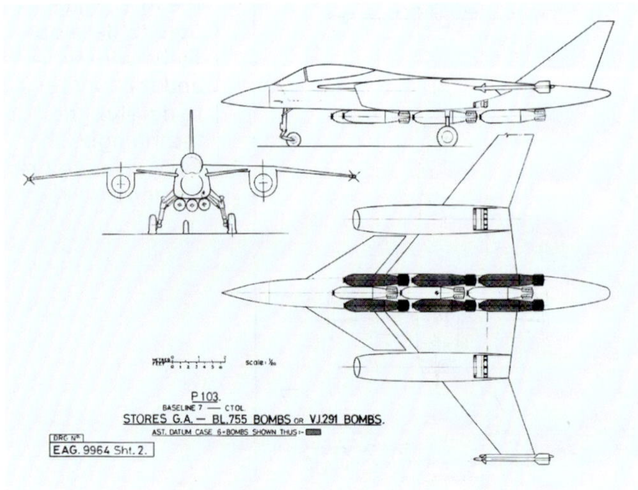

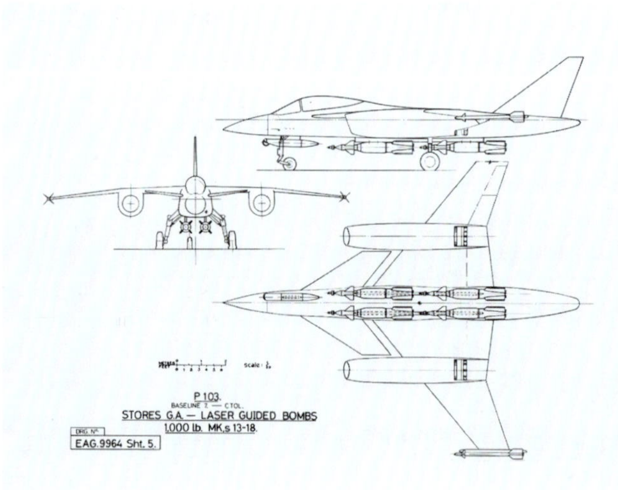

was intended to provide the short take-off and landing performance of the Harrier combined with the flight performance of a supersonic fighter aircraft. The solution adopted by Warton was to use the jet deflection of the earlier P.103 designs such as EAG.9910 combined with tilting the nacelles themselves, through 0° to 75°, with thrust modulation used to provide directional control when aerodynamic controls were ineffective. As can be imagined, the P.103 would have required a highly advanced flight control system (FCS) to enable the aircraft to be flown, especially in the USTOL phases of a sortie. Papers on the subject state that the P.103 would be flown with a side-stick and the control system would be fly-by-wire to maximise the benefits of the FCS.

Further developments of the P.103 incorporated tilt-wing and swivelling nacelles to provide VTOL performance with the combination of the nacelle swivelling through 75 and the wing tilting to 15 would provide the vertical thrust vectors required for VTOL. This variant also sported a butterfly tail, but another proposal, shown only in model form, saw the P.103 fitted with forward-swept outer panels on the wings.

The forward-swept variant of the P.103 followed the trend for forward swept wings that led to the Grumman X-29 flown by NASA.

ACT research for AST.403

Any aircraft to meet AST.403 would benefit from the latest in systems, particularly the flight control system. Electrical signalling systems (Active Control Technology, colloquially known as fly-by-wire) were first employed on the Avro CF-105 Arrow and in the UK, the Avro 707B in 1960 as 'manoeuvre on demand'. Analogue 'manoeuvre on demand' systems were fitted to the F-111 and F-8 Crusader, while the Hunter (and Concorde) continued development in the UK. All these had manual reversion which used mechanical linkages but restricted designs to stable configurations.

By the 1970s, computer technology had advanced to the point where a full active control system could be fitted to an aircraft, with a NASA F-8C Crusader having full-authority digital fly-by-wire control system. The F-16 became the most famous early fly-by-wire aircraft, complete with 'fixed' sidestick controller. The Jaguar (ACT) demonstrator was to 'establish confidence in the use of a digital ACT system without manual reversion' for an AST.403 aircraft. A control system without the mechanical systems allowed the full use of the aircraft's performance 'within aerodynamic and structural restrictions'. Therefore, there were advantages to be gained from using a digital system without manual reversion.

Why the Jaguar rather than the Tornado, a more modern design with ACT? The Tornado's

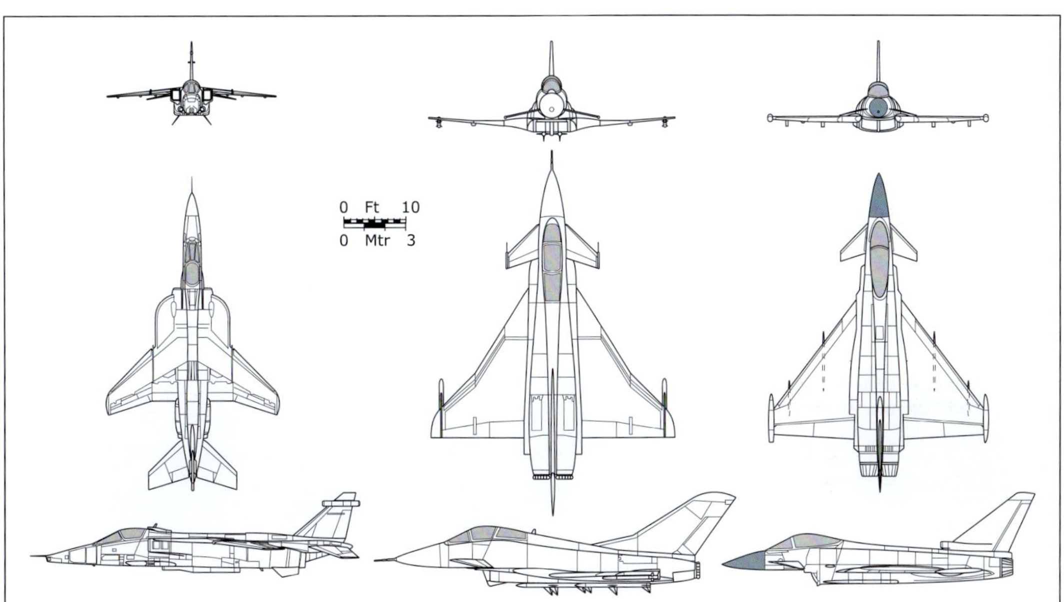

Milestones in the development of the Typhoon were the ACT Jaguar used to develop fly-by-wire systems and the EAP used to develop the technologies that would lead to the Typhoon.

ACT was analogue with manual reversion on the tailerons and would have to be replaced, thus delaying the ACT programme. In 1977 the Jaguar's flight envelope was better known than the Tornado (first flight in 1974) and BAC had been working on an ACT system based on the Jaguar for a few years. The flight programme would require a dedicated aircraft and there would not be a Tornado available for the ACT programme as all were involved in development work for service entry.

The ACT Jaguar, XX765 was an RAF aircraft withdrawn from service and converted by BAe to have fly-by-wire controls and unstable configuration with large strakes forward of the inner wing leading edges. These moved the centre of lift forward while ballast in the rear fuselage moved the centre of gravity backwards. The result of these changes included improved lift/drag and made the tailplanes more effective which would allow smaller engines and a lighter structure.

Flight trials commenced in 1981, providing improved manoeuvrability, and the computer-in-the-loop control system allowed the unstable configuration to be put to maximum effect known as 'carefree handling'. The hope, according to Vice-Controller, Aircraft, LF Nicholson in April 1977, was that this would 'allow the pilot to concentrate on the vital task of attacking airborne and ground targets' and reduce pilot workload. The ACT Jaguar was operated until 1984 and now resides in the RAF Museum at Cosford.

Fourth Generation Genesis

The various generations of fighter aircraft have been debated by amateurs and professionals alike and the aircraft to meet AST.403 and AST.410 have been described as 4th, 4.5 or 4+ Generation. Some categorise the Generations by capability (avionics, agility or networking), others by weapons while some observers merely place the generations in set time periods. However, the 4th Generation might be delineated, the broad requirements were that they entered service post-1990, had multimode radar, a certain degree of stealth and swing-role capability. Some observers take the view that the fighter generations are marketing nonsense.

The swing-role requirement was of most importance as the capacity to switch from air-to-ground to air-to-air at the flick of a switch or rather the push of a button on a multi-function display. The days of 'Not a pound for air to ground' were long gone, even for the aircraft the expression was coined for, the F-15, which was gaining an air-to-ground capability in the F-15E.

There was one particularly knotty problem for the British: the need to replace the Harrier. While they could delay a replacement for the Jaguar on cost grounds, the Harrier's V/STOL capability really did push the performance envelope for the aircraft to, in the words of the AST.403 title '...replace Jaguar and Harrier' without compromising performance. An aircraft with the Harrier's performance was required for 'direct support of NATO forces. As

The underside of a Harrier GR.7 lights up as it 'pops' flares. The Harrier, along with the Jaguar, was to be replaced by AST.396 and the later AST.403. The Harrier replacement Staff Target was split off from AST.403 as AST.409, resulting in the Harrier GR.5, which led to the Harrier GR.7 and GR.9. *MoD/ Open Government Licence*

a result, the Harrier replacement was split in early 1979 from AST.403 as AST.409 and led to the adoption of a mixed ground attack force for the future with the Harrier GR.5 entering service in 1987. By this time AST.403's future was looking decidedly ropey.

Having shed the Harrier replacement aspects, AST.403 was re-assessed and '1st Revise' issued to cover a Jaguar replacement and incorporated improvements to the air combat role. Concurrent with this, the western intelligence services acquired information on the MiG-23M *Flogger-B* which had *High Lark* look-down/shoot-down radar and Vympel R-23R (AA-7 *Apex*) beyond visual range (BVR) missiles, making the *Flogger-B* on a par with the F-4E/F Phantom, but probably more agile. This information led to the P.96F and HS.1204-2E being compared with the *Flogger-B*, an examination that supported the need for a highly manoeuvrable aircraft that could be armed with a BVR weapon such as the AIM-120 AMRAAM or Skyflash. Meeting these demands would be an expensive prospect and with the ongoing Tornado programme, plus the given the Government policy on aerospace projects, a bi- or multinational programme would be required. Alongside assessments of the UK design studies, three foreign types were examined; Mirage 2000, F-16 and the F-18L (land-based version of the Hornet to be produced by Northrop) but like the British proposals, none of the foreign designs progressed farther than paper analyses, although these suggest that the P.96F was the preferred option.

Alongside the AST.403 work in the UK, discussions commenced between UK, France and West Germany on a European Combat Aircraft (ECA) with AST.403 forming much of the UK contribution. Any progress on ECA foundered when France insisted on including carrier capability in the ECA, which would impact the other versions in a variety of ways such as increased airframe weight, high sink-rate undercarriage and catapult/arrestor gear. This prompted France to leave the group in 1979 and the UK and West Germany to reassess the situation and commence discussions on the European Fighter Aircraft (EFA) in 1981, but these soon fell apart.

AST.403 was effectively cancelled in the 1981 Nott Defence Review *'The Way Forward'* as the UK could not afford to replace the Jaguar but work on AST.403 continued until 1984. Interestingly, although the Royal Navy bore the brunt of the Nott Review, which is widely considered to have contributed to the Argentine invasion of the Falklands, the RAF saw its air defence assets improved. However, there was a view in Whitehall that there was a lack of a 'harmonising national requirement' for AST.403. In the fallout from the Nott Review (and before the Falklands Conflict impacted British military thinking), April 1982 saw AST.410 issued, having been under discussion for the previous year.

As issued, AST.410 saw a return to the ground attack aircraft with secondary air combat capability last seen in the AST.396 era. Rather than using the BL.755 cluster bomb as its primary weapon, the guided weapon to meet ASR.1238 (became Brimstone) was to arm the AST.410 type, which was to be capable of killing four, preferably up to seven, T-72 MBTs in a single pass in the battlefield interdiction role. AST.410 was to be day/night capable, possess reduced

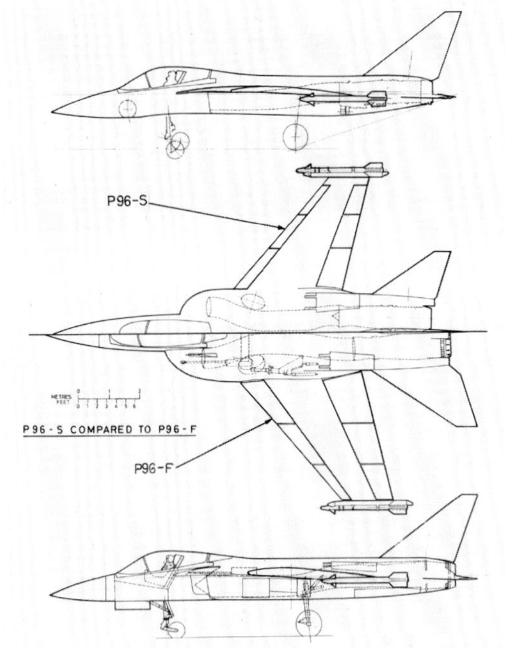

The BAC larger P.96F was considered a better option for AST.403 once the V/STOL requirement had been relaxed but better agility was required to tackle the new MiG-29 *Fulcrum-A* and MiG-23 *Flogger-B*. The larger control surfaces, such as the leading edge flaps and tailerons improved manoeuvrability compared with the P.96S *North West Heritage Group*.

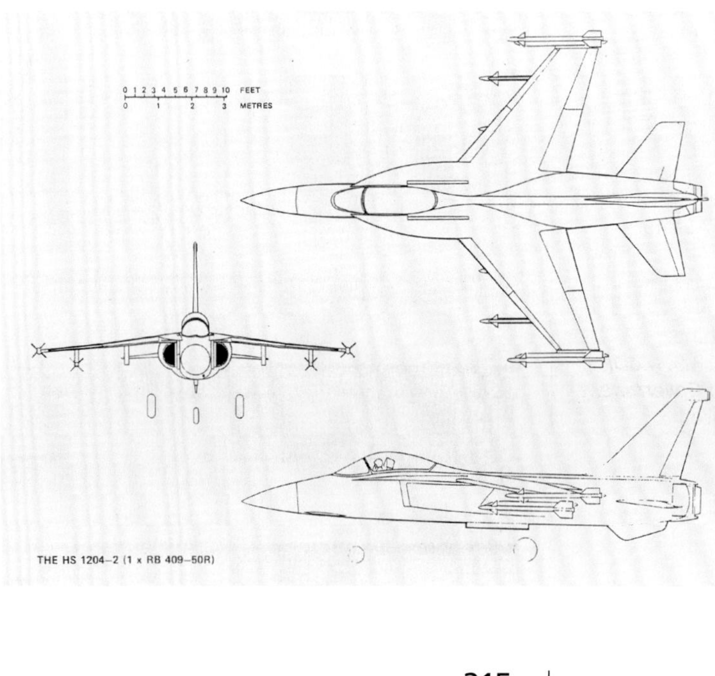

Hawker Siddeley addressed the agility requirement with the HS.1204 studies that incorporated a long leading edge root extension LERX.

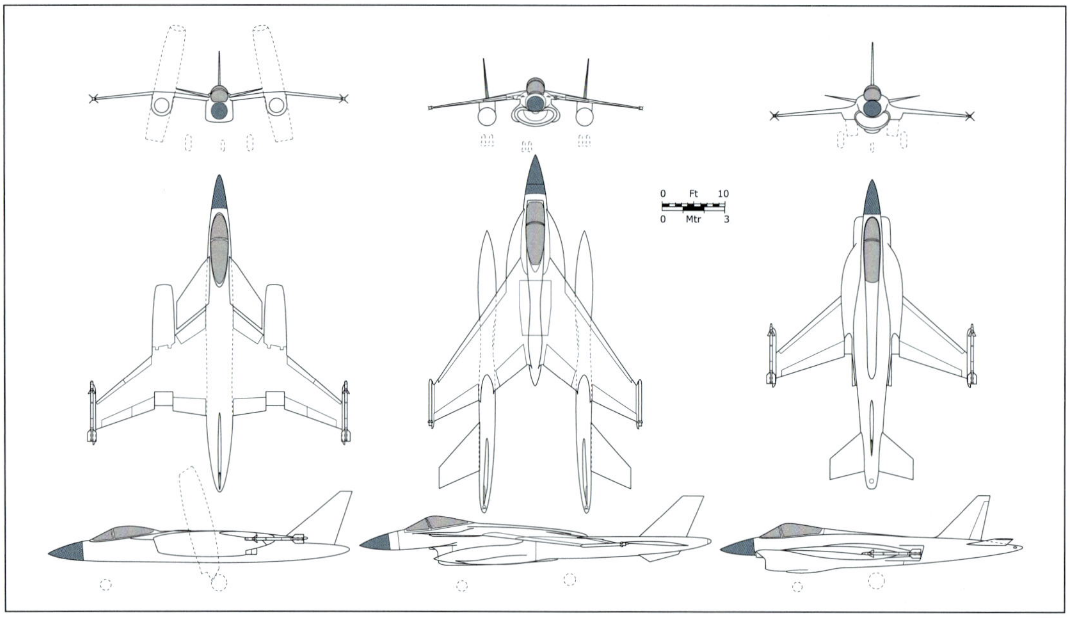

Three ASTOVL types proposed for AST.410 were (L-R) the P.103 from Warton, the P.1216 from Kingston and the P.109 from Warton. The P.1216 and P.103 reached mock-up stage.

radar and IR signatures to reduce vulnerability to Warsaw Pact mobile air defence systems and possess STOVL capability. Another factor in the transfer of effort to AST.410 was the introduction of the MiG-29 *Fulcrum*, which was thought to have performance on a par with the F-16.

The hope was that AST.410 could supersede AST.403 and AST.409 as a single multi-role ASTOVL type for the 1990s with better performance than the Harrier GR.3 and GR.5. The P.109 was BAe Warton's proposal for this, but the main work on AST.410 was carried out at BAe Kingston with the P.1216, and this type appears to have been the preferred programme for AST.410. The P.1216 was called an advanced short take-off and landing aircraft and was powered by an RB.422 turbofan with plenum chamber burning. The RB.422 was a 'three-poster' with two vectoring nozzles for bypass flow and a single nozzle for 'core' flow, although there was some mixing of the flows in the rear section. The single rear nozzle was more efficient than the split flow of the Pegasus on the Harrier, but rather than carry the empennage on a single boom-type rear fuselage, with attendant problems caused by noise and vibration from the efflux, HSA adopted a twin-boom configuration. The booms were mounted on the wings at mid-span with a tailfin and one tailplane on each, with the main undercarriage housed in the boom and a Mauser BK-27 cannon in the forward section. The booms were fitted with hard points for pylons and stores.

John Nott stepped down as Defence Secretary in January 1983, replaced by Michael Heseltine, who had a very European-oriented view of the defence industry. As noted above, various committees and discussion groups had been formed to examine European combat aircraft. A STOVL aircraft such as AST.410 was of no interest to European air forces as they had no requirement for such an aircraft and Heseltine, and the BAe management, fell into line with this thinking. BAe's rationale was that their plant at Warton would need a programme to ensure continued work after Tornado production finished. May 1984 saw AST.403 officially cancelled and AST.410 held in abeyance, subsequently superseded by AST.414 which called for an Agile Combat Aircraft. There would be no direct replacement for the Jaguar per se, but a new class of combat aircraft that could turn its hand to any role that in time would become known as a swing role type. And it looked like being European.

Back in 1981 the UK /West German ECF programme collapsed due to differences in the

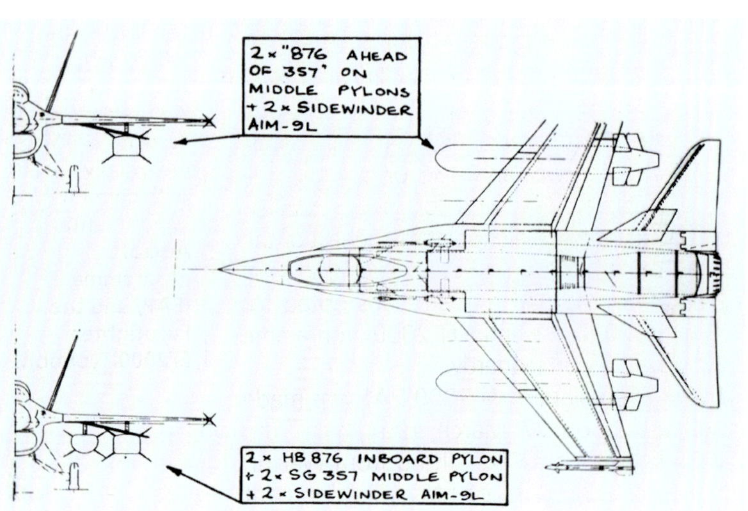

As with the P.1200, the P.1202-6 was powered by a single RB.431-10R, with bucket-type thrust reverser that required the aircraft to have twin fins. It is seen here in counter-air configuration with components of the JP.233 weapon either in a single pod (top) or split between two pods (bottom). *Brooklands Museum*

roles that the type would fill. By 1982, Panavia, comprising BAe, MBB and Aeritalia embarked on the Agile Combat Aircraft (ACA) as a private venture. This suited the British who considered Panavia a better prospect than any consortium that involved France, but soon discovered that West Germany and Italy were not so forthcoming with funds and that the ACA would not meet any country's requirement but could form the basis of a flying testbed. The initial plan was to produce two technology demonstrators under the Experimental Aircraft Programme (EAP), one built in the UK and another in West Germany, but the Federal German Government would not fund the work by MBB, so only the British EAP was produced. Although the design studies for the ACA, and the mock-ups shown at various airshows, had twin fins, the EAP had a single fin as it was based on the rear fuselage and RB.199 engine installation of the Tornado. The forward fuselage and wings were new, constructed using modern techniques and materials such as carbon composites and aluminium-lithium alloys.

The year 1983 was interesting year as it saw France back in the European fighter business with the launch of the Future European Fighter Aircraft (FEFA) programme with a consortium comprising UK, West Germany, Italy, Spain and France. This was fairly short-lived as France, once again wanted a carrier-capable aircraft so in 1984 the UK, Italy and West Germany left to found the European Fighter Aircraft (EFA) group, with the Turin agreement signed in August 1985. France meantime, embarked on the Avion de Combat Expérimentale (ACX) in 1985, which would ultimately become the Dassault Rafale.

The EAP, ZF534, was rolled out at BAe Warton in October 1985, making its first flight in August 1986 and embarking on an extensive flight test programme that proved the canard delta configurations and flight control system. In all ZF534 made 259 flights, greatly contributing to the development of systems and techniques that would subsequently be used on service aircraft.

Further action on the European fighter front occurred in June 1986 when Eurofighter Jagdflugzeug Gmbh (DASA, BAe, CASA and Aeritalia) and EuroJet Turbo Gmbh (Rolls-Royce, MTU, FIAT and ITP) were formed to develop the fighter aircraft and its engine, with Euroradar formed in 1990. Development of what was catchily named Eurofighter EFA commenced in 1986 and the aircraft was renamed Eurofighter (EF) 2000 in 1992. German reunification had an impact on the programme as the country sought to withdraw or develop a cheaper aircraft based on

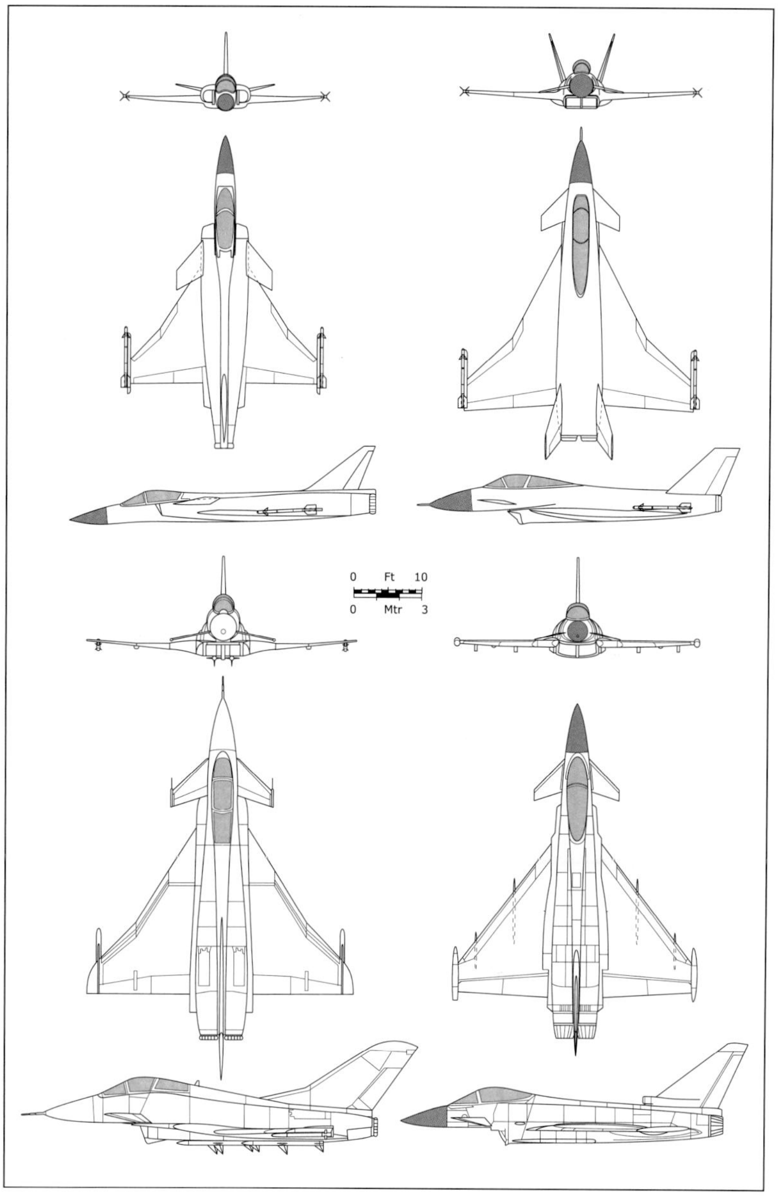

The road to Typhoon. (clockwise from top left) P.106 with a single RB.199 engine; Agile Combat Aircraft (ACA) essentially a P.110 with chin intake; Experimental Aircraft Programme (EAP) and the Eurofighter EF2000 Typhoon.

work already carried out on EF 2000. Germany had been offered a couple of American types instead of the EF 2000 including the McDonnell Douglas Hornet 2000 which was described as having 90% of the EF 2000 capability at 30% of the cost and the Agile Falcon. The Hornet 2000 was a F-18 with a new cranked-delta wing while the Agile Falcon was an F-16C or D with 25% greater wing area, aiming for greater agility. These types were developed at the behest of the US government to counter the potential sales of the EF 2000 and had the Germans opted for the Hornet 2000, the entire EF 2000 programme could have been in jeopardy.

The maiden flight of EF 2000 DA1 was made at Manching on 27 March 1994, with the first British example, DA2, flying from Warton on 6 April 1994. Both of these development aircraft were powered by the RB.199 but on

With the French Government deciding on a national solution to its fighter needs, especially the carrier-borne aspects, Dassault conducted a series of design studies, including the ACX shown here. Dassault's work led to the Rafale, which serves with l'Armée de l'Air and l'Aéronavale. *Blue Envoy Collection*

4 June 1995 DA3 flew with EJ200 engines from Turin. The first Spanish aircraft, DA6, flew from Getafe on 31 August 1996 becoming the first two-seater to fly.

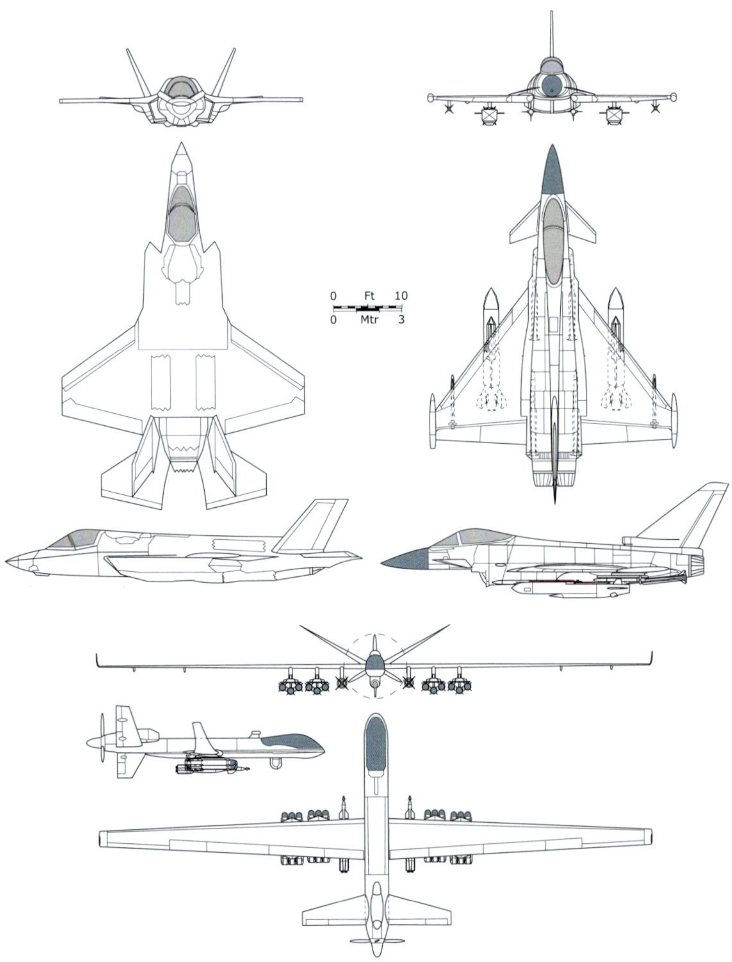

The RAF's strike aircraft for the 21*st* Century. Lightning, Typhoon FGR.4 and Protector RG.1. The long development of sensors and weapons make these aircraft some of the most lethal weapons platforms ever to serve with the RAF.

The development aircraft entered the programme, undertaking a series of trials with the various test establishments of the four participating countries. In 1998 the name Typhoon was adopted for the export market only, ostensibly because the name had been used during the Second World War for a Hawker fighter aircraft and the German government objected. This author has found no hard evidence for this, so can only assume it was an apocryphal tale.

The Typhoon entered RAF service with No XVII (Reserve) Sqn on 1 September 2002 as the Typhoon Evaluation Unit at Warton, taking delivery of its first Typhoon on 18 December 2003 with the Operational Conversion Unit, No 29 Sqn, forming in September 2003, also at Warton. No 3 (Fighter) Sqn became the first operational squadron at RAF Coningsby on 31 March 2006, taking over Quick Reaction Alert (QRA) duties from the Tornado F.3 at the end of June 2007. The first QRA interception of an 'X-ray' was by a pair of No XI(F) Sqn Typhoon F.2s that intercepted a Russian Air Force Tupolev Tu-95MS *Bear-H* on 22 August 2007.

The Typhoon's combat debut was in March 2011, patrolling the No-fly Zone over Libya as part of Operation Ellamy. A month later Typhoons, with targets spiked by Tornado GR.4s, delivered Paveway IV LGBs on a Gadaffi-loyalist forces 'Technical' laager. Typhoon FGR.4s were soon in action against ISIS/Daesh in Operation Shader from December 2015.

Weapons-wise the Typhoon had by 2017 been cleared to carry the full range of weapons, particularly those whose development is described in this work; Brimstone and Storm Shadow. Under Project Centurion the Typhoon FGR.4 can carry Paveway IV LGBs, Storm Shadow CASOM, Meteor BVRAAM and Brimstone ASMs, essentially making them as capable as the Tornado GR.4s they are replacing. The Typhoon had been undergoing trials for the use of SPEAR 3 in early 2019, with service entry set for 2020.

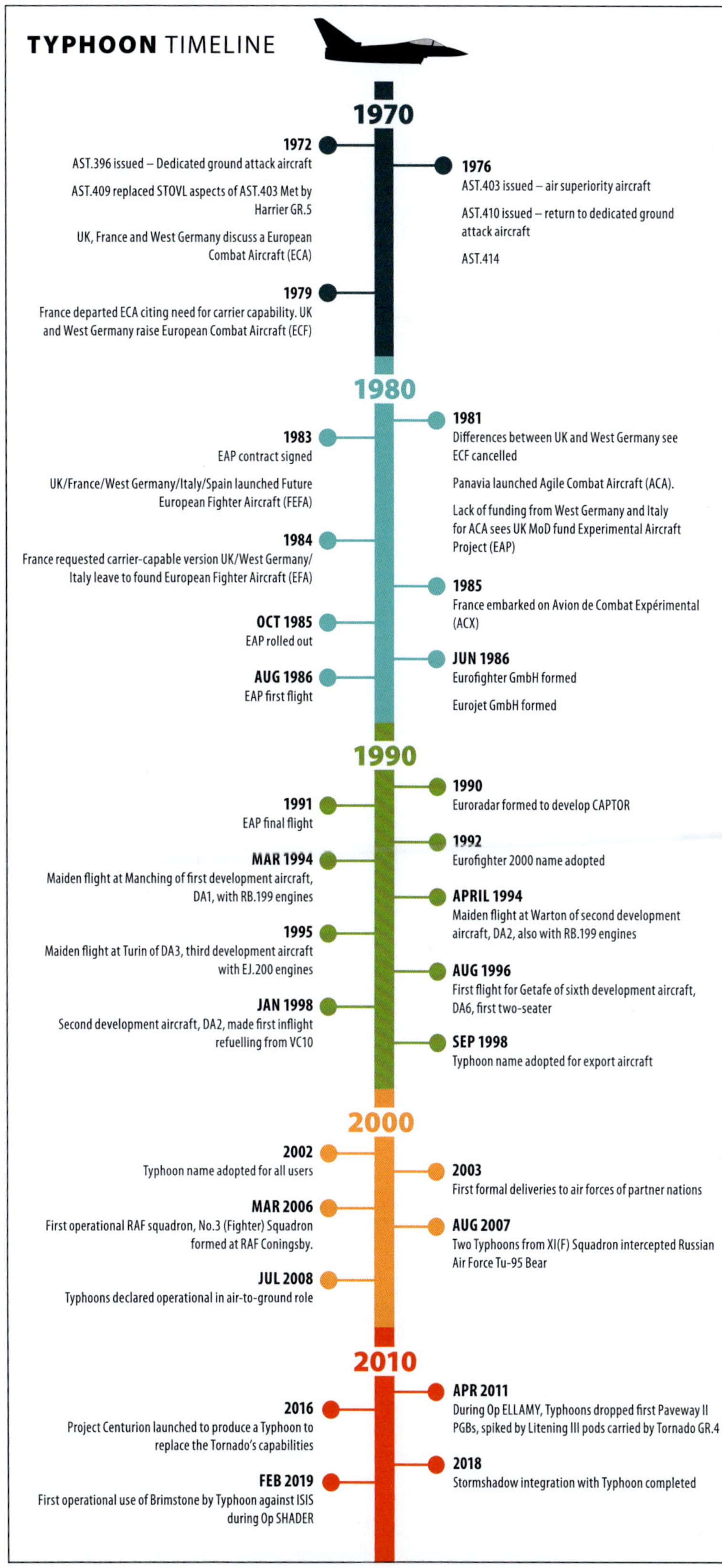

Beyond – Lightning and Protector

The UK was an early partner in the Joint Strike Fighter programme that led to the Lockheed Martin F-35 whose development can be traced back to 1992. The three main variants of the F-35 are the F-35A (conventional take-off and landing), F-35B (short take-off, vertical landing) and F-35C (Catapult Assisted Take-Off But Arrested Recovery). The UK has ordered 138 F-35s, although the precise mix of variants is still, as of June 2019, to be decided. The first F-35B entered service as the Lightning with No 617 Sqn in June 2018 (declared 'combat ready' in January 2019) and will be followed by the Fleet Air Arm's 809 Naval Air Squadron in 2023. Lightnings commenced operations in June 2019 against IS/Daesh during Operation Shader, flying missions from RAF Akrotiri in Cyprus.

The Lightning is intended to be the RAF's primary strike aircraft, having replaced the Harrier GR.7 and GR.9 plus the Tornado GR.4. The Lightning can carry up to 5,600 lb (2,540kg) internally to minimise its radar cross-section while if fitted with six wing pylons, plus the internal stores, in so-called 'Beast Mode' can carry up to 22,000 lb (9,979kg), which is the weight of a Grand Slam bomb from the Second World War. One important weapon earmarked for Lightning is SPEAR 3, which confers a stand-off precision strike capability on the Lightning, with up to eight SPEAR 3 carried in the internal weapons bay.

In Chapter 8 the RAF's UAV operations were outlined but for future operations the MoD in 2016 ordered 16 General Atomics Protector RG.1 UAVs and a suite of ground stations to replace the MQ-9A Reaper systems used in Afghanistan and Iraq. Protector RG.1 is an enhanced variant of the General Atomics MQ-9B SkyGuardian and provides increased endurance, possibly up to 40 hours, and payload capability compared with the Reaper. First delivery of the Protector scheduled for 2023 and it is the first UAV capable of operating in civilian airspace.

The Protector will be armed with the same weapons as the Reaper, including Paveway IV LGBs although the RAF plans to replace the Hellfire on its UAVs with Brimstone and possibly SPEAR 3. The Protector RG.1 can carry up to 18 Brimstone missiles on six triple racks, but the usual weapons load will be two Paveway IV LGBs and twelve Brimstone, with the SPEAR developments of Brimstone a possibility for the Protector.

Conclusion

Air Chief Marshal Sir Richard Johns' observation on single role aircraft opens this work. Hopefully what has been shown herein is that there has quite probably never been a single role aircraft. Spitfire? Interceptor, fighter escort, dive-bomber, reconnaissance, brewer's dray. Hunter? Interceptor, ground attack, reconnaissance, trainer. Vulcan? Bomber, tanker, maritime patrol, Counter-air, SEAD. Jaguar? Close support, reconnaissance, nuclear strike, trainer. Typhoon (Hawker or Eurofighter)? Interceptor, bomber, anti-tank, defence suppression, close support. Even the epitome of interceptors, the English Electric Lightning, was festooned with bombs and rockets for 'mud moving'. Perhaps the closest to a single role type would be the Harrier, but that is a subject for further discussion, in a pub or on Welsh hillside.

From a position that the RAF's ground-attack aircraft were merely superannuated, or failed, interceptors, this work has shown that such types served the RAF well. As of September 2019, the RAF's core combat aircraft are the Typhoon and the Lightning; both can suppress enemy air defences, attack ground targets and fight any air opposition they encounter. Neither can be described as failed or superannuated, but a lot of their capability relies on the weapons they carry.

Avro's Vulcan, during two months in 1982, carried out just about every role that its successor the Tornado would in the 21st Century. SEAD with Shrike (seen here beside the less than satisfactory AS.37), counter-air with 1,000 lb (454kg) bombs. The Vulcan could also conduct long-range strike with Blue Steel and the possibility of precision strike with Paveway II. *Blue Envoy Collection*

Appendix 1
The Gun/Armour Spiral

The objective of any anti-tank weapon – a knocked-out tank. A burned-out Iraqi T-72 lies in a roadside ditch along a road leading to Al Iskandariyah, Iraq, during Operation Telic. *DoD*

Until 1990 the main concern of British forces in West Germany was Soviet armoured forces; their destruction and/or restriction of their advance to the west. Any discussion of anti-tank warfare in Cold War Europe, must include some discussion of armour and anti-tank weapons. What follows is but a brief introduction to the field, not an in-depth analysis or description of a highly complicated and secret aspect of warfare.

During World War Two and up until the 1970s armoured vehicles were built from the same materials used on the dreadnoughts of Edwardian navies – steel – specifically rolled homogeneous armour (RHA). Steel is hard but can be made even harder and shock resistant by forging (or rolling in the case of armour plates) which removes imperfections and elongates the grains to increase the material's strength. Elongation of the grain structure also allows stresses to 'flow' away from the seat of any impact.

RHA worked well against kinetic munitions, such as high-velocity armour piercing (HVAP) rounds which could be defeated by increasing the thickness of the armour, as evidenced by the increase of armour thickness over the course of World War Two either by increasing the physical thickness of the armour plate e.g. from the 15mm (0.6in) of the Panzer I Ausf. A vs the 100mm (3.9in) of the Panzer VI Ausf. E (Tiger I). Added to the physical thickness of the armour was the effect of sloping the armour plate, most famously seen on the Soviet T-34. The T-34/76's glacis plate was 60mm (2.4in) thick but when sloped at 60° presented a thickness of 120mm (4.7in). By the war's end the formindable Pz. Kfw Tiger Ausf. B (*Königstiger* or Tiger II) was fitted with 150mm (5.9in) thick armour sloped at 40°, an effective thickness of 197mm (7.75in).

These tanks shared one particular feature – high velocity guns – that drove a solid shell of hard metal such as tungsten alloy at high speed to punch through the armoured plate. These 'kinetic' rounds evolved rapidly until the Armour Piercing Capped Ballistic Capped (APCBC) round with improved ballistics appeared. The word 'capped' does appear twice: the first cap protects the hardened core from damage, the second cap improves aerodynamics. Such rounds were in turn superseded by the armour piercing discarding sabot (APDS), that comprised a sub-calibre tungsten alloy penetrator encased within a sabot that was shed as

soon as the round left the barrel, thus applying the maximum pressure from the firing charge to the minimum area of the projectile, thereby producing maximum velocity for the penetrator. This technique was initially used on anti-aircraft guns to allow their shells to reach high altitude. Further reading on high-velocity guns and discarding sabot rounds for anti-aircraft use can be found in *Battle Flight*.

The increase in armour thickness produced a gun/armour spiral that saw Allied tank gun calibres increase from 40mm (1.6in) 2-pounder on the British Matilda to the 122mm (4.8in) on the Soviet JS-3. But as ever in warfare, there was more than one way to beat an enemy. The shaped-charge uses the Munro effect, whereby a cavity in the explosive focuses the power of an explosive charge and if that cavity is combined with a metallic liner, the result is the high explosive anti-tank (HEAT) warhead. This relies on a plasma jet formed when the explosion 'melts' the metal liner and focusses the resultant jet to burn through the armour. RHA provided less resistance to HEAT rounds and was no guarantee of protection against such 'chemical' rounds.

Another innovation in anti-tank warheads was high explosive squash head (HESH) whereby an explosive charge is propelled at fairly low velocity and on impact is squashed against the armour before detonating, sending shockwaves through the plate, spalling steel from the opposite face of the plate, i.e. inside the tank. HEAT and HESH did not require the high velocity of solid shot and so were suitable for use in low energy weapons such as the PIAT (Projector, Infantry, Anti-Tank) or Panzerfaust with a HEAT warhead and postwar British tank guns that used HESH shells. Postwar research revealed that in the Normandy campaign, the much-maligned PIAT destroyed more panzers than the much-vaunted Hawker Typhoon, which is no doubt testament to the difficulty in hitting a tank from the air.

By 1962 the Soviet Army was fielding the T-62 with a glacis plate of 102mm (4in) sloped at 60° which equated to 204mm (8in) and to defeat it required a big gun, such as the Chieftain's 120mm (4.7in) L11A5 gun that could fire HESH and APDS rounds. Similarly, the Chieftain's glacis was 120mm (4.7 in) sloped at 72° equating to 388mm (15.3in) other ways to beat the gun included placing the engine in the front of the hull of the Israeli Merkava, for increased crew protection.

Above left: The Soviet T-34 with its sloped armour, 76mm gun and wide tracks came as a surprise to the German Army in 1941. Why sloped armour was a surprise is a mystery as the German Sd.Kfz 251 half-track series had sloped armour. *Wiki Commons*

Above right: King of the gun/armour spiral with well-sloped thick armour and a powerful 88mm gun, not much could beat a Tiger II at the end of World War Two. Apart from lack of fuel. This is the only running Tiger II, held in the Musée des Blindés at Saumur, France. *Author*

Opposite, top: Armour-piercing, fin-stabilised, discarding sabot (APFSDS) rounds work by surrounding a finned, sub-calibre projectile (penetrator) made of a hard and dense metal (such as depleted uranium) with a full calibre housing (sabot) comprised of a light alloy and is shed on exiting the gun barrel. This allows the full pressure of the propellant charge to be applied to the round, giving the penetrator maximum velocity. The fins stabilise the penetrator in flight. On impact the velocity is such that, due to the hydrodynamic effect, the penetrator and the material(s) it hits act as fluids. The denser 'fluid' of the penetrator moves through the armour and penetrates to the target's interior.

Opposite, upper: High Explosive Anti-tank (HEAT) or shaped charge works by applying the Monroe Effect whereby a cavity in the explosive charge focuses and amplifies the explosive effect. If that cavity is lined with metal such as copper, the explosion turns the metal into a plasma and the Monroe Effect focuses the plasma into a jet. This jet then burns a hole through the armour.

Opposite, lower: A high explosive squash head warhead comprises a thin-cased shell filled with explosive and triggered by an impact fuze. The round is fired at low velocity and on impact deforms, spreading across the face of the armour plate. On detonation, a series of shockwaves form and, due to the large area of contact, these fracture the armour. This causes the inner face of the plate to spall, causing fragments to fly around the vehicle's interior.

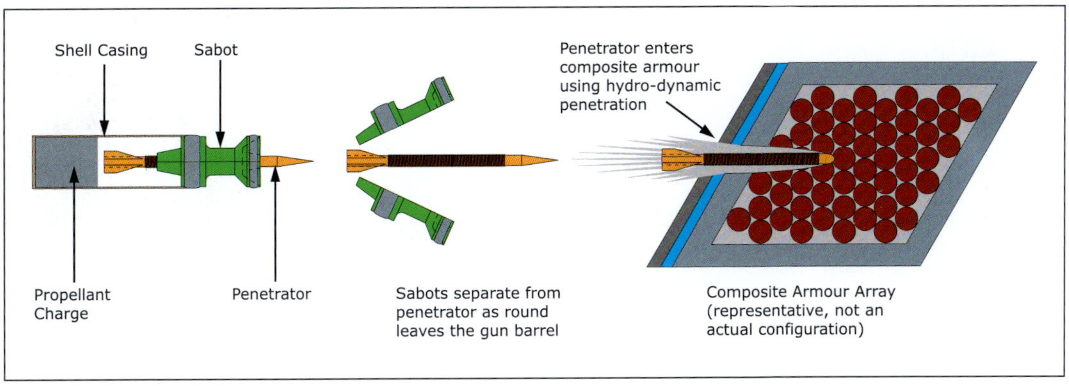

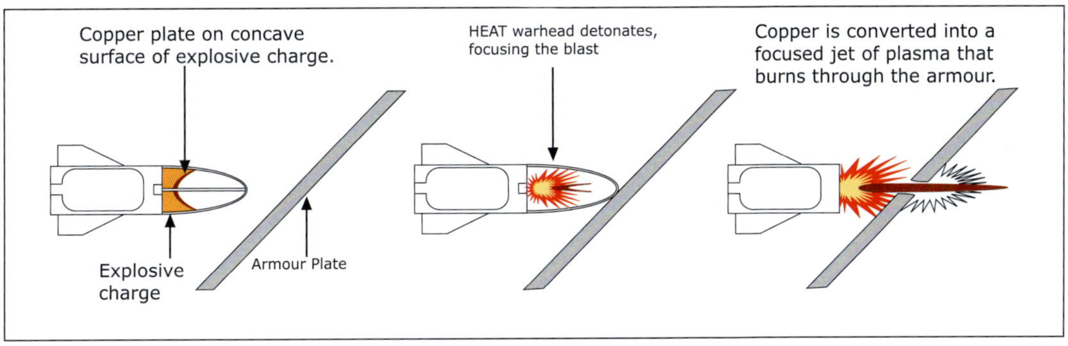

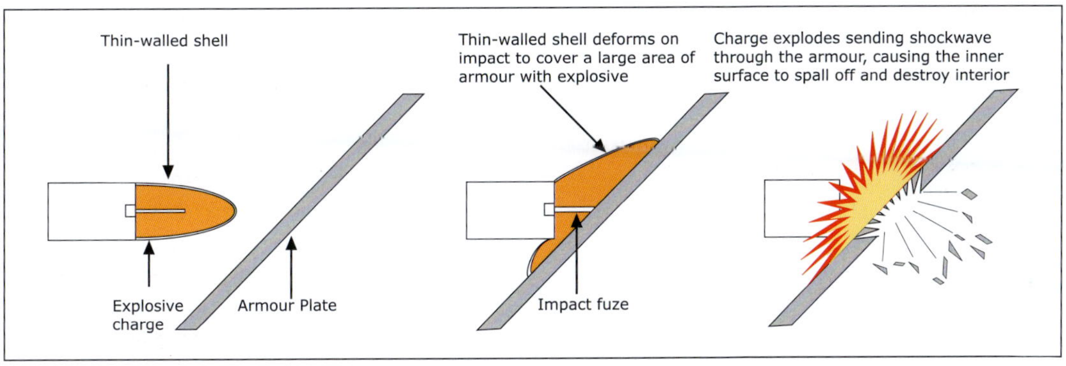

While sloping the armour allowed better protection for lower weight, the HESH and HEAT warheads (and APDS) were penetrating RHA despite the increased thickness and slope. Spaced armour reduced the effect of HEAT and HESH but not APDS. The answer came not from harder and thicker metals alone, but by combining materials such as glass to produce composite armour. In the mid-1950s the US Army fitted a T95 tank with armour plate that comprised glass sandwiched between RHA producing increased resistance to HEAT rounds. Ceramics were known to be resistant to penetrators as far back as the Great War but were too brittle for combat use. When in the 1950s they could be incorporated into the armour itself, ceramics were found to defeat tungsten penetrators by shattering them and defeating HEAT rounds by dissipating the plasma jet.

The Soviets introduced composite armour to service on the T-64 that used K Combination,

Above: The best tank in the World – for the Israeli Army. The Merkava has a low profile, highly sloped armour, Blazer ERA and its engine at the front. The Israeli Army prized crew survivability. These Merkavas are hull down behind a ridge to present the smallest possible target while being able to fire its main gun. *Wiki Commons/Black Mammba (sic)*

Improvised composite armour in the form of rocks and house bricks piled inside the bar armour of a Syrian Army T-72. In reality, such measures merely boost morale and damage the suspension. *Wiki Commons*

comprising glass-reinforced plastic between RHA. Soviet experiments with composite armour included filing cavities within armour castings with ceramic spheres or according to some sources, corundum (crystalline aluminium oxide, used in abrasive wheels and cutting disks, or if gem quality, emerald and ruby) or silica (crystalline silicon dioxide aka quartz). The name 'K Combination' may allude to the use of quartz as the Russian for quartz is *kvartz* although the silica may be in the form of fused silica (glass) rods arranged within the armour.

Interestingly, this use of minerals was not restricted to custom-made armour. Sandbags had been strapped to tanks since the tank first ventured onto the battlefield, usually to the detriment of the tank's suspension. During the Syrian Civil War T-72s were fitted with bar armour (also known as slat armour), a cage mounted on stand-off supports that surrounded the vehicle with bars spaced to prevent HEAT warheads reaching the vehicle hull. The Syrian Army went one step further by filling the space between the bar armour and the hull with rocks, house bricks or sandbags. Moving around a pulverised city like gigantic caddisfly larvae, the tanks might also find the rubble armour useful as camouflage.

Meanwhile in the UK, the Fighting Vehicles Research and Development Establishment (FVRDE) was developing composite armour using ceramic plates within a framework and the results of this work became known variously as Burlington and Dorchester armour but became better known as Chobham Armour. This armour was fitted to the US M1 Abrams, and British Challenger types and lurking beneath the angular green shapes of the turret and hull lie some of the most secret material combinations on the planet.

The angular shape of the armour on this Challenger 2 are due to the use of Chobham/Dorchester composite armour. The panels on the flanks and glacis plate are explosive reactive armour. *MoD/Open Government Licence.*

With the rise of the man-portable anti-tank guided weapon such as the Vickers Vigilant the tables were turned on the MBT. General Harold 'Pete' Pyman, a leading tank man in the War Office and General Officer Commanding, I Corps BAOR, famously chased two Vickers engineers from his office for having the temerity to suggest that a mere squaddie with a Vigilant ATGW could knock out one of 'his' tanks. They could, and they did. On a regular basis.

The first man-portable ATGW used in combat was the 9M14 Malyutka (NATO reporting name AT-3 *Sagger*), deployed by the North Vietnamese Army against the Army of the Republic of Vietnam (ARVN, South Vietnamese army) tanks and APCs. The South Vietnamese soon discovered that the best countermeasure was to open fire on the missile launch position, thereby preventing the operator guiding the missile. This worked because the separation between launch post and operator was only 15m (49ft). Just 18 months later the Arab armies employed *Sagger* against Israeli armour during the Yom Kippur War of October 1973. The Israelis lost 800 armoured vehicles to the *Sagger's* HEAT warhead, but soon adopted countermeasures similar to the ARVN, including firing on the ground between the tanks and missile positions to produce clouds of dust, which obscured the tanks.

In the intervening years man-portable ATGWs became simpler, smarter and lighter, culminating in the US Javelin, a fire-and-forget, top-attack weapon with an imaging infrared (IIR) seeker. This allows the operator to track the target with the Command Launch Unit, lock onto a target image and launch the Javelin missile, which homes in on the target using the stored image, overflying the target and firing its top-attack HEAT warhead.

Again, it was the Soviets who addressed the threat from the man-portable HEAT warhead ATGW by developing explosive reactive armour (ERA). In its simplest form ERA is a series of boxes arranged around the tank structure with each box comprising an explosive charge sandwiched between two metal plates. When a HEAT warhead impacts the ERA, the plasma jet detonates the explosive as a counter-charge, pushing the external plate into the path of the weapon. Additionally, ERA can also be used against penetrators, solid or explosively formed, by dissipating their momentum and thus reducing their penetrative effect. As ever, in the weapon/armour spiral, reactive armour

The T-72 was well armoured with composite armour and, on this Indian Army example, explosive reactive armour modules on the glacis plate and turret. *Wiki Commons*

Explosively Formed Penetrators (EFP) or self-forging warheads are a variation on the shaped-charge or HEAT warhead. The metal liner or plate in an EFP is less concave than in a HEAT warhead and may use variations in the explosive or multiple detonators to tailor the explosive effect across the back of the plate. The effect is to form the plate into a projectile that can take the form of fragments, a single slug or a projectile similar to the long rod of APFSDS.

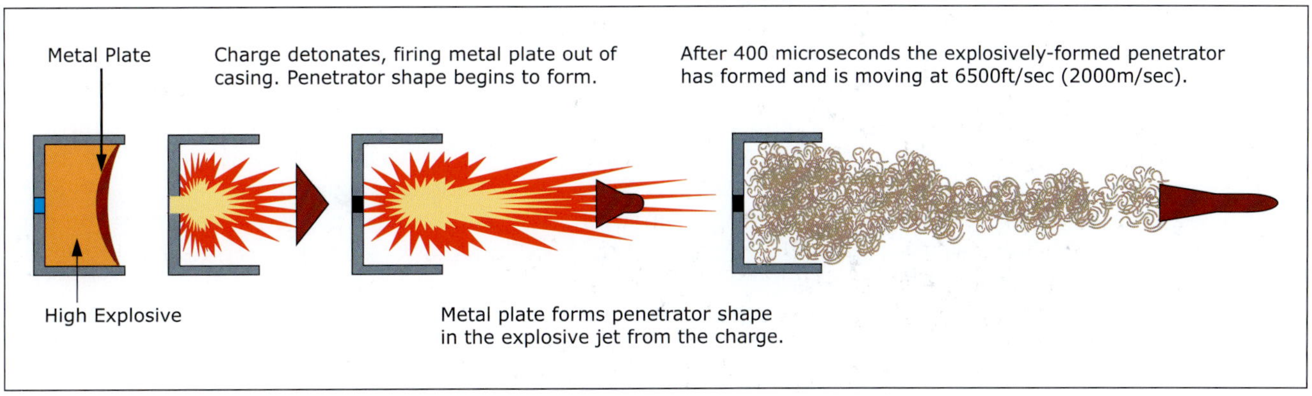

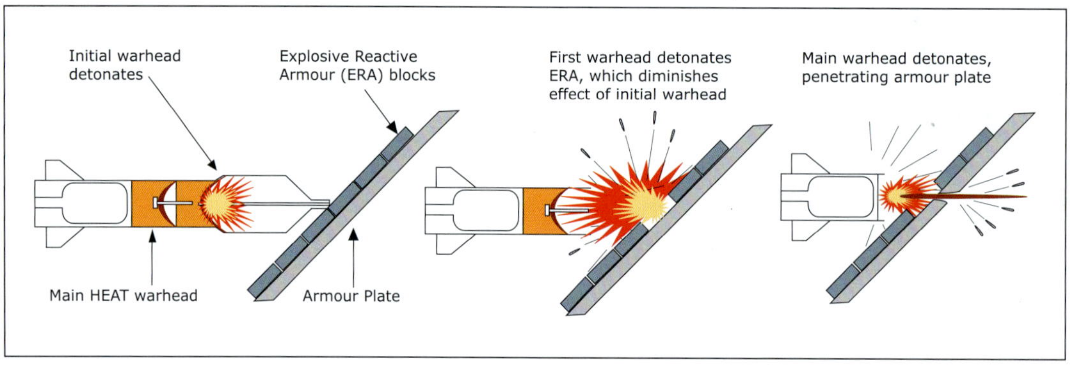

To defeat Explosive Reactive Armour (ERA) missile designers turned to the tandem charge warhead. The stand-off fuze detonates the initial HEAT warhead which in turn triggers the ERA. The ERA explosion and metal cover plate acts to diminish the effect of the initial warhead and exposes the vehicle's primary armour. The missile's main warhead detonates in turn and penetrates the newly exposed armour of the vehicle.

The weapon/armour spiral in the flesh. A British Army Challenger 2 MBT equipped with (at least) three types of armour to defeat the range of weapons. The basic composite Chobham/Dorchester-type armour on the hull and turret to defeat penetrators; bar/slat armour, seen on the rear quadrant and ERA boxes on the sides of the turret and hull to defeat HEAT rounds. A future upgrade will include the IMI Iron Fist active armour system. *MoD/Open Government Licence*

can be defeated by tandem charge warheads whereby an initial charge detonates the ERA followed by a second charge that penetrates the main armour.

With the arrival of the top-attack anti-tank missile, especially those with explosively formed penetrators (EFP), the missile did not need to hit the target, merely fly over it and fire the charge. This concept dated back to the SG 113A Förstersonde of 1945: six 77mm (3in) barrels arranged behind the cockpit of a Focke-Wulf Fw 190, firing downwards and triggered by magnetic induction or radar as the Fw 190 flew over. The system used to counter these is known as active armour, that uses a short-range radar system to detect incoming weapons. This in turn initiates a counter weapon which can be a small missile to intercept the threat, a charge to trigger a HEAT warhead before it can form its plasma jet or a shotgun type weapon to shred the incoming threat. Very James Bond.

The Merkava mentioned above has also been fitted with the Windbreaker active protection system using the shotgun type system whereas the Russian Afghanit uses a guided warhead that is said to be capable of countering APDS penetrators, although its performance against top-attack missiles is unclear.

The gun/armour spiral still exists as the weapon/armour spiral, but despite that, a tank is a formidable weapon and the embodiment of a show of force. Prime Minister Harold Wilson's instruction to union leader Hugh Scanlon to 'Get your tanks off my lawn' has gone down in history as a metaphor for reluctance to succumb to undue pressure.

Pundits have predicted the end of the main battle tank as a battlefield asset since the first ATGWs were developed in the 1950s. The MBT is still the ruler of the battlefield and continues to match, if not fend off, usurpers. Perhaps Pete Pyman had a point.

Appendix 2 Base Burning – No Use or Not Used?

'Although the method appears to be unattractive at first sight, preliminary study tends to be more encouraging.'
Summary on Base-burning, NGTE, Pyestock

What is base-burning and why was it being considered for aircraft such as the Advanced Strike Aircraft, MRCA and AST.396? The origins of the technique may lie in the mid-1960s with work done by the Swedish Försvarets forskningsanstalt (FOA, Swedish National Defence Research Institute) aiming to increase the range of the Svenska marinen (Swedish Royal Navy) coastal defence guns. Aside from the drag of the artillery shell's body as it moves through the air, another source of drag is the vortices forming aft of the flat base of the shell. Aerodynamic shaping of shells is restricted to a boat-tail as a more aerodynamic shape would affect its ballistics to the detriment of accuracy.

The FOA found that if a gas generator was built into the base of the shell, the expanding gas would produce little or no thrust but would reduce the differential pressure between the zone behind the shell and the atmosphere the shell was moving through. Range increases in the order of 30% could be achieved and the system was soon in service with the Swedish Royal Navy. The rights to the technology ultimately landed with the Space Research Corporation (SRC), and base bleed technology found its way into US Army and Israeli Army artillery pieces as part of the Extended Range Full Bore (ERFB) artillery shells in the early 1970s.

Meanwhile in southern Africa, the South African Army was operating in Angola and found its World War Two vintage 5.5in (140mm) Medium Guns consistently outranged by the Angolan and Cuban forces' Soviet-supplied M-46 130mm (5.1in) artillery and BM-21 Grad MLRS. Despite the sanctions in place at the time, SRC helped the South African company Armscor develop the 155mm G5 that used base bleed technology. Without base bleed shells the G5 had a range of 19 miles (31km) whereas with base bleed shells a range of 25 miles (40km) was possible. While the Space Research Corporation might not be familiar to readers, its founder, Gerald Bull, will as the designer of Project Babylon, the Iraqi supergun.

When applied to aircraft, the principle was similar. Base-burning involved increasing the effective thrust available by alleviating the base drag on the rear of an aircraft fuselage by burning fuel in the low pressure recirculation zone formed behind the base. Base-burning worked best on a bluff rear surface that has poor drag characteristics although it can also work on streamlined rear areas but shows fewer bene-

Hawker Siddeley at Brough conducted a series wind tunnel tests with various sizes of bases, different combustible gasses and incrementally increasing Mach Numbers. Brough's engineers were ready to move to flight testing burning bases on aircraft.
Brough Heritage

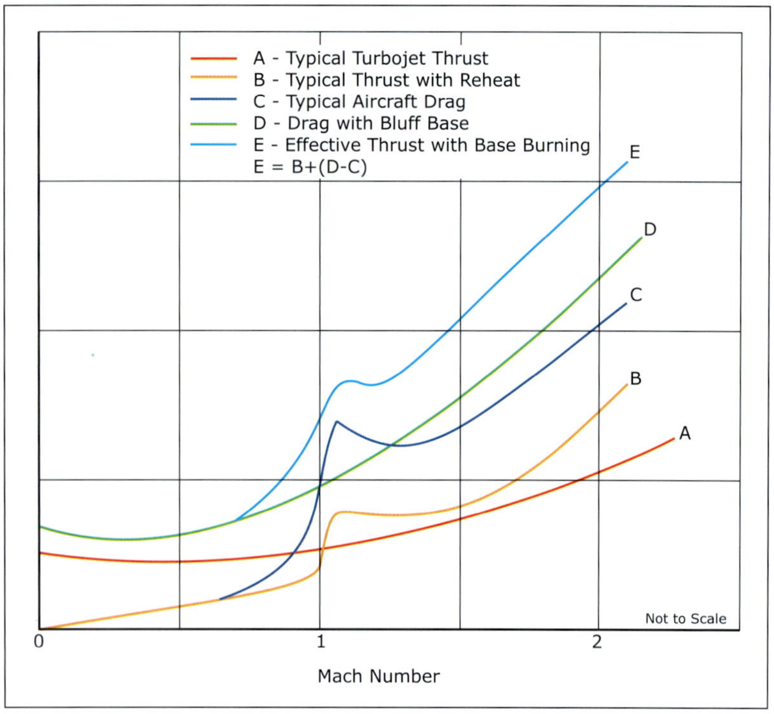

This graph shows how the variables involved in base burning combined to reduce drag and produce an effective thrust increase.

fits. One of the benefits of base-burning is that it allows an increase in fuselage cross-section and therefore internal volume without the need to extend the airframe to maintain fineness ratio. This increased volume can be utilised for fuel or weapons.

Base-burning works by replacing afterbody wave drag with base drag which in turn is reduced by base-burning: injecting fuel into the recirculation zone formed aft of the base, igniting it and the expansion of the gasses cancels out the drag and provides a modicum of thrust. This begs the question: why not use a bigger engine? A larger engine would no doubt be a more efficient means to burn fuel, but would require a redesign of the aircraft, triggering a 'vicious spiral' of size/weight escalation. Aircraft with 'oversized' engines suffer from poor efficiency at cruise whereas base-burning in combination with a reheated engine improved performance for the same size engine and is most efficient at transonic Mach numbers.

Base-burning was viewed as most beneficial in the transonic acceleration and supersonic regimes, although there is little benefit at low subsonic speeds. The maximum flight Mach number for a given aircraft/engine combination could be increased by the use of base-burning. When specific fuel consumption (sfc) was considered, it had been found that 90% of the base drag could be eliminated when burning 50% of the fuel required to eliminate 100% of the base drag. If the sfc of base-burning and reheat were compared, it was noted that a simple bluff-based cylinder would produce sfc values that exceeded that of a reheat system by a factor of two. However, base-burning performed best with a high drag rear such as an elliptical base with a central jet exhaust.

In its simplest form base-burning effectively provided a thrust boost to an aircraft with an engine that is already providing the maximum reheated thrust. At first sight the concept appears unattractive, but it allows aircraft designers the freedom to consider a bluff back end for a supersonic aircraft, thus increasing the internal volume. Base-burning also allows a power boost that would otherwise require a larger or additional engine but at a much lower weight penalty.

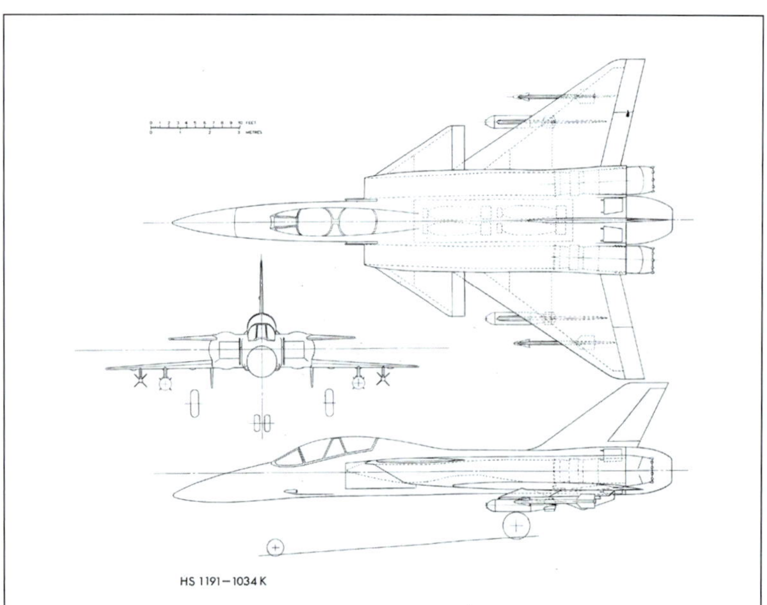

Wind Tunnel Work

Research work covered aircraft design studies and wind tunnel work under a contract, K7A/14/A let to HSA Kingston on 6 April 1970, which was related to a contract for Advanced Fighter Concepts, K7A/01/A/CB7A. This contract covered studies towards five basic 'Advanced Fighter Concepts' that HSA would examine to assess the benefits, if any, of base burning. The first was a fixed wing, conventional layout with external stores that was to act as the datum for the other four studies. Study 2 was a fixed wing type with base-burning and internal stores while Study 3 was a variable geometry type with internal stores but without base-burning. Study 4 was also variable geometry but with base-burning and internal stores while Study 5 was a VTOL type with-base burning and internal stores. As well as work on Study 1, the Datum Aircraft, Study 2 had received most attention by the time the base-burning contract was let in April 1970.

Brough had conducted wind tunnel work on a base-burning model as a private venture before the contract was let, with their 27in (68cm) high-speed wind tunnel being used during 1969 with further work, under contract, planned at the National Gas Turbine Establishment's Cell 1 at Pyestock or, if unavailable, at Bristol Siddeley Engines Ltd's High Altitude Test Plant (HATP) at Patchway. Meanwhile, work on unclassified aspects of base-burning was being undertaken by a PhD student at Southampton University.

The Brough work involved a 3in (76mm) diameter hollow body with a bluff base and a conical nose that was machined to have a peripheral slot around the base, fed with fuel through pipework in a pylon that held the body in the centre of the tunnel. The model was also tapped to accept six pressure transducers, five on the base at 'centres of equal annular areas' with the sixth, reference, transducer 3in (76mm) forward of the base. Three fuels were assessed: hydrogen, ethylene and propane and the initial tests showed that as the molecular weight of the gas increased, it became 'progressively more difficult to ignite' at transonic speeds, with the tests covering speeds from Mach 0.7 to 2.0.

Propane was used as it possessed combustion properties similar to atomised kerosene. The test showed that propane could not be ignited at speeds above Mach 1.4 but more significantly that 'full base relief was not achieved at any Mach No.' However, if the tests were restricted to the transonic regime, later trials showed reductions in base drag of 90-100% with hydrogen and 70-85% with propane at Mach 1.1. Encouraged by this, the model was modified to burn kerosene 'from which surprisingly good results were obtained' up to Mach 1.1. The Brough team considered scale as the problem when it came to maintaining combustion at speeds above Mach 1.1 and advised scaling up the model.

Meantime, other suggestions for more realistic tests for base-burning came from the NGTE's Dr DI Dawton who suggested free-flight rockets tests, captive rocket sled tests and the NGTE's Cell 1 or Bristol's HATP, which was used to test ramjets, as the NGTE's facilities were 'heavily committed'. Hawker Siddeley proposed a 10in (25cm) diameter model, with peripheral or axial fuel injection available and so the existing contract was extended to cover this work at Pyestock.

Underwing Base-burning

While the tunnel work had showed that base burning was feasible, in small scale models under controlled conditions and at transonic speed, the feasibility of applying it to an aircraft was far from proven. The next stage in development was to scale up the burning bases and fly an experimental system on an aircraft using kerosene. Hawker Siddeley had been building the F-4K and F-4M Phantoms for the RAF and FAA, so had a Mach 2 capable aircraft available in the shape of XT595, the first Phantom FG.1 for the Royal Navy.

The objectives were to prove that the base-burning system could not only use kerosene but be lit in flight, assess flame stability and measure base pressures at a range of speeds. Analysis had shown that a pylon mounting would be best, to keep the base-burning unit free of aerodynamic interference and that sparked discussions on the type of pylon and its position on the aircraft. If a 20in (50.8cm) diameter burning base was required, an extendable pylon would be required to provide sufficient ground clearance, particularly if a tyre burst on landing. An extension of 15in (38cm) was required. Telescoping, 'parallelogram' and folding pylons were considered, but simplicity prevailed and a fixed pylon carrying a 15in (38cm) diameter burning base and equipment pod was selected.

The 550 lb (249kg) pod was to be carried like a store on a standard ejector rack to allow it to be jettisoned if necessary. The 15in (38cm) diameter burning base was installed at the rear of a 10ft (3m) long pod whose forward third

Opposite, bottom: Base-burning was proposed for one of Hawker Siddeley's submissions for ASR.392 (MRCA), the canard delta HS.1191-1034K. This fairly large two-seater was fitted with a single nickel alloy base between the two RB.199-42R turbofans. Two pairs of BL.755 could be carried in the internal weapons bay. *Brooklands Museum*

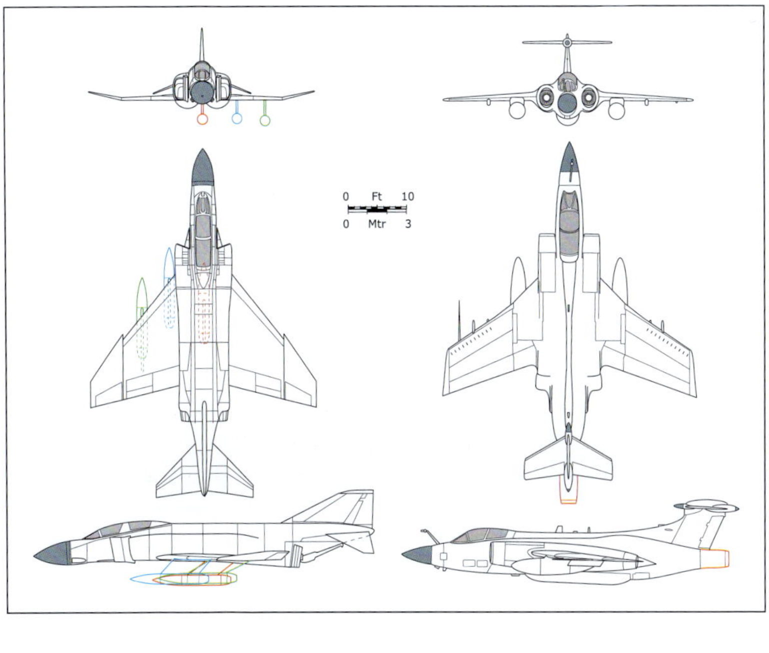

Below: Two HSA types were considered as testbeds for base-burning trials. Burning bases are shown in red. Buccaneer was too slow but the Phantom was favoured for simplicity of installation as the test article was effectively a store.

comprised a ogival nose enveloping a bay that contained instrumentation. The central section was cylindrical and held a fuel tank for 35 gallons (159 litres) of kerosene. Aft of the fuel section was an equipment bay holding fire suppression systems and fuel metering systems. The fuel/equipment section was separated from the burning base by an insulated heat wall. The burning base itself was at the rear of the pod and surrounded by a ring of fuel atomisers to feed the burning base. The atomiser on the 15in (38cm) pod would be arranged radially, but the intention was to have the atomisers inject axially to keep the flame in the pod's wake.

The base itself would need to be resistant to temperatures up to 1,700°C (3,092°F). Between 1,000 and 1,200°C (1,832 – 2,192°F) Nimonic could be used but as temperatures increased, more exotic refractory materials would be required such as tungsten or molybdenum. These would be not only expensive, but difficult to work into the shapes required. Higher temperatures would call for the heat-resistant steel to be coated with ceramic such as aluminium oxide (alumina), which could operate at temperatures up to 2,000°C (3,623°F).

Next concern was the thermal effects on the aircraft itself because although the flame was far enough away and would not impinge on the airframe, the radiated heat would affect the aircraft structure. Two solutions were suggested: fit heat shields to the airframe or limit the time the system was in operation. Of course, this would not pose a problem in an operational aircraft as the burning bases would be at the rear of the aircraft. One problem that afflicted jet aircraft was acoustic effects from the fast-moving propulsive exhaust gasses. Since base-burning produced little or no thrust, there were no acoustic effects on the airframe.

Two ignition systems were examined; spark generator or a torch, with spark ignition considered the simplest as the torch would require a separate fuel system. Some means of confirming ignition was also required, possibly a temperature sensor on the aircraft. Film and photographic coverage could be provided by installing cine cameras in the aft missile well. These would have 10mm lenses and cover the rear of the pod and the flame plume.

As for positioning, a centreline position was thought most feasible but aerodynamic interference was still a possibility, so the inboard and outboard wing pylons were considered. The centreline position was selected as wing mounting offered no experimental advantage and might lead to aeroelasticity problems. A further reason was that ventral carriage could be cleared by Brough whereas wing mounting would have required clearance from McDonnell Douglas in St Louis.

Much of the research work on base-burning was conducted under a Ministry of Technology (MinTech) contract with Hawker Siddeley's Military Research Department at Kingston. On 10 April 1970 RH Francis, Executive Director of Military Research at Hawker Siddeley Aviation gave a presentation at Kingston-upon-Thames to an audience of HSA engineers and aerodynamicists.

Francis outlined how the initial wind-tunnel work had been carried out at the Hawker Siddeley plant at Brough using a variety of models, with bases of 3in (76mm) in diameter that burned hydrogen, ethylene or propane. The Brough models were constructed with interchangeable bases with an atomiser in the centre of the base or towards the periphery. The tests showed that with hydrogen and ethylene injection from the central atomiser gave better drag relief than injection from a peripheral atomiser. The tests also showed that propane couldn't be burned on the central atomiser at speeds above Mach 0.5 but burning could be sustained up to Mach 0.95 with the peripheral atomisers.

As noted above, larger bodies, with 10in (254mm) diameter bases were tested in the wind-tunnel at the National Gas Turbine Establishment (NGTE) at Pyestock, again with hydrogen or propane. By August 1969 wind-tunnel work had shown the feasibility of base-burning in models with gases as fuel but there was little to be gained by further wind tunnel work. What was required was a demonstration that kerosene could be used as fuel and it could be ignited reliably in flight, although reheat from the aircraft engines was suggested. Other areas to be examined were how the base-burning combustion would perform with asymmetric flow or at incidence, aspects that had previously caused problems with another propulsion system: ramjets. The logical next step would be a flight research aircraft.

As ever, a testbed based on an existing aircraft would make sense. Its flight characteristics would be well documented and comparison with the testbed possible. The bases could either be 'scabbed' onto the aircraft, built into the aircraft itself or mounted on a pod. Four types were considered: The BAC.221 that had been used for research into the ogival planform, BAC Lightning F Mk.3, Phantom FG Mk.1 and Brough's own Buccaneer S.2. Given that base-burning appeared to work best at high

Mach numbers, the Buccaneer might seem an odd choice, but the base could be fitted in place of the tailcone airbrakes, be integrated with the airframe and fuel systems and, more importantly, allow a larger diameter base, 41½in (105cm) providing an area of 9.4ft^2 (0.87m^2). It would occupy a position and be of similar size to that later proposed for a strike aircraft.

The Phantom, another type Brough was familiar with as they built the British F-4K and F-4Ms, could be fitted with a pylon-mounted pod described above. However, that could only be 15in (38cm) in diameter with an area of 1.2ft^2 (0.11m^2), or if a folding or telescopic pylon was used, 20in (51cm) in diameter with an area of 2.2ft^2 (0.20m^2). One benefit of pylon mounting the burning base was that it could be jettisoned in an emergency.

While Buccaneer and Phantom came from the Hawker Siddeley stables, another two runners came from the other side of the country, the British Aircraft Corporation at Filton and Warton. The BAC.221, a development of the Fairey FD.2, had been used as an analogue for Concorde wing development. The engineers at Brough proposed fitting the BAC.221 with a pair of burning bases and fairings on the upper rear quadrant of the rear fuselage, one each side of the tailfin. These bases were self-contained, with the fuel and associated systems installed forward of the 20in (51cm) diameter burning bases, which could be changed to test different base and atomisier systems. The BAC.221 required many engineering changes including a triangular section cut out of the elevators to avoid fouling on the burning bases. One concern was the need for ballast in the forward fuselage to maintain CoG with the burning bases installed but the BAC.221 lacked the space for ballast, having a single ballast bay. Useable spaces for test equipment were also limited and the somewhat cramped cockpit could only accommodate the extra equipment to control the burning bases with difficulty.

As for the Lightning F Mk.3, it also carried 20in (51cm) burning bases on the rear fuselage, but unlike the BAC.221 the bases were not fixed in position and could be 'offset' to determine the optimum position. Ballast-wise the Lightning had many locations where ballast could be fitted, including gun and radar bays. This author recalls a former RAF Lightning engine fitter describing how 'souvenirs' from foreign deployments could be stashed, away from HM Customs officers' scrutiny in the Lightning's many 'Top Secret' bays. One problem the Lightning did have was its lack of a suitable location for a camera. While the Buccaneer and BAC.221 could carry a camera in a fin-tip pod and the Phantom carried one in the missile recess, the Lightning had no suitable location. The solution would be to have a chase aircraft filming the trials, probably another Lightning such as Lightning T Mk.4 XM968 used for TSR.2 trials.

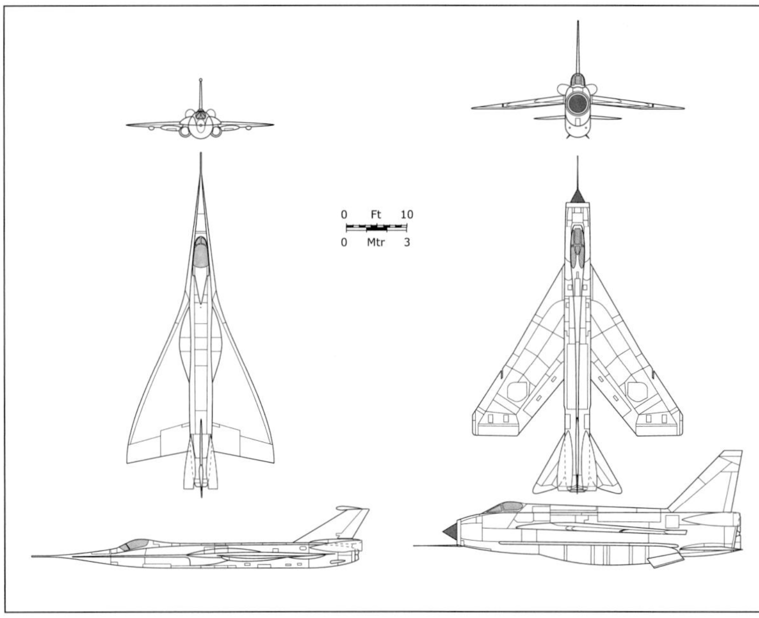

Two BAC aircraft were proposed for base-burning tests. Burning bases are shown in red. The BAC.221 lacked space for the required telemetry kit. The Lightning F.3 was considered best of the lot as it was more representative of a service aircraft.

When it came to select the type most suitable for the trials, the Buccaneer and BAC.221 were quickly dismissed. The Buccaneer was limited to its maximum speed of Mach 0.954 and although the BAC.221 was capable of Mach 1.8 on paper it was fuel-limited to Mach 1.5 and lacked endurance. It also had a two-position reheat, rather than the variable reheat on Lightning and Phantom. The burning-bases on the Lightning, BAC.221 and Phantom were removable, while the Buccaneer's was fixed but more representative of the installation on a service aircraft.

Oddly enough the operating airfield for test flights was under scrutiny because much of the test flying would be at supersonic speeds which should be conducted over the sea. Due to the BAC.221's endurance, it would need to undertake supersonic flights over land if operated from RAE Bedford and as a result the Blackburn airfield at Holme-on-Spalding Moor, a few miles west of Kingston-Upon-Hull, would be more suitable to avoid broken windows.

The choice lay between the Lightning and the Phantom. Both possessed the required performance and the configuration, and position, of the burning bases could be changed as trials progressed. The Phantom was easiest to modify – it was effectively a store – but that made it less attractive than the Lightning which was considered 'more representative of a service aircraft'.

The Case for the Fat Fuselage

The RAE Aerodynamics Dept's RK Page presented a paper on the *raison d'être* for base burning – the fat fuselage strike aircraft. The term 'fat fuselage' referred to 'a fuselage of appreciably greater cross-sectional area than the minimum required for the sums of the areas of: engines (or their intake ducts), undercarriage, service ducts and wing carry-through structure'. From the aerodynamic point of view the 'salient feature is that the finesse ratio is decreased'.

In a fat fuselage, the additional area and resultant volume could be used for more fuel, weapons or lift engines if these can be used to improve the performance over conventional types that carry these items externally i.e. pylon mounted fuel tanks or weapons or internal lift engines that displace fuel or equipment. The disadvantage of the fat fuselage is increased afterbody (base) drag.

Base burning, to reduce, if not remove, the afterbody drag appeared to offer advantages at high subsonic and transonic speeds, at which much of a strike aircraft sortie would be conducted. Page assessed the effect of base burning on each of the three additional 'items'. While the old adage is that you only have too much fuel when you're on fire, Page explains that providing a strike aircraft with extra fuel may rob the aircraft of speed and manoeuvrability while leading to 'a bomber of near-strategic range but only a tactical bomb-load.' Fuel was probably the most easily accommodated item, as it can be 'stashed' in the aircraft's nooks and crannies, making a fat fuselage specifically for more fuel less desirable, especially if drop tanks can be fitted.

As for weapons, internal carriage gives less drag and a benign environment, 'particularly with respect of kinetic heating'. There may be problems associated with weapons release from internal bays, with separation easier with external carriage while there could be restrictions on weapons size. Another problem could be with guided weapons that need to acquire the target before launch and would need to be exposed to allow this.

Lift engines were other items that could be accommodated in a fat fuselage. Page describes how a MRCA type could be converted to VTOL by fitting deflected nozzles on the propulsion engines and installing six XJ.99 lift engines in the fuselage. Page advised that the engines would increase the fuselage width by 2ft 6in (0.76m), producing a 14ft^2 (1.3m^2) increase in cross-sectional area but the attendant increase in drag could be countered by base-burning. Page took the view that the fat fuselage and attendant base burning would only be advantageous in the lift engine case.

In the presentation he delivered at Kingston, Francis gave the impression that he was keen on base-burning and that it held advantage for a strike aircraft, mainly due to allowing internal carriage of a good weapons load. To demonstrate this, Francis proposed developing a strike

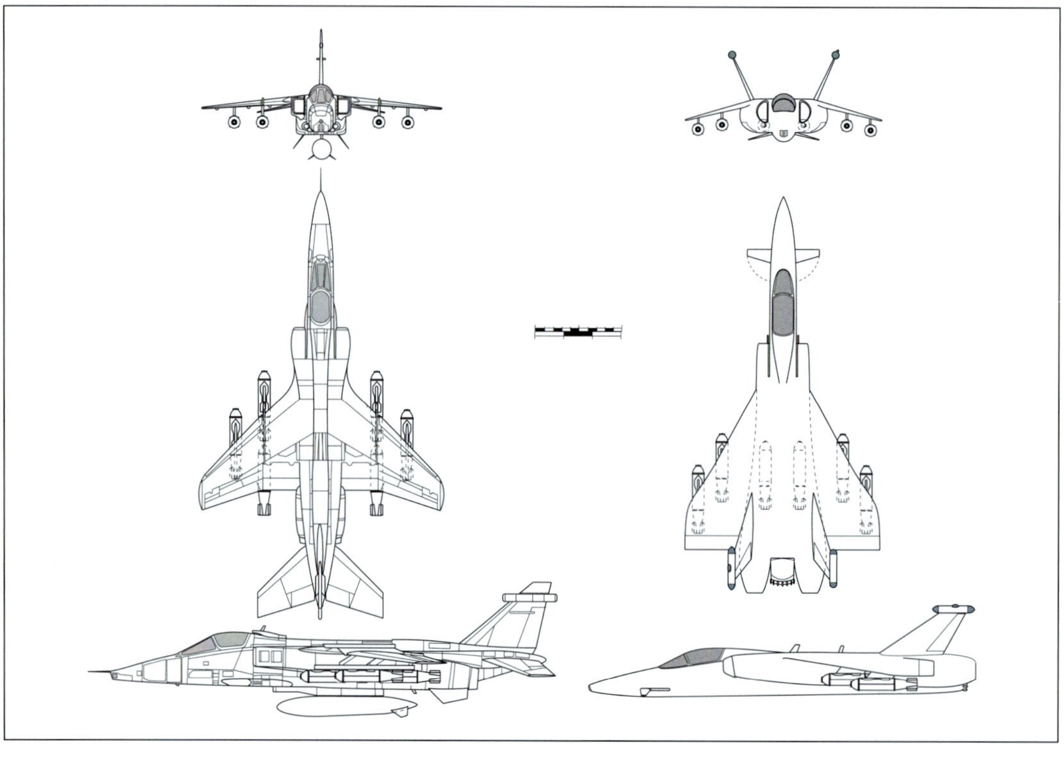

This page: Comparison of the HS.1191-1 with the Jaguar GR.1. the base-burning aircraft was slightly smaller but much broader thanks to the burning bases. BAC addressed the penetration/ escape boost requirement with liquid fuelled rocket engines on their P.69 study.

Opposite, top: The HS.1191-1 was a compact, Jaguar-sized, strike aircraft aimed squarely at AST.396. It carried two of its six BL.755 cluster bombs in an internal bay made feasible by the nickel alloy bases on either side of the RB.199-42R jetpipe. The HS.1191-1 also had retractable foreplanes to improve manoeuvrability. *Brooklands Museum*

aircraft incorporating base-burning. This aircraft was to be a small, 11,000lb (4,990kg) AUW delta aircraft powered by a single Rolls-Royce Turbomeca Adour, rated at 7,200lbf (32kN) reheat, and fitted with base-burning. This aircraft would be capable of Mach 1 flight for 8½ to 9 minutes. With reheat and base-burning, Francis stated that the aircraft could reach Mach 1.8; with reheat alone, Mach 1 and with dry thrust (no reheat or base-burning) Mach 0.8. As for the cost, Francis advised that this flying testbed could be produced for £5M (£78.5M in 2018) with the possibility of using it as the basis for a strike aircraft.

This 'light strike fighter' would be in the 17,000lb (7,711kg) AUW class, powered by an Adour with increased thrust, rated at 9,000lbf (40kN), the type could carry three BL.755 cluster bombs externally and a pair of internal guns, probably ADEN cannon. Of course, the larger fuselage would allow internal space for equipment or more fuel. Its field performance could be enhanced by fitting 'Dassault type foreplanes...giving some 25% increase in lift'. This aircraft may have been the precursor of a Kingston's proposal for AST.396, the HS.1191-1, was in the 20,000lb (9,000kg) class Kingston's designers drew up a small delta with small flip-out canards powered by a single RB.199-42R turbofan rated at 16,900lbf (75.2kN) with a base-burning body either side.

The ASR.392 requirement called for a strike aircraft in the 40,000lb (18,000kg) class and this led to MRCA and ultimately the Tornado, a requirement that Hawker Siddeley hoped to meet with the HS.1191-1034K. The powerplant for the HS.1191-1034K study comprised two RB.199-34R engines rated at 15,000lbf (66.7kN) each, separated by a single base-burning body. Base-burning was to be used during the penetration to and egress from the target area, providing an extra boost for escape after delivering the weapons. The base-burning unit comprised a flat nickel disk with a series of fuel injection ports around its circumference.

Both types could carry six BL.755 cluster bombs, with two internally on the HS.1191-1 and four on the larger HS.1191-1034K. The -1034K was to carry its bomb load as two pairs arranged fore-and-aft. While this would mean a wider weapons bay, it was thought that two stacked pairs, while allowing a narrower bomb bay, would require a deeper bay. The problem with the stacked pairs was two-fold – more complex suspension and release systems and the effects of a deep bay in the underside and associated aerodynamic problems. Other weapons included internal cannon, probably 30mm ADEN or BK-27 27mm and a pair of AIM-9 Sidewinders. Another gun considered for MRCA aircraft in the early days of the programme was the Oerlikon 304RK 30mm cannon. This became the KCA cannon and was one of the heaviest-hitting cannon available, and as such it was also examined as an anti-runway weapon.

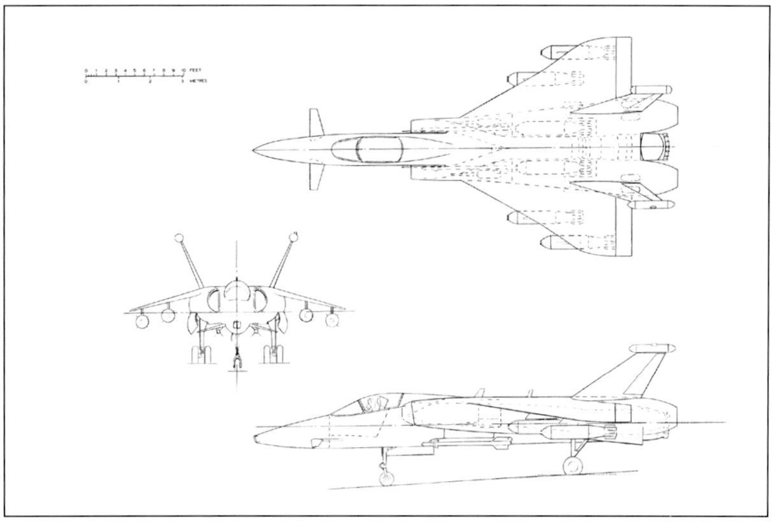

Base-burning was an innovative and interesting exercise aimed at increasing the performance of strike aircraft without the need to increase the engine size but allowing extra equipment, particularly lift engine to be added with minimal drag penalty. Interestingly there appears to have been a 'Pennine divide' on the matter with HSA Brough in the East Riding of Yorkshire being positive on the subject while across the Pennines in north west Lancashire at BAC Warton the technique was dismissed almost out of hand. Perhaps, like Handley Page's work on laminar flow and boundary layer control that has been adopted by Airbus, base-burning may return.

Below: **The HS.1191-2 dispensed with the foreplanes and had its wings set lower on the fuselage. All its BL.755 were carried on wing pylons as the weapons bay had given way to four RB.277 lift engines, two per side to improve airfield performance.** ***Brooklands Museum***

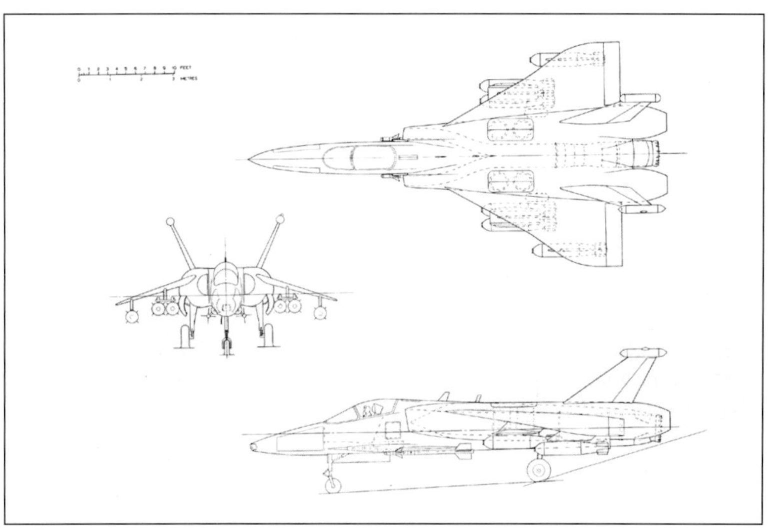

Appendix 3 Spooky Spectres Rule the Night

'Guns. Lots of guns.' Neo, *The Matrix*, 1999

Having absorbed many of the lessons the British learned in Malaya, the US forces in Vietnam were faced with a new challenge in the form of the interdiction of materiel being moved from North Vietnam to South Vietnam. The Ho Chi Minh Trail, famously portrayed as a peasant army pushing shell-laden bicycles through the rainforest, was more mechanised that the propaganda let on. Trucks, supplied by the Soviet Union, carried the heavier loads and these had to be stopped. Since these operated at night, any operation to interdict the Ho Chi Minh Trail required the ability to attack ground targets in the dark. As noted in Chapter 9, the USAF developed sensor to enable Tropic Moon III B-57Gs to attack trucks with Paveway LGBs. There was another approach.

Prior to autumn 1964 any commander of 'troops in contact' facing the prospect of having his position over-run had two choices when it came to calling for fire support – one if it was night time – to repulse the enemy: 'fast air' or artillery. Fast air was fighter-bombers operating on a similar basis to the cab rank system but unable to operate at night or in bad weather, while artillery was very much range-limited, typically less than 10 miles (16km) and therefore only useful if the situation unfolded near a gun position. There was also the prospect of the incoming shells falling short or being off target and impacting on the friendlies.

An AC-47 Spooky provides fire support for ground operations around Tan Son Nhut Air Base during the Tet Offensive in 1968. This time-lapse photograph captures the tracer rounds fired by the Miniguns. Typically, every fifth round was tracer. *DoD via Terry Panopalis*

Until the late 20th century and arrival of guided munitions, Artillery, Stalin's 'god of war' was not accurate enough to deliver explosive close to friendly forces, nor was fast air. Interestingly one type of heavy artillery was very accurate – naval gun support. Designed to hit ships at long range on the high seas, naval gunnery was a very exact science and with the demise of the capital ship, the big guns were seemingly redundant. However, naval gunnery had been key to amphibious landings during World War Two and has provided fire support on many occasions around the world since 1945, particularly in Korea, Vietnam and in the Falklands. The US Navy famously used the *Iowa*-class battleships and their 16in (406mm) guns to bombard North Vietnamese forces, especially when bad weather grounded fast air. The Royal Navy has a long history of shore bombardment and used the 4.5in (114mm) guns to good effect during Operation CORPORATE in the Falklands campaign.

What was required was a means to provide fire support by day and especially by night, that could react to the situation on the ground. The solution was to install ten 0.3cal Browning AN/M2 machine guns in the cabin of a C-47 Skytrain, but the guns and their World War Two era ammunition proved unsuitable and ten AN/M2s only produced the same rate of fire as one Minigun – a new gun developed in the early 1960s.

Developed to as a pod-mounted weapon for COIN aircraft or on a pintle mount to provide supressing fire from helicopters landing at 'hot' landing zones in Vietnam, the 7.62mm Minigun used the same Gatling principle as the M61 Vulcan. Electrically-driven, the Minigun could fire at a rate of 6,000 rounds per minute. Trials under Project Tailchaser involved fitting a Convair C-131 with a minigun pod mounted to fire out of the port side cabin door. This proved that the weapon could be accurately aimed using a rudimentary sight said to be a cross drawn on the cockpit glazing, with the aircraft in a pylon turn to port. The effect of this firing in a turn was to keep the target under fire longer than was possible in a strafing attack by a fighter aircraft. This led to Project Gunship I and trials with the C-47 in 1964.

With the trials successful, three Miniguns, in SUU-11A podded weapon guise, replaced the ten M2 Brownings in the C-47, producing the FC-47, later changed to AC-47, to placate fighter pilots who objected to the C-47 being designated as a fighter. Initially three SUU-11A aircraft pods were fitted in the cabin of the AC-47, one mounted in the cabin door and one in each of the last two cabin windows. Later AC-47s carried General Electric MX-470/A miniguns in bespoke mounts rather than pods. The AC-47s, callsign Puff but known as Spooky, performed so well that up-gunning was the logical progression for the role to allow engagements with heavier weapons and at longer ranges. Adding sensors could also expand the missions that could be undertaken by what was now being called a gunship.

By 1967 the USAF had clarified the requirement, identifying a need for a gunship with increased endurance, firepower, speed and ability to carry a suite of sensors. Having examined the AC-119 under Project Gunship III, which was underpowered, the USAF turned to the workhorse of the USAF: the Lockheed C-130 Hercules. A most unlikely combat aircraft, the C-130 did have the payload, endurance, performance and capacity for sensors the USAF sought and under Project Gunship II, a JC-130 was selected for conversion as AC-130A 54-1626.

The AC-130As were fitted with four 7.62mm miniguns and four 20mm Vulcan cannons, but the AC-130 also allowed for fitting of sensor arrays for target acquisition and aiming, rather than the AC-47 technique of dropping flares or have a 'flare ship' drop them to illuminate the target. Amongst the sensors were a Starlite scope, AN/AAD-4 forward looking infrared (FLIR) sensor for low-light observation, a searchlight, sideways looking radar, beacon tracker and a computer for fire control that was designed and built by an RAF Officer, Wing Commander Pinkerton. In addition to supporting troops under attack, one of the AC-130A's intended roles was the destruction of trucks on the Ho Chi Minh Trail, a task that required endurance firepower and some means of finding the trucks.

The next stage in the AC-130 story was aimed at the interdiction of trucks and was tested with the Surprise Package, a modification in which

The AC-47 Spooky was armed with four 7.62mm Miniguns. The AC-47's weapons were aimed by the light of flares dropped by a 'flare ship' but later a jury-rigged Starlight scope was used. *Terry Panopalis Collection*

the two Vulcans and two miniguns in the rear cabin were removed and replaced with a pair of Bofors L/60 40mm guns. A new AN/ASQ-145 low light level television (LLLTV) system and an APQ-133 sideways looking radar for beacon tracking were fitted and when combined with the FLIR, Surprise Package proved successful in the truck interdiction role. Building on that success came Pave Pronto which combined the armament and systems of Surprise Package with a new sensor called Black Crow.

Developed as the Pave Mace, the AN/ASD-5 Black Crow sensor used a sensitive flux-gate magnetometer derived from the magnetic anomaly detector used in anti-submarine warfare. Black Crow detected changes in the earth's magnetic field caused by the emissions from a vehicle's ignition systems (many Soviet trucks used petrol spark-ignition engines) and these were used to cue the targeting sensors. The Pave Pronto led to the original AC-130A fleet being upgraded and C-130E and -H models converted to AC-130E and AC-130H to replace the old high-time AC-130As and the updated airframes gave scope for further development. The new programme was called Pave Spectre and retained the pairs of Miniguns, Vulcans and Bofors of the Pave Pronto but improved internal layout of the sensor consoles and an observation blister on the tail ramp improved crew comfort. The blister allowed the tail ramp to remain closed rather than have a crewman lying on the tail ramp with their head over the back to watch for SAMs and AAA.

The latter would become increasingly effective along the Ho Chi Minh Trail and the USAF looked at a weapon with greater range to allow attacks from stand-off ranges. The choice fell on the M102 105mm howitzer that could engage targets at ranges up to 12,000 yards (10,972m) with the aid of a trainable mount and computer aiming system. This programme,

Above left: The original AC-130 Spectre was fitted with four 20mm Vulcan cannons and four 7.62 Miniguns as a dedicated truck hunter. The Spectre also carried a suite of sensors to 'see' in the dark. This variant carries the twin Bofors 40mm L60 and 20mm M61 Vulcan. *Terry Panopalis Collection*

Above right: The sensors on the Spectre included the Black Crow ignition emissions detector, ground-mapping radar, infrared sensors and, shown here, the AN/ASQ-145 low light level television system. *Author*

Pave Aegis, saw the removal of all the Miniguns and one of the Bofors replaced with a M102 Howitzer showing the AC-130E and H Spectres were tailored more to the anti-material role rather than anti-personnel and in effect the AC-47s had handled that role since the AC-130A had arrived in Vietnam.

The heavier weaponry of the Pave Aegis Spectre proved pivotal to operations against North Vietnamese forces during the NGUYEN HUE campaign. The Spectres were re-assigned to ground support and escort duties in support of South Vietnamese fires bases under siege. Bases such as An Loc required resupply and fire support with resupply coming in the form of air-landed stores but the C-123 Providers used for this came under mortar, artillery and small-arms fire. The Providers, and later USAF C-130s, were escorted by Spectres which suppressed enemy fire while also providing support for the hard-pressed troops on the ground.

The Pave Aegis configuration became standard in what became the AC-130H Spectre from its introduction in 1972 until 2000 when the Vulcan was replaced with a five-barrelled 25mm Equaliser cannon on a trainable mount. This armament suite was first fitted to the AC-130U Spooky II, based on the C-130H airframe. The AC-130W Stinger II was also based on the C-130H airframe, but only carried a single 30mm ATK GAU-23/A Bushmaster cannon, although the underwing pylons can accommodate AGM-114 Hellfire missiles and GBU-39 Small Diameter Bombs, four per hard point.

The USAF's faith in the Spectre/Spooky II/ Stinger II saw the role transition to the new C-130J Ghostrider, a modified MC-130J Commando II, fitted with a single 30mm ATK GAU-23/A Bushmaster cannon and a 105mm M102 Howitzer. Where the J-model gunship differs from its predecessors is the ability to carry the Gunslinger weapons system on the rear ramp. The Gunslinger includes AGM-176 Griffin missiles and GBU-44/B Viper Strike glide bombs in a dispenser on the tail ramp. As a result, the Ghostrider is more artillery platform than gunship in the Spooky mould. The application of a 30mm cannon and the 105mm shells (albeit combined with guided missiles) marks a return to the guns and rockets used by ground attack aircraft since the Forties, but with everything on one day/night capable aircraft. The Gunslinger system also reflected the doctrine adopted by Western armed forces since the 1991 Gulf War: avoid collateral damage where possible.

As AC-130 armament changed, so did the sensors. The AC-130H Spectre was fitted with the AN/APG-66 radar from the F-16 in its ground-to-air mode while the AC-130U used the F-15E Strike Eagle's AN/APG-70 radar. Optical sensors have kept up with the pace of technology with LLLTV and FLIR systems being updated as and when new equipment became available maintaining the AC-130 status as a prized asset wherever US forces operate, and to protect that asset a comprehensive defensive countermeasures suite was installed. Of course, shooting at a Spectre more or less invites it to shoot back, with inevitable results.

Over the years, many aircraft, ranging from the Cessna Bird Dog to the Boeing B-47 have been proposed as gunships with many to carry 20mm Vulcan cannon in ventral turrets. The

AC-47 saw service with a number of air forces around the world and as of 2019 was still in service with the air forces of El Salvador and Colombia. The AC-47Ts in service with Colombia are actually Basler BT-67 turboprop conversions so not strictly a Spooky but operated with success against FARC (Fuerzas Armadas Revolucionarias de Colombia) rebels. The 'Fantasma' (Spooky in Spanish) used its FLIR to seek insurgents in the bush at night, and having told the locals to stay indoors, Fantasmas hunted down the FARC. While many countries have cast an envious eye on the AC-130 series, Royal Saudi Air Force expressed an interest in the Spectre, no other country has acquired the Spectre.

Facing similar conditions in Vietnam, the Australian armed forces also looked at a gunship, but rather than using their C-130s the RAAF looked at using some of their DHC-4 Caribou fleet, tentatively called 'Dragonships' in support of troops in contact. The South African Air Force, fighting the Border War in Angola and what is now Namibia, fitted Hispano HS404 or MG.151 20mm cannon to C-47s called Dragon Daks. In Britain the only known proposal for a Spooky-type platform came from Britten-Norman who drew up studies to fit the Turbo Defender with four FN MAG 7.62mm machine guns in the cabin, firing to port. The proposal had no takers.

Only the USAF operates a fleet of large gunship aeroplanes, but many other armed forces operated another type of gunship – armed helicopters. By the start of the 21st Century a new type of aircraft, one that also had its origins in the colonial policing actions of the 1950s and 60s, was in service around the world, providing support for troops in contact. The armed transport helicopter (the gunship) and the attack helicopter both began life as escorts for troop transports, but rather than being a troop carrier fitted with weapons, the agile and heavily-armoured attack helicopter was designed to carry support weapons such as rockets and a big cannon and could get in close to support the troops. While they may have lacked the persistence and weapons of Spooky and Spectre, the attack helicopter had a similar effect on insurgents.

For troops in contact, be it US Army in a protected hamlet in Vietnam, Red Army in a hilltop post in Afghanistan or British Army in a forward operating base in Helmand the appearance of a Cobra, *Hind* or Apache could literally turn the tide. However, when you're in a situation, you want guns, lots of guns, and for the US and its allies, that's what Spooky and Spectre have provided for half a century.

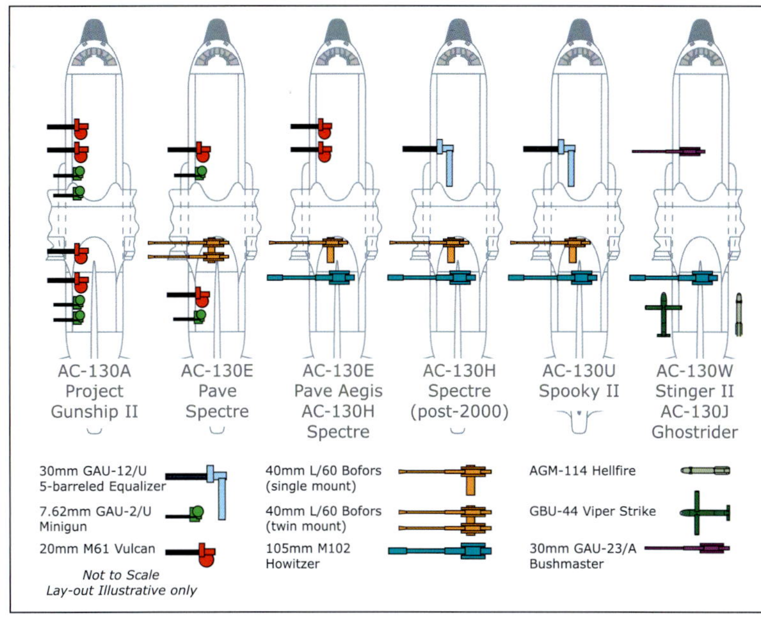

The Spectre's weapons fit has changed over the decades since the 1970s from a truck hunter to a fire support platform that operates wherever US ground forces are in action. The latest Stinger II is fitted with precision guided munitions.

Lockheed Martin AC-130U Spooky of the 4th Special Operations Squadron. Note the sensors on the port side of the lower fuselage and undercarriage sponson. The armament, a 30mm Bushmaster cannon, Bofors L60 40mm gun and a M102 105mm howitzer, can be seen. *DoD/USAF*

Glossary

2ATAF Second Allied Tactical Air Force. Formed in 1958 as a NATO force tasked with air support on NATO Northern Army Group.

2TAF Second Tactical Air Force. Formed in 1943 as an air arm to support the Army in the field. Became RAFG in January 1959.

ACAS Assistant Chief of the Air Staff. Various positions covering aspects of the RAF. ACAS(OR) deals with Operational Requirements. Post established in 1985.

Admiralty Senior officers who run the Royal Navy

Afterburner see reheat

AFV Armoured Fighting Vehicle. Catch-all term for vehicles that are armoured and carry weapons - tanks. Also includes engineering plant and air defence vehicles, if armoured

Air Staff The senior officers who run the RAF

APFSDS Armour Piercing Fin Stabilised Discarding Sabot. Anti-tank round mainly used by main battle tank guns.

ARM Anti-Radiation Missile

ASM Armstrong Siddeley Motors

ASR Air Staff Requirement – outline of what the subject has to do. The basis of the development programme.

AST Air Staff Target – formed the basis of a feasibility study for the Requirement.

Avro AV Roe aircraft company

AWA Armstrong Whitworth Aviation

BAe British Aerospace, became BAE Systems

BAC British Aircraft Corporation

Base-burning Means of reducing drag by burning fuel at the rear of an aircraft to reduce base drag. See Appendix 2

BSEL Bristol Siddeley Engines Ltd

CA Controller, Aircraft – Senior RAF officer charged with clearing an aircraft for service.

CAS Chief of the Air Staff – most senior military officer in the RAF.

Counter-Air Attacks on an enemy air forces' infrastructure

DCAS Deputy Chief of the Air Staff. Post abolished in 1969, replaced by ACAS.

DH De Havilland – aircraft company

DHP De Havilland Propellers - Guided weapons branch of De Havilland. Became Hawker Siddeley Dynamics.

DOAE Defence Operational Analysis Establishment

DOR Director, Operational Requirements

ECM Electronic Counter Measures

EEA English Electric Aviation

EECo English Electric Company

Elint Electronic Intelligence

ESM Electronic Support Measures

EW Electronic Warfare

FAA Fleet Air Arm – Royal Navy's air branch

FLIR Forward Looking Infra-Red

FVRDE Fighting vehicle Research and Development Establishment

General Staff The senior officers who run the British Army

HEAT High Explosive Anti-Tank. Anti-tank round mainly used by anti-tank missiles and cluster bombs.

HESH High Explosive Squash Head. Anti-tank round mainly used by main battle tank guns

HSA Hawker Siddeley Aviation – aircraft division of Hawker Siddeley

HSD Hawker Siddeley Dynamics – Guided Weapons division of Hawker Siddeley. Formerly De Havilland Propellers.

IFV Infantry Fighting Vehicle. Troop carrier with weapons mounted in a turret e.g. FV510 Warrior, BMP-2 or M2 Bradley

JATO Jet Assisted Take Off – original acronym, now RATO.

LLLTV Low Light Level Television – night vision device.

Mach Number A speed divided by local speed of sound.

MAD Magnetic Anomaly Detector

MBT Main Battle Tank.

Ministry of Supply (MoS) The ministry in charge of everything from 'boot laces to atoms'. Responsible for aerospace contracts and management thereof. Dissolved with the creation of the MoD in 1958.

MOD/MoD Ministry of Defence

NGTE National Gas Turbine Establishment

NPL National Physical Laboratory

OR Operational Requirement

PGM Precision Guided Munitions

RAE Royal Aircraft Establishment

RAF Royal Air Force

RAFG Royal Air Force Germany. Formed in 1959 as the British component of 2ATAF. Commanding Officer of RAFG also commands 2ATAF.

RATO Rocket Assisted Take-Off

RCS Radar Cross Section. Radar reflectivity of a target expressed as an area.

Reheat Thrust augmentation by injecting neat fuel into the exhaust flow between the turbine and the propelling nozzle. This fuel burns thereby increasing the temperature and the velocity of the gas as it leaves the nozzle. British term, American equivalent is afterburner.

RHA Rolled Homogeneous Armour. Type of armour plate used on tanks. Latterly used as a quantifier for composite armour i.e. 6in (15cm) RHA equivalent.

RN Royal Navy

RPV Remotely Piloted Vehicle. Now called UAV or UAS.

RRE Radar Research Establishment/Royal Radar Establishment

RSRE Radar and Signals Research Establishment

SACEUR Supreme Allied Commander, Europe. Officer in command of NATO operations in Europe. Traditionally held by an officer of the United States armed forces.

SAM Surface to Air Missile.

SEAD Suppression of Enemy Air Defences. Also known as Defence Suppression. Attacks or countermeasures against enemy radar and SAM installations.

SHAPE Supreme Headquarters Allied Powers Europe

SLAR Sideways Looking Airborne Radar

SLBM Submarine-launched ballistic missile

ST(A) Staff Target (Air). Also (Land Air) covering joint requirements with Army.

STOL Short Take Off and Landing

STOVL Short Take Off Vertical Landing

TFR Terrain Following Radar

TRE Telecommunications Research Establishment, became Radar Research Establishment in 1953, but renamed Royal Radar Establishment. Became Royal Signals and Radar Establishment in 1980 when Signals Research and Development Establishment was merged with RRE.

UAS Uninhabited Aircraft System

UAV Unmanned (or Uninhabited) Air Vehicle

VCAS Vice Chief of the Air Staff. Senior assistant to the CAS. Abolished in 1985

V/STOL Vertical/Short Take Off and Landing

VTOL Vertical Take Off and Landing

WARLOC War Location. Dispersed sites for Harrier operations.

Wing loading Total weight of the aircraft divided by area of wing

Index

SEPCAT Jaguar of No 20 Sqn on display with its range of weapons. One notable absence is the WE.177 Lay Down Bomb.